ENDEAVORS of ART

Frontispiece to *Andria* from Strassburg Terence, 1496
(*See pages 174–75*)

ENDEAVORS of ART: A study of form in Elizabethan drama ❧

By MADELEINE DORAN

MADISON
THE UNIVERSITY OF WISCONSIN PRESS
1963

*To my mother
and the memory of my father*

Published by
THE UNIVERSITY OF WISCONSIN PRESS
430 Sterling Court, Madison 6, Wisconsin

Copyright © 1954 by the
Regents of the University of Wisconsin

Second Printing, 1963

Printed in the United States of America

Preface

THIS BOOK IS an essay in historical criticism. It is based on the premise that to know and understand the frame of artistic reference within which the practising dramatists of the Elizabethan and Jacobean periods worked is to understand better their artistic achievement. They were limited in some directions, freed in others, by the artistic possibilities open to them in their own time, those possibilities that were shaped for them by their literary heritage, their predominantly rhetorical education, the commonplaces of renaissance aesthetic and poetic, and contemporary taste. To see both the weakness and the strength of the Elizabethan drama from this perspective is a corrective against anachronistic expectations. At the same time, though the setting of this study is historical, the point of view is aesthetic. The plays are regarded, not as documents illustrative of social or intellectual history, but as plays; the assumption is that their lasting value depends upon the degree of their success as works of art.

When Thomas Nashe in 1589, at the age of twenty-two, undertook to write a preface to his friend Robert Greene's pastoral romance, *Menaphon,* he made it the occasion of a remarkable survey of the contemporary state of English letters. With the intolerance of a gifted young man (and a new-made Cambridge Master of Arts to boot) he girded at upstart and ill-educated writers who sought to cover their lack of talent with imitations of classical and continental poetry and drama—"a sort of shifting companions, that run through every trade and thrive by none," that "leave the trade of *Noverint* whereto they were born, and busy themselves with the endeavors of art, that could scarcely Latinize their neck-verse if they should have need." The consequence of their activities is that

English Seneca read by candle light yields many good sentences, as *Blood is a beggar,* and so forth: and if you entreat him fair in a frosty morning, he will afford you whole *Hamlets,* I should say handfuls of tragical speeches. But o grief! *tempus edax rerum,* what's that will last always? The sea exhaled by drops will in continuance be dry, and Seneca let blood line by line and page by page, at length must needs die to our stage: . . .

This passage, because of its allusion to an early *Hamlet* and because of its supposed reference to Kyd, is generally quoted for itself out of context and is far better known than the rest of the essay. The preface as a whole is a plea to let English letters stand on their own feet, and is an attack on the inkhornists, the rackers of rhetoric, the makers of epitomes, and the slavish imitators of classical and foreign styles. It is a plea for originality, and by implication seems a plea for naturalness. So, in a sense it is; but it is not a defense of "nature" against "art," that is, a plea for naturalness without artifice. Nashe admires both scholarship and rhetoric when put to the proper use by men like "that aged father Erasmus," who "invested most of our Greek writers in the robes of the ancient Romans," and like Sir John Cheke, "the exchequer of eloquence," "a man of men, supernaturally traded in all tongues." In the passage quoted on the imitators of Seneca, Nashe is not scorning "art," or even "endeavors of art," but only the endeavors which he considers pretentious, misplaced, and unjustified. Towards the end of the essay, he tries a number of English writers —notably Chaucer, Gower, Lydgate, Spenser, Peele, and Warner— by "the touchstone of art," and finds them not wanting.

His praise of Greene's romance, which is modeled in part after the *Arcadia* and written in a euphuistic style, tempered but still patterned, is instructive:

I come (sweet friend) to thy Arcadian *Menaphon:* whose attire though not so stately, yet comely, doth entitle thee above all other, to that *temperatum dicendi genus,* which Tully in his *Orator* termeth true eloquence. . . . give me the man whose extemporal vein in any humor will excel our greatest art-masters' deliberate thoughts; whose invention, quicker than his eye, will challenge the proudest rhetorician to the contention of like perfection, with like expedition.

Greene appears to be one of those valued for his extemporal vein and his inventive genius; Nashe evidently despises neither imitation nor rhetorical formalism when they are used with originality.

The preface to *Menaphon,* then, perfectly illustrates a characteristic renaissance way of looking at poetry; though "nature" is given primacy, it is not "nature" undisciplined by "art." Until we understand the art, we can scarcely understand renaissance conceptions of naturalness. In examining the art of the dramatists and assuming that as educated men they were aware of its principles and that, according to individual temperament and interest, they paid more or less heed to them, we shall be in no danger of overweighting theory at the expense of practice if we keep in mind Nashe's own emphasis, ironically put: ". . . the private truth of my discovered creed in this controversy is this, that as that beast was thought scarce worthy to be sacrificed to the Egyptian Epaphus who had not some or other black spot on his skin: so I deem him far unworthy of the name of a scholar, and so consequently, to sacrifice his endeavors to art, that is not a poet, either in whole or in part." My book is an attempt to bring to the Elizabethan drama such a touchstone of art as the poets themselves would have understood and used.

It is not at all the book I set out to write when I began these studies some years ago. I had in mind a book on Shakespeare's architectonic power and his growth in mastery of dramatic structure. But for that book I found that I needed prolegomena, and, as prolegomena have a way of doing, they grew into a book in their own right. Much of the ground I have traversed is already familiar through many special studies, a number of which have come out since I began my own work. This is particularly true of the subjects treated in the chapters of general background on renaissance aesthetic, poetic, and rhetoric. But to understand what I was doing and where I was going I had to work through these matters myself and state them for my own purposes. The first and last chapters of the book give the point of view, the matters dealt with, the materials drawn upon, the procedures followed, and the conclusions reached. Anyone who reads these two can decide for himself where else in the book he wishes to look for full treatment of particular subjects.

One matter of form needs comment. With some reluctance and with occasional exceptions, I have modernized the spelling of quotations from English texts where the copy text was unmodernized; in such quotations I have altered the punctuation as little as possible consistent with clarity and ease of reading. It would not have been economical of time to handle editorial problems in unedited texts, but the standard texts of Elizabethan authors vary greatly in editorial practice; Lucas' *Webster,* for instance, is not modernized, Parrott's *Chapman* is, and all edited texts of Shakespeare, except the latest New Variorum volumes, and the incomplete and seldom found *Old Spelling Shakespeare,* are modernized. It is hardly fair to make Shakespeare seem less "quaint" than his fellows. In renaissance French and Italian, however, there is less difference from modern spelling than in English, and less individual variation among authors and printers. Therefore with quotations from works in these languages, and in the classical languages, I have followed the copy text, except to disregard printing conventions in the use of *i* and *j*, *u* and *v*, long *s*, and *ae* and *oe* ligatures in Latin and Greek.

Permission to reproduce the illustrations used from the Strassburg *Terence* of 1496 and from the Ulm *De claris mulieribus* of 1473 was generously given by the Huntington Library, San Marino, California. For their always courteous assistance I wish to thank the staffs of the Huntington Library, the Widener and Houghton Libraries, and the University of Wisconsin General Libraries.

For two semesters of leave from the university, I am most grateful to the Research Committee of the Graduate School of the University of Wisconsin, and to Dean Mark Ingraham of the College of Letters and Science; for another year of freedom, to the Fellowship Committee of the American Association of University Women, which awarded me the Marion Talbot Fellowship for the year 1946–47; and to my colleagues in the English Department for their constant encouragement and their assistance with many academic burdens during the long time this book has been in progress. My particular debts are many and gratefully acknowledged: to my graduate assistants, Mrs. Marie Cochrane and Mr. Yucheng Lo, for help with references and checking; to Mrs. Lo for her preparation of the typescript; to my student Mr. Angelo De Vitis for his review of my translations from the Italian critics and for his helpful suggestions; to Professor Allan Gilbert of Duke University for useful advice on my first plans for the book; to Professor Norman C. Stageberg of Iowa State Teachers College and Professor Paul Kocher of the Claremont Graduate School for criticism of some chapters in their early stages; to my former student Miss Mildred Munday, now of Bucknell University, for her assistance in the tasks of proofreading and indexmaking; to Miss Anne King, Professor Herbert Howe, and Professor Gaines Post, all of the University of Wisconsin, for invaluable aid in the interpretation of postclassical Latin texts. My former pupil, Mrs. Edgar W. Lacy (Margaret Swanson Lacy), besides doing many dull chores for me *con amore,* read the completed manuscript with an attentive eye for muddy passages and graceless phrasing, and with the needs of a graduate student in mind. To my colleague Professor Ruth Wallerstein I am deeply indebted, not only for her acute and constructive criticism of the book, but also for much more in the way of selfless friendship that went into its making. My deepest and dearest debt is to my master, Professor Hardin Craig; it must appear on every page.

MADELEINE DORAN

Madison, Wisconsin
January, 1953

Contents

xi

List of Illustrations

ENDEAVORS of ART

1 The Materials and the Problem

A CHARACTERISTIC of the multiple unity of the sixteenth century is that the separate things in the picture are felt to be relatively equal in material value. The narrative certainly distinguishes between main and secondary figures. We can see—in contrast to the narration of the primitives—from far off where the crucial point of the event lies, but for all that, what have come into being are creations of that relative unity which to the baroque looked like multiplicity.

—HEINRICH WÖLFFLIN, *Principles of Art History* [1]

THIS BOOK is an attempt to reconstruct some part of the context of ideas, assumptions, and predispositions about literary art in which Shakespeare and his fellow English dramatists, at the height of their country's Renaissance, must have worked, and to suggest ways in which these things may have helped shape their art.

One way to come at the problem of their artistry is to view them in relation to the artistic possibilities of the age in which they lived, for aesthetic interpretation gains depth from such historical perspective as we are able to achieve. Apart from textual study, English renaissance scholarship of our time has largely been concerned with the imaginative rebuilding of contexts in which to view the great literary figures—contexts that are religious, political, ethical, social, scientific, or psychological. The rebuilding of the artistic context is just as important. For Shakespeare could not have worked outside a frame of artistic reference any more than he could have worked outside a frame of personal or social reference. That frame, it is evident, must have consisted, not merely of the ideas of artistic purpose and form to which he could give a name, but also of the tastes, interests, assumptions, and attitudes to which his age would have predisposed him whether he thought about them or not. These assumptions and attitudes would have limited him in some directions, freed him in

3

others. Before I clarify this point further, it may be well to make two cautionary statements.

The first is that my position should not be confused with that extreme and critically dangerous one which implies that Shakespeare has only one "right" meaning, the meaning he had for men of his own day. If that is true, we had better put him away, once and for all. We cannot turn ourselves into Elizabethans; we should not fool ourselves by thinking we can. Even if we could, we should still have to ask which Elizabethans, for *Hamlet* cannot have meant the same thing to Burleigh as to Burleigh's cook, or to Jonson the poet and critic as to Gresham the merchant. The best we can hope to do through learning more about Shakespeare's age is to try to induce a sufficiently sympathetic frame of mind to see his plays in a new perspective which will reveal new meanings and modify those we may have anachronistically assumed. I think the effort is worth making, for the greater enrichment of our artistic experience.

The second caution is that by focusing attention on what his age had to contribute to his artistic development I do not mean to minimize his own artistic independence. On the contrary, Shakespeare achieved architectonic greatness after starting from a heritage that did not predispose artists towards structural form. We do his genius no injustice by understanding what it had to work with.

We have much to learn about both Shakespeare and his fellows as artists from viewing them in relation to the artistic possibilities of their age. An original development of this point of view with respect to painting, sculpture, and architecture is to be found in Professor Heinrich Wölfflin's *Principles of Art History*. His thesis is that alterations from age to age in the mode of vision, or of imaginative beholding, alter the formal possibilities open to the artists of any given period. "The historian has to reckon with stages of the imagination. . . . Instead of asking 'How do these works affect me, the modern man?' and estimating their expressional content by that standard, the historian must realise what choice of formal possibilities the epoch had at its disposal. An essentially different interpretation will result." [2] Professor Wölfflin compares two great periods of art, the High Renaissance and the Baroque, and shows that one achieved effects the other did not, not because of relative superiority of technique, nor because of differences in national development, nor even because of any difference in desire for naturalness of representation, but because the artists of the two periods had different standards for seeing. Leonardo, Raphael, Dürer, Holbein, for instance, saw things in a linear, tactile way with clarity of outline, the multiple parts independent and complete yet related to the whole, the shadows colored the same as the objects shadowed, the figures and objects diminishing in perspective in flat planes, the whole tied together in closed form with strong vertical and horizontal lines. Rubens, Rembrandt, Tiepolo, Velasquez, on the other hand, saw things in a painterly, visual way, with color and light giving strong emphasis to some parts, leaving others relatively unclear and without independence, the plastic forms not arranged in planes but diminishing in size in sharp recession, diagonals emphasized to break the rectangle, the necessary verticals and horizontals minimized to open the whole. Wölfflin considers any change in representational content from one period to the other to be less important to the effect of difference than the change in style arising from difference in decorative principle; each type of vision is bound up with a certain idea of beauty. This is an idea we shall find useful when we come to assess Elizabethan standards of "naturalness."

Wölfflin's general position, that the art of one age differs from that of another because the artists have different modes of imaginative beholding, seems to me as applicable to literature as to the graphic and plastic arts, if one allows "beholding" a wider connotation. Shakespeare saw with the eyes of the late sixteenth century, not with the eyes of the late seventeenth. I doubt if it would be possible to draw up as neat a set of parallel and contrasting categories for the literature of the age of Shakespeare and of the age of Dryden as Wölfflin did for the fine arts of the sixteenth and seventeenth centuries. Since ideas as well as forms and techniques are involved, the relations are more complicated. Words add a special complexity. For instance, renaissance critical theory furnishes a similar set of terms to both periods for talking about art, but as a formative influence on the art itself this theory is far less important in Shakespeare's period than in Dryden's. We must not, therefore, be misled by terms. We shall have to look for the special sixteenth-century meanings of common counters like "art," "nature," "imitation," "verisimilitude," and "decorum." Nevertheless, allowing for all the interactions and ambiguities, the general point is clear enough: Dryden worked in a frame of artistic reference sufficiently different in its limitations and its possibilities from that in which Shakespeare worked to make their respective artistic products immediately recognizable as belonging to different periods.

One particular difference is worth noting here, for it will recur all the way through the book as the major problem of form English renaissance dramatists had to solve. The clue to it is in Wölfflin. One of the chief points of difference between renaissance and baroque painting he finds in the "multiple unity" of the former, the "unified unity" of the latter.[3] He means that renaissance art "achieves its unity by making the parts independent as free members, and that the baroque abolishes the uniform independence of the parts in favour of a more unified total motive. In the former case, co-ordination of the accents; in the latter, subordination." [4] Now multiplicity is one of the first things that strikes us as characteristic of sixteenth century literary art. Rabelais, Ariosto, Cervantes, Spenser, and Shakespeare saw beauty in multiplicity of detail. Abundant variousness was a way of seeing the world in the sixteenth century that no longer had the same meaning or value at the end of the next century. To understand how Shakespeare achieved unity in respect to that multiplicity we need first to discover what choice of formal possibilities he had at his disposal. That discovery is the business of this book.

WE KNOW ALREADY a good deal about the context of controlling tastes and ideas in which Elizabethan dramatists must have worked. Intensive studies of parts of that background—of critical theory, rhetorical theory and education, inherited literary forms, theatrical conventions, ideas about style, and so on—are constantly being made. It is just because so much descriptive and analytical work has been done that we need a synthesis which will put the various parts of the field in relation with one another. My own efforts are directed toward giving some of the parts coherence.

Clearly, one of the most important determinants of the form of Shakespeare's plays, and therefore to be regarded as part of his frame of reference, was the theater in which he worked: its physical attributes, its conventions, its actors, its management, its audience. I shall say little about it systematically, and assume that my readers will not be likely to lose sight of its critical importance. The line I am following in this book is primarily dramatic rather than theatrical, a distinction which the concrete reality of the plays, written for stage production, proclaims as an academic abstraction. But it is a simplification necessary to bring my problem, even then appallingly complex and extensive, within compass; we may counter the dangers of this simplification by keeping the other abstraction, the theatrical aspect of the plays, constantly in mind as a check—or, to put it differently, by letting the concreteness of the plays as acted, in which both dramatic and theatrical aspects are realized, be the standard of appeal.

In our search for the significant ideas about poetry and drama that helped shape Elizabethan drama, we have to look both for formulated ideas and for implied interests and attitudes. Where do we look?

For explicit statement we have a considerable body of renaissance critical theory. I need not remind my readers of the foundation of this criticism in ancient criticism, principally in passages of Plato's *Republic, Ion, Gorgias,* and *Laws,* in Aristotle's *Poetics,* in Horace's *Art of Poetry,* in Quintilian's *Institutes,* and in various treatises and essays of Cicero's.[5] Nor need I remind them of the greater importance for our purposes of what renaissance critics made of these classical documents than of the documents themselves. An influence not so generally taken account of is that of the postclassical grammarians. The essays on ancient drama of Diomedes, Evanthius, and Donatus were frequently published during the Renaissance, the latter two usually as accompaniments to editions of Terence; the commentaries of Donatus and Servius on Terence appeared in many editions of the plays.[6] And the point of view of these grammarians is everywhere reflected in contemporary critical theory.

Of new criticism in the Renaissance itself, the output of the Italians bulks largest and is the most impressive in range and subtlety. In addition to the familiar monuments, like the poetics of Trissino, Robortello, Giraldi, Scaliger, Minturno, Castelvetro—some of them translations of, and most of them commentaries on, Aristotle—we should not forget the essays on special topics, like Fracastoro's dialogue on the imagination, or Lionardi's dialogues on the relations of poetry, rhetoric, and history; the prefaces to plays, like Giraldi's to *Orbecche,* and Della Porta's to some of his comedies; or the polemical essays of the literary controversies over *Orlando Furioso, Gerusalemme Liberata,* and *Il Pastor Fido.* From these controversies came two full-length *apologiae* of great importance, Tasso's *Discourses on the Heroic Poem* and Guarini's *Compendium of Tragicomic Poetry*, and many minor works less illumined but no less significant in revealing contemporary attitudes.[7]

French criticism is interesting to us chiefly in being confirmatory of what we find in the Italians. When it is not concerned like Du Bellay's *Defense* with special linguistic problems, it has nothing much to add. This is true both of the general treatments of poetry (as in the poetics of Sebillet, La Fresnaye, Laudun, and Peletier) and of particular statements about the drama, whether found in the *arts poétiques* or in prefaces to dramatic work like Grévin's, La Taille's, or De Baïf's.[8] Ronsard, in his *Abbrégé de l'art poétique*, is important in his approach to the problem of the imagination.

Of other European criticism, the commentaries on Plautus and on Terence have probably the most significance for the English drama.[9] Lope de Vega's *New Art of Making Comedies* [10] is interesting only as indicative of a parallel freedom from critical domination in Spanish as in English drama.

English criticism, scattered and fragmentary, has to be picked up from many places.[11] Much of it is polemic and controversial, with three main focal points: the question of the adoption of classical meters in English, the question of how the language is to be expanded and used, and the Puritan attack on the stage. The first is irrelevant to our purpose, the second exceedingly important, but outside the immediate scope of this book. As for the third, the skirmishings of Gosson, Lodge, and Nashe are valuable to us in defining attitudes, but give us slight help with problems of dramatic form; Heywood's *Apology for Actors* gives a little and Sidney's *Defense* more. There is no full-length treatise on the drama comparable to Trissino's, Giraldi's, or Minturno's in Italian. But we can gather a good deal that is useful to us from prefaces and prologues (like Jonson's, Marston's, Heywood's, or Webster's) and from critical plays (like Jonson's *Every Man out of his Humour* or the plays produced in London and the universities during the War of the Theaters). The two works most important to us for their bearing on general poetic questions are Sidney's *Defense of Poesy* and Puttenham's *Art of English Poesy*.

For clues to prevailing literary tastes and attitudes the best place to go is to the theory and practice of Tudor education.[12] The dominant interest in sixteenth-century education was rhetoric. The rhetorics, then, must be added to the poetics, partly as sources of critical concepts, more as sources of attitudes and of techniques. We shall find the rhetorics useful both in the beginning of our study when we are indicating the general directions and emphases of problems of form and later on when we touch on particular problems of style.

For implications as to taste and interests we must go also to the works chosen for imitation or adaptation, as sources either of useful techniques or of stories convertible into drama. The most important dramatic sources are Roman drama; medieval drama, particularly miracle plays and moralities; and contemporary Italian drama, especially comedy. The most important nondramatic sources are metrical tragedies, like the *Mirror for Magistrates;* historical chronicles; the chief medieval classical authors, Ovid and Virgil; and tales of all sorts, but especially Italian *novelle,* original or translated, Greek romances and their adaptations, and pastoral romances. Finally, we have the immediate context of Elizabethan drama in the process of finding direction and form.

I assume that the usefulness of literary sources is obvious enough and shall comment on only three main points: what we may expect to get from the critics, the spirit in which we should regard renaissance classicism, and the inheritance of narrative from the Middle Ages.

CRITICAL THEORY

For formal principles about renaissance poetry and drama, we naturally go to the critics, whose business it was to formulate ideas. Yet our first reaction to them is apt to be one of impatient rejection; they seem to us to be on a cold scent, while the quarry is over the hills and far away. We see Shakespeare writing for a living theater, taking traditional materials, shaping his instrument empirically as he goes, and creating something pleasing to a popular audience. What has *Hamlet* to do, we ask, with the earnest rules of the neo-Aristotelians, telling us that a play must be written in five acts, that it must keep to a single place and a day's time, that it must not intermingle the comic with the tragic or show deeds of horror on the stage, that it must purge us for our moral good of the weakening passions of pity and fear, and that it must teach us to fear to do evil lest we suffer a like fall with the hero?

Nevertheless, the critics have a good deal to tell us, even if much of it is beneath the surface. It is true that English drama stands in a different relation to renaissance criticism from that of Italian literary drama. For one thing, criticism in England was far less highly developed than in Italy; for another, criticism in England, as in Spain, where the drama was likewise national and popular, lagged behind rather than ran ahead. Criticism was not so largely informing of English drama as it was of the Italian drama of the academies, or as it came to be of French classical drama and English Restoration tragedy. We may agree with Toffanin that D'Ancona has overdone the classical influence on Italian drama and made insufficient allowance for the popular, romantic elements in it, and even so recognize that critical theory stood in a more influential relation to it than it did to English drama.[13] All the same, it is not true that the ideas enunciated by the critics, continental as well as English, were without any effect on English drama, whether they reached the dramatists directly from the critical treatises, or more dispersedly through other channels. Certain of the critics' general ideas about poetry— *imitation, decorum, verisimilitude,* and the like—are commonplaces met with everywhere. Some of their particular ideas about the drama were, as we shall see, also commonplaces derived from the fourth-century grammarians. The professed aim of the critics was usually to elucidate Aristotle, whose ideas of tragedy might at first glance seem remote enough to a world that had in its immediate background the mystery play and the dramatized saint's legend—episodic, narrative in spirit, essentially romantic. But the critics could not even interpret Aristotle without talking in terms of the world they knew, and in certain persistent biases (like the enthusiasm for variety, which gives Aristotle's unity of action a most peculiar look) or in misinterpretations (like the moral explanation of tragic catharsis), they betrayed the dominant tendencies and interests of their own age. One significant place to look, then, for ideas that may have helped to shape English drama is in the critics' misinterpretations of Aristotle.

Here, the Italian critics are more helpful than the English and as safe to use, since their biases are seen to be as applicable to English as to Italian art. In considering the availability of Italian criticism to English critics and poets, it should be remembered how great was the literary commerce between England and Italy in the sixteenth century.[14] My point, however, does not depend on any theory of direct influence, something almost impossible to assess. What is important is that the Italian critics, wrestling with the problem of making Aristotle available to their own age, give away the fundamental interests and predispositions of that age. We might of course deduce most of these from the literature itself. But the critics furnish us with the formulated concepts in which the age thought.

An object lesson taken from a related art will serve to make my point clear. In March, 1945, *Harper's* reprinted some excerpts from William M. Woollett's *Old Homes Made New,* published in New York in 1878. In considering the remodeling of a dwelling, the author says that the same principles should apply as would apply to new work. The principles he sets down are that the convenience of the plan, adapted to the particular inhabitants and to the site, is of first importance; that the exterior should grow naturally from the plan; that the exterior should "be a consistent following out of the proper and natural uses of the materials of which it is built"; that the architectural effect should be obtained from the structure, not from additions, from variety of outline rather than from richness of detail; and, finally, that the greatest work of art in architecture is that which produces the least expenditure of labor and detail in design—in short, principles of functionalism, adaptation, structural emphasis, and economy that we should regard as unexceptionable architectural principles then, now, or at any time. But when we look at the views Mr. Woollett furnishes of houses before and after remodeling, we get a rude shock. A simple, well-proportioned two-story frame house, rectangular, with a hip roof and a plain verandah, blossoms out with new arched piazzas at front and rear, an outside chimney, a many-gabled roof, dormer windows, and, over the front piazza, a bay window surmounted first by a balcony with spindled posts and then by a dormer projecting like the "heavens" in the Globe Theater. Of another alteration of a Georgian hip roof into a many-gabled, many-dormered affair, the architect remarks that the owner wanted a "French" roof, but that in his compromise the views of the owner were met and his own "sense of right saved from outrage." He was evidently not able to see in his Victorian swellings and excrescences any violation of his own principles of structural emphasis and economy. We have no right to argue that he could not see it because of any stupidity on his part. The lesson to be drawn is Wölfflin's lesson, that artists can see only what their own age predisposes them to see.

In the same way, the Italian critics insist repeatedly on unity of action for tragedy and heroic poem; and then they illustrate it with Ariosto! They loved his dozens of characters, his hundreds of incidents, his teasing interruptions and resumptions without motivation or transition, his movement from place to place in an instant of time, his wonderful multiplicity; and by ingenious effort some of them made him out to be as unified as Virgil.[15] We must not, then, take them at their word, at least at its face value. If we look always at their enunciated principles in the light of the applications they make of them, we get valuable indications of the really effective underlying formal possibilities by which the authors of the age were governed.

RENAISSANCE CLASSICISM

Another thing we have to remember is that the critics are only part of that passionate classicism which helped give shape and color to everything in the Renaissance. They state ideas which we know to have been available, indeed inescapable, through education; and they refer to literary modes which were equally inescapable.

There is a tendency in contemporary scholarship to minimize classical influences in favor of medieval influences. It is a healthy tendency in so far as it seeks to redress a balance that has been too heavily weighted on the other side. But the counterpoise can also be too heavy. The very metaphor of counterpoise I am using is a key to the difficulty, that is our constant attempt to make quantitative assessments of influence. The relations of the component elements are not additive but mutually modifying; the elements soon lose their identity in something essentially new. They are not even compounded in a chemical sense, for they cannot be altogether recovered by analysis, even figuratively. We cannot draw classicism off in a vapor and have medievalism left as a residue. All these metaphors of static quantity applied to literary process leave out the controlling factor of mind, which is not merely combinative but creative. In these attempts at assessment of influence, two important points should be kept in mind, one the tendency to oversimplify the terms "medieval" and "classical," the other what the Renaissance understood by classical.

Convenient as it is for analysis to separate the medieval from the classical, we need to remind ourselves of the oversimplification. The Elizabethans were heirs to a most complex artistic tradition composed of many strands, some separately interwoven, some knotted or fused with others: the late medieval interest in diversity and detail, the medieval interest in story for its own sake, the medieval emphasis on rhetoric and style founded on a debased tradition of classical rhetoric, the medieval conception of tragedy, new emphasis directly from the classics on structural form and on what were understood to be Aristotelian and Horatian principles of epic and drama, but at the same time a renewed emphasis from Cicero on rhetoric and style. It is not possible to make any clear separation of medieval from classical influence, because much of medievalism itself is classicism transmuted. Most medieval ideas about literature are themselves classical in ultimate origin. They have gone through a modifying experience that makes them distinctive, of course—for example, the medieval conception of poetic as now a part of grammar, now a part of rhetoric, even a part of logic.[16] But when they mingle with influences from the newly revived classics, they may no longer be certainly identifiable; for example, is Lyly's brand of rhetoric a remnant of the late medieval cultivation of stylistic preciosity, or is it a sign of the new humanistic interest in rhetoric? In one of the dominant ideas of early Elizabethan tragedy, the idea that fortune is a goddess not to be trusted, how shall we separate medieval Stoicism from renaissance Senecanism?

The best we can do is sometimes to distinguish the older influences of the Middle Ages (whether themselves ultimately classical or not) from the newer influences of the revived classics. But even such lines are by no means always clear. For instance, literary historians speak of the Elizabethan dramatists as learning form in comedy from Plautus and Terence; but Terence, generally sounder structurally than Plautus, had been known throughout most of the Middle Ages and was indeed a favorite school author. The truth is, writers learned something about structure only when they were ready to learn it. The whole picture is full of contradictions and resistant to clear analysis.

The second point is that what looked like classicism to men of the Renaissance often does not look so to us. They thought of themselves, correctly or not, as rediscoverers of classical wisdom and beauty. It is, after all, from the Renaissance itself that comes the idea of the period as a "rebirth" of art and letters, a rebirth inter-preted as mainly the consequence of rediscovering classical art and letters. If, in its neglect of medieval tradition and of medieval classi-cism, this view is a simplification and distortion of what actually happened, it nevertheless gives evidence of the effective vitality of the contemporary interest in classicism.[17] Admiration of the classics in general and of certain classical authors in particular is an un-deniable fact; attempted imitation of these is another. Imitation of classical models was both a basic educational discipline and a critical test applied in the evaluation of contemporary literary works.[18] We must be willing to look, therefore, at what these admirers of the classics were aiming at, and entertain the possibility of imitation with-out too swift a rejection even when the final result seems to us very different from the model. It seems probable, for instance, that new light can be thrown on English romantic comedy from an attempt to understand what the Renaissance found in Terence and in Plautus.

That the ideas of the academic classicists sometimes had effect in directions we have become accustomed to think remote has been shown in recent investigations of the renaissance stage. There is good reason to think that the attempt to revivify the Roman theater as described by Vitruvius was not confined in the sixteenth century to the Italian academies, but was made as well, at least in respect to scenery, in academic, court, and private theaters in England; moreover, and this is what is startling, that Vitruvian influences were not without effect even on the public theater: i.e., in the matter of the amphitheatrical shape, in certain aspects of the stage, and in the use of machines.[19] Certainly, the more we learn about the Elizabethan public stage, the further we move from the old conception of it as something bare, makeshift, and primitive towards a conception of it as well equipped and sophisticated.

A valuable clue as to how the Renaissance understood the classics is found in the particular authors admired. One interesting thing in what it reveals of contemporary taste is the admiration of Euripides. A search through prescriptions and permissions of Greek authors in English school and college curricula shows a neglect of Aeschylus in favor of Sophocles and Euripides; and if only one tragic dramatist is mentioned he is more likely to be Euripides than Sophocles.[20] The same thing is seen in the Italian critics. The attention they pay to Sophocles is suspect because of the prominence given to *Oedipus*

Rex in the *Poetics;* if Aristotle treats the play as if it were the perfect tragedy, his renaissance followers must of course do likewise. But except occasionally for *Antigone* they rarely mention anything else of Sophocles. In contrast, many of the plays of Euripides come up for allusion or analysis: *Hecuba, The Trojan Women, The Phoenician Women, Medea, Orestes,* the two *Iphigeneia* plays, *Helen, The Cyclops.* And it is Euripides who was most translated and imitated by continental authors; in England, the few translations of Greek drama that were made are of him.[21]

In his emphasis on psychological states, his heightened theatrical effects, including violence on the stage, his occasional mingling of comic and tragic tones, his rhetorical qualities, we can see why the Renaissance responded to Euripides more fully than to Aeschylus and to Sophocles. But these qualities are precisely the things in him we think of as "unclassical" when we use "classical" in opposition to "romantic" to mean order, proportion, structural emphasis, and economy. Perhaps, therefore, the Renaissance did not think of "classical" as implying quite these things, or, if so, did not recognize the violations of them in Euripides. Note that the renaissance preference is chiefly for those plays of Euripides that are structurally the least tight. It is the weak *Hecuba,*[22] the lyrical *Troades,* and the ambiguously tragi-comic *Orestes* which are most popular, not the great structural masterpieces of *Hippolytus, Hercules Furens,* or *Bacchae.* It is interesting that Ovid preferred Euripides to the other Greek tragic dramatists, that Cicero recommended him for his sententiousness, and that Quintilian recommended him as the most useful to the student of rhetoric.[23] Whether these references would direct men of the Renaissance, interested as they were in rhetoric, to the reading of Euripides, or whether they would have discovered him anyhow, the approval of three of their favorite Roman authors would certainly have confirmed them in the rightness of their preference.

But of course, as everybody knows, even if Euripides was preferred to the other Greek tragic dramatists, he generally had to take second place in men's admiration to Seneca.[24] In reaction against the exaggerated views of the followers of Cunliffe who saw Seneca as the major influence on Elizabethan tragedy, some contemporary criticism has sought to reduce him to minor importance.[25] But Seneca cannot be so reduced, whether what we see in *Gorboduc* or *The Spanish Tragedy* looks precisely like what we see in *Phoenissae* or

Medea or not. We have too much contemporary evidence of interest in and admiration for him to dismiss him, too much evidence of men's sympathetic response to his attitudes and techniques. *Hamlet* is certainly not much like any play of Seneca's one can name, but Seneca is undoubtedly one of the effective ingredients in the emotional charge of *Hamlet*.[26] *Hamlet* without Seneca is inconceivable. Not much Elizabethan Latin sounds like Ciceronian Latin either; but the schoolmasters certainly thought they were teaching it.[27]

It may be true that Elizabethans did not have to learn from Seneca their taste for the violent and the horrible, true that Virgil had taught them about the classical underworld, true that they had their own ghosts and their own impulses to revenge, true that their preachers had long been warning them against the dangers of worldly ambition and the folly of trust in slippery chance. It is just because of this community of interest that Seneca spoke to them with such authority. Moreover, in putting into words with such fluency these things they knew, he gave them the authentic excitement of great literary experience. It is idle for us to be superior about their bad taste in preferring him to the Greeks. He spoke to them as the Greeks did not, and in so doing loosed their own tongues. Loosed them in deplorable ways, we are inclined to say after wading knee-deep in the gory and Stygian vocabulary of some of the early tragedies, and after growing giddy with the monotonous turning of Fortune's wheel. Nevertheless this crude imitation, as I think we are justified in calling it, is apprenticeship for mighty things:

> 'Tis paltry to be Caesar;
> Not being Fortune, he's but Fortune's knave,
> A minister of her will; and it is great
> To do that thing that ends all other deeds,
> Which shackles accidents, and bolts up change,
> Which sleeps, and never palates more the dug,
> The beggar's nurse and Caesar's.[28]

As for the comic dramatists, Terence and Plautus are the undisputed favorites. An Elizabethan schoolboy could not have escaped Terence, and along with Terence a good many ideas about the drama: [29] how it should aim to improve morals, what comedy and tragedy were, how characters should be conceived according to certain ideas of decorum, and, perhaps, though less certainly, how a play should be built. He would certainly have witnessed, or taken part in, performances of Terence or Plautus, or plays in imitation of these written by his schoolmaster. If he went to the university—as did Marlowe, Lyly, Greene, and Peele—or studied Greek on his own, as Jonson did, he must have read some Aristophanes. But Aristophanes, with his topicality, his complicated special form, and his slight interest in story, had little to offer of structural use to Elizabethan dramatists,[30] whereas Plautus and Terence had a great deal. Menander, the principal source of the Roman dramatists, might have been a favorite if his plays had survived as wholes. Erasmus thought that Menander, if he could be recovered, would be worth all the rest of the comic dramatists.[31] He and the two Romans had something of a "romantic" element in their plotting that we are apt to regard as one of their least essential features, but which the Renaissance seized on for its own uses. Again, the lesson is that we have to try to see what Elizabethans saw in the classical authors they admired, and to recognize that it was often not precisely what we see as most significant or most characteristic.

MEDIEVAL NARRATIVE

The Renaissance could only see the classics, of course, through eyes that had been conditioned by their ways of seeing in the past. In matters of form, inherited medieval tastes and habits were still so attractive that what could be learned from the newly revived classics acted only as modifying influences on these older habits, never as entire replacements of them.

There are a number of ways in which the later Middle Ages made formal contributions to English renaissance drama, either in attitudes towards form, like the fondness for rhetorical ornament or the conception of what tragedy should be, or in survivals of particular forms, like the technique of debate literature. One of the most significant contributions to the drama was the renaissance inheritance of narrative from the Middle Ages. It is not so much the transmission of actual stories as source material that is in question, though there was a good deal of this, as it is the survival in drama of habits of form that were characteristic of some types of medieval narrative. There are two habits in particular, what I shall call multiplicity and sequential action. The example of the classics did not suffice to alter these fundamentally.

By multiplicity I mean number and variety of events, characters, scenes, times. By sequential action I mean action *ab ovo* developed in historical sequence or natural order as opposed to the "crisis" action or artificial order, beginning *in medias res,* of Greek drama and Homeric epic. Multiplicity and sequential action are both characteristic of medieval romance, and the natural order is characteristic of *novelle* whenever they have a plot and are not merely anecdotal. English dramatists followed the romances in fondness for plentifulness of action, and almost without exception adopted the method of historical sequence. This meant that to achieve satisfactory dramatic form, they had to face especially difficult problems of selection, coherence, and emphasis. Medieval drama had served to establish in stage practice these preferences for the looser techniques of fiction. The problems of English renaissance dramatists, then, were partly set for them by their inheritance of a strong narrative tradition.

THE LINES of a possible synthesis have perhaps been suggesting themselves. One way of looking at the development of renaissance drama is to see it as the attempt to resolve tensions between various expressive interests the dramatists had as men of their times and the need to achieve satisfactory dramatic form. These expressive interests were primarily interest in story and interest in language. The desire merely to tell a good story, for instance, might conflict with a selective attitude which is either "tragic" or "comic."

The critics were partly aware of these tensions and sought to impose on expressive lawlessness inherited "classical" forms of tragedy and comedy; they made the forms more rigid than their models and drew up rules in an authoritarian spirit. But in their often unconscious misreading of classical theory to favor present habits, they betrayed the presence of these tensions in themselves as well, especially the tension between, on the one hand, the delight of the age in variety and in ornament and, on the other, the need to master larger structural forms. Some of the critics managed to find in Aristotle warrant for abundance of episode, for violent deeds on the stage, even for tragi-comedy.

English dramatists did not so readily adopt the critics' way out as did Italian and French dramatists, but neither did they altogether reject it. In the long run they achieved their own distinctive ways of imposing order, but they did so not without influence from what they understood as classical forms and not without response to the organizing ideas about art that were commonplaces in their time.

This much of preface should make clearer what from the dramatists' point of view the various tensions were. There were tensions between the aim of entertainment and various formal restraints. This aim might be met in a number of ways: in a lively or romantic story, scenes of heightened passion, or scenes of violence; or in comic episodes, witty humor, or horseplay. The formal restraints might be one or more of the following: *a tragic or comic point of view,* which would limit in certain conventional ways the handling of the story; *the idea of decorum,* which forbade the mingling of tragedy and comedy, limited the social class of characters treated, provided for the treatment of characters according to their type, set the styles of speech; *the idea of verisimilitude,* which would affect the conception of character, the use of the supernatural and the fanciful, the handling of historic sources; *belief in the moral aim of drama,* which would demand certain attitudes towards the subject matter, the meting out of proper justice to the characters, the introduction of plenty of sententiousness; *problems of dramatic construction,* demanding coherence in the plot, concentration, and emphasis. There were tensions, besides, between verbal expressiveness (fostered by belief in the persuasive powers of rhetoric, admiration of a highly decorated style, fondness for wit) and the functional restraints that had to be imposed if words were not to run away with the play. And there were various tensions between different kinds of formal restraint, such as that in the handling of character between the Horatian idea of types and some theories of contemporary psychology.

Generalized, the tensions are those which art at any time must solve, of course; they are either between formless impulse and formal restraint, or between different and conflicting formal restraints. The particular impulses and restraints that Elizabethan and Jacobean dramatists were subject to and the means by which they sought to resolve the tensions between them are what we are setting ourselves to discover.

Their great problem was the achievement of unity out of diversity. This, too, is the problem of art at any time. But it had a special acuteness for men of the Renaissance because of their delight in variety and their intense expressiveness in multitudinous ways. Achievement of minor stylistic form came easy, achievement of major structural form came hard. Success in structural form was never very uniformly achieved in English renaissance drama; when it was, it was never at the sacrifice of variety. Elizabethan and Jacobean drama is always a teeming drama.

This is true no less of Jonson's drama than of Shakespeare's. Certainly each solved the problem of achieving unity out of variety in a different way. Jonson did it by exclusion and repetition, Shakespeare by inclusion and complex harmony. In Jonson—Volpone, Voltore, Corvino, Corbaccio, and Mosca; in Shakespeare—Prospero, Miranda, Antonio, Trinculo, Caliban, and Ariel. But within the narrower field of vision selected, Jonson loves variety as much as Shakespeare.[32] (He does not, indeed, always exclude enough to keep his plots clear; *Every Man in his Humour* and the two Roman tragedies fail in emphasis because of unsubordinated detail.) He likes abundance of words, incidents, and characters. Think of the rich gallery of rogues and gulls in *The Alchemist* and *Bartholomew Fair,* of the complicated troubles they get into, and of the ripe and full language they speak! Jonson is fond of one theme, or of two sharply contrasting themes, restated many times and subtly varied in development, but always in closely related keys. Shakespeare is fond of many themes, related but different, and of modulations into many keys.

We are likely to call Jonson's method "classical," Shakespeare's "romantic." If we are careful enough not to make the terms imply too much, they have a certain convenience. But Jonson is classical only in a general sense of strong consciousness of form; the particular form he achieves is distinctly his own. And Shakespeare has likewise a stronger sense of form than has generally been allowed him. Moreover, it is a mistake to see these two as heirs to separable traditions. One cannot simply equate impulse and variety, for instance, with the medieval heritage, and formal restraint with the classical; the relations are far more complicated. Besides, some of the forms most fruitful for the development of English drama came from the Middle Ages (e.g., the pattern of ethical conflict in the morality play), and much of the variety came from the newly realized riches of the classics. Jonson's method of concentration is certainly "classical" in a way Shakespeare's multiple variety is not. But Jonson owed as much to the technique of the morality play as Shakespeare did and probably more; and Shakespeare followed Roman comedy in ways that Jonson early abandoned.

MATERIALS AND PROBLEM 21

FOR CONVENIENCE in analysis and without prejudice to the older
terms of dramatic form (plot, character, etc.), we can restate the
Elizabethan dramatist's problem of achieving form in a set of useful
terms borrowed from modern criticism. In his "Lexicon Rhetoricae,"
included in *Counter-Statement*,[33] Kenneth Burke defines form in
literature as "an arousing and fulfilment of desires"; the reader is
led "to anticipate another part" and "to be gratified by the sequence."
Mr. Burke discusses form under five aspects: syllogistic progression,
qualitative progression, repetitive form, conventional form, and
minor or incidental forms. Syllogistic progression, the form of a
perfectly conducted argument, means in a plot progression of events
in causal relationship. Mr. Burke gives as one of the best examples
of syllogistic progression the peripety, or reversal of the situation,
discussed by Aristotle. Qualitative progression means a sequence
of qualities which induce states of mind that may appropriately follow each other: e.g., "the grotesque seriousness of the murder scene"
in *Macbeth* "preparing us for the grotesque buffoonery of the porter
scene." Repetitive form is the restatement of the same thing in different ways: e.g., a succession of images each evoking the same lyric
mood; "the sustaining of an attitude, as in satire"; "a character repeating his identity"; "the rhythmic regularity of blank verse." Conventional form, involving "the appeal of form as form" (e.g., as in
a sonnet), means in drama expectations of what a tragedy or a
comedy should be. As examples of minor or incidental forms, which
may be discussed as "formal events" in themselves, but whose "effect
partially depends upon their function in the whole," Mr. Burke gives
metaphor, paradox, disclosure, reversal, contraction, expansion,
bathos, apostrophe, series, chiasmus. These, of course, are rhetorical
"figures" in the classical sense, if we include both *tropes,* involving a
change of meaning (metaphor, metonymy, etc.), and *schemes,* involving the patterning either of sentences (*figures of sentence* like
repetition, balance, etc.) or of larger units of discourse (*figures of
thought* like interrogation, description, etc.).[34]

Stated in these terms from the "Lexicon Rhetoricae," how do the
formal problems of Elizabethan dramatists look? The taste of the age
and intensive training in rhetoric combined to give literary men
special interest in minor forms. The Elizabethan drama is always
eloquent. The achievement of major forms was on the whole less
successful.

The conventional dramatic forms of tragedy and comedy inherited from ancient times were modified first by the interpretations of the postclassical grammarians, then by medieval misunderstandings, and finally by renaissance interpretations of the recovered classical drama and classical theory. Other workable conventional forms, notably the morality play, were immediately inherited from the late Middle Ages. Tudor drama used these old conventional forms in the process of developing new forms distinctively its own. Often, considerable hesitation between forms resulted in weakness until a new set of formal expectations could be established. One of the best illustrations of this is in the development of tragi-comedy.

The mastery of syllogistic progression, was, as it must be in drama, the biggest problem—the mastery, that is, of plot so that it should not be merely episodic but should move with causal progression from beginning to middle to end. The crisis plot of classical tragedy proving unattractive, the problem was to develop a satisfactory form out of the chronological "narrative" type of story. The intrigue plot of classical comedy was used more readily, but again with a preference for chronological sequence. Ways of handling dramatic opposition came from the morality play, from the technique of the debate, from revenge on the Senecan pattern.

The problem of repetitive form in character was also an important one. The doctrine of types provided a means of achieving it, but English dramatists followed this doctrine much less consistently than did continental dramatists. Psychological theories of the humours reinforced it, and gave Elizabethan dramatists a means of developing their own repetitive patterns in "humour" comedy. But there were also strong pulls against the doctrine. One came from the theater; the temptation was great to make an immediate effect by a striking scene of violent passion or of repentance at the expense of total consistency of character. Another came from current theories of psychology at variance with humour theories. The belief that one passion drove out another combined with a tendency to view passions as detached from character—that is, a tendency to regard any man as subject, under the proper stimulus, to any passion. Hence, apart from or along with theatrical reasons, the sudden repentances on the Elizabethan stage.

Qualitative progression, because of the fondness for variety, was especially difficult of achievement. The unrelated mingling of tones —raucous horseplay, for instance, in the midst of the gruesome or

the pathetic, or romantic sentiment in the midst of satire—is commonplace. Sidney's protest is right enough; [35] the modern excuse of
"relief" does not suffice to save mere juxtaposition of different qualities from artistic badness. One quality must be handled in such a
way as to make the introduction of a different quality seem right.
One of Shakespeare's chief strengths as a formal artist lies here, I
believe. His achievement of unity from diversity is as much a matter
of adjusting a variety of tones to each other as in dominating the
problems of action and of character.

THE PRESENT BOOK will seek to define and examine the problems of
form that Shakespeare and his fellow dramatists had to face and try
to solve. It will attempt, as has been said, to reconstruct imaginatively
some part of the context of artistic ideas, attitudes, tastes, and interests in which they worked, and to define their problems in the light
of these. The discussion will be centered on Shakespeare's period,
beginning with his immediate predecessors, and ending with the
Jacobeans who were at least starting to write before his death. There
will be presented, first, a set of limiting renaissance attitudes towards
and ideas about literary art generally, then the important ideas about
the drama particularly, and finally, resulting from these, a set of
problems faced by dramatists in writing their plays. The first three
chapters are general. "Eloquence" is treated first because it seems to
be the major defining characteristic of renaissance literature. Next
comes a cluster of related ideas (imitation, verisimilitude, decorum),
followed by the didactic theory of poetry; these ideas are the general
principles in terms of which the Renaissance sees its literary problems. After these general matters come specific problems of the
drama: first, the concepts of kinds of drama, and the conflicts revealed between inherited conventional forms and the development of
new ones; next, problems of character (varying conceptions of character, modes of depiction, techniques of motivation); then, problems
of plot construction (the problem of securing unity without sacrificing the variety the taste of the age demanded, and the problem of
securing coherence in adapting episodic narrative to drama); finally,
the problem of achieving form adequate to meaning—in short, the
problem of successful artistic creation. [36]

2 Eloquence and "Copy"

Now AS speech makes a man more excellent than a beast, so eloquence makes the professors thereof more excellent than other
men. For this is the profession or art of speech: it is a more
exquisite communication of discourse and reason, the stern or
roother [rudder] of our souls, which disposeth the heart and
affections, like certain notes, to make a melodious harmony.
  Eloquence is not only a purity, and elegancy of speech, a discreet choice of words properly applied, ended in a true and a
just fall, but it must likewise be full of ornaments, graces, motions. . . .
                     —PIERRE CHARRON, *De la Sagesse* [1]

THE UNDERSTANDING of renaissance drama requires an understanding of certain renaissance assumptions about art in general and
literary art in particular that in some degree affected all forms of
literary expression. These assumptions are, first, the assumption that
discourse is the outward sign of man's peculiar property, reason,
hence that eloquence should be cultivated both as an educational
discipline and as a literary ideal; secondly, the assumption that art
is representational, hence that it must be judged by carefully formulated standards of verisimilitude and appropriateness; and, thirdly,
the assumption that poetry should be instructive as well as delightful,
indeed that it instructs by means of delight. These assumptions are
familiar enough to anyone at all conversant with renaissance aesthetic
theory, and scholarship is now centering a good deal of attention on
at least the first two matters, the belief in the importance of eloquence
and the imitative theory of art. The contemporary critical bent towards style has made the subject of rhetoric, with its influence on
sixteenth-century style, especially attractive to modern students.
Nevertheless, in order to examine fairly the bearing on the English
drama of these characteristic renaissance assumptions and attitudes,

24

I shall have to take the risk of going over sometimes very familiar ground. It is not self-evident that Shakespeare in learning how to parse and translate Terence in the Stratford grammar school should have made himself a master of English vocabulary and English construction, nor that after often hearing of the commonplace definition of comedy as the imitation of life, the glass of custom, and the image of truth [2] he should have created the world of Arden and Illyria. There is always in the period we are considering a difference between artistic theory and dramatic fact, but it is never one of rebellion or of mere negation. There is usually evidence, on scrutiny, of some sort of complex adjustment between, on the one hand, theoretical assumptions about art, poetry, and drama, and, on the other, the practical frame of traditional dramatic habits, physical stage, and the like, in which the Elizabethan drama was shaped. How this adjustment came about, I am not wise enough to know. But I can at least put assumptions and results together and exhibit them for inspection. In order to let the picture be seen as a whole, with the drama in perspective against its background, I shall have to sketch in the background rather fully, and may, therefore, repeat in this and the next two chapters a good many well-known things about renaissance rhetorical theory, the theory of imitation, and the didactic theory of poetry.

The Ideal of Eloquence

Above all things, the Renaissance is an age of eloquence. But its verbal eloquence is only part of an intense expressiveness that manifests itself in many ways: in dress, in ceremonies of all kinds, in the arts, in the violent expression of emotion, in the readiness to quarrel, in the general turbulence of life.[3] Like its times the drama is first of all eloquent. Even with its not infrequent crudities of motivation and gaucheries of construction, it never stammers for want of words— from the interminable speechifying of Gorboduc's counselors or the horrid reminiscences of Senecan ghosts to the moving eloquence of Faustus' terror in the face of death, the cosmic images of Chapman's heroes, or the salty objurgations of Jonson's "inspired vessel of kitchen-stuff," Ursula the Pig-woman. In exuberance of language, the "disciplined" Jonson plays no poor second to the "spontaneous" Shakespeare. No greater drama of sheer verbal display was ever written than *The Alchemist*. The opening is a high-colored flyting among the three crooks, the trickery is three-quarters verbal hocus-pocus, Sir Epicure Mammon's luxuriant visions, are, alas, realized only in words: a cascade of abracadabra from Doll overwhelms them.

To UNDERSTAND the Elizabethan drama aright we need to see it against the background of rhetoric that is one of the distinctive features of the age. To the Renaissance rhetoric was a discipline, a tool, the expression of an ideal. It formed the central core of human-istic education, it seemed to teach the means of moving men to virtuous ends, it embodied an ideal of the dignity of man. For speech, as the manifestation of reason, was taken as the measure of man's difference from the beasts.

Kynde onto man hath yoven elloquence.[4]

Only man can talk about the magnificent universe that God has created, or about God's purpose for man, or how, through the culti-vation of virtue, he may fulfill it. Quintilian had asked: "Why, there-fore, should we not consider that the special virtue of man lies just as much in eloquence as in reason?" [5] Speech is the great civilizing force. It is given to man, says Lionardi, echoing Cicero, "to be able to point out the useful, the harmful, the just, the unjust, the honest, and the dishonest. From it is born civil life ('la civiltà'), and public and private government." [6] Speech, therefore, is the measure of man's power. For it is through eloquence that men are won to virtue. Again Quintilian: "Nay, even the principles which should guide our life, however fair they may be by nature, yet have greater power to mould the mind to virtue, when the beauty of things is illumined by the splendour of eloquence." [7] Skilful persuasion, indeed, was be-lieved to be irresistible. As Wilson puts it, in his *Art of Rhetoric* (1560):

Such force hath the tongue, and such is the power of eloquence and reason, that most men are forced even to yield in that which most standeth against their will. And therefore the poets do feign, that Hercules being a man of great wisdom, had all men linked together by the ears in a chain, to draw them and lead them even as he lusted.[8]

The cultivation of beauty in discourse, then, is a legitimate means to move men to virtue. Since, to win and hold his hearers, a man must delight them, "every orator," says Wilson again, "should earnestly labour to file his tongue, that his words may slide with ease, and that in his deliveraunce he may have such a grace, as the sound of a lute, or any such instrument doth give."

IT IS EASY to see how this persuasive aim of rhetoric might be transferred to poetry. To Horace's two ends of poetry, to profit and to delight, many renaissance critics added a third, to move. Moving might be thought of as an inevitable accompaniment of the other ends. But to the Renaissance the term had a purposive connotation. It came, apparently, from Cicero's formula for oratory: *docere, delectare, permovere,*[9] and may be found in Pontano, Lionardi, Scaliger, Minturno, Sidney, and Jonson.[10] A very full renaissance treatment on the relation between poetry and oratory occurs in Alessandro Lionardi's *Dialogi della inventione poetica* (Venice, 1554). One of the things he discusses at length [11] is how the poet may move the passions by using such devices of the rhetoricians as diminution, amplification, similitude, comparison, example, conversion, exclamation, prayer, and other kinds and figures of speech. He must know the nature of men and the accidents (logical sense) which arouse them. All this, of course, is ancient lore from Quintilian and Cicero, ultimately based on Aristotle's rhetoric and psychology. The moving is viewed by the academic critics as being in the service of the useful. Minturno's interpretation of the catharsis of tragedy shows this: the business of the tragic poet is "so to speak in verse that he may teach, and delight; and move in such a way as to purge the minds of the spectators of the passions." [12] Although Sidney exalts moving above teaching, nevertheless it is the greater efficacy of poetry than philosophy for teaching that he is seeking to prove:

... that moving is of a higher degree than teaching, it may by this appear, that it is well-nigh both the cause and the effect of teaching. For who will be taught, if he be not moved with desire to be taught, and what so much good doth that teaching bring forth (I speak still of moral doctrine) as that it moveth one to do that which it doth teach? [13]

The moving of men to virtuous action is of course an aim identical with one of the aims of oratory. The assimilation of the ends of oratory and of poetry is well shown in the often repeated fables of Amphion and Orpheus:

. . . it is feigned that Amphion and Orpheus, two poets of the first ages, one of them, to wit Amphion, builded up cities, and reared walls with the stones that came in heaps to the sound of his harp, figuring thereby the mollifying of hard and stony hearts by his sweet and eloquent persuasion. And Orpheus assembled the wild beasts to come in herds to harken to his music, and by that means made them tame, implying thereby how by his discreet and wholesome lessons uttered in harmony and with melodious instruments he brought the rude and savage people to a more civil and orderly life, nothing, as it seemeth, more prevailing or fit to redress and edify the cruel and sturdy courage of man than it.[14]

Occasionally, a critic like Pontano or Fracastoro endeavors to express a more aesthetic conception of poetic eloquence. Castelvetro's bold refusal to see anything but delight as the aim of poetry is well known. To Fracastoro, the poet's eloquence differed from other men's in that theirs was always restricted to one particular end, such as teaching or persuading; whereas the end and function of the poet is

to express himself simply and appropriately on every subject. From this definition it is clear that no one else gifted with the art of eloquence can equal the poet since all the others speak well and appropriately indeed but not simply. For all of them, whatever serves their immediate purpose is enough; the poet alone speaks simply.

But the poet as a poet is inspired by no other aim than simply to express himself well about anything that proposes itself to him. He indeed wishes also to teach and persuade and speak of other things, but, restricted as it were by his aim, he does not develop the matter enough to explain it, but making a different idea for himself, of untrammeled and universal beauty, seeks all the adornments of speech, all the beauties which can be given to it.[15]

Fracastoro has some difficulty in defining "simpliciter bene dicendi" (not of course "speaking well without adornment" but "speaking only well, without other end"), because he can never quite break free of the traditional concepts of teaching and persuading, of imitation and the universal. But it is clear that he is trying to get at a concept which makes beauty of style, in some undefined way appropriate to the subject, the true differentia of the poet. Professor Bundy, in his introduction to Miss Kelso's edition of *Naugerius*, suggests that Fracastoro represents renaissance tastes and aims better than do the more academic critics. His beauty is the beauty of the craftsman: "adequate expression in terms of sense and imagination of the characteristic features of the subject."

THE RENAISSANCE interest in style, then, is not barren. If one is thinking about questions of form, perhaps the most obvious thing to occur to him about the literature of the Renaissance is its neglect of form in the large, its cultivation of form in the small. Texture is opulent; structure is relatively weak. I do not mean that there is any poverty of matter—far from it; but in so far as attention is given to form, and a great deal is, it is more apt to be centered on style than on organization. Think of Rabelais, Ariosto, Spenser, Marlowe. But we must be on our guard against the assumption that interest in rhetoric necessarily means emptiness in content. I make the point because it is easy to equate rhetoric with decadence—quite rightly so with reference to the late Roman period or, perhaps, as De Sanctis does, with reference to Italian literature after the Council of Trent; he says it "was rhetoric, that is to say a lie, the pompous expression of conventional sentiments." [16] But this part of the century is a late stage of the Renaissance in Italy, whereas in England it marks the height of the period. There, interest in style means something very much alive. If we accept the idea that thought and language are only different aspects of the same mental activity, we may perhaps see in the formal features of Elizabethan literature the qualities of Elizabethan thought: e.g., the habit of reasoning by analogy finds its stylistic counterpart in the fondness for the figures of metaphor, simile, and *allegoria;* the fondness for debate in the frequent use of antitheses; the earnestness of life in the hortatory quality of much literature.[17] The Elizabethan interest in style is in part a search for every possible means of persuading men to know the truth and to follow it, in part a search for an adequate response to a most various world.

Even as by the power of the sunbeams, the nature of the root is shewed in the blossom, and the goodness of the sap tasted in the sweetness of the fruit, even so the precious nature and wonderful power of wisdom is by the commendable art and use of eloquence, produced and brought into open light.[18]

This same sense of the relation between richness of expression and the richness of life seems to me what Fracastoro is trying to say, only without Peacham's slight ethical implication. Considering whether ornaments of style are extraneous or essential, he says:

... if columns and peristyles and other things are added to houses, they will be extraneous, for the barest structure will serve the purpose of a house, which is to protect us from storm and cold. But, indeed, if he consider objects as they should be, and look for perfection, these additions will not only not be extraneous but essential. Or ought we to think splendid garments extraneous because poor ones are sufficient. Do you not see that just as perfection and ornament are a real part of the things which nature produces, so they are of the things which art produces? What perfection and beauty are, only the great artists know. And if you take them away from the subject, assuredly you have somehow taken away life itself. Therefore what the painters and the poets add to things for perfection is not extraneous, if we mean by "thing" not the bare object such as common artificers, or those who are controlled and restricted by some purpose, make, but the object perfected and given life.[19]

If an explanation other than the expressive vitality of the age and the intense cultivation of the vernacular [20] is needed for the disproportionate attention to style at the expense of structural form, the one most easily found lies in the particular kind of rhetorical training humanistic education provided for. The place of rhetoric in the Middle Ages and the Renaissance has been much studied of late, and I shall not attempt anything like a summary of so complicated a subject. I shall consider only a few points that illuminate our particular problem.

Education in Rhetoric: Its Emphasis and its Effects

The original aim of education in the Renaissance, as conceived by humanists like Erasmus, Melanchthon, Sturm, Cheke, and Ascham, was a noble one: [21] it was nothing less than to prepare men to use rational discourse and persuasive eloquence in the service of truth and the public good. "Nihil est aliud eloquentia nisi copiose loquens sapientia": [22] eloquence is nothing else but wisdom speaking copiously. The humanists were moved by the great classical treatises: Aristotle's *Rhetoric,* with its lucid analyses of the means of persuasion through argument and through appeal to the emotions; Cicero's *De oratore,* with its eloquent vision of the power of oratory to civilize men; Quintilian's *Institutio oratoria,* with its moral conception of the good orator as a good man, and its humane, sensible attitude toward the teaching of rhetoric. But the orator described by Cicero grew out of the conditions of public life in democratic Athens and republican Rome, and the rhetorical art which he knew reflected actual practice, primarily in forensic debate and political oratory, secondarily in ceremonial speaking. The highly formalized art which was finally developed became, with Latin grammar and a little logic, the substance of an educational program in an undemocratic and politically illiberal age. In Henry's and Elizabeth's England a program designed to turn out moral young Tullys ready with silver-tongued eloquence to make the truth prevail seems to us unreal. In preparing young men to be militant Protestant ministers, or persuasive Jesuits, it was evidently not so. Yet except for sermons, we do not think of the age as one of great public speaking. There were famous debates like Ramus' in defense of his thesis against Aristotle; but these were in the tradition of the medieval disputation,[23] as were university debates generally. We do not think of the age as one of great pleaders, although there were many trials. Contrast the trials of Mary Stuart, Campian, and Essex with the Roman trial of the Catilinian conspiracy, and you will see the measure of the difference in the pleader's importance. Nor do we think of it as an age of great parliamentary debates, although by the end of Elizabeth's reign debates over subsidies and the royal prerogative were preparing the way for the more active parliaments under James.[24] None of the specimen deliberative orations in Wilson's *Art of Rhetoric* is on a political subject. Jonson praised Bacon as an orator,[25] and Bacon was certainly a skilful speaker in parliament and in court; but you have only to compare him with Pericles, Demosthenes, Cicero, Burke, or Lincoln to realize how slight was the political influence he had by virtue of that particular power. We recall that Sidney had to *write* as a prose discourse to Elizabeth what is in form a deliberative oration urging her not to marry Anjou, and that afterwards he deemed it prudent to retire for some months to the country.

The type of oratory Aristotle and Cicero were least concerned with, ceremonial oratory, was most cultivated by the Elizabethans, as it had been by the postclassical rhetoricians. There are many records of funeral orations, of university declamations, of addresses on diplomatic occasions.[26] But one wonders maliciously if ceremonial oratory were not chiefly exercised on occasions of Elizabeth's expensive visits to her nobles and to the two universities. Anyhow, the ceremonial or demonstrative oration tended to put a premium on showy ornament and compliment rather than on solid processes of logical thought. It is interesting that Wilson gives relatively much more attention to demonstrative oratory than does either Cicero or Quintilian.

But the faith was not lost, as might be shown by dozens of illustrations from literature. Puttenham gives us a pleasantly intimate glimpse of Bacon's father:

I have come to the Lord Keeper Sir Nicholas Bacon, and found him sitting in his gallery alone with the works of Quintilian before him; indeed he was a most eloquent man, and of rare learning and wisdom, as ever I knew England to breed.[27]

Daniel states the faith in eloquence in a passage in *Musophilus* (1599):

> Power above powers, O heavenly eloquence,
>   That with the strong rein of commanding words
>   Does manage, guide, and master th'eminence
>   Of men's affections more than all their swords,—
>   Shall we not offer to thy excellence
>   The richest treasure that our wit affords?
>
> .   .   .   .
>
> Or who can tell for what great work in hand
>   The greatness of our style is now ordained?
>   What powers it shall bring in, what spirits command,
>   What thoughts let out, what humors keep restrained,
>   What mischief it may powerfully withstand,
>   And what fair ends may thereby be attained?[28]

Consider the prominent place in the determination of policy given to deliberative and forensic oratory in the *Arcadia*. Perhaps we should not dismiss this as a poor substitute for the real thing. Perhaps education in rhetoric was less unreal than it seems to us, since it was one of the tools of that expressiveness that so informs Elizabethan life. Nor was the spirit of the humanists' vision lost if the training they prescribed helped produce such men as Sidney, Hooker, and Bacon.

IN PRACTICAL education, however, the humanistic ideal was seldom fully carried out. As will appear in the course of the following pages, what the schools actually taught fell far short of the program laid down in the *Institutes* of Quintilian. It is perhaps inevitable that it should have done so, and that rhetoric should have found its way, for the most part, into other channels than those for which it was originally shaped. Sermons, of course, were a most important channel. Letter-writing was another. This had likewise been an outlet for rhetoric in the Middle Ages, when the *ars dictaminis* had been much cultivated; so was it in the sixteenth century, as the great epistolary activity of the humanists and the number of manuals on letter-writing show. The amazing thing is to observe, in some manual like Angel Day's *English Secretary* (1586, etc.), how the divisions and patterns of oratory have been clamped down on an activity so essentially different: letters are divided into judicial, deliberative, and demonstrative; they are to contain as many of the traditional parts (exordium, narratio, propositio, etc.) as are necessary; they are to be eloquent with the figures of word and of sentence. Some few escaped this Procrustean bed through the omnibus classification of "familiar letters." Written composition in general became an outlet for rhetoric, as it no doubt had always been to a greater or less extent. Cicero had discussed the prose style of historians and of philosophers along with that of orators.

Since much of the art is applicable to either spoken or written discourse, such a shift in itself is natural, unobjectionable, and inevitable. But to see a poet's problems, dramatic, epic, or lyric, primarily in terms of the three kinds of oration and their parts, as Lionardi does in his first dialogue on poetic invention, is simply to court confusion. Erasmus remarked: "What especially delights me is a rhetorical poem and a poetical oration, in which you can see the poetry in the prose and the rhetorical expression in the poetry." [29] In school texts, such as those of Terence, the accompanying commentaries, when provided, are either moral or rhetorical, or both. Melanchthon's brief analyses of the plays of Terence, appended to Erasmus' edition of 1534,[30] are a good example. For four of the comedies he gives, besides a summary of the action, a comment on the moral implications of the play and one on its rhetorical type; *Andria*, for instance, full of consultations, consists almost wholly in the deliberative type, *Eunuchus*, in which there is more expostulation and accusation, chiefly in the judicial. R. B.'s *Terence in English* (Cambridge, 1598) is another interesting school edition, containing Latin and English text, the argument scene by scene in both languages, marginal annotations beside the Latin text on rhetorical matters, moral reflections on nearly every scene, *formulae loquendi* (Latin phrases from the text, with translation), and *sententiae* (sometimes from the text, sometimes just suggested by it). More elaborate commentaries, with detailed analyses of rhetorical effects, like the ancient commentary of Donatus or the humanistic one of Willichius,[31] would almost certainly have been used by university trained masters if not by grammar-school students themselves. None of the renaissance critics, not even the rather independent Giraldi, himself a playwright, or Sidney, a literary amateur, ever quite frees himself of the terms developed specifically for ancient oratory. Perhaps that is one of the reasons why style came to be emphasized at the expense of "invention" (the finding and conduct of arguments) and "disposition" (organization); it was so obviously hard to make the structural form fit a different type of discourse, so easy to deal with the minor forms in common terms. Here we see, then, how the cultivation of rhetoric tended towards that emphasis in Elizabethan literature we are considering.

SEVERAL other aspects of the cultivation of rhetoric during the century seem to me to tend in the same direction, towards a disproportionate emphasis on style. Two certainly do—the inheritance from the Middle Ages and Ciceronianism; and a third, Ramism, might unintentionally sometimes have that effect.

THE SOPHISTIC TRADITION

First, for the inheritance from the Middle Ages. The story of the sophistic tradition of rhetoric, which continued unbroken down into the sixteenth century, is too well known to be repeated.[32] Because, during the Middle Ages, rhetoric could hardly be exercised in its original function, it had taken certain specialized directions, just as it was to do in the Renaissance, in the *ars dictaminis* (mainly applied to official letters) and in the *ars praedicandi*. But aside from these, its concern was mainly with style. Since the ornaments of style might be the same in poetry as in prose, this concern led to a confusion of rhetoric with poetic: poetic came to be regarded as versified rhetoric and rhetoric as inclusive of poetic. Medieval *Po-*

etics, like those of Geoffrey of Vinsauf (1208–13), well known to Chaucer, were primarily applications to poetry of rhetorical techniques such as *dispositio* (here, methods of beginning and ending a poem) and *elocutio* (here, mainly stylistic ornament). The flourishing of the vernacular in the fourteenth and fifteenth centuries was one of the influences leading to a heightened interest in rhetoric in the fifteenth century. The aureate style was cultivated both in English and in Latin. Chaucer, who because of his ridicule of the "hauteyn" manner might not have appreciated the compliment, was praised as "the fader and founder of ornate eloquence"; and Lydgate, who cultivated ornateness, was valued for "his colours freshe on every side" and his "depured rethoryke." The Renaissance, in emphasizing style as the primary formal element in both prose and verse, in valuing an aureate style above other kinds, and in frequently treating poetry as versified oratory, was in part, therefore, only continuing a very old tradition. It revived, moreover, various textbooks of the sophistic tradition: grammars like those of Donatus, Diomedes, and Priscian; rhetorics like those of Hermogenes and Aphthonius.

The medieval conception of rhetoric as primarily stylistic decoration is revealed in a favorite representation of Dame Rhetoric that had long currency. Martianus Capella in his *De nuptiis* (ca. 410–27) had depicted Rhetorica allegorically as one of the seven handmaids presented by Mercury to his bride, Philologica. Rhetorica is a stately woman, handsomely armed and robed. Her garments are embroidered with all the figures of speech, her jewels are the "colors" of rhetoric. She enters to the blare of trumpets, and as she moves her accoutrements clash like thunder.[33] Dame Rhetoric, so represented, is a familiar figure down into the sixteenth century. She appears, for example, in the anonymous *Court of Sapience* (fifteenth century) and in Stephen Hawes's *Pastime of Pleasure* (1509). In Hawes's poem one of the things Rhetoric shows the poet is the "redolent well of famous poetry" from which spring four rivers, one of which is Carbuncles (the brilliant "colors" of style), shining fair in the dark night:

> Amyddes of whom the toure is so goodly
> Of Vyrgyll standeth most solacyous,
> Where he is entered in stones precyous.[34]

Praise of Virgil in similar terms appears in a little treatise by Domenico Delfino in the medieval encyclopaedic tradition (*Sommario di tutte le scienze,* Venice, 1556). His Rhetorica is a "donzella" less sharp intellectually than Logic, but more immediately impressive in manner and appearance. She is richly clothed, her golden hair is elaborately dressed, her face is rosy (falsely so, one sees on closer inspection), her words are delightful to hear, her gestures and expressions are strongly emotional; on the hem of her robe she carries the words "Ornatus" and "Persuasio." Although Delfino follows good humanist tradition in attributing to her, by virtue of her power over speech, a great civilizing force, he cannot shake the more superficial conception. Together with the ancient rhetoricians and orators depicted on the walls of her house are the poets; the greatest, Virgil, so much excels the other poets in his florid style that he seems like a parrot, adorned in his fine feathers, standing out among the other birds.[34a]

Ronsard is speaking in the same tradition when he says:

Elocution n'est autre chose qu'une propriété et splendeur de parolles bien choisies et ornées de graves et courtes sentences, qui font reluire les vers comme les pierres précieuses bien enchassées les doigts de quelque grand seigneur.[35]

CICERONIANISM

The second influence tending towards this excessive interest in style was the cultivation of Ciceronianism as a humanistic ideal. The fresh stimulus from the classics did not bring with it generally a return to the emphasis on thought and structure characteristic of the best classical rhetorics. Except by the early humanists, Aristotle seems not to have been much read at first hand. It is perhaps not a sign of neglect in England that although a number of Latin editions of the *Rhetoric* were published on the continent during the century, none was published in England until 1619, and that no English translation was published until 1686; for editions of the classics, generally, came from the continent. But other indications point to the neglect of the *Rhetoric*. Precise knowledge of it shown in the rhetorical treatises of the century is rare.[36] In spite of ideal educational schemes like those of Vives (1523–24), and of Laurence Humphrey (1560), one would hardly expect the book to appear in the grammar-

school curriculum, and it does not, in any of the numerous grammar-
school courses of study Professor Baldwin has found. One *would*
expect to find it in the university, but though it appears in various
college statutes, it is only permissive, not prescriptive.[37] John Rainolds' lectures at Oxford on the *Rhetoric* appear to have dealt chiefly
with textual exposition, not with rhetorical theory. If his emphasis
can be judged by his *Oratio in laudem artis poeticae,* it must have
missed the spirit of the *Rhetoric* entirely. In the *Oratio* Rainolds
speaks of rhetoric, in the tone of denigration found in Plato's *Gorgias*
(and repeated by humanists like Vives and Agrippa), as an art of
empty and deceptive ornamentation.[38] Edward VI and Elizabeth
did not escape the *Rhetoric,* but their education, directly adminis-
tered by ardent humanists like Cheke, Cox, Grindal, and Ascham,
is hardly typical. Sidney's interest in it, which led him, if John
Hoskins is right, to make a partial translation of it,[39] seems to be
indicative more of his own inquiring mind than of a general use of
the *Rhetoric.* At any rate little of its emphasis on the rational processes of persuasion, with its examination of different degrees of
probable truth, appears in the actual rhetorical training of the century. A reassertion of that emphasis had to wait for Bacon.

Cicero was on the whole more congenial to the Renaissance than
Aristotle. But the Renaissance, in valuing him chiefly for his praise
and his use of "Asiatic" eloquence (the aureate or grand style),
somewhat distorted his position. He always recognized style as a
living expression of ideas and feelings, never thought of it as ornament to be cultivated for its own sake: "But in oratory as in most
matters nature has contrived with incredible skill that the things
possessing most utility also have the greatest amount of dignity, and
indeed frequently of beauty also." As an example he describes the
structure of the universe in Ptolemaic terms and then observes:

This system is so powerful that a slight modification of it would make it
impossible for it to hold together, and it is so beautiful that no lovelier
vision is even imaginable. Now carry your mind to the form and figure
of human beings or even of the other living creatures: you will discover
that the body has no part added to its structure that is superfluous, and
that its whole shape has the perfection of a work of art and not of accident.[40]

And so through the rest of the memorable passage in which he points
out the beauty of structure of human beings, trees, ships, temples:

"In temples and colonnades the pillars are to support the structure, yet they are as dignified in appearance as they are useful." The same is true of a speech: "virtually unavoidable practical requirements produce charm of style as a result." Moreover, of the three styles (the plain or Attic; the middle—polished, but charming rather than vigorous; the grand or Asiatic—so-called because developed by Alexandrian and Rhodian rhetoricians), he did not give exclusive place to the grand style. The plain style was for proof, the middle for pleasure, the grand for persuasion.[41] Hence, one might begin a speech in the middle style, "sweet, fluent, copious . . . with bright conceits and sounding phrases" to win the good will of the audience, present the arguments in plain style, and rise in the conclusion to the grand style, rich with the figures of prosopopeia, apostrophe, and the like, in order to move the auditors to pity or to anger. But the choice of style would vary with the theme, the line of thought, the temper of the audience. An orator of the grand style must train himself in other styles. Against those like Brutus who would restrict the term "Attic" to the plain style, he appealed to the practice of Demosthenes, surely an Attic, who used all three. One wonders how much the *De oratore,* the *Brutus,* and the *Orator* were read in the sixteenth century; they appear only occasionally among the books named in the grammar-school curricula, whereas the *De inventione,* the *Topica,* and the pseudo-Ciceronian *Rhetorica ad Herennium* (all schematized textbooks) are common. Even in the universities, lectures on Cicero's mature oratorical works seem, like those on Aristotle's *Rhetoric,* to have been permissive rather than prescriptive; there is no way of knowing how often or how well the permission was followed. Certainly renaissance Ciceronianism was linked with preference for an Asiatic floridity of style. In the actual practice of Latin composition, where Cicero was the constant model, one would suspect that the culling out for future use of moral sentences, apt similitudes, and striking examples of the colors of rhetoric, would lead to an exaggerated emphasis on style at the expense of organization.

The third of the great classical rhetorics was Quintilian's. The *Institutes,* not as often named among school books as the *De inventione* or the *Rhetorica ad Herennium,* but everywhere thought of as a perfect rhetoric and apparently widely known, supplied an elaborate treatment for every detail of rhetoric: the three kinds of oratory, the parts of an oration, the topics or places to be developed and the methods of development, the several styles and the various tropes and figures; yet Quintilian, in his amiable, sensible way, despised formalism and was always warning against it. One doubts that John Lyly's schoolmasters heeded his spirit.

What Cicero and Quintilian meant to the Renaissance is seen in Thomas Wilson's *Art of Rhetoric* (revised edition, 1560), the most popular English rhetoric in this older tradition. Like them he sees rhetoric as a complete and independent art of persuasion. The "places," or lines of argument, common to it and logic, are not, however, examined in detail; the reader is simply reminded that he must know them. Persuasion is more by emotional than by rational appeal. More space is given to examples of orations than to analysis, which is presented briefly and systematically. And there is a shift in emphasis. The demonstrative, or ceremonial, oration, only lightly touched on by Cicero and Quintilian, is treated at length; the judicial or forensic oration, the most important type in the early treatises, is dealt with rather summarily; the deliberative oration, most useful for politics, is limited to private persuasion and exhortation. Elocution or style, which "with such beauty commendeth the matter, that reason seemeth to be clad in purple, walking afore both bare and naked," gets full consideration.

Leonard Cox's *Art or Craft of Rhetoric* (1524), from Melanchthon, is the only other English rhetoric published during the century in the tradition of the classical rhetorics, and it contains only invention. The other English rhetorics are either revivals of the late sophistic tradition (e.g., Richard Rainolde's *Foundation of Rhetoric,* 1563), or are merely handbooks of style. This latter is true whether they only give lists of figures after the pattern of the old manuals of Mosellanus and Susenbrotus still widely used in grammar schools, or whether they are new Ramist rhetorics. The principal handbooks of figures are Richard Sherry's *Treatise of Schemes and Tropes* (1550), his *Treatise of the Figures of Grammar and Rhetoric* (1555), and Henry Peacham's *Garden of Eloquence* (1577; revised 1593); the principal Ramist rhetorics are Dudley Fenner's *Art of . . . Rhetoric* (1584) and Abraham Fraunce's *Arcadian Rhetoric* (1588). The spirit of Capella's Rhetorica still walks in all these manuals.

Saturated with the formalism of the rhetorics and with such pane-
gyrics on style, a reader finds Montaigne's disparagement of Cicero
something of a tonic. Montaigne thinks Cicero's prefaces, definitions,
partitions, etymologies, before coming to the point, tiresome: "la
plus part du temps je n'y trouve que du vent." [42] Bacon, too, makes a
return to the classic spirit; he views rhetoric as a complete and independent art of public address, and he puts the whole weight of his
consideration on the handling of ideas rather than on style.[43] Even
before Bacon, Sidney seems to have understood Aristotle's *Rhetoric*
as few of his contemporaries did, and to have made an attempt, at
least partially successful, to return in his own writing to its emphasis
on thought and organization.[44] But in spite of a number of protests
by various men against the excesses of rhetoric, Montaigne is not
speaking in the loud voice of the century. The protesters are themselves not always to be looked to for unadorned simplicity and clarity
of statement: witness Nashe and Harvey, in both of whom much of
the fun is in the outrageous verbal variations on the theme of abuse
of each other's excesses. Indeed, Harvey's chief quarrel with Nashe
is that he overthrows the traditional eloquence ("fair rhetoric") of
the schools to substitute something worse:

I have seldom read a more garish and pibald style in any scribbling Ink-
hornist, or tasted a more unsavoury slaumpaump of words and sentences
in any sluttish Pamphleter that denounceth not defiance against the rules
of Oratory and the directions of the English Secretary: which may here
and there stumble upon some tolerable sentence, neighbourly borrowed,
or featly picked out of some fresh Pamphlet, but shall never find three
sentences together worth any allowance; and as for a fine or neat period,
in the dainty and pithy vein of Isocrates or Xenophon, marry, that were
a periwig of a Siren, or a wing of the very bird of Arabia, an inestimable
relic. Tush, a point: neither curious Hermogenes, nor trim Isocrates,
nor stately Demosthenes, are for his tooth, nor painting Tully, nor carv-
ing Caesar, nor purple-dyeing Livy for his humour. It is for Cheke or
Ascham to stand leveling of Colons, or squaring of Periods, by measure
and number: his pen is like a spigot, and the Wine-press a dullard to his
Ink-press. . . . The wit of this and that odd Modernist is their own; and
no such mineral of richest Art as pregnant Nature, the plentifulest womb
of rare Invention, and exquisite Elocution. Whist Art! and Nature advance thy precious Self in thy most gorgeous and magnificent robes! [45]

A "natural" style could be as showy as an "artificial" one, and was less
apt, Harvey thought, to show taste and judgment.

RAMUS

Finally, in the consideration of these influences seeming to make for emphasis on style, we come to Ramus. It is easier to describe what Ramus did to rhetoric than to assess the effect of what he did. Yet even accurate description is not easy. It is only a partial truth, and hence misleading, to say that he handed over to logic invention (the finding of arguments), disposition (the arrangement of material), and memory, leaving to rhetoric only style and, as a nonessential appendage, delivery. For his "invention" and "disposition," in being assimilated to logic, are not what they were in classical rhetoric. Nor is his "elocution," or style, the same. In Aristotle's treatment of the two arts of logic and rhetoric, each, though with some necessary duplication, was self-contained, since each had a function of its own: for logic, the investigation of truth, whether demonstrable or probable; for rhetoric, the persuasion of men to action through an appeal primarily to probable truth, secondarily to their emotions. In the shift and the changes Ramus made, much of rhetoric as anciently conceived (especially the detailed consideration of probability) disappeared altogether. No self-sustaining art of rhetoric was left. In constructing prose discourse according to his system one must take what one needed from the other arts and sciences: thought and method from logic, psychology from natural philosophy, questions of right and wrong from moral philosophy. What one could now get from "rhetoric" was only stylistic ornament. For *elocutio,* alone with delivery left to rhetoric, was deprived of considerations of correctness, clarity, and appropriateness, and was simplified to consist only of the ornaments of style. A consideration of prose rhythm had been common in classical rhetorics; to this the Ramus-inspired rhetoric of Talaeus [46] added (under figures of diction) a discussion of metrics, and so contributed further to the confusing idea that poetry was but versified oratory. One effect of these changes was to lose Aristotle's precise distinction between logic and rhetoric and to run them together as a practical art of argumentation. Another was to sheer rhetoric *per se* of its *raison d'être;* the residue permitted to it was left without functional relationship to thought. Logic found and arranged the material; rhetoric added pleasing ornament. [47]

The question pertinent to our problem is what was the total effect of Ramus' system on conceptions of style. The difficulty in answering it lies in the ambiguous implications of the system itself. On the one hand, Ramus declared that his concern was primarily with dialectic, "art général pour inventer et juger toutes choses," and naturally operative in all discourse. He took his examples as well from poetry and oratory as from philosophy.

Pour avoir le vray loz de logique, n'est pas assez de sçavoir caqueter en l'eschole des reigles d'icelle, mais il les fault et practiquer es poëtes, orateurs, philosophes, c'est-à-dire toute espèce d'esprit.[48]

The conclusion has been drawn from this fact that writers trained in Ramist logic would find their images in a search for logical "places": comparison, adjuncts, formal or material cause, and the like, and that their imagery would then presumably be logically functional. This is a debatable point, and I shall not enter into controversy here. On the other hand, the precise statement in the rhetoric Ramus sponsored and in the rhetorics derivative from his system is that style is ornament. The *Rhetorica* of Talaeus or Omer Talon, Ramus' alter ego, begins with Quintilian's definition, but with a different implication. "Rhetorica est ars bene dicendi": rhetoric is the art of speaking well. Quintilian, as the whole tenor of his treatise shows, meant to imply that only a good man could speak well; *ars bene dicendi* seemed to him a larger definition than the art of persuasion. To Ramus, *bene dicendi* is merely a contrast to *bene disserendi,* or disputing well, the end of dialectic. Talaeus says that Plato, angry with the Greek sophists and rhetoricians, had called rhetoric "a kind of trade of cookery (*obsonandi*), face-painting or cosmetic art (*fucandi*), fawning (*adulandi*), or bewitching (*incantandi*)"; and indeed "there is no kind of seasoning, of face-paint, of flattery, or of spell by which rude and uninformed auditors may more easily be led than by rhetorical ornaments accommodated to a fitting idea." [49] Style is the ornament of speech, and tropes are the chief seasonings of it, the chief cosmetics. The Ramistic rhetorics in English carry the same burden. To Fenner elocution is the "garnishing of speech," to Fraunce it is "bravery of speech." Since these little books contain nothing but elocution and delivery, and since elocution comprises nothing but tropes and figures, they would seem, like Sherry and Peacham, to invite the cultivation of style primarily as ornament.

On the one hand, judging from the Puritan preachers trained in it, Ramist logic promoted a plain style;[50] on the other, by giving style an independent and rather debased existence as a mere "cosmetic" art, Ramist rhetoric touched hands with the medieval rhetorical heritage. In any case, content and form appear to have been conceived of as separate.

LET US TRY to draw together the threads of this discourse before turning to a particular rhetorical ideal especially illuminating to the drama. Linguistic fecundity, shown in the intense cultivation of the vernacular tongues all over Europe during the Renaissance, was perhaps just one aspect of a general artistic fecundity. In any case, the interest in eloquence promoted the cultivation of rhetoric, which in turn promoted eloquence, or at least furnished particular modes in which eloquence might be realized. The revived ideal of Roman rhetoric, as a complete discipline and as a tool in the service of the good life, imported into such a different society did not fulfill itself. The practice of rhetoric was colored by the medieval attitude—itself a heritage from decadent post-classical times—towards rhetoric as primarily concerned with the gorgeous accoutrements of style. The transfer of a ready-made pattern for formal oral discourse to other types of discourse more vital than oratory in the sixteenth century was natural enough; but the difficulty of making the transfer perhaps tended to an emphasis on style as the element most clearly in common. Further, the revived interest in classical rhetoric, because it was centered on a not too well understood Cicero, joined hands with the medieval tradition in promoting the cultivation of style at the expense of structural form. The implications of Ramus' reform are, as I have said, ambiguous.

It is important to insist, however, that the preoccupation with style was not in Elizabethan England any sign of flagging creative power. The extraordinary vitality with which the dry formulae of rhetoric were converted into fruitful uses raises the question of whether formulated theory was ever quite adequate to the best literary practice. There is no simple answer. Suggestions of a concept of style which recognizes it as organically functional appear occasionally in critical theory, but the decorative concept is far more common.

Giraldi seems to have got hold of an idea of organic function when he defines *energeia* as the perfect fitness of expression to matter.[51] Fracastoro appears to be trying to phrase such a concept in his making beautiful and "absolute" expression the special attribute of the poet, and in his using the Ciceronian analogy of the colonnaded temple to show that the beauty of the building (or poem) is somehow intrinsic, not extrinsic.[52] The idea of speech as the simulacrum of the mind is not infrequent.[53] Puttenham enlarges on it with apparent acumen in his chapter on style. It is, he says, the image of man, *mentis character,*

for man is but his mind, and as his mind is tempered and qualified, so are his speeches and language at large, and his inward conceits be the metal of his mind, and his manner of utterance the very warp and woof of his conceits, more plain, or busy and intricate, or otherwise affected after the rate.[54]

But this discussion comes immediately after several passages on style as "exornation," the familiar conception of it as "pearl or passements of gold upon the stuff of the princely garment," or as "rich and orient colours" laid upon a portrait. Puttenham shows no awareness of having got hold of a fundamentally different notion. The same thing happens in Giraldi, whose perceptive passage on *energeia* follows a discussion of style as the *skin* (not the soul) of the organism which is the poem; the skin is visible beauty, but it cannot be said to be the informing principle of the body.

The idea of stylistic decorum, that is of appropriateness of manner to matter, is everywhere insisted on, but precisely what that doctrine implies as to the process of composition is a matter of dispute. Is it, as has been argued, a fully grasped theory of the organic function of style,[55] or is it simply a theory of decorative appropriateness—the idea that a humble subject requires a plain style, an elevated subject an ornate style? Is the familiar metaphor of style as a garment to be interpreted in the same sense as the similar metaphor of the soul as the garment of the body—that is, as the informing principle? Or is it to be taken simply to mean the decent and fit clothing of the body of thought? The crucial point to be decided is whether composition is conceived of as a complex process, in which style gives form to the thought, or as a compound one, in which matter is "found" and "disposed" and then set forth in an appropriate style? Again, probably no single answer can be given. The sophistic tradition in rhetoric rested on a theory of disjunction between the logical processes of thought on the one hand and the eloquent ornamentation of it on the other; and the multiplication, in the Elizabethan period, of the manuals of style, while Aristotelian rhetoric went relatively unregarded, testifies to the force of that tradition. The idea of disjunction in operation is implicit in the many comparisons of figures of speech to cosmetics, to condiments, to jewels sewn upon a garment. Comparisons to painting sometimes show the same conception of separable operations; a portrait is drawn and the colors are then laid on.[56] On the other hand, there are to be found passages like those in Sidney which deplore the superficial laying on of the "colors" of rhetoric and suggest some apprehension of the functional relation of style to thought.[57] But it is interesting to note that in trying to arrive at the way in which the style of a poem is expressive of its inner quality, Fracastoro distinguishes this quality of being beautiful *simpliciter,* or absolutely, from being beautiful appropriately, that is as following decorum; [58] he must have felt the distinction to be necessary because of the inadequacy of the concept of decorum as ordinarily used. My own impression is that a truly organic concept of style— one that we can surely understand as such—appears only fitfully in the critics, and that much of the time they appear to mean by decorum simply decorative appropriateness. Certainly the concept of decoration prevails in explicit statement. Or they may set down side by side, in unresolved and unnoticed conflict, two fundamentally different conceptions of the artistic process.

Nevertheless, I would not prejudice judgment against the ornamentation the critics call for by labeling it "mere" ornamentation. The decorative concept as entertained in the Renaissance is, as must be emphasized, no sign of an anaemic aestheticism. Decoration gives delight, and delight is most often regarded as a means of persuasion in the service of the moral end of poetry. Poets, says Sidney,

do merely make to imitate, and imitate both to delight and teach, and delight to move men to take that goodness in hand, which without delight they would fly as from a stranger, and teach to make them know that goodness whereunto they are moved.[59]

Perhaps more revelatory of unconscious attitudes than any such justifying theory is the excitement with which delight is generally discussed, an excitement which betrays the deeply vital root of the interest in it. In a passage which is typical of many to be found in the critics, Peacham says that the "figures and forms of speech are stars to give light, as cordials to comfort, as harmony to delight, as pitiful spectacles to move passions, and as orient colours to beautify reason." [60] Verbal proliferation was a form of vitality.

"Copy" of Words and Things

As one would expect, the prevalent ideal of style was copiousness. Fluency and variety as ideals of speech are natural extensions of the ideal of eloquence. However much Euphuism, Arcadianism, and Nashe's tumbling prose style differ among themselves in sentence patterns, in images, in figures of thought and in ornamental schemes —however much Marlowe's sonorous verse differs from the farced bombast of the translators of Seneca on the one hand, and from the subtly modulated verse of the mature Shakespeare on the other— all these styles are alike in verbal exuberance. A line of homely prose runs throughout the period in places like Deloney's prose tales, in Greene's and Harman's journalistic pamphlets on the habits of rogues, in some of the sermons, in many of the realistic comedies. But even those writers who are less ornate are likely to be just as copious. Among the greater literary figures Bacon, with his terse "Attic" style, is exceptional.[61] A sermon not good for at least a couple of hours was a meager thing indeed. Words come in pairs, for if one is good, two must be twice as good. They come in baker's dozens and in long tons.

That the taste was something wider than that given literary expression is suggested by the proliferation of detail in late medieval and renaissance graphic and plastic art: in fifteenth- and sixteenth-century illuminations, especially in ornamental initials and borders; in woodcuts, drawings, and engravings like Dürer's; in the elaborate window traceries, capitals, bosses, screens, tympana and other carved work of late Gothic architecture. Nor was profuseness altogether new in the sixteenth century as an ideal of literary art. Recall the *longueurs* of the romances, with their repetitions and their catalogues. Even a writer with so firm a structural sense as Chaucer liked amplitude and minutiae: consider the descriptive embroideries of the *Knight's*

Tale, the lengthily digressive discursus on dreams by Chauntecleer, the detailed analyses of sentiment in *Troilus and Criseyde*.

WE CAN HAVE no doubt, however, that renaissance rhetorical education gave fullness of style a fresh impetus. For copiousness was a persistent ideal of that education, and all the training tended to develop it. Whether an Elizabethan schoolboy ever used Cicero's or Quintilian's oratorical treatises or not, he was sure to work with Aphthonius and with Erasmus' *De copia.*

The regulations for grammar schools usually prescribe the use of Aphthonius [62] in one of the upper forms, when the boys were ready for work in declamation. Aphthonius gives fourteen minor types of oration, with examples of each. The boys use these examples as models for their own themes. The *chreia,* a discursus on a saying or deed of some famous person on an occasion, seems to have been oftenest prescribed. The interesting thing to observe here is that Lorichius, in a pamphlet supplementary to his first edition of Aphthonius (1537), showed how a *chreia* could be expanded to four times its size, and how a fable might be told in nine different ways. An English adaptation of Lorichius by Richard Rainolde (*The Foundation of Rhetoric,* 1563) carried this exercise in dilation still further; he wrote a theme on Aphthonius' fable of the ant and the grasshopper thirty times as long as the original.[63]

Erasmus' *De duplici copia verborum et rerum* (1511) was also universally required as a text in rhetoric; the aim of the book, as the title suggests, was to exercise the student in copiousness both of words and of matter. Although the author begins with a warning against a futile and deformed loquacity which obscures sense and burdens the ears of the listeners, it is a warning only against an abuse of what he considers a divine virtue: "nothing is more admirable or more magnificent than speech abounding in a full measure of thoughts and words, like a golden stream." [64] He relates with admiration how Apuleius both diminished and extended Aesop's fable of the fox and the crow, and how Cicero and Roscius were accustomed to argue which one could achieve more variety in the same *sententia* or aphorism, the former by words, the latter by gestures. Nothing is more to be feared than the ugly and tiresome vice of tautology or than the tedium we shall bring on our miserable hearers if we hesitate and stammer out the same words like children.

And he follows Quintilian in thinking that *luxuries* or prodigality of speech should not be feared in a child, for judgment and age will correct and restrain it; but thinness and poverty of wit ("tenuitas atque inopia") can in no wise be cured. Quintilian had said,

Exuberance is easily remedied, but barrenness is incurable, be your efforts what they may. To my mind the boy who gives least promise is one in whom the critical faculty develops in advance of the imagination. I like to see the first fruits of the mind copious to excess and almost extravagant in their profusion.[65]

Nature herself, Erasmus says, rejoices in variety; as the eyes are better held by the sight of diverse things, so the mind looks about as if searching for something new. Therefore, to avoid tedium one must change a sentence into many forms, "quam Proteus ipse se transformasse dicitur"—as Proteus is said to have transformed himself. Even if one wants to use a laconic style, he needs to practise varying. For no one can better achieve brevity and compression in his speech than he who knows what words and figures to choose from among a great variety. The student, therefore, should learn to vary a theme by constant practice: first once, then twice, then thrice, then oftener, until finally he can vary it a hundred or even two hundred times. He should paraphrase his reading, should turn poems into prose, and prose into verse, should store in memory and imitate the figures of writers who like Cicero, Aulus Gellius, and Apuleius excel in copious language ("copia dicendi").

The *De copia* is really a handbook to assist in this process of learning to vary. The first book, *De copia verborum,* treats of such means of varying as synonyms, enallages (alterations of sentences so as to change one part of speech to another or one case, tense, etc. to another), various tropes and figures of speech, and numberless formulae of connection, transition, cause, negation, distribution, prohibition, emendation, affirmation, etc. The second part, *De copia rerum,* treats of the heaping up, dilation, and amplification of arguments; of description, examples, *sententiae,* apologues, and so on. Many of the chapters in the book are simply lists of variant expressions under one heading or sentence: "Tuae litterae me magnopere delectarunt" and "Semper dum vivam, tui meminero" are varied an uncounted number of times; one guesses Erasmus' own aim of two hundred is fully achieved. Students could use the book, therefore, as a thesaurus in the composing of their Latin themes. There is abundant evidence that the other collections by Erasmus (*Similia, Apophthegmata, Adagia, Colloquia*) and the English commonplace books, often based on Erasmus, of Taverner, Udall, Baldwin, Palfreyman, and the rest, were so used.[66] Laurentius Valla's *Elegantiae,* a collection of Latin expressions making distinction between elegant and inelegant usage, was frequently prescribed in grammar school curricula; Erasmus also published it in a simplified form.

THE TREATMENT in Elizabethan rhetorics of the figure of amplification is indicative of the interest in "copy" of style. Although this meant strictly an augmentation or heightening of effect (*augendi* is Cicero's word) and was usually paired with its opposite, diminution, in effect it was often used synonymously with copiousness. For some of the means of amplification—comparison, example, description, repetition, periphrasis, digression—inevitably led to expansion of the theme. Although Wilson gives dilation as only one of the means of amplification ("examples enriched by copy help much for amplification"), he tends to assimilate the two in a statement like this: "Amplifying of the matter consisteth in heaping and enlarging of those places, which serveth for confirmation of a matter." And he says, "Yea, words that fill the mouth and have a sound with them, set forth a matter very well. And sometimes words twice spoken, make the matter appear greater." [67]

"Invention" often was used to mean, not merely cleverness in constructing arguments, but also dexterity in amplifying. Day thus defines invention:

. . . wherein plentifully is searched and considered what kind of matter, how much variety of sentences, what sorts of figures, how many similitudes, what approbations, diminutions, insinuations and circumstances are presently needful, or furthering to the matter in handling.[68]

When we know that writers had such training, we should not wonder at the punning changes played on words, at the constant synonymous variation of phrases, at the heaping up of detail, at the multiplication of epithets, at the elaborateness of descriptive pictures, at the fondness for figures of iteration, of analysis, of analogy or illustration, or at any feast of languages to which we may be treated.

"Copy" of style, as labored by Erasmus, seems to us dreary and trivial pedantry, and Shakespeare makes merry with it in the scraps Holofernes has stolen:

Novi hominem tanquam te: his humour is lofty, his discourse peremptory, his tongue filed, his eye ambitious, his gait majestical, and his general behavior vain, ridiculous, and thrasonical. He is too picked, too spruce, too affected, too odd, as it were, too peregrinate, as I may call it.[69]

But in the hands of genius, "copy" becomes the fresh and varied opulence of Rabelais, Marlowe, Jonson, or Shakespeare.

IT IS NOT only copy of words that is admired, but also copy of things. It is on the subject of variety that the Italian critics grow truly eloquent. If they had some difficulty in discovering just what Ariosto's unity consisted in, they had none at all in observing his variety and no qualms about praising him for it. Fornario da Rheggio says, in his exposition of *Orlando Furioso,* that if anyone wished to note in the poem the places where the passions and characters are treated, the "sentences," the words, and the other ornaments which are scattered through the work like precious gems, he would take away with him the impression of numbering the stars of heaven on a clear night, or the waves of the sea when it is most swollen in the midst of a wild and tempestuous winter.[70] The excuse for episodes and double plots was that a fable—epic, tragic, or comic—would not be long enough by itself; episodes must be put in for enlargement and for delightful variety. When Giraldi uses the analogy of a human body to discuss the parts of the epic (bones to represent the subject; sinews, the arrangement and articulation of the material; flesh, the amplification necessary to give the poem the right proportions; skin, the ornaments of style; soul, the energy given by the perfect union of expression and subject), it is with some zest that he describes the putting on of the flesh. After the skeleton is together, the poet must seek to fill up the holes and make proportionate the size of the members; this he does by amplifications ("riempimenti") in convenient and necessary places:

... such as loves, hates, tears, laughter, jokes; things serious, discordant, peaceful; things hideous and beautiful ("brutezze e bellezze"); descriptions of places, of times, of persons; fables feigned by him and taken from the ancients; navigations, wanderings, monsters, unforeseen events, deaths, obsequies, lamentations, recognitions; things terrible and pitiful; marriages, births; victories, triumphs, extraordinary battles, jousts, tournaments, catalogues, dispositions of troops ("ordinanze"), and other similar things, which by chance are so many that he who would recount them all one by one would grow not a little weary. For there is nothing above the heavens, or beneath, or in the depth of the abyss, that may not be handled at his discretion by a judicious poet ("che non sia tutto in mano, & in arbitrio del giudicioso Poeta"); nothing which cannot, with various ornaments, beautify the whole body of his composition and make it not merely a beautiful but also a lovely ("amabile") figure, giving to all its parts proper size and fitting ornament, with such proportion that one sees emerge a shapely ("regolato") and well-composed body.[71]

One reason for the renaissance critical preference for the epic over tragedy was that the former gave more opportunity for amplifying episodes and digressions. Nevertheless, plays as we know, at least in England, suffered from no dearth of "riempimenti." In this rhetorical ideal of copiousness, then, we have the justification (if not the actual cause) not only of the fluency of style, but of the double plots, the abundant intrigues, and the many characters of Elizabethan drama.

English renaissance drama is rhetorical from first to last. If a curve is drawn from the early Elizabethan period to the late Jacobean or Caroline period, conscious rhetoric will appear as a dominant characteristic of style at both ends—at one end because verse is stiff with the devices of the schools, at the other because, supple as it is, it draws attention to its own cleverness. If we are not so highly conscious of rhetoric at the height of the period, that is only because it has become thoroughly adapted to the matter it is used to express. Exuberance rather than economy remains characteristic of the plays of Jonson, Chapman, Marston, Webster, and Shakespeare. Jonson's firm structural hold in his best comedies does not restrain his fondness for verbal display. A sparser style, of course, sometimes appears, as in Middleton; simplicity, if not exactly economy, is frequent in Heywood and Dekker. It is true, too, that the greater dramatists in their best works show economy in the sense of adaptation of means to ends. *Faustus* (if we assume the horseplay to be not Marlowe's), *Othello,* and *Macbeth* are supreme examples. But my large generalization will be seen to be true, I think, if we put any of the great plays beside the best modern plays. There is a good deal of lengthy moral or psychological analysis in Shaw and O'Neill—if we take the most verbose of modern dramatists—but there is hardly verbal opulence in the sense that there is in Marlowe, Jonson, or Shakespeare. Whenever Shakespeare is acted on the contemporary stage, one of the most striking things, regardless of the play, is always the language—I don't mean its archaic flavor, of course, but its variety, power, and subtlety. We should get the same impression, if in less degree, from any other of the great Elizabethans or Jacobeans put on the modern stage. No modern playwright (except, of late, Christopher Fry) appears to take such delight in expression for its own sake. And no modern playwright conceives of such characters as Tamburlaine, Bussy, Sir Epicure, or Antony, in all of whom the essence is largeness of imaginative vision and of expressive power.

3 Verisimilitude

Ne 'l vero stesso ha più del ver che questo.
—POLIZIANO, *Stanze,* I. 119

PROBABLY THE most familiar of recurrent standards of judgment about a piece of literature is whether it is "true to life." As with all such large generalities we apply it more confidently than we are able to define it; yet we mean very different things by it in different contexts, as we know when we try to apply it as a touchstone to works as diverse as *The Divine Comedy* and *The Decameron; Agamemnon* and *Hedda Gabler;* the Psalms of David, the *Odes* of Horace, and Whitman's *Leaves of Grass.* Apart from its ambiguity, the phrase used as an aesthetic criterion is full of pitfalls. I shall mention only one, which is pertinent to the question of art and nature so much argued in the Renaissance. This pitfall is in being unaware of the extent to which our view of life is conditioned by the art we have grown accustomed to. We think that the nightingale sings a sad song because the poets have told us so ever since Greek mythology associated with the bird the gruesome tale of Procne and Philomela. There is a very literal and un-Platonic sense in which what Shelley says of Keats is true:

> He is made one with Nature: there is heard
> His voice in all her music, from the moan
> Of thunder to the song of night's sweet bird.

Nature since Wordsworth has not looked the same to men as it did before; yet they think they are seeing it with objective and unaided vision. Nature in renaissance poetry is often suggestive of those handsome French tapestries of *La vie seigneuriale* or *La noble pastorale,* in which courtly figures are posed, with a formal tree or two, and a few animals, in elegant grace against an over-all back-

53

ground of *fleurettes,* each single flower wrought in accurate and exquisite detail.[1] To renaissance descriptions of nature, the most intricate and purely decorative of the arts—those of the jeweler and of the goldsmith—often contributed the metaphors. To men of that time, nature could be described in terms of artifice foreign to our thinking. But if they could think of nature as imitating art, they also thought of art as imitating nature.

The degree of truth of that imitation is expressed in the concept of verisimilitude, the renaissance way of saying "truth to life." Verisimilitude is a concept we have especially to take account of in a consideration of renaissance aesthetic theory; for it was the primary standard of judgment applied to art by the critics of the time. We are faced with the interesting fact that though the dominant aesthetic was a representational theory of art, the most distinctive art of the time itself seems to us representational in no very narrow sense. Accustomed as we are to the types of "realistic" and "naturalistic" literature written since the mid-nineteenth century, we are not much tempted to call the literature of the Renaissance, by and large, either of these things—though, inconsistently, we use it freely as a social document to give us a "true" picture of life at the time. It is important to us to decide, therefore, just what the Renaissance itself meant by its representational theory. To understand "verisimilitude" we need to examine two constant themes of artistic discussion: the controversy over art *vs.* nature, and the idea of imitation.

Art *vs.* Nature

Educated men of the Renaissance were highly conscious of both decorative and symbolic effects. Artifice was everywhere apparent— in the ceremonies of court procedure, of civic occasions, of tourneys and pageants; in cookery; in gardens; in clothing and jewelry; in masques; in the music of the madrigal; in art rich in allegorical symbols like much of Dürer's (e.g., his three famous engravings of *Knight, Death and Devil; St. Jerome in His Study;* and *Melencolia I*).[2] In literature this consciousness showed itself in the fondness for elaborate allegory, in the cultivation of minor verse forms like the sonnet and of highly stylized prose like Euphuism, in the overworking of the more schematic figures of repetition, balance, and antithesis, in the exploitation of the pastoral convention. This is saying in another way what has already been said in Chapter II. Rhetoric was simply one of the means of studied effect.

In the light of all this artifice, it is interesting to find so much controversy over the relative importance of nature and art, and to find the debate so often decided, or apparently decided, in favor of nature. The theme is applied to various subjects: to woman's beauty, to science, to psychology and education (nature *vs.* nurture), to social and political life (simple country life *vs.* the life of the court). "Art," of course, has in these different contexts different connotations: in science or pseudo science, the means of control over nature; in education, training as opposed to natural talent; in the arts proper, both formal discipline and technique or artifice. With reference to literature the question has two aspects: the relative importance of natural gifts and of art (here, both knowledge of artistic principles and exercise of skill) in the production of a poem or a play; and the relative importance of naturalness of effect and artifice in evaluating the finished product. It is the latter, of course, that leads to the question of verisimilitude; but the first needs some preparatory examination, for the two are involved together. The question that ultimately concerns the drama is the question of verisimilitude—of realism in character and scene, of representation in style, and the like; but the more general assumptions about nature and art must be viewed first for the question of verisimilitude to have meaning. We shall find that, although there is a good deal of praise of nature both in considering the composition of poetry and in evaluating the finished product, the nature conceived of is never one undisciplined by art. In fact, a controlled art becomes the means by which nature is revealed.

COMPOSITION

The first of our two questions concerns artistic creation. The recurrent discussions of the relative importance of genius or inspiration and of artistic discipline in the composition of poetry are mainly important to us for their general bearing on characteristic renaissance attitudes towards nature and art. But we shall keep in mind the possible practical effects of these attitudes on the drama—whether

or not, for instance, the prevalent looseness of structural form reflects any depreciation of art in favor of nature. I think it does not.

Two limitations to the general discussion must be made at the
outset. First, to discuss theories of the precise nature of poetic inspiration, whether divine or natural, would lead into a long history
of interpretation and controversy not profitable to detail here.[3] Secondly, to put genius and inspiration together is a coarse generalization, but for my purposes a finer distinction would only confuse the
issue we are interested in. Genius and inspiration both stand together,
at least, against artistic discipline.

The issue of genius or inspiration *vs.* artistic discipline came to
the Renaissance already formulated by the most commonly read
classical critics and rhetoricians. The nice balance usually found in
statements of the issue is apt to be upset in implication. Although
Quintilian and Plutarch, thinking of orators, recognized the necessity
of natural gifts in the potential orator, they put their principal stress
on discipline. And Horace, writing specifically of poets, did the same.
Though his explicit statement makes them equal—

> ego nec studium sine divite vena,
> nec rude quid prosit video ingenium: alterius sic
> altera poscit opem res et coniurat amice— [4]

the tenor of the *Ars poetica* as a whole weights the scales in favor
of art.

A similar statement of balance is common in renaissance critical
treatises; compare Sidney:

A poet no industry can make, if his own genius be not carried unto it;
and therefore is an old proverb, *Orator fit, poeta nascitur.* Yet confess
I always that as the fertilest ground must be manured, so must the highest-
flying wit have a Daedalus to guide him.[5]

And of course as in Horace, the balance is not necessarily maintained
in implication. But there are perhaps fewer distortions of it in the
direction of training, like Varchi's position that if a man succeeds
without art it is by chance and he therefore deserves no praise,[6] than
in the direction of genius, like Giraldi's, Puttenham's, and Sidney's.[7]
These men are trying to form some conception of the poet's creative
power which is more fundamental than the mere talent enabling him
to understand and apply the rules with skill. Although not adopting
Plato's notion of a divine fury in any literal sense, as Scaliger and

Segni appear to do,[8] they are nevertheless, with the exception of Giraldi, touched by the inspirational doctrine of poetry set forth in the *Ion,* the *Phaedrus,* and the *Laws.* As Sidney puts it:

Neither let it be deemed too saucy a comparison to balance the highest point of man's wit with the efficacy of nature; but rather give right honor to the heavenly maker of that maker, who, having made man to his own likeness, set him beyond and over all the works of that second nature; which in nothing he showeth so much as in poetry, when with the force of a divine breath he bringeth things forth far surpassing her doings. . . .[9]

Many of the poets likewise respond sympathetically to the doctrine. Drayton, for instance, writes of Marlowe:

> Neat Marlowe, bathèd in the Thespian springs,
> Had in him those brave translunary things
> That the first poets had; his raptures were
> All air and fire, which made his verses clear,
> For that fine madness still he did retain
> Which rightly should possess a poet's brain.[10]

And Marlowe himself has given us one of the classic statements of the poet's vision as something beyond art. Tamburlaine exalts beauty both as a source of poetic vision and as something beyond the compass of art to express, something beyond the "heavenly quintessence" distilled from "immortal flowers of poesy":

> What is beauty, saith my sufferings, then?
> If all the pens that ever poets held
> Had fed the feeling of their masters' thoughts,
> And every sweetness that inspir'd their hearts,
> Their minds and muses on admired themes;
> If all the heavenly quintessence they still
> From their immortal flowers of poesy,
> Wherein as in a mirror we perceive
> The highest reaches of a human wit—
> If these had made one poem's period,
> And all combin'd in beauty's worthiness,
> Yet should there hover in their restless heads
> One thought, one grace, one wonder, at the least,
> Which into words no virtue can digest.[11]

As a consequence of such ideas of divine rapture, one might expect to find in the century examples of free-flowing, rhapsodic art— Whitman's type of poetry, let us say, as against Emily Dickinson's.

But not only is there no Whitman; there is even no Gray writing odes to inspired composition—

> Awake, Aeolian lyre, awake,
> And give to rapture all thy trembling strings.[12]

If Theseus' vision of the poet with his eye in a fine frenzy rolling suggests a figure like Gray's Bard—

> On a rock, whose haughty brow
> Frowns o'er old Conway's foaming flood,
> Robed in the sable garb of woe,
> With haggard eyes the Poet stood;
> (Loose his beard, and hoary hair
> Stream'd, like a meteor, to the troubled air)
> And with a Master's hand, and Prophet's fire,
> Struck the deep sorrows of his lyre—

to redress the balance we have only to recall the fate of the bard Glendower's visionary poetizings at the hands of Hotspur—"I think there's no better Welsh. I'll to dinner." There is, of course, danger of false pleading in wresting such an instance out of its dramatic context. Yet I think Shakespeare's amused handling of Glendower gives us an oblique hint of something of larger import than Glendower's immediate relation to the play and to Hotspur. If Gray's Bard, taken with Gray's seriousness, is unimaginable in the poetry of Shakespeare's time, it is because the Renaissance is too alert to the note of inflated self-love in such a creature. It gets a whiff in him of devilish brimstone, true or faked, and must therefore either abhor or make fun of him. To Shakespeare's age man is by his essence a rational being, and if poetic inspiration comes to him as a divine gift, it must yet be exercised through the medium of an exact discipline elaborated by his reason. As examples of his poetry, Shakespeare makes even Glendower boast only of lovely ditties framed at the English court, evidently according to the rules of art.

We must look again at the issue, therefore, to judge whether or not we have seen it aright.

ALTHOUGH so much sympathy in both critics and poets for "nature" would seem to conflict with the also widely held Horatian ideal of dispassionately controlled art, the conflict is, I believe, partly stated in terms we do not correctly apprehend; it is also off-center. The protest is against a mechanical conception which makes the poetic act only a skill and not an insight; but the protest is never against the application of skill to the insight. If someone theorizing does lean rather to the side of nature, he never does so to deny the validity of art, but only to assert the necessity of genius or of inspiration before art can be applied. Moreover, if one looks not merely at explicit statements but at the implications of the treatises on poetry, the question is seen to shift from the *degree* of control to the *quality* of control; that is, to the relative importance of invention, disposition, and style, to the kind of style, and so on.

To clarify this point, it will be useful to look in some detail at the position of George Puttenham, the author of that intelligent and thoughtful little book called *The Art of English Poesy* (1589). In his rather remarkable last chapter he considers seriously the function of art in relation to nature. He sees natural instinct as the first requirement. Though it is better, he says, to see with spectacles than not to see at all, yet the praise of the eye and the spectacle cannot be equal:

... no more is that which a poet makes by art and precepts rather than by natural instinct, and that which he doth by long meditation rather than by a sudden inspiration, or with great pleasure and facility than hardly and (as they are wont to say) in spite of Nature or Minerva, than which nothing can be more irksome or ridiculous.

Nevertheless, art is also essential. His resolution of the difference is like Polixenes' answer to Perdita, who will not plant "streak'd gillyvors," because, being artificially bred, they are "nature's bastards." Polixenes argues:

> Yet nature is made better by no mean
> But nature makes that mean: so, over that art,
> Which you say adds to nature, is an art
> That nature makes. . . .
> The art itself is nature.

Puttenham asks,

But what else is language, and utterance, and discourse, and persuasion, and argument in man, than the virtues of a well constitute body and mind, little less natural than his very sensual actions, saving that the one is perfited by nature at once, the other not without exercise and iteration?

The poet, in devising his subject, fashioning his poem, using metrical proportions, using language and style to achieve delight, is neither altogether like a craftsman, nor altogether unlike one. In using metrical proportions he is like a carpenter who borrows timbers from nature but who uses them otherwise than she could do; in what he speaks of the doings of another man (like Priam or Ulysses), he is like a painter or carver imitating nature's works; in speaking figuratively or arguing subtly or persuading copiously and vehemently, he is like a gardener fertilizing the soil and cultivating plants, using nature as a coadjutor to further her conclusions. In these things he is alterer, imitator, coadjutor of nature. But in that in him which issues from a quick invention, helped by a bright fantasy and imagination, he is not like these, but is a maker,

even as nature her self working by her own peculiar virtue and proper instinct, . . . [and] is then most admired when he is most natural and least artificial: and in the feats of his language and utterance, because they hold as well of nature to be suggested and uttered as by art to be polished and reformed. Therefore shall our poet receive praise for both, but more by knowing of his art than by unseasonable using it, and be more commended for his natural eloquence than for his artificial, and more for his artificial well dissembled, than for the same over-much affected and grossly or undiscreetly bewrayed, as many makers and orators do.

That this preference for nature over art means, however, no depreciation of the just claims of art is witnessed by the substance of Puttenham's treatise, which is essentially a craftsman's treatise, with full consideration of prosody, stanza forms, figures of speech, and even geometric shapes for verse. Does Puttenham catch a glimpse of the sound perception that a gifted man must be thoroughly trained in an art before he can attain the maturity to pass beyond its rules to an apparent "naturalness" that is sophisticated and controlled, not naïve? He uses the illustration of Sir Nicholas Bacon,

from whose lips I have seen to proceed more grave and natural eloquence than from all the orators of Oxford or Cambridge; but all is as it is handled, and maketh no matter whether the same eloquence be natural to them or artificial (though I think rather natural), yet were they known to be learned and not unskilful of th'art when they were younger men.[13]

"All is as it is handled." The passage on Bacon is a preface to Puttenham's statement that "good utterance . . . resteth altogether in figurative speeches"; and on a detailed treatment of figures, under the heading "Of Ornament," he now embarks.

In the attention paid to the devices of art, Puttenham's book is

characteristic of sixteenth-century critical treatises generally. There
are few concerned with the theory of poetry alone, many with the
craft. Whatever his temperamental bias in favor of nature, no critic
ever preaches a doctrine of libertinism. He may argue (like Giraldi
on the epic, Daniel on classical meters, or Jonson on comedy) [14]
that the rules of the ancients need not be binding for always, but he
never says that a poet can get along without some other form of
artistic discipline: the narrative technique of the romance, for instance, in place of the epic; English accent and rime in place of
quantitative verse; reasoned modifications of the rules of Roman
comedy to fulfill for a different age the true end of comedy. Free
verse, in the modern sense, would be inconceivable. Renaissance
critics never preach "self-expression," that shibboleth of so much
artistic and pedagogic theory. They always write on the basis of an
unquestioned assumption of the value of controlled form.

It is interesting to remark that all of Puttenham's attention, as
is Webbe's, is given to stylistic techniques, none to the organizing of
material. In other words, the important thing is, as I have indicated,
not the degree of control, but the kind of control—that is, where
the artistic emphasis is to be placed. The question of nature *vs.* art
in the production of poetry turns out to be mainly a theoretical one;
the practical question is where the poet shall exercise his formal
interests, and in this treatise as in the rhetorics the primary attention,
for reasons I have suggested in the two earlier chapters, goes to style
rather than to structural form.

Clearly, therefore, we cannot say, when we observe the looseness
of structure characteristic of so many Elizabethan plays, that a
doctrine of trust in nature rather than in art had anything to do with
it. The constant attention to rhetoric and style in the plays belies any
such theory. If a good many plays, particularly early ones, appear to
be put together without much art, they may sometimes be so through
sheer carelessness or naïveté. A more sympathetic view, however,
suggests that often their authors have insufficiently mastered the
problem of converting narrative to drama or of subordinating lyrical
and rhetorical effects to dramatic needs. Some dramatists perhaps
succeed no better because they have not fully defined for themselves
their central artistic problem. They are apt to let the story, perhaps a
good one in narrative form, take care of itself, and put their principal

attention on writing speeches. Such an emphasis is what their training in rhetoric would have prepared them for.

We are familiar with this question of the primacy of nature or art in the traditional contrast, inherited from the neoclassic period, between Shakespeare the child of nature, and Jonson the child of art. The neat, too readily made dichotomy, though springing from a truly felt difference of temperament and quality between the two men, makes a judgment equally false to both in its mutually exclusive assumptions. Jonson never minimized the primary importance of genius, nor should critics minimize it in him, whose range and fecundity, as distinct from his artistic control, are only in our time getting their proper recognition. In a passage in *Timber* Jonson says of poetry and painting: "They both are born artificers, not made. Nature is more powerful in them than study." [15] It is interesting to recall Drummond's comment that Jonson was "oppressed with fantasy, which hath ever mastered his reason, a general disease in many poets." [16] On the other hand, we are every day coming to recognize more fully the extent of Shakespeare's artistic discipline. Because Jonson has been so painstakingly explicit about his own artistic purpose and means, while Shakespeare has left his almost wholly to inference from the plays themselves, we should not therefore conclude that conscientious art in Jonson was a substitute for genius, or that, conversely, Shakespeare's genius made him indifferent to art. It is Jonson who is really to blame for the exaggerated contrast between himself and Shakespeare.[17] But we should not let him mislead us by his occasional impatience with Shakespeare, expressed as it is from his own temperamental bias and based sometimes on artistic assumptions that Shakespeare clearly did not share.

Shakespeare has given us many hints of his attitude towards nature and art, but they are not unambiguous. We think at once of the passage from *A Midsummer Night's Dream* on the poet, of imagination all compact, his eye in fine frenzy rolling. Uncalled for as it is in Theseus' mouth at the moment, it has the air of an *ex cathedra* aside by the author himself. Perhaps it is. But not clearly so. Nor is it certainly to be taken in a favorable sense. Professor Bundy thinks the very giving of the speech to the prosaic Theseus implies a derogatory view of this theory of poetry on Shakespeare's part; [18] it would not be derogatory, of course, of a deeper concept of imagination, but only of imagination viewed as a frenzy like the lover's or the madman's. We think, too, of the victory of nature and experience over pedantry, rigid discipline, and the affectations of art in *Love's Labour's Lost;* of the victory of Berowne's spirit over the spirit of Holofernes and Armado. It would be strange if the unbookish Shakespeare had not leaned towards Nature, who had given him so free-flowing a pen.

On the question of Shakespeare's intellectual position, however, we should for true perspective consider as well as *Love's Labour's Lost* the general import of plays in which is implicit the question of nature and art in a wider social and philosophical context than the merely literary: *As You Like It, The Winter's Tale, Cymbeline,* and *The Tempest.* In these comedies and romances, if nature is the well-spring of refreshment of spirit, it is also not the whole substance of man; the characters always return to the court at the end of the play. They put their new insights to work in the world formed by "art." In *King Lear,* nature has two aspects, one selfish, cruel, vicious, and chaotic; the other kind, beneficent, and productive of rational order. To abandon man's arts of civilization, which are the products of discourse of reason, is mere madness.

> O! reason not the need; our basest beggars
> Are in the poorest thing superfluous:
> Allow not nature more than nature needs,
> Man's life is cheap as beast's.

The moment at which Lear wishes to tear off his clothes and join Edgar, "the thing itself, unaccommodated man," is the moment of his complete loss of reason. The implication of *Lear* is suggestive of the position Cicero takes in the fourth and fifth books of *De finibus bonorum et malorum.* There, in a questioning of the Stoical postulate that happiness resides only in virtue, Cicero advances the position of the Old Academy that the material comforts and arts of civilization are also contributory, though in a lesser degree, to happiness.

Every natural organism aims at being its own preserver, so as to secure its safety and also its preservation true to its specific type. With this object, they declare, man called in the aid of the arts also to assist nature; and chief among the arts is counted the art of living, which aims at guarding the gifts that nature has bestowed and at obtaining those that are lacking.

[Wisdom] did not create man herself, but took him over in the rough from Nature; her business is to finish the statue that Nature began, keeping her eyes on Nature meanwhile.[19]

Montaigne's wonder at the virtues of the South American Indian cannibals is only speculative, an idea entertained temporarily for its value in criticizing the oversophistication of European culture. The noble savage either as an object of sentiment or as an ideal to be imitated had to wait for nearly another century. Caliban is not noble, nor does he, like Gray's savage, "repeat, In loose numbers wildly sweet" his "dusky loves." [20] He is

> A devil, a born devil, on whose nature
> Nurture can never stick.

And Ferdinand and Miranda are decidedly not Paul and Virginia. My point in all this is that to see Shakespeare as unappreciative of art, either in the literary sense of a controlled discipline of one's medium of expression or in the wider sense of a control over nature productive of the goods of civilization, is to see him as a non-renaissance man.

Whenever Elizabethan dramatists, even aside from Jonson, do make pronouncements on their own art, they show themselves thoroughly aware of Horatian artistic theory. Webster, for instance, apologizes that *The White Devil* conforms less to the rules than it should; he deplores the popular taste which compelled him to depart from them.[21] His position is not unlike that of Lope de Vega in *The New Art of Making Comedies,* who gives the same reason, but more cheerfully, for his "locking up the rules with six keys"; he says all but six of his 483 comedies sin against art.[22] If apologies like these are only sops to the Jonsons of the age, they still show us that "art" could not be lightly cast aside. Men wrote against a background of universal acceptance of the importance of artistic discipline.

The general attitude of the age, then, as shown in the legislative tone of most critical theory, in the pedagogical stress on formal rhetoric, in the cultivation of highly artificial forms of poetry and prose, showed no tendency to minimize the importance of art. Warm espousals of the claims of inspiration, whether natural or divine, may have been partly a normal reaction by gifted men against poetasters and obtuse critics, partly an assertion of the worth of poetry against detractors who found it only trivial artifice, partly a search for some conception of the creative imagination that seemed truer to experience than the rather mechanical one of the psychological treatises.

CRITICAL EMPHASIS

The second important feature, for us, of the debate over art *vs*. nature is the question it raises of critical emphasis. In the evaluation of poetry and drama is naturalness or artifice to be put first? The question has been answered partly in the preceding discussion, partly in the chapter on eloquence, and need be considered here only briefly. The renaissance concept of eloquence tended, as we have seen, to the cultivation of highly artificial styles, in both prose and verse. There were not wanting apologists for naturalness and simplicity. But their statements have to be viewed in the light of their own tastes or practices in order for us to understand what speaking according to nature meant. Sidney, for instance, inveighs with great good sense against some of the abuses of eloquence in his time—far-fetched words, "coursing of a letter," overworked figures, ornate-ness out of keeping with the subject, euphuistic schematic sentence patterns, and similes in multitudes from the herbarists and bestiaries. "So is that honey-flowing matron Eloquence apparelled, or rather disguised, in a courtesan-like painted affectation." [23] But we should set against this the revealing comment on a traditional and "artless" ballad which moves him:

I never heard the old song of Percy and Douglas that I found not my heart moved more than with a trumpet; and yet is it sung but by some blind crowder, with no rougher voice than rude style; which, being so evil apparelled in the dust and cobwebs of that uncivil age, what would it work trimmed in the gorgeous eloquence of Pindar? [24]

There is no perception of the fact that the old song moves him precisely because it is simple. As seen from his own Arcadian style, Sidney's standard of naturalness lies not in the reproduction of the rhythms of colloquial speech, but in what he considers appropriate-ness, a perfect wedding of style to thought, not overlaid with extraneous ornament. It is a carefully studied style.[25] Although it differs radically from Lyly's Euphuism in the employment of arguments from the "topics" as proof rather than as mere amplification, in the much less frequent use of figures of sound or of word (like allitera-

tion, assonance, *similiter cadens* or similar sounding terminations),
and in the relative freedom from ornamentation for its own sake,
Sidney's style is highly artful in the use of tropes (especially simile,
metaphor, irony), of the longer schemes that take a line or a sentence
to work out (such as balance, climax, the periodic sentence), and
of figures of thought (like personification, apostrophe, doubt, interrogation, parenthesis, exclamation).

Giraldi makes a protestation of naturalness in his apology for
Orbecche, where he has the tragedy, personified and speaking, dis-
claim swelling words and strong epithets, Acherontic horrors and
descriptions strewn with flowers, grass, shadows, caves, waves, soft
airs, rubies, pearls, topazes, and so on: "I have preferred to have as
a guide nature with due ornament than a feigned art with pompous
words." [26] Yet from our point of view this play and all his others
are highly rhetorical, and rhetoric we equate with artifice, not naturalness, of speech.

Exhortations to naturalness are accompanied with admonitions,
not to abandon art, but to use art to conceal art.

> He paints true forms, who with a modest heart
> Gives luster to his work, yet covers art. [27]

It is so in Sidney, in Puttenham, in Jonson:

> The true artificer will not run away from Nature as if he were afraid of
> her, or depart from life and the likeness of truth, but speak to the capacity
> of his hearers. And though his language differ from the vulgar somewhat,
> it shall not fly from all humanity with the Tamerlanes and Tamer-chams
> of the late age, which had nothing in them but the scenical strutting and
> furious vociferation to warrant them to the ignorant gapers. He knows
> it is his only art to carry it, as none but artificers perceive it. [28]

Better negligence nicely used, says Giraldi, than too great diligence.
Herrick is still expressing renaissance taste in his praise of "a sweet
disorder" in his beloved's dress:

> A careless shoe-string, in whose tie
> I see a wild civility,
> Do more bewitch me than when art
> Is too precise in every part.

"Wild civility" is the key to much renaissance description.

> My mistress when she goes
> To pull the pink and rose

Along the river bounds,
And trippeth on the grounds,
And runs from rocks to rocks
With lovely scattered locks,
Whilst amorous wind doth play
With hairs so golden gay;
The water waxeth clear,
The fishes draw her near,
The sirens sing her praise,
Sweet flowers perfume her ways,
And Neptune, glad and fain,
Yields up to her his reign.[29]

Poliziano's

Ma lieta Primavera mai non manca,
Ch'e' suoi crin biondi e crespi all'aura spiega,
E mille fiori in ghirlandetta lega [30]

might serve as a descriptive motto for Botticelli's *Flora*. And Botticelli himself might serve in this painting and in his *Venus Anadyomene* as the genius of the gracious Arcadian world of studied simplicity and careless elegance where "a belt of straw and ivy buds" has "coral clasps and amber studs." No sense of incongruence ever seems to be felt in the decorative juxtaposition of things natural and artificial.

Nothing is more common than the conventional paradox that the effects of nature and art are indistinguishable:

What guile is this, that those her golden tresses
She doth attire under a net of gold:
And with sly skill so cunningly them dresses
That which is gold or hair may scarce be told? [31]

The standard of highest excellence applied to any art object is the degree of its semblance to nature. Marina

with her neeld composes
Nature's own shape, of bud, bird, branch, or berry,
That even her art sisters the natural roses;
Her inkle, silk, twin with the rubied cherry.[32]

In describing Imogen's bedchamber, Iachimo says,

The chimney
Is south the chamber, and the chimney-piece
Chaste Dian bathing; never saw I figures

> So likely to report themselves: the cutter
> Was as another nature, dumb; outwent her,
> Motion and breath left out.

Yet nothing could well be less "natural" (if natural carries for us the connotation of simple or unaffected) than the scene the sculptor had executed or than the one woven into the tapestry hung on the walls:

> ... the story
> Proud Cleopatra, when she met her Roman,
> And Cydnus swell'd above the banks, or for
> The press of boats or pride.[33]

In Iachimo's praise of the tapestry, richness and bravery (showiness) are set side by side with exactness and "true life." Poliziano ends his long description in the *Stanze* of the splendid palace of Venus with this comment on the doors sculptured with the loves of the gods and with ornamental arabesques of intertwined acanthus, roses, and myrtles, and of birds so realistic that one seemed to hear them singing:

> Nè 'l vero stesso ha più del ver che questo.[34]

"Nor has the truth itself more of truth than this." For sheer gorgeousness of descriptive imagery it would be hard to surpass the cloth-of-silver and brocaded tissue of Marlowe's narrative poem, *Hero and Leander*. Even here the pretense that the most elaborately artificial is natural is kept up. Hero first appears in a veil of "artificial flowers and leaves, Whose workmanship both man and beast deceives"; she wears buskins of silvered shells and blushing coral to the knee,

> Where sparrows perch'd, of hollow pearl and gold,
> Such as the world would wonder to behold:
> Those with sweet water oft her handmaid fills,
> Which as she went would chirrup through the bills.[35]

What lies behind all this, of course, apart from a fondness for ornateness and for witty paradox, is the conception of nature as herself a great artificer. Desdemona is the "cunning'st pattern of excelling nature"—a prototype of beauty in the making of which nature has shown her greatest skill. The sculptor of the chimney-piece in Imogen's bedroom was "as another nature"; he competed with her in artistic design and execution. When this conception of nature is implied, it obviously prevents any connotation of artlessness, modifies the notion of simplicity, and completely resolves the opposition between art and nature.

We come easily, therefore, to the reverse of the paradox that artificial things may be so well made as to appear natural: namely to the paradox that natural objects may be so beautiful as to appear artificial. Hairs become golden wires or threads, brooks are crystal, water dripping from an oar is a rope of liquid pearl, meadows are enameled or adorned with dainty gems, birds make sweet division.

> Gli augelletti dipinti, in tra le foglie
> Fanno l'aere addolcir con nove rime.[36]

Drayton, a century and a half later, is in the same tradition as Poliziano.

> The flowers like brave embroidered girls
> Looked as they much desired
> To see whose head with orient pearls
> Most curiously was tired;
>
> . . . .
>
> No little bubbling brook from any spring that falls
> But on the pebbles plays me pretty madrigals.[37]

"Curiously" here means "with precise art." How much of nature in renaissance poetry is a glitter of jewels, a polyphony of madrigals!

"Nature" and "natural" clearly have different connotations as critical terms for the Renaissance than for us. In the light of all this paradoxical association of art and nature the ideal of naturalness in art, so often stated, so seldom, according to our criteria, achieved, suggests a kind of nostalgia bred of a highly artificial training and of a highly artificial society. It was an ideal like pastoralism, which is indeed an aspect of the same nostalgia. No one states this better than Sanazzaro, one of the fathers of renaissance pastoral, in the "Proemio" to his *Arcadia*. He says that many times tall and spreading trees produced by nature in wild ("orridi") mountains please us more than cultivated and trimmed plants in formal gardens; wild birds singing in green branches than trained birds in decorated cages; sylvan songs carved in the rough bark of beeches than polished verses written on the trimmed pages of gilded books; waxed reeds of shepherds sounding through flowery valleys than costly boxwood instruments of musicians in pompous rooms. And who doubts, he asks, that a fountain issuing naturally from among living stones, surrounded with green grass, is more pleasing than all the rest made by art of the whitest marble, resplendent with gold? "Certa che io creda, niuno." Surely no one, he thinks. Therefore he means to recite the rough eclogues, issued from a natural source, that he heard the shepherds of Arcadia sing in delightful shade beside the murmur of liquid fountains. The eclogues he recites are, of course, artistically intricate, as unreal as his pastoral landscape and his shepherds. How simple did he really suppose they were? Lope de Vega remarks in his own pastoral, *Dorotea:*

This business of shepherds is nothing but brooks and banks, and they and their shepherdesses are forever singing; some day I hope to see a shepherd seated on a bench, and not always upon a rock or near a fountain.[38]

Surely no one knew better than men of the Renaissance themselves how far from actual nature the "sweete sobs of Sheepheardes and Nymphes" were:

> Thy gowns, thy shoes, thy beds of roses,
> Thy cap, thy kirtle, and thy posies
> Soon break, soon wither, soon forgotten,—
> In folly ripe, in reason rotten.[39]

That did not prevent their assiduous practice of the pastoral as both a pleasant and a serious convention. But they showed little desire to take wild nature on her own terms.

Art as Imitation

In an age of so much artifice, what, then, does verisimilitude mean? It is best understood by examining the almost universally held theory of art as imitation. For clarity, it will be necessary to review rather summarily three different senses "imitation" was capable of carrying.

First, there is Plato's philosophical idea of the phenomenal world as an imitation of the world of forms and ideas. Secondly, there is his idea that poetry, in representing the phenomenal world, is but an imitation of an imitation.[40] Aristotle borrows the idea of "mimesis" as the defining characteristic of art, but develops it in his own direction. Aristotle seems to mean by imitation a representation of human habits, feelings, and actions in all their diverse modes of manifestation; yet he sees them in their particularity making manifest universal and general truth.[41] His "universal," however, is not quite Plato's "idea" and hence mimesis does not have for him the pejorative connotation it does for Plato; art is not for him the imitation of something better that is in itself the imitation of something better still. The idea of art as imitation seems to have been taken as almost axiomatic in the Renaissance, and was used as an argument by both the defenders and the detractors of poetry, the latter appealing to the authority of Plato for disprizing anything that was but the shadow of a shadow and a lie,[42] the former appealing to Aristotle's distinction between particular and universal truth. Thirdly, there is the use of the term so common in the Renaissance as meaning imitation of other men's work. In this sense it was both an important pedagogical principle and a critical touchstone in evaluating the work of authors ancient and contemporary.

The third sense does not concern us at this point. The ancient authors chosen by dramatists to imitate and the ways in which they were imitated will appear in the course of the book. It is the second sense, poetry as the imitation of human life, which chiefly concerns us in our attempt to understand verisimilitude; the first sense, Plato's philosophic sense, concerns us only in so far as it bears on the question of poetic truth.

Puttenham's definition of imitation may serve as a starting point for the consideration of the second sense:

... a poet may in some sort be said a follower or imitator, because he can express the true and lively of every thing is set before him, and which he taketh in hand to describe: and so in that respect is both a maker and a counterfaitor: and poesy an art not only of making, but also of imitation.[43]

Puttenham's definition is interesting because he so clearly associates making and imitating, creation and representation. Ascham, more specifically of the drama, says: "The whole doctrine of comedies and tragedies is a perfit imitation, or fair lively painted picture of the life of every degree of man." [44] The idea of poetry as a speaking picture ("ut pictura poesis"), generally borrowed from Plutarch, is so commonplace as to need no illustration; [45] and so is the comparison of poetry to an image or mirror of human affairs.[46] Hamlet's statement of the idea is only the best known of many; he says the function of playing is "to hold, as 'twere, the mirror up to nature; to show virtue her own feature, scorn her own image, and the very age and body of the time his form and pressure." No quotation was more common than the saying attributed to Cicero that comedy is the imitation of life, the glass of custom, and the image of truth: *imitatio vitae, speculum consuetudinis, imago veritatis.*[47]

But we shall be seriously misled if we give the metaphor of the glass too narrow a denotation by supposing that imitation was understood in any literally representational or naturalistic sense. That Aristotle did not understand it so is clear (1) from his idea of universal truth (poetry representing not what has happened, but what might happen, therefore more "philosophical" than history); (2) from his preference in the shaping of tragic plots for a probable impossibility to an improbable possibility; (3) from his theory of selection and emphasis, tragedy representing men as better than they are, comedy as worse; (4) from his remarks on propriety in character; and (5) from his prescription that tragedy should be written in verse and in an embellished style.[48] The Renaissance followed him in these ideas—with the usual personal interpretations, it is true, leading to much variation in emphasis and detail, but nevertheless with the essential ideas apparent through the modifications. The two leading ideas ultimately based on these points of Aristotle's are universal truth and decorum (that is, the doctrine of the appropriateness of expression to the subject), and they are the two great touchstones of verisimilitude.

UNIVERSAL TRUTH

The discussion in the first act of *Timon of Athens* between the poet and the painter shows how a work of art might be considered both as accurately representational and as ideally true.[49] The poet first praises the painter's portrait of Timon in the familiar terms of the lifelike:

> Admirable! How this grace
> Speaks his own standing! what a mental power
> This eye shoots forth! how big imagination

> Moves in this lip! to the dumbness of the gesture
> One might interpret.

And the painter complacently agrees:

> It is a pretty mocking of the life.
> Here is a touch; is't good?

The poet's reply, however, shows that, through some device of heightening, there is an idealized element in the lifelikeness; art surpasses nature:

> I'll say of it,
> It tutors nature: artificial strife
> Lives in these touches, livelier than life.

When the poet turns to a description of his own work, he makes the unmistakable claim of universal truth by denying a merely particular application of Timon:

> I have, in this rough work, shap'd out a man,
> Whom this beneath world doth embrace and hug
> With amplest entertainment: my free drift
> Halts not particularly, but moves itself
> In a wide sea of wax.

Although the poem is an allegory of the fickleness of Fortune, it is clearly thought of as representational of an actual state of affairs:

> Amongst them all,
> Whose eyes are on this sovereign lady fix'd,
> One do I personate of Lord Timon's frame,
> Whom Fortune with her ivory hand wafts to her;
> Whose present grace to present slaves and servants
> Translates his rivals.
>   *Painter.*   Tis conceiv'd to scope.
> This throne, this Fortune, and this hill, methinks,
> With one man beckon'd from the rest below,
> Bowing his head against the steepy mount
> To climb his happiness, would be well express'd
> In our condition.

After the poet has finished his account of the argument of the poem, which ends with the desertion of Timon's followers when Fortune has spurned him down the mountain side, the painter closes the conversation with the comparison of poetry and painting in terms of their moral efficacy. This makes an interesting footnote to the "ut pictura poesis" theme:

> A thousand moral paintings I can show
> That shall demonstrate these quick blows of Fortune's
> More pregnantly than words. Yet you do well
> To show Lord Timon that mean eyes have seen
> The foot above the head.

It is a comparison in which three commonplaces of renaissance critical thought join hands: the similarity of poetry and painting, the idea of art as a vehicle of universal truth, and the idea of art as a teacher of mankind.

The poet of *Timon* is prefigured in Sidney's statement of the aim and scope of the poet. Right poets, he says, "be they which most properly do imitate to teach and delight, and to imitate borrow nothing of what is, hath been, or shall be; but range, only reined with learned discretion, into the divine consideration of what may be and should be." [50] The description of ideal truth as "what may be and should be" raises the whole question of poetic fiction.

Sidney eloquently defends poetic fiction against those who call poetry the mother of lies. The essence of the defense lies, of course, in the conception of poetry as creative. If in one sense the poet is an imitator, in another he is a maker, "even," as Puttenham says, "as nature herself working by her own peculiar virtue and proper instinct and not by example or meditation or exercise as all other artificers do." But where must be placed the limits of the poet's "making"? It is easy to see that "what might or should happen" covers the invention of a fable in which the shapelessness of literal historical truth is replaced by an orderly concatenation of events, possible in human experience. This kind of fable appears probable (what might happen) by the very logic of necessary dependence, and it makes moral comment (what should happen) on the relation of men's deeds to the consequences that follow. Note that the use of *should* as well as *might* adds a moral connotation to Aristotle's merely logical subjunctive: ". . . it is not the function of the poet to relate what has happened, but what may happen,—what is possible according to the law of probability or necessity." [51] The addition gives a characteristic renaissance emphasis; it makes the defense of poetic fiction easier, but at the cost of some confusion of the central issue. What, however, of the invention of things impossible in human experience, the imaginary world of make-believe, where laws of reason and causality are in abeyance?

Plato had distinguished in the *Sophist* between icastic and fantastic images, the former of things actually subsisting, the latter of things only imagined; and he had deplored the latter as unsuitable for poetry.[52] But clearly, most poets, from Homer down, had made use of fantastic images. The problem, then, was to rescue this type of invention from Plato's stigma. In what sense, the critics ask, can fantastic images be "true"? There are two possible lines to take in the answer. One is that fantastic images are true in some higher sense, with a moral purpose of ultimate truth; the other is that they are true because they are credible within the framework of the poem. The difficulty of breaking away from the moral implication of "true" and "false" prevents most critics from taking the latter line with any boldness. They all say that a work of art must be either "true" or "verisimilar," that is, seeming true. The crux is in how they define the verisimilar. If they define it only in terms of universal truth, they are still within their circle of ethical implication.[53] They have not given the verisimilar any psychological differentia which will account for our acceptance of some fantastic images, our rejection of others. All they are saying is that the verisimilar is like the true, and the true is good, hence the verisimilar is also good; they are simply giving it a clean bill of moral health. On this line of reasoning, the only way in which fantastic images can qualify as verisimilar is by embodying truth in some allegorical form.

Occasionally an attempt is made to define the verisimilar in terms of artistic credibility. In an interesting passage in his second dialogue, Lionardi seems to understand Aristotle's preference for a probable impossibility to an improbable possibility in genuinely artistic terms; verisimilar things, Lionardi says, are those which are in keeping with the subject so that events in the story and digressions appear to come one from the other.[54] In his discussion of the marvelous, Minturno states this same principle of self-consistency and inter-dependency— the joining of things in the poem so that they appear to operate with the same necessity as things in the real world—as a thing which deceives the intellect and gives us marvelous delight. "Great praise is owing the poet who wins for things feigned a wondrous faith." [55] But both critics let this principle fade before the dominant ethical assumption that the verisimilar must in some sense be ideally true, hence morally useful.

Castelvetro, having declared delight to be the sole end of poetry, is free from this assumption. According to him, Aristotle is not concerned with the truth or falsity of things in nature, but only with their possibility and their credibility within certain limits.[56] In so far as Castelvetro sees these limits, as he partly does, in the rational conduct of the fable, so that one thing must seem to follow upon another, he is getting at the fundamental artistic principle. The poet's special concern, he says, is what is useful to the construction of the fable. Although it is impossible in nature that a dog live twenty years, yet, granted that condition, the recognition of Odysseus by his old dog is credible enough and useful to the story. Although Dido and Aeneas could not actually have met, since they did not live at the same time, yet the meeting, once their contemporaneity is assumed, is handled by Virgil with great verisimilitude. On the other hand, although it is possible (not in nature, but presumably in the imagined nature of gods) that Cupid might be transformed into the figure of Ascanius, it is incredible because Cupid could make Dido fall in love with Aeneas a simpler way, that is, by shooting her with golden arrows in the customary way. The transformation causes unnecessary difficulties in the story in taking care of the real Ascanius. But Castelvetro loses his grip on the idea of credibility as determined by structural consistency with the limitations he imposes on both the possible and the credible. Although actual fact in nature is not his criterion of the possible, a logical conception of potentialities rigidly based on the axioms of Aristotelian philosophy certainly is. The transformation of Aeneas' ships into nymphs is both impossible and incredible, incredible for no given reason, but impossible because insensate things cannot be transformed into gods! And Castelvetro insists that history or report is a limitation on the credible. That Pegasus or Daedalus could fly we may believe because legend tells us so, but not that any other man or horse simply invented by a poet can do so.

Lionardi, Minturno, and Castelvetro all appear to be groping after a statement of the problem in purely artistic terms. But the easiest solution of the problem of fantastic images is to see them as embodying some kind of moral lesson. Fracastoro makes a statement of the conditions of verisimilitude as typically understood: Nothing should be invented that is evidently incompatible with truth.

Everything allowed to invention must be true in one of the following senses: (a) it has the appearance of truth, (b) it has allegorical significance (the convenient back-door that lets in any amount of fantasy), (c) it is a common belief, and (d) it accords with the universal, the simply (i.e., absolutely) beautiful idea, and not with the particular.[57] The "verisimilar," then, generally implies the universal or the probable. Though it is sometimes used in the sense merely of the credible, the credible is likely to be referred to testimony (as in Castelvetro and Fracastoro) outside the limits of the poem.

DECORUM

The doctrine of decorum brings universal truth down from these speculative heights to a practical level. It gives directions for the embodiment of universal truth in poetic symbols. For it is a doctrine of the fitness of the means to the end.

One of its most important concerns is with the conception of character in drama and fiction. The proper place for a full discussion of this matter will be in the chapter on character. Here need be said only what is necessary to clarify the concept of decorum. Ideal truth asks for the invention of characters in terms of men not as they actually are in every respect of individuality but as they would be if they conformed only to some accepted notion of the type of miser, tyrant, lover, courtesan, father, pedant, or the like. The idea of propriety in character was in germ in Aristotle; as he put it, "There is a type of manly valour; but valour in a woman, or unscrupulous cleverness, is inappropriate." [58] By the sixteenth century, this had become an elaborate doctrine of types, recognized as established by the practice of Latin comedy and by Horace's insistent doctrine of decorum, and given enormous weight by the hierarchical structure of renaissance society.

Any renaissance critical treatise that deals with the epic and the drama has a good deal to say about the decorum of character. One of the fullest treatments is in Minturno's *Arte poetica,* where we learn that a character must act and speak according to his sex, his age, his fortune, his nation or city, his nature, his art or profession, his relations and associates.[59] We are told in detail, moreover, just what each of these conditions prescribes. A character is verisimilar if he is made

to behave and speak according to these conditions. Romeo, in love
with Rosaline, is verisimilar because he mopes and writes verses, as
young men in love are supposed to do; and, more seriously in love
with Juliet, he is verisimilar because he behaves with the headlong
impetuosity of youth, which is supposed to be more passionate and
less reflective than age. Capulet is verisimilar because he carries on
like the crusty fathers of Roman comedy. Hamlet ridicules Polonius
in terms of the decorum of character, pungently phrased. The
"matter" that he reads, or professes to read, is "that old men have
grey beards; that their faces are wrinkled, their eyes purging thick
amber and plum-tree gum, and that they have a plentiful lack of wit,
together with most weak hams."

Although character types do not appear with anything like the
same identifiable rigidity in Elizabethan plays as they do in Italian
ones, nevertheless the doctrine of decorum is the key to much puzzling behavior—the ease, for instance, with which virtuous women
succumb to temptation. They fall simply because they are women and
by nature weak. Mistress Frankford's swift yielding to Wendoll,
Mistress Shore's to Edward IV, Bianca's to the Duke of Florence,
are all examples of perfect "decorum." It is true enough that the
drama has its Castizas as well as its Gratianas; the chaste ones conform to the decorum of another, and perhaps rarer, type—the
woman proof against temptation. The doctrine had its possibilities
of accommodation.

The idea of decorum was not confined to conceptions of character.
It affected the conception of epic, tragedy, comedy, and pastoral—
the kinds of subjects appropriate and the classes of characters treated.
Aristotle's "better" and "worse" as distinguishing the characters of
tragedy and comedy had become universally "of superior" and "of
inferior social standing." [60] The idea of decorum affected style—the
choice between levels of diction, between verse and prose, between
different kinds of verse.[61] Certainly in style, as in the treatment of
event and character, conceptions of decorum so modify the doctrine
of imitation that it does not mean naturalism. Characters in drama
speak according to certain conventions that were thought to be in
keeping with poetic truth: e.g., the tragic style is more elevated and
"artificial" than the comic, the expression of strong emotion by
well-born characters requiring a rhetorical elaborateness that the

more prosaic sentiments of ordinary citizens do not. Naturalism as we know it, making men speak as nearly as possible as they actually do in life, was a slow discovery. It had a better chance in comedy than in tragedy, but even there any elevation in social rank made for formalism in style. Although Shakespeare in his comedies varies between verse and prose, and between different levels of verse, with far greater subtlety of purpose than the mere distinction in social rank modern critics too often fasten on as the sole purpose of variation, social rank is at least one of the purposes governing differences in tone and style. It is a relatively stronger purpose in early comedies like *Love's Labour's Lost* and *A Midsummer Night's Dream* than in more mature plays, both tragic and comic, in which he widens the use of prose and makes his stylistic variations a sensitive instrument to control differences of emotional tone. But of course the well-born characters in Shakespearean comedy are never permitted the linguistic gaucheries which are an established element in the fun made of the lowly-born: Costard, Mistress Quickly, Dogberry, Elbow, or Pompey.

BESIDES THE handling of character and style, the question of verisimilitude has special bearing on the drama in two other important ways: in the choice of, and the liberties taken with, historical subjects; and on the use of the marvelous and the supernatural.

HISTORICAL SUBJECTS

Aristotle had said that tragic writers clung to historic names and the stories of great families for the advantage of credibility; for what has happened is possible and the possible is credible. Renaissance critics generally express a preference for traditional or historical subjects for both tragic and heroic poetry. Giraldi is something of a radical among his fellows in favoring the use of new material for tragic plots and for romances, the modern descendants of the epic.[62] Had not Aristotle said that a wholly fictitious plot might be pleasing, as was the *Flower* of Agathon? Mazzoni likewise appeals to the authority of Aristotle for a poet's right to feign his action; he may feign the complete story of a king, if only it is of a country strange and remote.[63]

As for the liberty to be taken with the historical subjects chosen, critics persistently think of it in terms of the necessary moral to be aimed at. As Sidney puts it:

But if the question be for your own use and learning, whether it be better to have it set down as it should be, or as it was, then certainly is more doctrinable the feigned Cyrus in Xenophon than the true Cyrus in Justin, and the feigned Aeneas in Vergil than the right Aeneas in Dares Phrygius; as to a lady that desired to fashion her countenance to the best grace, a painter should more benefit her to portrait a most sweet face, writing Canidia upon it, than to paint Canidia as she was, who Horace sweareth was foul and ill-favored. If the poet do his part aright, he will show you in Tantalus, Atreus, and such like, nothing that is not to be shunned; in Cyrus, Aeneas, Ulysses, each thing to be followed.[64]

There is some awareness, however, of the essentially artistic aspect of the question, as Aristotle saw it, that is, how to manage the plot to secure the maximum of tragic effect. Giraldi sees that freedom in handling the plot, even if the material is from history, is essential to the poet, for it is by the fable that he enters into the mind of the reader, delighting him with his lively ingenuity.[65] That Fracastoro is aware of the artistic aspect of the problem seems to be implied in his discussion of whether additions for the beautification of a subject, like the Fall of Troy, are essential to it or extraneous.[66] He decides that they are essential because they give life to the subject; that he means by additions more than ornaments of style is shown by his discussion, already summarized on pages 76–77, of what feigned things may be added without violation of verisimilitude.

Whether the English dramatists did or did not know anything about critical opinion on the subject, they were in accord with it both in their tendency to choose true stories for tragedy and in their freedom in handling these stories. Even if they were more in line with the liberal Giraldi and more up to date than most continental writers, who liked to rehash Euripides and Seneca, the matter for English tragedies was still largely "historical." Marlowe's *Massacre at Paris* and *Edward II* are based on history, *Tamburlaine* and *Faustus* on half-history that passed for truth. Jonson's two tragedies are taken from Roman history; Chapman's *Bussy, Chabot,* and the two Byron plays from contemporary French history, his *Caesar and Pompey* from Roman history; Webster's two best tragedies from events in great Italian renaissance families. Examples might be multiplied. Of Shakespeare's tragedies apart from the English history plays (at least two of them distinctly tragic in form), three come from Roman history, one from Scottish history, one from Danish legendary history (again, perhaps regarded as truer than it was), one from legendary British history, two from Italian stories purporting to be true. The story of Timon rests on the authority of Plutarch and Lucian; *Titus Andronicus* at least makes a pretense of history.

The freedom Shakespeare takes with *Lear* and *Hamlet* is quite beyond the slighter alterations for dramatic fitness he makes in *Richard III* and *Richard II*. The problem for him, I think we are justified in believing, was not just one of the greater amount of factual material he had available for the more recent subjects, nor perhaps even one of any special fidelity to familiar history for its own sake, but also, and perhaps primarily, one of artistic verisimilitude. It was recognized that subjects remote in time gave more scope for invention just because they placed less strict limitations on credibility. Mazzoni says that when the history is not known in detail,

the poet has before him a wide field in which he can enlarge and particularize the history by introducing his own inventions without fear of transgressing the credible. This sort of regal story is better and more perfect than all the others.[67]

In seeking to prove that the *Gerusalemme Liberata* is a greater poem than the Homeric epics or than the *Aeneid*, one of the arguments Paolo Beni uses is that the subject matter is neither too old to lose the reader's faith (who knows that in antiquity many lies were born), nor too recent to stifle invention; the time—about five hundred years earlier—is just right for giving the action verisimilitude.[68] Although anything that is false is reprehensible to him, Fracastoro excuses Virgil's anachronism of making Aeneas and Dido of the same period in history by arguing that it was a falsehood not generally known; such falsehoods, not easily refuted because the facts are long forgotten or far off in time, do not injure verisimilitude. And Giraldi says that in writing of ancient times poets, who write of things not as they are but as they ought to be, for use and delight, satisfy men of their own age by introducing customs of their own times; Aeneas, for instance, sacrifices, not as in Asia in his day, but as in the Italy of Octavian.[69] Thus, even the anachronism so familiar to us in the Elizabethan drama gets critical approval; we are apt to take it as a sign of ignorance or of carelessness whereas it may often be the sign of a conscious attempt at verisimilitude.

We arrive at the paradoxical conclusion that both the choice of "true" subjects and the freedom in handling them may have arisen from the same feeling of the need to achieve verisimilitude.

THE MARVELOUS

As for the marvelous, I am again not sure that the justification did not come after the fact; that dramatists would not have brought in Friar Bacon with his glass and his Brazen Head, Sacrapant with his lantern, and Titania with her changeling boy, whether or not the critics had given their blessing to the strange and the fantastic. Nor did they all: Jonson would have no servant-monsters, like Caliban, in his *Bartholomew Fair,* nor "make nature afraid" like those who wrote of tales and tempests. It is interesting, however, to notice as a sign of the times that in some Italian critics Aristotle's treatment of wonder [70] in epic poetry and in tragedy, arising, he says, most strongly from the irrational, by which he means the coincidental or unexpected or ironic in event, becomes an apology for "the changes of men into trees, of ships into nymphs, of branches into ships, the union of gods with men." [71] Aristotle had said that a poet might justify his use of tales of the gods by appeal to custom: "This is how men say the thing is." But he did not say, with Giraldi, that "a composition cannot be pleasing in which these things do not appear," equating such inventions of the imagination with the right of the poet to be called a "maker." It is true that Giraldi is doing his best to legitimize as sisters of the epic, romances like Boiardo's and Ariosto's, crammed with all the *fatras* of the supernatural—magic horses, helmets and swords, monsters and magicians, strange disappearances and metamorphoses. But Mazzoni, speaking of poetry generally, not just of the epic, takes an even more extreme position:

If there were set before the poet two things equally credible, one of which was more marvelous than the other, though it was false, so long as it was not impossible, the poet ought to take it over and give up the less marvelous one.[72]

Tasso, who explicitly disagrees with Mazzoni in his position that a true poet is more properly an imitator of imaginary than of true things, nevertheless makes a place for the marvelous—as he must, if he is to justify his own poems. His reasoning is in keeping with his narrower conception than Mazzoni's of the verisimilar or credible: in new poems the marvelous must not be brought about by Joves and Apollos, whose marvels can be accepted in ancient poems because they were approved by ancient religion, but must appear wholly without probability in modern times; the modern poet can achieve credibility only by attributing the marvelous actions he invents "to God, to his angels, to devils, or to those to whom this power has been conceded by God or by devils, such as are the saints, the magicians, the fairies." "Because the men of our times drank in this opinion" of supernatural powers "with their milk when they were in their swaddling clothes, and were confirmed in it by the teachers of our holy Faith," such things will not seem to them beyond the limits of verisimilitude. Indeed they not only believe such things possible, but think they have often happened and will happen many times again.[73] Think how this applies to the Ghost in *Hamlet* and to the witches in *Macbeth* seen in contrast to the bookish Rhadamanthus of *The Spanish Tragedy!*

The verisimilar is usually stretched about as wide as it needs to be to allow for all the fantasies an imaginative age liked to entertain itself with.

WHAT THEN, finally, of imitation? It will be recalled from Chapter II that Fracastoro tried to define the special quality of poetic style as the "simply (or absolutely) beautiful"; he seemed to be trying to free himself of notions of usefulness and of representation and to formulate a principle which would express the sensuous delight in beauty characteristic of his age, the principle, that is, that a work of art is to be judged by the adequacy with which it expresses, in imaginatively beautiful form, the characteristic features of the subject. Fracastoro does seem to represent actual practice and taste. But it is hard to find anyone, even among practising poets, who can theorize very far on aesthetic aims (as distinguished from discussion of technical matters) except in terms of imitation and ideal truth and verisimilitude. I think of Giraldi, Tasso, Ronsard, Sidney, Jonson, Heywood, Lope de Vega, all of them successful, and four of them considerable, poets. Though Shakespeare does little theorizing, when he does he reflects the critical commonplaces (like the "ut pictura poesis" theme or the mirror concept of drama) of his time. These terms as used by the critics, however, can only be understood in the context of an age whose art shows such predominant delight in fantasy, in sensuous richness, and in highly wrought expression. A good deal of trimming was necessary to make the coat fit the wearer. But I am not sure that it was altogether conscious. "Truth to life" is the great critical trap into which most of us walk with open eyes at one time or another and never know we are caught.

4 Moral Aim

Let others task things honest: and to please
Some that pretend more strictness than the rest,
Exclaim on plays: know I am none of these
That inly love what outly I detest.
Of all the modest pastimes I can find
To content me, of plays I make best use,
As most agreeing with a generous mind.
There see I virtue's crown, and sin's abuse.
　　Two hours well spent, and all their pastimes done,
　　What's good I follow, and what's bad I shun.
　　　　　—CHRISTOPHER BEESTON, "To my good
　　　　　friend and fellow, Thomas Heywood" [1]

The Moral Aim in Theory

ANOTHER OF the great general ideas about art was the belief in the moral aim of poetry. It was nearly as axiomatic as the doctrine of imitation and is as troublesome to assess, since it appears so often divergent from actual renaissance practice. What honest moral excuse can be made for Ariosto's "golden cantoes," [2] the Elizabethan lyricists' carefree singing, or Marlowe's gilded and sensuous story-telling?

Nevertheless, statement of aims almost universally includes a didactic one. Horace's alternative ends "aut prodesse . . . aut delectare," are nowhere stated as either to profit or to delight, but everywhere as conjoined ends, to profit *and* delight. Indeed Horace's own intention, borne out by the phrases "miscuit utile dulci" [3] and "aut simul et iucunda et idonea dicere vitae," [4] warrants such equal stress. An even truer phrasing of prevalent renaissance opinion on the end of poetry, and true, too, to Horace, would be "to profit through delight." Lucretius' comparison of poetry to the honey with which a physician smears the edge of a cup of wormwood to be given to children, is everywhere copied or varied.[5] Sidney's passage is famous:

... he cometh to you with words set in delightful proportion, either accompanied with, or prepared for, the well-enchanting skill of music; and with a tale forsooth he cometh unto you, with a tale which holdeth children from play, and old men from the chimney corner. And pretending no more, doth intend the winning of the mind from wickedness to virtue; even as the child is often brought to take most wholesome things by hiding them in such other as have a pleasant taste, which, if one should begin to tell them the nature of the aloes or rhubarb they should receive, would sooner take their physic at their ears than at their mouth. So is it in men ... ; glad they will be to hear the tales of Hercules, Achilles, Cyrus, and Aeneas; and hearing them, must needs hear the right description of wisdom, valor, and justice, which if they had been barely, that is to say philosophically, set out, they would swear they be brought to school again.[6]

The theory of characterization implied in this statement will come in for fuller examination in the chapter on character.

Under this Horatian view of the aim of poetry one may range most renaissance critics, the English included. Indeed this is the one topic well represented in English criticism, partly, perhaps, because it was congenial to the temper of the English Reformation, partly also, perhaps, because it was capable of immediate practical application, especially to the stage. The extreme moralistic view led, of course, to an attack on poetry itself. The poets and the lovers of poetry, therefore, were bound to conduct their defense on the ground chosen by the attackers. The story of the attack and the defense is too well known to need repetition. And the same is true of the general didactic position of renaissance criticism. We may be content with two statements of rather different temper, those of Varchi and of Sidney.

Varchi gives a full and uncompromisingly logical statement of the position.[7] Starting from the axiom that philosophy comprehends all being, he proceeds by the scholastic method of definition and division to find that the place of poetic (the *art,* as distinct from the *act,* of making a poem) is under rational philosophy; yet rational philosophy, dealing with words and not things, is not truly a part of philosophy, but an instrument. Poetic is neither an art nor a science truly, but a faculty or instrument, and among the other faculties, it ranks above history and grammar, but below logic, dialectic, and rhetoric. Since poetic is a species of logic—taking logic, for the moment, as equivalent to all rational philosophy—no one can be a poet who is not also a logician. (Note the assumption also that one cannot perform the act of making a poem without knowing the art.) As with all the arts and sciences, the final cause of poetry is to make man perfect and happy; the only distinction is in the mode, which in the case of poetry is imitation. Poetry is the most effective means of teaching because it both delights and moves. The poet has the noblest end that could be, and performs his office, if not with the noblest, at least with the most useful instrument. But though poetry teaches by example rather than by syllogism or enthymeme (both nobler instruments than example), it has need of ethics and politics. Indeed no one can be a poet without moral and civil philosophy, and all who are not useful to men in dissuading them from vice and kindling them to virtue are not truly poets. There are four classes of poets who deserve the fire: the *plebei,* those who, like the romancers, write only to please the people (Ariosto comes in for a rap here); the *ridicoli,* who write with babbling and with banter; the *disonesti,* like Ovid, Propertius, and Tibullus, who write of lascivious things; and the *maledici,* the libelers, who write ill of others. Varchi's statement may be taken as presenting the didactic view in its strictest form. Happily, other Horatian critics are usually less rigid in their exclusions, not so severely logical as not to find, by ingenious rationalizing, a place for favorites like Ariosto and Ovid.

Sidney represents those critics, like Minturno and Daniello, who accord to poetry a position of greater dignity to begin with than does Varchi.[8] They regard it as the first great civilizing force, "the first light-giver to ignorance," symbolized by the stories of Amphion, the builder of cities, and Orpheus, the charmer of savage beasts. And, by virtue of its special activity of "making," they place it higher than the other arts and sciences, all of which rest wholly upon nature, either in describing nature or in giving rules for following it. The astronomer, for instance, describes the order of nature as set forth in the stars; the moral philosopher describes the natural virtues, vices, and passions of man and gives precepts of behavior based on them; and so on. "Only the poet, disdaining to be tied to any such subjection, lifted up with the vigor of his own invention, doth grow in effect into another nature, in making things either better than nature bringeth forth, or, quite anew, forms such as never were in nature. . . ." In Sidney's emphasis on the poet's creative activity, which he regards as the function in which man is nearest the divine image, lies the basis of an aesthetic fundamentally different from Varchi's. But he brings it back to the same premiss when he discusses the aim of poetry. The final end of all learning is said to be, as in Varchi, "to lead and draw us to as high a perfection as our degenerate souls, made worse by their clay lodgings, can be capable of." All arts and sciences are finally, if not immediately, "directed to the highest end of the mistress knowledge, by the Greeks called *architectonike,* which stands . . . in the knowledge of a man's self, in the ethic and politic consideration, with the end of well doing and not of well knowing only." Since "the ending end of all earthly learning" is virtuous action, it follows that those skills which most serve to bring it forth have the highest claim. History teaches virtuous action by example, philosophy by precept; poetry is superior in its effect to both, since it couples the general notion with the particular example. So even Sidney, with all his own love of poetry and all his awareness of its essence as a creative activity, must defend it as the best means of educating men to virtuous action.

Before we look for modifications of the didactic view, we should note what particular views of the drama follow from this assumption about the aim of poetry in general.

ONE OF THE results was to center critical interest in heroic poetry and drama at the expense of other forms. A moralistic aesthetic is apt to regard the romance as either trifling or morally dangerous and is bound to reduce the love sonnet and the pure lyric to lady trifles and immoment toys. Both Sidney and Puttenham are a little deprecatory of the English "lyrical kind of songs and sonnets." [9] De Nores dismisses from consideration odes, elegies, and epigrams as belonging to grammar rather than to poetry, whose aim he says is the furthering of civic virtue.[10] This view of the triviality of other forms puts a compensatory moral burden on epic and drama.

De Nores' stress on civic virtue is interesting. Although he is extreme in his position, basing his whole case for epic and drama on their political value, his exaggeration is only of what is a common tendency. In the view of nearly all the critics the drama is important not only because of its moral but also because of its political usefulness. In defending the commodity of plays, for instance, Heywood argues from the public good:

... plays have made the ignorant more apprehensive, taught the unlearned the knowledge of many famous histories, instructed such as cannot read in the discovery of all our English chronicles: and what man
have you now of that weak capacity, that cannot discourse of any notable
thing recorded even from William the Conqueror, nay from the landing
of Brute, until this day, being possest of their true use? For, or because
plays are writ with this aim, and carried with this method, to teach the
subjects obedience to their king, to show the people the untimely ends
of such as have moved tumults, commotions, and insurrections, to present
them with the flourishing estate of such as live in obedience, exhorting
them to allegiance, dehorting them from all traitorous and felonious
stratagems.[11]

The ethical aim tends to be interpreted more in a public than in a
private sense. By showing the evil fate of tyrants, tragedy teaches the
ruler to give his subjects a responsible government; by showing the
uncertainty of worldly glory, it teaches subjects to be contented with
their humble lot. By holding up to ridicule the follies of ordinary
men in their private affairs of business and love, comedy instructs
men in wisdom and sobriety, and hence helps them to be better citizens. Because it is a mirror of daily life, it teaches them what to
follow and what to avoid. As De Nores puts it,[12] the end of tragedy
is to make men abhor the life of tyrants and of the more powerful;
of comedy, to make men love private life, for the better conservation
of whatever well regulated commonwealth [13] they find themselves
in.

    One would hardly expect men with so solemn a view to allow as
"poetry" the popular drama of the market place, the *sacra rappresentazione* and the *commedia dell'arte;* and indeed the Italian critics do
ignore these forms as completely as if they did not exist. In paying
enough attention to the popular drama of his own country to tell
what is wrong with it, Sidney is less snobbish than his Italian masters;
but he, too, as one might expect, singles out for praise the academic
Gorboduc, noteworthy to him both for its poetry and for its serious
moral lesson.[14]

    Naturally, this utilitarian view affected the interpretation of Aris-
totle's difficult doctrine of tragic *catharsis.* Their ethical bias led most
critics to view it, as they did artistic credibility, in terms primarily
moral rather than psychological. Giraldi and Minturno both explain
it to mean that the mind of the spectator, by being moved to pity
and terror, is cleansed of the passions into which the characters of

the tragedy have fallen; he is thereby induced to become a better man.[15] Castelvetro makes a strange, but still moral, variation: the spectator is to be purged of pity and fear so that he will be changed "from vile to magnanimous, from fearful to staunch, from compassionate to severe." [16] Guarini likewise understands that the purging is to be of pity and fear, but only of the dangerous excess of these passions, which is an obstacle to virtue.[17] Varchi first extends the purgation to all passions *like* pity and fear, that is to all that move as they do; and then widens his generalization to include all passions, both irascible and concupiscible.[18] Segni, on the other hand, says that the purging is by pity and fear of *other* passions contrary to these and dangerous: anger and hate, also excessive joy, contrary to grief; excessive boldness, contrary to fear.[19] Sidney does not attempt to explain the catharsis itself. He merely says that tragedy, by stirring the emotions of "admiration and commiseration," teaches the uncertainty of this world; the emotions aroused by tragedy are viewed as the agents capable of effecting its didactic purpose.[20]

In a desire for a neatly schematic set of rules, the doctrine of catharsis was extended to comedy, the chief affection to be purged, according to Guarini, being melancholy, a highly dangerous emotion.[21] The social end of comedy, to make men love private life, De Nores says is attained by the purgation, through the delight born of imitation, of all those passions and discontents disturbing of their quiet that arise from the affairs of everyday life.[22]

One of the corollaries of the didactic bias was the allegorical theory of poetry, a theory not without important bearing on the drama. It would, it is true, be a shallow judgment to say that an uneasy awareness of the discrepancy between moral theory and much amoral practice was what kept allegory alive, both as a form for new poetry and as a device for interpreting ancient poetry. For the roots of allegorical symbolism were deep in tradition, and it remained a still vital habit of thought in other aspects of life than in poetry; the Renaissance was probably as rich in iconography, for instance, as the Middle Ages had been.[23] Nevertheless, the feeling of a need to bring poetry into line with the professed didactic aim might contribute to the long life of allegory. Such uneasiness betrays itself sometimes, as in Fracastoro's admission of allegory as the means by which apparently false things may be allowed as "true." [24] This is a commonplace attitude, of course; but it is interesting in Fracastoro because, after he has so long dwelt on the special quality of poetry as the absolutely beautiful, he must earnestly show that it is useful nevertheless. The use of the allegorical tradition by the critics finds more place, not unnaturally, in their treatment of epic, romance, and lyric than of drama. Yet the moralizing of Oedipus and Caesar as types of ambition, just as Achilles was moralized as the type of valor and Ulysses as the type of prudence, comes from the same allegorizing habit. And nothing in critical theory would run counter to the persistent practice of allegory in morality play and masque.[25]

OCCASIONALLY one meets with some modification of this utilitarian view of poetry, so generally held. In denying anything but delight as the aim of poetry, Castelvetro, it is true, appears to be a solitary rebel:

> The office . . . of the good poet . . . is after reflection to make a semblance of the truth from the happenings that come upon men through fortune, and by means of this semblance to give delight to his readers, leaving the discovery of the truth hidden in natural or accidental things to the philosopher and the craftsman ("artista"), with their own way, very remote from that of the poet, of giving pleasure or profit.[26]

> Those who will have it that poetry was invented chiefly either to give profit, or to give profit and delight together, should see that they do not oppose themselves to the authority of Aristotle, who here and elsewhere does not appear to assign any other end than delight; and if indeed he concedes some profit, he concedes it incidentally ("per accidente"), as in the purgation of terror and of compassion by means of tragedy.[27]

Several other critics, however, who are sensitive to taste and practice, take a less intransigent position than the more rigidly academic critics like Varchi and De Nores.

It is perhaps to Fracastoro that we should look for the profoundest attempt to get beneath the conventional didacticism. Though, as we have seen, he never quite frees himself from didactic assumptions, he struggles to arrive at a purely aesthetic differentia between poetry and other forms of discourse. He has some profound perceptions. Whereas the historian attempts to teach, the orator to persuade, condole, praise, or the like, the poet, Fracastoro says, aims primarily to express himself well about anything that proposes itself to him. The poet's business is to perfect and give life to his subject, and the great poets, especially those who seek to arouse wonder, do this. The beauties of style are "useful," because whatever makes manifest the perfection and excellence of the subject is useful.[28] In other words, Fracastoro attempts to define usefulness as adequate expression of the subject, and as the satisfying experience which such perfect and vitalizing expression furnishes.

Scaliger states an idea that makes of "usefulness" something more indirect and psychological, less direct and political than the cruder didactic theories.[29] He says that pleasure or gladness is a mental condition enjoyed by a perfectly healthy person, and is occasioned by an adequate object of desire; through poetry the spirit, turned back on itself, draws as from an inexhaustible spring that which inheres therein from the divine life. To illustrate how the Graces, pleasure, the Muses, and good health are related he tells the story of the Argive Telesilla, who, afflicted by a disease beyond medical art, was told by an oracle that she would be restored to health if she cultivated the Muses; she did so, and was not only cured but also endowed with vigor and the spirit of a general. Puttenham, likewise, sees a therapeutic effect in poetry. Although he justifies the minor forms of poetry on the grounds of their origin in some useful custom such as public ceremonies of rejoicing or lamentation, the justification is less ethical than Sidney's and more psychological:

Pleasure is the chief part of man's felicity in this world. . . . Therefore, while we may . . . to rejoice and take our pleasures in virtuous and honest sort, it is not only allowable but also necessary and very natural to man. . . . Therefore nature and civility have ordained (besides the private solaces) public rejoicings for the comfort and recreation of many.[30]

Lamenting is altogether contrary to rejoicing; every man saith so, and yet is it a piece of joy to be able to lament with ease, and freely to pour forth a man's inward sorrows and the griefs wherewith his mind is surcharged.[31]

The usefulness consists not in a sugar-coating to make a lesson palatable, but in an emotional release. Even here, the aim of such release is seen as the furthering of civic stability. But without pressing the social usefulness, this therapeutic interpretation, especially when applied to comedy, makes an easy and convenient defense.

In both their resistances and their partial surrenders, the critics are sign-pointers to the artistic directions of the time. For we should not imagine the didactic view of poetry to be confined to the academicians. Practising poets and playwrights and actors usually subscribe to it, at least in theory, without question. Sidney and Jonson, Tasso and Spenser come at once to mind. Among the English dramatists, those besides Jonson who have occasion to be explicit about their art—such as Chapman, Heywood, and Massinger [32]—are likely to make emphatic profession of adherence to the aim of profit in their works. The aim is implicit in the comment Shakespeare puts in Hamlet's mouth on the function of the players, to show the very age and body of the time his form and pressure. There are occasional disclaimers that anything but entertainment is intended,[33] but they are few and so far as I know confined to comedy. On a more modest level, the actors Robert Pallant and Christopher Beeston, who wrote commendatory verses to Heywood's *Apology for Actors*, probably represent the commonplace, uncritical view, stated without dogmatism or extreme claims.[34]

The Moral Aim on the English Stage

In England the didactic theory was given a great stimulus by the Puritan attack on the stage. The usefulness of tragedy and comedy as deterrents to vice—"sour pills of reprehension wrapped in sweet words" [35]—is repeated *ad nauseam* by every defender of the stage: Lodge, Nashe, Sidney, Webbe, Jonson, Heywood—to name only the principal ones. In retrospect the argument looks to us like defense for the wrong reason, partly because it seems to accord so little with predominant practice, partly because it implies such aesthetic confusion. But because drama treats of men living and acting in society, therefore in a moral and political frame, it does not offer easy rescue from an aesthetic of didacticism; and we should not too quickly dismiss the defenders as mainly interested in saving their own skins.

It is not altogether easy to judge the depth of preoccupation with moral issues in Elizabethan and Jacobean drama. Of sententiousness there is plenty. Yet when we try to recall general impressions of the whole of the drama of the period, we may remember principally the gaiety of much of the comedy, the passion for passion's sake of much of the tragedy, and the easily won happy endings of tragi-comedy and romance. Certainly we remember the dominant interest in lively story and lively people in all kinds of plays. Often tragedy treats its

horrors with a gusto that seems to accord little with the moral profession of the authors, as in *Cambises, Tancred and Gismund,* or
Selimus, among the earlier plays; *Antonio's Revenge* or *The Revenger's Tragedy* among the later ones. And comedy, light-heartedly
romantic or unabashedly indecent, often seems to be indifferent to
anything but good fun. Yet tragedy, if it is to be more than sensational violence, and comedy, if it is to be anything but froth, must
both be concerned with the values by which men live. It is for this
concern that we shall ultimately look. But ethical implication is one
thing, and explicit moral instruction another. And even ethical implication need not be so directly purgative as the defenders of the
stage claimed. Fortunately for the English popular drama, much of
it escaped the straitjacket of didacticism.

The problem of how poetry may organize our impulses and
thereby ultimately affect our morals I shall leave to Scaliger, Puttenham, and Mr. I. A. Richards. Certainly the effect is not such a simple
matter as either side in the Renaissance thought. The complaint on
moral grounds led the defense to take the obvious, but wrong, tack.
The Puritans had their opponents in a corner if the only good reason
the latter could think up for the *Ars amatoria* was that it taught
young men to shun lasciviousness. Webbe's argument is typical of
this position:

For surely I am of this opinion that the wantonest poets of all, in their
most lascivious works wherein they busied themselves, sought rather by
that means to withdraw men's minds (especially the best natures) from
such foul vices than to allure them to embrace such beastly follies as they
detected.[36]

This, of course, was the common defense made of the freedom of
manners in both ancient and contemporary drama. In his *Plays
Confuted in Five Actions* [36a] Gosson answers this line of argument
easily. Speaking of the incapability of the ordinary play-going audience to sit as dispassionate judges of the good and evil represented
before them, he says that "in the theaters they generally take up a
wonderful laughter, and shout all together with one voice, when
they see some notable cosenage practised, or some sly conveyance
of bawdry brought out of Italy. Whereby they show themselves
rather to like it than to rebuke it."

The entire position that plays teach because they imitate life comes in for a long and scornful rebuttal. Their substance is generally immorality:

The argument of tragedies is wrath, cruelty, incest, injury, murther either violent by sword, or voluntary by poison. The persons, gods, goddesses, furies, fiends, kings, queens, and mighty men. The ground work of comedies is love, cosenage, flattery, bawdry, sly conveyance of whoredom; the persons, cooks, queans, knaves, bawds, parasites, courtesans, lecherous old men, amorous young men. . . . The best play you can pick out, is but a mixture of good and evil; how can it be then the schoolmistress of life?

Tragedies, by inducing immoderate sorrow and making us lovers of dumps, undermine fortitude; comedies, by making us immoderate lovers of laughter and pleasure, undermine temperance. If not immoral, the matter of plays may be silly and unreal:

Sometimes you shall see nothing but the adventures of an amorous knight, passing from country to country for the love of his lady, encountering many a terrible monster made of brown paper, and at his return, is so wonderfully changed, that he can not be known but by some posy in his tablet, or by a broken ring, or a handkercher, or a piece of a cockle shell; what learn you by that? When the soul of your plays is either mere trifles, or Italian bawdry, or wooing of gentlewomen, what are we taught? Peradventure you will say, that by these kind of plays, the authors instruct us how to love with constancy, to sue with modesty, and to loathe whatsoever is contrary unto this.

He compares this kind of discipline to that used by a certain schoolmaster in Persia, who taught his scholars to lie and not to lie, to deceive and not to deceive; to do it to their friends for exercise, to their foes in earnest.

Wherein many of his scholars became so skilful by practice, by custom so bold, that their dearest friends paid more for their learning than their enemies. I would wish the players to beware of this kind of schooling, lest that whilst they teach youthful gentlemen how to love, and not to love; how to woo, and not to woo, their scholars grow as cunning as the Persians.

But indeed plays are no images of truth. "Either those things are feigned that never were, as Cupid and Psyche played at Paul's; . . . or if a true history be taken in hand," it is so altered to make places for tragical speeches, discourses of love, shows, and pomp, that "it is made like our shadows, longest at the rising and falling of the sun, shortest of all at high noon. . . . So was the history of Caesar and

Pompey, and the Play of the Fabii at the Theater, both amplified
there, where the drums might walk, or the pen ruffle." In summary,

the Palace of Pleasure, the Golden Ass, the Aethiopian History, Amadis
of France, the Round Table, bawdy comedies in Latin, French, Italian,
and Spanish, have been throughly ransackt to furnish the playhouses in
London. How is it possible that our playmakers' heads, running through
genus and species and every difference of lies, cosenages, bawdries, whore-
doms, should present us any schoolmistress of life, looking glass of manners, or image of truth?

Gosson also gives a pungent turn to the theory of the sugar-coated
pill:

Because the sweet numbers of poetry flowing in verse do wonderfully
tickle the hearer's ears, the devil hath tied this to most of our plays, that
whatsoever he would have stick fast to our souls might slip down in sugar
by this enticement; for that which delighteth never troubleth our swallow.
Thus when any matter of love is interlarded, though the thing itself be
able to allure us, yet it is so set out with sweetness of words, fitness of
epithets, with metaphors, allegories, hyperboles, amphibologies, similitudes; with phrases, so pickt, so pure, so proper; with action, so smooth,
so lively, so wanton, that the poison creeping on secretly without grief
chokes us at last, and hurleth us down in a dead sleep.

Neither the attack nor the defense distinguished with sufficient
acumen between levels of art [37]—between what we should call
music-hall bawdry on the one hand, where the direct appeal to
sensuality is the only intention, and more or less effective depending
on the state of mind of the listener, and, on the other, serious drama
dealing with an immoral theme, where the response demanded is
complex both emotionally and intellectually, and is satisfying in
itself. The problems of serious tragedies like *The White Devil,
Women Beware Women,* and *'Tis Pity She's a Whore* cannot be discussed on the level of Gosson and Webbe. And the defense weak-
ened its case for the portrayal of vicious subjects by invoking the
rule of poetic justice:

> But 'tis urged
> That we corrupt youth . . . :
> When do we bring a vice upon the stage,
> That does go off unpunish'd? Do we teach,
> By the success of wicked undertakings,
> Others to tread in their forbidden steps?
> We show no arts of Lydian panderism,

Corinthian poisons, Persian flatteries,
But mulcted so in the conclusion that
Even those spectators that were so inclin'd
Go home chang'd men.[38]

We are familiar enough, in the conventionally moralized sensationalism on screen, radio, and television, with the same implied argument from efficient cause and the same ethical and aesthetic confusions.

IT IS AGAINST this background of the nearly universally accepted aim of profit as the final end of poetry that we must set the Elizabethan drama, for it cannot have gone unaffected. When we look at actual practice, we have to make some distinctions. The first is between academic drama and popular drama, the second between explicit moralizing and moral implication. Academic tragedy, in Italy, France, and England, was heavily didactic; academic comedy, partly because it had better models to follow in Plautus and Terence than tragedy had in Seneca, partly because it was in closer touch with popular dramatic forms, partly because of the inevitable tendency of comedy to make diversion its first aim, was much less so or not at all. It is with popular drama, of course, that we are primarily concerned, but since in England its way was in no small part prepared by academic drama, we need not press the distinction. The second distinction, that between explicit moralizing and moral implication, is obviously of vital importance to the form of the drama. The distinction is useful to make if we do not think of it as an absolute dichotomy the terms of which must be exclusively applied to particular plays. We should think of the terms simply as representing the ends of a scale, along which there is every shading from directly announced meaning to meaning that is conveyed indirectly by the elements of dramatic form—fable, character, setting, and style.

First, for overt didacticism. This gives us no trouble in plays like *Gorboduc,* where story and statement coöperate to one explicit end. But actually there are few English plays so single-mindedly moral, or political, in aim as this. What we do find a good deal of is moralizing in the form of *sententiae* and apologues. Aristotle had made "thought" (*dianoia*) one of the requirements of tragedy, and this was usually interpreted narrowly to mean general reflection in the form of wise sayings; even without his supposed authority the general moralistic habit of the age and the educational training in collecting and using commonplaces would have doubtless led to the same result. But this sort of moralizing is not necessarily indicative of the dramatist's real artistic end, which may be to tell an entertaining or an arresting story; the sententiousness may be laid on—not necessarily hypocritically or cynically—in deference to a convention, and so appear accidental to the true organizing impulse of the play.

A good example of this is in *Friar Bacon and Friar Bungay*. In spite of the fact that Greene caps his play with Horace's line, "Omne tulit punctum qui miscuit utile dulci," we cannot seriously think that his end in exhibiting Bacon's fascinating magical powers—the crystal-gazing, the packing of the German magician off home on a devil's back, the production of the awful Brazen Head—was merely to prepare for the friar's pious abjuration of his art, any more than we can think that the author's first concern in telling the pretty Miles Standish tale of Prince Edward, Lacy, and the Fair Maid of Fressingfield was to celebrate the magnanimity of princes in giving up their sweethearts to lesser men.

It is not always possible to judge how much of this kind of extraneous moralizing is merely lip-service to the orthodox ideas about drama, how often a sign of artistic weakness, in which the desire simply to tell a story (the overwhelming motive force of the popular stage) and the uncritical acceptance of prevalent didactic theory pull in opposite directions. In view of the nearly universal assumption of the ethical purpose of literature, I should think the sententiousness more often honestly meant than not, at least in the earlier drama. In Middleton's sophisticated comedies, like *A Chaste Maid in Cheapside* and *A Trick to Catch the Old One,* it is suspect; suspect, too, very often in Fletcher, where the fine sentiments often have a hollow ring. In Chapman, Marston, Webster, and Tourneur, who are of a naturally reflective habit, the ethical generalizing is an essential element in the tone of their plays, not at cross-purposes with the major emphasis. It reinforces rather than wars with the ethical implications of the plays.

The greatest difficulty in judging didactic purpose comes, perhaps, with habitual moralizers like Dekker and Heywood. Much in the handling of *The Honest Whore*—in which in the main plot a prostitute is first reformed and then holds out against seduction by her erstwhile reformer, and in which in the subplot a patient man, a sort of male Griselda, is likewise made to hold his patience against the most trying provocations—suggests the witty manipulation of situations at least as much for theatrical effect as for moral intention. Heywood exploits a similar clever reversal of normal expectations in his two plays (*A Woman Killed with Kindness* and *The English Traveller*) in which an unfaithful wife dies from remorse at her undeservedly kind treatment. Of course it is a dramatist's business to be clever; and to raise the question of whether he is first of all writing a good play or trying to induce a more humane attitude towards prostitutes and adulteresses may seem beside the point. We should not indeed be any more concerned with intentions here than with Greene's if the authors themselves, by their frequent pointing of morals, did not ask us to be. Yet we must not let them put us off on the wrong issue. The real question for us is seen to be not degree of didactic intention but seriousness of artistic purpose, where the other question does not arise in so crude a form. The key to plays like those just named is probably the existence of a taste similar to that to which later sentimental drama was to appeal, a taste which likes the grim issues of tragedy tempered and stories of passion safely moralized. Dekker and Heywood write to such a taste uncritically—but not unseriously —doubtless because they share it.

Another less direct way than sententiousness to convey moral instruction is by the use of allegory, as in morality play and masque. In the drama the allegorical habit is seen in the long life of the morality. Even though it ceased in the eighties to be very common as a distinct form, its effect on the later drama, in the shaping both of attitude and of form, was profound. Even its precise techniques (e.g., motivation through abstract figures, psychological conflict externally represented, motivation by a Vice) did not entirely disappear. Long after satiric comedy had replaced the allegorical moral play, Jonson's *Staple of News* (1625) reverted to earlier methods. And of course in the court masque allegory continued to flourish.

But the effects of allegory need not be taken as confined to these extrinsic forms and the fragmentary survivals of their technique. More indirectly and profoundly, the attitude of mind induced by familiarity with allegory might result in an alertness to symbolism which a more realistic convention has partly atrophied in us. We know that ceremony, dress, and properties on the Elizabethan stage must have been used for symbolic value. A simple example is in the frequent use of a material crown as a symbol of power. Compare

Marlowe's rather naïve use of a crown in *Tamburlaine,* when Zenoc-
rate and the Turkish queen have a tussle over one after their husbands have fought out on the battlefield the issue of rule, and Shakespeare's more sophisticated use of one in *Richard II,* when Richard's
play with the crown in the deposition scene creates a dramatic moment rich in overtones of character, complex feeling, and irony of
theme. We also know that imagery could be used to carry symbolic
weight. But with this poetic symbolism, used often as much to induce a mood as an idea, we are at the other end of the scale from
naïve didacticism. Imagery was a form of implication that the greater
dramatists, especially tragic dramatists, were to exploit to great
effect.

   Finally, there is the ethical implication—or, one might better say,
the implication of meaning for men who must live and act in the
world—that is inherent in the action of the play and the behavior of
the characters. Here we enter a realm that we can approach more in-
telligently in the later chapters of the book. We need first to examine
the conventional notions of what tragedy and comedy were expected
to be, what they came in practice to mean to Elizabethan dramatists,
what other forms developed, what came to be the characteristic ways
of handling plot and character. The various ways in which a didactic
view of poetry may have affected the drama—in sententiousness, in
choice of subject and in attitude towards it, in the conception of
character, in the handling of the ending—will be apparent in the
consideration of these matters as we go along. Ultimately, the question of ethical implication becomes the wider one of form and meaning—that is, the question of seriousness of artistic purpose and the
adequacy with which that purpose is realized in dramatic form. That
is the final question of the book.

   With this chapter we leave the groundwork of assumptions about
literary art generally and turn towards those which concern the drama
alone.

5 Dramatic Forms

Now, sir, are you comedians?
Second Player. We are, sir; comedians, tragedians, tragi-
comedians, comi-tragedians, pastorists, humourists, clownists,
satirists: we have them, sir, from the hug to the smile, from the
smile to the laugh, from the laugh to the handkerchief.
—JOHN MIDDLETON, *The Mayor of Queenborough,*
V. i. 75–80

Shaping Influences

ANY ATTEMPT AT too fine a classification of Elizabethan dramatic
forms is bound to end in Polonius' kind of futile combination and re-
combination: "tragedy, comedy, history, pastoral, pastoral-comical,
historical-pastoral, tragical-historical, tragical-comical-historical-
pastoral." For the static labels mainly derived from forms achieved
in the past could hardly be expected to fit perfectly a new and fluid
art in the formative process. And Shakespeare was not the only
dramatist who poked fun at false precision in the use of conventional
labels.[1] Nevertheless, a comparison of the situation in the early days
of the Tudor interlude with that in the nineties and after shows that
certain forms had achieved a sufficiently recognizable identity to be
given reasonably satisfactory generic names. Heywood, for instance,
in the *Apology for Actors* (1612), describes "tragedy," "comedy,"
"history," "pastoral," and "moral." Our problem is to see how certain
dramatic habits and tendencies developed into accepted conventional
forms.

In the early days of the Elizabethan popular drama, in the sixties
and seventies, one has the impression that writers rarely had clear
distinctions in mind. When they tried to dramatize literal story, they
tended to graft on it the motivating machinery of the moral interlude.
In these early plays story and allegory run along side by side, some-

101

times without essential connection, as in *King Darius,* sometimes in combination, as in *Susanna, King Cambises,* or *Appius and Virginia.* But there is likely to be a hesitation of emphasis between story and moral, or between jollity and sensationalism. The Elders who tempt Susanna, Voluptas and Sensualitas, straddle uncertainly the realms of realism and allegory. The bawdry and slam-bang of the Vice, whose motivating function in *Cambises* is only slight, interrupt with insouciant high spirits the egregious horrors of the tyrant's reign.

> And though perchaunce some wanton word do pass which
>   may not seem,
> Or gestures light not meet for this, your wisdoms may it deem,
> Account that nought delights the heart of men on earth,
> So much as matters grave and sad, if they be mixt with mirth.[2]

Selective point of view, if there was one at all, was only the moral one. Without that anchor, or the anchor of a story well constructed to start with, incident for its own sake was apt to ride free and aimless; Peele's *David and Bethsabe* and *Edward I,* though much later than these interludes, are good examples of shapeless unselectivity of incident. Interest in abundant event remained characteristic of English dramatists to the end of the period. Nevertheless, they learned selection and bias in favor of a tragic or a comic point of view.

Not well enough by 1580, it is true, to suit the exacting Sidney.[3] Nor perhaps well enough to have altogether satisfied him twenty, or even forty, years later, for the mingling of hornpipes and funerals never ended. We must not forget that as important a phenomenon to remark as the gradual achievement of the separate forms of tragedy and comedy was the continued resistance to complete separation. Thus we have in English drama until the end of the period the habit of interweaving a tragic story with a comic subplot, sometimes quite unfused, as in Middleton and Rowley's *Changeling;* the use of comedy as an integral part of tragedy, as in *Hamlet* and *Macbeth;* a taste for serious romantic story with a happy ending, the kind of thing, practised from the start, that triumphed in Fletcherian "tragicomedy."

A QUICK REVIEW of the various lines of influence that helped the Elizabethan drama to take shape will clarify the problem.

The most important influence was that of romantic story. It was indeed the base and ground of Elizabethan romantic drama, the determinant of its essential structure. Other influences modified or adorned that structure somewhat, but never altered it fundamentally. Romantic story in dramatic form was not new in the Renaissance; it had already had a long life in the miracle play, or dramatized saint's legend. Although there are no English survivals of miracle plays except the late Croxton *Play of the Sacrament* and the Digby *Mary Magdalene*, the latter modified by morality play techniques, records testify to their ubiquitousness and to their early appearance and long continuance. Professor Manly [4] has found records of performances in many parts of England, the earliest dated 1097, the latest 1584, of plays on such subjects as St. Catherine, St. Hugh of Lincoln, King Robert of Sicily, St. Thomas à Becket, St. Dionysius, St. Andrew, and St. Eustacius. As Professor Manly has observed, the material in the Eustace legend is different in no essential way, except in its religious orientation, from the material of secular romances like *Eglamour* or *Sir Isumbras*.

The characteristics both of this type of saint's legend and of the romance of chivalry are strange adventures, separations, wanderings, rescues miraculously effected, dangers overcome and trials passed until the final triumph of reunion or martyrdom. Independent testimony to the ease with which romantic religious story could assimilate secular themes is furnished by some of the Italian *sacre rappresentazioni*. The heroines of *Santa Uliva, Santa Guglielma, Stella*, and *Rosana* remain constant under calumny and persecution, but at the end, instead of receiving the crown of martyrdom, they are reunited by the aid of the Virgin with husband or lover. The story of *Rosana* is the same as that of *Flores and Blancheflour* and of Boccaccio's *Filocolo*, a romance of separated lovers. The theme of the other three, of the faithful wife whose loyalty is sorely tried and triumphantly vindicated, is reminiscent of Griselda or of Constance. And indeed there is even a *sacra rappresentazione* on the story of Griselda, though by effecting the denouement without supernatural intervention it has lost its "sacred" quality.[5]

Certainly we know from the many titles of lost plays in the early days of the popular Elizabethan drama that the secular romances were a great quarry for material; of these only three survive—*Patient Grissell, Common Conditions* (both "contaminated" with morality play devices), and *Clyomon and Clamydes*, an episodic, yet not formless, play of chivalric love and adventure.[6] We suspect from the complaints of Gosson on moral grounds, of Sidney, Whetstone, and Jonson on artistic grounds,[7] and from Beaumont's parody in *The Knight of the Burning Pestle,* that the far-wandering tale of adventure was exceedingly popular on the stage. We may observe, too, that the characteristic English chronicle play—unless it was shaped by Marlowe or Shakespeare into tragedy—is primarily the *gestes* of a king, just as the miracle plays were often *gestes* of saints and martyrs.

The chief line of influence from the medieval drama comes then, if Professor Manly is right, from the miracle play. The mystery play, probably much less influential, was likewise neither tragic nor comic. Although individual plays might have comic or tragic moments, and although the Passion play had possibilities of developing into tragedy,[8] the conception of a mystery cycle as a whole was epic. The morality play, again, although it dramatized the perennial conflict within the soul of man between the vicious urgings of passion and the virtuous counsels of reason, and hence helped to shape dramatic motivation for later tragedy, was not in itself tragic; its concern was not to show the inevitability of failure in the contest, but the ever-renewed possibility of success—certainty, indeed, if one followed the formula. It was, therefore, nearer comedy in the medieval sense than tragedy;[9] but in the classical sense it was hardly comedy except occasionally and incidentally in the activities of the Vice, for it saw the cure of man's follies in terms not of laughter, but of sober reformation.

The inheritance of "tragedy" from the Middle Ages was solely the narrative *De casibus* tale, the tale of the fall of a man from power at the turn of Fortune's wheel.[10] Boccaccio's *De casibus virorum illustrium* fathered a long line of such narrative tragedies from Chaucer's Monk's Tale and Lydgate's *Fall of Princes* through the *Mirror for Magistrates* in its many versions down to Daniel's *Complaint of Rosamond* (1592) and even to some early seventeenth-century tragic narratives. "Comedy" as a formal term in the Middle Ages had implied merely the reverse of a tragic fall, but the renaissance inheritance of actual comedy was wider. Elements of comedy—horseplay, mockery, obscenity, and witty jesting—appeared in the religious drama and the morality. And independent farces, especially on *fabliau* themes, like *John John, Tib, and Sir John* attributed to John Heywood, perhaps had a greater currency than we can judge from surviving texts.[11] But for the conceptions of tragedy and comedy in a fully developed dramatic sense, as we understand the terms, we must look to renewed acquaintance with the ancient drama.

For practical purposes that meant in England the tragedy of Seneca and the comedy of Plautus and Terence. Terence, it is true, had been known and read throughout the Middle Ages; but misconceptions about the performances of his plays had prevented understanding of them as acting dramas.[12] As everyone knows, the imitation of classic drama did not dominate dramatic production in sixteenth-century England to the extent that it did in Italy and was later to do in France. Senecan tragedy was a powerful formative element that gave impetus to popular tragedy, but soon lost its identity in a stream composed of many currents. Roman comedy, also modifying and modified, left the pattern of its form to be more clearly recognized. The great service of ancient drama was to give English drama a point of view in handling story other than mere successiveness of event. To understand the terms in which the distinction between tragedy and comedy was viewed, we need to look beyond the plays themselves to some of the critical statements about them.

Conventional Theories of Tragedy and Comedy

Aristotle, of course, is not the first place to look. Nor, primarily, is the critics' interpretation of Aristotle. Apart from its abundant attention to language in Italy, France, and England alike, sixteenth-century criticism is largely one long exegetical exercise on the *Poetics*. But, as is often pointed out, its legislative spirit is more Horatian than Aristotelian. Moreover, how far the critics are from getting fully at Aristotle's fundamentally aesthetic point of view is shown in their continued confusion of rhetoric with poetic, their social interpretation of "better" and "worse"—Aristotle's terms of distinction between the characters of tragedy and comedy—their inability to get away from the moral implication of "truth" and "falsity" in their treatment of poetic fiction, and their predominantly moralistic rather than psychological interpretation of *catharsis*. The critics labored hard over all the terms of Aristotle's definition of tragedy, and produced a parallel and contrasting one to match it for

comedy. But all their interpretations were qualified by their inheritance of a much simpler, more schematic view of dramatic forms.
This scheme was far more widely available in the sixteenth century
than either Aristotle or the critics' interpretations of Aristotle; it was
indeed available to every educated man. It is to this scheme, therefore, that we must turn directly for an understanding of what tragedy
and comedy looked like to the sixteenth century.

In many of the early editions of Terence there is published, together
with his life, attributed to the fourth-century grammarian, Aelius
Donatus, an anonymous essay "De tragoedia et comoedia" also as-
cribed to him.[13] On examination this essay turns out to be actually
two essays, one following the other and partly repetitive of the same
ideas. The first is now generally regarded as by Evanthius, a contemporary of Donatus, and the second as probably but not certainly
by Donatus.[14] When referring without distinction to the ideas common to both essays, I shall use "Donatus" as a convenient collective
term. Still another essay written by an early grammarian, Diomedes,
and appearing in a miscellaneous collection of grammatical treatises
published at Venice by Nicolaus Jensen in about 1478, carries sub-
stantially the same account of tragedy and comedy. The three essays
are themselves evidently largely derivative from older accounts of
the drama, chiefly Alexandrian in origin.[14a] Their importance for us
is that they were the principal channels through which the Renaissance got its ideas of the history and forms of classical drama. The
Diomedes essay, through reprintings of the Jensen volume, was
fairly accessible in the Renaissance,[15] the "Donatus" was even more
so. It is a usual accompaniment to editions of Terence even when
the full Donatus commentary on the plays is absent. No one working
with Terence on the university level could have escaped it. Nor
would it have been unavailable even to grammar-school pupils.
Erasmus' school edition of Terence, for instance, contains it. So far
as one can judge, it is the standard account for the Renaissance of
ancient drama. Various brief accounts by other humanists are echoes
of these grammarians.[16]

The three essays are all brief histories of the drama, both Greek and
Latin. Diomedes treats equally of tragedy and comedy; Evanthius
and Donatus are primarily concerned with comedy. In all three, the
definitions of tragedy and comedy betray the grammarian's taste for
clear outline and rigid division. In the two fullest, those of Diomedes

and Evanthius, the differences are precisely balanced. The subject of tragedy, according to Diomedes (following Theophrastus, he says) is heroic fortune changed to adversity; of comedy, private affairs conducted without danger to life. In tragedy, the persons are leaders, heroes, kings; in comedy, humble and private citizens. The former treats of conflicts, exiles, violent deaths; the latter, of love affairs and the seizure of maidens. In the former, there is almost always a sad outcome to happy affairs, and a change of fortune for the worse; in the latter, the recognition of children and a happy outcome to sad affairs.[17] Evanthius says the principal difference is that whereas in comedy there are men of mediocre fortune, little violence and danger, and joyful endings to the action, in tragedy everything is contrary: great persons, great fears, mournful endings.[18] "Et illic turbulenta prima, tranquilla ultima; in tragoedia contrario ordine res aguntur"; as Heywood paraphrases it, "Comedies begin in trouble, and end in peace; tragedies begin in calms, and end in tempest." [19] Then, whereas in tragedy life is to be shunned, in comedy it is to be embraced. Finally, Evanthius adds the qualification that the plots of tragedy are often based on history, the plots of comedy feigned. The third essay—the Donatus proper—describes only comedy, but remarks on the distinction of its persons from those of tragedy.[19a]

The differences, then, are three, in persons, subject, and ending. But note that essential differences are distorted or neglected in the interest of schematic definition: tragedy, treating of the great affairs of kings and heroes, begins in happiness and ends in sorrow; comedy, treating of the lighter affairs of private citizens, begins in sorrow and ends in happiness. Possibly the formula for tragedy is a far-off echo of Aristotle's statement that a reversal from good to bad fortune makes the best tragedy, but it is shorn of his alternative suggestions and also of his qualifications on the degree of goodness and badness of the hero. Moreover, it is a strange simplification to make after Seneca, whose reversals are slight. As Professor Harsh observes of the normal pattern of Seneca's plays, "The situation is very bad at the beginning, and it rapidly becomes much worse." [20] In these brief treatments of the grammarians there are no fundamental questions raised, either, as in Aristotle, about the nature of tragic feeling and the conditions of its evocation, or about the irony in events that arouses wonder. To do Evanthius and Donatus justice, they are mainly concerned with comedy, and we have left of Aristotle's theory of drama only a full treatment of tragedy. Nevertheless, the schematized treatment of the grammarians was what the Renaissance knew well, and, I believe, in large part followed as understood. Since the difference in subject was taken for granted, the explicit distinguishing differences tended to resolve themselves into two: the social status of the characters, tragedy dealing with kings and heroes, comedy with ordinary citizens; and the ending, tragedy leading to ruin, comedy to a happy solution of all the troubles in the play.

Now these were the bare terms in which tragedy and comedy had been understood throughout the Middle Ages, when knowledge of their dramatic form was lost. Boccaccio's tales of the falls of princes from high estate were "tragedies"; Dante's serious poem, ending the hero's long pilgrimage from Hell with a beatific vision, in the heaven of light, of the "candida rosa" of the redeemed, was a "comedy." [21] Even with the recovery of considerable knowledge of how Greek and Roman tragedy had been acted, and a consequent return to a conception of tragedy and comedy as drama rather than as narrative, the Renaissance would have recognized in the grammarians something old and familiar. And the conception of the grammarians so far prevails that the critics generally distort Aristotle in its direction: they make distinction between the two forms rigidly social, and they draw up a parallel and antithetical definition of comedy to balance his of tragedy, giving it a full treatment to supply the absence of one in the *Poetics*. Whenever during the sixteenth century the drama is treated in more summary form, in Italy, France, or England, the terms of definition are almost always recognizably those of the grammarians. Peletier's statement in his *Art poétique* (1555) will serve as an example of many similar ones:

Au lieu des personnes comiques, qui sont de basse condition, en la tragédie s'introduisent rois, princes et grands seigneurs. Et au lieu qu'en la comédie les choses ont joyeuse issue, en la tragédie la fin est toujours luctueuse et lamentable, ou horrible à voir.[22]

I need not illustrate further, since the material is readily available. It is worth repeating the reminder, however, that in England there was no full-length critical treatment of the drama. Treatises devoted to it, like Lodge's or Heywood's, are defenses of its moral usefulness against the Puritan attack. Distinctions of form and purpose that appear either in these apologies, or in more general poetical treatises like Webbe's or Puttenham's, are very brief and follow the lines of "Donatus." [23] Even Sidney, though he has more to say on dramatic structure, hardly gets beyond the traditional formula on the essential characteristics of tragedy and comedy; he does include "the stirring affects of admiration and commiseration" in his treatment of tragedy, but gives them the usual moral bearing.

WHEN WE LOOK at the English drama of the Renaissance we see that the definition of the grammarians will apply to a good deal of it. Their view of tragedy is peculiarly suitable to the *De casibus* pattern, which is the basic pattern of much Elizabethan tragedy. But there are forms of tragedy which elude it, partly or wholly. One is the Italianate play of intrigue and crime, which may or may not treat of noble persons. Another is domestic tragedy, which is concerned with the private crimes of ordinary citizens that do not shake the body politic. The grammarians' view of comedy is sufficiently descriptive of the scores of comedies about artisans and merchants, lawyers and needy gentlemen, handled with greater or less realism; with emphasis now more on manners or character, now more on clever intrigue; with mood now satiric, now merry. That means most of the comedies of Middleton, Marston, Chapman, Jonson; some of the comedies of Shakespeare, Dekker, Heywood, Beaumont and Fletcher, and many lesser men. The definitions are wide enough to cover many plays of romantic intrigue; but there is no specific provision for the kind of romantic comedy we think of as characteristically Elizabethan, in which the characters are as likely as not to be dukes and in which sentiment is as important as comic imbroglio. There is none for Lyly's type of witty "conversation piece." Nor, at first sight, is there any for tragi-comedy and "romance." But what Aristotle and Diomedes had said about the Greek satyr play was to give important critical warrant for this renaissance tendency towards the mingling of forms. The satyr play was likewise appealed to as the ancestor of pastoral drama. Altogether unprovided for, of course, are the morality play, medieval in origin, but still surviving as a recognized type, and for the peculiarly English chronicle play, in which history is not treated as tragedy at all, but merely as a story of things that happened. The conventional definitions of the grammarians, then, even when they are stretched as wide as critics sometimes tried to stretch them, can never be made to cover all the modes of sixteenth-century drama. Nevertheless, these definitions, since they were so widely accepted as commonplace, are of fundamental importance in helping us to understand some of the major conventions of renaissance drama.

We shall consider in turn history, tragedy, comedy, and tragicomedy. It will be more convenient to treat "moral" and pastoral in relation to other forms than as separate forms in themselves. Pastoral plays, strictly defined, do not form a large class in English renaissance drama, but pastoralism is an important element in English comedy and the continental pastoral play did influence Jacobean tragicomedy. Morality plays, likewise, by the time of the great period of the drama beginning in the late eighties, have ceased to be interesting as a special class; they become chiefly important in their effect on the attitudes and techniques of tragedy and comedy. These we shall be constantly aware of.

All that needs to be said about the morality play as a separate form I shall say here.[24] Even though its heyday was over, the naming of the "moral" as a class by Heywood in his *Apology for Actors* in 1612 shows that it still had some independently recognizable existence. Occasionally one finds a play on the lines of an old-fashioned moral interlude, like *The Contention between Liberality and Prodigality* (1601),[25] or *Lingua* (1602–7), an academic play giving a serious lesson in ethical psychology. Robert Wilson, in his *Three Ladies of London* (ca. 1581) and his *Three Lords and Three Ladies of London* (ca. 1589), extends the technique from private to public ethics, and gives a lesson in the characteristic evils that beset the body politic and the saving ideals that should govern it. He even adds a topical flourish in the futile attempt of three Spaniards (Pride, Ambition, and Tyranny) to win the three Ladies away from the three Lords. The term "moral" may perhaps have been taken as well to apply to something like Lodge and Greene's *Looking-Glass for London and England* (ca. 1588–90), which, though without abstract figures, treats the threatened destruction of Nineveh as a dramatic exemplum to make Englishmen aware of their sins. The term might apply, too, to Dekker's *Old Fortunatus* (1599). This play is primarily a fairy tale, but as in a right morality the abstract figures of Fortune, Vice, and Virtue contend for dominance over the leading characters; reproof of folly is not primarily through laughter, but through a serious lesson couched in a tale half allegorical. It is interesting that

Jonson, after his triumphs in his own brand of comedy, should have experimented with some of the techniques of the obsolescent morality. In *The Devil Is an Ass* (1616) he tried his hand at a comedy set in a partial morality frame; and in 1625, in *The Staple of News,* which like *Liberality and Prodigality* has the proper use of money as the subject of the argument, he returned still further in the direction of the morality, to the detriment of his comedy. Of course as a form for pageants and masques allegory with moral intention showed no signs of decay. But our concern will be with the effect the morality had on the major forms of drama developed in the Elizabethan period.

6 History and Tragedy

quem dies vidit veniens superbum,
hunc dies vidit fugiens iacentem.
—SENECA, *Thyestes*, 613–14

For whom the morning saw so great, and high,
Thus low, and little, 'fore the even doth lie.
—JONSON, *Sejanus*, V. 902–3 [1]

The Chronicle Play

IT WILL BE convenient to begin this chapter with a brief discussion of the English chronicle play, because though it developed as a form distinct from tragedy it also provided for Marlowe and Shakespeare an important proving-ground for tragedy. The brevity of my treatment of the chronicle play is not to be taken as evidence of its unimportance, only of its relative lack of complexity from the formal point of view and also of the fullness with which other scholars have recently handled it.[2] Important as a class competing for public interest with tragedy and comedy was "history." Tragedy in the Induction to *A Warning for Fair Women* complains that Comedy and History are more popular than she.[3] Awareness of the distinction between history which is tragedy and history which is "chronicle," because it sets down history as such, is shown in titles: *The True Tragedy of Richard III, The Famous Victories of Henry the Fifth, The True Chronicle History of King Leir*. (Remember that this pre-Shakespearean play did not end tragically.) The editors of the Shakespeare Folio, it is true, put *Richard III* and *Richard II* into the category of the histories alongside *Henry IV* and *Henry V;* but to separate them would have broken a historical scheme which had achieved a kind of epical continuity. The rule, besides, could not be hard and fast, for a play with tragic overtones might yet not fully qualify as tragedy. The Henry VI plays are examples. And plays on recent history, handled with less freedom than subjects from remote times, might easily seem to lie across the dividing line.

In so far as history is viewed selectively and tragically, it meets the traditional conception of tragedy; in so far as it remains merely chronicle, it is a quite different genre and has no critical warrant. Authors might have appealed to ancient authority for it, if they had wished, in the *fabula praetextata* of the Romans, the serious play on historical subjects, not necessarily tragic and generally given in celebration of some religious and patriotic festival. Although the *fabula praetextata* was treated by Diomedes and "Donatus," no specimens of it survived except the *Octavia* attributed to Seneca, and that had a tragic bias. The English chronicle play is evidently of wholly native growth. It could grow because of the combination of a popular theater and an increasing new interest in English history. That interest was partly owing, of course, to the nationalistic feeling which followed the Reformation and which was being intensified by the war with Spain. It was owing likewise to the renaissance emphasis on historical studies as a source of enlightenment about the present. In England this took on special significance because of the memory of the internecine struggles throughout the fifteenth century and the fear that without settlement of the problem of succession the country would again lapse into civil war. Finally, history could be made to illustrate the view, cultivated by the Tudors, of a hierarchical and fixed social order as part of God's great rational plan of an orderly universe. It is interesting that the only other country which developed nontragic historical drama during the sixteenth century was Spain, a country which, like England, was developing strong national awareness, and in which the stage was even freer than the English of academic dominance.

As MIGHT BE expected, English chronicle plays are likely to be the most formless of the dramas. They have no dramatic models to follow, no organized narrative plots to borrow, only the abundant and undifferentiated material of history to draw on. One way to secure point and shape is to borrow the methods of motivation and opposition from the morality play; that is what Bale does with his *King John*. Another way is to imitate tragedy: that is what the early academic authors of *Gorboduc* and *The Misfortunes of Arthur* do; what

Marlowe does in *Edward II,* without the Senecanism and with deeper awareness of the springs of tragedy in character; and what Shakespeare does in *Richard III* and *Richard II.* Only too often the dramatists do nothing except to select enough striking incidents from a reign to fill up the time of a play and set them down as they come. The only selective point of view is liveliness of event, and the chief shaping attitude is patriotism. A familiar example of this type of play is *The Famous Victories of Henry the Fifth,* exploiting the legend of Henry's wild youth for comic purposes and of his French victories for patriotic ones. Another is Peele's *Edward I*—the wildest hodgepodge of romance, battle, rough comedy, *De casibus* morality (in the death of Elinor), and jingoistic patriotism in commemoration of the birth of the first Prince of Wales that the mind of man could conceive. Sometimes a single historical event provides a certain amoebic cohesion, as in *A Larum for London,* on the seige of Antwerp. But royal love and glorious war are not the only themes of the chronicle plays. Heywood makes an appeal to bourgeois sentiment in his *If You Know Not Me,* Part II, which is primarily a glorification of Sir Thomas Gresham, the wealthy London merchant who founded a school at Bishopsgate, built the Royal Exchange, lent money to the Queen, and qualified for the gallery of famous London citizens alongside Dick Whittington. Just to show what stuff a substantial Londoner is made of, when the news of one business reversal after another is brought to him as he is feasting the Russian ambassador and some lords from the court, he drinks the health of the Queen in wine enriched with a crushed pearl too costly for princes to buy. Such a man is obviously worthy of knighthood. Into the play for good measure are stirred the conspiracy of Dr. Parry, the comedy of Hobson the haberdasher, and the defeat of the Armada. Heywood always knows how to touch the sentimental chord. The First Part of *If You Know Not Me* is a rather sticky representation of the persecutions of the young Elizabeth at the hands of the wicked Mary Tudor and Philip of Spain; she is a saintly innocent over whom in her sleep guardian angels hover.

Shakespeare tried his hand at the nontragical history play with varying results. His solutions to the major problem of unity vary and he is not always successful. The Henry VI plays remain episodic, *King John* is not very well integrated, *2 Henry IV* falls apart into two separate interests—the Falstaff comedy and the serious history. The more successful union of comedy and history in *1 Henry*

IV is one solution; the treatment of history as epic pageantry in *Henry V* is another. But his great contribution is not so much in unifying any single play as in giving an epic sweep to the whole series beginning, in historical time, with *Richard II* and ending with *Richard III*. This plan, as the plays show, was clearly evolved during its execution and was not foreseen at the beginning. Nevertheless, the series completed, a partial design emerges. It is a development of what has been called the Tudor myth: the belief that Henry Bolingbroke's deposition of Richard II, an anointed king, was punished by God with a long train of civil discord that ended only with a providentially appointed savior, Henry Tudor, who could unite the two houses. Although both history and Shakespeare's sympathetic insights into opposing characters get in the way of a consistent design, and although Shakespeare's interest seems to me to be dramatically centered in character caught in political action rather than in a political lesson for its own sake,[4] the plays do have an underlying unity of emotional response to England's fate. In them are implicit the fear of civil war, the danger of rebellion, the necessity, above all things, of authority and order, and a deeply felt patriotism.

So much for the history play as such. But history according to critical opinion, and also according to much Elizabethan practice, formed the matter of tragedy. Two of the plays in his series Shakespeare handled as tragedies, and in so doing taught himself a good deal about the structure and motivation of tragedy. Throughout his life, history, with its recurrent theme of man in a position of power and responsibility, remained the primary source of his tragic material. *Julius Caesar* and the other Roman plays, *King Lear,* and *Macbeth,* are different only in depth and complexity from *Richard III* and *Richard II,* not different in kind. In this respect, Shakespeare, like Marlowe, Chapman, and Jonson, is following the dominant tragic tradition of the sixteenth century. To that tradition we now turn.

ELIZABETHAN tragedy may be roughly divided into three main types. according to theme and pattern: *De casibus* tragedy, or the fall of the mighty, with ambition as a chief motivating force; Italianate intrigue tragedy, with love or jealousy usually the central passion; and domestic tragedy, or the tragedy of crime in the lives of ordinary citizens. The first is derived from the traditional medieval conception of tragedy, and is perfectly consonant with Diomedes and "Donatus."

The second, if the persons are of rank, also fits the grammarians' definition. The third has no traditional warrant.

De Casibus Tragedy

Before we examine *De casibus* or "Gothic" tragedy in detail, we should scrutinize carefully the two emphatic features of the grammarians' definition of tragedy, the high rank of the persons and the unhappy ending.

The insistence on the social distinction of the persons is interesting. True enough that it has some historical basis in Greek drama. It would seem, however, to be owing more to difference in origin and function than to notions of propriety based on class. Certainly Aristophanes did not scruple to thrust into his comedies great men of public affairs like Pericles and Alcibiades. Tragedy, arising from the dithyrambic songs, a serious part of the ceremonies in honor of Dionysus, drew for its material on ancient legends of gods and heroes. Comedy, though probably also arising from the same religious festivals as tragedy, seems to have developed from the lighter side, the *kōmos* (κῶμος, L. *comessatio*) or festival procession ending in a phallic song. The songs naturally turned into indecent jests, and the jesting into commentary on contemporary men and manners. Later, the New Comedy of Menander, giving up the direct lampooning of actual men and events, continued to draw in a more general way on contemporary life and manners among Athenian citizens.[5]

Donatus found support for his view of a social distinction between the persons of tragedy and comedy in his derivation of *comedy* from *kōmē* (κώμη, L. *vicus*), the Megarian word for village or outlying hamlet; comedy was thus taken to mean in origin a song (*ōidē, ᾠδή*) of or about villagers. Aristotle, Diomedes, and Evanthius suggest this derivation side by side with another from *kōmazein* (κωμάζειν), to revel; a *kōmos* is a merry-making.[6] Either derivation is possible, since the most ancient traces of comedy have been found in the Dorian towns of Megara and Syracuse;[7] most modern scholars, however, accept the etymology from *festival-song* rather than from *village-song*. Donatus says comedy is ἀπὸ τῆς κώμης, that is "ab actu vitae hominum, qui in vici habitabant, ob mediocritatem fortunarum: non in aulis regiis, ut sunt personae tragicae"[8]—from action in the life of men who dwelt in a village on account of mediocrity of fortune, not in royal courts as do tragic persons. Moreover, the function of comedy in imitating humble life is precisely to correct its manners and morals.[8a] No statements quite like these are to be looked for in Aristotle. Analyzing Greek drama as he finds it, he says the most effective tragic hero occupies a mean between eminent virtue and depravity, and falls into bad fortune, because of some error of judgment; also, the tragic hero is "of the number of those in the enjoyment of great reputation and prosperity; e.g., Oedipus, Thyestes, and the men of note of similar families." [9] When Aristotle says that tragedy imitates men who are better and comedy men who are worse than those about us, he clearly has in mind, as the context shows, relative greatness and meanness of character.[10] When he says that poets of the graver sort imitated noble actions and the actions of good men, but poets of a lower type the doings of meaner men,[11] the ideas of distinction in social importance and of distinction in character may well both be present, simply because they would be involved together. But in any case, he is not making "class" as such the essence of the distinction.

In the Renaissance, with its undemocratic society, the critics are thoroughly in accord with Donatus and see the social distinction as fundamental in Aristotle; they take it as a rule, bound with the rule of decorum, essential to the concepts of tragedy and comedy.[12] Tragedy should not deal with persons of mean estate, not merely because we are more shaken at the fall of the mighty, though that is important to the tragic effect, but also because it would not be in accordance with verisimilitude. Terrible crimes of passion do not happen in the lives of ordinary citizens. The implication is that they are too mean-spirited to be moved by great passions. Only lords and kings and military heroes are capable of the emotions which produce tragedy. A citizen will not be moved to revenge by injuries done him, for he has no "honor." On the other hand, verisimilitude requires that any breath of comic fun which comes near the great be properly sweetened and disinfected. It is only the humble who may be subjected to the indecent jests, the horseplay, the compromising situations that make a man look foolish. A cuckolded citizen is the butt of jest; a cuckolded prince a righteous avenger. De Nores takes the revenge of the injured husband on his wife's lover in Boccaccio's story of Rossiglione and Guardastagno as an example that the enmities of illustrious and tragic persons are turned into deaths and killings, whereas those of private persons are turned into feastings and joy.[13] It is good for private men, of course, to be the subject of jest in comedy, for it teaches them to see their follies and to be better citizens. As Sidney puts it,

comedy is an imitation of the common errors of our life, which he [the dramatist] representeth in the most ridiculous and scornful sort that may be, so as it is impossible that any beholder can be content to be such a one.[14]

Lessons to the great must come not through laughter but through the spectacle of ruin. Tragedy, Sidney says,

openeth the greatest wounds, and showeth forth the ulcers that are covered with tissue, that maketh kings fear to be tyrants, and tyrants manifest their tyrannical humors; that with stirring the affects of admiration and commiseration teacheth the uncertainty of this world, and upon how weak foundations gilden roofs are builded.[15]

Ruin in tragedy meant death. Tragedy cannot end with the principal characters continuing to live in full, horrible realization of their state as so much of ancient tragedy ends (compare *Oedipus Rex, Choephorae, Prometheus Bound,* the *Hercules Furens* of both Euripides and Seneca), or with a serious upturn towards a redemption to be worked out in life (compare *Eumenides* and the evident intention of the lost third play from the Prometheus trilogy). Death is not merely a useful means of giving a certain finish to the action. It is an essential part of the *De casibus* conception of tragedy. It is both the wages of sin and the gruesome physical evidence of the corruption and instability of mundane things, on which most men are foolish enough to pin their hopes. Even with the renaissance recovery of more faith in the uses of this world, the *memento mori* and the *danse macabre* as artistic themes continued to have a profound fascination; indeed their very recrudescence in the sixteenth century was perhaps a testimony, by way of dramatic contrast, to the new urgencies of life.[16]

The view of tragedy as the prerogative of great ones is intimately bound up with the death motive. For what can better bring home to man the irony of his earthly hopes than a swift descent from the height of power, wealth, and glory to ignominious death? Death taps on the shoulder of emperor and plowman, grand lady and chamber-

maid; the coffin worm awaits all alike. The king's final progress is
through the guts of a beggar.

> Imperious Caesar, dead and turn'd to clay,
> Might stop a hole to keep the wind away.
> O, that that earth which kept the world in awe
> Should patch a wall t'expel the winter's flaw!

The conception of death as tragic in itself is seen in a crude form
in *Tamburlaine.* So far as this conqueror of kingdoms and scourge
of God knows any tragedy, it is only the tragedy of his impotence
before the universal fact of death. A dozen or so years later the theme
of death is developed in *Hamlet* in all its possibilities of tragic
subtlety. It is the *leitmotiv,* played in all keys—of grief, physical re-
pugnance, horror, grotesque comedy, stoic acceptance. Death bears
a tragic irony here far deeper and more complex than in the traditional *De casibus* story. For Hamlet, so bitterly disillusioned at the
beginning of the play, learns acceptance of life only in time to lose
it, and to lose it gallantly. The difference between *Tamburlaine* and
Hamlet is the difference between tragedy still strongly medieval, in
which death is a sufficient tragic fact, and mature renaissance tragedy,
in which the irony is in man's ennobling struggle against unfriendly
destiny.

THE NOTION OF tragedy as a fall from greatness lent itself especially
well to the treatment of ambition and its consequences. The typical
De casibus story told of the ascent to power as well as of the loss
of it, and so perhaps helped to establish the pyramidal rise and fall
structure characteristic of so much Elizabethan tragedy.[17] The shape
of such stories is clearly indicated in the image of the hill the Painter
and the Poet use to describe the rise and predicted fall of Timon:

> This throne, this Fortune, and this hill, methinks,
> With one man beckon'd from the rest below,
> Bowing his head against the steepy mount
> To climb his happiness, would be well express'd
> In our condition.

> .   .   .   .

> When Fortune in her shift and change of mood
> Spurns down her late belov'd, all his dependants
> Which labour'd after him to the mountain's top

Even on their knees and hands, let him slip down,
Not one accompanying his declining foot.[18]

We can watch the tragedy of power grow more complex. It starts with the medieval idea that tragedy is a fall from greatness resulting from the instability of all sublunary affairs. Descended from the Stoical pessimism of the late Roman world, this view of tragedy was formed as the *contemptus mundi* theme grew in medieval thought and found literary expression in narrative "tragedies" of the falls of princes. In some of Boccaccio's stories, however, and increasingly in the later Mirror literature, retribution for sin freely willed operated in the tragic fall side by side with unstable fortune. This association is well stated by Puttenham in his account of the origin of tragedy after tyrants came into the world:

... their infamous life and tyrannies were laid open to all the world, their wickedness reproached, their follies and extreme insolencies derided, and their miserable ends painted out in plays and pageants, to shew the mutability of fortune, and the just punishment of God in revenge of a vicious and evil life.[19]

In the Renaissance the *De casibus* conception took dramatic form after a new infusion of Stoicism from Seneca's tragedies. In them the constant theme is the uncertain stay of worldly power.

Quicumque regno fidit et magna potens
dominatur aula nec leves metuit deos
animumque rebus credulum laetis dedit,
me videat et te, Troia. non umquam tulit
documenta fors maiora, quam fragili loco
starent superbi.[20]

So Hecuba at the opening of *Troades*. But pride is unsafe not only because it stands on the uncertain ground of all things beneath the moon; it is also unsafe because it is the sin of Lucifer, the deadliest of the Seven. These two ways of regarding tragic catastrophe, the Stoic and the Christian, are both to be looked for in Elizabethan tragedy.

Actually, they do not form a simple contradiction. They can be, and sometimes were, reconciled theologically: since it was the sin of our first parents that brought the sway of irrational chance into the world, there is a sense in which even bad fortune is retribution. Fortune is a hampering circumstance of this world that men as children of Adam must live with; yet they have some choice in the degree of their subjection. To follow pride and to seek riches and power is to make themselves the more liable both to evil temptations and to the whims of Fortune; to live quietly and modestly, content with their lot, is to avoid the occasion of sins that accompany greatness and to stay clear of the realms where Fortune is most ready to operate. But we do not expect to find the dramatists often concerned with precise logical reconcilement. What is more important for them as poets is that these two views of tragic catastrophe, one regarding it as unavoidable bad fortune, the other as divine retribution for sin, were as much a matter of emotional response to the world as of philosophy. Both views were components of the Christian tradition; different men and different ages, or sometimes even the same man at different times, reflected more strongly now one, now the other, intuition about the world. In Elizabethan plays, we sometimes find the two views operating crudely, as in *Locrine*,[21] in what seems to us unassimilated juxtaposition. More often we find something more complex, with both views present, but with an emphasis of mood in one direction or the other. These matters of emphasis are very hard to define, and philosophical consistency is not to be looked for. More of this, with illustration, as we go along.

A way to intensify tragedy came by a shift of emphasis in the Christian ethical scheme from its theological to its psychological aspect. Aristotelian-Thomistic ethics saw the attainment of virtue as the active victory of reason over the will, which in turn governed the passions in the interests of reason. Potentiality for tragedy lay in the disruptive force of runaway passion. The more narrowly ethical side of this scheme had been expressed in the morality play, with its contest between the virtues and the vices for the soul of every man. And the forms and terms of the morality play were not to be forgotten in later tragedy. But it was the psychological side of the scheme, the conflict between reason and passion, that widened the possibilities for tragedy in the Elizabethan period. In the highly developed psychological theories of the passions in which there was at the time such great interest, dramatists found means of deepening motivation and of intensifying internal conflict.[22] This making of the conflict personal gave, in turn, new immediacy, poignancy, and subtlety to the moral problem. And the dramatists did not lose sight of the stage upon which this battle was fought. In Marlowe, Jonson, Chapman, and Shakespeare, all heirs of the *De casibus* or "Gothic" tradition, the simple old theme deepened into an awareness of the complex tensions between man's individual desires and the divine order, and hence into an awareness of profound tragic irony.

The central irony in old *De casibus* tragedy is the disproportion between the price man sets on worldly power and its actual worth. As the Elizabethans developed the theme, their sympathies and their moral emphases varied.[23] Ambition, as the sign of man's aspiring mind, could even be viewed as godlike; yet, however regretfully, it was rarely seen as other than ultimately dangerous. Even Tamburlaine, "the fiery thirster after sovereignty," found that

> The perfect bliss and sole felicity,
> The sweet fruition of an earthly crown

must yield before death. And Faustus'

> world of profit and delight,
> Of power, of honor, of omnipotence,

lasted but twenty-four years, a mere breathing moment before the eternity of suffering that, at the hour his term was up, he foresaw so acutely. But Tamburlaine, stilling our judgment, carrying us along emotionally on his joyous surge of magnificence, is at one extreme of the scale. At the other stands Sejanus, seen from the beginning as evil and dangerous in his arrogant impiety, holding power precariously in a world of cruel intrigue and rotten flattery; at the end, when his body is torn to bits by the mob, we are stunned by a retribution horrifying in its savagery, yet somehow fitting to the vicious and hollow world he helped to make:

> The whole, and all of what was great Sejanus,
> And, next to Caesar, did possess the world,
> Now torn and scattered, as he needs no grave—
> Each little dust covers a little part—
> So lies he nowhere, and yet often buried!

Sometimes, as I have suggested, the moral emphasis is more Stoical, sometimes more Christian. Chapman, not altogether consistently with his moral comment in prologues and speeches, suggests obliquely through the imaginative direction of his plays, that Bussy and Byron are somehow blameless in their passion for greatness—victims, like Seneca's heroes, of a world in which human aspirations count for little. This shift of sympathies is partly owing to Chapman's peculiar variation of the great man theme. His heroes are not clearly motivated by simple ambition for power. They seem to be moved as much or more by an intense ambition to be themselves in their innate greatness; they feel themselves caught in a world where man-made law is not true justice, where crooked policy takes the place of direct and honest action, where the holders of power are not always the great in spirit. But Bussy and Byron never recognize that their desire for an uninhibited exercise of "greatness" is inevitably a thrust at power. Since it is not easy to reconcile this absolute freedom to be great with any system of law and government, much less the authoritarian one Chapman himself allows, his heroes are doomed to bafflement and noble protest. Shakespeare, on the other hand, viewing ambition more traditionally, makes two of his insurgents a Richard III and an Edmund, evil troublers of the poor world's peace. A third, Macbeth, is no less capable of noble greatness than Bussy or Byron, but he is differently judged. He himself knows that he is putting his "eternal jewel" in jeopardy when he murders Duncan to get the power that lures him so fatally. But that danger seems a long way off. He has uneasy premonitions that he cannot trammel up nearer consequence:

> . . . that but this blow
> Might be the be-all and the end-all here,
> But here, upon this bank and shoal of time,
> We 'd jump the life to come.

What irony! For he loses both the here and the hereafter. We pity him, not because he cannot free himself from the shackles on his ambition, but that in breaking them he but binds himself to damnation.

Nevertheless, the ancient conception of tragedy as a fall from greatness underlies all these plays and, however differently the responsibility for failure is assessed, and however differently power and greatness are valued, the idea lends a constant irony of its own—to Bussy's tragedy no less than to Macbeth's. Worldly greatness is seen as both a fascination and a fatality.

Ambition (which is a thirst after honour and glory, a gluttonous and excessive desire of greatness) is a sweet and pleasing passion, which distilleth easily into generous spirits, but is not without pain got forth again. . . . *Natura nostra imperii est avida, & ad implendam cupiditatem praeceps: We are naturally greedy of authority and empire, and run headlong to the satisfying of our desires.* And with such force and violence do some men run, that they break their own necks, as many great men have done, even at the dawning as it were, and upon the point of entrance and full fruition of that greatness which hath cost them so dear.[23a]

IN A SOCIETY whose equilibrium was felt to be so precarious, the exercise of power was of the most vital concern. Think how many Elizabethan and Jacobean tragedies have some form of it as a theme—the lust for power, the corrupting effects of power, both on the holders of power and on their followers, the conflict between the drive and insight of a great man and the limitations of authority and of man-made laws. There are the early plays from legendary British history on the dangers of overweening ambition and of civil war (*Gorboduc, Misfortunes of Arthur, King Leir, Locrine*); the biographical Mirror plays on a simple rise and fall pattern (*Cromwell, Stukely,* the Jane Shore story central to Heywood's *Edward IV,* the Queen Elinor story in Peele's *Edward I*); the plays in which the reign of an English king is given a tragic pattern (*Troublesome Reign of King John, True Tragedy of Richard III,* Marlowe's *Edward II,* Shakespeare's *Richard III, Richard II,* and parts of the *Henry VI* plays); the "conqueror" plays owning *Tamburlaine* as a progenitor (*Selimus, Alphonsus of Aragon, Battle of Alcazar*); the many tragedies on Roman history, especially the exciting period of struggle for power at the end of the republic and the beginning of the empire (*Caesar's Revenge, Nero,* Chapman's *Caesar and Pompey,* Shakespeare's *Julius Caesar, Antony and Cleopatra,* and *Coriolanus,* Jonson's *Sejanus* and *Catiline,* Heywood's *Rape of Lucrece*); and the tragedies boldly drawn from the lives of contemporary, or nearly contemporary, historical figures (Marlowe's *Massacre at Paris,* Chapman's *Bussy d'Ambois, Chabot,* and his two Byron plays, the anonymous *Sir John Van Olden Barnavelt*). We must add, too, several plays that do not exactly fit into any of these categories: Marlowe's *Dr. Faustus,* Shakespeare's *Timon, Macbeth, King Lear,* and even, in part, *Hamlet.* Power in a far wider sense than the merely political is the motive of Faustus. *Timon,* though it is not concerned with the exercise of power, states in its barest terms the personal problem of the hollow service that goes with power and wealth—the service of the summer-birds that fly when winter comes; and the play is built on the great man pattern, the rise alluded to and the fall enacted. Though power is not the major issue of *Hamlet,* it is nevertheless a crucial issue, since it is responsible for the state of things that

Hamlet must set right; and the play, as I have already suggested, is full of echoes of the *De casibus* theme. *King Lear* is not so clearly recognized at first as of this progeny, for it is at the extreme of complexity from the old simple Mirror tale. Nevertheless, it has power as one of its principal themes and plays on it in different keys, as *Hamlet* does on death. *Macbeth* is the full flowering of *De casibus* tragedy, at the end of a straight line from let us say *Richardus Tertius;* deepened and enriched, but with the old elements clearly marked. Power is even one of the motives of *Titus Andronicus.* Except, then, for *Romeo and Juliet* and *Othello,* and in part *Titus Andronicus* and *Hamlet,* all of Shakespeare's tragedies are to a greater or less degree in the tradition of Gothic tragedy. Like Chapman and Jonson, Shakespeare carries over into a time when the focus in tragedy is shifting elsewhere.

There are two specially interesting things to remark about this tragedy of ambition or power. One is that it is based on history, real or imaginary. The reader will recall the critics' prejudice, ultimately based on Aristotle, in favor of historical subjects for tragedy because they have verisimilitude. The critics reasoned that an audience would expect to have heard of such great misfortunes and would not therefore find an invented story—or at least a story with imaginary names —credible. Since this rule for historical subjects appears in Evanthius, one can expect that it was thoroughly familiar.

The other point to be noted is the very un-Aristotelian conception of many of the tragic heroes in this list. The grammarians had nothing to say about the hero beyond his social position. There is no attempt in many of the plays to make the hero "midway between good and bad." In about a third of those I have listed above he is frankly bad, a dangerous seeker, through means ruthless or cunning, of tyrannous power. He may excite a good deal of admiration for his large imagination of power and for his boldness in going after it (as with Tamburlaine and Richard III), but he can hardly be taken as a good man erring through weakness or a mistake in judgment. There is no true *hamartia* in the Mirror tradition. The tragedy lies in the instability of power in itself. True, a man may commit crimes which provoke retribution and for which he will inevitably pay, but to induce him to commit crimes is only one of the tricks false Fortune plays on him. And the good, moreover, who trust to her fall as well. Very powerful reinforcement to interest in the careers of tyrants

came in the horrid fascination to Elizabethans of Machiavellian political doctrine. It gave new vividness of realism to the tragedy of
ambition, so long familiar. Judging by the standards of Aristotle,
who says there is nothing tragic in the fall of a wicked man, we do
not find Muly Morocco, King John or Richard III, Sejanus or Catiline, satisfactory tragic heroes. Macbeth is perhaps the only villain-
hero who fully arouses both pity and fear. This is only to say that
the Elizabethan tragedy of ambition is not in its conception Aristotelian. For we must, I think, admit that this type of hero had
immense fascination for the Elizabethans themselves. Puttenham
assumes, in the passage I quoted a few pages back, that tragedy
originated in the necessity of reproving the tyrannous abuse of power.

There are, of course, many heroes in this tragedy of power who
come near, or actually fit, the Aristotelian pattern—figures like Edward II and Richard II, Cassius, Antony, and Coriolanus, figures
whom we sympathize with as well as condemn, and whose ends,
exciting pity, as well as fear, give rise to a more complex irony than
do the falls of the merely wicked. But it is necessary to point out
the long endurance of a different tradition, and to point out, too, the
force of horror its simpler irony might have. Jonson with Sejanus is
in this respect closer to medieval tradition than Shakespeare with
Macbeth or Coriolanus.

MEDIEVAL TRADITION and the theory of the grammarians (partly by
its omissions) combined, then, to produce one of the major types of
Elizabethan tragedy, the tragedy concerned with ambition and power.
It received reinforcement, too, from revived classical tragedy, at
least as understood. The play of Sophocles most widely read—almost
certainly because Aristotle had discussed it so fully as a perfect
tragedy—was *Oedipus Rex.* To the Renaissance, Oedipus became,
in a most un-Greek interpretation, the classic type of dangerously
ambitious man, and his fall was read as a lesson to the mighty. The
lesson was thought to be clearly seen in his reappearance as old,
helpless, and blind in the *Phoenissae* of Euripides and of Seneca.
Very rarely do any references occur to the wonderful *Oedipus at
Colonus,* in which Oedipus has expiated his unwitting crime and
achieves in his death a mysterious power for good. Among the favorite plays of Euripides were *Hecuba* and *Troades,* both on the greatest
of all *De casibus* themes, the destruction of Troy; and *Phoenissae,*

on the fatal struggle between the sons of Oedipus, Eteocles and Polyneices, for the possession of Thebes. It is perhaps suggestive that the one adaptation of Euripides to be published in England was of the *Phoenissae,* Gascoigne and Kinwelmersh's *Jocasta* (1566). Lodovico Dolce's Italian version of a Latin translation of Euripides had Senecanized the play with gloomy reflections on the instability of Fortune, the dangers of ambition, and the superior desirability of the simple life; the English translators of the Italian further emphasized the same themes.[24] This play, with the theme of ambition centered in civil war, was clearly thought by Elizabethans to have a special relevance to their times. Their own early attempts at classical tragedy—*Gorboduc* and *The Misfortunes of Arthur*—make use of native subject matter to point the same lesson.

I said that Dolce's *Giocasta* was Senecanized. Seneca contributed, of course, the predominant classical influence to *De casibus* tragedy. Of the ten plays generally regarded in the Renaissance as his, one, *Troades,* is a straight tragedy on fallen glory, and four have ambition or tyranny as themes; it is central in *Phoenissae* and *Octavia,* subsidiary in *Oedipus* and *Thyestes.* All ten of the plays make much of the mutability of Fortune. English *De casibus* tragedy does not organize itself in Senecan fashion, but it finds in Senecan tragedy powerful reinforcement of familiar themes. As I have suggested in the first chapter, this is surely an important reason, among others, why the Renaissance took Seneca rather than the Greek dramatists to its heart. He talked about things Englishmen of the sixteenth century knew from historical experience and long moral discipline to be dangerous and fraught with possible tragic consequences. Moreover, he brought poetical power to the expression of that Stoical pessimism latent in much Christian thought. In a world in which the cards are stacked against men, a man must not look for amelioration in circumstance. His chance for happiness lies in learning to see the world for what it is and in enduring it courageously. This is not quite the way out of Christian asceticism; it was a way more acceptable to the Renaissance. A man may live in the world and yet be superior to its lures and its blows. The way lies in self-knowledge and self-dependence.

The Elizabethans would have found in Seneca, too, a warrant for the villainous hero. His characters are on the whole an unlovely lot. And they are un-Aristotelian, in having no flaw that can be rightly

interpreted in Aristotle's sense. Medea, Phaedra, Atreus, and Clytemnaestra are so possessed by furious passion that they are hardly
responsible agents. Modern taste finds it hard to respond to them
with pity. Yet Seneca probably conceived of them as pitiable in the
very helplessness with which they are driven by their passions of
jealousy, love, or desire for revenge. The relatively passive Hercules,
in *Hercules Oetaeus,* who merely suffers and commits no crime, is
instructive. The killing of Lichas in the extremity of torture he
suffers from the shirt of Nessus cannot count as a crime. Hercules
does arouse pity, yet his case is only an exaggeration of that of the
other Senecan heroes in that they are all essentially victims of misfortune, a misfortune which drives them to crime. Professor Craig
points out the element of titanism in the Hercules story and reminds
us of the fascination that titanism must have had for the Elizabethans.[25] This titanism is expressed in one mood in frankly villainous
heroes like Richard III and Selimus, in another in Chapman's more
complicated heroes, whose passionate drives are sympathetically
conceived and who, like the mighty Hercules, go down without surrender.

> Prop me, true sword, as thou hast ever done!
> The equal thought I bear of life and death
> Shall make me faint on no side; I am up;
> Here like a Roman statue I will stand
> Till death hath made me marble.[26]

Italianate Tragedy of Intrigue

Besides tyranny, Seneca has another repeated theme in his tragedies, revenge incited by jealousy, and this is a theme which leads us
into the second great class of English renaissance tragedy, the Italianate tragedies of intrigue centered about crimes of passion. The revenge theme furnished invaluable dramatic motivation to English
dramatists; though they shifted its moral implications, they never
let go of it as a dramatic device until the closing of the theaters.[27]
They did not have to look to Seneca for it, of course, for it was often
a component of narrative Mirror tragedies, it was familiar through
their favorite, Ovid, it was a notorious feature of contemporary
Italian *mores,* and it evidently had a good deal of vitality in their

The Tragedies of Jocasta and of Clytemnaestra from Boccaccio's *De Claris Mulieribus,* Ulm, 1473

De Clitemestra micenar regina. C. xxxiiij.

129

own turbulent lives. But that Seneca impressed them with its dramatic possibilities is clear enough from the early imitative tragedies like *Gorboduc, The Misfortunes of Arthur, Locrine,* and *Titus Andronicus,* and from the revengeful ghosts that continue to haunt the stage into the seventeenth century. Even in the most thoroughly Senecan of English plays, the imitation of the pattern of action is not close, as it is in continental Senecan tragedy, for Seneca was too narrow in plot, too static for English taste, which liked plenty of action as well as plenty of words. Nevertheless, Seneca furnished them with a motive for opposition and counter-action out of which exciting conflict might come.

Many Elizabethan tragedies apply this revenge motive, as Seneca does in *Thyestes,* to the favorite theme of ambition (e.g., the early academic tragedies, *Locrine, True Tragedy of Richard III,* Shakespeare's *Richard III* and *Julius Caesar*); and a few Jacobean tragedies do the same (e.g., *Hamlet,* Jonson's *Sejanus* and *Catiline*). But there is another longer-lived line of revenge play where the central themes are love and jealous hatred, as they are in Seneca's *Medea, Agamemnon, Phaedra,* and the two Hercules plays. With these revenge plays we may associate other plays of passionate crime and intrigue where revenge does not figure at all. I am not, that is, treating "revenge" as a class of tragedy, but as a motive which frequently operates in tragedy of two different sorts, the rise-and-fall tragedy of ambition, and the Italianate tragedy of intrigue. There is recognizable in the latter class a different line of tragic interest, with different emphasis. Professor Farnham makes *The Spanish Tragedy* the father of it.[28] A very early example is the Inns of Court drama of *Gismond of Salerne* (1567–68), later revised by Robert Wilmot, one of the original authors, as *Tancred and Gismund* (1591–92);[29] but *The Spanish Tragedy* appears to have started the new fashion on the public stage.

The Spanish Tragedy is primarily a lively play of intrigue, psychologically motivated, in which there is a love affair (as well as the motive of ambition) and in which revenge within revenge cleverly managed furnishes exciting action. Among Elizabethan plays of its descent I should include Kyd's *Soliman and Perseda,* the early *Hamlet,* Marlowe's *Jew of Malta,* Shakespeare's *Titus Andronicus* and *Hamlet,* Marston's *Antonio's Revenge.* The major Jacobean plays in this line are Shakespeare's *Othello,* Marston's *Insatiate Countess* and perhaps his *Sophonisba,* Tourneur's *Re-*

venger's Tragedy and *Atheist's Tragedy,* Beaumont and Fletcher's
Maid's Tragedy, Webster's *White Devil* and *Duchess of Malfi,* Middleton's *Women Beware Women* and *Changeling;* the major Caroline ones, Ford's *Broken Heart* and *'Tis Pity She's a Whore.* Many
lesser-known plays, besides, fall into this general class. There are
many differences, obviously, among the plays in this list. Some, like
Titus Andronicus, Sophonisba, and *Hamlet,* cross the lines of the
other big class, the tragedy of power. (*Bussy D' Ambois* and the *Revenge of Bussy,* which I put into the other class, might likewise, for
the same reason, have been included here.) Political intrigue is not
absent from many of these tragedies, especially the earlier ones, yet
it is usually only one among other motives, and the movement of the
action is not the rise-and-fall pattern. Most of the tragedies in the
list have love, lust, or jealousy as the motivating passion; but, though
none of these passions is dominant, though present, in *Hamlet* or
The Jew of Malta, both plays are clearly descendants of *The Spanish
Tragedy.* Revenge figures in most of the plays, though not centrally
in all. Nevertheless, all these plays belong in this same loosely conceived class because they are all tragedies of intrigue motivated by
passion, they nearly all have a romantic interest, and when they
achieve tragic irony it is of a different sort from that of the tragedy of
ambition centered about the theme of power. One may, with large
reservations, include even *Romeo and Juliet,* for though revenge does
not figure centrally in it and though it does not issue in crime, it is
at least a tragedy of love and intrigue quite unrelated to *De casibus*
tragedy.

THE TYPE OF story on which these plays are based is to be found in
the Italian *novelle,* which were turned out in quantities in the Renaissance. Although the major collections are familiar names to everyone, it may be useful to set down here in one place the most important.[30] The best-known rivals to the *Decameron,* still a perennial
favorite, though not translated as a whole until 1620, were Matteo
Bandello's *Novelle* (1554) and G. B. Giraldi Cinthio's *Ecatommithi*
(1565 etc.). For Englishmen who could not read Italian—and the
number of traveled gentlemen who could must have been great—
there was in French Boaistuau and Belleforest's much moralized
version of Bandello, *Les Histoires tragiques* (1559 etc.). Marguerite
of Navarre's popular *Heptameron* (1559) was less useful for tragedy.

In English there were numerous collections—free translations, usually with considerable moralizing additions, of Italian tales or their French versions. The most important were William Painter's *Palace of Pleasure* (1566–67, 1575), from a variety of authors including Boccaccio, Bandello (both direct and through Boaistuau and Belleforest), Giraldi, and Marguerite of Navarre; Geoffrey Fenton's *Certain Tragical Discourses* (1567), from Belleforest; George Turberville's *Tragical Tales* (1587), in verse, chiefly from Boccaccio; George Whetstone's *Rock of Regard* (1576) and *An Heptameron of Civil Discourses* (1582), with some stories from Giraldi and others, with some invented; Barnaby Rich *His Farewell to Military Profession* (1581), with sources, when they can be found, in the usual Italians. There were, besides, lesser collections and single tales. Spanish authors likewise translated and imitated the Italian tales and produced collections of their own, the finest being Cervantes' *Novelas ejemplares* (1613); this added to the Italian and French *novelle* a rich source, on the whole more suitable for romance than for tragedy, to be drawn on by later Jacobean and Caroline dramatists.

Another source of the same type of story was in Italian tragedy. Although Italian poets leaned pretty heavily on Seneca and on Roman history for themes, some, like Giraldi, went to the *novelle* for more up-to-date stories. Seven of Giraldi's nine tragedies (published posthumously in Venice in 1583) are based on his own prose tales. *Epitia,* for instance, is based on his fifth novel of the eighth decade; the story, through Belleforest, reached Whetstone and ultimately Shakespeare, who dramatized it as *Measure for Measure*. There is a probability that Shakespeare knew the Italian tale and even play as well as both the narrative and dramatic versions of Whetstone.[31] Another example is Luigi Groto's *La Hadriana* (1578), recognized as possibly influencing *Romeo and Juliet* through the medium of some intermediate English play. We are not very sure of the channels by which the Italian drama influenced the English. We know that Italian actors visited England; whether they acted anything but *commedie dell'arte* we do not know. But it is perhaps unlikely, since the tragedies and the *commedie erudite* were written for the academies and the courts. There is no reason, however, why some of the plays may not have been available in printed copies brought from Italy. Social and literary commerce with Italy was abundant, and animadversions against the influence, literary or moral, of Italian drama imply that it was widely known. Certainly, a number of English comedies are directly traceable to Italian originals. And many English plays, either tragedy or comedy, have features so like Italian plays that we are tempted to posit for their conception and design some immediate Italian source. On the whole, however, the evidence is more extensive and more convincing for comedy than for tragedy.[32] About the *novelle,* at any rate, we can be sure enough.

Now the *novelle* are particularly suitable for dramatic plundering —for comedy, tragedy, or romance. Any reader of Boccaccio's tales knows that those centered around romantic adventure are told chiefly for their narrative point. Complication leads to some sort of neat unraveling, happy or unhappy. They have, besides, an air of verisimilitude; they are located at a particular place, often at a particular time, and the names appear to be those of real people. Bandello and Giraldi specialize in tales of passion fit for tragedy, with emphasis on violence and horror, Giraldi especially so. All these things make the *novelle* acceptable to English dramatists. It is easy to see, however, how tragedy based on these stories takes on a different color and tone from the tragedy of ambition, and how it sometimes slips away from even that broad conception of tragedy formulated by the grammarians. For one thing, social position ceases to be so essential to the irony. For another, an invented plot may serve as well as a true one. For still another, a romantic intrigue plot may by a clever turn be brought to a happy conclusion. Indeed, that is the inevitable direction of this sort of tragedy, as seen in the tragi-comedies and romances of the later Jacobean and Caroline dramatists. Even revenge comes no longer to insure an unhappy ending; compare Middleton and Rowley's *Fair Quarrel* and Webster's *Devil's Law Case.* A rather verbal, posturing "honor" is often satisfied with something considerably short of killing. But this is at the end of things.

ITALIANATE INTRIGUE tragedy was bloody enough in its heyday in the 90's and early 1600's. And it was, too, generally satisfying to the traditional definition of tragedy in that it dealt with the turbulent affairs of illustrious persons and ended in death. It was also, we must believe, capable of satisfying renaissance notions of classical principle. An illuminating instance of this is found in De Nores' *Poetica.*

He is perhaps the most rigidly academic and the least imaginative
of all the Italian Aristotelians. He is at once so sure of his correct
classicism and actually so imperceptive that one can be certain his
departures from classical intention are wholly unconscious; they are
especially valuable, therefore, in revealing tastes of his time which
he did not recognize but from which he could not escape. For each
of the major literary forms, epic, tragedy, and comedy, he chooses
a tale from Boccaccio and shows how it might be worked up according to Aristotelian principles. The story he takes for tragedy is the
brutal story of Rossiglione and Guardastagno,[33] two noble knights of
Provence, in which Rossiglione, in revenge for his wife's infidelity
with his friend, first waylays Guardastagno and murders him, then
gives his heart, cooked and dressed as if it were the heart of a wild
boar, to his wife to eat. When, after she has eaten it, he tells her
what she has done, she kills herself by leaping from a window; he,
fearing reprisals from her family, takes flight. This story, De Nores
says, is suitable for tragedy by reason of the illustrious rank of the
personages, the characters midway between good and bad, the reversal from happiness to unhappiness with peripety and recognition,
the completeness and verisimilitude of the action, capable of arousing
pity and fear and of being restricted to twenty-four hours—in other
words, by reason of the terms of Aristotelian formula as typically
understood in the Renaissance. The story misses, of course, the very
essence of Greek tragedy, that is, its religious character, but is perfectly adapted for treatment in the best renaissance Senecan manner.
Although De Nores talks nearly always of Greek rather than
Senecan plays, it is clear from this choice of story and his suggestions
for handling it that he perceives no difference. True that the tale
does not surpass the revolting horror of many Greek myths: the story
of the Thyestean banquet, for instance, or the story of Philomela and
Procne. But Greek tragedy, except for some of Euripides (e.g.,
Bacchae, Hippolytus), rarely goes quite so far. Moreover, and this
is the important thing, the horror in Greek tragedy has its origin in
myth, not in casual brutal incident; the horror, therefore, is attended
by the issues of divine purpose and human destiny that myth is concerned with. Seneca, to do him justice, is concerned with the same
things; but in Seneca it is easier, because of his horrendous rhetoric
and his emphasis on violence for its own sake, to miss the point. And
De Nores appears to have missed it. There is nothing in his story

but a horrible tale of revenge asking for treatment in the most grue-some neo-Senecan manner.

It is interesting to note that the first tragedy of romantic intrigue in England, *Gismond of Salerne,* borrows a similar story from Boc-caccio,[34] the one in which Tancred revenges himself on his daugh-ter's secret love by having her lover murdered and his heart carried to her in a cup; she puts poison in it and drinks the blood. That the authors thought they were writing tragedy in the classical manner is suggested by their giving it a Senecan framework of choruses and a fury and a Senecan tone of moralizing rhetoric. Giraldi's *Orbecche,* enormously influential, is of the same type, a story of secret love and savage revenge appearing first in his *Ecatommithi.* If a renaissance dramatist was well enough read in the Greeks to know that violent deeds rarely appeared on the stage, and if he recalled Horace's prohibition, he could appeal in Seneca to Hercules' slaughter of his children or the piecing together of the mangled remains of Hippoly-tus. Whether Seneca's plays were written only for declamation or were actually produced is an unsettled academic question of no relevance here,[35] since in any case renaissance authors found example for their own deeds of horror in his. Giraldi was shrewd enough to per-ceive that Aristotle had not actually prohibited the showing of violent scenes and he used this omission as authority for following modern taste.[36] Horrible deeds, then, were a recognized component of trag-edy and the shock of bloody spectacle taken as an equivalent to Aristotle's tragic wonder. Shakespeare's *Titus Andronicus,* though complicated by the theme of ambition and not based on a *novella,* is clearly in this same line of tragedy.[37] It is second to none in horror and perhaps seemed as "classical," except in regard to time and place, as *Orbecche* or *Gismond.*

BUT THE Italianate tragedy of intrigue often fell away from the traditional conception of tragedy. The ways in which it did so may be briefly examined. In the first place, historical truth was of less importance than in the tragedy of ambition with political figures as characters. The prejudice persisted, however, and it is probable that many dramatists borrowing the plots of *novelle* thought they were following true tales when they were not. Giraldi and Bandello both told theirs for true. Bandello, by means of references to places and famous people he had met and of considerable realistic detail, invested his with an air of great verisimilitude. In translating Bandello's stories, Belleforest praised them especially for "la verité de l'histoire." Some few, of course, were based on fact, the story of the Duchess of Malfi, for instance. The interesting thing is that a story like this is indistinguishable from one that is pretty certainly fiction, like that of Romeo and Julietta. The central story of Bianca Capella in *Women Beware Women* is grounded in historical fact; the subplot is from a tale that makes the claim of truth—Alexander Hart's *True History of the Tragic Loves of Hippolito and Isabella, Neapolitans*. Middleton perhaps thought he was also using a true tale for *The Changeling*, borrowed from the story of Alsemero and Beatrice-Joanna in John Reynolds' *The Triumph of God's Revenge against Murder* (1621).[38] Perhaps indeed he was, for the source of Reynolds' story is not known. How can we tell if Giraldi's story of the Moor who at the instigation of his ensign murdered his Venetian wife Disdemona is true or not? If a fictional story can pass for true, then the inhibition against inventing plots for tragedy is removed. Later plays do, indeed, contain more fictional plots than earlier ones. Clearly, standards of verisimilitude are less exacting in the requirement of historical truth for tales of love than for tales of princely ambition.

The second way in which Italianate tragedy modified the traditional conception was in sometimes having heroes of lower rank. When the tragic irony is not centered, as in the tragedy of ambition, in the distance of a man's fall, his rank ceases to be of quite so much importance. Bianca Capella in *Women Beware Women* is a merchant's wife; for this reason Professor Adams treats the play as a domestic tragedy.[39] But Bianca's love affair is with Francesco de' Medici, Duke of Florence, and the management and tone of the play put it with other Italianate intrigue plays, e.g., *The White Devil*, where the same duke figures. It is not different in any essential particular of setting or handling of plot from *The Changeling*, where the characters are hardly noble either, but at least military and so outside the range of domestic tragedy. Similar observations about rank and tone might be made of Ford's *'Tis Pity*. I should treat it as somewhat debased romantic tragedy, whereas Mr. Adams treats it as decadent domestic tragedy.[40] Since these classes are in any case imposed after the fact, there is no reason to quarrel; it all depends from which end one starts. The difference of opinion is testimony to the point I am making, namely that in tragedies of romantic intrigue rank is of less crucial significance than in tragedies of power.

Most important of all is the movement towards the happy ending. An intermediate stage (not necessarily so in time, but so in logic) is the tragedy with the double ending that Aristotle deplores, punishment for the bad, reward for the good. Giraldi justifies it as being pleasing to the taste of his own day.[41] He tries it in at least two of his plays, *Altile* and *Selene;* they are still tragedies because they deal with the lamentable affairs of illustrious persons. In *Epitia* and several other "tragedies" he carries the process a step further and has the evil-doers forgiven; this is possible since no actual crime has been committed. In *Epitia* as in *Measure for Measure,* the heroine's brother, whom the perjured governor has ordered executed, turns out to be not dead after all; the heroine is so overjoyed to find him alive that she pleads for the villain's life and they all live happily ever after. This is instructive. We are in the region where tragedy and comedy are cut out of the same cloth. The major plot of *Much Ado,* for instance, is from a story of Bandello's in which malicious plotting on the part of a rival for the heroine's hand and of his evil accomplice is made to produce only mishap, not irrevocable criminal action, and therefore does not preclude a happy outcome.[42] Romantic plots which put a premium on the strangeness and complication of event for its own sake naturally tend towards this kind of solution. This type of plot had always been known and popular in England, but in the later years of Elizabeth's reign it yielded somewhat to more sharply distinguished tragedy and comedy. However, very early in James's reign, the current set strongly in the direction of tragicomedy.

BUT WHEN THE Italianate tragedy of intrigue is still tragedy, how does it differ in essential tragic feeling from the rise-and-fall tragedy of ambition? In the early tragedies of romantic intrigue, interests appropriate to the murder mystery—plentiful action, suspense leading up to a deed of horror, shocking crime—are apt to take the place of any deeper questioning about man's destiny. *The Spanish Tragedy, Soliman and Perseda, Tancred and Gismund, The Jew of Malta, Titus Andronicus,* and other Elizabethan tragedies of this sort strike us as primarily lively thrillers, although we sometimes catch glimpses of a deeper purpose, as in the pathos of the distraught Hieronimo or in the mordancy of Barabas. The exciting force in this kind of plot is frequently love or jealous hatred, mixed or not with political intrigue. Bandello's 214 tales contain sixty-six tales of adultery and kindred themes (excluding those involving the clergy) and nineteen tales of the tribulations of love ending unhappily. The largest class in Giraldi's collection is likewise illicit love—twenty-eight out of 110.[43] Here, of course, in the contemplation of the unhappiness that comes upon men and women in their relations with each other, is a chance to deepen tragic feeling, and this was done in the great Jacobean plays. The considerable interest in psychological studies around the turn of the century, especially in pathological mental states, gave dramatists the means of rendering human behavior more richly and subtly. Another line of interest growing strong at the same time, for social and literary reasons that I need not develop here, was the interest in satire; it helped set a tone in the treatment of problems of sex. Moreover, in their French and English versions, the source stories had to be quarried out from layers of moralizing on sin, especially on adultery. The interests in psychology and in satire joined hands in the favorite malcontent type, with his bitter wit exposing all the ugliness of the society around him. The result, at its best, of this amalgam of psychology, satire, and moral gloom is a tragedy of intensely conceived characters—not always attractive and often unbalanced emotionally—caught in an evil world of adultery, incest, and murder.

How are we to take tragedy like this? A tragic flaw will hardly describe what is wrong with heroes and heroines like Vittoria or Evadne or Bianca Capella, not to mention the Insatiate Countess, Brachiano, or Vindici. Nor is the response indicated so often one of pity and fear as of fascination or disgust or both together.[44] These attitudes are most strongly felt in Marston, Tourneur, and Webster, though in Webster with much qualification. Morbid fascination and disgust find their extreme expression in *The Revenger's Tragedy*. (If the tone of disgust at sexual licence is as strong in *Hamlet* as in *The Revenger's Tragedy,* it is less crude, less morbid, not exclusive of pity.) Though Middleton's world is as ugly as Marston's or Tourneur's, he has more emotional detachment than they in regarding it. In Beaumont and Fletcher plentiful statement of attitude takes the place of actual feeling about it. Ford has lost the disgust, but kept the fascination. As with much of the tragedy of power, it is evident that Aristotelian canons, either of the nature of the tragic hero, or of the emotions appropriate to tragedy, do not generally apply. Shakespeare in *Othello,* in the nobility of his hero, and in the catharsis of emotion he effects, is rather the exception than the rule. It is true that we feel a compelling admiration for the boldness and vitality of many of the principal characters in these plays—people like Beatrice Joanna, Evadne, Flamineo, and De Flores—but we should find it hard, I think, to pity many of them; nor are we usually asked to. The Duchess of Malfi, who has goodness and greatness in her as well as intensity, is a significant non-Shakespearean exception, and perhaps Vittoria is, too, in a different way.

Webster, though he is in this line of tragedy, is more complicated and harder to define than the others. His dark world is lit by a splendor that evokes something more than morbid fascination and disgust. Even creatures like Brachiano, Lodovico, and Flamineo shine in darkness. However wicked they may be, there is defiance and a kind of glory in the courage with which they meet death. In this respect Vittoria is akin to the Duchess. If the Duchess is Duchess of Malfi still, Vittoria in her death will not shed one base tear. There is something here, in a different realm of action, like the defiant courage of Chapman's heroes. Simple vitality asserts itself in a world that is doomed. The Duchess of Malfi cries out in justified protest against Ferdinand's jealously revengeful and diseased "honor," which she has supposedly violated by her clandestine marriage:

> Why might not I marry?
> I have not gone about in this to create
> Any new world, or custom.
>
> .   .   .   .
>
> Why should only I
> Of all the other princes of the world
> Be cased up, like a holy relic? I have youth
> And a little beauty.[45]

But Vittoria's defense, in so far as she deigns to make any answer to the charges against her of adultery and of complicity in murder, is akin to the Duchess':

> Sum up my faults, I pray, and you shall find
> That beauty and gay clothes, a merry heart,
> And a good stomach to a feast are all,
> All the poor crimes that you can charge me with.[46]

If the world is doomed, then such vitality and such courage must evoke pity, a pity that transcends the lines of good and evil. In Webster, there is a hint, afar off, that all the sons of men are to be pitied. In the tragic wonder he evokes, Webster, with Shakespeare, comes closer than his contemporaries to Aristotelian tragedy; but in his moral and philosophical implications he is far more Stoical than Aristotelian.

Different as these Jacobeans may be in their separate emphases, there is one way in which they can be viewed as part of a common tradition. In their tragedies, Death and the Devil are common symbols. As in the tragedy of power a little grave is the end man's glory comes to, so in the tragedy of sex the foulness of the skeleton is the end of woman's beauty. The ironic contrast is not to power, as in the other tragedy, but to the life of the senses, and, occasionally, to a beauty and love beyond that level. But in any case death opposes a different form of vitality from the energy of ambition. Death is present in the midst of life, and the Devil has taken over the world. There is a significant difference here, however, from the Christian tradition. The symbol opposed to Death in the morality plays (the Virtues in some form, or a Good Angel) and by whose aid man might save himself, has largely disappeared. Man, therefore, in these plays lives "in what a shadow, or deep pit of darkness." [47] If there is to be any assertion of value in such a world, it can only be endurance in life and courage in confronting death. Antony, Cleopatra, Clermont, and Cato in courageous death remove themselves beyond the caprice of Fortune:

> ... and it is great
> To do that thing that ends all other deeds,
> Which shackles accidents, and bolts up change.

As Clermont puts it:

> Since I could skill of man, I never liv'd
> To please men worldly, and shall I in death,
> Respect their pleasures, making such a jar
> Betwixt my death and life, when death should make
> The consort sweetest, th'end being proof and crown
> To all the skill and worth we truly own?

He will follow his admired master, the Guise:

> Now, then, as a ship
> Touching at strange and far-removed shores,
> Her men ashore go, for their several ends,
> Fresh water, victuals, precious stones, and pearl,
> All yet intentive (when the master calls,
> The ship to put off ready) to leave all
> Their greediest labours, lest they there be left
> To thieves or beasts, or be the country's slaves:
> So, now my master calls, my ship, my venture,
> All in one bottom put, all quite put off,
> All gone under sail, and I left negligent,
> To all the horrors of the vicious time,
> The far-remov'd shores to all virtuous aims,
> None favouring goodness, none but he respecting
> Piety or manhood—shall I here survive,
> Not cast me after him into the sea,
> Rather than here live, ready every hour
> To feed thieves, beasts, and be the slave of power?
> I come, my lord! Clermont, thy creature, comes.[48]

Cato by his suicide conquers conquering Caesar. Yet if the world is not just one of unhappy circumstance, but one of positive evil, actually the Devil's world, without chance of redemption, then there is hardly even a victory in stoical courage. The noble Pompey, treacherously caught and stabbed, questions eternal justice:

> See, heavens, your sufferings! Is my country's love,
> The justice of an empire, piety,
> Worth this end in their leader? Last yet, life,
> And bring the gods off fairer: after this
> Who will adore or serve the deities? [49]

He hides his face in his robe and submits to his assassins. Middleton's De Flores, in a Christian setting, takes his mistress boldly to Hell.

> Make haste, Joanna, by that token to thee [i.e., the
>   wound he had given her],
> Canst not forget, so lately put in mind;
> I would not go to leave thee far behind.

Alsemero has prepared the way with a grim image:

>   ... rehearse again
> Your scene of lust, that you may be perfect
> When you shall come to act it to the black audience,
> Where howls and gnashings shall be music to you.
> Clip your adulteress freely, 'tis the pilot

Will guide you to the *mare mortuum,*
Where you shall sink to bottoms fathomless.[50]

And Webster's Bosola dies in a mist, on a voyage of doom.

Shakespeare uses the same symbols of Death, the Devil, and Hell in *Othello,* and Othello makes a stoical speech of courage in the face of death. But the judgment on himself is without defiance. There is a note of humility in Othello scarcely to be found elsewhere in these plays, unless it is in Bosola. Above all, the play is different in effect from most of the others because in it there is goodness and redemption as well as ruin and death.

To SUMMARIZE the ironic implications of these two major lines of tragedy we have been considering: The special irony in the tragedy of ambition, where it is fully realized, is in the final helplessness of man, in spite of his godlike aspirations for power, before an inexorable universe. The special irony in the tragedy of sex is in man's betrayal by his passions to a world of evil. A supreme realization of this irony is in *Othello,* where a man rich in all that we most admire in character—emotional depth, integrity, idealism, frankness, and generosity—is led by his very largeness into self-betrayal by the basest of passions, and led by a man who is the epitome of meanness, cynicism, malice, and intelligence directed toward evil ends. A more characteristic realization of the irony, however, is perhaps found in other Jacobeans, where men less good and great are betrayed by vanity or lust or simply a desire for life, as with the Duchess of Malfi, to a world in which death is supreme.

Domestic Tragedy

The third major class of tragedy is domestic tragedy. It has been seen as a direct derivation from the morality play, especially of the Prodigal Son type.[51] The general theme of the Prodigal Son plays— e.g., *Mundus et Infans, Lusty Juventus, Nice Wanton,* Gascoigne's *Glass of Government*—is that the temptations of the world lead to sin, the wages of which are death, but that true repentance and reformation of life may move God to mercy. The hero in the plays is a young man or woman whose social position is not in itself important and whose problem of salvation is intensely personal. He is a descendant, of course, of Everyman, and, in this view, he prepares the way for the tragedy of common men.

Another way to look at domestic tragedy, however, is to see it simply as the dramatization of a class of stories, which, like chronicles, romances, *novelle,* or any other sort of lively story, looked like promising material to be put on the stage. Stories of contemporary crime would have a special appeal as thrillers, and it would have been strange if the popular stage had neglected to exploit them. On this view, the trace in many of these tragedies of a moral play or homiletic scheme of temptation, sin, repentance, and punishment looks less like the original impulse to the plays than like a conventional moral pattern such subjects would attract. This is not to say that domestic tragedy did not owe a good deal to the morality, but only to shift the emphasis in viewing the relationship. One cannot be dogmatic about the matter or make an inclusive statement about all the plays in the class, but certainly some of them, especially *Arden, Woman Killed,* and *The Witch of Edmonton* suffer distortion if viewed as dramatized homilies.

Domestic tragedy deals with the troubled affairs in the private lives of men of less than noble birth—gentlemen, farmers, merchants. It is a small and fairly well-defined class; the action is most frequently a murder, committed for greed or love, the setting is usually English and realistic, the basis for the story is nearly always an actual and fairly recent crime, recorded in a chronicle like Stow's or in ballad, chapbook, or pamphlet. The principal Elizabethan domestic tragedies conforming to this pattern are *Arden of Feversham, A Warning for Fair Women,* and Robert Yarington's *Two Lamentable Tragedies;* the principal Jacobean ones, *A Yorkshire Tragedy,* Heywood's *Woman Killed with Kindness* and *English Traveller,* Heywood and Rowley's *Fortune by Land and Sea,* Dekker, Rowley, and Ford's *Witch of Edmonton.*[52]

THAT SOME OF the authors of domestic tragedy were conscious of their boldness in attempting it is attested by their deliberate calling attention to its differences from orthodox tragedy. The curious framework of *A Warning for Fair Women* is evidently to be understood as an apology for this type of tragedy. The presenters of the play are Comedy, History, and Tragedy. The first two deride Tragedy with a description of the Senecanized variety: [53]

> How some damn'd tyrant, to obtain a crown,
> Stabs, hangs, impoisons, smothers, cutteth throats,
> And then a Chorus too comes howling in,
> And tells us of the worrying of a cat;
> Then of a filthy whining ghost,
> Lapt in some foul sheet or a leather pilch,
> Comes screaming like a pig half-stickt,
> And cries "*Vindicta!* revenge, revenge!"
> With that a little rosin flasheth forth,
> Like smoke out of a tobacco pipe, or a boy's squib:
> When comes in two or three like to drovers,
> With tailors' bodkins, stabbing one another.
> Is not this trim? is not here goodly things?

The attitude of Tragedy is ambiguous. She appears to take the description as maliciously libelous, not as a true account of an inferior type of tragedy:

> Thus with your loose and idle similes
> You have abused me: but I'll whip you hence,
> I'll scourge and lash you both from off the stage;
> 'Tis you [i.e., History and Comedy] have kept
>   the theaters so long,
> Painted in play-bills upon every post,
> That I am scorned of the multitude,
> My name profaned.

But when the play is done, she describes it in terms that form an unmistakable contrast to the earlier description:

> Perhaps it may seem strange unto you all,
> That one hath not reveng'd another's death
> After the observation of such course:
> The reason is, that now of truth I sing,
> And should I add, or else diminish aught,
> Many of these spectators then could say,
> I have committed error in my play.
> Bear with this true and home-born tragedy,
> Yielding so slender argument and scope
> To build a matter of importance on.

Nevertheless, perhaps to be on the safe side, in the first of the dumb shows between the acts (the division itself a noteworthy concession to classical form) the old standbys, the Senecan Furies, together with

Lust and Chastity, appear to motivate the action. Notice of a wedding between Senecan tragedy and native moral play could scarcely be more plainly given.

It was evidently felt, too, that decorum demanded a plain style for these mean and domestic subjects in place of the elevation demanded by great personages and state affairs. The author of *Arden* describes his play as "naked" and without "filed lines." Heywood characterizes *A Woman Killed* as "a barren subject, a bare scene," *The English Traveller* as composed of "bare lines."

> A strange play you are like to have, for know,
> We use no drum, nor trumpet, nor dumb show;
> No combat, marriage; not so much today
> As song, dance, masque, to bombast out a play.

In style, as in theme, domestic tragedy perhaps owed something to the morality play, which had helped establish a tradition of realism in scenes of common life. See the truancy scenes, for instance, in *Nice Wanton,* or the scenes between the young married couple in *The Disobedient Child,* in which, after the borrowed money runs out, bickering and recrimination succeed to the billing and cooing of the honeymoon scenes.

THE PECULIARITY of domestic tragedy to England at this period is an interesting testimony both to the relative freedom of the English stage from critical dominance and to the large middle-class element in its audience. Professor Harbage's revealing study shows that the public theaters must have drawn on a wide cross section of the population of London, excluding normally only the very poor.[54] Domestic tragedy has the characteristics of bourgeois literature in its heavy moral emphasis and in its combination of sensationalism and sentiment.

The ethical pattern of temptation, sin, repentance, and punishment that domestic tragedy inherited from the moral play was one widely familiar to everybody through persistent Christian teaching. It was given precise and elaborate form in the official book of homilies prescribed for weekly reading in every church, and it was echoed everywhere in sermons and moralizing pamphlets, even in the broadside ballads commemorating striking crimes that served in that day in place of sensational journalism.

The type of tragedy making use of this scheme lends itself to excessive emphasis on pathos tô the exclusion of more complicated feelings and of reflection. Pathos was a specialty of the writers of domestic tragedy. Their chances to develop it came in three places: the innocence of the victims (e.g., Beech and his boy in one story of *Two Lamentable Tragedies* and Pertillo the child in the other; Bean in *A Warning,* children and wife in *A Yorkshire Tragedy,* Susan in the *Witch of Edmonton*); the Christian forbearance of one of the characters (the young friend of Pertillo in *Two Lamentable Tragedies,* the injured husband in *A Woman Killed,* Geraldine the injured lover in *The English Traveller*); and the repentance of the guilty hero (in all the plays in my first list). While the repentances of Alice Arden and Calverly, both strongly conceived characters, have little of the pathetic in them, the good ends of Geraldine's lady, of Mistress Shore, and of Mistress Frankford are worked for all the pathos they are worth. Other plays range along the scale between these. The stern view of the preachers might be that man is essentially only worthy of damnation and can be saved only by the grace of God. But in the blurring of this view with the tears of innocence, forgiveness, and repentance the writers of domestic tragedy appeal to softer sentiment and lose the harsh edge of tragedy. An easily achieved divine mercy takes the curse off original sin.[55]

The tendency to the sentimental leads, as one would expect, to the happy ending. Heywood's *Woman Killed* and *English Traveller* are tragedies with double endings; only the guilty die. George Wilkins in his *Miseries of Enforced Marriage* takes the same story as in *A Yorkshire Tragedy,* and by omitting the commission of murder makes possible the complete reformation of the hero and a reconciliation with his wife. Dekker's two plays of *The Honest Whore* have affinities with domestic tragedy in this respect, though their courtiers, their love affairs, and their intrigues link them with Italianate romantic drama. But Bellafront is certainly less than noble in social position;[56] and her repentance, together with her persistence in the reformed state despite all the pressure on her to break down, is a declaration of possible goodness, even in a fallen woman. Although both plays end happily, Dekker's firm hold on character, his satiric humor, and his vivid realism in the portrayal of his rogues keep out sentimentalism.

WE MAY CONCLUDE our examination of the major types of tragedy by remarking on a traditional idea about Elizabethan drama, the idea that it was wholly free in its development, wholly scornful of critical theory. Free as compared with the Italian and later French drama it certainly was, and running ahead of criticism rather than behind it. But the dramatists were certainly not working in critical darkness. Whether or not they ever went to Aristotle or the Italian critics, they could not have avoided the traditional concepts of tragedy and comedy as formulated by the grammarians, and they could not have avoided acquaintance with Senecan tragedy and Roman comedy. We are often misled in comparing their tragedy with classical tragedy as we understand it by not seeing clearly enough how they understood it. They were sometimes imitating it according to their lights when they seem to us not to be. When they were actually trying to do something different, I believe they knew what they were doing.

7 Comedy

Mitis. ... the argument of his comedy might have been of some other nature, as of a duke to be in love with a countess, and that countess to be in love with the duke's son, and the son to love the lady's waiting-maid: some such cross wooing, with a clown to their serving-man, better than to be thus near and familiarly allied to the time.

Cordatus. You say well, but I would fain hear one of these autumn-judgments define once, *Quid sit Comoedia?* if he cannot, let him content himself with Cicero's definition (till he have strength to propose to himself a better) who would have a comedy to be *Imitatio vitae, Speculum consuetudinis, Imago veritatis;* a thing throughout pleasant, and ridiculous, and accommodated to the correction of manners.

—JONSON, *Every Man out of his Humour,* III. vi. 195–209

Jonsonian and Shakespearean Comedy

THE PROBLEM OF labeling types is even more difficult for comedy than for tragedy. The lines of its heritage—from medieval farce and juggling turn, from comic episode and realistic scene in mystery and morality, from chivalric romance and saint's legend, from Roman comedy, from Italian comedy both learned and popular, from Greek romance and Italian novel, from pastoral eclogue and pastoral romance—are complexly interwoven to issue in many new patterns. The mood of comedy shifts from raucous guffaw to gay good spirits, from biting satire to tender sentiment; it shifts, sometimes, so far in the direction of sobriety or sadness that it loses its identity as comedy and touches hands with tragedy.

One may make at least a gross division into two main varieties, Jonsonian and Shakespearean comedy. We have to watch the terms of opposition—"realistic" and "romantic"—applied to these, however, for they are misleading unless carefully qualified. There is prob-

148

ably as much realism, if we consider character as well as manners, in Shakespeare as in Jonson; and though there is little romance in Jonson, there is much in the way of contrived plot and drawing in caricature that is not at all realistic. Autolycus could more easily walk off the stage into the living world than could Mosca. "Classical," as descriptive of Jonson's great comedies, is almost less satisfactory, for they are as different in their own way from Plautus and Terence as are Shakespeare's great comedies in theirs. We must not categorize either Shakespearean or Jonsonian comedy too simply, for both are highly complex. Yet different they certainly are, and these labels, of course, are attempts to get at differences which we feel to be fundamental.

Jonson himself has described the difference in the conversation between the presenters, quoted at the head of this chapter, in the third act of *Every Man out of his Humour*. The comedy described by Cordatus in Ciceronian terms fulfills the inherited conception of comedy transmitted by the grammarians. Its sphere of observation is the real life of ordinary men and women, its attitude critical, its means pleasurable, its aim at least partially corrective. The realism in such comedy is apt to be, apart from motivation in human weaknesses, mainly realism of detail, or local color. The critical attitude leads, in the treatment of character, in the direction of satiric exaggeration and even caricature, and, in the management of the fable, to intricate manipulation in order to bring about a witty exposure of human folly. The other kind of comedy, the comedy described by Mitis, has a romantic rather than a critical emphasis. Its principal characters are well born, its theme is love, its aim is to delight with an adventurous story that ends well. The fable may be no less intricately contrived than in a social comedy, but it is so for a different reason: not to make a moral or satiric point, but only to give interesting suspense to progress along the rough path of true love until the moment when the lovers kiss and begin to live happy ever after.

The essential difference between the two modes of English comedy is not so much one of realism, although that is Jonson's implication, as it is one of attitude and tone. The emphasis is on a different set of human motives—on the one hand, on poetic longings for love and adventure; on the other, on the grosser appetites for women, money, or power. The defining difference of tone is the difference between lyrical sentiment sympathetically expressed and critical satire.

But Jonson's description throws into relief only the extreme points of difference. As a matter of fact, these clear differences in emphasis are seldom maintained in English comedy with any purity. Although it tends to divide into lines that are predominantly romantic and predominantly critical or social, little of it except Jonson's best is exclusively one or the other. Most of the social comedy, the comedy of bourgeois London life, is built on a central romantic plot. (Jonson's great comedies—*Volpone, The Alchemist, Bartholomew Fair* —are atypical; he found his own nonromantic formula.) How the romance is treated varies greatly. Sentiment may be prominent, and essential to the plot, as in Chapman's *Gentleman Usher* or Marston's *Dutch Courtesan;* it may be present, but awkwardly handled and felt to be *de trop,* as in Middleton's *Family of Love;* or it may be at a minimum, as in plays like *Eastward Ho* or Middleton's *Chaste Maid,* wherein the romantic story is only the frame on which to hang the more interesting comedy of fleshly passions and follies. Most of what we call romantic comedy, on the other hand, is full of admixture of other elements—realistic glimpses of manners high or low, satire, even slapstick. *Damon and Pythias, Endymion, The Old Wives' Tale,* and *Friar Bacon* are familiar examples. It is a mixture familiar to us in Edwards, Lyly, Peele, Greene, Dekker, and Shakespeare. *Twelfth Night* is a supreme example of it. Many comedies, like some of Chapman's, Dekker's, Heywood's, and Marston's, refuse to be put on either side of the line, so mixed are they of the adventurous, the poetic, the comic, and the satiric. These things testify both to the persistent interest in romantic story, which is the ground of nearly all Elizabethan drama, and to the delight in variety, which made singleness of effect rarely sought for.

Furthermore, both these lines of emphasis, the romantic and the critical, draw alike on Roman New Comedy for much that it had to offer, especially in the organization of the fable. *Volpone* and *Twelfth Night* seem nothing near allied; yet both have roots in Latin comedy, or more immediately in its renaissance Italian derivative. What Jonson and Shakespeare borrow from this tradition is partly different, and what they make of it completely different, not only from each other, but from the common source. Jonson borrows the method of the intriguer to manipulate his plot, Shakespeare the mistaken identities and fortuitous conclusion. But Jonson's satiric result is as unlike the mood of Roman comedy as is Shakespeare's tender and merry one. Nevertheless, both dramatists learned something essential about play-making from that comedy.

Roman comedy is seldom the primary ingredient in mature English comedy, but it is nearly always to some degree a modifying one. As a convenient way of organizing the discussion of the different modes of English comedy, I shall take as a point of departure the different uses Latin comedy was put to. It had in it various elements which led in different directions, depending on the attitudes of dramatists it influenced and on the other lines of dramatic interest they chose to blend it with. The elements in it which the Renaissance saw and which in various ways affected English comedy are the mechanism of the intrigue plot, the social element of character types, manners, and moral attitudes, the romantic element of love and adventurous background, and the rhetorical element of wit, sententiousness, and lyricism. As I comment on each of these, I shall show how they blended with other influences to produce varying results.

Eloquence, or the Rhetorical Element

I shall dispose of this quickly first, because I wish merely to raise a question about it. We know from the commentaries on Terence both of the post-classical grammarians and of the renaissance humanists, from the rhetorical apparatus in school editions, and from records of actual school practice how much attention was paid to Terence's style as a source of elegant Latinity for boys to emulate. His figures, his moral sentences, his metrics, were all given close attention. We have less surviving evidence of the same treatment of Plautus, because Plautus was a less constant feature of the school curriculum. Yet I think we may safely assume that whenever Plautus was studied he must have been subjected to the same treatment, for the method of rhetorical analysis and imitation was the general method of education. Now Plautus more frequently secures comical effects from bold rhetorical devices like alliteration, repetition, and play on words than does Terence. He is, besides, notably more varied in his meters than Terence, and fuller of lyricism. He adapts his style freely to character and situation, and so helps set the tone of a scene; *Rudens* is one of the best examples. *Casina* and *Persa* are so full of lyric elements that Professor Harsh speaks of the first as a musical farce and the second as close to comic opera.[1] The question I wish to pose is whether English comic dramatists did not learn something from Plautus of their manipulation of style to secure variety of tone.

It is not far-fetched to suppose that Lyly, in trying to develop an English comedy of wit and elegance, or that Peele, Greene, and Shakespeare, in learning to adjust style to theme and mood, should have taken some stylistic hints from the more versatile of the two Roman comic dramatists. As an illustration take the most obvious one, *The Comedy of Errors,* demonstrably indebted to *Menaechmi* and *Amphitryon* for the plot. In tone the English play is a mixture of knockabout farce, verbal wit, and moments of lyric sentiment; its style is very markedly varied, with prose or tumbling verse for the clowning parts, couplets or cross-rimes for the passages of light sentiment, blank verse for the staple of dialogue and for the more serious expression of feeling.[2] Furthermore, it is not unlikely that those dramatists who made such free use of song in their comedies for lyric effect—the "university wits" generally, Shakespeare, Dekker, Fletcher, and others—thought of themselves in so doing as in good classical tradition. Aristophanes could have taught a similar general lesson of wide stylistic variation to effect difference of tone, but we cannot count on any intimate acquaintance with him on the part of any English dramatist except perhaps Jonson.

One does not know what a close comparative analysis of Plautus' style with Shakespeare's would show beyond a possible similarity in certain general tendencies. It might show similarity in certain particular figures and rhetorical practices. It could not, of course, show precise similarities in movement of verse, not only because of the difference between quantitative and accentual verse, but because of the comparative crudeness of the means of variation at Shakespeare's disposal. Such a comparison applied to the early comedies, however, might throw light on the *motives* of variation from blank verse to riming couplets or to stanza patterns, and from the pentameter line to different meters.

The Intrigue Plot

Plautus and Terence, especially the latter, had more to offer a practical dramatist in the way of mechanism for successful stage comedy than did Seneca for tragedy. That is perhaps why English renaissance comedy, however English it is in characters, setting, and language, continues so often to have identifiable features of Roman comedy in the plotting.

The plots of Latin comedy are manipulated plots, with someone managing the intrigue—a man and his wife plotting against each other as in *Casina,* a parasite as in *Curculio,* most often a clever slave as in *Epidicus.* A typical intriguing slave, like Syrus in Terence's *Heautontimorumenos,* manages the affairs of his young master so as to trick a disapproving father out of enough money to buy for the young man the woman of his choice, not without getting himself and his patron into considerable trouble before he gets them out. The ingenuity of his devices, the narrowness of the escapes, the success of the execution, not realism, are the tests of excellence. It is only in a few plots, however, that the intriguer carries things to a conclusion without the help of good fortune. In Plautus often, and in Terence always, solution is only possible with a recognition by tokens of one of the characters: the girl the young man wants to marry is happily discovered to be of free Athenian birth, usually the lost daughter of one of the older men in the play; she may be revealed as the hero's sister in time to prevent his union with her; or she may turn out to be the woman he himself has unwittingly wronged and her child to be his own. This element of the fortuitous must be kept in mind, for it is the aspect of New Comedy that romantic comedy naturally chose to make use of. Where the plot is mainly built on intrigue, the comedy may become one of various things, depending on the purpose for which the intrigue is designed—to produce farcical situation, lively story for its own sake, revelation of character, or satire on manners. For the moment we are considering the nature of the intrigue plot itself.

English dramatists had as models in this type of plotting the modern Italians as well as the Romans. For the intrigue plot was a fundamental characteristic of renaissance Italian comedy, both academic and popular. It was often much complicated by disguises, mistaken identities, and subplots. Plautus' stories are usually single in action, Terence's double; those of Italian comedy may be triple. In *commedia dell'arte* the trick of duplicating groups of characters (two sets of lovers, two old men, two clowns) and of repeating stock situations, or of crossing parallel themes, makes complication relatively easy to achieve.[3] The intriguing slave of Roman comedy becomes the cunning servant; in *commedia dell'arte* he is often one of the *zanni*, and his line eventuates in Scaramouche and Figaro. Other intriguers special to the times, however, are added, like the fake necromancer in Ariosto's *Il Negromante*, who trades on everybody's gullibility but who is eventually too clever for his own good; or like the pair of idle students in Cecchi's *L'Assiuolo* (*The Little Horned Owl*), who send an old man off on a fool's errand after a young neighbor woman he has been coveting and who see that he is cuckolded in the meantime.

A great deal of English renaissance comedy is of this contrived sort, in which much of the fun comes from witty plotting.

> All your business must be compassed
> With winding plots, and cunning stratagems.[4]

Often, ancestry is clearly marked. Plots are sometimes borrowed directly from Plautus or Terence; frequently, in line with the renaissance habit of providing plenty of action, two plots are interwoven, just as Terence built some of his plays by "contaminating" one plot with another, both from Greek New Comedy. Jonson's *Case Is Altered* combines the *Captivi* and the *Aulularia* of Plautus; Chapman's *All Fools*, the *Heautontimorumenos* and the *Adelphi* of Terence. Sometimes, plots are clearly taken from contemporary Italian comedy: [5] e.g., *The Bugbears* from Grazzini's *La Spiritata*, Chapman's *May-Day* from Piccolomini's *Alessandro*, the minor plot of *The Taming of the Shrew* from Ariosto's *I Suppositi*, Marston's *What You Will* from Sforza degli Oddi's *I Morti Vivi*. And often some Italian plot is likely whether actually discoverable or not: e.g., in *Jack Drum's Entertainment* and *The Wit of a Woman*. Although Bond doubts the influence of Italian comedy on Lyly's *Mother Bombie*,[6] it is hard not to see it in the disguisings and the balanced duplication of relationships and situations. But all the plays I have named have the strong mark of their origin upon them and are only half anglicized. The test of the vitality of the method is its appearance in thoroughly English plays like Porter's *Two Angry Women of Abingdon*, Heywood's *Wise Woman of Hogsden*, Jonson's *Alchemist*, Dekker and Middleton's *Roaring Girl*, Middleton's *Chaste Maid* or *Michaelmas Term*. The structural basis of all these plays is ingenious intrigue. They depend on disguise, lies, clever excuses, manipulation to get characters together at the right time or to keep them

separate—as Ascham puts it, on "fine fetches." An element of the
fortuitous may be present in the solution, but it is not enough to
change the tone of the play.

The intriguer in English comedy is not often a servant; he is
more likely to be one of the principals. If the intrigue is a love affair,
the lover himself is apt to try to outwit his sweetheart's reluctant
father, as Touchwood Jr. does in *A Chaste Maid in Cheapside,* or as
Sebastian does in *The Roaring Girl.* A clever brother or friend, like
Rinaldo in *All Fools,* or Lodovico in *May-Day,* may help things
along. If the intrigue is the outwitting of a tight-fisted relative, the
hopeful heir is pretty sure to be the intriguer, like Witgood in *A
Trick to Catch the Old One,* or Sir Dauphine in *Epicoene.* If the
intrigue is the fleecing of fools, the rogue of course handles the trap:
e.g., Volpone and Mosca in *Volpone,* or Quomodo the draper in
Michaelmas Term. The manipulator may be a necromancer or magician, like Friar Bacon, Sacrapant, or Prospero. An intriguer of this
sort, however, is very apt to introduce elements of fantasy which
take us into another realm of comedy. But he need not if, like Jonson's Subtle, he is in the brotherhood of the impostors of Italian
comedy—Ariosto's *negromante,* Grazzini's quack astrologer in *La
Strega,* or Bruno's fake alchemist and fake necromancer in *Il Cande-
laio.*

It might be thought that the mischievous Vice of the moralities
would easily combine with the intriguing slave or parasite of Latin
comedy, and he does appear to have done so in some of the earlier
plays—in *Misogonus* unmistakably, in *Roister Doister* and *Gammer
Gurton's Needle* less obviously. But a thoughtful examination of the
long line of intriguers in Elizabethan comedy reveals relatively few
who bear much resemblance to the Vice. His line seems to be rather
that of the Fool, either as a butt or as a maker of jests, but not as an
active intriguer. The English intriguer is more apt to be a healthful
exposer of men's follies than a malicious instigator of them. If he is
not a lover furthering his own love affair or a rogue taking in gulls,
he may be a disinterested person merely exposing gullery for the fun
of it. Rinaldo in *All Fools* is of this sort:

> My fortune is to win renown by gulling.
> Gostanzo, Dariotto, and Cornelio,
> All which suppose, in all their different kinds,
> Their wits entire, and in themselves no piece,

All at one blow, my helmet yet unbruis'd,
I have unhors'd, laid flat on earth for gulls.[7]

Intriguing servants, as I have said, are rather rare in English comedy. The servants in Shakespeare's early comedies run about on
errands, talk wittily, confide their troubles to the audience, all in the
manner of New Comedy; but they are never active intriguers like
Syrus, Parmeno, Epidicus, or Pseudolus. When the servants *are* the
manipulators, they soon become unlike their models. The four in
Mother Bombie are drawn close to type; and Brainworm, in *Every
Man in his Humour,* though more anglicized in manner, still reveals
his ancestry. But Face, Lovewit's major-domo in *The Alchemist,*
is thoroughly of his own day and country. Jonson suggests for him
an obscure past history. Although by Subtle's account Face was "the
good,/Honest, plain-livery three-pound thrum" that kept his master's house for the vacation until Subtle got him into their present
profitable business of cony-catching, by his own account he was
the prime mover in the scheme. As Doll's "whoreson, upstart, apocryphal captain" he is altogether too accomplished to suggest an
innocent past. The ambiguity about him creates the illusion of a
rogue who has always lived by his wit in rough places, and is only
in service because he can make a good thing of it. He is as much like
Lazarillo or Guzman, the picaresque rogues, as he is like Tranio, the
impudent slave in Plautus' *Mostellaria,* a play which appears to have
suggested to Jonson the device of the servant brazenly outfacing the
master in order to prevent or delay the latter's discovery of what has
been going on in the house during his absence.

All these changes show the thorough way in which a tried and
useful type of plot management is adapted to new social conventions.
None of these changes in manners violates any of the accepted conventions of comedy as described by the grammarians. Indeed, in
making it reflect contemporary bourgeois manners, renaissance
dramatists but fulfill the old prescription that comedy be the mirror
of daily life. Middleton's comic plots are likely to be quite fantastic
in their manipulation; yet so vivid are his rogues and gulls and pictures of London life that we unhesitatingly call him a realist. This
leads us to a consideration of the elements found by English dramatists in Roman comedy that they could put to use in the service of
realism.

The Social Element: The Movement towards Realism

MANNERS AND TYPES

The ever-recurrent theme of New Comedy is the contest between high-living young men, deeply involved in an apparently discreditable love affair in which they are abetted by a faithful, clever slave, and their conservative fathers, who are of course anxious to have their sons settle down as sober householders. This universal theme is particularized with situations and codes of behavior that were characteristic of late fourth- and early third-century Greece: the peculiar status of the courtesan, the purchase of virtuous singing-girls from pimps, the exposure of girl babies, the importance of Athenian citizenship, the combined intimacy and subserviency in the relations of slaves to their masters, and so on. The characters, even if sometimes skilfully individualized, fall into easily recognizable types. Apuleius amusingly lists these as "et leno perfidus et amator fervidus et servidus callidus et amica inludens et uxor inhibens et mater indulgens et patrus obiurgator et sodalis opitulator et miles gloriator, sed et parasiti edaces et parentes tenaces et meretrices procaces" [8] (perfidious pimp and eager lover and crafty servant, frivolous mistress and bossy wife and indulgent mother, reproving uncle and companion-helper and soldier-boaster, gluttonous parasites and stingy parents and shameless courtesans). In adapting Menandrian comedy to Roman audiences, Plautus introduced a number of Roman touches, but for the most part, certainly in Terence, the situations and tone of Roman "fabula palliata" are predominantly Greek.[9]

It was to be expected, however, that at such a distance of place and time, renaissance dramatists imitating the structure of ancient comedy would seek to give it contemporaneity by bringing its manners and characters up to date. They must do, moreover, if they were to make it fulfill the accepted social function of comedy: by mirroring the customs and manners of civil life to teach us which to follow and which to avoid. Modern criticism allows that even Italian *commedia erudita*, the most dependent of all European renaissance comedy on ancient models, was much more contemporary in its pictures of manners than it has always been given credit for being. It was far more vital than academic tragedy, and the reason doubtless was that it drew more freely on contemporary life and on the types current in the popular drama.

In England, the first efforts to naturalize ancient comedy are marked by bold freedom. *Ralph Roister Doister,* with its English village setting, is not much like *Miles Gloriosus* or *Eunuchus* except in the possession of a cowardly braggart, in a wittily manipulated plot restricted in place and time, and in the division into five acts. (The latter was thought to be a characteristic of Roman comedy.) *Gammer Gurton's Needle,* except in these two latter respects, has no affinity at all with ancient comedy; it is strictly English farce. In point of fact, these early school dramas are almost more English in tone than some of the later imitations of classical comedy, like Lyly's *Mother Bombie,* Shakespeare's *Comedy of Errors,* and Chapman's *All Fools.*

Fortunately for English comedy, the movement towards realism was strong. One can, if one likes, trace out in New Comedy lines of ancestry for some of the types in English comedy. What seem perennial types of New Comedy recur, in a new guise fitted to sixteenth- or seventeenth-century London. The *miles gloriosus,* slightly musty from the schoolroom as Roister Doister, Sir Tophas (in *Endymion*) and Huanebango (in *The Old Wives' Tale*), is convincingly modern and alive as the fantastical Spaniard Armado, the solemn thief Pistol, the plausible Bobadill, the cynical Parolles, the sharking Quintilian (in Chapman's *May-Day*). Perhaps the *miles* is to be seen also in the old fat knight Sir John Falstaff,[10] though the tradition is so modified that it remains as just an echo, one allusion among many in the richness of Falstaff's composition. The crusty father who is so sure of himself and his own methods of education is not very distinguishable in Chapman's Gostanzo of *All Fools* from Terence's Chremes or Demea; as old Capulet in *Romeo and Juliet,* or as Yellowhammer in *A Chaste Maid,* he is so individualized as to make his possible type model easily forgotten. The elderly voluptuary, like Lysidamus in *Casina,* is even more frequent in renaissance comedy than in Plautus; though he tends to fall into the class of repulsive old creatures in Middleton and Marston whose names one has no desire to recall, occasionally he emerges as a memorably individualized character, like the rapacious Volpone, the magnificent Sir

Epicure, or the self-indulgent Falstaff. But the discomfited Falstaff of the *Merry Wives* is far nearer the type of amorous old man of Plautine and Italian comedy than is the more complex Falstaff of the history plays. The very number of models that can be claimed for Falstaff reveals the absurdity of the attempt to fit him into any pattern. The truth is that about most types it is idle to inquire whether they survive from classical comedy, since they would in any case have been invented anew. Puttenham lists the types of New Comedy with a significant comment: "marchants, soldiers, artificers, good honest householders, and also . . . unthrifty youths, young damsels, old nurses, bawds, brokers, ruffians, and parasites, with such like, in whose behaviors lieth in effect the whole course and trade of man's life." [11] Ovid's lines,

> Whilst slaves be false, fathers hard, and bawds be whorish,
> Whilst harlots flatter, shall Menander flourish,[12]

testify as much to the permanence of the types as to the permanence of Menander. The Doll Tearsheets and Mistress Overdones of London comedy are in general a much rougher lot than their ancient sisters and certainly need not be thought of as the perpetuation of a type. And though we may sometimes detect traces of the parasite of classical comedy in the roaring boys and swaggerers who are out to take in the innocent heir from the country, the gallant aspiring to be a gay dog, or the citizen's vain wife, we really have in them a new and more active type of leech.

It is in the comedies of London life that realism takes deepest root. A new social setting produces new themes and new types. The old theme of the high-living young man entangled in a love affair opposed by his father or guardian is as common in English as in Roman comedy. But the social pretensions of merchants, the infidelity of their wives, the attempts of gentlemen to live by their wits instead of their hands, the cheating of the rich and innocent by city sharpers and cunning lawyers, the piety and hypocrisy of Puritans, the attractions to the greedy and gullible of alchemy and astrology, are contemporary themes, fertile in the production of new types, especially a great gallery of rogues and fools.[13] The predominant themes are probably cuckoldry and gullery, neither one new, certainly, in the world's experience, but the former not a theme in New Comedy, and the latter much more narrowly applied.

This English comedy of London manners and types may seem a long way from Plautus and Terence. I think it is. Sometimes all that is left as a reminder is a plot wittily contrived and perhaps a type with distant echoes of the parasite or the *miles gloriosus*. But as Puttenham's remark and others like it show, the types in Roman comedy were regarded as significantly realistic and durable, and English comedy of contemporary London life must have seemed, in its fulfillment of the supposed Ciceronian dictum—*imitatio vitae, speculum consuetudinis, imago veritatis* [14]—in the same tradition. Moreover, I think we can see how at least one impetus towards the realistic depiction of contemporary life came from a typical renaissance attitude towards ancient comedy. This is the moralizing one, and it needs some attention.

MORAL INSTRUCTION

From the point of view of renaissance schoolmasters it did not matter that Terence, and to a less extent, Plautus, were reproducing the manners of Menander's Athens rather than of their own Rome. From a strict historical point of view, Roman comedy is not realistic. But it evidently seemed sufficiently so to the Renaissance to satisfy the conventional notion that comedy should be the mirror of daily life. And in their lessons drawn from the indiscretions of the young men, the injudiciousness of the parents, the deceitful trickery of the servants, and the extravagance of the courtesans, sixteenth-century schoolmasters seem not to have been hampered by any remoteness of manners from their own times. In his notes on how to teach Terence appended to Erasmus' school edition, Melanchthon is clear on the moral lesson to be learned from each play: [15] in *Andria,* modest and filial behavior on the part of a young man; in *Eunuchus,* the dangers of bad company, of courtesans like Thais and braggarts like Thraso; in *Heautontimorumenos,* the weaknesses of parents; and so on.

Elyot, in his discussion of the education of young men of the ruling class, advocates the reading of Terence and Plautus, despite the charges of immorality against them: "they be undoubtedly a picture or as it were a mirror of man's life, wherein evil is not taught but discovered." As a useful example to discover the snares of harlots, he cites *Eunuchus,* and quotes, in a free translation that gives greater generality to the moral, a speech of Parmeno's:

> In this thing I triumph in mine own conceit,
> That I have founden for all young men the way
> How they of harlots shall know the deceit,
> Their wits, their manners, that thereby they may
> Them perpetually hate. . . .[16]

Terence's *adulescentulus* in the second line, referring to the young Chaerea alone, has become in Elyot "all young men." Elyot has, moreover, violently wrested the speech from its context. In the play, Parmeno the slave makes this self-congratulatory remark on the false assumption that the girl he has assisted Chaerea in getting is a courtesan; but he is here on the point of discovery that she is a free-born Athenian citizen and that her brother is about to take a horrible revenge on the "adulescentulus." Although everything will come right in the end, it will be through no doing of Parmeno's; and at the moment, far from being Terence's statement of the moral of his play, this speech is merely an ironic preparation for Parmeno's getting caught by his own too-clever trick. Finally, Phaedria, the other young man in the play, is allowed by his father to keep his courtesan-mistress Thais!

It is evident that schoolmasters were not hampered by the frequent absence of any didactic point of view on the part of their authors. Most of Plautus and even much of Terence is surely meant to be primarily entertaining, and is without a deeply serious criticism of life. The scenes in Plautus of young men drinking and making love are rather delightful than otherwise. Two plays of Terence, however, *Heautontimorumenos* and *Adelphi,* the latter especially, are concerned with the problem of moral education: the degree of strictness a father should exercise in his son's upbringing, and the father's attitude towards his son's excesses. The solution suggested is a happy mean, with rather more leaning towards tolerance than towards severity. Plautus shows some seriousness in handling the problems of youth in *Trinummus* and *Truculentus.*

These Latin plays were useful to schoolmasters as they stood. But obviously, plays that brought the tavern and brothel scenes up to date, that showed a less indulgent attitude towards the sowing of wild oats, and that were unequivocal in their recommendation of parental discipline would be more useful still. The result was a "Christian Terence," extremely interesting because it shows the tradition of classical comedy combining with the tradition of the religious drama to produce a strong movement towards realism.

The history of "education-drama" is well known: [17] how Italian *sacre rappresentazioni* treated the Prodigal Son story, how German and Dutch humanists placed the Biblical story in a Terentian frame, most notably in Macropedius' *Asotus* (ca. 1510) and Gnapheus' *Acolastus* (1528), and how the writers of English interludes set the same story, or some other story of riotous youth, in the abstract frame of the moral play. Good examples of the latter are Thomas Ingelend's *Disobedient Child,* probably from Edward VI's reign, and *Nice Wanton,* published in 1560, but perhaps of earlier composition. *Misogonus,* of uncertain authorship and date, but evidently not written before 1560,[18] combines the three lines—Prodigal Son story, morality play, and Latin comedy.

It is worth demonstrating this combination in some detail. The scene of *Misogonus* is set in Italy, the names are partly Latinized Greek, partly English. Misogonus the prodigal, badly spoiled by his father, lives a godless life, in which he is abetted in part by two servant-companions but chiefly by Cacurgus the Fool. By posing as a "natural," Cacurgus is able to pull the wool over Philogonus the father's eyes about his son's evil ways. Remonstrance and threat of disinheritance have no effect on Misogonus. The father's prayer to God is answered by the revelation of two of his old tenants that his wife, now dead, actually bore him twin sons, Eugonus and Misogonus, but sent the "elder" away to be raised by her brother in Apollonia. The son Eugonus is sent for, arrives, is recognized through an extra toe on his right foot by three old women who had been present at his birth, is vouched for by a letter from the uncle, and is joyfully acknowledged as his heir by Philogonus. Misogonus, who has attempted through Cacurgus to prevent the recognition, is now abandoned by his ribald followers, repents, and is urged by Licurgus, his father's honest servant, to beg his father's pardon. Here the manuscript breaks off, but there is no doubt that, following the traditional story of the prodigal, the play must have ended with paternal acceptance of the son's repentance.

It is interesting to note that one of the most important elements in *Misogonus* borrowed from New Comedy is the romantic one—the child "lost" at birth, the fortuitous discovery of him at precisely the right time, and the recognition of him by physical signs. The element of contrast in Latin comedy between the characters of the young men and of the servants, and between two ideals of education, has been sharpened into clear black and white. I think we may see here the influence of the moral play, with its opposition of virtues and vices. I think we may see its influence, too, in Cacurgus, who has both the Vice's malice and his amusing mischief. In his attempt to live off Philogonus, he carries a suggestion of the parasite of New Comedy; in his assisting in Misogonus' affairs against his father, a suggestion of the intriguing servant. But though he is a fun-maker, as both these characters are, he is evil, as they are not, and as the tempting Vice is. As in the morality plays generally, it is the scenes of loose living that are depicted with the greatest realism. The tavern setting, with dicing, dancing, and whoring, is made contemporary and topical by the inclusion of Sir John, a merry and scandalous priest. *Nice Wanton* is another of the Prodigal Son plays memorable for its scenes of lively realism.

The theme of prodigal youth is also a favorite in Elizabethan and Jacobean comedy, and scenes of low life are frequently the liveliest in realistic representation. Sometimes, as often in Middleton, the sympathy of the audience is totally with the young heir in his attempts to wring his inheritance out of an unwilling guardian, and satire is wholly at the expense of the guardian. One may be skeptical, in plays like *A Trick to Catch the Old One* and *A New Way to Pay Old Debts,* of models other than those found in contemporary society. Since stage traditions are tenacious, however, it is not unlikely that Middleton and Massinger are faithful to an old line, made over so as to be nearly unrecognizable. In many plays, enough of the older moral attitude and enough of the old technique survive to be recognized as unmistakable links with Prodigal Son morality or Christian Terence, or both.

The tone of the plays varies with the proportion of the ingredients and the placing of the moral emphasis. Chapman's *All Fools,* for instance, is nearly straight Terence, significantly a combination of *Heautontimorumenos* and *Adelphi*. It is true that the portrait of Valerio, the sophisticated and extravagant youth whom his father supposes an innocent in the world's ways and a paragon of thrifty husbandry, is elaborated far beyond that of his prototype Ctesipho,

Demea's son in *Adelphi*. Chapman's young man is "contaminated" with the Lusty Juventus of the moral interludes. He has

> skill of dice,
> Cards, tennis, wenching, dancing, and what not,
> And this is something more than husbandry!

He is

> known in ordinaries, and tobacco-shops,
> Trusted in taverns and in vaulting-houses,
> And this is something more than husbandry! [19]

The tavern scene in Act V, in its display of Valerio's *savoir-faire* in ordering dice, tobacco, wine, and music, of his arrogance towards the servants, and of his impudence to his father, is especially reminiscent of similar scenes in *Nice Wanton* and *Misogonus*. To his father's remonstrance, "Oh, thou ungracious villain!" he replies,

> Come, come, we shall have you now thunder forth
> Some of your thrifty sentences.
>
> .   .   .   .
>
> Fill the old man some wine.

Nevertheless, the attitude of the author remains Terentian in that the moral is at the expense not of the young man but of the father, whose wisdom has overshot itself; at the discovery of his son's courses Gostanzo is the butt of much sarcastic wit. On the other hand, the combination of Latin comedy and morality play in the secondary action of Heywood's *English Traveller* produces less comedy of character and more serious moralizing. The story of the youth who is having a royal binge at home during the absence of his father, and whose servant pretends the house is haunted in order to delay the father's entrance on his unexpected return, is from Plautus' *Mostellaria*. But the introduction of an abstract character named Riot to be the active misleader of the youth turns the tale from jolly farce to semi-morality.

One of the most interesting witnesses, if not a very satisfactory comedy, to the amalgamation of elements is Jonson's *Staple of News*. The plot is one of complicated intrigue on the Latin-Italian model; but the hero, young Pennyboy Junior, is a prodigal who is led through a whole moral play apparatus of temptation and good advice before he is saved. One group of characters is composed of the city sharks and gulls of London comedy, drawn as humours, set in a realistic frame and treated satirically; another group is composed of complete abstractions—Mortgage, Statute, and the like, including Pecunia, the woman to be won. The "jeerers" or sharks are the tempters; Pennyboy Senior, disguised, the counsellor to virtue. The central moral argument is this: Pennyboy Richer, the miserly uncle, would have Pecunia, or Money, locked up, the jeerers would exploit her for their own ends, the prodigal would waste her on riot; but Pennyboy Senior, the father, teaches his son both to enjoy and to keep her by wise usage. Jonson, being always didactic about his art, likes to tell us what he is doing. The presenters of the play, in a conversation after the second act, give us this illuminating insight:

> *Mirth.*   . . . How like you the Vice i' the play?
> *Expectation.* Which is he?
> *Mirth.* Three or four: Old Covetousness, the sordid Pennyboy, the money-bawd, who is a flesh-bawd too, they say [all the same character].
> *Tattle.* But here is never a Fiend to carry him away. Besides, he has never a wooden dagger! I'd not give a rush for a Vice that has not a wooden dagger to snap at everybody he meets.
> *Mirth.* That was the old way, Gossip, when Iniquity came in like Hokos Pokos, in a juggler's jerkin, with false skirts, like the Knave of Clubs! but now they are attir'd like men and women o' the time, the Vices, male and female! Prodigality like a young heir, and his Mistress Money (whose favours he scatters like counters) prank't up like a prime lady, the Infanta of the Mines.

In another place, the presenters comment on the "catastrophe" and its position in the play.[20] Here we have Jonson's characteristic assimilation of elements: general theme, motivation, and device from the morality play, particular theme from the Prodigal Son variety of it, manners and setting from contemporary life, and formal structure from Latin comedy.

These plays with the labels so clearly attached perhaps give us clues to those in which the elements have undergone a more thorough transformation. We may find traces of the Prodigal Son theme, for instance, though lightly handled, in Heywood's *Wise Woman of Hogsden,* a play of intrigue and love, in which Young Charlton the wastrel is humbled for his wild courses. Nor can we miss the allusions to the theme in *Michaelmas Term* in the careers of Andrew Lethe, spendthrift son of old Walter Gruel, and of the country girl set up by him as his mistress. But in keeping with Middleton's characteristically sophisticated satire neither Lethe, when confronted with his mother, whom he has mistreated, nor the girl, so often admonished by her father, shows any signs of repentance. The prodigal theme is present in *Eastward Ho,* with its contrasts of staid and extravagant daughter and of virtuous and vicious apprentice; its plot is designed to show the outcome to be expected of the path in life a young person chooses to follow. Whether the moral is to be taken seriously, or tongue in cheek as a mirthful ribbing of a familiar convention, the play declares its ancestry. All these plays have the manipulated plots —with scheming, disguising, and implausible timing—characteristic of Latin and Italian comedy.

Professor Dover Wilson has brilliantly developed the thesis that the Prince Hal–Falstaff episodes in Shakespeare's history plays may be the better understood for seeing them in the tradition of the Prodigal Son moralities.[21] On this view, Hal is the prodigal, Falstaff the Vice—"that reverend vice, that grey iniquity, that father ruffian, that vanity in years," "that villanous abominable misleader of youth, Falstaff, that old white-bearded Satan." Hence he must finally be repudiated. There is some danger, however, in fitting the pair too narrowly into this pattern. One may lose the humor and reduce the complex ironies of the situation and of the relationship to a very simple irony—that vice is more attractive than virtue. As with seeing too much of the *miles gloriosus* in him, one may lose Falstaff himself. If we see this traditional pattern of the moralities, however, as only one shaping element in the total complexity of the character, we rather increase than diminish our awareness of its ironic tensions.

Regardless of how we think of Falstaff, there is enough evidence from other plays to show that the Prodigal Son tradition lived for a long time, and that it combined classical and native influences in a flourishing line of realistic comedy.

THE MOOD OF SATIRE

I have been considering the moral element in English comedy with no particular reference to satire, which may be used as a special mode of moral emphasis. I say "may be used as" rather than "is," because of the difference between such satire as Jonson's and as Middleton's. If we are to take Jonson at his insistent word, his intentions are serious; the seriousness of Middleton's is often very doubtful indeed. Middleton's satire is "moral" only in the wide sense that it implies a standard of judgment about what aspects of human behavior are ridiculous or not; but their ridiculousness appears to be in no wise disturbing to him.

Satire was a favorite mood of English renaissance comedy, especially Jacobean comedy. Renaissance dramatists might have found warrant for it in Latin comedy, as they found for so many other things. But we must make a careful distinction. In point of fact, although Latin comedy is often described as satiric, it is largely so only incidentally and by the way. The main emphasis is likely to be on witty plot and situation, with satire confined to good-natured ridicule of manners (like the silliness of Plautus' infatuated or drunken young men) or of ludicrous types (like the parasite in *Captivi* or Thraso the braggart in *Eunuchus*). Only occasionally is the spring of the comic plot satirically conceived. It is so conceived, seriously in Plautus' *Aulularia,* where Euclio, the miser, loses his gold through his overcarefulness of it; farcically in *Casina,* where Lysidamus schemes so hard to get for himself the slave girl his son is interested in that his wife sets a trap for him and neatly catches him. In Terence's *Heautontimorumenos* and *Adelphi* a mildly satiric intention governs the movement of the plot: overstern fathers come out worse in their bringing up of children than do the more indulgent parents. The same distinction should be made for Italian comedy. Of *commedia erudita* Ariosto's *I Suppositi,* with an ingenious plot of disguises and mistaken identity managed for the sheer fun of the contrivance, is probably more typical than Machiavelli's *Mandragola,* with a plot no less ingenious but with its motive force in the author's profoundly ironic conception of human stupidity and avarice. Ariosto's play, translated into English as *The Supposes* (1566), was one of the channels by which intrigue comedy came to England.

In English comedy as well, satire is apt to be incidental, concentrated on scenes or types of London life, or left to a minor plot, while the major action is one of ingenious intrigue, very often romantic, leading to a delightful conclusion. Two plays, one immediately dependent on Latin comedy, the other on Italian comedy, may be cited as examples of this type of structure. The first is Jonson's *Case Is Altered.* The main plot, adapted from Plautus' *Captivi,* is a story of romantic love, adventure, and intrigue; such satire as there is in it comes from the remarks of the "humorous" Onion and Juniper and is miscellaneous and nonessential. Satire arising from the action is confined to the second plot, from *Aulularia;* in it, a typical miser, through his greed, is made to lose his ducats and his daughter. The second play is Chapman's *May-Day,* a highly involved play of three actions taken from Piccolomini's *Alessandro,* and containing the usual ingredients of disguise, mistaken identity, witty manipulation, and happy accident. Two of the actions are romantic, each with a pair of young lovers having the usual difficulties in getting wed; the third is mildly satiric in being built on the stock situation of an old man in love, and in exhibiting the complacency of Quintiliano, a *miles gloriosus,* who cannot believe his wife will cuckold him. And there is a little good-humored satire on manners in tavern scenes. Even more instructive than these two plays is *The Roaring Girl,* by Middleton and Dekker, for here, with a local scene and a notorious contemporary character, the opportunities for realism and satire are unlimited. But the play is built on the usual formula. Moll Frith herself plays a romantic part in assisting a young man to win his sweetheart from a reluctant father; the realism is "atmospheric" in talk and scene and the satire left largely to a minor action in which a group of citizens and their wives are gulled by a set of smooth courtiers. This type of construction is quite normal with Middleton and Dekker, and in Jacobean "satiric" comedy generally. We think of Marston, for instance, as essentially a satirist, and rightly so. Yet in Marston's comedies the satire appears, partly in secondary actions subsidiary to a romantically designed plot, partly in biting comment, like Malevole's, that overlays the conventionally organized action.

Satire evolving from the action, of course, is only possible when character, especially character bred by a particular social scene, is conceived as the motivator of action. The intrigue must be more than a clever scheme for entertainment arbitrarily set in motion; it must be initiated by traits of human nature liable to ridicule and must work itself out to the discomfiture of its initiator. Chapman's Gostanzo in *All Fools* is so sure of his rightness in the strict hold he keeps on his son that he is due for the unpleasant revelation that his "innocent" son is far more accomplished in naughtiness than the son of his more liberal neighbor. Middleton's Quomodo in *Michaelmas Term* is so infernally clever in rooking young Easy out of his inheritance that he finds himself rooked in the end. The greatest of all overreachers are Volpone and Mosca. This control of the central design of a play by a satiric conception appears occasionally in Marston, Chapman, and Middleton, but as a thoroughly realized method of composition only in Jonson.

He is the great master in English comedy of the structural use of satire. He seems to be groping after a method of making it structural in *Every Man in his Humour* and *Every Man out of his Humour*. But in the first he hesitates between action motivated by humours and action arbitrarily complicated, with a resultant blurring of emphasis. In the second his humours are merely exhibited mechanically and motivate no genuine intrigue. The "plots" of *Cynthia's Revels* and *The Poetaster* are the flimsiest excuse on which to hang satire on literary foibles and types, often scarcely disguised portraits of his contemporaries. But in *Volpone* Jonson finds at last the way to make a satiric conception of human behavior produce exciting dramatic action. In the great comedies, the tightly managed intrigue and the outward shape of the plot are like Latin and Italian comedy; yet the motivation of the intrigue in satirically-conceived character, or rather in common human impulses of greed and folly, makes these plays fundamentally unlike Latin comedy. In their moral-psychological combination of motives they seem to me to have closer affinity with the morality play tradition. But essentially they are something new, a distinct form in themselves.

Jonson knew, I think, that his fundamental inspiration did not come from Latin comedy. The structural use of satire is more characteristic of Aristophanes than of New Comedy. And it is probable that Jonson thought of himself as Aristophanic. In the discussion by the presenters that precedes *Every Man out of his Humour*, Cordatus says of the play: " 'tis strange, and of a particular kind by itself, somewhat like *Vetus Comoedia:* a work that hath bounteously pleased me." I take *Vetus Comoedia* to be the Old Comedy of Aristophanes as distinguished from the New Comedy of Menander.[22] This statement appears especially important when we consider that Jonson's *Case Is Altered,* written earlier than the two humour comedies, had been built from two plays of Plautus. The present statement, therefore, sounds something like a repudiation of New Comedy. This is significant, as we shall see when we turn in a moment to romantic comedy.

Certainly Aristophanes contributed nothing to the normal plotting

of Elizabethan satiric comedy; nevertheless, in Aristophanes' fundamentally satiric intention Jonson would seem to have recognized a
dramatic kinship. In the "Apologetical Dialogue" appended to the
Folio text of *The Poetaster* he defends himself from the charge that
all his writing is "mere railing" by an appeal to the authority both
of Aristophanes and of the Roman satirists:

> Ha! If all the salt in the Old Comedy
> Should be so censur'd, or the sharper wit
> Of the bold *satyre,* termed scolding rage,
> What age could then compare with those, for buffons?
> What should be said of Aristophanes?
> Persius? or Juvenal? whose names we now
> So glorify in schools, at least pretend it.[22a]

On this point, it is interesting to note that Scaliger, whose *Poetices*
Jonson knew, also linked Juvenalian satire with Old Comedy: "In fact
we find in this Old Comedy the usage and theory which Latin satire
should accept as its law." [23] And it is, actually, the nondramatic
Latin satirists who are the acknowledged masters of English dramatic
satire. Marston tells the reader of *The Fawn:*

> If any desire to understand the scope of my comedy, know it hath
> the same limits which Juvenal gives to his Satyres,

> *Quicquid agunt homines, votum, timor, ira, voluptas,*
> *Gaudia, discursus, nostri farrago libelli est.*[24]

Jonson most frequently invokes Horace, even in *The Poetaster* adopting the name for himself; but he knew and freely used the other classical satirists as well. For example, the theme of legacy-hunting in
Volpone was suggested by Lucian and Petronius,[25] and was handled
with a sardonic bite more Juvenalian than Terentian. Like all of
Jonson's comic masterpieces, *Volpone* shows an Aristophanic richness of invention. It does not derogate from Jonson's felt indebtedness
to the classical satirists to discover, as Professor Baskervill has done,
that he owes as much or more to native tradition. Whatever his
sources, he worked restlessly until he achieved an original dramatic
form capable of carrying his satiric purpose.

The satiric mood in comedy, being emphasis on the critical side,
keeps it within the conventional lines laid down by the grammarians.
Its function is social. We may also put satire on the side of "realism,"

although of course if it moves far towards caricature, as with the Puntarvolos and Fastidious Brisks of *Every Man out of his Humour,* it becomes quite genuinely unrealistic in its simplification. It is realistic simply in springing from a desire to ridicule the follies of ordinary men, realistic in the sense that we call Daumier a realist in his satiric lithographs of *les gens de loi* and *les bons bourgeois.* Satire begins in realism but may go beyond it to the point of distortion.

The Romantic Element

The movement in English comedy towards realism and satire was complemented by one perhaps even stronger to romance and sentiment in the other direction. Indeed, one of my assumptions is that romantic story is the primary source of English renaissance drama. It was Jonson, as usual, who was vocal about the essential difference between comedy that was a charming dream of true love, unreal dangers, supernatural encounters, and lucky conclusions, and comedy that was an unflattering, if amusing, picture of the stupidities and rogueries of unregenerate man. And to him the former was not true comedy. *Quid sit comoedia?* What, then, is comedy? Not "some mouldy tale,/Like *Pericles,*" certainly; [26] or a lifetime story of miraculous adventure in which the knight travels between the acts to do wonders in the Holy Land, killing "Paynims, wild boars, dun cows, and other monsters"; [27] or the cross-wooing of a set of dukes, countesses, and waiting-maids. Comedy should show men's actual manners at the present time—

> . . . deeds, and language, such as men do use:
> And persons such as Comedy would choose
> When she would show an image of the times,
> And sport with human follies, not with crimes; [28]

observe the laws of decorum—

> The laws of time, place, persons he observeth,
> From no needful rule he swerveth; [29]

ridicule general vices and follies, not particular persons—

> And still 't hath been the praise of all best times,
> So persons were not touch'd, to tax the crimes; [30]

and improve men's manners while it delights them—

> But, when the wholesome remedies are sweet,
> And, in their working, gain and profit meet,
> He hopes to find no spirit so much diseas'd
> But will, with such fair correctives, be pleas'd.[31]

Whether Jonson saw that these two streams of social and romantic comedy were both fed from New Comedy we cannot be altogether sure, though we may suspect that he did.

The possibility that at least one of the lines that entered into the composition of romantic comedy was New Comedy seems to me interesting and important. It may have seemed to renaissance dramatists that their romantic plots were less unclassical than we think them. Critics often distinguish in *The Comedy of Errors,* the Shakespearean comedy most palpably imitative of Latin comedy, between the Plautine elements of farce and intrigue and the "original" element of romance in the recognition of Aegeus and Emilia at the end of the play. It is true that Shakespeare struck a vein here that he was to follow for the treasures of his later comedy. But a comparison with Jonson will be instructive. Which is Jonson's closest imitation of Latin comedy? Not *Volpone* or *The Alchemist* or even *Epicoene,* but the romantic *Case Is Altered,* made from a combination of two plots, the major one from *Captivi,* and the minor one from *Aulularia.* Satire is confined to the minor plot. The romantic elements of the main plot are similar to those in *The Comedy of Errors,* but they actually play a larger part in the plot—loss of children, far wanderings over many years, fortunate recognition at a moment of imminent peril, and final happy reunion of parents and children. These are common features, as everybody knows, of New Comedy. The girl the young man is in love with is recognized through some mark or token as the lost daughter of one of the Athenian citizens in the play, hence becomes an eligible wife for the young man; or a young man who is the slave-companion of another turns out to be of free birth, and the son, stolen and sold in infancy, of one of the chief characters. Jonson takes the latter motive from *The Captives;* Shakespeare, in having the parents as well as the children "lost" and discovered is only elaborating a familiar pattern.

The distinction in *The Comedy of Errors* from New Comedy can be found, if at all, not in the *device* of discovery, but simply in the poetic expression of sentiment on the occasion of it. Be it noted, however, that Jonson, who always knows pretty clearly what he is about, tries in his Plautine comedy the same things Shakespeare does in his; Jonson also enlarges the romantic element in the plot and tries sentiment, even though unsuccessfully. This suggests that to follow the invitation such a romantic theme gave to the expression of sentiment did not seem a violation of accepted models. Nor is it, altogether. There is, certainly, some appeal to pity in *The Captives,* in the harsh treatment given Tyndarus, the hostage, and some no-bility of sentiment in Tyndarus' sacrifice for his supposed master; and there is some pathetic sadness in *Rudens,* in the scene in which the girl and her attendant, thrown on shore after a shipwreck, lament their helplessness. Terence's *Hecyra* is serious throughout and shows considerable delicacy of feeling.

Nevertheless, it is true that sentiment in the treatment of romantic situations is largely absent from Plautus and Terence. The discovery of the romantic background of hero or heroine is merely a convenient device to untie the knot of complications. Even in a plot with such romantic possibilities as *Rudens*—a lost daughter, a shipwreck, ref-uge in a temple, an ardent lover determined to keep his girl from the pimp, the discovery of her parentage through tokens in a chest cast up by the sea—moments of sentiment are brief. Love in Latin comedy is nearly always simply an infatuation or an urgency of possession and is presented from the man's point of view; the girl, if a virtuous one, is wholly passive and rarely appears. The impossibility of finding in an English comedy an episode like the one in *Eunuchus* in which a young man violates a sleeping girl and then rushes out to make rhapsodically delighted comments to the audience is a measure of the difference in taste between republican Rome and Elizabethan England. If in Roman comedy any actual love-making is shown on the stage, it is frankly licentious, as in the scene between the slave Sceparnio and the slave girl Ampelisca in *Rudens;* or sentimental only in a comic way, as in the scenes at the opening of *Mostellaria* and *Curculio.* On the whole, Italian renaissance comedy follows Latin comedy in the absence of sentiment. In the attention paid to the character of the heroine, in the emphasis on romantic love, and in the expression of feelings—particularly of tenderness, affection, sadness, and pity—English comedy was to move quite away from Latin comedy in tone and spirit.

WHAT IS THE evidence, then, for thinking that English romantic comedy shows a significant kinship with Latin comedy? The Greek romances, of which there were so many translations and imitations in the sixteenth century, are generally given the principal credit for starting the romantic line in English comedy. Although I would put the ground of it farther back, in medieval romantic story,[32] I would agree that the Greek romances were indeed an important addition to the fund of stories at hand for dramatizing. *Theagenes and Chariclea, Clitophon and Leucippe,* and *Daphnis and Chloe,* were all available in English before 1597 and in French and Italian long before that.[33] And Italian *novelle* with similar plots of love and adventure, medieval stories like the tale of Gamelyn, and new romances like those of Montemayor, Sidney, Greene, and Lodge, ultimately derivative from the Greek type, were abundant and are demonstrably the sources of many plays. But the interesting thing is that such romantic elements as there are in Latin comedy, derivative as it is from Greek New Comedy, are of course the same as in the Greek romances. And there is good evidence, I believe, for thinking that to the Renaissance these romantic elements may have seemed to bulk much larger in Latin comedy than they do to us. My point is that for a dramatist to take a plot from a Greek romance or one of its derivatives might not have seemed like the opening of a new line in comedy, but simply the extension of an old, authoritative one, established by Menander, carried on by Plautus and Terence, and hallowed by the blessing of the grammarians. *Twelfth Night,* for instance, may have seemed quite Plautine. Professor Thorndike suggested the importance of Latin comedy for the development of the romantic line in English comedy, but he did not fully develop his point.[34] I shall give some substantiating evidence in contemporary attitudes.

Illustrations in the early editions of Terence.[35]—In the Strassburg edition of Terence of 1496, printed by Johann Grüninger, a full-page woodcut precedes each play. Unlike the illustrations in the Lyons edition of 1493, printed by Jean Trechsel, which show stage settings, the cuts in the Grüninger edition are illustrations of the story of each play. They are compositions in the manner of many illuminations and medieval paintings with narrative subject matter; that is, various incidents in the story appear within one frame, the same character reappearing in different parts of the picture wherever required by the episodes illustrated. The *Figur* for *Andria* is particularly interesting. Houses with the appropriate characters grouped around them appear in the foreground and in the middle distance. Crito, in the center, with a finger pointing towards Glycerium, Pamphilus' mistress, is indicated as the character who brings the clue to her identity and hence the solution to all difficulties. In the background at the top of the picture is a scene illustrative of Glycerium's romantic past, when, as Pasibula, the daughter of Chremes, she was lost in a shipwreck. The scene is a seascape showing an abandoned ship, the head of Phania, her uncle, near drowning, the child Pasibula afloat on a raft, and "Andria insula," fortified with towers and battlemented walls, in the midst of the waters.

In the play, of course, the action is confined in classical fashion to the critical moment in Pamphilus' affairs when his father is on the point of marrying him off to Philumena, his friend Charinus is suspecting him of breach of faith in taking her away from him, and his mistress Glycerium is giving birth to his child. The revelation of Glycerium's past comes in the last act as a means of untangling what looks to be a hopelessly complicated knot. The effect of the illustration, on the other hand, is to give the romantic background even more prominence than the critical action of the play. It is a narrative, not a dramatic, illustration, without focus on a single moment of action. The story, if not fully set forth, is at least implied from start to finish. The illustrations for the other plays are of the same narrative type, although no other carries the story so far back.

Grüninger issued a German *Terence* in 1499 with the same *Figuren*. And a French *Terence* printed in Paris by Antoine Vérard not earlier than 1500 contains an obviously derivative set of woodcuts. In the Vérard *Terence* the illustration for *Andria,* clearly imitated from the cut in the Grüninger *Terence,* is used over again for *Phormio,* with a mere change of labels for names; the seascape is here meaningless, but it was evidently thought good enough to suggest the pathetic passages in the history of Phanium before she was discovered to be the daughter of Chremes.

These early illustrators use the same type of illustration they might for a narrative of romantic adventure or a biographical chronicle of a saint's life.[36] The point to make here is that the plays of Terence were easily assimilated to the tradition of medieval romantic narrative. Sixteenth-century readers of these editions, accustomed to that tradition, would scarcely have thought anything untoward or out of balance in the illustrations.

The position of De Nores.—The first clue to this renaissance emphasis on the romantic element of Latin comedy came to me through De Nores. In his *Poetica* (1588) he gives for each of the three forms he discusses—epic, tragedy, and comedy—a story from Boccaccio suitable for modern treatment. De Nores is the most rigidly academic of all the Italian critics and is horrified at the slightest departure from classical principles as he understands them. Consequently, his interpretations, since they are unoriginal, and his deviations, since they are unrecognized by himself, are especially valuable as indicative of completely pervasive contemporary attitudes. In his choice of a story for tragedy we have seen the importance of this.[37] Now the story from Boccaccio he chooses for comedy [38] is not one of the tales of domestic life suitable for satiric treatment. It is the fifth novel of the fifth day, a tale of love, intrigue, lost children, mistaken identity, and fortuitous discovery. Two young men, Giannole di Severino and Minghino di Mingole, are in love with the same girl, Agnesa, the ward of Giacomino of Pavia, now a respected resident of Faenza. Since Giacomino will not listen to their suits, each one, in a hurry to outwit the other, connives with a different servant to get access to her. Giannole tries to carry her off, Minghino prevents him; they fight, cause a public scandal, and are arrested. When the kindred and friends of the young men press Giacomino for clemency, he reveals that the girl was taken at the age of two at the sack of Faenza and that her parentage is unknown; circumstances and a scar from a wolf bite behind her left ear reveal that she is the daughter of Bernabuccio of Faenza, father of Giannole. The solution of difficulties is now simple: Giannole and Minghino are released and reconciled, and Agnesa gains a brother in the one and a husband in the other. The dilemma of choice between suitors vanishes.

De Nores doubtless chose the story because its intrigue centered in a love affair and its resolution through a happily coincidental discovery was suggestive to him of Plautus and Terence. The discovery of a brother-sister relation occurs in *Epidicus* and *Curculio*. De Nores says the story is capable of being made into a perfect comedy, for it has action harassing ("travagliosa") in the beginning, agreeable in the end, and treats of private persons, midway between good and bad. The action is complete, has a reversal of fortune from unhappiness to happiness, intermingled with peripety and recognition, and can be treated within one revolution of the sun.

The important things to notice about his choice and his comments are these: (a) This type of story, with a love intrigue central and with solution in a fortuitous discovery revealing a past of romantic adventure, puts a premium on cleverly managed story for its own sake. (b) The same story might easily be handled tragically; the possibility that Agnesa will unknowingly marry her brother, or that the rivals will kill each other, is always present until the lucky discovery is made. De Nores emphasizes the bourgeois manners of the characters, especially in the fact that Giacomino is willing to let the scandal to the girl's honor be settled without revenge, which is proper only to noble characters and to tragedy. Nevertheless, the motivation of jealous hatred on the part of the young men, in its humorless intensity as Boccaccio handles it quite unlike anything in Plautus or Terence, brings them very close to killing one another. So far as the actual story in Boccaccio is concerned, its happy ending is owing merely to lucky accident, not to any difference in the characters from those in stories which end unhappily. Moreover, De Nores' own position that a comedy should have in it an element of the marvelous and a peripety with recognition, introduced to make his definition of comedy parallel that of tragedy, takes him closer to tragedy, or at least tragi-comedy, than he realizes. (c) The fun is to come in the manners of the servants, and apparently only there. Crivello, the servant who assists Giannole, and Agnesa's nurse, who assists Minghino, may be made comic, with *burle* (jests) introduced into their parts. But there is no indication that the principal characters are to be treated other than seriously. Satire, if any, will then be only incidental; there is no specific provision for any.

We have something, obviously, as easily treated as "romance" or tragi-comedy as comedy—and very likely to be, judging from the fate of this type of story in the hands of both Italian and English dramatists. If it were handled as comedy, it would lead to a comedy of different levels of tone, in which the main action of love and adventure, treated with sentiment and more or less seriousness, would be sharply set off from the low comedy in the parts of servants and clowns. English romantic comedy often added another level of comedy in minor actions giving realistic or satiric pictures of manners. This composite pattern is the pattern of Lyly's and Greene's comedies, and, with greater complexity, of most of Shakespeare's. The pattern of mixture persists, as we have seen, in much Jacobean comedy, only with a shift in the proportions and a change in tone, so that the realism and the satire tend to swamp the romance. The earlier emphasis reasserts itself, with differences, in Shakespeare's late "romances" and in Fletcherian tragi-comedy.

That De Nores himself was unaware of these implications is certain, for he regarded tragi-comedy as anathema and was Guarini's chief opponent when Guarini defended his *Pastor Fido* as tragi-comedy.[39] Moreover, all his illustrations, during his discussion of comedy, are from Terence; he clearly regards the story of Giannole and Minghino as perfectly susceptible of treatment as modern Terence. Evidently he saw the romantic element of Terence, therefore, as bulking very large. Further, he insists loudly on the social, indeed political, function of comedy, and yet does not at all perceive, as Jonson would have perceived, that in the emphasis he gives story for its own sake and in the neglect of satire, he is in the way of losing altogether the Horatian spirit of comedy.

Italian comedy.—Some of the practising dramatists among his countrymen did lose that spirit, or perhaps had never had it. Since Italian comedy stays so close to Latin comedy in basic patterns of plot and of character drawing, it shows very clearly the different directions in which that comedy could lead. Ariosto and Secchi illustrate the direction of witty plotting for its own sake, with incidental satire; Machiavelli, the direction of structural satire; Cecchi, the direction (among others) of farce; Della Porta, of romance and tragi-comedy.

The position of Della Porta is an interesting confirmation from a practising dramatist of the tendencies De Nores unconsciously reveals. Della Porta was rather fond of romantic comedies. One of them, *Gli Duoi Fratelli Rivali* (*The Two Rival Brothers*),[40] is worth looking at in some detail for the parallel it offers to *Much Ado about Nothing*. It is a story of an intrigue in a love affair, so handled that it might end as unhappily as Da Porto's *novella* of *Romeo e Giulietta,* if the author had not deliberately introduced an element of lucky chance to make possible a reversal to happiness. Two Spanish brothers fall in love with Carizia, a beautiful girl of Salerno, and with the help of their respective servants intrigue independently to win her. One of the brothers, Ignacio, wins her consent and her family's and arranges the wedding for the next day. Flaminio, the other brother, learning of this, tries to thwart the marriage by ruining the girl's reputation. This he does by bribing a parasite, friendly with her maid, to get some of her clothing and Ignacio's betrothal ring; these he shows to Ignacio as proof of her infidelity. Ignacio denounces her and breaks off the wedding; when her father also denounces her, she faints and apparently dies. Flaminio, now stricken with remorse, reveals the truth to his brother and to the girl's father. The Spanish Viceroy at Naples, uncle of the two brothers, adjudges that Flaminio shall marry Carizia's sister in order to make amends to the family, but Ignacio protests that he should be the one to have the sister. At this point, the mother comes in to announce that Carizia is living after all. In the general wonder, the brothers apologize to each other and swear friendship, and each gets a wife. The story is handled with great seriousness and intensity of passion. The only attempt at amusement is in the parts of a parasite and of a braggart soldier.

The parallels to *Much Ado* are obvious: the malicious slander of the heroine and the means of making it believed, the effect on the girl in her fainting and apparent death, the suggestion that the slanderer (in Shakespeare the lover, rather) marry someone like her, the solution with her restoration to life. In the handling of the Hero-Claudio story there is likewise little humor, which is largely reserved for other situations and characters. I am not suggesting that Shakespeare knew Della Porta's play. The origins of his story are usually located in Bandello's twenty-second *novella* (perhaps through Belleforest) and in Ariosto's story of Ariodante and Ginevra.[41] Della Porta's play, in point of fact, is very close to the *novella*. I am concerned, however, not with particular sources, but with common attitudes towards comedy.

Now the interesting thing is that in his prologue to the play Della Porta claims kinship with the masters of New Comedy. Addressing the "vil canaglia" who think they know what a play should be and judge it by arbitrary rules from Aristotle, he says the first thing to be considered is whether the fable is new, marvelous, and pleasing, and has all its parts agreeable to one another, for the fable is the soul of the play. One should consider the peripety, which is, in turn, the soul of the fable, the very soul of the soul, as it were.[42] Whereas the ancients used twenty scenes to make the peripety fall in one, in his play it falls of itself, without any wrenching, entirely in the fourth act, and if one looks more closely, he will see peripety born from peripety, and recognition from recognition. "If you were not blind in the eyes of the intellect as you are, you would see the shades of Menander, of Epicarmus, and of Plautus walking in this scene and rejoicing that comedy had arrived at that height and at that mark at which all of antiquity aimed." [43] The aim of the writers of New Comedy was, then, according to Della Porta, to work out a smoothly articulated plot with a high point in an unexpected reversal of fortune brought about by recognition, that is by an element of the fortuitous and the marvelous.

Étienne and "Gl'Ingannati."—The anonymous Italian play of *Gl'Ingannati* (*The Dupes*) performed in 1531 by the Society of the Intronati of Siena [44] is well known as a probable source, directly or indirectly, of *Twelfth Night*. The central situation—of separated twins, mistaken identity, and cross-wooing—is similar in both plays. When Charles Étienne published in 1552 a revised edition of *Les Abusez,* his translation of *Gl'Ingannati,* he made an interesting claim for it in his dedicatory preface, namely that it would give the Dauphin and the other readers a good idea of classical New Comedy. Although this comedy itself is not made by the ancients, but by modern Siennese, "studieux de toute antiquité et honnesteté," Terence himself, if he had written it in Italian, could scarcely have done it better. Étienne reprehends much modern French drama for following classical satire and Old Comedy in vilifying particular persons and taxing superiors. This was the reason the ancients abolished these follies as pernicious, and more instigative of rumors and debates than of pleasure and delight:

... instead of such follies, they invented the comedy which they called "new," in which they introduced only citizens, or persons of low degree, not treating of other events than marriages, love-affairs, and similar things; these things, to the end that they should be pleasing to the auditors, the authors managed in such a way and so skilfully—changing themes, introducing things unexpected and hidden, then disclosing them, leaving one matter to take up another, then returning to the first again, leading everything dextrously to the conclusion—that the whole gave incredible delight to the spectators.[45]

The emphasis here is on the skilful conduct of the fable as the essential characteristic of New Comedy, and on the harmlessness of the stories it deals with. And *Gl'Ingannati,* he says, is the best example of modern Terence yet written.

We might assemble more evidence of the same sort, such as Scaliger's description of the plots of New Comedy:

> In the New Comedy, marriages and loves have the chief place. Rivalries abound; virgins are bought from panderers that they may be free, and those found free are bought with a ring, an amulet, or a garden-plot, of father, mother, lover, or brother; and invariably the panderer is discomfited.[46]

(Think of Marina in *Pericles* rescued from a brothel.) The common denominator in all these views is the stress on the importance in New Comedy of a well-managed romantic story with a happy ending. This element had been allowed for by the grammarians, for all their stress on the civic usefulness of New Comedy.[47]

The position of Jonson.—Most significant of all for our purposes, since he is English, is the evidence implicit in the attitude of Jonson. The seeds of disruption of the Ciceronian view of comedy as a mirror of daily life and of the Horatian view of it as a means to satirize contemporary manners were present in the romantic features of New Comedy. That Jonson saw these features bulking large seems evident in the romantic treatment he gave his early Plautine play. That he also saw whither they tended is evident, I believe, in his rejection of them and his attempt to find a different medium for wholly satiric comedy. Viewed in the light of the earlier *Case Is Altered,* which he did not, by the way, include in his 1616 Folio, his appeal to "Vetus Comoedia" in the prologue to *Every Man out of his Humour* looks like a declaration that New Comedy would lead him away from what he regarded as the true social function of comedy.

IT DID LEAD others away. Or, to put the matter the other way around, they were led by the old romantic interest in story-telling to warp New Comedy in the direction of this interest. Playwrights grounded in the structure of Latin comedy assimilated it to the romantic story-telling line. As a result, they produced a distinctive comedy which did not achieve in its time a new critical definition except in Jonson's slurring comments, and which ran counter to the academic view of comedy in several ways: in a primary emphasis on delightful story rather than on social criticism; in the emphasis on the purely fortuitous in the plot, especially in the unraveling, so that the effect of a startling peripety was sought rather than the effect of intelligent manipulation on the part of an intriguer to bring his scheme to a head; in the cultivation of pleasurable sentiment, not to the exclusion of the satiric and the comic, but enough to give major emphasis to feeling (lyricism in the verse and in the introduction of actual songs were means of emphasis); in the use of themes from fairy tale and myth, and in the creations of fantasy; in the failure to live up to the academic requirement that comedy treat only the affairs of common men. Most of these tendencies should be clear enough from what I have already said. Emphasis on delightful story brought the admission of the melancholy maidens disguised as pages, the busy magicians, the "servant-monsters" and "nests of antics" Jonson deplored.[48] These elements of marvelous adventure in turn reinforced the preference for chronological treatment over the crisis action of Latin comedy. They also invited the cultivation of danger to the point where only semi-miraculous intervention could save the situation. Moreover, the disregard of the directly critical function of comedy made possible the presence of characters of a higher rank. The lovers of romantic comedy could be given noble rank without violation of decorum because they were not made fools of. Although he had done this very thing in *The Case Is Altered,* Jonson had a sour word to say on the matter in *Every Man out of his Humour.*[49] Latin comedy merely served as a useful frame in which to handle the "tales and tempests" Jonson liked to make fun of.

The Mingling of Tones in English Comedy

This analytical separation of social and romantic comedy of course falsifies actual English practice. There is far more mingling of the two kinds than there is separation. Jonson's comedy is the "purest" on the social side; Peele's, perhaps, on the romantic side. Nearly everybody else's, even Shakespeare's, is more or less mixed, with emphasis on one side or the other depending on temperament and interests. Predominantly social comedy, like Middleton's, is apt to have a central romantic affair with the lovers sympathetically handled and even with some little expression of sentiment. Predominantly romantic comedy, like Shakespeare's, has its realistic pictures of manners made the subject of delightful laughter. Moreover, its criticism of life may be profound, though its methods of criticism are indirect. I shall illustrate with only one point.

One of the means of complicating romance is by expressing it in the pastoral mode. We think of pastoralism as the essence of romantic escape. But an escape convention may be used as an instrument of criticism. There lies behind renaissance pastoralism, not only the pastoral novel, with its origin in Greek romance, and the medieval *pastourelle* or love-dialogue, but also the whole history of the eclogue, with its tradition of social and political criticism. Pastoralism lends itself, therefore, to the expression of a wide range of attitudes, from the simplest to the most complex.

English drama puts the convention to various uses.[50] On the simplest level, it is exemplified in Peele's *Arraignment of Paris;* although that is a mythological play, not a strict pastoral, it has in setting and treatment the mood of uncomplicated pastoral, in which prettiness and charm are their own reason for being. These qualities may be taken so, too, with differences, in Jonson's *Sad Shepherd,* which naturalizes classical pastoral in Sherwood Forest, or perhaps simply reverts to medieval tradition. The differences in tone largely come with the change of setting: Robin Hood's hunting horn is oftener heard than the shepherd's pipes, and the Scottish witch Maudlin and her sprite Puck-Hairy are rather more malicious in their mischief-making than the nonmoral satyrs of traditional pastoral. It is true that the play is touched with criticism of the Puritans, "the sourer sort of shepherds," who decry the "Pagan pastimes" of a happier age, yet practise worse sins under cover of zeal:

> *Robin.* I do not know what their sharp sight may see
> Of late, but I should think it still might be
> (As 'twas) an happy age, when on the plains
> The woodmen met the damsels and the swains
> The neat'ards, plow-men, and the pipers loud,
> And each did dance, some to the kit, or crowd,
> Some to the bag-pipe; some the tabret mov'd,
> And all did either love, or were belov'd.
>
> .   .   .   .
>
> *Lionel.* And all these deeds were seen without offence,
> Or the least hazard o' their innocence.
> *Robin.* Those charitable times had no mistrust.
> Shepherds knew how to love, and not to lust.[51]

But direct criticism in the play is momentary, and even implied criticism (perhaps in the Merry England theme) is quickly forgotten in the dominant mood of fairy tale.

As something more than the creation of a mood or the vehicle of a story, pastoralism is used by Daniel and Fletcher. Daniel's *Queen's Arcadia* puts the convention to the service of social criticism, not, perhaps, to be taken too seriously; a group of city people—Colax "a corrupted traveller," Techné "a subtle wench of Corinth" whose "art" defines itself, Adlon a quack-salver, and Lincus a pettyfogger—corrupt with gossip, suspicion, jealousy, vanity, and hypochondria the hitherto simple and morally sound Arcadian shepherds. Fletcher's *Faithful Shepherdess* anatomizes, in the relations of the various characters, the many aspects of love, sensual and chaste; the final glorification, not merely of chastity, but of virginity, is not precisely in Theocritan vein. Even though Fletcher's Platonism is perhaps more a pretty exercise in poetry than a serious examination of morals, it certainly sophisticates the mood of pastoral romance.

Finally, there is Shakespeare's use of the pastoral convention as a very oblique device in the service of comedy. The charm is always there for its own sake. Yet criticism comes in by the way, and is double-edged; for, if the fresher air of the woods and fields blows a healthful breeze through the close atmosphere of the court, the sophisticated court dwellers also show up the crudeness of rural life. "Ay, now am I in Arden, the more fool I!" cries Touchstone, regarding himself as honest Ovid among the Goths. Escape is never more than temporary and restorative, and the place escaped to is never a place where rough reality can be denied.[52] The pastoral dream is itself one of the things laughed at. The laughter, however, is never cynical. For there is always more than dream. Perdita's flowers are as real as Autolycus' light fingers. The reality of nature is precisely the source of its refreshment. There are indeed tongues in trees and sermons in stones. With Shakespeare the pastoral is only one of his ways of approach to the larger question of nature and art, nature and civilization, that fascinated him all his life.

With the pastoral dream, moreover, is linked the dream of the Golden Age, so often represented in painting and poetry as a time of pastoral simplicity.[53] It is a note often touched by Shakespeare, and always delicately. His lovely visions of the Golden Age are without

Keats's melancholy pang for lost romance; Shakespeare's visions are glimpses into the green places of the human spirit.

> O, fellow! come, the song we had last night.
> Mark it, Cesario; it is old and plain;
> The spinsters and the knitters in the sun,
> And the free maids that weave their thread with bones,
> Do use to chant it: it is silly sooth,
> And dallies with the innocence of love,
> Like the old age.

Perdita and Florizel, in their innocence and assurance, recover for Polixenes and Leontes their lost simplicity, trust, and love. Ferdinand and Miranda have not like Porphyro and Madeline fled away into the storm, ages long ago. They are alive, in the bright morning of the day. Perhaps they will arrive at Prospero's troubled doubts by the end of it, but their present moment of wondering discovery is as valid as his loss of illusion; and he can himself only hope to achieve his beneficent purposes by putting the future into their hands.

8 Tragi-Comedy

No merry tale, my boy, nor yet too sad,
But mixed, like the tragic comedies.
—SAMUEL DANIEL, *Hymen's*
Triumph, IV. iii

Romantic Story

UP UNTIL THE years immediately preceding the close of the theaters, "tragi-comedy" for English plays was a term only fitfully and rather uncertainly applied. That is understandable enough in an age whose dramatic tradition was fundamentally one of romantic story. In the earlier stages of its use the term was a betrayal of critical uneasiness rather than an accurate description of an identifiable form. It actually misrepresented the historical process. For "tragi-comedy" implied an anomalous mixture of distinctive forms, whereas romantic story, neither tragic nor comic in the classical sense, was not a breakdown of these forms but antecedent to them in medieval and early renaissance stage practice. It was romantic story which, under the influence of inherited conceptions of ancient drama, got pulled about and shaped into the separable forms of tragedy and comedy. Nevertheless, the history of the term "tragi-comedy" is not negligible, for it provoked one of the most famous critical controversies of the age, that over Guarini's *Pastor Fido,* and it came finally to be applied to drama with definable characteristics as a form.

As a conventional form, we usually mean by English renaissance tragi-comedy the Beaumont-and-Fletcher sort of thing,[1] typically represented by either *Philaster* or *A King and No King,* the former more pathetic, the latter more melodramatic, but alike in the high rank of the principal characters, in a certain solemnity of sentiment, and in the clever management of plot so that a surprise recognition or change of heart brings about a dramatic reversal from extreme peril to good fortune. Fletcher's own definition recognizes the importance of this reversal:

A tragi-comedy is not so called in respect of mirth and killing, but in respect it wants deaths, which is enough to make it no tragedy, yet brings some near it, which is enough to make it no comedy, which must be a representation of familiar people, with such kind of trouble as no life be questioned; so that a god is as lawful in this as in a tragedy, and mean people as in a comedy.

Although this description was intended specifically for his pastoral drama, *The Faithful Shepherdess* (ca. 1608), at least the first half of it applies as well to the courtly tragi-comedies; they want deaths, yet bring some near it, and their whole tone is controlled by that fact.

We may think of this Fletcherian form as a softening of both tragic and comic attitudes, alike as a weakening of tragic stress and as a dilution of comic salt. From one point of view, it looks as if tragedy and comedy had been melted into a new amalgam. Other types of Jacobean plays besides romantic tragi-comedy also suggest the crumbling of the edges of the traditional conventional forms of tragedy and comedy: for instance, domestic tragedies with happy endings or some of Marston's satiric-romantic plays. The important thing to remember, however, is that these different modes of assimilation towards the end of the curve of English renaissance drama are only a final yielding to pressures there from the beginning. The tendency to inclusiveness is far older, indeed, than the academic movement towards a classically rigorous separation of forms and persists against this movement throughout the sixteenth century, both to prevent the developing forms of tragedy and comedy from becoming narrowly exclusive and to produce mixed plays that the academically minded were sometimes moved to call tragi-comedies.

It is true that there is a great difference between a formless mixture of adventure, idealism, and horseplay like *Damon and Pythias* and a formally satisfying blend of serious trouble, adventure, sentiment, and humor, as in *The Winter's Tale* or *Philaster*. It is probably also true that Fletcherian tragi-comedy would not be quite what it was if Shakespearean tragedy and comedy had not preceded it. Fletcher's own definition testifies to an awareness of assimilation of separable forms. Nevertheless, with our eye on a long history, we may conclude that this distinguishable Fletcherian form represented primarily the attainment of skill in manipulation of a type of story characteristic of romantic drama from its remote beginning in the trials of knightly lovers or of holy saints. We recognize the kinship in the name "romance" we sometimes use in place of "tragi-comedy," in spite of the sophisticated tone of the plays.[2]

In writing a history of English tragi-comedy, one would traverse the same ground as in writing a history of romantic drama generally, with special emphasis on romantic comedy. *Susanna,* an early Elizabethan interlude (pr. 1578) based on the story of Susanna and the elders, *Much Ado about Nothing* (ca. 1598), and *Cymbeline* (ca. 1609), are all stories of calumny on a woman's honor and of her final triumphant vindication; although they are variously blended of seriousness and humor, so that the tone of each is different, they are all in the same tradition of the romantic tale of trials successfully overpassed. The labels we attach to them—"moral interlude," "romantic comedy," and "tragi-comedy," respectively—should not be allowed to obscure this fact. Romantic story and variety of interest are the essentials of all three. How the variety is blended determines the labels. When our focus is on tragi-comedy alone, we are tempted to distinguish a stage of inartistic nonselectivity (applicable to *Susanna*) from a stage of conscious artistic assimilation (applicable to *Cymbeline*) that comes only after a period of selectivity has given definition to forms distinctively tragic and comic. But no date can be set when one stage passes into the other, for plays that one might feel to be artistically sophisticated are written concurrently with those that are not, and precisely what they are to be called is often an idle question. We have always to remember both the fondness for romantic story, which tends to an exaggeration of dangers undergone leading to an ultimately happy solution, and the strength, throughout the period, of the impulse to variety that leads to many different blendings of tone, sometimes successful, sometimes not. Think of the many interludes combining the seriously moral and the ludicrous; of the romantic comedies of Lyly, Greene, Peele, Shakespeare, and Dekker, with their variety of adventure, sentiment, fantasy, and humour; of the half-satiric half-romantic plays of Marston, Chapman, and Dekker; of Shakespeare's "problem" comedies; of the domestic dramas of Heywood and others in which tragedy is considerably modified. Fletcherian tragi-comedy is simply one type of blending of interests and tones. It is the success of the blending that entitles it to be called a form.

Lyly has two statements that are interesting in showing this resistance to narrow selectivity and rigid definition of form. In describing *Endymion* (?1588), he says:

We present neither comedy, nor tragedy, nor story, nor any thing but that whosoever heareth may say this, Why here is a tale of the Man in the Moon.

In the prologue to *Midas* (?1589–90), he comments on the variety in all things that is the fashion. The drama is no exception:

At our exercises, soldiers call for tragedies—their object is blood: courtiers for comedies—their subject is love: countrymen for pastorals —shepherds are their saints. Traffic and travel hath woven the nature of all nations into ours, and made this land like arras, full of device, which was broadcloth, full of workmanship.

Time hath confounded our minds, our minds the matter; but all cometh to this pass, that what heretofore hath been served in several dishes for a feast is now minced in a charger for a gallimaufrey. If we present a mingle-mangle, our fault is to be excused, because the whole world is become an hodge-podge.

If we are to believe Lyly, this making of minces and stews is something recent. Actually, he is only expressing an old and continuing taste; it probably looked new to him since he saw it displacing the academic conventions he was familiar with. Two very early statements of a similar kind and from different countries help to put Lyly's remarks in clearer perspective against the background of his age.

In 1486, Nicolò da Correggio published his *Cefalo,* the Ovidian myth of Cephalus and Procris, with embellishments and alterations, the chief of which is Diana's intervention at the end to restore the dead Procris to life and a happy future with her husband. The plot structure is that of the episodic *sacra rappresentazione,* or popular Italian religious drama, and the intervention of Diana is like that of the Virgin in the plays of saints' lives; but *Cefalo* is divided into acts, provided with choruses of nymphs and satyrs, and infused with reminiscences of Plautus. The prologue recognizes the difficulty of description in the conventional terms:

Non vi do questa già per comedìa,
Chè in tutto non se observa il modo loro;
Non voglio la crediate tragedìa,
Se ben de Ninfe gli vedrete il coro.
Fabula o historia quale ella se sia,
Io ve la dono, e non per precio d'oro.[3]

Toffanin suggests the importance of the combination of the words "tragedy" and "comedy" as unconsciously anticipatory of a characteristic renaissance form. It would seem more accurate to emphasize the rejection of the conventional terms in favor of the noncommittal "history" or "fable."

In 1502, the Spanish Rojas said his *Celestina,* or *Tragicomedia de Calisto y Melibea,* a pseudo drama or dramatic novel in twenty-one acts, was regarded by some as a "historia toda junta." (James Mabbe translated the phrase in 1631 as "a history, huddled, I know not how, together, a kind of hodgepodge or gallimaufrey.") Not knowing what to call it—for some said it should be termed a tragedy on account of the sorrowful ending, and "the first author" [4] would have called it a comedy from its pleasurable beginning—Rojas had divided it in the midst and called it a tragi-comedy. By the tone of his Prologue one suspects Rojas of a careless Plautine "Take it as you please" attitude, for indeed the work is unclassifiable.

Certainly the "What you will's" and "As you like it's" of Elizabethan romantic comedy are recognitions of this unabashed eclecticism that achieved successful dramatic form.[5]

The Term "Tragi-Comedy" and Its Connotations

The term "tragi-comedy" had a long history. Used for a long time, sometimes apologetically, sometimes abusively, to describe plays which had no recognizable conventional shape, "tragi-comedy" came to have towards the end of the century more precise connotations. This was partly the result of a good deal of critical concern with the term. As usual, critical controversy was provoked by something existent in fact, romantic drama which was not rigidly adherent to academic conceptions of tragedy and comedy; and, as usual, criticism found a way, despite its classical pretensions, to justify the compelling tastes of the age—this time the taste for variety, for romantic story, and for happy endings.

As we should expect, it is to Italy primarily that we must look for critical arguments and definitions. There, where the distinction of conventional forms was sharper and came earlier than in England, and where, consequently, the "artistic" stage of tragi-comedy came earlier, the use of the term and the legitimacy of such a kind of drama was much disputed.

But Italy was not different from England in having a flourishing popular drama. Plays one learns nothing about from the critics, but which must have exerted at least an indirect influence on renaissance drama, were the *sacre rappresentazioni,* plays on Biblical subjects and the lives of saints and martyrs, episodically organized and romantically treated; as these continued in popularity in the fifteenth and sixteenth centuries, they often adopted secular themes from chivalric romance and popular tale. Examples are *Guglielma, Uliva, Stella,* and *Rosana,* all of which belong to familiar patterns of romantic folk tale. Although the heroines of the first two are accorded sainthood, they are not to be found in any authentic hagiography. In all four the heroines are good and faithful; their chastity is called in question or they are otherwise persecuted—by a brother-in-law, mother-in-law, or stepmother; after many trials, during which their goodness and perseverance never falter, they are triumphantly reunited with husband or lover through the miraculous intervention of the Virgin.[6] Many of the early plays on profane subjects written by and for the *litterati* were organized, despite classical externals, on the frame of the religious plays: [7] e.g., Poliziano's *Orfeo* (1471), Nicolò da Correggio's *Cefalo* (1486), Baldassare Taddone's *Danae* (1496), Bernardo Accotti's *Virginia* (1494), from Boccaccio's tale of Giletta of Narbonne, the same as Shakespeare's *All's Well.* And later on, although the *sacre rappresentazioni* were ignored in critical circles, the taste they represented found expression in romantic modifications of classical form in the academic drama.

In the forties and fifties Giraldi wrote romantic plays with happy endings (*Epitia,* one of the sources of *Measure for Measure,* is an example),[8] and was willing to have them called tragi-comedies, though he himself thought of them as tragedies. But in going even so far, he was braver than most. In the third quarter of the century the grave and sentimental plays of Raffaello Borghini and Sforza degli Oddi were called comedies, and by the latter defended as such.[9] Della Porta, as we have seen, thought of his tragi-comic *Duoi Fratelli Rivali* as in the tradition of Menander and Plautus. Few men writing for that learned, hypercritical society of the Italian academies would cut themselves loose from the authority of classical tradition even if in practice they yielded partially to contemporary tastes. No one before Guarini, in the controversy over *Il Pastor Fido,* a "pastoral tragi-comedy," defined tragi-comedy in such a way that it had a chance to be regarded as a legitimate species distinct from comedy and tragedy, not merely as an amorphous mixture. The definition and the species won no easy victory. The *Pastor Fido,* in process of composition from about 1580 and published in 1589, was argued over for nearly forty years. The chief documents in the controversy are De Nores' attack in his *Discorso* (1587) and *Apologia* (1590); and Guarini's defense in *Il Verato* (1588), in *Il Verato Secondo* (1593), and, in definitive form, in *Il compendio della poesia tragi-comica* (1601).[10] Guarini's influence reached England. Fletcher was to describe his own pastoral tragi-comedy of *The Faithful Shepherd-ess* (written about 1608, published in 1609 or 1610) in terms taken from Guarini but reduced to a neat formula.

Guarini's final critical treatise is a triumph of the rationalizing process. It must be given close examination; but it will be better understood after we have looked at the variety of connotations "tragi-comedy" had throughout the sixteenth century.

THE GRAMMARIANS had transmitted no formula, as they had done for tragi-comedy. Of course they could not transmit one, for tragi-comedy had achieved no recognition as an independent form in ancient times. Euripides' plays with happy endings, like *Alcestis* and *Iphigeneia in Tauris,* had still been tragedies in the Greek sense. Although "comoedotragoedia" [11] had occasionally appeared as a title to Greek plays, now lost, the Renaissance appears to have known the term chiefly from Plautus' use of "tragi-comedy" to describe *Amphitryon:*

... then you shall hear the argument of our tragedy. What? Frowning because I said this was to be a tragedy? I [Mercury] am a god: I'll transform it. I'll convert this same play from tragedy to comedy, if you like, and never change a line. ... I understand your feelings in the matter perfectly. I shall mix things up: let it be tragi-comedy. Of course it would never do for me to make it a comedy out and out, with kings and gods on the boards. How about it, then? Well, in view of the fact that there is a slave part in it, I shall do just as I said and make it a tragi-comedy.[12]

Plautus would seem to imply that he was creating a mixture in two ways: in treating a potentially serious affair humorously, and in putting together with the gods normally found only in tragedy the mischief-making slave of comedy. He may also, however, have been using the term with a special connotation lost for us, that is to mean a mythological travesty.[13] But making comedy of gods and heroes was to later Christian times a matter of concern, and the Renaissance generally took Plautus' humorous characterization of his jolly farce quite seriously.

Although the sixteenth century is free with the term Plautus supplied, there is no easily definable common usage before Guarini, and, as Professor Ristine remarks, no general sense will cover the different shades of emphasis except the mere coupling of the tragic and the comic.[14] This passes into the even vaguer sense of mere freedom from any sort of formal rules. Thus, Marc de Papillon uses the term of his farce, *La Nouvelle tragicomique* (1597):

> Je n'ensuy en cette œuvre icy
> La façon de l'ardeur antique,
> C'est pourquoi je la nomme aussi
> La Nouvelle tragi-comique.[15]

The general sense of "mixture," however, we may break down into these specific meanings: (1) a mixture of tragic and comic episodes, and of the feelings appropriate to these; (2) a mixture of social classes, or a violation of the distinguishing class lines of tragedy and comedy; (3) a combination of the serious action of tragedy with the happy ending of comedy. Although these meanings are rarely used singly, since they usually involve each other in some measure, sometimes one gets the principal emphasis, sometimes another.

MIXTURE OF TRAGIC AND COMIC EPISODES

It was to plays like *Cambises* (1569–70), "a lamentable tragedy, mixed full of pleasant mirth," that Sidney evidently meant to apply his scornful epithet of "mongrel tragi-comedy." [16] Although many plays contained such a mixture, and although authors or publishers often advertised it, Sidney's sense of the term did not in the end obtain. The normal thing came to be to call a play either tragedy or comedy according to its chief intention. Sidney, unless he had been won over to a more liberal view by the power of mature tragedy, might still have called *Faustus, Romeo and Juliet,* and *The Changeling* tragi-comedies in his pejorative sense.

Edwards' description of his *Damon and Pythias* (ca. 1565–68) as "a tragicall commedie" seems most obviously to imply a mixture of the grave and the merry; the comic episodes of Grim the Collier interrupt the earnest and sentimental adventures of the two friends:

> Lo here is Syracuse th'ancient town which once the Romans won,
> Here Dionysius' palace, within whose court this thing most strange was done.
> Which matter, mixt with mirth and care, a just name to apply
> As seems most fit, we have it termed a "tragical comedy." [16a]

But of course the play is also tragi-comic in senses (2) and (3), of a social mixture and of a happy ending.

Maybe "tragi-comedy" as a description of *Celestina* should be taken no more precisely than to mean a loose association of the tragic and the comic, mere registering of the awareness of some anomaly in the form, though it comes under (2) and (3) in curious reverse senses. With a tragic theme, its characters are the private citizens of comedy; with a light and pleasant beginning, it yet ends in tragedy. "Tragi-comedy" in either of these senses is abnormal usage. The shortened English form of the "play," however, published by Rastell, probably in the twenties, was described as "A new comodye—in maner of an enterlude," and did actually end without catastrophe. Whatever the description given it, this wonderful piece of realistic fiction was widely known.

MIXTURE OF SOCIAL CLASSES

Among the critics, "tragi-comedy" was regularly applied to a mingling in one play of the persons of elevated rank proper to tragedy and of the persons of middling or lower rank proper to comedy. This was universally taken to be Plautus' primary meaning of the term for *Amphitryon.*[17] Yet the mingling of ranks almost inevitably implied the mingling of tones. By "mongrel tragi-comedy" Sidney meant not only a matching of hornpipes and funerals, but also a mingling of kings and clowns. And Bishop Hall complained:

> Now, lest such frightful shows of Fortune's fall,
> And bloody tyrant's rage, should chance appal
> The dead-struck audience, midst the silent rout
> Comes leaping in a self-misformed lout,
> And laughs, and grins, and frames his mimic face,
> And justles straight into the prince's place.
> Then doth the theatre echo all aloud,
> With gladsome noise of that applauding crowd.
> A goodly hoch-poch, when vile russetings
> Are match'd with monarchs, and with mighty kings.
> A goodly grace to sober tragic muse,
> When each base clown, his clumsy fist doth bruise,
> And show his teeth in double rotten row,
> For laughter at his self-resembled show.[18]

The point is this. Whereas the question of rank in tragi-comedy seems to us an accidental feature, less important artistically than the mingling of tones, to the Renaissance it was an essential feature of any precise definition. For, ideas of decorum being so strongly held, a mingling of tones followed from a mingling of ranks. Tragedy and comedy were partly defined in terms of rank. Given characters of a certain rank, there were certain accepted ways to treat them. Without shocking violation of decorum one could not make princes ridiculous or peasants noble. Hence, when people of different classes were included in important parts of the action—allowances being made for the messengers and supernumerary menials of tragedy—the tone of treatment must vary. This variation occurred to a certain extent, of course, within a comedy on the Latin model, in which the grosser comedy was reserved for the servants. In a play in which, however, the masters were not private citizens, always regarded as the legitimate subjects of comic correction, but noblemen and princes, the variation must be much wider and would lead to tragi-comedy. For how should the affairs of the great be represented as other than important and serious? Yet the temptation, when associating them with the affairs of meaner persons, was to treat them lightly as well; Jupiter, in *Amphitryon,* could hardly escape the taint of comedy. To the more severe critics either the association in one play of the weighty affairs of the great with the trivial affairs of the humble, or a light handling of the great, was deeply offensive. The social and the artistic were inextricably involved together. Hence, though *Amphitryon* was appealed to as an authoritative example by the defenders of tragi-comedy, by the attackers it was deplored as a sign of Plautus' inferiority to Terence, who was never offensive to taste.[19] The solution of the difficulty, of course, lay precisely in a skilful mingling of different tones, as Guarini was to see, just as in romantic comedy offense was avoided by treating characters of different rank on different levels of comedy.

The mingling of rank was also almost never discussed, either, apart from the happy ending. Again, ideas of social and artistic decorum were inseparably united, this time resulting in a confusion unperceived by the critics themselves and hard for us to understand.

Giraldi, for instance, in discussing the tragedy with a happy ending, the form which gives most pleasure to the spectators, includes the mingling of rank as a matter of course.[20] He would have us believe that Plautus is describing this form in the prologue to *Amphitryon* when he says that in his play there are persons less noble mingled with the great and royal, and that Plautus gets the idea from the "mixed" tragedy Aristotle discusses in the *Poetics:* i.e., the tragedy with the double ending, one for the good characters, another for the bad.[21] There is no use looking in Aristotle for any such association of ending and social rank, and no use either to try to reduce these sentences of Giraldi's to logic. The difficulty lies in a concealed ambiguity. On the one hand, he is taking Aristotle's "better" and "worse," characterizing the persons of tragedy and comedy respectively, to mean socially "superior" and "inferior"; on the other hand, he is taking "better" and "worse" to apply to the morally good and bad characters to be differently disposed of in the tragedy with a double ending. He uses "migliori" and "peggiori" indifferently in both senses. He does not perceive that this unconscious equation of social and moral meanings, if followed to its logical conclusion, would lead to "tragedy" in which the serious troubles of the great, because the persons were "better," would have to end happily; and to "comedy" in which the petty troubles of the humble, because the persons were "worse," would have to end unhappily—in other words, to a complete reversal of the conventional decorum of tragedy and comedy.

This same unperceived fallacy is revealed unmistakably in Guarini when he discusses Aristotle's allowance of a tragedy with a double ending, from which he regards tragi-comedy as legitimately derived.[22] I shall not ask my readers to thread through the ambiguities of the argument. No more than Giraldi does Guarini perceive where the logic of his position leads: to "tragedy" in which "i migliori" are socially and morally "better," deserve no punishment, and come to a happy end; to "comedy" in which "i peggiori" are socially and morally "worse," do evil, and are justly punished. Of course he means nothing less.

On the importance of rank as a defining characteristic of tragi-comedy, another instructive point can be found in Guarini. De Nores objected to the *Pastor Fido* not only because anything trying to be both tragic and comic must be a monstrosity, but also because a pastoral could be neither one, let alone both. Shepherds, being simple country people, were fitting neither to comedy nor to tragedy. They were capable neither of the banter and clever sayings necessary to comedy—for these things were a sign of "urbanity"—nor of the vehement loves leading to atrocious conclusions which were the subject of tragedy. In the slight difference of manners between master and servant, their society was unlike civil society. Hence, a play based on their lives had no civic usefulness.[23] Guarini's reply to this charge is most interesting. He did not say that the rank of the characters was unessential. Far from it.[24] What he said was that since in Arcadia there had been an entire society of shepherds, there must have been ranks among them, rulers as well as ruled, "i migliori" as well as "i peggiori"; that they did not all perform the menial task of actually tending sheep; and that as the examples of Abraham, Isaac and Jacob, Moses and King David prove, the pastoral society characteristic of the early days of the world was capable of producing illustrious persons. His title of "pastoral tragi-comedy" was justified. Since some of the persons in the *Pastor Fido* were noble and others not, the former produced the tragedy, the latter the comedy, and both together the tragi-comedy; "pastoral" described the condition of life of all of them.

Although before Fletcher there is no application to a particular English play of the term "tragi-comedy" with the unmistakable implication of a violation of the conventions of rank, remarks like those of Sidney and Bishop Hall already quoted show us that it was an implication commonly understood.[25]

AVERTED CATASTROPHE

The third meaning, the reversal to a happy ending of an action apparently moving to catastrophe, is the sense in which we ourselves most commonly use the term, and it came to be the sense finally dominant in the seventeenth century. It was, however, as we have seen, involved throughout its history with the other meanings. Moreover, it was applied to two different types of drama: on the one hand, to plays in the religious tradition having a serious theme of temptation to vice and ending with repentance and reformation of character; and, on the other, to romantic plays of love and peril in which tragedy is narrowly averted by some fortunate discovery.

The humanists started using the term for neo-Latin school drama which was a blend of miracle or morality and Latin comedy. Nicholas Grimald explained why he called his *Christus Redivivus* (1543), a miracle play in the style of classical comedy, *comoedia tragica:*

As to the question how the play itself may defend its title, it is evident that the first act ends in tragic misery, but the fifth and last is turned to joy and gladness: thus there is variety enough; now sadness, now joy is sown among all other intermediate parts.[26]

Gascoigne used the term for his *Glass of Government* (ca. 1575), a moral play in the Prodigal Son tradition, with the difference that the evil sons do not repent. Gascoigne's explanation of the term is moral. The play is "a tragical comedy so entituled, because therein are handled as well the rewards for virtues as also the punishment for vices." "Tragical" must be taken in the sense of the extreme danger of eternal damnation in which the souls of the wicked sons lie, "comedy" in the sense of certain spiritual salvation for the good sons. Possibly "R. B." used "tragi-comedy" of his *Appius and Virginia* (1567–68) with this same connotation of moral triumph, even though the virtuous characters actually perished.[27] The play is also, however, tragi-comic in sense (1), in that it is a mixture of tragic story and of unrelated farcical episodes. Another application of the term suggesting the morality background was to Greene and Lodge's *Looking-Glass for London and England* (ca. 1590),[28] a play which ends in God's mercy for the sinful, but repentant, Ninevites. The moral play tradition may have had something to do with the forming of Marston's kind of serious, satiric-romantic play.

Another point needs remarking. *The Glass of Government* is actually a play with a double ending, one for the bad, another for the good, not with a happy ending for all. But the two types of ending cannot be considered separately. The movement towards the double ending, which mitigated the harshness of tragedy, was felt especially in English domestic tragedy—e.g., in *A Woman Killed* (1603), *The English Traveller* (?1625), *The Witch of Edmonton* (1621). The two latter were even designated as tragi-comedies on their title pages. Geraldine's unfaithful mistress, in *The English Traveller,* and Frank Thorney the murderer, in *The Witch of Edmonton,* receive a just reward in death, but save their souls by repentance. Wilkins' *Miseries of Enforced Marriage* (1607) goes a step further by making the hero's repentance lead to a happy ending for everybody. In all these plays, tragedy is averted by a spiritual reformation on the part of the sinner.

In the romantic tradition, the aversion of tragedy is more likely to be either a lucky accident, or the culmination of some beneficent schemer's plans: a lost child is found, a disguise is thrown off, someone believed dead comes to life, a god comes down in a machine. Perdita is found in a sheepcote, Marina in a brothel; the youth Bellario shows himself to be the lovesick maiden Arethusa, Hermione's statue breathes, Jupiter descends on an eagle's back. If a change of heart averts catastrophe, the change is not motivated by a long moral struggle, but is a mere technical device to bring about the necessary happy ending—e.g., the king's repentance for his lust in Fletcher's *Humorous Lieutenant.*

Again, the history of the term "tragi-comedy" as eventually applicable to this kind of drama cannot be considered apart from the tragedy of the double ending. Giraldi did not separate the two, although he wrote both kinds. In his prologue to *Altile,* he suggests that those who object to calling this play with a happy ending (actually double) a tragedy may call it a tragi-comedy. He himself called it a tragedy, as he did all the rest of his plays with either double or happy endings.[29] His authority was what he considered Aristotle's allowance of such a kind of tragedy (even though Aristotle had regarded it as inferior to tragedy with an unhappy ending), and his plea was that modern taste preferred such endings to the more rigorous tragic ending for all. To Giraldi an ending was evidently "happy" if it was happy for the deserving characters. The source of the ambiguity is probably to be looked for in Aristotle himself. In the section in which he is discussing tragedies of the second rank, that is tragedies with opposite catastrophes for the good and the bad, he goes on to say that the pleasure derived from such tragedies is proper to comedy, "where those who, in the piece, are the deadliest enemies—like Orestes and Aegisthus—quit the stage at the close and no one slays or is slain," [30] i.e., where evidently neither good nor bad suffer. Guarini, like Giraldi, relies for authority on the same passage in Aristotle, but understands him to be talking only about "mixed" tragedy with a double ending; tragi-comedy, Guarini says, is superior in unity because it has a single happy ending.[31]

Further warrant for the serious play with a nontragic conclusion came from *Alcestis, Ion, Orestes, Helen, Iphigeneia at Aulis,* and *Iphigeneia in Tauris.* Critics were more apt to regard these as the tragedies with happy or double endings given second rank by Aristotle than as any such miscegenation as tragi-comedies. Vauquelin, for instance, protests against "tragi-comedy" by an appeal to the authority of Euripides:

On fait la Comedie aussi double, de sorte
Qu'avecques le Tragic le Comic se raporte.
Quand il y a du meurtre et qu'on voit toutefois,
Qu'à la fin sont contens les plus grands et les Rois,
Quand du grave et du bas le parler on mendie,
On abuse du nom de Tragecomedie;
Car on peut bien encor par un succez heureux,
Finir la Tragedie en ebats amoureux:
Telle estoit d'Euripide et l'Ion et l'Oreste,
L'Iphiginie, Helene et la fidelle Alceste.
Tasso par son Aminte aux bois fair voir d'ailleurs
Que ces contes Tragics ainsi sont des meilleurs.[32]

De Nores insists that the endings of *Electra* and of *Iphigeneia at Aulis* are not really happy. As for *Orestes,* he says, it is at fault in having a happy ending; one should not appeal to bad examples for authority.[33] Still, the plays were there to be argued over, and Giraldi and Guarini could use them in their cause. The method of dramatic and happy solution Euripides was fond of was undoubtedly one of the reasons, among many, for his popularity in the Renaissance.

The exciting plot, grave in tone, with an ingeniously effected happy ending, was an important part of the meaning of tragi-comedy to Fletcher: it wants deaths, yet brings some near it. In England his was the one precise statement on tragi-comedy after Sidney's. But there came to be an increasing use of the term, as Caroline title pages show, for plays of this kind.[34]

THE SATYR PLAY

A fourth connotation of tragi-comedy, one cutting across these other lines, must be taken into account. That is the association of the term with pastoral and satirical drama. Although the grammarians had not approved of tragi-comic mixtures,[35] they had allowed, however, for a third form of Greek drama, the satyr play, which was to be appealed to by renaissance critics and the more learned dramatists as authority for tragi-comedy, especially pastoral tragi-comedy. The satyr play originated in Dionysiac revels, presenting the god accompanied by satyrs and sileni. In describing the form, the grammarians and later critics sometimes spoke of it as tragedy in which satyrs were introduced to enliven the serious matter with coarse jests,[36] sometimes as comedy having a civic corrective function of "satiric" raillery and as being eventually abandoned, as Old Comedy was, because it grew too licentious and personal.[37] In this ambiguity they were justified, not only by the obscurity of the early history of Greek drama, but by the evidences of common origin of all three of its types—tragedy, comedy, and satyr play. Diomedes was perhaps not altogether wrong, either, in comparing the satyr plays with the Sicilian *Rhintonicae* and with the Atellan farces.[38] Whether or not the specifically Dionysian representations of Athens had any influence on these later entertainments of Sicily and Italy, mythological travesty appears to have had a place in all three. The chief business of the Sicilian and Atellan farces, however, was indecent burlesque and satire on domestic matters. And it was the confusion of *satura* with *satyr* that fixed, if it did not originate, the idea of a connection between Latin popular satiric drama and the Greek satyr play. The confusion of terms persisted into and beyond the Renaissance; *satire*, indifferently spelled *satyre*, was thought to be so called because the satyr chorus of Greek drama had the function of ridicule and scurrilous jesting.[39]

The confusion of *satyric* with *satiric* led to the further confusion of the pastoral with both; for satyrs and shepherds seemed to belong together in the same far-off Arcadian world, and the eclogue, or shepherd's song, had the authority of Virgil behind it as a vehicle for satire. This connection is interesting for the history of tragi-comedy, since the pastoral setting, through the influence of Tasso's *Aminta* (1573) and Guarini's *Pastor Fido* (1580–89) became a favorite one for renaissance tragi-comedy. Although Guarini recognized that pastoral drama was something new in the Renaissance, he found ultimate authority for it in the Greek satyr play.[40] Italian pastoral tragi-comedy, too—hence European pastoral drama generally—seems to have owed something to the notions of the satyr play suggested by the Vitruvian bosky stage setting for it, and by Serlio's elaboration of this.[41]

Now all this matter of the satyr play was obscure, as much so to the Renaissance as to us. The brief accounts of it given by Horace and the grammarians yielded no clear formula for a type that could be called tragi-comedy. The satyr play was to serve mainly as a not very convincing analogy to be appealed to for authority after renaissance tragi-comedy had established itself in fact. Euripides' *Cyclops,* the one surviving example of the Greek satyr play after it had attained an independent literary status, was to rival *Amphitryon* as an authoritative precedent for tragi-comedy.[42] It is interesting to note, as evidence of this thinking of tragi-comedy as a third dramatic form associated with pastoral and satyrical drama, the appearance of Tragicomoedia along with Tragoedia and Comoedia on Hole's engraved title page to the 1616 Jonson Folio.[42a] Tragicomoedia is shown with the simple dress and socks of Comoedia, the cloak, crown, and scepter of Tragoedia; and she is significantly flanked on the one hand by "Satyr" and on the other by "Pastor." This is only one of many attempts by men of the Renaissance to put themselves under the classical aegis. The influence of the ancient satyr play, however, was surely never more than directive, not initiative—and directive, too, only of a limited kind of tragi-comedy, the pastoral. This was a form that never flourished in England, although it is significant of the association in men's minds of tragi-comedy with pastoral that Fletcher applied his definition to his pastoral, not to his other tragi-comic plays. Nevertheless, the impulse to tragi-comedy was far wider and deeper and had been long at work before Vitruvius and the *Cyclops* were appealed to as authorities.

Guarini and Formal Theory

Just as the rank of the characters and the ending were the key points in the conventional formulae for tragedy and comedy, so the same points came to be the defining characteristics of tragi-comedy, at least of the romantic kind, which was the only kind that achieved full recognition as a distinctive form. Subject matter was not usually the focus of critical attention, because it was taken to follow upon the rank of the characters included. Guarini was the critic who saw most clearly that there was something more involved in tragi-comedy than the mere graft of a happy ending on a tragic action about noble characters; that, indeed, the whole play must be of a piece in subject and tone, so that the happy ending would force no wrenching of the material. Although Guarini's theory was evolved in defense of his pastoral tragi-comedy, for our purposes the parts of it concerned with the pastoral may be neglected. He himself insisted that the pastoral element was not the defining element of tragi-comedy, but merely an accidental qualification.

Others before him were partially aware of the formal problems inherent in tragi-comedy, whether or not they used the term. Sforza degli Oddi, who wrote sober, sentimental plays that he called comedies, has an interesting prologue to his *Prigione d'Amore* (published in 1590, but probably written in the seventies) in which "Commedia" defends this new, serious type of comedy against the complaint of "Tragedia" that it is usurping the honors due to her. Oddi shows himself not unaware of the artistic problem of the necessary blending of tones, though his answer to it is the renaissance commonplace on the beauty of contrast. To Tragedia's charge that Commedia has taken over pity and other emotions proper to her sister, Commedia replies:

In the bitterness of tears there is yet hidden the sweetness of delight; and I who wish in every way to give delight often make thus a most lovely mixture of both tears and laughter, and the bitterness of weeping makes more joyous the sweetness of laughter.[43]

Della Porta gets close to the problem of the kind of plot most suitable when he praises his tragi-comic *Duoi Fratelli Rivali* for its neatly managed peripety, the essence, he says, of the plot. Giraldi had seen and stated the same thing much more clearly. An intricately knotted action that the readers can see being unknotted little by little but of which they cannot foretell the exact outcome, and which will be finally untied by a dramatic recognition, is especially appropriate, he says, to the tragedy with a happy ending.[44] Double plots, like Terence's comic plots, make for more complicated action and more pleasure in the solution. He puts emphasis, that is, on complication, suspense, fortunate and surprising discovery, and dramatic reversal—all the things that, from the examples of Shakespeare, Beaumont and Fletcher, and Lope de Vega, we know help to make successful tragi-comedy.

GUARINI, LIKEWISE, sees that this kind of plot is the best for tragi-comedy. He says there should be a strong element of the wonderful in the loosening of the knot. The thing that induces wonder is that the change to good fortune grows out of the very accidents that appear entirely inimical.[45] In his own *Pastor Fido,* the reversal to happiness comes from Amarilli the heroine's being condemned to death. Who would think, he asks, that such confusion and sorrow would turn into the contrary? Who is of subtle enough wit to discover with what art, in what way, such an accident, so far from likelihood, could ever succeed? The surprise reversal, of course, is one of the major conventions of romantic tragi-comedy, and it is especially successful when ingenious plotting makes it appear to come from the events themselves.

But Guarini saw the problem still more deeply in terms of the tone of the play. For, clearly, a surprise reversal would not succeed if the feeling induced by the incidents did not in some way prepare for it. He puts the difference in terms of pity and terror, the essential emotions of tragedy. Laughter is destructive of both of these. But laughter is not incompatible with pity in the sense that the two may not be included in the same story "under diverse conditions and persons." Menedemus in *Heautontimorumenos* moves the spectator to pity, whereas the astute Syrus, who deceives Chremes, moves us to laughter. Terror, however, cannot coexist with laughter in the same play:

There can therefore be in the same fable, I do not say happiness and sorrow, but pity with laughter. And thus the whole sum of this contradiction might be reduced to a single difference, that is the terrible, which can never occur except in a tragic fable, nor can anything comic ever be mixed with it, because terror never comes about except by means of grave and mournful representations [of events]; and, where it is found, there is no place for laughter or joking.[46]

Although this may seem to us to be a rather cautious, formalized distinction, it is, I think, based on the acute perception that the pathetic rather than the terrible is the proper subject of tragi-comedy.

Guarini makes another attempt to define the tone of tragi-comedy in terms of its end. The proper end of tragedy is to purge pity and terror, the proper end of comedy to purge sadness. The effect of purging in the one is to sadden and constrain, in the other to gladden and relax. Tragi-comedy has the same aim as comedy, to purge melancholy, hence to delight. But since the makers of tragi-comedy wish to elevate it above the tedium and triviality of much contemporary comedy—following the footsteps of Menander and Terence, who sought to raise the dignity of comedy—they have undertaken to mingle with pleasing things those parts of tragedy which can go with the comic in so far as they are conducive to the purgation of sadness; they temper comedy with tragic gravity. Tragi-comedy is

the mingling [temperamento] of tragic and comic delight, which does not allow the hearers to fall into an excess either of tragic melancholy or of comic relaxation. From this results a poem of the most excellent form and harmonious composition [temperatura].[47]

Tragi-comedy is actually nobler than either simple tragedy or simple comedy, for it neither subjects us to horrible and inhumane sights of blood and death nor makes us sin against the modesty and decorum of breeding by dissolving us in laughter.

One of the ways to avoid the peculiarly tragic feeling of terror is to avoid blood, deaths, and atrocious events. Tragi-comedy gets some of its special effect by keeping the danger of death without death itself.

And what is tragic pleasure? The imitation of serious actions of illustrious persons with new and unexpected accidents. Now if terror is removed and peril alone left, a new fable and new names feigned, and the whole tempered with laughter, there will remain the delight in the imitation, which will be tragic in potentiality, but not in action, and there will remain the husk only, not the emotion of terror [lit., which constitutes the terrible] to bring about the purging, the which cannot be induced except by all the tragic parts. . . .[48]

De Nores laughed in bitter scorn at the logical and psychological absurdity of such an idea. How could one keep the danger without experiencing the terror? [49]

Guarini tells how. In his analysis of his own *Pastor Fido* [50] he gives the most precise directions for controlling the expectations of the listener, so that he will be kept in suspense and unable to guess at just how the danger is to be averted and yet made aware that it will be averted. Guarini stresses two things that must be done at the very beginning. One is to make a clear exposition of the initial situation from which all the action is to evolve. In the *Pastor Fido* it is a dilemma arising from a projected marriage which seems to fulfill the conditions of a riddling oracle, but which will give the heroine an unwilling bridegroom and leave her true lover hopeless. Guarini is evidently counting on the conventions of romantic narrative to put the listener in the proper state of expectancy. Clearly, the fulfillment of an oracle must solve dilemmas, not create them; and a wise audience will know that after all the thrills it is entitled to expect, everything will come out right in the end. (The ambiguous oracle in *The Winter's Tale* or in *Cymbeline* is a comparable example.) [51] The second point Guarini makes is that the tone of the opening scene must warn the listener that he has to do with a tragi-comedy, not a pure tragedy. Therefore, just as Plautus opened *Amphitryon* with Mercury's joking and trickery at the expense of Sosia, Guarini begins the *Pastor Fido* with the comic reluctance of Silvio to marry Amarilli; and throughout the first act he alternates scenes serious and joyous ("festose") so that the listener will know what kind of play to expect. Guarini continues with detailed instructions on the effective conduct of the plot and on the blending of tones. All these are ways, obviously, to create an attitude on the part of the listener which is receptive to what will be tragedy only in possibility, not in fact.

A further attempt at definition of the tone of tragi-comedy, and of course at the same time a further indication of how to control the response of the listener, comes from Guarini's discussion of the style proper to tragi-comedy.[52] Like the subject and the social class of the characters the style should be mixed. Although Demetrius of Phalerum teaches that the humble and the magnificent styles cannot mix, he allows that the polished and the grave can, even when associated with one or other of the first two. Accompanied by the grave, the magnificent style is proper to tragedy; the magnificent accompanied by the polished, to tragi-comedy. To the latter the humble is inappropriate because of the great persons, and the grave is unsuitable because of the absence of the terrible and the horrible. Tragi-comedy has sweetness, rather, which tempers the sublimity proper to tragedy. The discussion continues at some length on the right degree of figurativeness, of ornament, and of lyricism appropriate to an Arcadian subject.

Guarini rightly argues that there is no question, in the tragi-comedy he is seeking to define, of a mere compound of the unchanged elements of tragedy and comedy; for these are not found in tragi-comedy as entire forms, but only as qualities that, like heat and cold, moist and dry, in interaction lose their own proper forms and conspire to make new ones. Copper and tin are mixed to make bronze; but bronze is different from either. The composer of tragi-comedy

takes from the one [tragedy] the great persons and not the actions, the fable verisimilar but not true, the affections moved but blunted, the delight but not the melancholy, the danger but not the death; from the other [comedy], the laughter that is not too relaxing, the modest amusements, the feigned complication, the happy reversal, and above all the comic order. ... These components, corrected in this way, can stand together in a single fable, especially when they are handled with the decorum and quality of manners that are fitting to them.[53]

These tragic and comic parts that can coexist in verisimilitude and decorum are put together in a single dramatic form with a single aim: to purge with delight the melancholy of the hearers. This is done

in such a way that the imitation, which is the instrumental end, is that which is mixed, representing a mingling of tragic and comic things. But the purgation, which is the architectonic end, exists only as a single entity, restricting the mixture of the two qualities to one aim: the freeing of the listeners from melancholy.[54]

This form actually sins less against unity, he says, than the tragedy with a double ending allowed by Aristotle, for tragi-comedy has one knot, one unraveling, one end.

The scholastic cast of Guarini's argument should not blind us to his originality. In this brief digest, I have not done justice to the subtlety of his perceptions or the closeness of his argument. What he saw were three fundamental principles of form: that the parts of a poem are mutually modifying, that the diverse parts must be so handled as to contribute to a total unity, and that a listener's or reader's satisfaction can come only from a fulfillment of expectations aroused. As for the first principle, I have seen nowhere else in the Renaissance quite such awareness of the qualitative relationship between different parts of a play. The second principle, that unity must come from diversity, is of course often enough stated in the Renaissance, but not always with understanding of what it means in terms of actual problems of composition. Guarini's distinction is in his full realization of it in terms of a particular dramatic form. His awareness of the third principle, the necessity of arousing only expectations that can be fulfilled, is especially interesting, since it might seem to conflict with the surprise reversal on which he lays so much stress. Actually it does not, for the expectations are not necessarily conscious; they are matters of attitude and receptivity.

THE ONLY OTHER full apology by a great practitioner of it for the kind of romantic drama we are discussing is Lope de Vega's *Arte nuevo de hacer comedias en este tiempo* (1609).[55] (Lope's and Calderón's *comedias de capa y espada* are tragi-comedies or "romances" in character, if not in name.) But the *Arte nuevo* is not at all comparable to Guarini's *Compendio,* being partly an excuse for not following the rules, partly a set of practical observations on what makes good theater. We deduce from these that what is most important is an exciting or ingenious plot, with a surprise reversal held up until almost the very end of the play; otherwise, says Lope cynically, the audience will walk out before the play is over.

Guarini's prescription for a harmonious blending of tones seems to be echoed by Daniel in the passage quoted at the head of this chapter from *Hymen's Triumph,* the second of the pastorals he wrote in imitation of Italian pastoral drama:

> No merry tale, my boy, nor yet too sad,
> But mixed, like the tragic comedies.

But the only important attempt at definition in England is Fletcher's, prefixed to his *Faithful Shepherdess,* which was written in imitation of Guarini's by then widely known pastoral play and published some time before the end of 1610. The definition may be repeated:

A tragi-comedy is not so called in respect of mirth and killing, but in respect it wants deaths, which is enough to make it no tragedy, yet brings some near it, which is enough to make it no comedy, which must be a representation of familiar people, with such kind of trouble as no life be questioned; so that a god is as lawful in this as in tragedy, and mean people as in a comedy.

This is clearly derivative from Guarini. It is interesting to note, however, that in Fletcher's reduction of Guarini to a brief formula, the subtler points have fallen out and prominence is given to social position and ending, the key points in the old conventionalized formulae for tragedy and comedy. The statement makes no special prescription for pastoral tragi-comedy, although the "mean people" probably carries a pastoral implication. Except for this phrase and except that "royal or noble person" might be substituted for "god," the prescription is generally applicable to the courtly type of tragicomedy Fletcher wrote.

Fletcher's advertisement in this way of the term "tragi-comedy" did not bring it into any immediate general use on title pages in England; he did not use it again for his own tragi-comic plays. Nevertheless, there was certainly an increasing recognition of the independent status of such a form. The appearance of Tragicomoedia on the title page of the Jonson Folio of 1616 is one interesting piece of evidence.[56] As the courtly form itself flourished and grew more conventionalized and as it replaced in the years before the closing of the theaters all other dramatic forms in popularity, it came more often on the title pages of Caroline dramatists to carry the designation of tragi-comedy.

Tragi-Comic Mixtures of Various Sorts

What we customarily call tragi-comedy, then, is a sophisticated end product of renaissance delight in variety and resistance to the simplicity of classical form. But tragi-comedy is, at best, always elusive as a conventional form. Tragi-comic mixtures are various and the lines between heroic tragedy on the one hand and romantic comedy on the other are often very thin. And there are other mixtures in the Jacobean period—mixtures of romance and realism, of satire and sentiment, that do not so well qualify for Guarini's definition but are nevertheless in some sense tragi-comic. These plays are sometimes less formally successful than the best Fletcherian tragi-comedy, but they are not the less interesting, and they are quite as characteristic of the period. Examples are to be found in Chapman, Dekker, Marston, and Shakespeare. They are serious plays, with serious issues; but they elude conventional definitions. In Shakespeare we call them, not too happily, "problem" plays. Since they raise acutely the question of the relation of form and meaning, I shall reserve for the last chapter a fuller treatment of some of these plays. Here, I wish merely to complete the picture of "tragi-comedy" by setting beside the smooth Fletcherian variety that has earned the name those less classifiable plays that have much of the form of romantic comedy without its mood.

A review of the major tendencies to tragi-comedy will perhaps be the best way to throw into relief the differences in the final expression of these tendencies.

The tradition of the medieval drama.—There is, primarily, the inherited tradition of mixture in the medieval drama of the serious and the ludicrous, the pitiful and the farcical, that made for a resistance to the rigorous selectivity and economy of classical form. It is often said that this mingling, in both medieval religious drama and renaissance secular drama, of emotions and attitudes is an expression of realism. From one point of view it is. The sixteenth-century justification usually given, indeed, for such a mingling was its naturalness. Guarini, for instance, does not see why actions great and not great, serious and amusing, public and private, should not be included in the same play, for the mingling is not contrary to nature.[57] Lope de Vega echoes the pedantic point of view when he admits that the mingling of the tragic and comic, of Terence with Seneca, produces a monster like the Minotaur; but he pleads with the voice of honest contemporary taste when he says that the variety in such a mixture of the grave and the absurd is pleasing, and that the example of it comes from nature, whose beauty is owing to such contrasts.[58] Naturalness resists conventional standards of decorum. From another point of view, therefore, this mixture of subjects, attitudes, and tones may be regarded as "romantic," not as opposed to "realistic," but as opposed to "classic." Realistic episode or character is often a component in a romantic mixture: e.g., Sancho Panza in *Don Quixote,* Falstaff in *Henry IV.* Great romantic writers have often been, like Ariosto, Cervantes, Shakespeare, and Dickens, masters of realism as well. It is idle, however, to force such terms. What we can see beneath all the mixture is an intense creative vitality that proliferates in a varied abundance of ways.

Perhaps we should put with this fondness for variety the literary heritage of both classical and medieval forms. Dramatists laid hands on whatever was useful, and they had a good deal to choose from.

The interest in story-telling.—Secondly, there is the interest in story-telling. Emphasis on story for its own sake leads to plots crowded with action, exciting situations, clever entanglements and solutions, long suspense and pleasing surprises. The storehouse of medieval narrative was enhanced by a great sixteenth-century production of tales and romances. To the Greek romances and Italian and French *novelle* as sources of plots for English plays, one must add the Spanish tales that were produced in great numbers around the turn of the century; their emphasis on gallantry and honor made them especially useful for tragi-comedy and high-flown romance, and they were freely drawn on for plots, as in *The Spanish Gipsy* by Middleton, Ford, and Rowley, and in *The Island Princess, The Spanish Curate, The Custom of the Country,* and *The Fair Maid of the Inn* by Fletcher and his collaborators.

Only a difference of emphasis—a lessening of the witty jesting or the comic trickery, the deepening of the seriousness, real or pretended, the increase of sentiment at the expense of humor, the sharpening of the contrast between vicissitude and happy outcome— turns the same type of story from comedy to tragi-comedy: *Much Ado,* for instance, to *Cymbeline.* It takes a much greater change to turn tragedy into tragi-comedy (e.g., *Othello* into *Cymbeline*), but the change must be worked in the same way, with increase of emphasis on story and theatrical device: sentiment must mitigate passion, and manipulation reverse the irony inherent in the situation. "Oh, the pity of it!" must become "Oh, the wonder of it!" Fletcher's highly extravagant tragedies, like *Valentinian, Bonduca,* and *Thierry and Theodoret,* through their emphasis on device, are more nearly akin to his and Beaumont's tragi-comedies, like *Philaster* and *A King and No King,* than to earlier Jacobean tragedy.

Others in England tried this tragi-comedy of romantic plot before Beaumont and Fletcher—Chapman, for instance, in *The Gentleman Usher* (ca. 1602), Marston in *Antonio and Mellida* (ca. 1599) and *The Malcontent* (ca. 1604), Shakespeare in *Measure for Measure* (ca. 1604). These plays, however, are heavily shaded by satire, wrenched by a violent change of tone, or suffering from a disjunction between seriousness of moral problem and frivolousness of device. The harmony prescribed by Guarini, which makes not monstrous combination of tragedy and comedy but a new form, often seems better realized in the smoother, if less interesting, romances and tragi-comedies of Fletcher and his collaborators, of Massinger, of Ford, and of Shirley, and in the more subtly complicated late romances of Shakespeare. The real success of Fletcherian tragi-comedy, however, comes not from a lessening of the distance between the handkerchief and the laugh,[59] but from the very sharpness of the transition between them. The completeness of the reversal and the ingenuity with which it is brought about become ends in themselves. Fletcher's best entanglements are managed in such a way that, although the spectator cannot guess at the precise outcome, they will solve themselves when the right key is touched. Della Porta might have been describing Fletcher's plots when he said of his own *Two Rival Brothers* that peripety is born from peripety, and recognition from recognition. Cassilane's repentance in *The Laws of Candy* causes a whole series of interrelated potential catastrophes to collapse like a house of cards. The concealed key block in a Japanese puzzle, once found, causes the whole interlocked structure to come apart. The concealment of the key in romantic tragi-comedy is an exciting and necessary part of the game, for the very concealment is a warning to the spectator that he may expect a surprise and that the surprise will be delightful. Giraldi, Della Porta, Guarini, and Lope all knew this, and the most successful English writers of tragi-comedy discovered it in practice.

The tradition of the morality play.—Thirdly, there is the tradition of the morality play, with its focus on a serious moral problem that is brought to a happy ending in at least spiritual salvation. We have seen how the Prodigal Son theme was a continuing tradition in serious plays on domestic themes: straight tragedy like *A Yorkshire Tragedy,* tragedy with a double ending like *A Woman Killed* or *The English Traveller,* and tragedy with a happy ending like *The Miseries of En-*

forced Marriage or *The London Prodigal.* Plays like the latter two, with realistic emphasis, obviously belong to a very different order from Fletcherian tragi-comedy. Both kinds are tragi-comedy because they refuse the special emphasis of pure tragedy. But the domestic plays replace this emphasis with serious realism and sentiment, Fletcherian tragi-comedies with exaggerated romantic adventure and sentiment. The blend is of course very different. Other plays that are more romantic in the externals of the plot than these domestic plays, but like them in having a serious problem central in the action—plays like Marston's *Dutch Courtesan* or Dekker's *Honest Whore*—may also reflect something of the old moral play tradition. I shall have more to say of these in Chapter XII.

The mood of satire.—Fourthly, there is the mood of satire so prominent in the early seventeenth century. We have seen it giving a special tone of bitterness and disgust to the tragedy of sex, and operating as the architectonic motive of Jonsonian comedy. It leads, too, to tragi-comedy; for it can either take the bloom off romantic comedy or freeze the normally expansive emotions aroused by tragedy. Perhaps Shakespeare's *All's Well* can be taken as an example of the former, Shakespeare's *Timon* or Marston's *Insatiate Countess* as examples of the latter.

A mixture of romantic story and satire is one of the commonest in English renaissance drama. It has a tragi-comic flavor in Chapman's *Gentleman Usher,* in Dekker's *Honest Whore,* both parts, in Shakespeare's *Measure for Measure* and *Troilus and Cressida,* and in several plays of Marston. Marston, restlessly experimental if not ever conspicuously successful, is one of the most interesting of the early Jacobeans. His plots, whether in comedy or in tragedy, are generally of the manipulated Italian sort, with much use of intrigue, disguise, and surprising discovery. But they are usually so strongly qualified with satire as to be neither deeply tragic nor gaily comic. *Antonio and Mellida,* with perhaps the least satire, is tragi-comedy with a seriously romantic plot and a violent reversal to a happy end. Marston had not learned Guarini's lesson of how to prepare the audience for what was to come. *The Malcontent,* based on the same type of story, is far more successful formally because the mordantly satiric attitude of Malevole binds it together in unity of tone. In *What You Will* Marston has, surprisingly for him, lightened the tone of his tragi-comic original, Oddi's *I Morti Vivi,* and turned into farcical satire the situation of the supposedly dead husband returning home to find another impersonating him. But *The Dutch Courtesan,* for all its lively slapstick in the Cocledemoy episodes, is tragi-comedy in the main plot. *The Insatiate Countess,* ostensibly tragic, is actually tragi-comic. It is a strange medley of three stories: the story of the nymphomaniac countess, who repents before her hanging in the best morality tradition, and only one of whose victims does not finally escape; the story of Mendoza and the Lady Lentulus, a tale of idealized honor pushed to fantastic lengths of near tragedy before the situation is saved; and the story of two married couples involved in a Boccaccesque plot of cross-cuckoldry. Marston's editor, H. Harvey Wood points out that "the reduction of tragedy in emotional power to something more like heroic intensity, and the informing of comedy with a moralising and satiric purpose, is the means by which these jarring elements are made to unite." [60] The repetition of the themes of lust, jealousy, and hatred, viewed both grimly and satirically, but never with deep emotion or with much laughter, makes tragi-comedy of a most un-Fletcherian kind. Fletcher's comic underplots, as in *The Spanish Curate,* may be touched with satire on the usual Jacobean themes of jealous husbands, rascally lawyers, or foot-licking courtiers, but the satire never has Marston's moral earnestness.

The tradition of the pastoral.—There is, finally, the tradition of the pastoral. As I have pointed out in the chapter on comedy, it is a tradition ambiguous in its implications; for, on the one hand, if pastoralism suggests the innocence of the Golden Age and is, therefore, specially apt as setting for romantic story of the Rosalind-and-Orlando sort, it suggests, on the other, the sometimes reflective or critical mood of Virgil's *Eclogues* or the mood of comic raillery the satyr plays were supposed to have. An excellent statement of this ambiguous tradition is in Puttenham.[61] After stating the theory that "pasturage was before tillage," and agreeing that the civilizing arts of social intercourse must have originated in early pastoral societies (that their meetings when they kept their herds was "the first familiar conversation," "their babble and talk under bushes and shady trees the first disputation and contentious reasoning," "their songs made to their mates or paramours either upon sorrow or jollity of courage, the first amorous musics," and so on), he continues:

But for all this, I do deny that the eglogue should be the first and most ancient form of artificial poesy, being persuaded that the poet devised the eglogue long after the other dramatic poems [i.e., tragedy and comedy], not of purpose to counterfeit or represent the rustical manner of loves and communication, but under the veil of homely persons and in rude speeches to insinuate and glance at greater matters, and such as perchance had not been safe to have been disclosed in any other sort, which may be perceived by the Eglogues of Virgil, in which are treated by figure matters of greater importance than the loves of Tityrus and Corydon.

On the whole, following the lead of *Aminta* and *Il Pastor Fido,* renaissance tragi-comedy that made use of the pastoral setting leaned rather more towards the romantic than towards the satiric. But pure pastorals like Fletcher's *Faithful Shepherdess* and Daniel's *Hymen's Triumph* are outside the main line of English drama. Our concern with the pastoral is chiefly with its effect on Shakespeare, for he absorbed all aspects of the tradition, though he wrote no strictly pastoral play. His last three romances are all to some degree affected by pastoralism, although its effects are more transmuted than in *As You Like It. The Winter's Tale,* especially, is informed by the whole complex tradition. On the one hand, the charm of the Golden Age becomes the charm of youth and a restoration of hope and goodness to older people who have spoiled their lives with suspicion and discord; but, on the other hand, we are not allowed to grow sentimental over Perdita's sheepcote. As usual, Shakespeare's view of Arcadia is not simple. It is true that Autolycus, who counters the idyllic mood, is neither shepherd (like Audrey's William) nor "wild man" [62] (as in a measure Caliban is); he is a knowing "rogue," a member of a specialized profession incident to a highly developed society. Nevertheless, more even than Tasso's or Guarini's naughty satyrs, and certainly more than Fletcher's rather benevolent ones, Autolycus is the true heir of the Arcadian-satyric tradition, for in his sophisticated unregeneracy he is the comic critic of the play.

9 Character

Face. . . . .
My part a little fell in this last Scene;
Yet 'twas *decorum*.
              —JONSON, *The Alchemist,*
                    V. v. 158–59

ONE OF THE delights of the Elizabethan drama is its variety of vivid and memorable figures—its salty Dolls and Cocledemoys; its foolish Druggers and Yellowhammers; its bitter Malevoles, Vindicis, and Flamineos; its poetical Lacys and Orsinos; its pretty and resourceful Luces and Rosalinds; its lawless Vittorias and Livias; its gorgeous Tamburlaines and Antonys. For comedy one can draw up categories of favorite romantic types—maidens witty or pathetic, lovesick youths, heartless fathers; or of more realistic social types—of gullers and gulled, of boastful talkers and sharp doers, of suspicious citizens and wanton wives, of spendthrift heirs and stingy parents, of canting Puritans and ignorant parsons, of courtly fops and malcontent observers. Yet for all that, English renaissance comedy, even realistic bourgeois comedy, does not strike us as being so thoroughly a comedy of types as Roman comedy or its Italian and French derivatives. The people of Elizabethan comedy more frequently transcend their basic type or lose its outlines in vividly original speech and behavior. In tragedy, type characters are less to be expected; but the characters of English drama are less often than the stagy heroes and heroines of continental renaissance tragedy mere declaimers of passion, more often convincingly real as imaginary persons. The figures of Elizabethan drama, even the minor ones, are abundantly possessed of that *energeia* which Aristotle had praised and which renaissance critics recognized as the *sine qua non* of successful imaginative writing.

Lively individuality, however, is only part of the impression we have of the characters of Elizabethan drama. Another, nearly as strong, is of inconsistency, a disconcerting unpredictability that some-times militates against a coherent total impression, whether of type or individual. The appallingly hard Evadne suddenly repents of her deception of her husband and kills her royal lover; the conscienceless Vittoria Corombona gains our sympathies against her justified, if un-scrupulous, accusers; Hippolito, upright enough to win Bellafront in the first part of the play from her life of prostitution, is the very one, in the second part, to tempt her again to ruin.

We have to inquire, therefore, what were the formal conceptions of character current at the time, and to what extent English drama-tists were guided by them, to what extent governed by the always compelling urge for immediate dramatic effect.

Verisimilitude, Consistency, Propriety

In creating or judging a fictitious character our customary modern standard is realism or "truth to life." The critical standard of the Renaissance was also "truth to life"—expressed as "verisimilitude"—but more precisely defined than our vague phrase and raising a rather different set of expectations. Since "verisimilitude" carried the im-plication not of naturalism but of ideal or universal truth, the appli-cation of the principle exaggerated the typical in all theories of character-drawing. There was, besides, a practical usefulness in the principle, since to follow a type pattern is an easy way to achieve consistency in a character, and to achieve consistency, or at any rate coherence, is the first problem of character-drawing. The standard of judgment about what was verisimilar was *decorum,* or the doctrine of appropriateness.[1] Speech and behavior must be appropriate to the person, the place, the time, the circumstance, the end or purpose:

And there is a decency to be observed in every man's action and be-havior as well as in his speech and writing. . . . And this decency of man's behavior as well as of his speech must also be deemed by discretion, in which regard the thing that may well become one man to do may not become another, and which is seemly to be done in this place is not so seemly in that, and at such a time decent, but another time undecent, and in such a case and for such a purpose, and to this and that end, and by this and that event, perusing all the circumstances with like considera-tion.[2]

Although Puttenham here makes the determination of "decency" a matter of "learned and experienced discretion," resting in the discerning part of the mind, the signs of appropriateness could be, and were, elaborately codified for the aid of the less discerning. In this same passage Puttenham refers the poet to the orator's art, especially to speeches of praise and dispraise, and refers to a book he has himself written *De decoro.* The lore of decorum was abundant in such forms as the four (or seven) ages of man, the four humours or temperaments, the differences in the sexes, the trades, the social classes, the characteristics of different nationalities, and so on. We apply sufficiently shopworn tags to similar distinctions of genus in our own day, but the renaissance distinctions were more detailed and formalized than with us and were brought home more sharply in the visible signs of color, dress, insignia, and ceremony both public and private. Every renaissance man must have absorbed these things as a commonplace background to his own judgments about people. And everything he learned in school or read in critical theory—if he concerned himself with that—would have confirmed the habit of identifying class by signs.

The more wonder that Elizabethan dramatists so often went beyond the merely typical in their characters. Possible reasons for this individualizing I shall suggest after examining the background of thought contributing to the doctrine of types. I shall consider in turn critical theory, the teaching of Plautus and Terence in the schools, the teaching of minor rhetorical forms, the medieval literary tradition, and psychological theory.

CRITICAL THEORY

First, for critical theory. The theories of decorum of character, so ubiquitous in the Italian critics, go back directly or indirectly to Aristotle's doctrine of appropriateness in the depiction of character, briefly expressed in the *Poetics,* more fully in the *Rhetoric.* In the *Poetics,*[3] he says that in respect of character in tragedy four things are to be aimed at: moral goodness, propriety, resemblance (truth to life? resemblance to prototype?), consistency. In the *Rhetoric,*[4] he describes the characters of men according to their emotions, habits, ages, and fortunes, and says that character (ἤθη, *ēthē*) may be expressed by signs, because to each class (e.g., age, sex, country) and habit (ἕξις, *hexis*, moral state forming character) belongs an appropriate style. As usual, however, the critics echo Horace's more dogmatic mood and they follow Cicero's or Quintilian's more detailed list of "places" for helping to categorize a person. In discussing the argument from the person to be used in the *confirmatio* of an oration, Cicero lists the following "attributes" to be considered: *nomen* (name); *natura* (nature: such things as sex, race, country, family connections, age, inborn physical, emotional, and intellectual endowment); *victus* (manner of life: education, masters, associates, trade or profession, domestic habits); *fortuna* (circumstances: whether enslaved or free, rich or poor, private citizen or official, etc.); *habitus* (a stable constitution of mind or body, such as a capacity, an art, some special knowledge, a bodily skill, acquired by training or practice—"studio industriaque"—as distinct from native endowment); *affectio* (an unstable condition, literally a sudden change in mind or body owing to some cause—"animi aut corporis ex tempore aliqua de causa commutatio"—such as joy, desire, fear, annoyance, illness, weakness); *studium* (interest: assiduous application of mind to some interest like philosophy, poetics, geometry, letters); *consilium* (reason for doing or not doing a thing); *facta* (things done); *casus* (things befallen); *orationes* (things said).[5] (The last four matters, of course, relate to the deed or crime under consideration in a judicial oration, and are adaptable to portraiture only when a character is shown in a particular situation.) Quintilian gives a somewhat variant list of attributes, less schematized, more fully illustrated.[6]

It may be observed, of course, that the more of these identifying attributes one applies and the more precisely one applies them the closer one comes to making a character only that character and no other, that is, to an individualized portrait. But the word the Italian critics use for characters in fiction and drama—"i costumi"—shows that the emphasis remains general. The word, generally used in the plural, suggests manners, morals, and habitual actions, and is closer to Cicero's and Quintilian's *habitus* and *mores* than to our *character*. Under the heading of "i costumi," the Italian critics repeat the commonplace variations of character according to sex, age, fortune, and the rest; and they severely enjoin the unbreakable rule of decorum. This means appropriateness of speech and behavior applied consistently throughout the play. They all cite Aristotle's condemnation of Euripides, in the passage just cited in the *Poetics,* for the change in Iphigeneia (at Aulis) from timid supplicant to resolute heroine. The critics give lists of types appropriate to tragedy and comedy and instructions for varying the style of speech according to the character as determined by the Ciceronian "places."

In a brief and popular form Wilson's *Art of Rhetoric* repeats the same doctrine.[7] It tells us that "a man of good years is counted sober, wise, and circumspect; a young man wild and careless; a woman babbling, inconstant, and ready to believe all that is told her"; that "by vocation of life a soldier is counted a great bragger, and a vaunter of himself; a scholar simple; a russet coat sad, and sometimes crafty; a courtier, flattering; a citizen gentle"; that Englishmen are known "for feeding and changing of [8] apparel, the Dutchman for drinking, the Frenchman for pride and inconstance, the Spaniard for nimbleness of body and much disdain, the Italian for great wit and policy, the Scots for boldness, and the Boeme for stubbornness"; and that "in describing of persons, there ought always a comeliness to be used, so that nothing be spoken which may be thought is not in them." English allusions to decorum show that the doctrine and the lore of types that went with it were entirely commonplace, so commonplace as to make further illustration superfluous. A passage from Whetstone's Epistle Dedicatory to *Promos and Cassandra* (1578) may be singled out, however, since it applies the doctrine to drama:

Many times (to make mirth) they make a clown companion with a king; in their grave counsels, they allow the advice of fools; yea, they use one order of speech for all persons: a gross *Indecorum,* for a crow will ill counterfeit the nightingale's sweet voice; even so affected speech doth misbecome a clown. For, to work a comedy kindly, grave old men should instruct, young men should show the imperfections of youth, strumpets should be lascivious, boys unhappy, and clowns should speak disorderly: intermingling all these actions in such sort as the grave matter may instruct and the pleasant delight; for without this change the attention would be small, and the liking less.[9]

Familiarity with the traditional signs illuminates the behavior of a good many dramatic characters. Romeo and Mercutio, for instance, divide between them the characteristics of Aristotle's typical youth. Mercutio has the sensuality, the sociability, the hot temper, the touchiness which cannot endure to be slighted, the insolence, the desire for superiority, and the ambition for honor; Romeo has the intensity and variety of passion, the inconstancy (at the beginning), the heedlessness of the future, the directness of action, the courage, the generosity, the high-mindedness. Similarly, Friar Laurence and old Capulet part between them the characteristics of Aristotle's old man. The Friar shows the lack of passion, the uncertain view of the future, the caution and prudence, the timidity; Capulet shows the fondness for recalling the past, the loquacity, the tendency to outbursts of anger, hot but soon over.

Giraldi tells us [10] that according to the general rule young girls should be shown as shamefast and timid, matrons as chaste and solicitous; he implies that none should show special intelligence. The women of tragedy, however, may be allowed a greater latitude than the women of comedy. That is because women of high position are less constricted by household duties, more familiar with the world, and hence more apt to show prudence and sagacity than the bourgeois women of comedy. Moreover, the women of tragedy may reveal great licentious passions indecorous for the respectable women of comedy, partly because the great are capable of greater passion, partly because tragedy teaches the dangers of these mighty passions. Happily for us, the women of Elizabethan comedy, even the good ones, are less subdued and abide by freer rules of decorum than the critics would have approved of. But Giraldi's word about the women of tragedy points up for us the passionate and sometimes even terrible heroines of Elizabethan tragedy. The convention of women's weakness, moreover, is observed in at least one way in English drama. Women, even good women, generally yield quickly and easily to persuasion. Anne's yielding to Gloucester, whom she loathes, Mistress Frankford's to Wendoll, whom she can hardly be said to love, are typical examples. It is against that rule of decorum that we must set striking exceptions like Bellafront in *The Honest Whore* and Isabella in *Measure for Measure;* they gain force through our awareness of the convention. Isabella's resistance to Angelo is a sign of superior strength and nobility of character, not of prudishness, as modern readers are likely to feel. In Part One of *The Honest Whore,* Dekker subjects Bellafront to a piece of persuasive oratory from Hippolito that turns her, as an audience would expect it to, to repentance and reformation of life. In Part Two, he stages the reverse situation in

having Hippolito try to persuade her to be his mistress.[11] Any Elizabethan audience would recognize this as normally the prelude to
her fall.

> *Hip.*   . . . with one parley
> I won you to come in.
> *Bell.*   You did.
> *Hip.*   I'll try
> If now I can beat down this chastity
> With the same ordnance. Will you yield this fort,
> If with the power of argument now, as then,
> I get of you the conquest: as before
> I turned you honest, now to turn you whore,
> By force of strong persuasion?
> *Bell.*   If you can,
> I yield.

But Dekker varies the situation by having her match her own eloquence against Hippolito's and turns the tables by not letting her fall.
Nevertheless, he is careful not to strain verisimilitude too far, for
when Hippolito refuses her victory she suddenly retreats:

> *Bell.* . . .
> Let the world judge which of us two have won.
> *Hip.* I!
> *Bell.*   You? nay then as cowards do in fight,
> What by blows cannot, shall be saved by flight.

Another thing Giraldi has to say about decorum has an interesting
bearing on Hamlet's behavior. In discriminating between the necessary and the probable in the depiction of character, he uses as an
example the courageous man.[12] It is *necessary* that he not be made
to sustain injury without seeking to avenge it; it is *probable* (*verisimile*) that he will not seek it by trickery ("con insidie"), but with
sword in hand ("con la spada in mano") without any exterior advantage that is not customary or reasonable. Shakespeare's Hamlet
is preëminently noble and courageous. In an Elizabethan audience
would not the expectation have been raised that he would seek his
necessary revenge sword in hand, not with the treacherous means
that Claudius used in killing his father? Hamlet, armed for revenge
in the prayer scene, puts up his sword, not that he may perfect a
studied scheme, but that he may seize his sword at a fitter time:

> Up, sword, and know thou a more horrid hent.[12a]

That Shakespeare means us to mark the difference between revenge "con insidie" and revenge "con la spada in mano" is shown by the unmistakable contrast between Hamlet's openness and Laertes' disingenuousness at the end.

In critical application this theory of typical and static character, allied with the didactic theory of the purposes of poetry, resulted in simplified interpretations of the familiar characters of the classics. "There is found in Aeneas the excellence of piety; in Achilles, of military courage; in Ulysses, of prudence." [13] The world of nature, Sidney says,

> is brazen, the poets only deliver a golden. But let those things alone and go to man, for whom as the other things are, so it seemeth in him her uttermost cunning is employed, and know whether she have brought forth so true a lover as Theagenes, so constant a friend as Pylades, so valiant a man as Orlando, so right a prince as Xenophon's Cyrus, so excellent a man every way as Virgil's Aeneas. [14]

One of the advantages the poet has over the historian is that the poet can simplify and idealize, "where the historian, bound to tell things as things were, cannot be liberal (without he will be poetical) of a perfect pattern." [15]

The result of composition according to such a theory of types and of ideal truth may be seen nowhere better than in Sidney's own *Arcadia,* where the characters are conscientiously constructed—there is no other word—according to the plan of ideal truth Sidney wished to convey and according to the strictest rules of decorum. If we are in any doubt about this judgment, John Hoskins, Sidney's admirer and possible acquaintance, confirms it from the point of view of a contemporary reader. In his *Directions for Speech and Style* (1599), under the heading of Illustration (description), he states the right method for creating character: [16]

> ... he that will truly set down a man in a figured story must first learn truly to set down an humor, a passion, a virtue, a vice, and therein keeping decent proportion add but names and knit together the accidents and encounters.

He praises Sidney for having done this most excellently and attributes part of his success to his being acquainted with Aristotle's *Rhetoric* and perhaps Theophrastus' *Imagines.*

But to our purpose—what personages and affections are set forth in *Arcadia*. For men: pleasant idle retiredness in King Basilius, and the dangerous end of it; unfortunate valor in Plangus; courteous valor in Amphialus; proud valor in Anaxius; hospitality in Kalander;

and so on through a long list of the characters of the *Arcadia*. He ends with a praise of their decorum and perfect consistency.

Now in these persons is ever a steadfast decency and uniform difference of manners observed, wherever you find them and howsoever each interrupt the other's story and actions.

Castelvetro shrewdly perceived that the great characters of literature were created in no such way.[17] He argues that if, as Aristotle says, the end of tragedy (and so of every sort of poem) is the representation, not of men, but of action and of life, and if the exhibition of character is accessory to the action, not the reverse, then many well-regarded authors, including Julius Caesar Scaliger, have prated nonsense ("ciancie") in saying that the aim of good poets, like Homer in the *Iliad* and the *Odyssey* and Virgil in the *Aeneid,* has been to show to the world a perfectly drawn commander ("capitano"), valorous leader ("valoroso conduttiere"), or wise man ("savio huomo"). Such a point of view would not be poetic, but philosophical, like that of Theophrastus in his *Characters*. Therefore good poets, like Homer and Virgil and others, have understood how to compose a fine story and let it control their choice of persons and of suitable behavior; they have achieved greater beauty, that is more wonder and more verisimilitude, than if they had followed the contrary method. Castelvetro's opinion, however, is less typical than Scaliger's and Sidney's. We can be glad that the thorough rooting of the Elizabethan drama in story-telling saved its characters from Sidney's frigid method, at whatever cost of consistency or even, sometimes, of disconcerting formlessness.

THE TEACHING OF PLAUTUS AND TERENCE

Reinforcement to ideas of decorum in character came from the study of Plautus and Terence. Since this subject has been treated so fully elsewhere in the book,[18] nothing more than a reminder is needed here. The theory of types enjoined by Horace was thoroughly exemplified in the classical plays most congenial to renaissance taste.

The rather few types of New Comedy are monotonously repeated in Roman comedy, with only minor individual variations, and renaissance schoolmasters, interested in laying bare the core of moral truth in all their pupils read, saw to it they did not miss the essence of these types.

Melanchthon's method, prepared for schoolmasters, of studying *Andria,* included a study of the types of characters: "judicious old men, Davus grown old and clever, the youth Pamphilus honest and filial." He suggested a comparison of Pamphilus with the very dissimilar Carinus: the latter has nothing of moderation or of prudence in him, whereas almost everything about the former "is more moderate than either his age demands or his love allows." [19] This same method appears in Maurice Kyffin's English translation of *Andria,* published in 1588:

> By heedful reading, and diligent marking, the due *Decorum* observed by Terence in his comedies, the scholar shall gather very much pleasure and profit, as for example, in this comedy of *Andria,* he opposeth several speakers, of several natures, and contrary conditions, one to another: as, Simo being hot and testy, is opposed unto Chremes, a mild and moderate man. Pamphilus, a staid and shamefast young man, is opposed unto Carinus, a harebrained fellow void of discretion. Davus, a sly and subtle servant, is opposed unto Byrria, a slothful and rechless fellow. Mysis, a sober maid, is opposed unto Lesbia, a drunken gossip. Crito, honest and poor, is opposed unto Chrysis, dishonest and rich. These persons are of set purpose thus placed by Terence, to the end that the undue demeanor in the one may the sooner be seen by the contrary in the other.[20]

Sidney, well instructed, tells us how comedy handles the filthiness of evil and the beauty of virtue in private and domestical matters so that

> with hearing it we get as it were an experience, what is to be looked for of a niggardly Demea, of a crafty Davus, of a flattering Gnatho, of a vainglorious Thraso, and not only to know what effects are to be expected, but to know who be such by the signifying badge given them by the Comedian.[21]

THE TEACHING OF MINOR RHETORICAL FORMS

Schoolboys were taught the decorum of character not only by a study of the Roman comic dramatists, but by practice in their compositions. We have already noted the important contributions of the classical rhetoricians to ideas of character in their analysis of the "places" to be observed in argument from the person in a forensic oration of accusation or defense, or in a demonstrative oration of praise or dispraise.[22] Rhetoric had other contributions to make to the theory and technique of character drawing that were more readily adaptable to theme-writing, the daily staple of instruction.[23]

Many of the figures of thought gave practice in brief delineation of character, all of them handled by the rhetoricians in such a way as to emphasize the typical in character or in emotion. We must note briefly what these were before observing how they were adapted to composition.

Charactera, characterismos, descriptio, effictio, and *notatio* were figures of description; by the Roman rhetoricians the first three terms were applied to descriptions of the characteristic conduct of moral types; the latter two, in intention at least, to descriptions of individual persons, *effictio* giving the physical appearance, *notatio* the moral characteristics. Another term, *descriptio personae,* though not used by Cicero himself, was later applied to the detailed description making use of Cicero's list of topics covering the subject's appearance, nature, and way of life.[24] But, through shifts in meaning and through the illustrations used, the term *notatio,* and *descriptio personae* as well, came to be used generally to mark the defining characteristics of a type. The figure *notatio,* for instance, comes from the *Rhetorica ad Herennium,*[25] where the definition calls for the description of an individual, but where the illustration, the portrait of a man ostentatious with his small wealth, stresses the typical characteristics of a class of men. Erasmus refers in the *De copia* to this type portrait under the heading *personae descriptio.* Under the figure of *descriptio* Wilson gives a portrait of a typical pinch-penny.[26]

Ethopoeia and *prosopopoeia* are figures of impersonation rather than of description, so that the person being depicted is made to reveal his character in an imaginary speech. Quintilian's distinction between the figures is not wholly clear, *ethopoeia* being called *mimesis* (the imitation in speech of other men's characteristics in word or deed), *prosopopoeia* being called *fictiones personarum,* the provision with feigned speeches of persons real or imaginary, gods, dead persons, cities or peoples.[27] How these and the other terms were varied in their particular meaning by the sophistic, medieval, and renaissance rhetoricians is less important for us to observe than how they were put to practical use.

The way in which these figures were adapted as forms of short themes we know from the rhetorics used in sixteenth-century schools. Quintilian prescribes the *ethologia,* or theme delineating character, and seems to mean by it the description of a type; for in another place he appears to refer to a similar exercise, which he calls *ethos:*

There is also good reason for giving the name of *ethos* to those scholastic exercises in which we portray rustics, misers, cowards and superstitious persons according as our theme may require. For if *ethos* denotes moral character, our speech must necessarily be based on *ethos* when it is engaged in portraying such character.[28]

Aphthonius in his *Progymnasmata* gives among his types of short orations, used actually as forms of written themes, the *ethopoeia* and the *descriptio.*[29]   *Ethopoeia,* imitation which expresses the nature of someone, is either "passive," when it expresses the subject's emotions on particular occasions, or "moral," when it expresses his nature (*mores*), or mixed, when it does both. The example given is passive, Niobe "all tears" addressing her fallen children. Lorichius, whose edition of Aphthonius was the one most commonly used in grammar schools of the sixteenth century, makes up a number of additional examples, including a speech of Hecuba's on the fall of Troy and one of Andromache's on the death of Hector.[30] And in his *scholia* Lorichius refers to a number of speeches in literature which may be taken as *ethopoeiae.* The models provided are significant, since they are all imitations of imitations, imitations, that is, of literary figures in classically typical situations of grief, anger, jealousy, or some other passion.

Descriptio, in Aphthonius, is of persons, things, time, places, brute beasts, and plants. The only example provided is a description of place, and though Lorichius contributes other illustrations, he gives none of a person. But in the *scholia,* he defines the description of a person, or *prosopographia,* as the depiction of the person of a lover, a lecherous person, a miser, a glutton, a parasite, a bawd, or some other moral type, as in Terence's description of Thraso. Rainolde's English adaptation of Aphthonius gives as an example of *ethopoeia* "what lamentable Oration Hecuba Queen of Troy might make, Troy being destroyed"; of a *prosopopoeia,* Cicero's feigned speech of Rome against Catiline; and of the *description of a person,* "a description upon Xerxes," illustrating his pride and his cowardice with events from his Grecian campaign.[31]

Schoolboys, therefore, had practice in the description of character, the value of their exercises depending, then as now, on the extent to which their master demanded of them actual observation of the life around them, the extent to which he was satisfied with the monotonous reappearance of Terentian Demeas, Thrasos, Davuses and Bacchises, and with the rehashing of the eternal griefs of Niobe, Hecuba, and Andromache.

It is doubtful that schoolboys had any help from Theophrastus, at least until late in the century. Although several editions of the *Characters* in Greek were published during the century, "characters" on the Theophrastan model did not become a literary vogue until after Casaubon's Latin translation of 1592. What effect that vogue may have had on the increasing number of social types in Jacobean comedy is not easy to assess, for the influence may well have worked both ways, the writers of "characters" as freely borrowing from the dramatists as the other way about.[32]

MEDIEVAL LITERARY TRADITION

As so often happened in the Renaissance, the fresh study of classical literature and literary theory only helped to interpret and justify something already familiar in living literary tradition.[33] The art of portraiture was thoroughly familiar in medieval and early renaissance satire, *exemplum*, and morality play. The literature of virtues and vices and the literature of "estates" both helped develop an art of depicting types. The personification of vices and virtues in the moralities, or the illustration of social evils in sermons or satires, called for the depiction of moral and social types, often given great artistic vitality, as in Barclay and some of the best moral interludes, by realistic and individualized detail, but always strongly marked with the lines of the genus. Chaucer's characters in the *Prologue* are the great exemplars of social portraiture; some more typical in outline, some more highly individualized in behavior, but all full of energetic life. The strength of this tradition and continuing habit no doubt contributed to the vitality of the social types of Elizabethan drama—helped keep them realistic and contemporary, rarely just echoes of the already second-hand types of Roman comedy. There is a great affinity, for instance, between the rogues of Elizabethan satiric and cony-catching pamphlets and the rogues of London social comedy.

PSYCHOLOGICAL THEORY

Finally, literary example and theory were bolstered to a certain extent, or seemed to be, by the teachings of physiological psychology. Renaissance psychology was a great synthesis of Galenic physiology with Aristotelian psychology and with Christian ethics, the latter in turn a synthesis of many currents of classical and medieval thought. The particular aspect of renaissance psychology which contributed most to a doctrine of types was of course Galen's theory of the four humours and the resultant doctrine of the four complexions or temperaments. Although this theory was no new rediscovery in the sixteenth century, it was expanded and refined upon and subtly complicated. It furnished writers with a vocabulary and gave an apparently scientific basis to their distinctions of human behavior according to age, sex, climate, race, temperament, and the rest of the Ciceronian places. This whole subject is so familiar that I need not develop it,[34] only point out a bearing on our topic that may easily be overlooked.

Although such a theory favors up to a certain point a classification of men according to typical aspects of their behavior, so that, for example, we can identify Tamburlaine by his physical signs as choleric,[35] or Sir Andrew Aguecheek as phlegmatic, beyond that point the theory actually leads to the blurring of typical lines. More and more refined cross-classifications of physical signs cancel each other out. The humours vary, not only according to natural temperament, but according to race, climate, season, time of day, the disposition of the stars, sex, age, disease, temporary states of passion, and many other accidents. To resolve the inevitable contradictions that arise means an elaborate system of physiological adjustments, of relative dominance and submergence of humours according to circumstances; in the end the system must fall of its own weight. The best psychologies of the period, fortunately, are undogmatic and tolerant of inconsistencies; their empirical descriptions of men's behavior, as distinct from their explanations, are often brilliant. The constant variation of and refinement on symptoms, especially in the detailed studies of melancholy, led away from typicality to particularity. This was all a gain from the dramatic point of view, as the varied gallery of melancholic characters, from Jacques to Bosola, shows. The great service of Elizabethan psychology to dramatists was to furnish them less with a set of rigid types than with a readily intelligible descriptive vocabulary and with a wonderfully flexible frame in which their empirically created characters might move with freedom and life.

The peculiar development in English comedy of the "humour" character is usually represented as a means to depict types. But it is so only to a limited extent. If it is pushed very far, it becomes a move towards extreme particularity, towards caricature rather than towards typicality.[36] The Theophrastan method reveals a class of moral behavior (like flattery, boasting, officiousness, cowardice) through the behavior of an imaginary individual; the humour technique, on the contrary, starts with the person and makes an individual excess, sometimes a vice or passion, but more commonly a mere eccentricity of behavior, the essence of the character. In his humour plays, Jonson has humours of both sorts, humours of character (like the jealousy of Kitely, the anxiety of the elder Knowell, the envy of Macilente) and humours of affectation (the affectation of melancholy in Stephen, the affectation of gallantry in Matthew). In the Induction to *Every Man out of his Humour* Jonson has Asper comment on the distortion of meaning "humour" has undergone from its metaphorically psychological sense of a general disposition to its present fashionable sense of a trick of singularity:

> But that a rook, by wearing a pied feather,
> The cable hat-band, or the three-piled ruff,
> A yard of shoe-tie, or the Switzer's knot
> On his French garter, should affect a Humour!
> O, 'tis more than most ridiculous.

When Asper says the play is meant to "scourge those apes," he surely means that the apes are those who are affecting humours. These apes are individualized to the point of caricature.[37] Puntarvolo's affectation of the manners and language of chivalry, Fungoso's attempt to be in style by copying Fastidious Brisk's clothes to the last ribbon, Sordido the countryman's perpetual consultation of the almanac, hopeful for foul weather—all focus attention on some piece of socially idiosyncratic behavior. Shakespeare uses the same device in

Nym's rather tiresome identifying catch-phrase, "That's the humour of it," and in Pistol's tags from old-fashioned plays. Humour characters of this sort are unlike the broad types of classical comedy; they are narrower and sharper.

It is possible to arrive at satiric caricature by either means, but the effect is different. In the satire of types, some general feature of a class is satirized—the unscrupulousness of pimps, the miserliness of some kinds of old men, the lasciviousness of others, and so on; in the satire of the humour, satiric emphasis is thrown on some particular departure from the norm. Jacques the miser in *The Case Is Altered* is a type on classical lines; he does what misers are expected to do, hides his gold, worries about it everlastingly, and cries the loss of it aloud to the world. Morose in *Epicoene,* on the other hand, with his obsession against noise, is a specialized humour character; the obsession is not characteristic of a class of men. The two methods of characterization are often combined, the humour being thrown into high relief against a typical background; the humour serves to rescue the type from flatness of outline. Macilente belongs to the general class of sour melancholics, but he is particularized by the humour of envy of those with less brains than he who have better positions in the world. Jealous husbands are a type; but the jealousy of Cornelio (in Chapman's *All Fools*) is treated as a humour, since it has reached a diseased extreme. After his early comedies, Jonson does not usually follow so narrow a means of individualizing his types. Volpone, Face, Sir Epicure, Ananias, Zeal-of-the-Land Busy, Ursula, and Judge Overdo are conceived in ampler terms.

The humour character seems to me to be the reverse of the personified abstraction of the morality play. I have already spoken of Jonson's use of the two forms of character in his *Staple of News*.[38] They do not sort well together. Their juxtaposition makes for something of a conflict in form, since they represent contrary methods of securing universality, the one by giving concrete embodiment to an abstraction like money (Pecunia), the other by giving peculiar whims of behavior general significance as the marks of typical playboy, wise father, and sharper.

To sum up: Since the concern of literature was with universal truth, critical theory taught that the persons of fiction and drama should be represented in their typical aspects. Rhetoric provided method; Roman drama, models; and psychology, theories of temperament and many descriptive terms. To mark a character with the signs of some class to which he belongs (miserly old men, prudent old fathers, jealous husbands, young men afflicted with love melancholy, and so on) is a simple way to give him consistency and propriety and a certain kind of verisimilitude. Such emphasis on type makes for quick recognition on the part of reader or spectator, arouses expectations that can easily be satisfied, gives a coherent total impression. But of course even a consistent and appropriate and verisimilar character, to be interesting, must also seem alive, and to do that he needs identity as an individual, not merely as a member of a class. The long native tradition of satiric portraiture was a tradition of types, but it was also a tradition of realism based on observation of vitalizing and individualizing detail. One of the special Elizabethan developments of this tradition, aided by physiological psychology, was the humour character. The impulse to this development may have been chiefly one of social satire, and that means emphasis on the typical. But the result was a definable method of individualizing a character, usually against a strongly typical background—that is, by means of an idiosyncratic trait constantly exhibited. It is a rather crude method in itself, leading, if unvaryingly applied, to simplification and caricature rather than to complexity and realism of character. What Elizabethan psychological theory contributed, besides the humour theory, to conceptions of character and to techniques of character-drawing is not an easy matter to assess. In its more developed form it lost its cruder emphasis on simple physical types, centered more of its concern in aberrations from the norm, and became more complex and varied in its description of them; this was a concern, in fact, if not in name, with the problem of personality and its variations. Formal psychology, then, especially the psychology of melancholy, was able to furnish dramatists with a language at least as useful for suggesting individuality in a character as for categorizing it. The extent and manner of the use of this language varied greatly, of course, with individual dramatists.

Ethos and Pathos

There is no comparable set of critical and pedagogical tendencies towards the depiction of individuals as toward the depiction of types.

We should not expect one. In the first place, emphasis on the typical in character followed as a corollary on the renaissance interpretation of imitation as the imitation of universal truth. The critics had no word for "personality." In the second place, to carry conviction an imagined character must, above all things, seem alive, and no clear set of rules can be made for that inwardness of perception and for that expressive gift which can animate with the illusion of actuality an imagined character. The presentation of the character must be informed with the quality of style which the rhetoricians called *energeia,* variously translated as energy, force, vigor, life, actuality, vividness. The renaissance critics could recognize *energeia,* and analyze it, as a quality of style in speeches or in descriptive passages,[39] but they could not see, or did not appear to see, its relevance to the problem of the whole conception of character. At least they did not see that all they urged about the depiction of character according to a set of rigid formulae made against this very quality of vitality. Regardless of the shape of current artistic theories, or even the absence of any, there have always been great characters in literature who carry the conviction of life—from Achilles and David to Captain Ahab and Leopold Bloom. Perhaps we should content ourselves with saying about the Elizabethan dramatists that they were specially alert to the life around them and specially blessed with the great poetic gift of *energeia,* which enabled them to give that life expression.

That they operated by no formal theory of individuality of character, except perhaps the humour theory, is shown by the frequent failure of coherence of character—what we might call the failure of repetitive form—I have already spoken of.[40] This of itself need not mean a lack of expressive energy, for although that is the quality, the sense of living wholeness, we recognize in the depiction of all successful individual characters, it may be present merely in intensely realized situations and fail of that final sense of cohesion. An illustration from the Bible will make clear what I mean. Samson, as he appears in Judges, is hardly a "character" in the modern sense at all; he is presented wholly objectively, in a number of different situations, most of them suggestive of a Heraclean mighty man of folklore, rather at odds with the introduction of him as a Nazarite vowed to certain ascetic practices and dedicated to the service of the Lord. It takes Milton to bring the strong and the moral Samson together as a character. In the Biblical story, we can grasp no "character," properly speaking, yet nearly every episode is possessed of zestful actuality, especially the woman of Timnah episode, the betrayal by Delilah, and the mighty last revenge on the Philistines. In the same way, much of the remembered vividness of human beings in action we carry away from the Elizabethan drama comes from moments of display in single scenes, though of course far less simple in presentation than Samson's in the Biblical narrative—such scenes as Faustus' tortured conflict before his damnation, Vittoria's courage at her trial, Brachiano's bitter death struggles, Evadne's brutally cynical revelation to her newly married husband that she is the king's mistress. Often the reason for a failure of total coherence at the expense of the vitality exhibited in single situations may be no more than a dramatic one: focus on an immediate striking effect rather than on a total impression.[41] This is the sacrifice of a formal aspect of the play as a whole to formal success within a smaller unit, and perhaps, judged by the effect on the spectators, it is an entirely defensible sacrifice. Perhaps we are more troubled by what seems the failure of repetitive form in many Elizabethan dramatic characters because we have been rendered too sophisticated in our expectation by the characters in modern fiction. Moreover, in reading Elizabethan plays instead of seeing them we are the more easily led to judge them by a set of standards foreign to them.

Even allowing generously, however, for this practical dramatic motive for presenting character *ad hoc,* I believe there were other reasons why dramatists and audiences would have been less perceptive of what to us seem failures of unity and coherence. One lay in psychological theory, the other in ethical tradition.

PSYCHOLOGICAL THEORY

One highly developed aspect of Elizabethan psychology, the psychology of the passions, complicated the theory of temperaments, indeed cut straight across it. The passions, those temporary states of change affecting body and mind, were classified and analyzed, each one for its motives, symptoms, and effects. Of course it was recognized, and said, that men of different temperaments were liable to different passions—"choleric men be subject to anger, melancholy men to sadness, sanguine to pleasure, phlegmatic to sloth and drunkenness." [42] Yet the tendency to view all men, by virtue of their being men, as in some degree subject to any passion, was inevitable. The reason for this assumption was partly psychological and partly theological: all men, like beasts, are subject to passion because passion is a function of the vital or sensitive soul; and all men are subject to passion because they are the children of Adam and beset by the Devil. On this view, the *passion* becomes the controlling standard of judgment instead of the *temperament*. The divisions become horizontal, cutting across all mankind, instead of vertical, separating men by types one from another. The effect, in the depiction of character, is a generalizing one. Any man, by reason of the effect of his senses on his imagination, and of his imagination on his vital spirits, can experience any passion, and if he gives it heedless way, it is liable to growth on its own accord, for it quickly blinds the reason and seduces the will; once it gets the better of him, he will behave like any other angry or lustful or frightened man. A man possessed by anger or jealousy is liable to run amuck and kill another; one possessed by love or grief, to destroy himself. In this emphasis on the passion at the expense of temperament, an emphasis the drama was prone to follow, a man's principles, the standards of conduct by which he has been raised, a life-long habit of moderate behavior count for nothing against the terrible onslaught of passion got out of hand. As Chapman puts it,

> You know, besides, that our affections' storm
> Rais'd in our blood, no reason can reform.[43]

By definition, an emotion is a temporary change of bodily and mental state. But scenes of passion in the Elizabethan drama often have an exaggerated *ex tempore* quality, as if nothing had prepared for the onset of the passion.[44] Moreover, since violent passion affects the humours of the body in their composition and motion, it will, during the time of its sway, affect a man's very nature. Hence, the normally good men in Elizabethan drama who succumb, with unrealistic haste, it seems to us, to temptations to lust or anger or ambition—Wendoll to his desire for his friend's wife, Arbaces to his infatuation for his supposed sister, Leontes to his diseased jealousy of Polixenes. Not only can one passion grow quickly in a good man to criminal proportions, but another can displace it with equal swiftness. Indeed, a man whose fortifications of prudence are down under the onslaught of one passion is all the more liable to succumb to another.

> Frailty is fruitful, one sin gets another.[45]

Witness the onslaught of degrading passions in Macbeth, the explicit linking of lust and murder in plays like *Women Beware Women* and *The Changeling*.

Join this theory with the belief in the enormous persuasiveness of eloquent speech, especially if accompanied by expressive countenance and gesture, and it is as easy to explain the swift repentances as the swift falls of the heroes and villains of Elizabethan tragedy. Once the eloquent vituperation of Melantius gains access to Evadne's heart, shame sweeps over her. It is true that his words are assisted by the threat of the sword; but her repentance goes beyond fright to honest recognition of her "soul-sickness" and determination to redeem her sin by killing her adulterous lover. Gertrude swiftly loses her grief for her dead husband in her attraction to Claudius; and just as swiftly, moved by Hamlet's eloquence, she is recalled to shame and remorse. As a woman, in whom reason is relatively weak, she is especially subject to the sway of the affections:

> But, look! amazement on thy mother sits;
> O! step between her and her fighting soul;
> Conceit in weakest bodies strongest works:
> Speak to her, Hamlet.

We are never made to feel that she is actually bad. In Gertrude, admittedly, there is no loss of coherence as a whole, as there not infrequently is in other dramatic characters. Fortunately, the Elizabethan genius for observation of detail and for verbal originality often rescued from perfunctoriness these scenes of conventionally swift change. Within the immediate scene, if one does not look too curiously for consistency in the character as a whole, the persons usually move and speak with intensely convincing vitality.

A basis for the distinction between temperament and passion lay in Aristotle's distinction in the *Rhetoric* between *ethos,* a man's natural bent, disposition, or moral character, and *pathos,* emotion in a given situation.[46] Quintilian debated the meanings of the terms at length.[47] He thought *mores* rather too wide a term for *ethos,* and treated both *ethos* (untranslatable, he said, in Latin) and *pathos* (*adfectus*) as aspects of emotion: *ethos,* being permanent, is usually a relatively mild state; *pathos,* being temporary, a violent one. Sometimes they are of the same nature, only differing in degree, love, for example, coming under the head of *pathos,* affection of *ethos.* Aphthonius and Priscian [48] gave the distinction between the two a practical rhetorical application in the division of the *ethopoeia,* or speech of impersonation, into three classes—moral, "passive" or pathetic, and mixed. A speech in the moral mode reveals a man's nature, habits, or the like (e.g., a speech by a rustic on first beholding the sea); a speech in the pathetic mode reveals an emotion on a particular occasion (e.g., Andromache's grief on the death of Hector); a speech in the mixed mode naturally combines both (e.g., Achilles' speech on the death of Patroclus, which is pathetic in expressing grief, moral in expressing his determination to fight).

Minturno's lengthy treatment of character is a good example of a renaissance man's response to these distinctions. He knows the whole background and weaves it all into his discussion of "i costumi" and "i passioni," both of which he treats, like Quintilian, as aspects of "gli affetti." [49] But then he sets down first the Ciceronian topics (nature, fortune, etc.) for the distinction of "i costumi," secondly a description of the major passions, each considered in and for itself, without reference to a particular context of temperament or personality. In another place,[50] in the discussion of the characters of tragedy, he gives first a list of appropriate characters (merely those in family relationship—mother, sister, daughter, father, lover), then of appropriate passions (fear, grief, terror, hate, lamentation). Thus, although he has made an attempt at reconciliation of the two modes of imitation, pathetic and moral, the effect of his classifications and illustrations is one of disjunction. It is just such an effect as one sometimes gets from the speech and behavior of the characters in Elizabethan tragedy.

If it should be found that in general the characters of Elizabethan comedy behaved with more consistency, or were at any rate more coherently organized than the characters of tragedy, it would not be a surprising discovery, for *ethos,* as Quintilian remarks, resembles comedy, *pathos* resembles tragedy.[51] The distinction to be made is not merely between the milder and the intenser emotions, though that is implied; or between greater and less conformity to a social type, though that follows. A distinction in the psychological basis on which the dramatist builds a character is also in question, and consequently the way that character is to be judged artistically. Why should we suppose Elizabethan dramatists not to have known this distinction and not to have shifted, at least partly, the basis of judgment in tragedy from character to passion, from something permanent to something temporary? Shakespeare certainly knew the distinction and counted on his audience's knowing it. Yet only too often modern readers refuse to believe him when he tells us that Othello was not naturally jealous, but, being moved, jealous in the extreme. There lies in Othello's justification the implication of a whole background as well of artistic as of psychological theory.

ETHICAL TRADITION

This *ex tempore* conception of the passions was reinforced by, indeed partly grounded in, ethical tradition, with particular dramatic expression in the morality play. In that convention, men are viewed in general with regard more to particular passions or particular virtues and vices than to individual "character." The emphasis is on common humanity, all alike subject to the old Adam, or law of the flesh. A character called Mankind, Humanum Genus, Infans, or Juventus is placed in a situation of temptation, and, before he is saved, drama requires that he behave with the weakness all flesh is heir to; for the Christian's whole life is a warfare upon earth against "his domestical enemy,"

which never permits him to be quiet, but molesteth in prosperity, dejecteth in adversity; in pleasure makes him dissolute, in sadness desperate, to rage in anger, to tremble in fear, in hope to faint, in love to languish.

The passions carry

their stratagems, and continual incursions, even unto the gates of the chiefest castle of his soul, I mean the very wit and will.[52]

This tradition makes it inevitable that Faustus, for all his intellectual gifts, should listen rather to the Evil than to the Good Angel. It is Marlowe's profound insight into tragedy that makes Faustus, unlike Mankind,[53] never able to surrender self long enough to trust the message of the Good Angel. Elizabethan audiences expected good men and good women to fall before strong temptation; they expected

them to be carried headlong into crime, and not because Aristotle
had propounded a theory of "tragic flaw," but because they knew
that temptation to sin was the way Satan had for encompassing the
ruin of mortal man.

> Will you, I pray, demand that demi-devil
> Why he hath thus ensnar'd my soul and body?

So Othello in horror-struck discovery of "honest" Iago.

The distinction between *ethos* and *pathos* was well understood.
The bold concentration on *pathos* in Elizabethan tragedy, often at
the expense of *ethos,* may be destructive of consistency in character,
even of special identity. Perhaps because of our intense concern with
personality, we find this disconcerting. But it had its basis in the psychology of the passions and in traditional ethics, which emphasized
the common humanity in every man and his danger from a common
enemy.

The Influence of Rhetoric in Exhibiting Character

The depiction of character in drama of course involves more than
psychological theory and literary doctrine. It involves as well practical techniques of exhibiting character on the stage. A full study
of these techniques in the Elizabethan drama has yet to be made.[54]
All I shall do here is to suggest some lines of inquiry, and some problems of form Elizabethan dramatists had to face.

MINOR RHETORICAL FORMS

The possible influence of minor rhetorical forms on the depiction
of character through speech is clearly one line of inquiry. Apart from
action, character must be exhibited through description by other
persons or through the speech of the person himself, either by direct
self-explanation or by implication. The question, as always with
Elizabethan dramatists, is how much they learned in the handling
of these modes from formal principles, rhetorical training, and classical models, how much from trial and error in the actual business
of making a story come alive on the stage. It is never a wholly
answerable question, even for any particular dramatist. Certainly

we can believe that the common experience they all had in school
with certain rhetorical exercises and with the reading of Terence
would not always have been without practical effect. For depiction of
a character in speech, his own or another's, the figures of thought
discussed earlier—*effictio, notatio, descriptio, ethopoeia*—would
have been preparatory. To test whether training in them were actually operative in any given dramatist's work one would need to look
for formal indications: for static portraits with indications of general
similarities to a type and particular individual differences, perhaps
with hints of Cicero's "places"; for set speeches declarative of character or passion in the stilted moral and passive modes of Aphthonius.
One would expect the flavor of school rhetoric to be stronger in Kyd
than in Fletcher; stronger in Shakespeare's early plays than in his
late ones. Yet this expectation, based on casual impressions, would
need careful checking, since one might be misled by a sophisticated
art which better conceals and transmutes what it uses.[55] Moreover,
one would have to make two important allowances: one for the
vogue of the Character, modified from the Theophrastan type, in
the Jacobean period and later;[56] and one for the conscious use of
formal devices, even in late plays, for special effect.

That Shakespeare appears to have had a knowledge of these forms
of description a few random examples will show.

Viola's account of the nature and function of an "allowed fool,"
Jacques' account of the same and also of himself as a professed melancholic, are perfect examples of *ethologia,* or *characterismos.*[57]
Othello's last speech, in which he relates to this present deed of
murder the past and the future and makes evident his character, precisely distinguishing *ethos* from *pathos,* is an *ethopoeia moralis* put
to fine dramatic use. The purpose of the moral *ethopoeia,* to reveal
the essential nature of a man, shows through more obviously in some
of Richard of Gloucester's bald soliloquies, especially those in the
first act in which he declares his determination to prove a villain, and
the final one, after the vision of the ghosts, in which he has a debate
with his conscience. When we read Iago's or Claudius' or Macbeth's
more realistically managed self-declarations, or Hamlet's ambiguous
musings, we are inclined to forget what they started from. *Richard II*
is interesting as being a bridge between Shakespeare's earlier, more
academic use of rhetoric for the depiction of character, and his later,
more indirect use of it; the play is in its way a triumph, because in the

speeches of Richard Shakespeare made a perfect union between formal rhetoric and psychology.

Shakespeare's descriptive skill is at its best in brief scenes of action, a form of description recommended by Aphthonius. Shakespeare's are often used as means to throw highlights on a character, as in Richard's description of Bolingbroke's departure, off-bonneting to an oyster-wench,[58] or in Scarus' account of Cleopatra's flight from Actium, and Antony's following like a doting mallard.[59] These, and many like them, are so easily and racily done as to leave no mark of school training. Where we find evidence of that is in the more artificial, more static pieces, carefully framed in a heightened figurative style for emphasis—as in Gertrude's description of Ophelia's drowning, or in the Gentleman's description of Cordelia's receipt of the news about her father's sufferings:

> . . . patience and sorrow strove
> Who should express her goodliest. You have seen
> Sunshine and rain at once; her smiles and tears
> Were like a better way; those happy smilets
> That play'd on her ripe lip seem'd not to know
> What guests were in her eyes; which parted thence,
> As pearls from diamonds dropp'd.[60]

These are artfully designed pieces, putting rhetorical device to a very special use, and at the last remove from naïve imitation. To be certain that Shakespeare knew what formal school-taught *descriptio* was, and could at need turn out a piece in the right inflated manner, we have only to look at the speech on the fall of Troy so much admired by Hamlet: [61]

> The rugged Pyrrhus, he, whose sable arm,
> Black as his purpose, did the night resemble
> When he lay couched in the ominous horse,
>
> .   .   .   .

Brief *effictiones* give us the physical appearance of the raging Pyrrhus and the distracted Hecuba, and the action is set forth with precise detail. I shall return to the speech in the discussion of style to follow.

CONCEPTS OF STYLE

Another line of inquiry into the influence of rhetoric on the techniques of depicting character is into the concepts of style.

Energeia.—I have suggested that the supreme excellence of Elizabethan dramatists is in their gift of *energeia,* the quality of style which gives animation to description and to speech. It was a quality much studied and defined by rhetoricians and critics, though what it resided in precisely was a matter of dispute. Although Quintilian treats *energeia* as a quality of style applicable to the oration generally, and although Aristotle treats it only in connection with description, it is specially relevant to the depiction of character, whether in descriptive passages or through the character's own speech.

Aristotle uses the term in his discussion of metaphor in the *Rhetoric.*[62] He says that things are set before the eyes by words that signify *energeia* and that *energeia* is *kinesis,* or movement; Homer's descriptions, his metaphors, and his similes—since he so often uses the animate to describe the inanimate—especially exemplify it. Quintilian treats it as one kind of force, a near relative of the other kinds —sublimity, imagination, completeness of effect; *energeia* "derives its name from action and finds its peculiar function in securing that nothing that we say is tame." But *energeia* is not always in the rhetoricians and critics clearly distinguished from *enargeia,* distinctness or vividness of description, and indeed vividness may be taken as one of the forms of energy in style. Quintilian, always helpful in these matters, discusses *enargeia* in connection with the statement of facts in a case, where vivid illustration is needed. He defines *enargeia* as *repraesentatio, perspicuitas,* or *evidentia,* a quality beyond mere clarity in that it forces itself on the attention, not merely lets itself be seen; the facts are displayed before the eyes of the mind— "oculis mentis ostendi." [63] Demetrius likewise treats of *enargeia* as something more positive than clearness. Like clearness, it is one of the requirements of the plain style; it arises from such things as exact narrative omitting no detail, from repetition, and from suspense in narration. To force of style, which he calls *deinotēs* rather than *energeia,* Demetrius devotes a separate book.[64]

An interesting renaissance attempt to describe the quality of *energeia* appears, with some assimilation of the connotations of *enargeia,* in Giraldi's *Discorso de i romanzi.* He denies that *energeia* resides simply in the manner of speaking or in gesture, as some say, since it is as well perceived by a reader as by a hearer, and he denies that it consists, as Trissino thought (evidently following Demetrius on *enargeia*), in minutely setting down every little detail ("cosuccia") in a description. The soul of an oration or poem is

nothing else . . . than that force and that power of the work whence the affections enter into the heart of the reader, as if a living voice were speaking. . . .[65]

It seems to come from the words that are most significant, thus most apt to mirror the ideas in the poem; these they imprint in the mind of the reader with so much efficacy and so much vehemence that the mind feels itself moved by those passions contained under the veil of words. This is "l'energia," which consists not in minute particulars, but in placing the matter clearly and forcefully before the eyes of the reader, and in the ears of the listener. *Perspicuousness* is given with established, familiar words, "as if born together with the matter"; [66] *force* with metaphors, comparisons, similes, epithets or adjectives, and hyperbole.

The Player's Hecuba speech in *Hamlet* illustrates all these features of style very deliberately chosen: the setting of the action *clearly* before the eyes by precise detail and familiar words ("run barefoot up and down," "a clout upon that head," "spokes and fellies from her wheel"), and *forcefully* by the metaphors that animate inanimate things—

> Then senseless Ilium,
> Seeming to feel this blow, with flaming top
> Stoops to his base, and with a hideous crash
> Takes prisoner Pyrrhus' ear;

by the Homeric simile—

> But, as we often see, against some storm,
> A silence in the heavens, the rack stand still,
> The bold winds speechless and the orb below
> As hush as death, anon the dreadful thunder
> Doth rend the region; so, after Pyrrhus' pause,
> Aroused vengeance sets him new a-work;

by the epithets conspicuously selected to give the proper murkiness of atmosphere—"rugged" and "hellish Pyrrhus," "sable arm," "dread and black complexion," "coagulate gore," and so on; by the hyperbole—

> But if the gods themselves did see her then,
> . . . .

> The instant burst of clamour that she made—
> Unless things mortal move them not at all—
> Would have made milch the burning eyes of heaven,
> And passion in the gods;

finally, by the uncommon diction—"total gules," "impasted," "coagulate gore," "bisson rheum." As Polonius knew, " 'mobled queen' is good," since a heroic subject calls for fitting epithets. This is "energy" of a very academic sort, intentionally so, and not much to our taste; but it is well to recall it when we delight in the great imaginative passages of Marlowe, Shakespeare, Chapman, and Webster in which the figures leap and all is alive with motion.

We recognize as productive of energy, nevertheless, something besides imaginative extravagance; for it can reside as well in Falstaff's simplest prose as in Antony's most golden verses. It resides, as Giraldi says, in whatever carries the affections into the heart of the reader, "as if a living voice were speaking" ("come se fosse una viva voce che parlasse"). The Elizabethans could have learned from the rhetoricians and the critics all about what energy of style consisted in; whether that is altogether how they learned it is of course another question.

Amplification and extenuation.—The Hecuba speech is also a reminder of the renaissance fondness for amplification, or heightening of effect. Amplification has a special bearing both on vivid description and on speeches of passion, or *ethopoeiae* in the mode passive, for the classical rhetorics treated it as belonging to the persuasive aspect of oratory, which principally rests on appeal to the emotions. The passions, therefore, were studied as a province of rhetoric; they were treated especially in connection with the peroration of a speech and with amplification as a device.[67] The heightened expressions of passion so common in the Elizabethan drama would have been a natural consequence of rhetorical theory and training. In Hieronimo's

> What outcries pluck me from my naked bed,
> And chill my throbbing heart with trembling fear,
> Which never danger yet could daunt before?

or

> Oh eyes, no eyes, but fountains fraught with tears;
> Oh life, no life, but lively form of death;
> Oh world, no world. . . .[68]

the devices for amplification—repetition, antithesis, hyperbole, interrogation, exclamation, and the like—are painfully obvious, and were laughed at by the more sophisticated taste of a few years later. But the taste for amplification itself, though achieved less manifestly by the pedant's rule, did not die out. Compare, when they are speaking at the crest of passion, any of the brilliant figures of Elizabethan or Jacobean tragedy. Of course, in many of the characters most memorable for heightened speech—characters like Tamburlaine, Sejanus, Bussy, or Byron—the amplification in speech is only the rhetorical expression of the fundamental conception of *De casibus* tragedy, namely, that the magnitude of a man's ambition leads him to knock with his "advancèd head" "a star out of heaven" [69] before he is tumbled into the dust. Lear, Antony, and Coriolanus, all great speakers, though they are complicated by other motives than pride or ambition and taught no such simple lesson, are still in the same tradition.

Though "extenuation," the diminuendo balancing the crescendo of amplification, was also stated to be a means of moving the passions, it was relatively neglected. And the playing down of passion was far less common in the drama than the playing up, no doubt partly because it was infinitely harder to do, but also probably because there was less taste for it. It is hard to recall in Elizabethan plays many of those profoundly moving moments of understatement of which Shakespeare is master—phrases like "Well, Juliet, I will lie with thee tonight," or "Master Shallow, I owe you a thousand pound," or "I am dying, Egypt, dying."

Decorum of style.—Enormously important as well is the whole doctrine of the appropriate style. The Italians worked out for their own language elaborate analyses of metrics and of levels of diction. Minturno and Giraldi consider such questions as the greater suitability of rimed verse or of Trissino's "versi sciolti" (normally eleven syllables, unrimed) for tragedy, and the relative merits of rimed verse, unrimed verse, or prose for comedy; and they examine at length the effects of various meters, hence the places where they are to be used.[70] Minturno describes in detail, with many subdivisions, seven different "forms" or styles of speech expressive of different purposes and moods.[71] Although one finds nothing like these analyses in England, any educated person must have known the characteristics of the three levels of style—the elevated, the suave or elegant, the plain—and the doctrine of their use according to the time, the place, and the person.[72] The great subtlety which the better Elizabethan dramatists displayed in the use of style, not only for the suggestion of character, but for the suggestion of feeling and tone, was doubtless a matter of independent discovery and of empirical achievement in the practice of writing prose and verse for the stage. But it can only be understood against a background of universal renaissance assumptions about style.

English dramatists never were slaves of decorum. But their violations of it, according to critical standards, are not the lawlessness of ignorance; the general observance of the rule gives the exceptions emphasis and daring.[73] In making Hamlet so often speak prose, Shakespeare breaks the rule of the person, because Hamlet is a prince; the rule of the dramatic kind, because he is the hero of a tragedy. But these infractions only strengthen the consciousness of the rule of time and place: Hamlet speaks prose chiefly in the humorous scenes ridiculing Polonius and Rosencrantz and Guildenstern; these are scenes with more of manners than of passion, and the style of comedy is therefore in order. At times, however, even this rule is broken, as in the jangling tension of the nunnery scene. The point is that Shakespeare gains not only in range but in emphasis by taking emotional expression beyond the normal expectation of verse. The changes of key in this variation between verse and prose, especially when the modulations from one into another are gradually done, as in the nunnery scene or the duel scene in *Hamlet,* or as in the storm and heath scenes in *King Lear,* affect our emotional ear as our physical ear is affected by the variations of accent, pause, and rhetorical structure against the recurrent undertone of the stable blank verse line.

A similar awareness of appropriate diction gives pungency to violations. Shakespeare knows what he is doing when he uses of Cleopatra epithets so indecorous as "riggish," "gypsy," and "royal wench." We do not forget that it is "royal Egypt," Cleopatra glorious in her triumph on the Cydnus over Antony (one of the triple pillars of the world) and more glorious in her final triumph over Caesar ("sole sir o'th' world"), who is at the end "lass unparallel'd."

In all these considerations of style in the drama the thing chiefly to be remembered is that style was regarded as more an expressionistic than an impressionistic instrument. Verisimilitude did not demand naturalism, although it did not altogether disallow it. Naturalistic speech, for instance, was felt to be more fitting to comedy than to tragedy, since comedy dealt with manners rather than with passion, and generally with people of lower rank, hence with fewer of the ceremonial aspects of life. But Elizabethan romantic comedy, being full of sentiment, was also full of poetry. The modern taste for the literally imitative tends to confine speech in fiction and drama to the relatively poverty-stricken level in daily use; its bareness has to be made up for—when it is—by other means of suggestion. For of course a man expresses himself in a thousand ways besides verbally— by bursting out in song in the bathtub, by tossing the baby in the air, by dropping or forgetting things, by crossing the street to avoid meeting someone. Naturalistic fiction, Hemingway style, describes the acts and gestures; we must supply the feeling ourselves from the situation. This is an external, objective way of representing the world. Young people in love do not on moonlight nights chant litanies in figured and measured verses:

> The moon shines bright: in such a night as this,
> When the sweet wind did gently kiss the trees
> And they did make no noise, in such a night
> Troilus methinks. . . .
>   In such a night
> Did Thisbe. . . .

But they would if they could. Elizabethan dramatists had a means of giving verbal expression to that impulse; modern writers committed to naturalism can only make them say, "I love you," or "Nice night, ain't it, kid?" It is impertinent to ask which is truer to life, the poetic or the prose statement, since the matter is not one of truth, but only of focus. That focus on what can be seen objectively, however, restricts us to a very partial view is proved by the rebellion against it by the writers of our time who have tried again—until Eliot and Fry, more successfully in the novel than in the drama—to look from the inside out. Why else should Virginia Woolf say of Galsworthy and Bennett, who are such masters of verisimilitude, that they are all wrong? [74]

Nothing better illustrates Wölfflin's principle that different ages have different representational possibilities in art because their vision changes than this difference between sixteenth-century poetic eloquence and twentieth-century prose lack of it, a difference that is also expressed in our taste for informality. We have lost part of the key to Elizabethan eloquence because we have lost the meaning of formality and ceremonial. We wear formal dress on fewer and fewer occasions, and are less and less sure when it is expected of us. Costume is for holiday times, like lodge conventions, when we can relax the rules of utility and drabness without social censure. And since no one knows certainly any more the occasions and the times for ceremony, indulgences in it are likely to be merely wanton and without style; they become the bad taste of excessive display. Perhaps the chief difficulty with *Hamlet* in modern dress is that the language does not match the dress and the manners.

Even Elizabethan prose dialogue that has the rhythms of natural speech is full of wit and eloquence. Falstaff speaks great and simple prose, but Falstaff can grow lyrical and talk of "Diana's foresters, gentlemen of the shade, minions of the moon," "for we that take purses go by the moon and the seven stars, and by Phoebus, he, 'that wandering knight so fair.' " Pistol habitually speaks in heroic fustian, and Marston's wonderful, unquotable Cocledemoy plays with epithets and oaths with as much zest as he tricks honest citizens out of their plate and their wives. His final apology for his practical jokes is in rhetorical terms:

No knave, worshipful friend, no knave, for observe: honest Cocledemoy restores whatsoever he has got, to make you know, that whatso'er he has done has been only *euphoniae gratia,* for wit's sake: I acquit this vintner as he has acquitted me; all has been done for emphasis of wit, my fine boy, my worshipful friends.[75]

His wit has been both verbal and practical. How much of all this sort of thing is true representation of the talk of Elizabethan rogues, how much the sheer fun of play with racy speech? It will be remembered that the point in Prince Hal's teasing of Francis the drawer is to expose the poverty of his invention, which must make "Anon, anon, sir!" serve for all occasions. "His industry is upstairs and downstairs, his eloquence the parcel of a reckoning." Elizabethans would seem to have put a value on eloquence that we do not. Since speech was taken to be the outward manifestation of man's essence, that is, his possession of intelligence and an immortal soul, his eloquence was perhaps what chiefly seemed worth representing. The stumbling inadequacy of so much human speech, when a man seemed least to mark his difference from the beasts, and being least himself was least interesting, perhaps did not strike Elizabethan ears with the same accent of truth as it does ours.

An excellent illustration of style used expressionistically rather than imitatively is in the speeches of Hotspur. Hotspur despises poets and poetry from the bottom of his heart, yet who in the play speaks more wonderful poetry than he? It is a mistake, however, to smile indulgently at Hotspur and say that he is a poet whether he knows it or not. He is not, and Shakespeare does not mean him to be. As he is conceived, he could not sit down and speak sad epitaphs on the death of kings, as Richard, a true poet, does; imaginative as he is, he yet has no gift either of reflection or of controlled composition. The poetry he speaks is Shakespeare's poetry, a device for giving us all the color and vitality of Hotspur's bodily expressive temperament. It is an oblique device of style, completely unavailable when convention forces literal reproduction of the spoken word.[76] Caliban, the brutish Caliban, incapable of being taught moral or spiritual beauty, is another example of the same thing; it is Caliban as a part of the island, not as a character, who helps make us aware of its natural beauty and of the mysterious sounds in its temperate air.

Shakespeare's apprenticeship was capable of some pretty dreadful stuff. But we need not deplore too much the painful fancy of

> come, loving, black-brow'd night,
> Give me my Romeo: and, when he shall die,
> Take him and cut him out in little stars,
> And he will make the face of heaven so fine
> That all the world will be in love with night,
> And pay no worship to the garish sun;

or the ineptitude of

> O woe! O woeful, woeful, woeful day!
> Most lamentable day, most woeful day,
> That ever, ever, I did yet behold!
> O day! O day! O day! O hateful day! [77]

Shakespeare did not arrive at the masterly artifice of his late lyric expression by imitating the familiar triteness of everyday speech in moments of strong feeling. Juliet's strained metaphor is preparation for Cleopatra's gorgeous hyperbole:

> His face was as the heavens, and therein stuck
> A sun and moon, which kept their course, and lighted
> The little O, the earth. . . .
> His legs bestrid the ocean; his rear'd arm

> Crested the world; his voice was propertied
> As all the tuned spheres. . . .[78]

The frigid wailing around Juliet's bed is the beginning of something that ended in the incomparable lyric movement in the scenes of Antony's death.

> *Second Guard.*   The star is fallen.
> *First Guard.* And time is at his period.
> *All.*   Alas, and woe!

> *Cleopatra.*   O sun!
> Burn the great sphere thou mov'st in; darkling stand
> The varying star o' the world. O Antony,
> Antony, Antony!

> *Cleopatra.* . . .
>   My lord!
> O! wither'd is the garland of the war,
> The soldier's pole is fall'n; young boys and girls
> Are level now with men; the odds is gone,
> And there is nothing left remarkable
> Beneath the visiting moon.
> *Charmian.*   O, quietness, lady!
> *Iras.* She is dead too, our sovereign.
> *Charmian.*   Lady!
> *Iras.*   Madam!
> *Charmian.* O madam, madam, madam!
> *Iras.*   Royal Egypt!
> Empress!

Ways of Exhibiting Motive

Character in action involves questions of motivation and opposition which will be better handled as elements of structure. But some dramatic problems arising out of ways of exhibiting motive may be mentioned here.

The main problem of form is the fusion between story and characters. The tendency of dramatists to borrow the plots of *novelle,* which are primarily stories for the story's sake, not character studies, left them with the task of giving depth and vitality to the persons of the story. These may sometimes be vividly realized in particular situations without being made adequately to motivate the required story. Elizabethan audiences were apparently less bothered by this sort of weakness than we. But understanding their expectations of motive may help us to adjust our own expectations and make us fairer judges of whether or not there is a real failure of form.

A certain type of person would be expected to do certain things, a certain passion to result in certain actions, and no explanation would be necessary. What we are inclined to label lack of motivation may often be only our failure to recognize a reason for action clear to an Elizabethan audience. This has been made sufficiently clear in the discussion of decorum and of the psychology of the passions.

Sometimes we are troubled by lack of motivation in character when an Elizabethan audience would take the story for its own sake without expecting motivation at all. Our oversophistication in fiction leaves us disconcerted by the methods of pure story so often operative in Elizabethan romantic comedy. The motives are often the non-individualized motives of fairy tale, which are taken for granted. They reside in a conventional problem, whose terms have to be literally met, as a riddle's terms are met. One of the best illustrations of this technique is in *All's Well that Ends Well,* a play that post-Romantic critics turn into a "dark" or "bitter" or "problem" comedy, and wholly falsify. The only "problem" in it is Helena's problem of getting the man she wants for a husband. There is nothing gloomy or bitter either about the problem or about its solution. It is a problem in wit, not in manners or morals. The clue to it is in Boccaccio's heading to the tales of the third day, from the ninth of which Shakespeare's plot was taken:

... beginneth the third in which, under the rule of Neifile, discourse is had of the fortune of such as have painfully acquired some much-coveted thing, or, having lost, have recovered it.[79]

It is a fairy-tale problem, with certain conditions understood or given that must be fulfilled: a difficult task to be accomplished and a promised reward; the reward at first denied, making necessary the accomplishment of a still more difficult task before the reward is secured; the reward itself quite naturally a husband. It is partly Shakespeare's fault, of course, that we are thrown off the track. He gives us far more character in Helena and her mother-in-law than we have need of for the story, and so we look at Bertram with the same expectancy and are shocked at what we find. But Bertram is only fulfilling his necessary part in the story: at the beginning he must be churlish, and at the end he must be delighted at Helena's victory and behave like a good sport. Fairy-tale solutions are always brought about to the mutual satisfaction of the interested parties. Anyhow, since Helena has proved her resourcefulness and her resolution, and given him an heir to boot, why shouldn't any sensible man be delighted to have her? Bertram's "character" is not in question, and Helena is meant to be congratulated for winning her man, not sympathized with for what we mistakenly take him to be. The same is true of Julia and Proteus in *The Two Gentlemen*. Proteus fulfills the part the story requires; character analysis is beside the point.

Again, we may fail to allow for the exigencies imposed by the Elizabethan fondness for a narrative technique in drama—that is, for presenting a story sequentially from beginning to end with as much action along the way as possible. With so much action compressed into so short a space, motivation must often be quickly suggested rather than fully presented. There may often be as much a practical dramatic reason as a psychological reason for the swift conversions to villainy and the equally swift repentances in Elizabethan drama.

A common method of quick suggestion is the soliloquy. Giraldi defended the soliloquy against the charge of unnaturalness.[80] He maintained that it was quite as verisimilar for an audience to pretend to overhear a man's private communion with himself as to overhear the conversations he had with others. True enough. But so far as the Elizabethan drama is concerned, by no means all the soliloquies sound like a man really talking with himself. Hamlet's soliloquies are probably less typical of general Elizabethan practice than Richard III's or Iago's or Edmund's, in which fewer pains are taken to be realistic than to give the audience in the most economical way some necessary information about the character and the moves he is going to make. Direct self-explanation is a dramatic short cut, useful when action is full and complicated and characters are many. Momentous conflicts of passion and of purpose that change the course of the speaker's life are set down in the barest terms and decided in a moment. When Faustus determines to devote his life to black magic, and thus takes the first step on his way to damnation, he arrives at the decision after the most perfunctory review and rejection of all the other fields of learning—logic, medicine, law, divinity. In the same swift way Calverly, in *A Yorkshire Tragedy*, has a moment of repentance for his wasted youth and of tenderness for one of his children before suddenly beginning his mad course of slaughtering his family. The scene actually reveals brilliant insight into the alternate clarity and confusion of an unbalanced mind; but it is done almost in shorthand, without preparation or without sequel, without any suggestion that such a state was typical of many in Calverly's experience. It is a kind of synecdoche of construction, a commonplace of Elizabethan dramatic technique; unless we understand it so, we condemn the plays for lack of realism, where literal realism is not intended.

Sometimes a dramatist omits consideration of motive altogether, perhaps because he is choosing to concentrate on something else and has not time for both. Leontes' jealousy in *The Winter's Tale* is a good example. Unlike Othello's it appears suddenly, unmotivated and full blown. But *Othello* is a study in motivation—that is, in the movement of a man to tragedy; *The Winter's Tale* is not. Shakespeare is not interested in the reasons for Leontes' jealousy, only in its consequences. The jealousy is simply the most important motivating element in the dramatic situation he chooses to develop. It must be accepted as "given," just as are the fairy-tale elements of romantic comedy, like the shipwreck and separation of twins or the enmity of an elder brother who drives a handsome and nobler younger one from his inheritance. There is a difference in *The Winter's Tale* from these conditions, of course, in that Shakespeare uses with great accuracy all the symptoms of psychopathic jealousy, and so denies us the mood of fairy tale. But the very suddenness with which Leontes' jealousy begins is a way of revealing, in heightened fashion, a truth about it: that it is a diseased state of mind, without external motivation. Shakespeare sacrifices strict realism, which would show a gradual development of Leontes' pathological condition, to an arresting and emphatic statement of the situation from which all the near-tragic consequences of the story are to unfold.

With slightly more shading, he does a somewhat similar thing in *King Lear*. How Lear, in his old age, came to stage the foolish love contest between his daughters, is not Shakespeare's first concern; the consequences of it are. The amount of motivation he does show—the illusion created in a few swift touches of a passionate, autocratic, nonreflective, self-dramatizing temperament grown more difficult in old age [81]—though not sufficient to satisfy many critics, was sufficient for his purpose. Beneath the enlivening of the character and the changes in the terms in which the characters speak, the old fairy-tale frame is there, sufficiently recognizable to give an Elizabethan audience the right start. It is the story of the Clever Lass and of Cinderella combined.[82] The father proposes a testing question and the daughters answer it, the wicked daughters openly but falsely, the good daughter riddlingly but truly. Though the heroine's "I love you as much as salt" has gone through the metamorphosis of Geoffrey's epigrammatic "Quantum habes, tantum vales," [83] into Shakespeare's

> I love your majesty
> According to my bond; nor more nor less,

the marks of the riddle have not disappeared, as any Elizabethan audience, understanding the law of Nature and the force of its bonds would know. The terms of the story demand that the father not understand the riddle and cast out the good daughter to suffer Cinderella-like until the day when he discovers the answer and she is vindicated. How else, then, except on such clear and evident lines, should Shakespeare start his play?

Finally, motivation is sometimes exhibited rather baldly in ways not familiar to us, or at least, not customary in modern dramatic usage. The aside and the soliloquy are such conventions. Another, going out of fashion in the Elizabethan period, is interesting as a survival of the morality. That is the representation of internal conflict in an external way, through personified abstractions of the forces contending within the character's soul. The best-known example of this is the Good and Evil Angels which alternately appeal to Faustus.[84] This device seems to us perhaps psychologically crude. But its dramatic effectiveness is undeniable. The external debate had the merit of sharp emphasis, and because of the familiar background not only of the morality play but of ethical and psychological teaching generally, it was in no danger of being misunderstood. Since every man's soul was known to be a battleground between the promptings of the bestial part of him to vice and the promptings of the divine part to virtue, nothing more natural than to dramatize this struggle in a contest between Virtues and Vices, between Good and Evil

Angels, or between a hero and a devilish tempter like Othello and Iago or Macbeth and the Witches.

Even the debates a character is made to stage within himself often carry the flavor of the externally represented debate. Richard III's, on the eve of Bosworth Field, is just as dialectically conceived as if two external forces were contending for his soul.

> Is there a murderer here? No. Yes, I am:
> Then fly: what! from myself? Great reason why:
> Lest I revenge. What! myself upon myself?
> Alack! I love myself. Wherefore? for any good
> That I myself have done unto myself?
> O! no: alas! I rather hate myself
> For hateful deeds committed by myself.
> I am a villain. Yet I lie; I am not.
> Fool, of thyself speak well: fool, do not flatter.
> My conscience hath a thousand several tongues,
> And every tongue brings in a several tale,
> And every tale condemns me for a villain.

Indeed, the debate is just a movement to the inside of his mind of something externally initiated by the ghosts of his slaughtered victims. Although the ghosts are real enough, Shakespeare gives them as well the function of dramatizing the bad conscience and the good, respectively, of Richard and of Richmond.[85]

The most subtle development of this method of representing internal conflict by external means, far removed from the crude technique of its origin, occurs in *King Lear;* for at least one of the Fool's several functions is to exhibit to us Lear's tortured conscience. The Fool may be viewed simply, it is true, as teacher and taunter of Lear, instructing him in his folly and helping to drive him insane by turning the knife in the wound. But the torment in Lear's mind gains in its effect of terror and pity if we heed his admission, before he leaves Goneril's house, that he has made a tragic mistake in judgment and done Cordelia a grave injustice:

> O most small fault,
> How ugly didst thou in Cordelia show!
> Which, like an engine, wrench'd my frame of nature
> From the fix'd place, drew from my heart all love,
> And added to the gall. O Lear, Lear, Lear!
> Beat at this gate, that let thy folly in,
> And thy dear judgment out! [86]

and if we recognize the Fool as the worm of conscience, the ayenbit of inwit, gnawing within him.

Some Dramatic Problems

The dramatic problems arising out of Elizabethan conceptions of character and the techniques of exhibiting it may be summarized.

The problem of individuality vs. *typicality*.—Although theories of character, the doctrine of decorum, rhetorical training, and classical models tended to stress the typical in character, Elizabethan dramatists, for whatever reasons of creative vitality, were not inhibited by these influences. The social types in realistic comedy, where type characters are to be expected, were many and varied, and they spoke with the accent of contemporary London. The humour character, so much in vogue at the turn of the century, was a means to individualize a type by the sharpness of caricature, but it was a more mechanical means than the freshness of observation and richness of language that gave to so many of the characters of the drama the illusion of life.

The problem of repetitive form, or consistency.—Elizabethan dramatists often seem weak to us in this respect. Their emphases on story and action, on the immediate dramatic situation, and on the passions (an emphasis which both psychological theory and rhetorical taste sanctioned) make against the formal consistency so much insisted on by the critics. But what the characters sometimes lose in singleness of impression they often gain in vividness in individual scenes, or in a more complicated, less easily described, conviction of life.

The problem of static vs. *dynamic, or developing, character*.— This is closely related to the former problem. The critics saw artistic coherence, evidently, only in absolute consistency, or in the perfectly static character; this is one reason for their emphasis on types. With static characters, whether typical or not, the dramatic problem is how to rescue them from monotony by progressive revelation of character. With characters that develop, the problem is how to show change without loss of coherence and unity. For perfect consistency is of course not a necessary condition of either. The problem of static characters is primarily the problem of comedy, the problem of developing characters primarily of tragedy. It is not certain whether either problem was fully understood. Certainly, there are many failures—on the one hand, in the monotonous tricks of speech and manner by which comic characters, especially humour characters, are made to identify themselves; on the other, in the emphasis on scenes of passion that give a character a momentary brilliance but leave him unrealized as a whole. Shakespeare is preëminently successful with both methods: the characters in *Twelfth Night* are instances of the former, the gradual revelation of basically unchanged character; the great tragic figures are instances of the latter, the developing of a character under stress. But there are other successes besides Shakespeare's. One reason for the vitality of the best of Jonson's comic characters—like Volpone, Mosca, Face, Sir Epicure, Ursula, and Busy—is that their resources of character and of language are gradually called into play by the variety of situations in which they appear. And some of the memorable figures of tragedy—like Marlowe's Edward II, Middleton's Beatrice Joanna, Webster's Duchess of Malfi—deteriorate or are ennobled in the course of the action without loss of the illusion of a living personality.

The problem of motivation.—This is primarily a problem in structure, in the coherence of character with story, hence a problem in syllogistic form, if we use Burke's term. Elizabethan dramatists were undoubtedly often careless of motive. But when we think a particular dramatist has failed to supply sufficient motivation in character for the actions that follow, we may be entertaining false expectations. Either we fail, through ignorance of Elizabethan psychological theory or inattention to dramatic conventions, to recognize adequate motives, or we ask for motivation in character when the dramatist is not concerned much with character but simply with story. The latter situation is especially true in romantic comedy.

The practical problems of exhibiting character and motive in speech.—These are in part problems in the handling of minor forms: rhetorical figures of thought and types of discourse suitable for imitation in dramatic speech; and the conventions of the soliloquy, the aside, the external debate to represent internal conflict, etc. They are also problems in the adjustment to practical need, of controlling conceptions of style: *energeia*, amplification, decorum, and verisimilitude interpreted as the significant expression of inner truth rather than as the exact imitation of external impressions. It is against a background of formal rhetoric and of the doctrine of the appropriate style that we must understand the supreme stylistic achievement of the Elizabethan dramatists. These traditional conceptions did not stultify their great expressive vitality; but they did give it something to start from, something to work both with and against. Style in English renaissance drama, therefore, is not lawless; partly through and partly against a controlling norm, its wonderful variety in verse and prose speaks with a living voice.

10 *The Fable: The Unities*

IF BY these rules ... we should judge our modern plays, 'tis probable that few of them would endure the trial; that which should be the business of a day takes up in some of them an age; instead of one action, they are the epitomes of a man's life; and for one spot of ground which the stage should represent we are sometimes in more countries than the map can show us.
—LISIDEIUS, IN DRYDEN'S *Essay of Dramatic Poesy* [1]

The Fable in Classical and Elizabethan Drama

THE TWO MOST fundamental differences between ancient classical drama and Elizabethan drama are probably in the relative economy with which materials are used and in the conduct of the fable. The two tend to go together. In theme, event, number of characters, emotional tone, a classical play is economical, and usually concentrated in its effect; an Elizabethan play, lavish and multiple. (For example, *King Lear* compared with *Oedipus Rex*.) The plot of a classical play typically begins *in medias res* and follows the "artificial" order; the plot of an Elizabethan play normally follows the "natural" or historical order of events. The exceptions and modifications on both sides do not invalidate the large generalization.

Even at the risk of repeating commonplaces of knowledge, a fuller statement of the second point of difference, the conduct of the fable, is necessary for our understanding of the problems of unity, coherence, and emphasis to be taken up in this and the succeeding chapter. Both classical tragedy and classical comedy of the New Comedy sort have "crisis" plots. A crisis plot in tragedy begins with the point of critical decision preceding a crucial action; we are informed only through interpolated exposition of antecedent action. Since the motivation of the action to be developed has already occurred, we have only to watch the making of the decision or discovery

259

and its culmination in fatal action. As Dryden puts it, the audience is set at the post, where the race is to be concluded.[2] Before the play opens, Jason has already determined to put Medea aside and marry Creusa; Oedipus has committed the terrible deeds of unwitting patricide and incest which are to lead him to doom. We witness, then, not the moving of Medea to revenge, but only her decision as to the form it shall take, and her accomplishment of it; only Oedipus' ruinous discovery of his deeds. Sometimes, as in *Agamemnon,* even the decision has been made. The reason for Clytemnaestra's hatred of Agamemnon—his sacrifice on the eve of departure for Troy of their daughter Iphigeneia, itself a link in a long chain of reprisals and counter-reprisals involving divine as well as human enmity—and her decision to kill him are outside the play; we are asked to share only in the mounting tension as Agamemnon, returning from victory, is welcomed by his wife and her lover to his fatal bath. The beginning *in medias res* is not restricted to tragedy. Greek New Comedy, hence the imitative Roman comedy of Plautus and Terence, although different in organization from tragedy in the greater part taken by intrigue, is yet similar in focusing on a crisis. If the plot centers on a young man in love, as it generally does, his affairs are always at their most desperate state. Indeed, the favorite critical moment to choose is the day on which his mistress, either secretly loved or disapproved of by his father as a wife, presents him with a child—the most flagrant possible evidence of his trouble. Our concern is not with how all this happened, but with how it can possibly be straightened out. We are always shown the darkest moment before daylight breaks.

Elizabethan drama, on the other hand—tragedy, comedy, or history—generally begins at the beginning and proceeds straight through in chronological order until the end. This means that the motivation of action is within rather than precedent to the action of the play. We follow Tamburlaine's long career from his irruption into Asia Minor as a Scythian shepherd until his death after the conquest of much of the eastern Mediterranean world; Faustus' twenty-four years from the moment of his willing pact with the devil until its term is up; Brutus' rise and fall from the first temptings of Cassius to consider the assassination of Caesar until his defeat at Philippi at the hands of Caesar's avengers; the Duchess of Malfi's love and marriage through the birth of three children before her brothers' slow revenge is accomplished; Macbeth's career of crime from the moment of temptation by the witches until his death on the battlefield at the hands of Macduff. Even when the time covered by the action is reduced, antecedent events are usually only very quickly sketched in and something of the process of motivation is left for the play itself. When the play opens, Hamlet already has known reasons to hate his uncle, but he is moved to plan action against him only by the revelation of the Ghost in the fifth scene. The overt reasons for Iago's hatred of Othello are given as immediately antecedent to the play, but the deeper motivation in character is skilfully and powerfully presented in the first act; and Iago's moving of Othello to jealous hatred and revenge makes the action of the play. In romantic comedy, though the time is often much compressed, we are frequently shown, nevertheless, the start of the love affair which has to be carried through many vicissitudes to a successful conclusion: for example, Campaspe's and Apelles', Margaret's and Lacy's, Portia's and Bassanio's, Rosalind's and Orlando's, Perdita's and Florizel's, and so on.

The strength of crisis drama is in concentration, hence intensity. By stopping down a lens, you sharpen the focus. The weakness of crisis drama is in the halting of action on the stage for the narration of action secondhand, during which the play may go dead. The weakness and strength of historically ordered drama are the converse of these. The weakness is in its liability to diffusion; a play so organized easily becomes episodic, loose, and lacking in emphasis. The strength is in the maintaining of lively interest by plentiful action on the stage.[3] English dramatists usually got plentiful action at all costs. Their problem was to learn to keep variety and liveliness without sacrificing unity, coherence, and emphasis.

In these differences, of course, each type of drama reflects the differences in its origin and development. For Greek drama took story only secondarily into a lyric frame, and let it expand under control; Elizabethan drama was founded upon story. These fundamental characteristics of Elizabethan drama, multiplicity and sequentially presented action, are survivals of medieval narrative habits, exemplified both in actual narrative and in drama, and they posed certain problems in the achievement of satisfactory dramatic form.

Narrative of any length can take its time, begin at the beginning, move straight along or follow a tacking course, interlace a number of

actions, bring in any number of characters, halt the story to describe
or moralize, move about as freely and quickly in time and place as
the mind moves. It need not do these things, of course, but it has
the freedom to do them, whereas drama has not. And it took English
dramatists a long time to learn, when faced with getting a story on
the stage, that it had not. There are possibilities, that is, of multiplicity, diffusion, and amplitude that need not wreck a story as they will
wreck a play. Consider Malory, for instance, or Ariosto. All long
medieval narrative, certainly, is by no means multiple and diffuse
in action. *Sir Gawain and the Green Knight* and Chaucer's *Troilus
and Criseyde,* for instance, have unified actions, with lines strongly
marked; their plots, shorn of description and lengthy analysis of
sentiment, are readily convertible into drama. And of course short
narrative of the type of the fabliau, the beast fable, or the exemplum,
where sharpness of point is the aim, often excels in economy of effect.
But English dramatists followed the romances in fondness for plenty
of action; that being so, they had to struggle with problems of
emphasis and coherence that would have been solved beforehand had
they always had an eye for more sharply drawn stories. Nor was
this fondness for multiplicity confined to the English; how the Italian
critics, "classical" as they were, supported in some degree what was
evidently a general renaissance taste we shall see.

   Action in historical sequence, beginning with the first motivation
of it and continuing until it is concluded, was called "natural" order
by the renaissance critics in opposition to the "artificial" order of
Greek drama and Homeric epic, in which action is climactically centered, with antecedent and contributory action introduced exposi-
torily and narratively. The artificial order was also called "ordine
turbata" or "perturbata." Unsophisticated narrative of any age is
pretty sure to be of the "once upon a time" sort, beginning with the
egg and developing in a leisurely way; doubtless the perception of
this had something to do with Horace's unequivocal condemnation
of the natural order. But of course, by skilful use of compression in
the right places, of differences of pace, of suspense and climax, the
sequential method can become highly sophisticated, as it does in
Chaucer's *Pardoner's Tale.* In the tales of the *Decameron* which have
a plot, not merely an anecdotal point, Boccaccio usually starts from
the beginning and sketches in the circumstances necessary to understand the story. It is the regular method of the *novelle,* his and his

followers', and these prose tales are one of the richest stores of plots the dramatists had to tap. But drama needs to make a quicker and more emphatic start. If dramatists insist on telling a story from start to finish, obviously they create major difficulties for themselves in the way of selection and emphasis. Yet English dramatists almost without exception adopted the sequential method of action, and all the weight of classic drama did not prevail to change their minds about it—not even the mind of the "Horatian" Jonson.

Both of these aspects of narrative form—abundance of action and sequential action—were characteristic of medieval religious drama. The mystery plays tended to be episodic, even individually considered, apart from their great cumulative episodic effect in cyclic form. Even more important for the tradition of romantic drama, dramatized saints' legends must usually have been quite as episodic. There is no reason to suppose they would have been better organized than the source material from which they were drawn. We can get some notion of what they were like from the legends they made use of, from the French miracle plays, from the two surviving fifteenth-century English miracles (the Croxton *Play of the Sacrament* and the *Mary Magdalene* of the Digby MS),[4] and from Italian *sacre rappresentazioni* on similar subjects.[5] One example will suffice here. Though *Mary Magdalene* is half a morality, it is also a saint's legend, and has fully succumbed to the looseness and multiplicity biographical material is liable to. It covers the life of Mary from the time of her girlhood in Bethany until her sanctified death in the wilderness. It includes not only the Magdalene's temptation, fall, and repentance, her conversion of the King and Queen of "Marcylle" to Christianity, and her subsequent holy life, but also scenes exhibiting the power of Tiberius, Herod, and Pilate, and of the World, the Flesh, and the Devil; scenes from the life of Christ, like the raising of Lazarus, the Resurrection, and the Harrowing of Hell, the last of which is not even tangential to the Magdalene's life; and scenes from the pilgrimage of her converts to the Holy Land. The fifty-two scenes into which Dr. Furnivall has divided the text often follow one another with only slight causal connection, or none. In the dramatic presentation of the life of a saint like this and of the life of a knight-errant there is no need for formal difference. As survivals like *Common Conditions* (ca. 1576 or earlier) and *Sir Clyomon and Sir Clamydes* (ca. 1570) show, the material of the secular romances which went to form a great number of plays on the early Elizabethan stage was just as hard to organize into coherent dramatic form.

Nevertheless, we cannot regret the Elizabethan continuance of medieval methods when we look at the frigid plays turned out by the French and Italian academicians of the sixteenth century. How disastrous attempts might be to put romantic narrative into the strait jacket of classical form is well illustrated by Cecchi's religious drama of *Tobia*.[6] The Apocryphal story of Tobit is of the usual pattern for saint's legend or miracle play—the woes of old Tobit, a Jewish captive in Nineveh, and the adventurous travels of his son, young Tobias, all leading to the final miracle in which the old man's faith is rewarded and his sight restored. It had been the subject of a Florentine *sacra rappresentazione* handled in loosely episodic and sequential order.[6a] Cecchi turned it into a regular five-act piece, with unity of time and place, and action concentrated on the final episode. Tobia and his wife are at home in Nineveh just preceding the return of their son, whose arrival brings about the happy catastrophe of the play. This demands that "Tobia vecchio's" wife reveal all their former troubles, and that a series of improbable messengers who arrive during the course of the day narrate all the adventures "Tobia giovane" had on his journey. Absolutely nothing happens on the stage until the young man returns in the last act with his bride and with his incognito traveling companion, who is the *deus ex machina* to make old Tobia's scales fall from his eyes and to reveal himself as the Angel Raphael. We can all be thankful that Marlowe, Shakespeare, and Webster were moved to work in more traditional ways. As distinct from his *drammi spirituali*, Cecchi's comedies, modeled, like most Italian *commedie erudite*, on Roman comedy, are lively enough. The reason, probably, is that the preparation for the crisis in Roman comedy is filled with bustling intrigue. English dramatists, very likely because it involved no sacrifice of action, were far readier to adopt some of the plot techniques of Latin comedy than they were of classical tragedy, Greek or Roman. Resistance to the pattern of organization of classical tragedy is shown even in conscious academic attempts at some sort of classical form, like *Gorboduc* and *Gismond of Salerne*. Both of these tragedies follow a natural order and cover an undefined period of time.

By clinging to these traditions of abundance of action and of chronological sequence, Elizabethan dramatists had to find a different method from the classical in two central problems of form: how to get concentration, and how to achieve organic structure, that is, how to achieve an action causally connected from beginning to middle to end. The two are involved together, but I shall deal specifically with the first problem in this chapter, and with the second in the following chapter.

Unity of Action: The Critical View

The problem of concentration is the problem of the unities. We can learn something about a subject even as apparently outworn as this by looking afresh at the critics. Although a good deal has been said about the critics' formulation of the unities, little has been said about how, beneath their school-driven logic and formalism, their genuine enthusiasm is for the variety and multiplicity characteristic of the age they live in.[7] As with the history of science, where there is always a tendency to distort the state of things in a given period by singling out for emphasis those attitudes and ideas which were fruitful for later developments, so in the history of criticism we have tended to distort the position of the renaissance critics in relation to their own times by seeing them primarily as forerunners of the rigid doctrines of the neoclassical period.

Aristotle's statement that drama is an imitation, not of men, but of the actions of men,[8] struck a sympathetic note in the Renaissance. The critics were fond of repeating Aristotle's metaphor that the fable was the soul of the play.[9] They put in some of their best efforts in insisting on the unity of action, in explaining structural terms like *peripeteia*, recognition, complication, and unraveling, in working out a pattern for comedy similar to that for tragedy, and in analyzing the plots of standard classical favorites like *Andria, Oedipus Tyrannus, Antigone,* and *Hecuba*. Nevertheless, nothing better reveals the distance of these men from the spirit of classic art than what they have to say about the matters of plot which form the core of Aristotle's treatise. For everywhere seeming to agree with him, they are actually always implying quite different ways of seeing. And in spite of themselves those ways of seeing were formed by the narrative and dramatic traditions of the Middle Ages. Even in the act of insisting on Aristotle's "one action, and that a whole," [10] they nearly always managed to make provision for "plenty" of action, either by extending the sense of "unity," or by finding ways to admit extraneous action. In this fondness for plenty of action they were at one with the least scholarly-minded of popular dramatists.

The controversy over *Orlando Furioso* that went on during most of the century, even though it immediately concerned heroic poetry and not drama and therefore involved somewhat different problems, is instructive of more general attitudes towards unity and variety. We are helped to understand the doctrine of the unities in the drama by seeing it in a wider frame; I shall take a little time, therefore, to look at the controversy over Ariosto's poem. *Orlando Furioso* was a major irritant in the flesh of the critics, and the attempt to save Ariosto in spite of himself, both for his lack of moral purpose and for his violation of epic form, stimulated an enormous amount of critical activity. Several of the pearls produced were of general value, notably Giraldi's *Discorsi dei romanzi* (1549) and Paolo Beni's *Comparatione di Homero, Virgilio, e Torquato* (1607), the final lecture of which was on Ariosto.

That *Orlando Furioso* was the greatest Italian poem of the time, at least before *Gerusalemme Liberata* offered competition, was an undeniable fact. Equally undeniable was the lack in the poem of any apparent unity of action, the *sine qua non,* as laid down by Aristotle, of an epic as of a tragedy. Minturno sadly admitted the defect and said Ariosto had deliberately chosen a bad method in order to give pleasure to many.[11] But his point of view was not the usual one. The critics generally found one of two ways out of their embarrassment. One way was to find the nonapparent unity and insist on it, the other was to admit the lack but find a creditable excuse for it.

If the poem had a single subject, what was it? The madness of Orlando? the love and heroic adventures of Ruggiero and Bradamante? the wars against Carlo Magno of Agramante and his Saracens?[12] In spite of the title it was hardest to defend the first, less hard the second, and perhaps least the third. Fornario da Rheggio and the Florentine Academy took a stand on the third[13] and claimed that the wars of Agramante against Charlemagne were made the subject of the poem in imitation of the *Iliad,* which was thus understood to have its center in the Trojan War, not just in the quarrel between Achilles and Agamemnon. Moreover, taking the wars of the Moors as the chief action gave Ariosto's poem a central heroic figure in

Charlemagne and gave it a central unity of moral purpose in showing that deeds undertaken rashly, as were Agramante's, are bound to end badly. Some of the more perceptive critics, who saw that the poem could not be unified in a single action, found cause for praise in its very multiplicity. Beni declared that the argument of the poem was what Ariosto said it was: "l'Arme, gli Amori, le Cortesie, e l'audaci imprese di Donne e Cavalieri" [14] (the arms, loves, courtly doings, and bold undertakings of ladies and knights), and that Orlando and Ruggiero were simply the most important examples of these. The wars of Charlemagne were the background, and were necessary in holding the poem together, but could not be said to give singleness of action. Beni quoted a number of passages from the poem which stated explicitly Ariosto's intention of variety.

The important thing for Beni and other defenders of the multiplicity of action in *Orlando Furioso* was the recognition that the poem was a romance and therefore something not precisely comparable to the epic as discussed by Aristotle and not subject to his laws. Giraldi, the critic always most ready to allow for changing taste, and his pupil Pigna, both discussed the romance as a new form and took as its central characteristic the imitation of many actions of many men. Pigna said in effect that since the business of the romance was to imitate the wanderings of many paladins, the more wanderings the better. [15] In saying that a romantic poem would naturally reflect in its organization the wanderings of its subjects, he was guilty of what Mr. Yvor Winters, in discussing *The Waste Land,* calls the fallacy of imitative form. [16] Minturno recognized the fallacy and regretted that Ariosto had used his great genius on so barbarous a form; it was only his wonderful style, Minturno said, that gave the poem beauty. [17] But since the other critics had found a way to remove Aristotle's heavy hand, they could rather defiantly praise the variety they, and everyone else, enjoyed. Giraldi said that the romance was liked in modern times for the very reason that it allowed many actions and many digressions. [18] This attitude parallels, as we shall see, his leaning towards multiplicity of action in the drama.

But of course just liking variety was never quite a sufficient reason for allowing it. In addition, therefore, to the argument from imitative form, the critics found other good rhetorical or philosophical or artistic justifications for it. In saying that many actions avoided the danger of satiety in the reader that a single action was liable to cause,

Giraldi was talking like Erasmus, who had been so concerned about
furnishing, in *De copia,* rhetorical methods of avoiding tedium in the
hearers. And in making a long catalogue of the variety of things that
might be treated in a romance Giraldi was showing he had learned
well the kind of lesson Erasmus had taught.[19] Paolo Beni thought
Ariosto superior to Homer in this very matter of avoiding satiety, for
Homer, with his simplicity and directness, sometimes bored his
readers, whereas Ariosto never did.[20]

Another defense of Ariosto's multiplicity was in the familiar analogy to the multiplicity of nature. Beni argued at some length the
question of whether art should imitate nature in her multiplicity or
in her uniqueness. He concluded in the ambidextrous style of medieval debate that, since nature produces better effects when they are
single or unique ("un solo"), unity in art is certainly preferable, but
that, on the other hand, since nature does not exclude plurality,
multiplicity in art is a good thing too.[21] This kind of impasse
comes as the penalty of following too rigidly an imitative theory of
art.

Still another defense was found in the skill with which Ariosto
interlaced his many actions and yet maintained suspense. In dropping his action at a critical point, and leaving it in suspense while he
took up another, Ariosto had developed the technique of the serial
long before the day of serialized fiction. Beni marveled at the way in
which he passed the various actions from hand to hand, teasing the
reader by letting go of one at a crucial point and turning to another,
yet never losing any of the threads, but finally picking them all up
and following them to the end.[22] Now since Aristotle had said that
the perfection of a fable consisted in the skill with which it was complicated and untangled, the intricate knotting and untangling in
Orlando Furioso, not of one knot, but of many, qualified it as of
special excellence and Ariosto as a superior artist, superior to Homer.
For one "bel nodo e solutione" in Homer, there were ten in Ariosto.
In this passage of Beni, there is revealed an unfeigned delight in
richly varied and skilful story-telling. One of the episodes he singles
out for praise is the fable of Ariodante and Ginevra, one of the ultimate sources of the Claudio-Hero story in *Much Ado About Nothing.*
He says that nothing ancient or modern is so wonderful and moving,
or better entangled and untangled; for these reasons it might serve
as form and idea of a most beautiful tragi-comedy. It is worth noting

that Beni attributes Ariosto's skill in handling his "gentilissimi nodi" to his experience in drama, in which the fine knotting and untying contain the beauty and good of the action. The same admiration for intricacy is in Giraldi and carries over to his views of dramatic plotting.[23] For instance, a shrewd statement he makes about tragedies with double or happy endings suggests at least one reason for his preference for them over the orthodox tragedy with an unhappy ending; he says they are better adapted for intricate knots.

Tasso was easier to defend on grounds of unity of action than Ariosto. Indeed Beni had no trouble in demonstrating that he surpassed both Homer and Virgil in this respect. But Tasso, too, was especially admired for the episodes with which he diversified his main story.[24]

It is interesting that Sidney, the intransigent English defender of unity in the drama, should betray the ubiquitous fondness for variety when he had what he evidently considered a proper opportunity. It is certain that in his *Arcadia* he tried to embody the conception of the heroic poem as defined by the Italian critics.[25] He selected one action centered about one person, the abrogation of his public responsibilities by King Basilius, to form the core of his story, and then complicated it with many subsidiary episodes of love and combat. They may seem to us to put a considerable strain on the structure, but there is no doubt that the "poem" would have satisfied the critics not only in its organization around a single center of action, but equally in its variety of situations, passions, moral problems, wise sentences, displays of rhetoric, pastoral interludes—that is, in such delightful "riempimenti" or fillings-in as Giraldi catalogues in the passage quoted above in Chapter II or such as Fornario da Rheggio lists specifically for *Orlando Furioso*.[26] It is clear from Spenser's letter to Raleigh that he likewise conceived of a heroic poem as having a single action enriched with diverse episodes; but since Spenser had a less firm hold on structure than Sidney, in *The Faerie Queene* the episodes submerge the central action even more completely.

All that the critics say about unity of action in discussing *Orlando Furioso* and *Gerusalemme Liberata* is indicative of their delight in romantic material and in romantic methods of narrative. Even though they clearly feel freer in treating romance than in treating drama, we shall see that similar attitudes of mind qualify what they say about unity of action in the drama.

Two OTHER observations with bearing on the drama should be made before leaving this question of the heroic poem. Both Giraldi and Beni showed some preference for a "natural," that is a chronological order, as against the "artificial" order of beginning *in medias res.*[27] The interesting thing about this for our purposes is that they both recognized the fitness of the natural order for narrative material covering a length of time and that both saw that such an order demanded condensation, omission, changes of pace, if emphasis and suspense were not to be lost. Neither went so far, it is true, as to advocate this order for drama, where singleness of action and dramatic climax seemed to call for the "ordine perturbata." But they did recognize the essential difference in form between the "expository" organization of classical drama and the "narrative," chronological organization of medieval romance. If they had not been quite so conservative, they might have taken one further step and justified a natural order for drama as for romance. But they could not escape the double authority of Aristotle and Horace for a form they were not able to rescue by its novelty, as they could romance. It is seldom that even the most liberal of the critics flies full in the face of authority; except occasionally in Castelvetro, we must look for explaining away, not defiance. Giraldi showed more independence than most of the critics, but it is untrue to say that he was not an Aristotelian. He was occasionally bold enough to dispense with Aristotle's authority if he had to in defense of modern taste, but he much preferred to have the master behind him, and by dint of a certain amount of misunderstanding and ingenious argument—not, evidently, at all dishonest—he usually managed to seem to.

The second observation is on the position of Castelvetro. The man who gets the credit for the final formulation of the doctrine of the unities, which had been in process of shaping since early in the century, is nearly the most revealing of all. In his commentary on Aristotle's passage comparing a well-organized epic poem to a living organism, Castelvetro takes Aristotle to task.[28] There is no special beauty in a single animal just because it is single. Everybody knows that many animals are more delightful to see than one, for variety gives delight, as singularity does not. What Aristotle should have said was that a single animal having in itself the beauties which many other animals have separately—this one having one beauty, that one another—gives more delight than they. The longing eye of a judicious man would take far more pleasure in seeing the Helen of Zeuxis or Crotona if she were brought to life than the five women from whose separate beauties the sculptor drew the sum total of Helen's beauty. Therefore, an epic poem like one of Homer's pleases, not because the action is single and about a single person, but because the poem combines in this single action the delights of many actions and many persons. This seems like a statement of the important aesthetic principle that unity must come from diversity. But the composite animal of many beauties, even though it is a commonplace figure for the principle of universality in art, in the present context makes one uneasy. By the form of his statement Castelvetro appears to be putting more value on the mere aggregation of separable and numerous beauties than on the realization of a universal beauty. And another passage of Castelvetro's on unity of action [29] makes one doubt if he fully understands Aristotle's principle of organic form and if multiplicity might not please him better than unity if he were not driven somehow to find the rationale of all of Aristotle's "rules."

In his treatment of unity of action in tragedy and comedy, he denies, by implication, that there is any organic necessity for such unity either in the drama or in the epic. His argument starts from a comparison of history and poetry. For history, he says, represents a single action of a whole people (illustrated in Sallust), many actions of one people (Livy and many Greek and Latin historians), many actions of one person (Plutarch, Suetonius, Cornelius Nepos), and many actions of many persons (Trogus Pompeius and others). Now poetry is like history and follows in its footsteps. Except for verse, the only difference is that poetry represents actions that might happen, history those that have happened; Aristotle says so. If we praise historians who do these various things contrary to Aristotle's rule for a single action of a single person, then why should not we praise a poet who does them too?

Notwithstanding, Aristotle, here and elsewhere, obstinately commands that the action filling up the fable be one, and of one single person; if, however, there should be more actions, [he commands] that one depend on the other; nor does he adduce reasons, or any proof whatsoever, except the example of tragic poets and of Homer, who have held themselves to this singleness of the action of one person in composing the fable.[30]

Once again Castelvetro rescues the exasperating master from his imagined predicament and tells us what he should have said. Aristotle could see, Castelvetro says, that a tragedy or comedy must have only one action of one person, or two actions which by dependence on one another could be reputed one, because the limitation to twelve hours of the action to be represented and the confinement ("strettezza") of the place wherein the action was shown did not permit the treatment of many actions of many persons. This is one of the famous passages formulating the unities, and I shall return to it later; also to the matter of two actions in a play. The point to be made here is that Castelvetro flatly states that the limitation of place and time is the only reason for the limitation of the action. In this passage he shows no perception of any organic necessity. He goes on to say that of course this reason (the limitation of time and place) cannot apply to the epic fable, which Aristotle had perversely used to illustrate his point about tragedy. The reason for limiting the epic fable to one action of one person is that to delight one's hearers by writing about many things and persons is so easy that there is no special credit owing to the poet for holding their attention. The very things that command their interest are the multitude of actions, of new events, of persons and of peoples, and the delight and amplitude and magnificence of such a narration. The poet can show his skill properly only by doing the much harder thing of delighting them with a single action of one person. In sum, therefore, Castelvetro argues that a dramatic fable has unity of practical necessity, an epic fable has unity in order to demonstrate the poet's skill. In neither does he admit it as a necessity of form.

Judging by their insistence on it for drama and epic, the critics generally would seem to perceive the necessity of unity of action; judging by their discussion of the necessary dependence of the parts in the composition of the whole, they would seem also to understand what it consists in. Yet statements like those of Castelvetro just summarized, or like some made by the defenders of Ariosto's multiplicity, would seem impossible of entertainment if unity of action were fully understood as a principle of organic structure. We may be sure, at any rate, that it is the most complex kind of unity, Wölfflin's "multiple unity," [31] that the critics want; they have no taste for simplicity or economy. What really moves them are those multitudinous beauties of Ariosto which, to number, would be like numbering the stars of heaven or the waves of the sea.[32] And, as will be clear from their treatment of episodes in drama, they do not confine the idea of beauty in multiplicity to epic and romance.

As I HAVE said, the critics had less freedom to strain the principle of unity of action for the drama than for the heroic poem. What they could do, however, to warp it to contemporary taste they did, even if unconsciously. They came at it on the flanks, and modified the Aristotelian conception in two ways. One way was in the interpretation of episodes, the other was in the recommendation of double plots and intricate action.

"Episode" is used in more than one sense in the *Poetics*. In the passage, possibly interpolated, on the quantitative parts of a tragedy, the nonchoral parts are given as *prologos, epeisodion,* and *exodos*.[33] The prologue is the part before the entrance of the chorus, the exode the part after the exit of the chorus, *the episode the part between.* Since there are several choral songs dividing this middle part of the dialogue, the episodic part is broken into several portions. The word is used in this passage in its literal sense of being something "added to" the songs, since the dramatic part of Greek tragedy was an accretion to the original lyric element.

Since the parts of the dialogue between the choral odes are in some sense organized sections of the plot, by extension and abstraction an episode may be taken as *any developed situation in a play, any "chapter" of action having some coherence in itself.* This is a familiar modern sense of the term. Aristotle does not use the word precisely in this sense by itself; but he does imply it in a passage which carries a further qualification: he says that *an "episodic" plot is one in which the episodes* (i.e., *the developed situations or chapters of action) succeed one another without probable or necessary sequence.*[34] Such a plot is "episodic," presumably, because in it the episodes are not subordinated as parts of a whole logically organized plot.

In the section in which he says the poet should first sketch in the general outline of the plot and then fill in the episodes and amplify in detail, he is using "episode" in the sense *of particular incidents, motives, and the like, which help the telling of the story and are relevant to it, but are yet outside the main action.*[35] He illustrates by outlining the plot of *Iphigeneia in Tauris.* The plot demands that Iphigeneia's brother appear at Tauris, where as priestess she is obliged to sacrifice all strangers to the goddess; but the particular reason why the Oracle commanded Orestes to go there, or his own purpose in coming, are outside the general plan of the play. This sense of episode implies not developed situations which are essential parts of a whole, but *variable particulars or details* as distinct from the general essentials of the action, and it suggests the sense of *something subsidiary or additional to the plot*—relevant, and useful to clarify or amplify it, but not absolutely essential. Episodes of this kind in the drama, Aristotle says, are short, whereas they are needed in the epic to give it extension. In the statement that Homer admits as episodes in the *Iliad* many events from the general story of the war, such as the catalogue of the ships, Aristotle carries the sense of extraneousness still further.[36] Here, episodes may be taken to mean *parenthetic additions* of any sort to the plot. Compare Dryden's "episodical ornaments, such as descriptions, narrations, and other beauties which are not essential to the play." [37]

The word, with varying emphasis on these several implications—the sense of *developed situations,* the sense of *particulars* as distinct from the general outline of the action, the sense of *things extraneous* to the action—is applied in certain special ways in the Renaissance. *Episode,* for instance, is often used to refer to *secondary plots* in either epic or drama; [38] in this usage, all the senses of the word are implied. The warlike undertaking of Goffredo to free the Holy Sepulchre is the main action of *Gerusalemme Liberata;* the affairs of Raimondo, Rinaldo, and Tancredi are episodes. The love of Pamphilus for Glycerium constitutes the main action of *Andria;* the love of Charinus for Philumena, an episode.

Episode in the sense of *incidents outside the dramatic action of the play* is defined rather carefully in terms of place and time.[39] The doctrine of verisimilitude led to a distinction between what might be allowed to happen within the action of the play and what might happen outside it, that is, at a different time or place. There was thought to be less strain on credulity, for instance, in making supernatural events happen outside the fable. This exaggerated stress on what was happening before the eyes led to the connotation of "unity of action" as action happening here and now; therefore, *anything that had happened before it, or that would happen after it, or anything happening in a different place,* even if causally connected to the present action, was in this sense of physical or temporal remoteness extraneous and therefore an episode. So, says Castelvetro, the discussion at the beginning of a play of preceding events, news brought by messengers of happenings off stage, revelations in dreams or by spirits are episodes.[40] This definition would make Prospero's account to Miranda of their expulsion from Milan, Edgar's account of the death of Gloucester, King Hamlet the Ghost's account of his poisoning, "episodes" in a rather special sense.

Episode in the sense of *particulars as distinct from the action in summary form* is the sense Castelvetro gives to define Aristotle's use of the term in his condemnation of episodic plots; he qualifies this by saying that he means only the accidental particulars, not those depending on the action by probability or necessity.[41] Even so, this application is rather confusing. Aristotle does not appear to be thinking at this point of an organized plot to which extraneous details are attached, but rather of a fable which is only a sequence of essentially unconnected episodes and therefore is not, in his sense, a plot at all.

Most interesting of all, these derivative abstract senses of the term were used by renaissance critics most unhistorically in explanation of the original concrete sense as a purely quantitative part of the play (Aristotle's first sense). That is, the parts of a play between the first choral ode and the last (or, in the Latin system, Acts II–IV) were said to be episodes *because* they were the parts in which the details and the things subsidiary to the main action occurred. Castelvetro said these acts were commonly filled up ("si riempono") with the episodes of the play both in the sense of *things happening outside the play in place and time* and in the sense of *particulars of the action not known by the summary treatment of the action in Acts I and V.* Giraldi said these central acts contained *the things needed to fill out the fable to proper length,* for the plot required by the unity of action would not be long enough by itself.[42] This notion carries over to the drama the idea found in all discussions of the epic that the central action needs enlargement—partly to give magnificence to the subject, partly to give delight to the hearers. Episodes are necessary as "flesh" to fill out and give grace to a subject.[43] On this interpretation, the middle of a play, as well as of an epic, is "filled in" with details, crowded with amplification. Now of course the critics realized that the drama, without the extension of the epic, had less room for filling in, and they also stipulated that these details be joined to the argument so as to appear to arise from it according to verisimilitude. But to describe a play as treating the action in summary form at the beginning and the end and filling in the middle with episodes is to give Aristotle's passage in Chapter XVII (his third sense) a most peculiar look. The critics' way of putting the matter suggests not a plot in which the main events have been expanded with the particulars of motivation and conflict, but a plot in which these main events are briefly treated and the parts between are filled in with all sorts of "episodical ornaments, such as descriptions, narrations, and other beauties which are not essential to the play." It suggests, in fact, a play like *Dr. Faustus,* in which the critical events—namely, Faustus' motivation, his decision, his inner conflict, and his damnation—are treated rather briefly, and the play is filled out to an acceptable length with the many episodes displaying his magic powers. The critics would certainly condemn these for being an intrusion into tragedy of the debasing matter of comedy, but would they reject them as destructive of the unity of action? One can indeed show the magic episodes to be joined to the argument so as to appear to arise from it according to verisimilitude. But they hardly appear to be the kind of filling in Aristotle was thinking of in his discussion of *Iphigeneia in Tauris.* With *Faustus* contrast *Macbeth,* which, in the songs of the witches, the prophetic pageant of kings, the narration of the murder of Macduff's family, has "episodical ornaments," certainly, yet ones which all serve the central tragic conception of the play.

The crux of the matter lies in what latitude would be allowed in the interpretation of "filled in" and "linked according to verisimilitude." When one thinks of the rhetorical training of the age, of the enthusiastic extension of "riempimenti" in epic and romance beyond anything suggested by Aristotle on the epic, and of the general taste for multiplicity and amplitude in art, one strongly doubts that these phrases were applied to the drama in quite their Aristotelian sense.

The effect of these modifications and extensions of the sense of "episode" is to narrow the interpretation of "the action" to the main outline of the story and to enlarge the sense of "episode" to include all the detail, whether extraneous or not. And the logical consequence of this interpretation is that far from constricting anyone's impulse to variety, it enlarges it. For if there is no restriction on the number of episodes, so long as they can be called episodes, not actions, and if these episodes need be there only to give delight, not to clarify the fable, then you may have as many episodes as the physical length of your play will allow you. To do the critics justice they do not actually push the logic of their position to this extremity in their discussions of the drama. But I think the paradox needs statement in order to correct the too easily formed conclusion that all is "unity" in the critics. Though they talk constantly of unity, their unrecognized assumptions are sometimes at variance with it.

FONDNESS FOR plentifulness of action expressed itself in a fondness for double plots and in a justification of these by the critics. They were helped by the example of Terence, the ancient comic dramatist they knew best and most admired. Minturno's interpretation of the unity of action held it so strictly to mean singleness of action that he always regarded one of the actions of Terence as *the* action, the other as an episode attached to it. This description fits *Andria* clearly, *Eunuchus* somewhat less certainly; but it requires some wrenching to be made to fit *Phormio, Heautontimorumenos,* and *Adelphi.*[44] Guarini and others saw that the double actions of Terence were so skilfully interrelated as to constitute no violation of the principle of organic structure, even if they could not be described precisely as one action of one person.[45] This perception gave these critics a chance to indulge their taste without an uncomfortable violation or distortion of the rules.

Castelvetro startlingly makes the outright claim that tragedies and comedies, unlike epics, should have two actions, not one, and that, indeed, all the well-ordered ones do.[46] He then adds that the second action is not always dependent on the first by probability or necessity and gives as examples the *Hercules Furens* of Euripides and of Seneca and the *Andria* of Terence. The killing of Lycus by Hercules in revenge of his attempt on Megara, Castelvetro says, has no connection with the madness of Hercules, brought on by Juno, which leads him to kill his wife and children. In *Andria,* the love of Charinus for Philumena has no connection with the love of Pamphilus for Glycerium. (This is not strictly true, for the happy outcome of Charinus' affair depends on the success of Pamphilus'—that is, Charinus obviously cannot marry Philumena if Pamphilus is forced to marry her himself; but it is true that there is no reverse dependence of Pamphilus' affair on Charinus'. Castelvetro recognizes that the episode constitutes, therefore, no genuine complication.) The implication of

these illustrations is not clear, since he does not say whether he regards these plays as well-ordered or not. A few pages further on,[47]
however, he assumes interrelation of the actions to be necessary when
he says that the restricted time and place of the stage require either
one action or two actions which by dependence can be reputed one.
This point of Castelvetro's about double action in the drama is worth
emphasis, since we usually hear only about his insistence on the
unities, not about his insistence on variety and complication. Scaliger,
likewise, another of the contributors to the doctrine of the unities,
likes a play as varied and manifold as possible, as well as concise.
The illustration he gives is *Hecuba,* a loose play of two independent
actions.[48]

We have seen how Della Porta, Giraldi, Castelvetro, Guarini, and
Beni all praised intricate action skilfully manipulated. The critics
were quite in line with the actual practice of Italian comedy, which
followed the general pattern of Roman comedy, but further multiplied its complications and intrigues. In the light of all this, we can
be assured, I think, that the variety of action of Elizabethan drama
would not have disqualified it for critical approval provided the
threads of action were skilfully knotted and untied. Diffuseness,
failure of direction and emphasis, and lack of coherence were the
weaknesses of that drama, not variety in itself. The variety might
be, and sometimes was, its strength. As I have emphasized before,
Jonson's great comedies, well organized as they may be, are truly of
the Renaissance both in number of lines of action complexly interwoven and disentangled and in general richness of detail—in character, in language, in observation on things and people. Dryden praised
Jonson, significantly, for "the copiousness and the well-knitting of
the intrigues." [49] The pairing is interesting. Dryden recognized that
variety of action, if well ordered, gave English plays much of their
vitality.[50] Whether English dramatists learned anything about structural unity from the Italian critics, either directly or through Sidney,
Whetstone, and Jonson, is impossible to say. The important thing,
as usual, in assessment of the critics, is to observe how their distortions of Aristotle give us keys to contemporary taste. Whatever the
degree of critical influence, English dramatists must have worked out
their problems empirically in a popular theater and have been in
part governed by its audience and its physical conditions. These conditions of the theater must have been especially important in deter-

mining the handling of place and time, and to these, in their relation
to our problem of unity of action, we now turn.

Place, Time, and Action: Stage Practice

It is customary to say that had Sidney lived to see the drama in its
heyday he would not have been so severe as he was about 1583 in
his strictures against its naïve plotting, its violation of the unities of
time and place, its mingling of merriment and sadness. We cannot
be sure. For Sidney, however much he overlaid it with copiousness
of matter and style, had a strong sense of form, as Professor Myrick
has convincingly demonstrated. What would he have said of Tamburlaine's bloody but morally uncomplicated progress through kingdoms and years to the catastrophe of mere death? What would he
have said of the dragging attempts of Alice and Mosby to kill Arden,
taken with scarcely any selection from Holinshed's account of the
actual murder? Or, if these examples seem too early or too crude, take
some of the acknowledged best among the later plays: *The Duchess
of Malfi, The Revenger's Tragedy, Women Beware Women, The
Changeling,* or *The Winter's Tale.* In the handling of the birth of the
children and of the lapse of time, Webster is utterly careless of plausibility; in the tale of revenge within revenge, Tourneur has too many
dispersed climaxes for the play to have a sharp center; in silly and
only fortuitously connected comic subplots, Middleton, with or without the help of Rowley, dilutes the intensity of his tragic main plots.
Shakespeare's leap of sixteen years between two acts and from one
country to another breaks his play into parts which require a *tour de
force,* albeit a brilliant one, to bring together again.

By the terms in which he puts it, we can see that Sidney's merry
scorn of plays in which Asia is of the one side and Afric is of the
other, and in which lovers beget a child who by the play's end is ready
to get another,[51] is more than mere disapproval of the unconcern for
formal conventions, though it is of course that too. It is recognition
of the general looseness of structure of which the neglect of time
and place is often symptomatic. Adhering to an arbitrary rule of action within one city and within one day is not in itself important, but
paying some attention to time and place, if only to make a deliberate
decision to leave them indeterminate for a special effect (as in *King*

Lear), and coming to whatever terms with them a unified action requires, *is* important, for they are both physical conditions of the
dramatic medium. The critics in their formulation of the unities of
time and place may only have been driven by the academic logic of
consistency, but it is possible that they were groping for some principle that would express such a concomitant relationship between action, time, and place as I have stated, and they mistakenly found it in
a formal prescription which they took to be classical.

Castelvetro illuminates the problem for us by standing it on its
head. To say that action has to be unified only because of the limitations the stage imposes on place and time seems to be putting first
things last.[52] But if we modify the statement to say that a stage which
imposes a strict limitation on time and place makes the achievement
of unity of action, not necessary, but distinctly easier, there is some
truth in it. And if we take the mental leap Castelvetro gives no indication of taking, and suppose a stage that by tradition allows us as
much freedom in place and time as our imaginations are capable of,[53]
then we may make a proposition the converse of his: namely, that
such a stage predisposes the action to multiplicity. We can at least say
that it is much harder to achieve unity and economy of action when
the stage itself imposes no control.

It is usually said that the narrative romantic tradition of English
drama forced a free handling of place and time.[54] That is doubtless
true; but the relation must have been one of mutual reaction rather
than of pressure only in one direction. For the tradition of freedom
in place and time, inherent in medieval methods of staging, helped
produce a physical stage in Shakespearean England which perpetu-
ated the same possibility of freedom as in medieval drama. That
being so, imposition of the severe limitations on place and time of
the renaissance-Roman stage might well have seemed an unnecessary
sacrifice of the opportunities the stage provided. Just as romantic
story asked for a loose treatment of time and place, so, conversely,
freedom from temporal and spatial restriction in staging meant no
imposition of limits on the choice of romantic story. The process must
inevitably have been circular.

What a classical restriction imposed on the Elizabethan stage
would have meant we may imagine by an analogy drawn from our
own times. In the early days of the talking films, when the problem
of adapting dialogue to the scenically fragmentary character of the

moving picture had not been solved, the easiest thing to do was to film stage plays, and they brought with them a constriction that seemed very strange, and was indeed a loss of the special potentiality of scenic range and variety the moving picture has. The films have now pretty generally returned to their earlier freedom of place and time, and with it to a relatively looser structure than characterizes modern stage plays, unobservant of the unities in a strict sense as even they are.

Just as Castelvetro thought of the unity of action as consequent on the unities of time and place, so Beni thought of the artificial order of classical plays as consequent on Aristotle's restriction of time.[55] In arguing against the artificial order for the epic, he says that distortion of the natural order of events is allowed comic and tragic actions, because they are bound to a single revolution of the sun, but such distortion is not tolerable with the fullness of time allowed an epic action. Again, the converse of his proposition, in so far as it applies to the drama, namely that the free convention of the Elizabethan stage with respect to time imposes no necessity for artificial order, illuminates for us English stage practice. Certainly the natural order established itself so firmly that it was not to be rooted out. And it predisposed the drama to looseness. Even when English drama was successful in achieving unity of action, it nearly always followed the chronological order of events which the possibilities of the stage allowed. Jonson is a good example to cite as proof of the weight of stage tradition. One might expect him, as a good Horatian, to have adopted the artificial order and to have kept to the severe rule of time. He did not. Although he did not make his actions jump continents or consume Odyssean numbers of years, he did follow the principle of natural order and did make use of a succession of scenes in various places. In *Sejanus* the action follows the hero from his first emergence as a power in Rome until his death an indefinite length of time later; in the sources this was a period of about eleven years. In tragedy, Jonson, as well as others of his contemporaries, achieved unity without the aid in definition and selection the artificial order gives.

A CONSIDERATION of the differences in theatrical history in Italy, France, and England will show, I think, the intimate connection between the type of stage and the relative speed with which the unities were adopted as an operating rule. In England a flexible stage and loose structure both lasted longer than on the continent. It will be necessary first to review briefly the three fundamental principles of staging available to the Renaissance.[56] We shall keep in mind for each principle its implications with respect to place and time, hence to the handling of the action.

The first was the principle of *décor simultané*. When the place of performance was stationary, the religious drama had used a "multiple" stage. A number of places were present to the spectator's eye at once in the form of structures variously called *domus, loca, sedes, luoghi deputati,* "mansions," or "houses," arranged along the sides of a rectangle in a cathedral or public square; in a circle, as in the Cornish "rounds"; or in a line, as on a raised platform seen from the front.[57] In this principle of *décor simultané,* whether the actor is at a given place from the start or comes to it during the action, he localizes a place by acting or speaking at it. If all the places of the drama are equally present to the spectator at once, localization is merely a matter of focus. With this conception of place, the conception of time is intimately connected. For if a man may move from Jerusalem to Rome in a moment, so may he move from one day to the next, or from year to year; movement from place to place may bring a definite lapse of time into focus just as it brings a particular place. The *platea* or open "place" in front of or between the mansions is neutral ground, which may either remain unidentified or be whatever place it needs to be at the moment; it is also neutral with respect to time, for the imaginary duration in traversing it from place to place may either be specified or left indeterminate. The fixed stage set with stations was the common method of the religious drama in France and Italy. In England at least one cycle, the so-called *Ludus Coventriae,* was evidently so presented.[58] We may assume that the miracle plays, or plays based on saints' lives, were staged in some such way. Although the absence of texts leaves us without much detailed information, enough records of performances and payments remain for us to infer that structures and machines were freely used.[59] The Digby *Mary Magdalene* calls for a number of stations, which may have been arranged in a circle. A diagram of staging accompanying *The Castle of Perseverance,* with stations so arranged,[60] shows that a morality play, likewise, was sometimes planned for a performance more elaborate than the bare platform stage often posited for school or hall.

The second principle was that of *décor successif.* The English mystery cycles were commonly performed on "pageants," or wagons, drawn in turn into a square or market-place. At first sight, this would seem to mean a single set scene, hence a rigidly limited place, for at least each play; variation would come only with the next play. Actually, however, the simultaneous principle was frequently combined with the successive one. Sometimes action on the two stories of the pageant is indicated, as in the Norwich *Creation,*[61] where the upper stage is Eden, the lower, Earth outside it; sometimes two or even three stations are called for on one level: e.g., the Burning Bush, a throne for Pharaoh, the Red Sea in the Towneley *Pharaoh;* an apple tree, Hell-mouth, the Sepulchre in the Cappers' Resurrection pageant at Coventry.[62] The principle of the unlocalized *platea* also appears: many plays which seem to have a good many scenes, with a good deal of coming and going, as in the Chester *Nativity,* or in the Coventry Shearmen and Taylors' Nativity group of plays, actually reveal only one or two specific places calling for a structure, such as a manger, on the pageant; the rest of the action—the wise men stopping in their journey at the sight of the star or talking with Herod, Herod seeking learned advice from his doctors, his soldiers slaughtering the innocents—is essentially unlocalized. The pageants, then, generally combined the principles of succession and simultaneity; they were often themselves multiple stages, though of a limited sort.

The third principle was that embodied in the single and fixed place of the Roman stage. One of the great landmarks of the Renaissance is the publication in 1486 of Vitruvius' *De architectura.* The Vitruvian description of the Roman stage [63] was interpreted in two quite different ways scenically, but each interpretation embodies the same principle of fixed place.

One interpretation, worked out in designs by Serlio [64] and enormously influential, was the stage with perspective scenery, the nearer portions built as practicable two-sided houses of lath and plaster, the farther painted in perspective on a back cloth. The decorum of the three several types of play—tragedy, comedy, and satyric play—required a stock set appropriate to each type. The tragic represented a street of palaces and magnificent buildings:

Houses for tragedies must be made for great personages, for that actions of love, strange adventures, and cruel murthers (as you read in ancient and modern tragedies) happen always in the houses of great lords, dukes, princes, and kings. Wherefore in such cases you must have none but stately houses. . . .

The comic scene represented a street of citizens' houses, and

specially there must not want a brothel or bawdy house, and a great inn, and a church; such things as are of necessity to be therein.[65]

The satyric scene was a woodland scene with rustic cottages. The action of a Terentian comedy or a Senecan tragedy went on, therefore, at the house doors or in the street between the houses. Shift of place was impossible and time naturally tended to be continuous or nearly so. Lapse of time of any length was possible only between scenes, when the characters were off the stage, not while they were in view, as on the multiple stage, walking from one place to another. Just as the place of the action was restricted to the visible setting, so the imagined time of the action during a scene tended to be restricted to the actual elapsed time of the dialogue. And the return of each scene to the same place tended to hold in the imagined time between scenes to the brief periods necessary for short errands to different parts of the same town.

The other and truer interpretation of the Vitruvian stage, that embodied by Palladio and Scamozzi in the Teatro Olimpico in Vicenza,[66] was of a fixed architectural façade with three doors opening on the stage, through each of which might be seen a set perspective view. As with the Serlian stage, the conception was of an unchanging place and fairly continuous action. Italian stage designers also worked out in the later Renaissance elaborate techniques for changes of scene, but these were mainly used for the *intermedii* between acts.[67]

THE ITALIANS recovered—figuratively, at least—classical drama and Vitruvius at the same time, so that imitation of the ancient drama and the ancient stage went hand in hand. Plays written for either the Serlian or the Palladian types of stage, as were Italian academic plays, naturally followed these rigid conventions. Even if there were no other reasons, this is a good one why the theory of the unities should have been developed in Italy.

In France, the triumph of the unities in the late seventeenth century as a regular principle of composition came only after the Roman principle of staging had, not set aside, but gradually absorbed and restricted, the old multiple stage of the religious drama. The multiple stage easily lent itself to such conversion and one may see it happening. Some of the illustrations in early editions of Terence, for instance, show how the classical stage was thought of in terms of the stations or mansions of the medieval stage. In the Lyons *Terence* of 1493, each of the plays is illustrated by a series of woodcuts showing a structure with four or five curtained rooms or stalls, like confessionals, next each other; each is the "house" of the principal character, for the name is given above each entrance.[68] The Serlian stage was really an adaptation of the houses of the medieval stage to the classical notion of a fixed place. In France, in mid-sixteenth century, Passion plays were still using the *décor simultané* on a large scale, even in indoor theaters. Hardy and Corneille, in the Hôtel de Bourgogne, inherited the stage of the Confrérie de la Passion, that is, a stage habitually set with fixed stations. As the designs of Mahelot for the mid-seventeenth century reveal, plays at the Hôtel de Bourgogne continued to use the stations, though they were restricted in range and number.[69] A design for Hardy's *Clidament* is a multiple stage with three stations, or "compartments," as they came to be called: an open central room flanked by a curtained doorway on one side and a ship on the other. A setting for *Pandoste,* a play on the same theme as *The Winter's Tale,* has four compartments: the Palace of Epirus across the rear, a prison to the right, the Temple of Delphi and a painted sea to the left. The *Cid* (1637) must have had similar compartments, but it also followed the successive principle in making the whole stage, unchanged, stand for different places in different scenes: the specific location of one of the compartments, that is, such as the house of Chimène, evidently extended itself to the open stage. Corneille claimed he was adhering to the unity of place by having all his scenes at least within the walls of Seville. But in making a set scene represent a succession of different places, first the house of Chimène, next the apartment of the Infanta, then a public place, then the apartment of the king, he laid himself open to legitimate criticism on the grounds of lack of clarity.[70] The three principles of simultaneous, successive, and fixed scenes meet in this play, not without confusion. French staging was moving towards the single tableau of Racine.

WE CAN SEE ON the English academic and court stages of the sixteenth century the same hesitation as in seventeenth-century France between the medieval multiple stage, with its numerous stations having as wide a suggestive range as need be, and the renaissance-classic stage, with its few houses sharply restricted to a literally representational range. The setting for *Campaspe* (1580–84) has a classical narrowness. It calls for the studio of Apelles, open so that some action may go on inside it, the tub of Diogenes, and the portico of Alexander's palace. Time is clearly meant to be restricted also. *Endymion* (ca. 1588), on the other hand, calls for a multiple stage of stations imaginatively far apart—ranging from Cynthia's palace and Endymion's lunary bank near by to the castle in the desert where Tellus is imprisoned and the fountain that Eumenides apparently takes twenty years to find, and another twenty to return from.[71] Here the extension of place carries with it extension of time. Professor Chambers speaks of the court stage as breaking down its principle of renaissance staging under the pressure of romantic taste cultivated in the public theaters; he regards the multiple place and time of *Endymion,* that is, as a breakdown of the academic principle embodied in the setting of *Campaspe.*[72] He says the University Wits widened the "conception of locality to a city and its environs instead of a street," and then romantic narrative forced them to make the stage "foreshorten leagues or cross the ocean." But this type of foreshortening is what romantic drama had always required. It may be true that the academic stage followed first the renaissance-classical principle of staging and then began to follow the medieval principle, but in so doing it was hardly *widening* a conception of locality; it was simply reverting to an older tradition to which in the meantime the newer Serlian conception had been adapting itself. The miracle plays for which Professor Manly has found records of performance down to 1584 must almost certainly have been staged on the old principle.[73] Even on the academic stage, the two principles seem to go along pretty much side by side; the multiple setting is now more medieval in its range, now more classical. The order just of Lyly's plays shows this fluctuation. *Campaspe* (1580–84), very early, and *Mother Bombie,* very late (1587–90), are the two that are classically restricted in place. (But the setting of *Campaspe,* as indicated above, is also perfectly traditional and medieval.) The others in between and *Midas,* probably latest of all (1589–90), show varying degrees of freedom and foreshortening.

Some effect of the renaissance stage was felt, almost certainly, on the Elizabethan public stage. If Professor Campbell and Professor Nicoll are right, the Globe may owe as much to the renaissance-classical theater as to the innyard.[74] That is, in placing as a background to his projecting stage a *frons scaenae,* with a prominent central entrance and flanking doors, Burbage may have been imitating the fixed Palladian façade. Nevertheless, with its possibilities of both localized and unlocalized action, of rapid shifts from inner stage to outer, of action both upstage and downstage and on several levels at once, the Elizabethan public stage kept the freedom of the medieval stage and at the same time added to its richness. Although the Elizabethan stage followed chiefly the principle of successive scenes, probably in the interests of verisimilitude and variety, it did not lose the fluidity of the multiple stage. For not only could succession be quickly managed; simultaneity was also possible. In plays such as *George-a-Greene, Arden of Feversham, Stukeley,* and *Faustus,* all plays of the early nineties, there are still traces of that medieval ease with which an actor traversed miles in plain sight and in a minute or two. The most striking use of simultaneity, however, is in Shakespeare's *Richard III.* By setting up the opposing tents of Richard and of Richmond on the two sides of the stage, and by making the ghosts of Richard's victims appear simultaneously to both, Shakespeare could give visible dramatic contrast to the characters and fortunes of the falling villain and the rising hero.

On that stage, deliberately to retreat from such flexibility to the rigidity of the renaissance fixed setting would have been indeed a strange sacrifice. There is nothing at all to wonder at in the freedom with which Elizabethan and Jacobean dramatists continued to treat place and time and even action. Moreover, with the scenic principle dominantly successive, the chronological order in the action is the normal one to expect.

The unities did not win out completely in any country, even in the neoclassic period. Ingenious devices for changes of scene were worked out for masques, *intermedii,* and operas, and they came to be freely used for "machine" plays, in which novelty of spectacle made the chief appeal.[75] And in the end, the principle of successive scenery, allowing more freedom of place than on the renaissance-Roman stage, but less than on the medieval multiple stage, became the normal thing for plays generally; it is the type that we have inherited.

Elizabethan Solutions to the Unity of Action

To achieve an organic structural form under such temptations to freedom as a fondness for romantic story prompted and as a flexible stage urged cannot have been easy, and many dramatists never did achieve it fully. When they did, it was never, except in rather early academic attempts, by mere imitation of classical or continental drama. They got it in several ways.

One way, which showed itself early, in chronicle play and tragedy, was in the domination of a single striking figure, like Tamburlaine, Selimus, Richard III, or Alphonsus. The danger here, of course, was that the unity would be only of the hero, and not of the action, that many of the events of the plot would stand together in the accidental relationship of biographical chronology rather than in the necessary relationship of cause and effect. Some means of bringing all events together in at least a loose connection lay in the Mirror theme: the cyclic conception of the rise and fall of a great man at the hands of Fortune or of Providence. This is the unity the Queen Elinor story has in the midst of the episodic variety of Peele's *Edward I,* and that the Jane Shore story has in the less confused but still disunified matrix of action in Heywood's *Edward IV.* The Margaret-and-Suffolk and Margaret-and-Clifford episodes of the *Henry VI* sequence emerge as minor unified actions within the chronological episodic whole. The rise-and-fall pattern takes over and successfully unifies the central action in *Richard III, Richard II,* and *Edward II;* it becomes, with greater moral complication, one of the basic patterns of Shakespearean tragedy—of *Julius Caesar, King Lear, Macbeth, Antony and Cleopatra,* and *Coriolanus.* But "greater moral complication" is the crucial proviso. The theme of itself offers no great resistance to the serially episodic construction of a plot. *Tamburlaine* is unified in theme, but not in Aristotle's sense of complex action. These are problems calling for further discussion in the next chapter.

Another and more successful way in which Elizabethan dramatists tried for unity of action was through concentration on some one action, such as, in tragedy, a crime and its avenging, or, in comedy, a troubled love affair and its successful outcome. This might be called a thematic unity as against the biographical unity of the first type. Favorite unifying themes in tragedy were revenge, the danger of political disunity, illicit or star-crossed love; in comedy, the difficulties in the way of a love affair because of the rivalry of other suitors, the calumny of the heroine, the lack of fortune, or the opposition of parents.

For this type of unification in tragedy, the tradition of the morality play was important, with its focus on a problem in which moral choice had to be made—a choice, moreover, which was conceived of in terms of a psychological conflict between the reason and the passions.[76] *Faustus,* compared with *Tamburlaine,* is a great illustration of the superior dramatic possibilities of this method of organizing events in a nexus of choice and its consequences. *Edward II* combines the two methods, biographical and thematic. And Shakespeare's tragedies in the Mirror tradition, like *Julius Caesar, Macbeth,* and *Coriolanus,* are not episodic, because Shakespeare conceives of rise and fall not merely as a succession of fortunate and unfortunate events, but as a pattern of complication and solution centered in a fatal choice.

The only way, then, to secure this strictly Aristotelian unity, whatever the theme, was to learn how to complicate and untie the action, to learn, that is, the problem of necessary progression from beginning to middle to end.[77] This is the problem to be discussed in the next chapter. It is enough to include here a reminder of the great usefulness in this respect of New Comedy and of the tradition of story-telling which stemmed from similar sources. The intrigue technique affected tragedy as well as comedy, as plays like *The Spanish Tragedy* and its successors show. The technique was especially helpful in tying in intricate knots the several actions Elizabethan dramatists were fond of. *Titus Andronicus* and *The Revenger's Tragedy* are good examples.

For the problem was not merely to learn to unify the episodes in a single story; it was also to learn to put several stories together. The dramatists did not often achieve that harmony described by Dryden in his figure of the main plot as the *primum mobile* whirling about the underplots like the orbs of the fixed stars and the planets, each with its own motion, yet each moving as part of the whole design:

That similitude expresses much of the English stage; for if contrary motions may be found in nature to agree, if a planet can go east and west at the same time—one way by virtue of his own motion, the other by the force of the first mover—it will not be difficult to imagine how the underplot, which is only different, not contrary to the great design, may naturally be conducted along with it.[78]

The several actions, as we know, were more commonly allowed to run parallel courses than made to work together; for example, in *A Woman Killed,* where the rivalry of Acton and Mountford, without essential connection to the Frankford story, follows even a quite different time scheme from the main plot. The separate actions might sometimes be caught together only at the end, as in *The Dutch Courtesan,* where Malheureux and Mulligrub are simultaneously saved from the gallows. Lisideius, in Dryden's *Essay,* justly remarked of such plays that

the one half of our actors are not known to the other. They keep their distances as if they were Montagues and Capulets, and seldom begin an acquaintance till the last scene of the fifth act, when they are all to meet upon the stage.[79]

BUT IN SPITE of a not infrequent failure to bring their different actions together in a unified piece of plotting, Elizabethan dramatists often achieved a kind of unity which is one of feeling or tone rather than of structure. This may be called a qualitative unity.[80] They got it by throwing the different actions into some relation of reinforcing, complementary, or contrasting tones: for example, in repeating the same theme in different keys, as in the three love stories in *The Insatiate Countess;* [81] in making the comic action parody the serious one, as Sir Tophas' burlesque romance does the sentimental ones, in Lyly's *Endymion.* Or they got it by poetic means of controlling feeling— through setting, iterative imagery, lyrical devices, prosodic variation. Of course in the best plays, this kind of unity is made not a substitute for the involvement of several actions, but a reinforcement of it, as in *Twelfth Night* or *Lear.* Some of these qualitative means I wish to examine in more detail.

In unifying different actions, the method of associating parody, humor, and satire with serious subjects is an old one, common in medieval life, and we need not trace it. It is interesting to mark its appearance, however, in the only early secular romantic play we have, *Fulgens and Lucres*.[82] In that, the servants parody the earnestness in love of their masters. It is the line followed by Lyly, Peele, and Shakespeare. One of the reasons why Elizabethan romantic drama is never insipid is that it is usually well salted with laughter at the expense of its lovers and its aspiring courtiers. The method is Shakespeare's *par excellence,* from the Syracusan Dromio's *contretemps* with the gross kitchen wench and Titania's dalliance with the long-eared Bottom, to Stephano and Trinculo's aiding and abetting of Caliban in rebellion against Prospero.

Humor with a more sharply satiric edge complements the romantic plots of Chapman, Marston, and Middleton. The achievement here of qualitative unity is more difficult than in Shakespearean romantic comedy. There, where sympathy is pervasive, both the love-making and the laughter are fun. But disgust or sneers or cynical laughter have no common denominator with tenderness. The result is apt to be that any kind of romantic sentiment is felt to be out of place. This is well illustrated in Middleton's *Family of Love,* where the romantic dialogue of the young lovers, in contrast with the talk of the satirically handled members of the "family," is stiffly unconvincing. Even in the much superior *Malcontent,* the affairs of the hero in his "true" role as the high-minded Altofront hardly seem of a piece with him in his much more vital disguise as the scheming, scurrilous court-critic, Malevole. Satiric comedy most nearly achieves qualitative unity when the satire so completely takes over the play that the romance remains nothing but a neutral frame on which to hang a plot, as in Middleton's more successful comedies, like *A Chaste Maid* or *A Trick to Catch the Old One.* If an unblended mingling of tones disturbs us less in comedy than in tragedy, it may be because we are more willing, in comedy, to take a little of everything for good measure. "Who is offended, let him not go to see comedies!" [83]

There is little Elizabethan tragedy that is unrelieved or single in tone. We have seen how the critics adjusted their rigid notions of tragedy and comedy to the tastes of the time by developing a theory of tragi-comedy. This theory allowed the mixture of thrills of fear, of pathos, of sentimental satisfaction at a happy ending, even of a little comic satire, but hardly the mixture of horror and laughter. Following medieval tradition, however, few Elizabethan dramatists appear to have been bothered by this juxtaposition. One of their great achievements was in learning to put comedy at the service of tragedy. And I do not know where they learned it except through intuitive perception and experience. Some never tried very hard. From *Cambises* to *The Changeling* there are plays in which the association of tragic and comic action is casual and irresponsible. A theory of comic relief will not save such plays as *Locrine* (ca. 1591), or Heywood's *Rape of Lucrece* (ca. 1606). But many tragedies give evidence of serious artistic purpose in the way the comic elements are handled. The most common method of bringing comic relief into relation with the tragic action is through satire on the court, nearly always the scene of action in romantic tragedy. This is the Jacobean method—Chapman's, Jonson's, Marston's, Middleton's, Beaumont and Fletcher's. In Webster the "relief" is too somber to be called comic at all. Marston's use of it is extremely interesting, for his pervasive satire qualifies both the tragic and the comic parts of his plots. I have discussed this characteristic of *The Insatiate Countess* in Chapter VIII. In tragedy, as in romantic comedy, it is Shakespeare who most successfully achieves a varied harmony of tones. The bad taste of the distressing comic relief in *Romeo and Juliet* is succeeded by Falstaff's successfully ironic, yet not destructive, parody on Hotspur's theme of honor. In *Hamlet* and *Lear* the comedy is thematically related to the tragic action; though the comedy means a relief of tension, it is always something more besides—an ironic commentary, an insight into character, a set of subtle variations on the theme of death or of man's pride. These plays are triumphs of qualitative form.

The use of setting to bring a varied action together in feeling is no doubt part of the Elizabethan romantic heritage. I do not mean the physical stage setting as such, although that might be contributory, but the suggestions of place in the dialogue. Such feeling may come not only from descriptions of place, but also from details of local color, allusions to common associations, and poetic suggestions. Lyly gives few suggestions in his dialogue of the atmosphere of a particular place, partly, perhaps, because he does not need to. Place is visibly defined by the "houses" where the action takes place. But in *Galathea* and *The Woman in the Moon,* faintly, and in *Love's Metamorphosis,* more strongly, he does contrive in the dialogue to give a sense of the over-all woodland-pastoral background. Peele, in *The Old Wives' Tale*, with the same kind of multiple stage, uses setting to order and control the varied action. In *The Arraignment of Paris* the setting is, much more than in Lyly's mythological pastorals, made a poetic means to achieve feeling. *George-a-Greene, Friar Bacon*, and *The Two Angry Women of Abingdon* have a strong feeling of their country or village settings, just as so many Jacobean comedies, like *Eastward Ho, The Roaring Girl, A Chaste Maid in Cheapside*, or *Bartholomew Fair*, are steeped in the atmosphere of London. In some of the great plays of the period, setting becomes a means both of organizing action and of unifying emotional tone. Shakespeare is preëminent in this structural use of setting: he discovered it in *A Midsummer Night's Dream* and *Romeo and Juliet* and used it thereafter in various ways to the end of his life: in the forthright way of local color in *The Merry Wives;* more poetically in the romantic comedies of *The Merchant of Venice, As You Like It*, and *Twelfth Night;* with profound tragic significance in *Othello, Lear*, and *Macbeth;* and with very great subtlety in the union of theme and mood in *Antony and Cleopatra* and the late romances, *The Winter's Tale* and *The Tempest* especially. But Jonson's *Bartholomew Fair* is another masterpiece in this structural use of setting. The Fair is not just a place where people are conventionally assembled for action, as before the city houses in a Serlian setting. It is both a place and an idea. It provides an important part of the motivation of the action and the means of its complication and solution. And it is the visible symbol of the themes of human sensuality and folly on which variations are played throughout the comedy.

A detailed consideration of the stylistic means, through syntax, diction, figure, imagery, and prosody, of achieving unity out of great diversity is outside the scope of this book. They can be given only a word of comment here. In this field, Shakespeare is once more the master. He learned how to relate his songs in theme or tone to the action of his plays, how to give a play its own peculiar emotional coloring with the dominant imagery, how to weave a pattern of echoes and contrasts in words and images which everywhere works with the action, how to vary verse and prose not merely with the rank and nature of the characters, according to the rules of decorum, but also with changes in attitude, in emotional tension, in the tone desired for the scene. One of Shakespeare's greatest architectonic gifts was in his mastery of various means of qualitative form. Other dramatists are apt to be either more rigid in their applications of poetic means (as in Dekker's adherence to rule in the assignment of verse and prose in *The Shoemaker's Holiday*) or more uncertain (as in Webster's and Middleton's frequent haltings between prose and verse for no apparent reason). Nevertheless, the greater Elizabethan and Jacobean dramatists—especially Marlowe, Jonson, Chapman, and Webster—show considerable command of these stylistic means to achieve qualitative unity. They all deserve closer study than they have had. Jonson, particularly, though less spectacular than Shakespeare because he deals less in contrasts, within his narrower range manipulates language and meter with complete assurance.[84]

UNITY FOR THE Elizabethans, then, was hard to come by. For few were willing to sacrifice any variety to get it. In consequence, when it was achieved, it was a kind of multiple unity of many parts. It was bustling, lively, and generous. The motto seems to have been never to throw anything away that could possibly be tucked in somewhere. One of the reasons for Shakespeare's superiority to his fellows was that he had a genius for finding a way to bring all this variety into harmonious relationship.

11 The Fable: Complication and Unraveling

IF THEN the parts are managed so regularly that the beauty of the whole be kept entire and that the variety become not a perplexed and confused mass of accidents, you will find it infinitely pleasing to be led in a labyrinth of design where you will see some of your way before you, yet discern not the end till you arrive at it. And that all this is practicable I can produce for examples many of our English plays, as *The Maid's Tragedy*, *The Alchemist*, *The Silent Woman*.

— NEANDER, IN DRYDEN'S *Essay of Dramatic Poesy* [1]

Experiments in Plotting

UNITY OF ACTION in Aristotle's sense also implies coherence of action. When he said that the plot should represent one action, and that a whole, he meant what might be called a moral nexus of events, progressing in a coherent structure of cause and effect from beginning to middle to end.

In the conversion of romantic narrative into drama, the achievement of such organic structure cannot have been easy for Elizabethan dramatists. The persistence of episodic structure testifies to this difficulty. Episodic structure is essentially serial, a stringing together of events in mere temporal succession; each complication is solved as it arises, and a new one succeeds it. This may well have been the pattern of most early plays based on the deeds of a hero, whether a saint or a secular figure, just as it was the pattern of so many later chronicle plays like *The Famous Victories of Henry the Fifth*, biographical plays like *Cromwell*, and conqueror plays like *Tamburlaine*. Some of the early plays more organically put together, like Thomas Garter's *Susanna* (1568–69 or earlier) or R. B.'s *Appius and Virginia* (ca. 1567–68), are perhaps so because the story chosen was well organized to begin with.[2] Susanna's story, for instance, moves just as it does in the Apocrypha from a beginning through a complicated middle to a solution: the attempt of the elders, stirred by her beauty, to seduce her, is met by her refusal; this provokes their attempt to traduce her, and this in turn brings about near catastrophe, which is avoided by the timely appearance of Daniel to vindicate her innocence and turn the tables on her accusers. The solution here does not come as the result of the inevitable logic of events; nevertheless, it is coherent with the central idea of the play, evident in the talk of the abstract moral figures, that God champions the innocent who trust in him. *Appius and Virginia,* a story from Livy familiar in Chaucer's *Physician's Tale,* has a more perfectly logical structure: the lust of Appius for Virginia, countered by her chastity, initiates his attempt to get possession of her through a legal fiction; her father's counter-attempt to block his action produces an impasse which is solved by a tragic denouement—the father's stabbing of his daughter to prevent her disgrace and Appius' suicide in despair of his wickedness. Stories like these were ready-made. In being converted into drama, they were overlaid with sententiousness, enlivened with the usual unrelated comic episodes, and equipped with motivating machinery in the way of morality figures (True Report, Ill Report the Vice, Voluptas and Sensualitas the wicked judges, in *Susanna;* Haphazard the Vice, Justice, Conscience, Rumour, Memory, and Reward in *Appius and Virginia*). The effect of all this is to blur the emphasis on the stories proper. The author of *Appius and Virginia,* besides, follows the simpler version of Chaucer rather than Livy's more involved and dramatic original.[3] In Chaucer and the interlude, there is no complicating resistance to Appius of a lover of Virginia, no appeal to his army by Virginius, no civil disorder or political issue. But the author of the interlude stands up badly, too, against Chaucer, as does Garter against the Apocrypha. Even so, the stories themselves are so good that they cannot be altogether spoiled; they do hold the plays together in a coherent pattern.

The suspicion that the source material is often the chief determinant of whether or not a play is well organized is borne out by an examination of later plays. If the story chosen is tightly knit then the play is apt to be—though the introduction of a secondary plot interlaced through the main one (as in *The Changeling* or *The English*

Traveller) may dilute the effect of the principal story. If the source is diffuse, then the play very often is. Contrast different plays by the same author—for instance Peele's rather shapeless *Edward I* or *David and Bethsabe,* both from chronicle sources (if *2 Samuel* may be counted as chronicle), with his orderly *Arraignment of Paris,* based on a familiar mythical tale having few characters and centered about an essentially dramatic problem.[4] The difference is even well illustrated by Shakespeare's *Antony and Cleopatra* and *Coriolanus,* both of which strongly reflect their sources in Plutarch, the one extensive and loose, the other intensive and tight. Shakespeare's noteworthy achievement of coherence in *Antony and Cleopatra* was made not by the exclusion or even reshaping of much of his source material, but by the exploitation of character and of setting to emphasize dramatic conflict and by the use of various poetic devices to secure the harmonious repetition and contrast of emotional tones.

Plays based on *novelle* are, naturally enough, apt to be better organized than plays based on chronicles or similar material. If Shakespeare first wrote a version of *Romeo and Juliet* as early as 1591, the superiority of its structure to that of the *Henry VI* plays may be partly attributed to the differences in source. All the sentimental, moral, and rhetorical padding of Bandello, Boaistuau, and Brooke could not obscure the strong lines of the old Da Porto story. Most important, the handling of the Romeo and Juliet story may have helped teach Shakespeare lessons of plot construction for later use,[5] such things as the clear joining of an issue, the moving of action towards an ironic reversal, the inevitability of catastrophe in the logic of events. The play satisfies the requirements of the critics that the conduct of the fable, especially of the *peripeteia,* should produce wonder, the wonder that arises when seeming accident brings about a reversal that is yet seen to be prepared for in the logical sequence of events.[6] Shakespeare marks this fatality of the apparent accident by Romeo's cry, when he has stabbed Tybalt: "O, I am Fortune's fool!" Although Shakespeare greatly intensifies the irony of the reversal by telescoping time and dovetailing events,[7] he is exploiting with brilliant insight the irony inherent in the original story. Holinshed naturally furnished nothing so clearly plotted. Although Shakespeare learned to build coherent plots from the chronicles, the variety of solutions he attempted suggests that he did not find the problem easy, and none of his English history plays except perhaps *1 Henry IV* is without some structural weakness; even *Richard III* and *Richard II* are not. Jonson's tragedies illustrate the difficulty a dramatist we are accustomed to think of as a master of structure had with the abundant material of history. Although the plots of both *Sejanus* and *Catiline* are built on a logical sequence of events, with a controlling design behind it, they are crowded with incidents and people from the sources and hence are lacking in strong enough emphasis on the main lines.[8]

The typical problem faced by an Elizabethan dramatist was the shaping into a two- or three-hour stage play of a narrative of some sort, whether historical or fictional, which began at the beginning and took events in order. The story might or might not be well plotted to start with; it might need pruning and organizing to reduce to size and order, it might need padding with incident to fill up the time. Actually, to put the problem in these terms is to oversimplify it; for generally the problem decreed by taste was not, as has been sufficiently emphasized, just the conversion of one story into a play, but the combining of two or three stories. How, if the source story or play did not itself teach them, did dramatists learn to build a coherent plot structure? We may admit at once that only a few ever did learn the lesson with any thoroughness. The tendency to organize events around several episodic centers, with the connections falling slack between them, curses such otherwise fine plays as those of Chapman, Tourneur, Webster, and Ford. Nevertheless, dramatists did learn something, even much, about plotting, and I propose to examine some of those means which gave Elizabethan drama its characteristic shapes.

WE CAN SEE the groping for structural cohesion even in early episodic plays. The simplest sort is given, of course, by the unity of the hero. Yet in a play like *Cambises* (before 1570) the various actions of the hero have no connection beyond their motivation in his tyranny. Twice the reproof, by someone in his court, of the cruel deed in one episode brings about the reprisal from him which constitutes the next. But this slight thread of connection does not make the succession of the larger episodes less accidental; any other order would do as well. There is an improvement on this structure even in the simple organization of *Tamburlaine,* for the episodes are at least links in a chain; Tamburlaine's successive conquests have a necessary order, controlled by geography as well as by time. Yet any complication in one episode is usually solved before the next one begins. It is only the assertiveness of Tamburlaine's personality and the rush of his poetry continually sounding in our ears that obscure for us the loose structure of the play.

Something rather more intricate is found in the much earlier *Clyomon and Clamydes* (ca. 1570), one of the few surviving plays based on the popular material of chivalric romances. Judging by allusions, plays on such subjects must have been common in the early days of the secular drama. It is interesting to compare *Clyomon and Clamydes* with *Common Conditions* (1576 or earlier) [9] to see how early dramatists met the problem of plotting stories from the romances. *Common Conditions* has a kind of intricacy in that one complication leads to another, but progression is wayward and digressive. The banishment from Arabia of Galiarbus, followed by his son and daughter in search of him, starts the play. But Galiarbus disappears inconspicuously and for good, the son disappears temporarily, and we are left with the affairs of Clarisia, the daughter, as the main interest. Her search for her father is forgotten and we see her smitten with love for one Lamphedon, suddenly introduced "out of Phrygia"; their true love now becomes the theme of the play. The disguised brother turns up momentarily as Nomides and falls in love with his sister, whom he fails to recognize. Nomides, in turn, is loved by Sabia, whose father, a Spanish doctor, is supposed to assist her in winning him. But after the introduction of the situation, we hear no more of these two, and Nomides himself drops out without finding out the identity of his sister. Other characters along the way who complicate the affairs of Clarisia and Lamphedon simply disappear. The chief agency of complication is the ambiguous "Common Conditions," who is sometimes the malicious Vice of the piece, sometimes the faithful servant of the heroine. The play is brought to an abrupt end, with no clarity of intention—whether the poison drunk by the faithful lovers is real or not we cannot be sure. Action in the play progresses tangentially; one thing leads to another, but old interests fall out without ever being developed or concluded. The end of the play has no relation to the beginning. No doubt "the most famous history of Galiarbus, Duke of Arabia," which, according to the title page, the play was taken from, brought the threads together, but the adapter of the story for the stage huddled things up very badly indeed.

The author of *Clyomon and Clamydes* does better. Here, likewise, one episode gives rise to another in a chain sequence, and new characters and motives are constantly introduced, but the end resolves the issue joined at the beginning. The parallel and opposing stories of the two knights are made the means of achieving such crude complication as there is; the ending of the antagonism between the two started at the beginning of the play enables them to combine to bring to a happy solution each other's love affair, which each has been pursuing independently. Sir Clyomon, Knight of the Golden Shield, son to the King of Denmark, and Sir Clamydes, the White Knight, son to the King of Swabia, are at enmity with one another because Clyomon does Clamydes out of his knighthood by slipping in at the ceremony and receiving the blow of the mace intended for the other; Clamydes is charged by his father to avenge his lost honor. Throughout most of the play the two knights are in search of one another to settle accounts in honorable combat. Suspense is sustained by an early meeting in which they agree to fight publicly before King Alexander in Macedon on the fifteenth day ensuing; by complications which prevent each one from keeping the appointed day; by rumors each hears of the other; and by a renewal of the search for each other. Each, of course, has a lady, and in seeking to win her has many independent adventures, including those of Clamydes with the wicked giant "Brian sance foy"; but these adventures lead to a meeting before Alexander in which each knight appears disguised as the champion of opposing sides in a quarrel over a title. The meeting in turn leads to a revelation of the hitherto undeclared identity of Sir Clyomon and therefore to a reconciliation, since Sir Clyomon is found to be none other than the brother of Sir Clamydes' lady. The final events, with Clyomon assisting Clamydes, take place in Denmark, where the giant is worsted, both love affairs are settled, and double nuptials are planned. The Vice, "Shift," is much less responsible for motivating the action than is "Common Conditions" in the other play. In this play, things mostly just happen according to the conventions of romance and fairy tale. The pattern of the play is like a French braid, in which new strands of hair are constantly brought in from the sides to enter a continuous structure.

Peele's *Old Wives' Tale* (ca. 1591–94) is put together in a similar way, except that setting is used as an important device of unification; the placing of Erastus at the crossroads, where all the separate groups of characters come in turn to hear his riddling prophecies, gives the play a radial rather than a linear effect. Moreover, the whole pattern appears to be deliberately chosen for humorous effect.

The pulling of new and hitherto independent strands into the main line of action continued as a method of plotting. It can be seen, for instance, in Ford's *'Tis Pity* (ca. 1627). Each of Annabella's suitors has a story of his own, yet each is drawn, for no good reason, into the central confusion. The essentially episodic character of the plotting is concealed by a specious appearance of complication; specious because the chain of complication involving Richardetto-Hippolita-Grimaldi-Soranzo-Bergetto has nothing really to do with the main issue, the love of Annabella and her brother.

What dramatists needed was a way not just of tightening episodes in a series, and of bringing them round in a circle to the beginning, but of achieving a genuinely complicated structure, the "favola intrecciata" of the Italian critics, in which all lines, whether of one action or several actions, lead into and out of a central knot. To achieve such a well-knit fable meant a grasp of the problem of dramatic opposition—how to initiate an action which would lead to counteraction and how the two could be made to move progressively towards a solution. This is Aristotle's problem of $\delta\acute{\epsilon}\sigma\iota\varsigma$ and $\lambda\acute{\upsilon}\sigma\iota\varsigma$,[10] the tying and untying of the knot, which he treats as the only two essential parts of a play.

If the suggestion is correct that the sources were chiefly responsible for teaching these principles of plotting, then we should expect to find the models for the familiar patterns of dramatic opposition in the materials converted into drama. And we do, in fact, find in romance, *novella,* morality play, medieval narrative tragedy on the Mirror theme, Senecan tragedy, and Roman and Italian comedy the few major patterns of conflict that persisted throughout the course of English renaissance drama. Familiar as these influences are, they need to be examined in the light of our immediate problem, the movement of the fable. We need especially to see how motivation in character was made to fit into, or altered, these traditional molds. I shall consider first the complication, then a special mode, the debate, of exhibiting dramatic opposition, and finally the unraveling.

The Complication

The problem of complication is centered in the problem of conflict, whether externally or internally considered. Dramatic conflict in its simplest form is of course the physical opposition of opposing forces, St. George and the Dragon, for instance, or Tamburlaine and Bajazet, or even Punch and Judy. The general movement, with the sophistication of English drama, was towards subtler methods of opposition in character—Edward II against Mortimer, Hal against Hotspur, Feste against Malvolio. For English drama became more and more a drama of personalities. The movement was also, especially in tragedy, towards inner as well as outer conflict—Hamlet against himself as well as against Claudius. At one extreme stands the hand-to-hand combat, in fairy tale, romance, or village pageant,[11] of a hero with a giant or dragon or wicked knight, the emphasis almost wholly physical, the element of moral conflict nothing but the simple one of a traditional champion overcoming a traditional enemy, right overcoming wrong in a large and general way, with no questions raised and no decisions to be made. At the other extreme stands the tortured Othello, who, to conquer evil, must kill, not his outward adversary, Iago, but his inner adversary, himself. Or Lear, who brings to focus in the mind-devastating conflict between his pride and self-knowledge a whole world of conflict between the elements, between men, between nations, and between the gods and men.

One of the things directly contributory to this complexity was an increasing skill in realizing character in a dramatic medium—showing interesting people in some way, not always so clearly defined as in Shakespeare or Jonson, affecting and being affected by the world of the play they are set down in. This lively perception of individual people did not always make for better plotting, much less for easier plotting. Not every dramatist had any formulable philosophy about the interaction of character and event. If he did not greatly care, he simply gave his story the lead and illuminated it with flashes of vivid personality along the way; if he took the matter seriously, and struggled with the problem, his own uncertainties might prevent his ever achieving a smoothly motivated plot.[12] Even so, as in Chapman and Webster, the spectator or reader usually has a sense that the characters as people count. Hence, one of the principal differences between English and Italian renaissance drama, the plots of which are more mechanically run. The more individual the characters, the more difficult to build a perfectly integrated plot.

FOR HELP IN plot-making the English relied on traditional types of story and motive. Underneath the sophistication and the complexity of mature Elizabethan drama we may still see a few familiar patterns of conflict that began early and lasted long. I shall discuss four of the commonest themes and techniques of dramatic opposition—the opposition of good and evil, the cyclic rise and fall pattern of *De casibus* tragedy, the motivation of action and counter-action by revenge, and the intrigue technique of Roman comedy.

Conflict between good and evil.—Opposition between good and evil was a theme both of romance and of moral play. Medieval romance was not very helpful, as we have seen from *Common Conditions* and *Clyomon and Clamydes,* in teaching coherence of dramatic action. It had one aspect, however, which deserves remarking in this connection. Conflict was typically between a noble hero and a malignant adversary—giant, dragon, enchanter, Saracen—symbolic in a rather general, conventional way of right and wrong, good and evil, beauty and ugliness, or the like. Emphasis was on the story and the contestants in their own right; the ethical implications were simple and might be taken for granted, though they were sometimes pointed up in Christian terms. Saints' legends, for all their nonsecular emphasis, were cut out of the same cloth. To this kind of thing was readily assimilable the explicit opposition of virtues and vices in the morality play. We can see the joining, unfused, in *Mary Magdalene,*[13] *Common Conditions, Appius and Virginia,* and other early plays in which conduct in stories of romantic origin and flavor is motivated by abstract figures from the moralities.

Satan, usually through a subordinate devil or a representative vice, was of course the principal adversary in the moralities. But he was hardly a new figure on the stage. In the grand scheme of the mystery cycles—the fall of man and his redemption—the conflict between good and evil had always been implicit, though doubtless not much attended to by the ordinary viewers of the plays; sometimes, in plays on particular subjects like the Fall, the Temptation of Christ, or the Harrowing of Hell, in which Satan must appear as a visible antagonist, the conflict had become actual and immediate.

The conception of the evil adversary never altogether died out of English renaissance drama, either comedy or tragedy. Romantic comedy and tragi-comedy continued to have their malicious villains. If Sacrapant and Friar Bungay seem too old-fashioned and anachronistic to be good examples, consider Don John of *Much Ado,* Antonio of *The Tempest,* Megra of *Philaster,* the Queen and Iachimo of *Cymbeline.* Don John is a specially illuminating example, because he appears to have no adequate reason to destroy Hero and is hence unsatisfactory to modern taste. But he need not be particularly motivated, for he belongs to an ancient and familiar convention, that of the malicious worker of evil who throws obstacles in the path of true love and virtue.

Nor did Satan ever wholly desert English tragedy. Although the old external conflict of the moralities between the virtues and the vices—the former instigated by reason as the instrument of God, and the latter prompted by the uncontrolled passions as the instrument of Satan—became in part internal and psychological and no longer so simple in its issues, the sense of an evil adversary to man's good persisted. The adversary appears in *Faustus* in a literal way, and the conflict within Faustus is exhibited in the old morality form of external debate between the contenders for his soul. The adversary appears in *Othello* more masked in symbolism, but none the less recognizable:

> I look down at his feet. But that's a fable.

And the conflict is expressed in terms of the passions warring within Othello's breast.

The protagonist's realization of how he has been deluded into doing evil is put in similar terms in other plays. At the sudden reappearance of her lover Wendoll, the repentant Anne Frankford cries out:

> Oh, for God's sake, fly!
> The devil doth come to tempt me, ere I die.[14]

And Byron, caught in his treasons, in torment at the end of his mighty conflict between loyalty and ambition, starts back in disgust and horror at the sight of La Fin, the instrument of his betrayal. To Byron he appears a "damn'd enchanter" who has tempted and bewitched him, a monstrous issue of hell.

Sure he call'd up the devil in my spirits,
And made him to usurp my faculties:
Shall I be cast away now he's cast out?
What justice is in this? [15]

In Jacobean tragedy generally, the adversary is reduced to imagery, but the imagery of the Devil, death, and hell is so persistent and pervasive—especially in Marston, Tourneur, and Webster—as to give to that tragedy an overwhelming sense of an unknowable, unconquerable evil set in eternal enmity against the happiness of men.

In Shakespeare there is a much stronger sense of responsibility in character than in some of his contemporaries, especially Chapman and Webster, in whom there is, hardly more pity, but certainly more apology, for irrational passion. Even in Shakespeare, however, the foe is without as well as within. Othello's goodness is sufficient to meet and conquer any recognizable evil; the terrible thing is that the evil he meets is not recognizable for what it is.[15a]

Medieval romance and pageant, then, furnished the conception of dramatic conflict between a hero and a malignant adversary; the morality play, the same thing expressed in theological and ethical terms and with the conflict external in representation but in implication internal as well. The religious drama generally, both mystery and miracle play, had for centuries given representational vividness to the conflict between man in his fallen state and his sleepless enemy.

Rise and fall in De casibus *tragedy.*—The medieval conception of tragedy as the fall of a man of wealth or power at the hands of adverse fortune was inadequate in itself for drama unless the evil fortune was made to appear in the form of external enemies. But the germ of complication lay in the cyclic pattern of *De casibus* tragedy, with one man rising as another fell. All that was necessary for drama was to make the rise consequent upon the fall, that is, to present the fall of the hero as engineered by a climbing rival. The motive of ambition countered by ambition, and perhaps by revenge as well, produced a perfectly characteristic and recognizable pattern: a curve of rise and fall for the protagonist, with the fall of the protagonist crossed by the rise of the antagonist. This is the pattern of *Edward II, Julius Caesar,* and *Sejanus.* It was one of Shakespeare's favorite patterns; he used it, with modifications, in many of his histories, in all his Roman plays, and in *Macbeth.*

One of the ways to increase the dramatic intensity of this theme was to motivate opposition in the clash of personalities as well as in circumstances—to pit the insolent assurance of Mortimer, for instance, against the scolding vacillation of Edward; the shrewd self-control of Bolingbroke against the self-pitying irresponsibility of Richard; the cold, rather mean, competence of Octavius Caesar against the warm extravagant rashness of Antony. Such clash of character complicated the old simple pattern of Fortune's turning wheel. It did not necessarily rob her of her power, only gave her a plausible means to work in a world of men's wills, mutually irritant, jealous, or emulous, and perpetually at variance.

Revenge and counter-revenge.—The motive of revenge, sometimes present in *De casibus* tragedy, has to be considered in its own right, since it was to prove one of the most fruitful of all motives for dramatic opposition. Senecan tragedy appears to have given it its impetus on the English stage, but it was a rather ubiquitous motive to be found as well in Mirror stories, in Greek drama and myth, in modern Italian *novelle* and plays, all familiar as source material. Doubtless with Seneca's *Thyestes* and *Thebais* [16] in mind, Sackville and Norton used revenge as a major complicating motive of their politically directed, pseudo-historical plot in *Gorboduc* (1562). Thomas Hughes imposed a more obviously Senecan variety of revenge on the Arthurian legend in his *Misfortunes of Arthur* (ca. 1587). Into *Gismond of Salerne* (ca. 1567–68) revenge came with the source story from Boccaccio.[17] In all these plays the movement is rather simple: one action provoking a counter-action of revenge, that in turn leading to catastrophe either directly or through a further act of counter-revenge. There is little, if any, manipulation by intrigue. But the Gismond story, with its motives of love, honor, and jealousy, and its action of secrecy, surprise, and deadliness, is of a type that invited exploitation of the revenge motive. This sort of situation and motivation would develop towards more and more intricate knots of revenge and counter-revenge, plotted by intrigue— in short, towards *The Spanish Tragedy, Titus Andronicus,* and *The Revenger's Tragedy.*

Greater tragic meaning came with the shift of emphasis from the mere problem of getting the revenge done to the impact of revenge on the character of the revenger. The handling of the ghost as motivator throws this shift into relief. In the simplest pattern, following *Thyestes,* the necessity of the revenge action somehow resides in the ghost; revenge is first of all his concern, and it is enough for him to appear for the action to begin. In Seneca's play, the spirit of Thyestes is tormented by Megaera so to inspire his nephews with rage, fury, and discord that they will continue the chain of crimes begun by him. In *The Misfortunes of Arthur,* the ghost of Gorlois, wanting vengeance on the family of Uther Pendragon for the seduction of his wife, prophesies the events which lead eventually to the mutual self-destruction of Arthur and Mordred. In *Locrine* (ca. 1591) the ghost of Albanact drives Humber, his slayer, to commit suicide. Although *The Spanish Tragedy* keeps the outward frame of this pattern, in that the ghost of Andreas calls for revenge and sits on the stage to watch the destruction of his enemies, the real motivation has changed. There is something of the conventional assumption of inevitability, it is true, in the way in which Bel-Imperia, on hearing of the death of her sweetheart, begins automatically to set about to revenge him. But with Hieronimo's problem of avenging his murdered son, we are wholly in the realm of human trouble and human character. Perhaps written under the influence of *Hamlet,* the later additions to the play intensify the element of conflict in Hieronimo between unnerving and distracting grief and desire for revenge. Even in the first form of the play, however, revenge is a problem in character as well as in action; it is the germ of the thing that leads to Hamlet. In *Hamlet* the ghost is once more a genuine inciting force, but what he incites is not just the act of revenge; it is a devastating conflict in Hamlet's soul. Later ghosts—Bussy's in *The Revenge of Bussy,* Brachiano's in *The White Devil,* Alonzo's in *The Changeling*—can at best be taken only as symbolic reminders of duty to the revenger, or of guilt to the murderer. With their need as motivators gone, they have degenerated into mere mechanical survivals of an old tradition. They are the pallid ghosts of ghosts. Montferrer's ghost, in *The Atheist's Tragedy,* has the distinction of charging his son Charlemont *not* to avenge his death, but to follow the Christian ethic of forgiveness.

Why the motive of revenge should enjoy such popularity from the early days of Elizabethan down to Caroline times naturally provokes speculation. That it had deeply sympathetic affinities with the conditions of actual life we must suppose.[18] Yet its very endurance, even after it had lost its vitality, as the commonest counter-motive in tragedy, suggests something besides imitative realism. Its persistence may have been to some extent owing to its great usefulness for play construction in furnishing so practicable a method of counter-action.

Comic intrigue.—The counterpart of the intrigue plot in tragedy motivated by revenge is the intrigue plot of Roman and Italian comedy, in which the complicating motive is the outwitting of somebody. Again, as with the revenge motive, though the conditions of London life produced plenty of types of rogues to do the outwitting and of fools to be outwitted, one may suspect that this pattern of opposition had a dramatic usefulness irrelevant to its realism. It was a workable frame, easy to use over and over—as the monotonously repetitive situations of Italian comedy prove.

The best English comedies of this sort are freshened with many Bobadills, Cocledemoys, Lampatho Dorias, Sir Petronels, and Overreaches, who make their fantastic rogueries or stupidities seem of the stuff of human sharp practice or silliness. But characters as individual as these are, in a sense, an agreeable bonus; for the most conventional motivations in stock types, as Latin comedy illustrates, will serve to pull the strings of the intrigue. And, since the fun is in the cleverness of the manipulation, a few threads of nicely calculated coincidence to make the knot more intricate will help the plot rather than hinder it. Shakespeare's *Comedy of Errors, Taming of the Shrew* (the Bianca story), and *Merry Wives;* Porter's *Two Angry Women of Abingdon;* and some of Middleton's and Chapman's comedies are the happiest examples of this sort of witty plotting.

When, with the manipulated plot, character is made the genuine and nearly sole motive force, Jonsonian comedy is the result. The intrigue pattern is built into a whole world, satirically conceived, of gullers and gulled. Yet though the motives are few and repeated— self-love, sensuality, greed, witty intelligence, and credulity—they are not monotonous, for they are embodied in characters as subtly varied as Volpone and Sir Epicure, as Mosca and Face, or as Ananias, Tribulation Wholesome, and Zeal-of-the-Land Busy.

Intrigue was useful, too, in the manipulation of plots of romantic adventure. For the hazards and lucky chances of fortune—the separations of twins and sweethearts, the shipwrecks, the captures by pirates, the recognitions by rings and by chests of baby garments— which are the stuff of romantic story, need something to pull them out of the straight line of successive episodes into a knot of complication. A wicked magician (or even a Prospero) to rile up the sea at an opportune moment will work wonders for a plot.

In a purely romantic story, character in any individualized sense is no more a necessity than in a story of roguery largely worked by intrigue. For a romantic plot can coast on the conventional expectations of story for story's sake. The element of the fortuitous is generally much larger than in a plot of more "domestic" intrigue; and the characters themselves must meet standard expectations of motive: love at first sight, the pangs of jealousy or separation, natural malice or benevolence, and so on.[19] When character is deepened, therefore, in a romantic story, it ought not to be allowed to alter the motivation seriously. Caught in the fantastic and exaggerated situations of the plot, the characters should behave convincingly; yet they must still be largely moved by the accidents of their fairy-tale world. Viola, in disguise as a boy and as an unwilling wooer of her own beloved's mistress, behaves with all the embarrassment, pertness, ruefulness, and wit a real Viola would in such an unlikely situation; but Viola can be extricated from her predicament only by several even more unlikely chances—the arrival on the spot of her twin brother, supposed drowned, the mistaking of him for her by the woman who loves her, and his willingness to walk into matrimony with a strange woman in the very instant of meeting her. What happens in Shakespearean romantic comedy is that fully-conceived characters give an illusion of reality to the most fantastic situations; we are presented, therefore, with a delightful and rather zany world that we yet believe in. More of this in the section on the denouement.

To ACHIEVE greatness with any of the traditional themes and modes of plotting we have been discussing, a dramatist needed to have some ideas about the causes and consequences of action, about the cooperation of character and circumstance in event, about the rôles of fate and fortune in the affairs of men—in short, some view of the relation of men to the world they live in. We have gradually been assembling material and establishing points of view from which to consider these deeper questions of the relation of form to meaning. And more that is helpful will emerge, I hope, in the remainder of this chapter. I wish to discuss in some detail an important technique for exhibiting conflict, whatever its theme or its motives. For this technique greatly affected the achievement of satisfactory dramatic form; it was contributory both to the strength and the weakness of Elizabethan drama. This is the technique of the debate.

The Technique of the Debate

The debate is dramatically familiar, of course, in the morality play, but was actually of so much older and wider use as to be thoroughly engrained as a habit of thought. The method of formal disputation did not end with the Middle Ages; it was still in the sixteenth century the chief method of intellectual discipline in the universities. And although the heyday of the *débat* as a form of literary composition was over by then, its influence survived in various ways. One excellent example is in the contentious habit of Euphuism, whether in full-length debates over such questions as the rival claims of love and friendship, love and war, nature and nurture, or whether in the groundwork of dichotomy and antithesis on which so much of the prose is built:

Couldest thou, Euphues, for the love of a fruitless pleasure, violate the league of faithful friendship? Diddest thou weigh more the enticing looks of a lewd wench, than the entire love of a loyal friend? [20]

Either you think there are no gods, or I must think ye are no men. You build as though you should live for ever, and surfeit as though you should die tomorrow.[21]

Aye, but she is beautiful; yea, but not therefore chaste. Aye, but she is comely in all parts of the body; yea, but she may be crooked in some part of the mind. Aye, but she is wise; yea, but she is a woman! . . . It is thought wonderful among the seamen, that mugil, of all fishes the swiftest, is found in the belly of the bret, of all the slowest: And shall it not seem monstrous to wise men, that the heart of the greatest conqueror of the world, should be found in the hands of the weakest creature of nature? of a woman? of a captive? Ermines have fair skins, but foul livers; sepulchres fresh colors, but rotten bones; women fair faces, but false hearts. Remember, Alexander, thou hast a camp to govern, not a chamber. . . .[21a]

Now the characteristics of a model scholastic debate are that the two sides of a question are stated with equal force and ingenuity. Skill at marshalling arguments in one's favor and at discrediting the arguments of one's opponent through tricks of sophistry count more than ultimate truth. Since the thing is a game of wits, the moderator must decide in favor of the cleverest, not the truest, argument; or, if both are equally clever, he must sidestep the real issue and award partial honors to both sides. The familiar medieval literary *débats* are generally organized to set forth opposing lines of equally persuasive argument, and decision is often evaded either by being left to the reader or by some adventitious device. In debate on such favorite themes as the relative merits of the owl and the nightingale, winter and summer, water and wine, no conclusion is possible, for these contraries are only conventional symbols of familiar oppositions in experience, and if these can be reduced to genuine issues for debate they admit only of practical decision in the course of living, not of theoretical and absolute conclusion. The owl and the nightingale, in the early thirteenth-century English poem of that name, having raised many insoluble questions about the useful and the beautiful, the serious and the joyful sides of life, fly away to one Master Nicholas to have their claims adjudged, and the author ends:

> Then with these words away they flew
> Alone, nor followers with them drew;
> To Portesholme, I trow, they came,
> But how they fared at that same
> That can I you in no wise tell,
> I know no more of what befell.[22]

It is the airing of the issues that has been important, not the conclusion.

Many of the French *jeux partis* in which questions of love are wittily and sophistically debated, are submitted at the end to a judge or arbitrator, but no judgment is ever given. Evidently none is meant to be, for the questions posed are unanswerable dilemmas abstracted from the actualities of any particular situation: Who might be expected to make the most beautiful songs, the unhappy lover or the favored lover? Which is preferable for a lover, the death or the marriage of his beloved? Of two lovers, which is the least unhappy, the one who loses his sight, or the one who loses his hearing? Of two husbands, which is the more to be pitied, the one who has his suspicions, or the one who has his proofs? Who is the more to blame, the lover who boasts of the favors he has received from his lady, or the one who boasts without having received them? [23]

But the matter was not wholly one of witty game. The same habit of mind was put to quite serious uses, and these were continued in the Renaissance. Rhetorical training, for instance, emphasized the technique of setting contraries against each other, or of being able to handle either side of a subject—the useful or the harmful course of action in a deliberative oration, the accusation or defense in a forensic oration, the praise or blame in a demonstrative oration. In his discussion of the poet's need of oratory, Lionardi [24] uses as an illustration of forensic oratory Petrarch's *canzone* in which he first accuses Love and then defends him. Lionardi is concerned at this point, not with the resolution of the question, but with the beauty and ingenuity and judgment with which the opposing arguments are set forth. Yet his ultimate concern, like all the serious-minded men who wrote on rhetoric in the Renaissance, was with the discovery of truth. Rhetoric if properly used was thought to be, like logic, an instrument for its discovery.

Euphuistic balancing contrasts, like those illustrated above, show in extreme form the fallacy of seeking truth through sophistical debate. Euphues argues as well for the greater fickleness of women as on another occasion he does for their greater constancy. The decisions of Lyly's characters, after such Gordion knots have been tied, either must be arbitrary and dictated by the demands of the story, as they largely are in *Euphues;* or else they must be rooted in a plausible conception of the character, as in *Campaspe,* when Alexander decides to return from love to the pursuit of military glory. The debates themselves decide nothing.

How profoundly this technique affected the structure of Elizabethan drama we shall see presently, but first it will be helpful to note some early instances of the incorporation of the recognizable literary *débat* in plays, and to see how it is used in different ways.

ONE MAY REMARK on the comic debates in John Heywood's farces— *Witty and Witless, A Play of Love, The Play of the Weather, The Four P's.*[25] The debates may end in a stalemate, as in the argument in *The Four P's* as to whether the Palmer, the Pardoner, or the Poticary does the most for the salvation of man's soul. They may end in a diversion that leaves the question still in the air, as with the song in *Love* that interrupts the debate as to which is in the worse case, the Lover not Loved or the Loved not Loving; or as with the horseplay of the Vice that stops the dispute between the Lover Beloved and the Neither Lover nor Loved as to which is the more fortunate. The debates may end in a moral, as when Jerome settles the argument in *Witty and Witless* between John, who is pleading the case for the Wise Man's life, and James, for the Foolish Man's; he changes the question to: "Whether would ye be a reasonable man or an unreasonable beast?" This does not admit of argument. These plays are dramatic only in the most limited sense of being spoken dialogue on some subject of argument. They contain no situation which debate complicates and which decision can resolve.

More interesting for our purpose is the form of Medwall's *Fulgens and Lucres*.[26] Usually regarded as the earliest surviving secular romantic play (ca. 1497), it is, most significantly, constructed on the lines of a debate. The dramatic issue is whether Lucrece should marry a rich, worldly young man of noble family or a poor, studious young man of low birth. The issue is generalized into a question— whether true nobility consists in birth and family honors or in the practice of virtue—and each suitor pleads his case in the fashion of the *débat* or the disputation. Aside from some farce in the servants' parts, this is the only action in the play, and suspense consists merely in awaiting the choice of Lucrece, who is moderator of her own fate.

The choice is a genuine one, not an evasion of the issue, since Lucrece chooses Gaius Flaminius, the poor but virtuous young man, who she thinks will make her a better husband than Publius Cornelius, the descendant of the Scipios. But since there has been no complication, dramatically the choice is arbitrary, not the inevitable working out of a problem. Interestingly enough, in the *débat* from which the argument of the play was drawn, Caxton's English version of Bonaccorso's *De vera nobilitate*,[27] the decision is referred to the senate, whose verdict we do not hear, and the reader is left to judge for himself. The dramatist, however, is forced to make a choice, and Medwall makes his on the romantic side. Although Lucrece does not appeal explicitly to love, the greater worth of Flaminius' love is implied, and the situation is clearly the forerunner of the dramatic convention in which decision must be on the side of true love.

The love-debate was sometimes incorporated in old dramatic or semi-dramatic forms used for or derived from folk festivals—wooing games, May games, Robin Hood plays, eclogue dramas. There is, for instance, a debate in the fourteenth-century French eclogue play of *Griseldis*. And court pageants and interludes based on love allegories and mythological motives must often have employed the debate; such themes as *Love and Riches* (an interlude performed at

Greenwich on 6 May 1527) imply its use.[28] The influence of these entertainments survives in Elizabethan semi-allegorical plays like *The Rare Triumphs of Love and Fortune* (pr. 1589).[29] In this play the verbal debate between Love and Fortune over their respective authority is insoluble; hence each is given a chance by Jupiter to display her power in the lives of a pair of lovers. Each act ends in alternate triumphs, until Jupiter, foreseeing only general trouble for the world out of this endless contention, urges them to agree to conditions which will leave each goddess equal.

> *Venus.* Whom Fortune favors I will not despise.
> *Fortune.* Whom love rejects by me shall never rise.

Each contributes to a happy ending for the lovers in the play; thus arbitration has ended in a traditional compromise. In her last speech, Fortune resolves the dilemma by giving the palm to a third power:

> Wisdom ruleth Love and Fortune both:
> Though riches fail, and beauty seem to save,
> Yet wisdom forward still unconquer'd goeth.

In this type of debate, the judgment must be nicely calculated to give each side its due. The outcome is conventional and expected. If it evades the issue, no one is troubled; for no one expects the debate to settle anything. Peele's *Arraignment of Paris* is in this tradition. The Judgment of Paris was a theme long a favorite for love allegories, since the rival attractions of wisdom, wealth, and beauty—or love— could be set forth in dramatic form. If the decision in Peele's play is novel, it is yet in the spirit of court-debate in its neat side-stepping of the issue: the apple is finally awarded, not to one of the three goddesses, but to Elizabeth, who is adjudged to possess all their qualities in a superior degree.

Lyly's plays exhibit not a little of the influence of the court show, with its elegant and unreal debates, designed more to charm by pageantry, wit, and compliment, than seriously to enlighten on moral issues. *Galathea* perhaps illustrates this technique best. The principal action concerns the ideal friendship of two young girls, both disguised as boys to avoid the risk of the annual sacrifice to a sea monster; each falls in love thinking the other is a boy. The secondary action concerns the revenge Cupid takes on four of Diana's nymphs, who have scoffed at him, by making them fall in love; here, there is an implicit opposition between love and chastity. The play ends with a debate between Venus and Diana; and Neptune, who acts as moderator, solves it by a compromise which makes a concession to both goddesses and provides a denouement for both plots. Venus wins in part, being given the opportunity to turn into a man one of the two young shepherdesses, so that they may love each other happily. Diana wins in part in that she gets back her nymphs, and in that Neptune agrees to give up his annual demand of the sacrifice of a virgin. It is hard to find this play an "idea play," as Professor Baldwin does,[30] and to take seriously the issue between love and chastity. It is not an issue in the main plot until the end, and it produces no great complication in the minor one. Indeed, although the two actions of the play and the scenes of comic interlude progress in a balanced movement of figures on the stage, it is merely a pattern of display, like a dancing pattern, and involves no genuine conflict or knotting of the action. I should regard the play as a pretty myth of love and metamorphosis, the embodiment of which in drama brings with it some of the techniques of the court pageant. A deficiency in genuine dramatic opposition and complication is made up by the mere appearance of drama in the final debate. The issue between love and chastity is not settled, but it need not be; the whole thing is only a game. In *Love's Labour's Lost,* on the other hand, a somewhat similar issue, also subjected to much debate, is settled in a genuinely dramatic way.

In contrast to debate in the court pageant, debate in the morality play and moral interlude was more crucial. It formed the core of the play; for the forces of good and evil, set in dramatic opposition to one another, had to attempt to win the hero by cleverness in persuasion. Perhaps in the background of this type of drama one may place medieval *débats* on such serious themes as the Church and the Synagogue, the Body and the Soul, Heaven and Hell.[31]

As has been sufficiently pointed out,[32] the moral play technique of debate persists in the later drama, both in the external debates between the counselors of the hero to good or evil, or to prudent or imprudent action (as in *Gorboduc*), and in the debates within the conscience of a character. Even the latter are often presented with all the formality of statement, counter-statement, rebuttal, and counter-rebuttal characteristic of school debate. Though in the later drama the forms of the debate disappear under greater informality and naturalness, we may suspect a continuous line of tradition. We know how Shakespeare, for instance, went through an apprenticeship in the artificial form, as seen in Richard III's debate with himself on the eve of Bosworth Field, before arriving at the "natural" form of self-examination of a mind divided against itself, as shown in the soliloquies of Claudius and Macbeth.

The debate stemming from the morality play had this advantage over the debate on purely academic questions: it allowed of a genuine, not a specious or even merely conventional solution. When the debate is between some form of good and evil, obviously the right choice can only be of the good; if it is of the evil, tragedy must follow, as in *Faustus* or *Macbeth*. The morality play itself and romantic comedy or tragi-comedy mitigate the harshness of a wrong choice by allowing an escape if a change of heart and a reversal of choice come in time, as in *Mankind* or in *Measure for Measure* or in *The Winter's Tale*. But tragedy keeps its inexorability and its irony by making its reversals of choice, as in *Coriolanus,* always too late. In any case, the impasse created by the presentation of opposing points of view may be broken only by genuine choice.

The issue may be simple and the right way evident, if unattractive, as in the appeals to Faustus of the Good Angel and of the Old Man, or as in Macbeth's clear-sighted apprehension of "the deep damnation" of his killing Duncan. These are tragedies in which a man knowing the good chooses the evil. Or the issue may be between actions neither of which is simply good nor simply evil; good and evil appear as different faces of the same thing. Then we have arrived at such great moral dilemmas as are faced by Brutus and Hamlet and Coriolanus. Here, moral ambiguity lies in the nature of things corruptible, and is the source of tragic irony.

BUT THE HABIT of double direction, disconcertingly engendered by the academic or courtly debate, persisted in the drama in more than one way: both in actual debates on the stage, and in ambiguous attitudes towards the characters or the action.

Debate within or between characters is a device for exhibiting conflict that is capable of great effectiveness. It is generally a means of heightening suspense, and should be a means of making vocal motives of action and counter-action. Numerous examples will suggest themselves: excellent ones are the two debates between Hippolito and Bellafront over the wickedness and misery of the harlot's life *vs.* its attractiveness—the first debate, in Part I of *The Honest Whore,* leading Bellafront to abandon her way of life; the second, in Part II, seeking to win her back to it. But only too often on the Elizabethan stage, these stated motives are not the real determinants of the action, which proceeds as the story demands, with motives only obscurely indicated, if at all. The effect of a debate that does not really motivate the subsequent action is mere forensic display and the dilemma created by it is a cheat. The dilemma is shown to be false when it must be broken arbitrarily so that the story can continue on its own lines of logical or conventional development. One of the best examples of this sort of thing is the dispute in *Troilus and Cressida* between Troilus and Hector over the return of Helen to the Greeks. Shakespeare lets interest in the debate momentarily run away with the necessities of his plot. Though Hector appears to have the best of the argument, that Helen is not worth losing any more lives for and that the Trojans have no right to her anyhow, he gives way anticlimactically to Troilus' argument for honor.

> . . . these moral laws
> Of nature, and of nations, speak aloud
> To have her back return'd; thus to persist
> In doing wrong extenuates not wrong,
> But makes it much more heavy. Hector's opinion
> Is this, in way of truth; yet, nevertheless,
> My spritely brethren, I propend to you
> In resolution to keep Helen still;
> For 'tis a cause that hath no mean dependance
> Upon our joint and several dignities.[33]

Of course, the story demands that Hector go on with the war and be slain by Achilles. Shakespeare has let the debate go forward on its own and lose its dramatic function as exhibition of the genuine complicating motives of the play.

Although we are apt to feel something unreal about the debates of potential villains with their consciences, there is usually a different problem here, the problem of swift motivation in a story crowded with action. This problem has been discussed fully in the chapter on character.[34] The motives of such self-examining villains are usually genuine enough, only too unextended in time to be realistically convincing.

THE HABIT OF mind fostered by the debate leads, I believe, to greater structural defects than mere runaway speeches like Hector's. It may be responsible for the unresolved oppositions in *The Merchant of Venice, Richard II,* and *Julius Caesar;* in *The Revenger's Tragedy,* in *The White Devil,* and in the Bussy and Byron plays. All these plays are characterized by a puzzling failure of direction because two or more different ethical or political points of view are unreconciled. On the one hand, we see Vittoria, without explanation or apology, guilty of adultery and at least connivance at murder, if nothing worse; on the other hand, we see her in the trial scene nobly at bay. We readily adopt with Vindici the ethic of revenge; yet we are asked to displace it on the instant with the ethic of legal justice which suddenly appears at the end of the play. Bussy steals Montsurry's wife, yet self-righteously feels put upon when Montsurry comes to take his revenge.

An especially good example is furnished by the two Byron plays, for in them more of actual verbal debate occurs than in the others. The case for and against Byron as a traitor to King Henry IV of France is never really solved. He and the King argue their respective points of view with equal persuasiveness and seemingly equal justice.[35] The King's speeches always set things right for the time being, but as soon as Byron begins to talk the hearer loses his grip on the issue. The King argues for law, for a sovereign's right to expect obedience of his subjects provided he himself abides by the law; Byron argues for the right of the subject to rebel when courts are debased, kings corrupt, and merit unregarded. The difficulty is that Henry does not fit Byron's charges; yet we can never be sure that Byron is meant to be wholly deluded. He indubitably commits acts of treason, and is as indubitably perjured in denying these acts to the King. His complaint that he has been tricked and bewitched into treason does not clear him of perjury. Yet he is treated as such a man of integrity and his speeches are so eloquently innocent that we seem meant to believe them. Indeed we wish to. But what we feel for Byron is not the sympathy accompanied by adverse judgment that we feel for a man like Brutus, who has pursued a good end with the wrong means, or for a man like Coriolanus, who has lost his integrity in trying so hard to keep it; what we feel, caught between the two sides of the debate, is a troubled uncertainty as to how we are meant to feel. For it is never settled whether the end Byron pur-

sues is a good end or not, or even whether he has lost his integrity
or not. There is no clarity here about the coöperation of character
and event, no certainty about motivation. The confusion, we may
suspect, lies in a conflict in Chapman's own philosophy, since it
haunts all his tragedies.[36]

Although Shakespeare in his later plays is without this weakness in
handling opposing points of view that besets some of his greatest
contemporaries, he shows it in some of the earlier plays, notably in
The Merchant of Venice, some of the histories, and *Julius Caesar.*
But his confusions are never so deep or so fatally damaging to play
structure as are Chapman's. Sometimes they arise from the sources,
and, for whatever reason, are allowed to stay. Sometimes they may
arise from his ability to put himself into any man's shoes in any
imagined situation. But they do not stem from any confusion about
matters of ethics.

Whatever led Shakespeare to present the case for Shylock as eloquently as he did the case against him got the dramatist into difficulties, for his comedy demanded Shylock's downfall, and not a
tragic downfall, either. I would not deny that Shakespeare's great
gift of imaginative sympathy was chiefly responsible for all that is
favorable in the portrayal of Shylock. At the same time I would suggest that the habit of mind fostered by a disputatious age would
make such an unresolved presentation of opposing points of view acceptable, and perhaps less recognizable as harmful to dramatic structure than to us.

Shakespeare's histories—the "epic" series to a certain extent, and
King John more obviously—suffer somewhat from the same double
direction. John is both something of a cruel tyrant and something of
a pre-Protestant hero and martyr. These are contradictions of the
sources; but it is noteworthy that Shakespeare has taken no trouble
either to eliminate one of the conflicting attitudes, or to resolve the
two. I shall not diagnose the weaknesses of the Yorkist-Lancastrian
tetralogy, except to remark that the rival claims of the two factions
are equally well argued; to see the series as an apology for the
triumph of the predominantly Lancastrian house of Tudor raises as
many problems as it settles. *Richard III* pulls the three earlier plays
together with a satisfactory conclusion, but the issue, in retrospect,
is seen to be not the superior claims of one family over the other,
but the danger of rebellion against properly constituted authority.

Even this issue gives Shakespeare trouble in *Richard II*. The difficulty is, what constitutes proper authority? It is hard to reconcile a theory of Divine Right with the pragmatic theory that *de facto* possession of power, however come by, makes proper authority; yet the two ideas were both tenets of Tudor political philosophy, and both operate in *Richard II*, to the detriment of its structure. For if Richard is king by divine appointment, then Bolingbroke, in wresting the crown from the Lord's annointed, can only be an unjustified usurper, regardless of Richard's unfitness to rule; but in the episode of Aumerle's rebellion against Henry, at the end of the play, Shakespeare makes York, hitherto the chief spokesman for Divine Right, take the pragmatic position: no rebellion is justified against Henry, now he *is* seated on the throne. The very insistence on the point, by playing up the episode of York's demonstration of loyalty to the new king, suggests that Shakespeare was aware of the dilemma and was seeking to solve it by transferring the sacredness from the man to the office. But in political terms there is no satisfactory resolution of the play.

Neither is there a perfectly satisfactory one in terms of the opposing characters. We are at first in sympathy with Bolingbroke when he returns to claim the inheritance of his duchy, even in sympathy with his move for the throne, since he is obviously so much more fitted to rule than the capriciously tyrannical, effeminate, self-centered, and ineffectual Richard. Yet by the end of the play, the pathos and the brilliant poetizing of the falling Richard make sustained sympathy with Bolingbroke difficult. The explanation of this double point of view on Shakespeare's part is not, I think, so much in historical detachment, as in the focus of his interest on Richard's character as it progressively reveals itself with his changing fortune. Since Bolingbroke, on this view, is only a foil to Richard, a shift in point of view towards Richard inevitably entails one towards Bolingbroke, however unjustified it may be if he is considered purely for himself and his own position. The cyclic pattern of Mirror tragedy may also have something to do with the failure wholly to resolve the divided sympathy in the play. Pity must be for the victim of Fortune as he swings down with the turn of her wheel. So Bolingbroke, down at the beginning, while Richard is at the crest, wins our sympathy; but as Bolingbroke begins to mount, we transfer it to the now declining Richard. This suggestion is not at odds with the point I am making about the habit of unresolved oppositions bred by the technique of the debate. Indeed, they both may well be part of the same mental habit of thinking in antitheses and paradoxes.

The same political dilemma as in *Richard II* arises in *1 Henry IV;* but this time Shakespeare solves the structural problem it poses. Has Henry, the usurper, the right to be king and to enforce obedience to his government? His final word on the Percy rebellion, "Thus ever doth rebellion find rebuke," must seem ironic in view of his own earlier rebellion against Richard. But Shakespeare's perception and even exploitation of the irony saves the play. There is no uncertainty about Henry's position; he is king in fact and a good one. Yet his strong consciousness of both his duties and his prerogatives as king overlays an uneasy memory of how he came by the throne and of how Richard died. He is one of the most complex and subtly realized of all Shakespeare's historical figures. The absorption of all the complexity arising from the political issue in the character and attitudes of Henry leaves unclouded by political ambiguity the dramatic opposition of Hal and Hotspur. The political issue there can be taken for granted; the issue to be solved lies in the opposition of character between the two young men, and Shakespeare needs no help with that kind of problem. Thus Shakespeare finds his way out of the contradictions of political philosophy by attending to character.

But as in *Richard II* Shakespeare was to have trouble again with the problem of political opposition. A similar *De casibus* theme of interchanging power and a similar ambiguity occurs in *Julius Caesar.* The first half of the play pleads the case of the conspirators, the second half, indirectly, the case of Caesar. The Orson Welles production, which sought to turn the anti-Caesar note of the early part of the play into left-wing revolutionary propaganda against dictators, was of course wide of the mark; it left the latter part, in which the spirit of Caesar, "ranging for revenge," helps defeat the conspirators, an anticlimactic and irrelevant appendage.[37] Nevertheless, Mr. Welles could only have achieved the powerful effects he did out of the first half because there was something there on which to base his distortion. Caesar at the summit of his power, smitten with *hybris,* is undeniably an unsympathetic figure, and Cassius' plea for "beauteous freedom" [38] sounds like the voice of truth. But the play can no more be turned into an apology for tyrannicide than it can into an apology for tyranny. Nothing more clearly reveals than this play that Shakespeare, for all his adherence to the main lines of Tudor political philosophy, was no political propagandist. The disjunction in attitude in the play is undeniable, and it can only be bridged by looking elsewhere than to political theory for a solution. One solution is to recognize once again the cyclic pattern of opposition in *De casibus* tragedy, here with a motive of counter-revenge. Yet, as in *Richard II,* there is a certain structural crudeness in making the opposing points of view alternately dominant, debate-fashion, in the two halves of the play. The other solution is to focus attention on the tragedy of Brutus, whose impractical idealism puts him into the power of a world of base motives and sordid methods. As in *Richard II,* the center of interest is in a particular man's response to the political situation he is in, not in the political situation itself. Shakespeare's dominant interest is ethical, not political.

None of Shakespeare's later tragedies runs the risk of breaking in two as these earlier ones did, perhaps because he has thoroughly learned his structural lesson, perhaps because the issues are primarily ethical, only secondarily political. There is no mistaking where our sympathies should lie, however well Shakespeare may play the devil's advocate for his villains. The plausibility of Iago's, Edmund's, and Goneril's self-justificatory speeches masks a wickedness that wholly invalidates their superficially rational pleas. Nor does Shakespeare's habit of seeing both sides of a question lead to any uncertainty of direction in handling complicated characters and issues of mingled good and evil. For if he perceives that men are often doomed to a tragic destiny because of the involvement of good and evil one with the other, so that choice of the wholly good is not possible, he also perceives that men must be judged by the motives of their choice. Shakespeare is never ambiguous on the fundamental bases of ethical judgment.

In any consideration of the degree to which in the Elizabethan drama meaning receives adequate structural form, the habit of mind induced by the debate is of first importance.

This discussion of the debate technique in drama, whether used as a precise form or reflected in the structure, has continually raised the question of the resolution of the action.

The Unraveling

The critics generally gave the denouement a good deal of attention. Guarini observed that the untying of the knot was harder than the tying, and Castelvetro complained that Aristotle had not taught how to make both the knotting and the untying equally pleasing to the spectators.[39]

The chief distinction in methods of denouement is of course between the solution that seems to come inevitably from the direction of events and the solution that is brought about arbitrarily. Following Aristotle and Horace, the critics universally condemned the *deus ex machina*.[40] Yet a careful examination of their qualifications shows that they were not at all averse to the fortuitous solution provided it could be plausibly enough handled. Quite the contrary.

Aristotle had said that the accidental was a source of wonder if it seemed to have the effect of design, e.g., as when the statue of Mitys in Argos fell on the murderer of Mitys and killed him.[41] The critics stress the importance of the "meraviglia" or "mirabile" which arises from this way of handling incident, and they generally seem to understand it in Aristotle's sense. As usual, however, their applications of the principle betray a shift of emphasis. Discussion of tragedy usually takes the regular line. It is the discussions of comedy and of tragi-comedy that are most illuminating of renaissance taste.

Following their general habit, the critics analyze the plotting of comedy in the same terms of reversal and recognition as for tragedy.[42] Though they define wonder as arising from an unexpected change of fortune that is yet seen, on examination, to arise out of the constitution of the fable,[43] they do not actually rule out that element of the marvelous discovery of long-lost relatives that plays so large a part in the solutions of New Comedy. For instance, though the forms of recognition (by natural bodily signs, by artificial signs, by memory, etc.) are discussed and arranged in order of plausibility, the far greater implausibility of situations arising that call for these signs is not considered—the implausibility, that is, of lost daughters, exposed at birth, turning up at all, much less getting involved with one's friends' sons. Of course the daughters must then be recognized by one of the approved means; but it seems a little late in the day to raise the issue of plausibility. Though Giraldi condemned Euripides and Plautus for the arbitrariness of their solutions, he praised Terence for his skill in the denouements of *Andria* and *Adelphi*, the first of which rests on the usual recognition of lost daughters; and Giraldi himself used the same device of infants lost and discovered in his romantic tragi-comedies of *Altile* and *Gli Antivalomeni*.

At the base of all these critical analyses, especially those by Giraldi and Guarini, of the endings of comedy and tragi-comedy, is the admiration for abundant action intricately knotted. Several things follow from this admiration. The first thing is a special emphasis on the denouement. For an intricate knot demands skilful untying. Guarini remarks that as in the head resides the intellect of man, so in the denouement is placed the major sinew ("il maggior nervo") of the plot;

for to know how to tie the knot is difficult enough, but how to loose it much more, so much does the untangling call, in the change of fortune, for the wonderful to be joined with verisimilitude. There is nothing in dramatic art either more difficult or more valuable than this combination.[44]

With such an emphasis, the element of improbable accident is not in itself felt to be objectionable so long as its improbability can be skilfully enough concealed. Verisimilitude comes to lie in the management of the revelation rather than in the fact revealed. The emphasis on the clever denouement puts, in turn, a premium on surprise. The better the coming reversal can be concealed, the greater the delight in the discovery. Further, the greater the reversal from unhappiness to happiness the greater the pleasure in the solution.

The second important thing that follows from this admiration for intricately knotted action skilfully untied is that the methods of comedy are advised for tragedy, and such application leads, of course, to tragedy with a happy ending, or tragi-comedy. As we have seen, Giraldi recognized that the double plots, the intrigues, the clever denouements of comedy are especially applicable to the tragedy with double endings or happy endings.[45] Guarini correctly observes that in general the knots of tragedy are more open, less artificially contrived than in comedy.[46] For that very reason, he likes tragi-comedy, which has something of the seriousness of tragedy, yet which is managed with all the dexterity of comedy. There is nothing more instructive on this subject than his detailed analysis of his own *Pastor Fido*.

Thus, even in the Italian critics, relatively conservative and academic as they are, is revealed that interest in romantic story which characterizes the century. It is partly an interest in story well told for its own sake, partly a disposition to take a more relaxed view of the world than either tragedy or satiric comedy allows. It is precisely that relaxed view that delights us in Shakespeare.

THERE IS NO need to enlarge on the fortunate arrivals and discoveries —the reunion of shipwrecked twins, the discarding of page-boy disguises, the discoveries of lost wives in nunneries and on strange seacoasts and even at home—which play so large a part in the denouements of English romantic comedy and tragi-comedy. Since Shakespeare is the chief practitioner of this sort of thing, it is interesting to observe how he learns to handle it, and to compare the implications of his use of it with the implications of the very different endings of Jonsonian comedy.

Shakespeare's problem, as indicated in the discussion of complication earlier in the chapter, was to fit his not altogether tractable characters into a pattern of romantic story, with its usually large admixture of strange adventure and wonderful chance. To make the two seem to move harmoniously was the problem, perhaps even more difficult to achieve in the unraveling than in the complication. *The Comedy of Errors* gives no trouble since character is slight. The lucky recognition of Aegeus and Emilia at the end may be touched with un-Plautine sentiment, but it is essentially Plautine in device. It has no more serious implications than the usual New Comedy recognition. The problem stands out sharply, however, in *The Two Gentlemen*, where story and character rather frown at one another. The device of the Robin-Hood outlaws to bring the four lovers together and the dilemma of love and friendship they face at the end are in approved romantic tradition. Though Valentine, to have his loyal and generous friendship set off against Proteus' betrayal, must *make* the offer of Sylvia to Proteus, Proteus must not, of course, take it, but must repent. For in the end the true lovers, Valentine and Sylvia, must have each other, and the faithful and pathetic Julia must have her Proteus. Yet we protest at the fickle Proteus' having *her*. Too much "character" in Julia has fouled up the conventional lines of Shakespeare's story.

A similar situation of cross-wooing—of shifting triangles of relationship that have to be sorted out into pairs of lovers at the end— comes up again in *A Midsummer Night's Dream*. This time Shakespeare avoids the difficulty of the *Two Gentlemen* by making the motivation—both of complication and of unraveling—almost entirely owing to a combination of chance and magic. Since Puck's juice relieves Demetrius partly and Lysander altogether of responsibility for their fickleness, Shakespeare can play freely with the comic imbroglios it causes without risking the loss of sympathy for his young men. Moreover, within the arranged situation he can develop the individuality of response of the characters as fully as he likes—as he does with Hermia and Helena. The effect is to make agreeable fun of the desperate vows and jealousies and changeabilities of young lovers without these things ever being viewed as serious "problems."

The handling of still another situation of two pairs of lovers involved in cross-wooing is done in *Twelfth Night* in yet another way and with masterly skill. Both in the complication and in the solution there is a nice adjustment of character and chance. The fortuitous element is there in the supposed drowning and lucky rescue of Viola's twin, Sebastian; he holds the key to the solution, for he need only be present on the stage at the same time as Viola for all difficulties to be resolved. Yet he is fitted so smoothly into the scheme of the play, which is built around the various suits for Olivia's hand, that he does not seem obviously devised—as does Emilia in her convent in *The Comedy of Errors*. As for the part character plays in the situation, Olivia's is so imperious and Sebastian's is so conventionally acceptable as the right kind of young man that we are willing enough to take, as he does, his being summoned into matrimony as a pleasant waking dream. The really important question of character, the Duke's transfer of his affections from Olivia to Viola, is handled with such lightness and subtlety that we do not think of being offended or of blaming him for Protean fickleness. The secret is in the delicate balance between the mood of cultivated hopeless sentiment, of falling strains and banks of violets, that always attends the scenes of his courtship of "the cruel fair," Olivia, and his affectionate interest from the start in his "boy," Cesario. Until the end we never see him with Olivia, only listen to his loverly moodiness about her, and we always see him with Viola-Cesario, who we know could charm a bird off a bush. Therefore, we always believe more in his relations with Viola than with Olivia. There is no quarrel in this play between our wanting the heroine to have her man and the kind of man he is.

The final touch in *Twelfth Night* is Shakespeare's making fun of the very convention he is using. When the great scene of discovery comes, which is to untie every knot, and it is time to bring forth the "signs" of recognition upon which the proof of Viola's and Sebastian's twinship must rest, Viola laughs to Sebastian,

> My father had a mole upon his brow.

And Sebastian caps this with indubitable proof: "And so had mine."

The appearance of manipulation increases in the exaggerated discoveries of the late romances of *Cymbeline* and *The Winter's Tale,* with their larger admixture of surprise and theatrical device. The solutions are not actually more arbitrary than in the earlier comedies, since the untangling is worked out independently of Jupiter's descent on an eagle's back and of the statue's coming to life. But the effect of the oracles and the visions and the lengthier explanations is to diminish the amused insouciance of the earlier endings and to increase the wonder. Shakespeare, of course, puts this effect to serious symbolic use in the theme of loss and recovery which runs through all the late romances. The great structural triumph is in *The Tempest,* which is all discovery; the complication within the play—the shipwreck and its consequences of conspiracy among nobility and servants alike—is only a mirror of that earlier complication of conspiracy and sea voyage and tempest which put Prospero upon his island and is the cause of his now having his enemies in his power. The action of the play is Prospero's discovery to his enemies, their discovery of themselves, the lovers' discovery of a new world of wonder, and Prospero's own discovery of an ethic of forgiveness and the renunciation of power.

> In one voyage
> Did Claribel her husband find at Tunis,
> And Ferdinand, her brother, found a wife
> Where he himself was lost; Prospero his
>   dukedom
> In a poor isle, and all of us ourselves,
> When no man was his own.[47]

Structure and idea are one.

The logical climax of development of dramatized romantic story is, as Giraldi and Guarini saw, to build a play towards the denouement. Fletcherian tragi-comedy, with its elaborately contrived and carefully staged surprise discoveries, represents this sort of thing at its most skilful, though without Shakespeare's seriousness. One of the things Caroline admirers of Beaumont and Fletcher single out for praise is precisely this achievement. In his commendatory verses in the 1647 Folio, Cartwright says of Fletcher:

> None can prevent the Fancy, and see through
> At the first opening; all stand wondring how
> The thing will be until it is; which thence
> With fresh delight still cheats, still takes the sense;
> The whole design, the shadows, the lights such
> That none can say he shews or hides too much:
> Business grows up, ripened by just increase,
> And by as just degrees again doth cease,
> The heats and minutes of affairs are watcht,
> And the nice points of time are met, and snatcht:
> Nought later than it should, nought comes before,
> Chymists, and Calculators do err more.[48]

An important difference between the Shakespearean and the Fletcherian discovery is the difference in the handling of the suspense with which one waits for a solution. We know from the start that Cesario is Viola. The suspense with which we watch for a solution to her difficulties is complicated by dramatic irony: we enjoy the predicament in which ignorance of her identity involves the other characters. The same is true of Imogen disguised as Fidele, though the enjoyment is in a different mood. But in *Philaster,* though we may guess through our experience with the habits of romantic tragi-comedy that Bellario is a girl, her identity is carefully kept concealed. Hence, in exchange for dramatic irony extended throughout the play, we are given the concentrated pleasure of finding, at the last desperate moment, the thread that will loosen the knot. In *Twelfth Night* and *Cymbeline* we know which the right thread is, though we do not know just when and how it will be pulled; in *Philaster,* we are confident, through experience, that there is a right thread, but we are not supposed to be able to tell which it is. The surprise in *Philaster* is nevertheless prepared for, in the manner approved by Guarini, in the constitution of the fable: since the predicaments in the story are largely owing to Euphrasia's disguise as Bellario, her discovery will largely solve them—only we are not supposed to know that she holds the key.

In contrast to these solutions in which marvelous chance is made to play so large a part, the solutions of Jonson's best comedies are strictly what Aristotle called for in tragedy, namely, solutions which come from character itself.[49] By his type of nearly complete motivation in character, Jonson builds a closed world; the passions and the engineering wit which complicate the action, also, by the logic of the same process, work out its solution. Greedy credulity and wit in the service of greed alike dupe themselves in the end. The best example of this is in the remorseless and ironic logic by which all the intriguers in *Volpone* destroy themselves. The rapacious "birds of prey" intrigue against each other and against Volpone; Volpone, as rapacious but more witty, uses their own intrigues as the keystone of his intrigue against them; Mosca, wittiest of all, in assisting Volpone in the intrigue against the birds of prey actually intrigues for himself against Volpone; but Mosca's success brings his own ruin, for Volpone, with nothing to lose, since all is lost, discovers the truth about Mosca and himself. In "the uncasing of a fox" all go down together. It is in the nature of things that the rapacious birds of prey should fall prey to cleverer predators. But it is also inevitable that these cleverer ones should destroy themselves by their own prideful wit. Volpone's pride over his and Mosca's success in making Vulture, Crow, and Raven sing in unwilling consort blinds him to Mosca's threat to himself. The scene of the inventory, in which Mosca as Volpone's heir turns off the suitors one by one and the "dead" Volpone gloats over their disappointment, reveals the wonderful double irony of Mosca's part. Now that we see him, seemingly playing Volpone's game, really playing his own, we realize that he has never played anything else. The feigned playing up to Voltore and the others was no falser than his playing up to Volpone has been; he has never played other than himself, the parasite, and Volpone had all the clues to know it. So the clever Fly springs the trap on the Fox. But the irony is not done. Mosca's security has rested only on the ingenious but flimsy contrivance of his lies and his tricks; one true word from Volpone is enough to pull it down.

In this world of human baseness and its consequences, accident is allowed, to be sure, in a not illiberal use of coincidence, but it becomes simply part of the data which the intriguer manipulates. It is the accident of the fly entering the spider's web. Nothing but chance, for instance, impels Drugger, Dapper, Kastril, and his sister all to arrive at the Alchemist's on the very morning that Sir Epicure and the Anabaptists are pressing for "projection"; but as the lesser dupes come in, Face weaves them into his scheme with brilliant improvisation. In the same way the unlucky arrival of his master Lovewit on that same busy day is used by Face to save his face. The ending, even though Face goes unpunished, does not therefore break the logic of the design.

Nor does the rather jolly ending of *Bartholomew Fair*, when dupers and duped gather together in a feast at Justice Overdo's. The fools have already got what they deserved or learned a lesson: through running after gingerbread and hobbyhorses, Cokes has lost his cash and his fiancée; through too much attention to his "art," Littlewit has come too close for comfort to being cuckolded; and Justice Overdo likewise, through worrying about morals farther from home. We should be sorry to see Ursula carted for helping to corrupt women whose silliness asks for a fall, or Nightingale hanged for picking the pockets that open themselves to be picked. Without the viciousness and positive evil of *Volpone*, and with a shift of responsibility from gullers to gulled, both *The Alchemist* and *Bartholomew Fair* call for lighter endings.

The denouements of Jonsonian satiric comedy, therefore, lie in the logic of events, produced as character manipulates the situations that present themselves; the solutions are generally ironic in that the end achieved is the reverse of the one aimed for. In contrast, the denouements of Shakespearean romantic comedy are worked out by a combination of character and pure luck; the irony is the reverse of Jonsonian irony in that the very things that seem to work against the end wished for are often the things that bring it about—for example, the banishment of the Duke and the flights of Orlando and of Rosalind in *As You Like It*, the exposure of the infant Perdita in *The Winter's Tale*, the casting adrift of Prospero and Miranda in *The Tempest*. A specially good example is in *Much Ado;* the stupidity of the watch, though it first works to assist the malicious conspirators, eventually blunders into confounding them. The effect of this kind of irony is to give an impression of a not wholly explicable world, in which good intentions count even against intelligence when that is applied to the wrong ends. It is a very different world from that of *Volpone*. There the innocence of Celia and Bonario is helpless in itself; its triumph is purely negative, incidental to the mutual self-destruction of the evil characters. Although Jonson set up his own comedy against the comedy of romantic adventure as something closer to real life, the realism is neither more nor less, only differently placed; and the distortion is as great, only in a different direction. It is as easy to believe in the shipwrecks and happy reunions of Shakespearean comedy, given the delightfully credible people who experience them, as in the perfect rationality of cause and consequence in Jonson's closed world. In fact, some tastes may find it easier. For most of us would admit to a large mixture of apparent irrationality in ourselves and the world we daily experience, a world in which we do not always perceive the links in the causal chain, one which we have to take on faith, yet one in which we know we can make a life. At any rate, Jonson's simpler, more explicable, more intransigent world is harder to take. There are times when we like to believe that for the well-meaning and the kind of heart there is a share of luck that's good.

IN TRAGEDY, as we should expect, the fortuitous ending is less frequent than in comedy. The expected catastrophe was death, and the traditional patterns of tragic opposition, combined or separate—the Falls of Princes theme, the revenge theme, the conflict between forces of good and evil—were all easy to lead to that conclusion, although, as we have seen in the section on the debate, a wrench might come in an attempt to resolve conflicting points of view. The tragedy of power was expected to follow its curve of rise and fall; ambition in the protagonist inevitably generated an opposing counter-action of ambition or revenge that, with or without the aid of fortune, would bring him low. The conflict of other passions—love, jealousy, or hate —was expected to set in motion a chain of crime and of revenge for crime that would lead inevitably to a fatal catastrophe. When a moral problem entered in a simple choice between good and evil, the tragic choice, the choice of evil, could lead only to death. The great moral insights of Marlowe and Shakespeare and Chapman framed dilemmas of choice, so that a man like Faustus, to obtain an ambiguous good, must coöperate with an evil he does not fully reckon with; or, like Hamlet, be forced through no fault of his own to choose between two evils; or, like Othello or Brutus or Byron, be persuaded to choose an evil he thinks he can transform by calling it an act of justice. Irony was deepened by catastrophe which came no less inexorably because the face of truth had been hidden when choice was made. Difficulties of resolution came, when, in the handling of these more complicated problems, opposing points of view, political or ethical, might both be justified.

Certain conventions often used to assist the denouement should not mislead us. We should not too hastily condemn as arbitrary the sudden changes of attitude, like Evadne's repentance in *The Maid's Tragedy* and her consequent vow to kill the king, which help to precipitate catastrophe. Elizabethan psychological theory, as we know, allowed for such dramatic changes, and certain situations by convention demanded certain responses. One must, of course, agree that these conventions of sudden repentance or sudden response to the promptings of evil passion were exceedingly convenient to a hard-pressed dramatist. Another common device that need not be arbitrary is the masque, dance, play, or duel under cover of whose movements the final catastrophic killing is done. The great usefulness of the device is attested by the frequency with which it is employed in the best plays: e.g., in *The Spanish Tragedy, Hamlet, Antonio's Revenge, The Revenger's Tragedy, Women Beware Women*. But though this device has an affinity with the carefully staged surprise endings of tragi-comedy, in all the plays named except *The Revenger's Tragedy* the logic of the plot demands the killings, and the audience is aware of the sinister use to which the entertainment is to be put; the only surprise is to the victims. The dance in *The Broken Heart* provides a genuine surprise; but since the knot has been nearly untangled with the deaths of three of the principal characters, Calantha's amazing death merely cuts the last thread. The play is significantly late.

The fortuitous and the arbitrary were more apt to be used to avoid an ending in death than to bring one about. But there was actually little place in anything that could qualify as tragedy for the Euripidean solution of the type used in *Medea*, which, by divine intervention, mitigated the consequences of crime. Solutions "by machine" had their place in tragi-comedy, but the tone of such plays is not at all like *Medea*, or even like *Andromache* or *Orestes*. For in the romantic world of English tragi-comedy, the intention of crime is rarely fulfilled in act. (Cf. the Queen's frustrated attempts to poison Imogen or Philaster's to stab Arethusa and Bellario.) Hence there is no genuine sense of tragedy, and no moral shock in a happy ending. Domestic tragedy tended to soften the catastrophe by the wrong-doer's repentance before death (as in *Arden, A Yorkshire Tragedy,*

A Woman Killed, The Witch of Edmonton). His soul is saved, like Mankind's in *The Castle of Perseverance*,[50] though his body is dead; pious sentiment replaces tragic irony. But the effect of arbitrariness modern readers get from the last-minute repentances was probably not the effect on Elizabethan audiences; the conventions of the gallows speech was a convention in life as well as in art. *The Revenger's Tragedy,* with the sudden appearance of Antonio to execute justice on Vindici and Hippolito, appears quite as arbitrary in the other direction. This kind of double ending, so much liked by Giraldi, wherein the solution differs for the good and the bad, requires a good deal of preparatory ingenuity to manage plausibly. Even so, the air of manipulation clings to it; and by confining the catastrophe to the evil doers it lessens tragic irony.

The deeper problem of the ending in the great tragedies is not how well various conventions are manipulated to avoid the appearance of arbitrariness. It is the degree to which acts of moral choice bring about the ending and the degree to which chance is used to heighten the effect of inevitable tragedy. We think of Shakespearean tragedy as the tragedy of character *par excellence*. Yet Shakespeare's tragic world is not, any more than his comic world, a world of perfect logic, in which every act is motivated in character and has a strictly proportionate consequence. It is Iago's and Edmund's mistake to think it so. The world of uncontrollable circumstance always operates to heighten the mystery and deepen the irony. Shakespeare employs accident in his denouements, in the way approved by Aristotle, to heighten tragic wonder and to raise the question of human destiny. In a simple way he does it in *Romeo and Juliet*. The advancement of the wedding date and the accident which prevents Friar John from delivering Friar Lawrence's necessary message to Romeo increase the sense of unfriendly destiny that has pursued the young couple from the beginning of their love. But that play is primarily a tragedy of circumstance. In a profounder way, Shakespeare uses the device in *Lear,* a play in which the hero's pride and unwisdom have unmistakably set in motion the widening circles of tragic consequence. The failure of Edmund's countermanding order to reach the jailer in time to save Cordelia from hanging and Lear from resultant heartbreak sustains the question of theodicy the action of the play has already raised: Are the gods just? Why, if so, do they permit suffering out of all proportion to guilt? Why do they permit the wholly innocent to suffer at all? The effect of this final blow of Lear's death, coming as it does after Albany's remark,

> All friends shall taste
> The wages of their virtue, and all foes
> The cup of their deservings,

is to give one a sense of a world, like Job's world, beyond the reach of men to know. Albany's pious judgment is palpably false. A man can draw up no simple equation of suffering and deserts, reduce to no easy formula the ways of divine justice.

In the tragedy of Shakespeare's greatest Jacobean contemporaries, Chapman and Webster, unfriendly fortune plays a much larger rôle. Yet how it does so is hard to define in terms of the plot. It is not brought in just as a trick of the denouement, to force an unhappy ending, which in most of their plays grows logically enough out of the constitution of the fable. Bad fortune is mainly something always talked about or felt, an atmosphere of fatality surrounding the central characters. Different as are Bussy, Clermont, Byron, Vittoria, and the Duchess of Malfi, they all exhibit a kind of passivity. Action swirls around them and they are involved in it and die, yet no one can ever say with certainty, at least of any of Chapman's three, as one can say of Brutus, Othello, Macbeth, or Antony, that he made a free choice which led him to doom. If this can be said of Webster's Vittoria and Duchess, it is nevertheless qualified by a note of defiance that they had a right to the choice.

This passivity leads to a heightened emphasis on the way in which death is met, for this is the climax of the suffering, the last blow of fate. There is something of this Senecanism throughout Jacobean tragedy, in Shakespeare as well as the rest. But in general, though the stoicism of Shakespeare's last scenes emphasizes the hero's courage and increases our sense of the mystery of man's lot, it does not confuse our awareness of the values by which we must judge the actions of men. Othello's final speech should surely not be taken as defiant apology or as cheering himself up.[51] With dignity it puts things straight, as they need to be put straight, so that we do not confuse motive and deed. He does not ask to be saved from the consequences of his act. The speech must be viewed in the entire Christian context of the play. When he first realized what he had done in the killing of Desdemona, it seemed to him that he had made eternal

separation between himself and her—that she was in heaven, whereas
he had doomed himself to hell:

> . . . when we shall meet at compt,
> This look of thine will hurl my soul from heaven,
> And fiends will snatch at it. . . .
> Whip me, ye devils,
> From the possession of this heavenly sight!
> Blow me about in winds! roast me in sulphur!
> Wash me in steep-down gulfs of liquid fire!
> O Desdemona! Desdemona! dead!

Consequently, when he takes his sword at the end to execute a true
act of justice on himself, in commutation for the false act of justice
on her, he is, so far as he knows, sending himself to eternal damnation. This is not at all the same as Byron's frantic protest of innocence
or as Bussy's Herculean stance, in which he is solely concerned to
meet with the right gesture the death he feels dishonoring, not to
recognize what he did to bring it on himself:

> Prop me, true sword, as thou hast ever done!
> The equal thought I bear of life and death
> Shall make me faint on no side; I am up;
> Here like a Roman statue I will stand
> Till death hath made me marble. Oh, my fame,
> Live in despite of murder! . . .
> . . . fly where men feel
> The burning axletree, and those that suffer
> Beneath the chariot of the snowy Bear:
> And tell them all that D'Ambois now is hasting
> To the eternal dwellers; that a thunder
> Of all their sighs together (for their frailties
> Beheld in me) may quit my worthless fall
> With a fit volley for my funeral.[52]

He forgives Montsurry for killing him; he does not ask Montsurry's
forgiveness for taking his wife. Even Antony's end, although it reflects Plutarch's Stoicism, including the use of the Hercules symbol,[53]
is different from Bussy's. For with Enorbarbus we have watched Antony making "his will lord of his reason" and are in no doubt of the
assistance he has given Fortune in his fall. Webster's dying brave ones
are less protesting than Chapman's, more contemptuously pessimistic.

> O, I am gone—
> We are only like dead walls, or vaulted graves,
> That ruin'd, yields no echo.[54]

But they are not like Shakespeare's freer characters, either. In Webster's strange and terrible world, courage in the face of suffering and death becomes the one positive value.

Summary

Since the last section has ranged considerably beyond the technicalities of the denouement, it may be helpful to return to plot structure for a survey and a pointing up of several matters.

The sources and plot structure.—One of the controlling elements in plot-building by Elizabethan dramatists was certainly the source stories they chose to dramatize. In general, though with many exceptions, plays based on *novelle* or on Roman or Italian plays are better knit, more unified and coherent, than those based on chronicles or episodic romances. That is to be expected. Material of the latter kind is hard to restrict and organize; in any case it appears to have been liked for its liveliness and variety. Sir Edmund Chambers remarks on the episodic looseness of the mystery cycles, which were hardly obsolete in Shakespeare's day, and on the persistence of the same sort of thing in the chronicle plays. He also shrewdly observes: "One need not expect that this desultory temper should have offended against the popularity of the type. It is at all times your literary man, and not the public of the theater, that calls for the plain issue." [55] That is probably true. For most Elizabethan dramatists, doubtless, success in the theater was of first importance, and if a lively and bustling parade of scenes satisfied, perhaps that was enough.

Nevertheless, a well told story is liked by an audience at any level of sophistication. One reason, among others, why Shakespeare was more popular than Jonson, may have been that he is a better storyteller; compare, for example, *Catiline* with *Julius Caesar.* And many dramatists, in different degrees and with varying success, did put some effort into plot-building. To see that this was so one has only to compare Marlowe's *Edward II* with *Tamburlaine,* both taken from episodic sources; Peele's *Old Wives' Tale* with *David and Bethsabe;* Dekker's *Honest Whore* with *Old Fortunatus;* Shakespeare's *Richard III* with *Henry VI;* and so on.

Traditional means of complication.—A number of traditional means of dramatic opposition were available and were fully exploited to help control the dramatic fable. Three of these, sometimes separate, but often combined in richly varied ways, lent themselves to the purposes of tragedy.

One was the conflict between a hero and a malignant adversary, common in medieval pageant, romance, legend, and religious drama; in the morality play the conflict was explicitly one between good and evil and was internal as well as external. Much of English tragedy, from *Dr. Faustus* to the *The Changeling,* kept the coloring of this background, with evil, both outwardly and inwardly conceived, as the antagonist. The deepening of motivation in character did not replace, but rather enhanced (in plays like *Othello* and *The Duchess of Malfi*) the sense of a wider evil active in the world and forever antagonistic to the happiness of men. This conception of evil as adversative provided a focus of dramatic conflict, but did not limit the plays in which it appeared to a particular pattern of plot movement.

A second means of dramatic opposition, one which did provide an identifiable plot movement, was the cyclic pattern, from medieval narrative tragedy, of the Falls of Princes theme, in which the fall from power of the hero was crossed by the rise of the antagonist. It shaped, for example, the structure of *Richard III, Richard II, Sejanus,* and Shakespeare's Roman plays. The motivation in all these plays, of course, varies greatly, and with it the tragic implications. In quite different ways, *Richard III, Sejanus,* and *Macbeth* show what might be done with the *De casibus* scheme when the motive of ambition was combined with the motive of evil. In *King Lear* this combination reaches the ultimate in complexity, both in plot structure and in tragic conception.

A third means of dramatic opposition was the motive of revenge, familiar from many sources, but stimulated by fresh acquaintance with Seneca and well supplied from Italian novels. Revenge was to prove one of the most fruitful motives for complicating tragic plots. It was used in plots of the *De casibus* type like *Richard III* and *Julius Caesar,* but even more in the intrigue plots of love, lust, and jealousy so popular after the turn of the century. It especially lent itself to the development, by some of the greater Jacobeans—Shakespeare (in *Hamlet*), Marston, Tourneur, Webster, and Middleton—of a tragedy of evil.

A fourth method of dramatic complication, the method of comic intrigue, thoroughly familiar in Plautus and Terence and known as well from Italian comedy, was to prove useful in the handling of all kinds of comedy, even that based on romantic story. *Twelfth Night* and *Every Man in his Humour* exemplify the very different comic purposes to which the method might be adapted. But the looser techniques of traditional romantic story continued to have their way, as in popular plays like *Fair Em;* Peele's *Old Wives' Tale* is a delightful parody of these techniques.

The debate.—Another thing that may well have been important in shaping the Elizabethan drama was the debate—the habit common for centuries in folk play and pageant, in cultivated literary forms like the *débat,* in rhetorical training, and in academic disputation. Debate, as Professor Baskervill has emphasized in his studies on the popular background of the Elizabethan drama, is the core of drama, since it is a means other than physical of exhibiting opposition. But it has its liabilities as well as its advantages, and I have suggested that some of the weaknesses of logical progression found in the Elizabethan drama are owing to a habit of posing both sides equally well in formal debate, with the solution missing or arbitrary. The necessary forward movement of the story is not always clarified or decided by the debate; it may even be impeded.

The denouement.—The untying of the knot, as the critics knew, is harder to manage than the tying, and an arbitrary cutting of it by a *deus ex machina* or by a liberal use of coincidence and chance is an easy way out of difficulties. I have not tried to survey the methods of denouement of Elizabethan dramatists, or to discuss their individual clumsiness or skill at it; I have made only casual mention of special techniques, such as the dance, masque, or play so frequently used to manipulate the tragic catastrophe. I have concentrated, instead, on three matters which seem to me of special interest and importance.

One is the difference between the characteristic denouement of Shakespearean comedy, with its use of sustained suspense, and of Fletcherian tragi-comedy, with its use of late surprise. The latter type is quite in line with critical approval of the cleverness which manages a "favola intrecciata" so that though the solution is prepared for in the logic of the fable, the means to it is concealed until the latest possible moment. Fletcherian tragi-comedy, with its emphasis on plot manipulation, smooth timing, and stage effect, is one of the best examples of the movement of Stuart drama in the direction of dramatic "art" as critically defined. The preference of the critics for intricate plots, deftly solved, would lead, if followed, precisely to the Caroline style of tragi-comedy. Critical theory and dramatic practice fuse in the Restoration period, and Beaumont and Fletcher become, significantly, the favorite playwrights from the earlier period.

The second matter is the rôle played by accident, coincidence, or luck in the management of comedy, especially in the ending. Jonsonian and Shakespearean comedy illustrate the extremes of method and implication. Jonson, at his best, constructs a perfect Aristotelian plot of beginning, middle, and end in causal progression; he creates a wholly logical world in which the interplay of the interests of his characters moves the plot towards a necessary conclusion. Though there may be a plentiful use of coincidence in the plot, it is part of the data the author makes his characters manipulate in solving their problems; it is not itself made the solvent. Shakespeare, on the other hand, takes a romantic story, with all its traditional conventions and its improbabilities, animates it with his characters (more realistic in effect, usually, than the story), and lets happy chance have a large part in the outcome. There is actually no less skill in Shakespeare's management of his plots than in Jonson's of his, but the effect of management is less. And, more important, the impression of the two worlds of comedy is quite different—the one ordered and rather remorseless, even when it is funny; the other irrational, a bit haphazard, and full of good luck. Again, as with Beaumont and Fletcher, it is interesting that Jonson's logical, intricate plotting had its day of glory in the neoclassic period, when critical principle triumphed on the stage.

The third matter is the part that the irrational may play in the outcome of tragedy, and here again I have chosen to look at the deeper implications of the denouement rather than at details of its technical management. A logical bias, the same thing that led Giraldi and Guarini to admire the intricate knot skilfully tied and untied, was undoubtedly one of several attitudes that led Giraldi to favor tragedy with the double ending, tragedy in which the evil suffer and the good are rewarded according to their deserts. This rationally conducted tragedy is the kind that triumphs in the Augustan age. The greater Elizabethan and Jacobean tragic plots are always more than the working out, according to a strict rule of poetic justice, of the logical consequences of the hero's misjudgment or frailty. The sense of unpredictable circumstance, of evil destiny, of unrecognizable evil, or simply of the widening circles of consequence that take in the good and the bad alike is always there in some degree to suggest that man is not wholly master of his fate. It will be recalled how Tate in 1681 and Coleman a century later mutilated the ending of *King Lear*. The temper that understood and asked for the strict meting out of poetic justice in tragedy evidently could not endure the terror and the pity of that awful catastrophe.

12 Endeavors of Art

Why, hark you, honest, honest Philomuse
(You that endeavor to endear our thoughts
To the composer's spirit), hold this firm:
Music and Poetry were first approv'd
By common sense; and that which pleased most
Held most allowed pass: your rules of art
Were shapt to pleasure, not pleasure to your rules.
    —JOHN MARSTON, *What You Will*, Induction

WE COME TO a final assessment of English renaissance drama in its achievement of characteristic and satisfying artistic forms. The problems in such an achievement were met with varying degrees of success, but at least they were met well enough by the end of the century so that we can talk about "Elizabethan tragedy," "Elizabethan comedy," "the Elizabethan chronicle play" and know we shall be implying sufficiently characteristic and recognizable forms for our terms to have meaning; and we know, too, that if we talk specifically of "Jacobean" or "Caroline" comedy, tragedy, or tragi-comedy, the ways in which we are refining on the earlier terms will be understood in at least a general way.

The central structural problem in achieving these forms was, as we have seen in Chapters X and XI, the conversion of narrative into drama. This was mainly a practical problem, of course; but it was not wholly so, uncomplicated by theory. Nearly universal assumptions about the aims and methods of literary art played their part in the shaping of even so popular a form as the Elizabethan drama. This was true whether these assumptions were explicitly held and formulated, or whether they were less critically entertained as a set of familiar terms and attitudes. These assumptions, as I have tried to suggest in Chapters II–IV and V–VIII, helped shape the drama in both a positive and a negative way, as they coöperated with or pulled

341

against the story-telling impulse. The final English dramatic achievement, then, needs to be reviewed in its relation to the three major ideas of renaissance poetic: namely the ideas of eloquence, of mimesis, and of moral purpose.

Eloquence, Imitation, and Moral Purpose

As for the belief in the value of eloquence, so deeply inculcated, there is no conflict at all between theory and taste. Whatever else it may be, the Elizabethan drama is always eloquent. The artistic conflict, not always recognized by the dramatists, or if it was, not always resolved, was of course between the taste for rhetorical fullness and the demand drama makes for economy. Eloquence is both the strength and the weakness of Elizabethan drama, for it gives it its richness of texture at the expense, often, of clear structural emphasis. We need not rehearse illustrations. Marlowe and Chapman are perhaps the most conspicuous of the major dramatists whose glories and whose defects take root in the same impulse to splendid speech. But even Jonson, with all his skill in manipulating a complex fable, was liable to let the strong framework of his structure be obscured by the heaping up of detail. More so, in fact, than Shakespeare, for all of Shakespeare's fondness for variety and "copy."

I have always thought that *Richard II, Romeo and Juliet,* and *Love's Labour's Lost* were remarkable disciplinary pieces for Shakespeare. (I hold with the dating of *Love's Labour's Lost,* at least in revised form, as late as 1594, and of the final form of *Romeo and Juliet* as 1594 or 95.) The conception of each allowed him considerable rhetorical freedom and at the same time channeled the rhetoric to a central dramatic purpose. *Love's Labour's Lost* throughout, and *Romeo and Juliet* in the young-men-about-town scenes, allowed him both to indulge in and to make merry with the linguistic artifice he and his age were so fond of. *Romeo and Juliet* and *Richard II* allowed him to exploit highly formal poetry, in the one as a device of heightening the poignant beauty of youthful tragic love, in the other as the quintessential expression of a character for whom reality dwells in the hypnotic suggestion of words and the images they evoke:

> *Boling.* The shadow of your sorrow hath destroy'd
> The shadow of your face.

Rich.   Say that again.
The shadow of my sorrow? Ha! let's see!
'Tis very true: my grief lies all within;
And these external manners of laments
Are merely shadows to the unseen grief
That swells with silence in the tortured soul.

So Richard takes the lure. But Shakespeare, enjoying the verbal game, never lets it run away from its function in exhibiting Richard's weakness. He always ends one of these rounds of verbal play with a clarifying comment that marks it as a pitifully ineffectual game in a world of political realities:

Mock not my senseless conjuration, lords,

or

                    Well, well, I see
I talk but idly,

or

                              But my time
Runs posting on in Bolingbroke's proud joy,
While I stand fooling here, his Jack o' th' clock.

After these plays, though the eloquence is as great, the evidence of rhetorical device becomes less; style is put to more oblique uses. The artifice and the simplicity together become Cleopatra and the world she makes for Antony; they become *King Lear, The Winter's Tale,* and *The Tempest.*

With other dramatists as well as Shakespeare, after the turn of the century one becomes generally less aware of an eloquence that breaks dramatic bounds. Sometimes the control may come from a focus of attention on dramatic technique, as in Beaumont and Fletcher, so that temptation grows less to let eloquence run riot. Sometimes, as in Middleton, the change comes from the development of a sparer style, closer to prose speech. Yet in one of the greatest of the Jacobeans, Webster, poetic eloquence is still packed, and sometimes unruly.

THE AESTHETIC OF imitation, interpreted as the imitation of universal truth and governed by rules of decorum, partly helped control the subject matter and the point of view of tragedy and comedy, the conception of character, the social level of the characters, and the levels of style. But though the various formulae applicable to drama were seldom questioned in critical theory, they were constantly questioned in English practice. Since I have not treated except incidentally the levels of style, I shall confine this review to the matters discussed in the book, namely the conventional forms of drama and the handling of character.

The accepted universal truth for tragedy was catastrophe befalling persons, preferably historical persons, of high place and fame; of comedy, the commonplace misadventures in love and business, ending in happiness, of fictitious persons of middling rank. The recurrent statement of these formulae, by practising dramatists as well as critics, and the numbers of plays that satisfy them testify to their importance and to the long and deep-rooted tradition behind them. Yet the many ways in which English drama did not conform testify quite as strongly to other interests and pressures.

In practice romantic comedy, grounded in romantic story, the staple of which was the adventure and the true love of characters quite apt to be well born, was as popular as the comedy of bourgeois manners and social criticism. Indeed, it was probably more so. Testimony to this popularity exists in the long life of *Mucedorus,* which went into more editions than any other play of the period.[1] It is a play of a fair princess, a disguised prince, unwelcome wooers, elopements, missed meetings by wells, escapes from bears and "wild men," and of course a happy-ever-after ending. Except for Jonson largely, and for other Jacobeans occasionally, romantic comedy supplied the frame, not always very happily, even for the comedy of critical realism. And though satiric realism was the order of the day in the first decade of the seventeenth century, taste shifted back to romantic comedy in the refurbished form of Fletcherian tragi-comedy. It was Jonson who understood the issue and returned to it again and again in his prefaces and prologues. For Jonson, the countesses and their cross-wooings, the knights and their slaughter of paynims, the magicians and their squibs, could not fulfill the true function of comedy, since its function was to imitate men as they are and the sphere of its imitation was men in the market place. It is interesting to remark that Beaumont, who so gaily mocked in *The Knight of the Burning Pestle* the romantic tastes of the London citizens uninstructed in the true function of comedy, became a partner of the famous team that helped set the style for Stuart tragi-comedy—more sophisticated and elegant, of course, than Ralph's naïve taste could have risen to, yet in its own way quite as much a world of dream as his.

On the whole, tragedy stayed closer to the conventional idea of what it ought to be, and this was largely, I think, because the theme of tragedy inherited from the Middle Ages, the *De casibus* theme, fulfilled, or seemed to fulfill, the expectations of tragedy as defined by the critics. Moreover, in an age when the spectacle of changing fortunes among the great was everywhere before the eye, the universal truth of the theme could hardly be questioned. But, again, the story-telling impulse led tragic dramatists to borrow from prose tales and this contributed to the development of the Italianate tragedy of crime and intrigue, where affairs of public moment were replaced by more narrowly domestic matters and in which the characters might be fictitious. In the same way, contemporary murders among ordinary people furnished exciting plots, and so led to what has been called "domestic tragedy," tragedy of a different social milieu and style, and for which critical apology was often made.

Interest in dramatized story, interest in history, especially English history, and a lively nationalism, helped develop a new type of play, the "chronicle," which was able to sustain itself vigorously in its own right. Marlowe and Shakespeare tried to pull the English chronicle play into the orbit of tragedy; this involved no conflict, since the falls of princes were in any case thought to be the essence of tragedy. But the untragical chronicle, without much attempt at critical justification, continued to be written—by Shakespeare himself, by Heywood, and by lesser men. Some of these plays (for example, *Henry IV, Henry VIII*, and *Edward IV*) echo the Mirror tradition in some degree, but are yet not shaped into tragedy. *Henry VIII*, most interestingly for its late date (1613), presents eloquently a whole series of falls—Buckingham's, Katharine's, Wolsey's; but the play ends with the baptism of the infant Elizabeth and Cranmer's fulsome prophecy of England's greatness. The whole effect is of a pageant of history, now pitiful, now grimly ironic, now splendid.

Finally, traditional sorts of plays, some derived from morality and interlude, some (like *Fair Em the Miller's Daughter*) with no discernible form, continued to be presented and evidently enjoyed.

THE ISSUE OF universal truth is of course especially acute with respect to the handling of character, and the classical rules of decorum provide for the critics the touchstone by which the success of the imitation of this truth can be judged. The careful application of these rules leads to characters constructed as types. But although there are certain recurrent types in Elizabethan drama—braggart soldiers, city and country gulls, roaring boys, vain city wives, fawning courtiers, and so on—the total impression is more of an active and individual life, sometimes showing itself in momentary flashes, sometimes sustaining a whole character, than of a gallery of consistent and typical portraits. As I have indicated in the chapter on character, there is no literary theory to provide for this individuality except for the theory of *energeia* in style, and no very adequate psychological theory except for the one that any person is capable of any passion given sufficient stimulus, and except for the extension of the theory of humours to account for any individual excess or idiosyncracy. There is, besides, the important idea from rhetoric that *ethos* is the business of comedy, *pathos* of tragedy. If followed through in practice, this would lead to the depiction of types in comedy, the depiction of passions—not necessarily of individualized characters—in tragedy. All these notions, sometimes coöperating, sometimes contradictory, appear to have their part in the varied characters of Elizabethan drama. Assessment of particular influences is difficult, and perhaps futile. In the end one may feel that eloquence— the sheer delight in playing with language—combined with a lively observation of detail, has more to do with our sense of living people in the drama than any theories of character consciously applied. And indeed, one may sometimes feel in moments of bafflement that the whole matter of character is a haphazard affair, and that success, when it comes, comes unlooked for.

There are hundreds of characters in plays that have no "character," properly speaking, at all; they exist only for their function in the story. Here we have evidence once again, I think, that the main roots of Elizabethan drama lie in traditional medieval narrative. In story told for its own sake, the fable is dominant and the characters fulfill the rôles cut out for them. These rôles may be quite conventional, as in fairy tale, and so in a sense they are universal—as a prince charming, a wicked stepmother, a bloodthirsty pirate are universal; but such characters, though sometimes "true" in a mythical sense, are not really good illustrations of the decorum of types. Their function is to move a story in expected ways, not to hold a mirror up to the varieties of human beings as they operate in society. The perception of this may have been another of Jonson's reasons for rejecting the narrative technique of romantic comedy; its characters would seem to fulfill no critical social function.

When the characters of Elizabethan drama come alive, it is not because their conventional outlines are painstakingly filled in with more detail, but because they are given some intimate and realistic touches of motive or response that make them spring to life, perhaps only for a scene or two, perhaps for a whole play. Sometimes the individualizing touch is disconcerting because it gives the character a dramatic moment of life that pulls against the direction of the plot, like Shylock's *apologia*. Sometimes it is in excess of the demands of the story and embarrasses the improbabilities of the fable, especially when the other characters merely fulfill their plot functions; so Julia seems to sort ill with Proteus, Helena and the Countess with Bertram. But when it is successful—as with Greene's Margaret of Fressingfield, who has a wit and independence beyond that called for by her rôle as charming dairymaid; Heywood's Master Frankford, whose grief at the sight of his faithless wife's lute is not in the pattern of jealous husbands; Dekker's bravely pathetic Bellafront, impudently callous Matheo, and crusty Friscobaldo, who follow no regular pattern of reformed prostitute, high-flying rogue, or benevolent father—we have universality of another sort than the universality of type.

This is Shakespeare's kind of universality. His way of handling characters is like Greene's, Dekker's, and Heywood's—and like many others of his contemporaries—in the sympathetic awareness of the situation they are in and in the individualizing accent he knows how to provide them with. Apart from greater range and sometimes greater subtlety of perception, Shakespeare's difference from his romantic contemporaries is largely a matter of degree; he is more often able to sustain his conceptions, more able to make one character seem of a piece (without resorting to repeated tricks of phrase or mannerism), more able to endow all the characters of a play with life, and, most important of all, more able to make them work together functionally. For this sustained interplay of character works towards an architectonic end. Some might say that Shakespeare's greatest triumphs are in those highly individualized characters that have proved endlessly resistant to critical analysis and description, and that yet convey a sense of integrity and vitality in spite of their exasperating inconsistencies—characters, that is, like Falstaff, Hamlet, and Cleopatra. Is this impression of integrity the result of intentionally subtle complication on Shakespeare's part, or merely a lucky illusion produced by many separate touches of vitality? Perhaps that is like asking whether one of Cézanne's apples, composed of many strokes of color laid on side by side is "really" the picture of an apple. It is at least what it is, and nothing else.

Type characters in Elizabethan drama naturally found their place in the imitations and adaptations of Roman and Italian comedy. But this method of characterization fell in with the traditionally familiar one of satiric portraiture in poem, pamphlet, and morality play. The socially critical comedy that came to be so popular in the Jacobean period owed at least as much to this tradition as to the classical one, fortunately for the vitality and immediacy of the plays. The liveliest gallery of types is of the rogues and gulls of contemporary life. But not all the types come to life with the necessary individualizing touches. Surely Stuart drama is at its stalest and dreary worst in its numberless senile husbands, obsequious courtiers, smirking female bawds and pimps, and appalling nymphomaniacs.

The special Elizabethan invention to secure individuality was the device of the humour, the caricature of some excess usually against the background of a type. But a humour endlessly applied can be the dullest and most limited form of characterization. Jonson, who most fully exploited the fashion, also showed the best way to transcend it, in the individualizing richness of attitude and language with which he endowed his great comic characters. Volpone, for instance, has more than the humour of lust for money; he has also a humour of wit and a humour of epicurism. The combination, expressed through Jonson's wonderfully precise and subtle sense of language, is quite unlike the ordinary flat humour character.

Type characters appear fitfully in all kinds of English plays, comic and tragic, whenever there is some reason of social satire or observation of manners to have them. It is only Jonson who fully realizes their function in satiric comedy and makes their interplay of motive the spring of his comic action. The others who are most skilful at types—Marston, Middleton, and Chapman—are usually ready to fall back in some degree on a romantic frame story (romantic at least in externals) and use their satiric types only in a limited way in relief against it. It is Jonson, then, who most completely achieves the imitation of universal truth in comic drama as it was understood by the critics. But he does it less by the imitation of Roman comedy than by the working out of a new and sure organic relationship between plot and character.

THE THIRD GREAT tenet of Elizabethan poetic, that the aim of poetry was didactic, is the most difficult, in the degree and quality of its effect on the form of Elizabethan drama, to define and handle. I reviewed in Chapter IV the nearly universal statement of the didactic aim, both by critics and by practising dramatists, and noticed the more casual, hardly polemic questionings of it on the part of a few dramatists; I also stated the very great difficulty of assessing this aim in practice, since it can operate in so many different ways.

We can recognize easily enough the straight didactic plays written for some special purpose—for instruction to students, like *Lingua;* for political warning on a particular issue, like *Gorboduc;* for the statement of literary theory, like Jonson's *Poetaster;* for topical satire, like Middleton's *Game at Chess.* But these plays are special and occasional, written explicitly for instruction or for the airing of particular issues. It is a more general didactic aim that the critics had in mind—namely, that plays should make men better, both in private and in public affairs. Their concern would therefore have been with the plays—tragedies, comedies, histories—that were the daily fare of the theaters. And these plays were chiefly dramatized stories, true or fictitious, by and large giving the impression of having been written for entertainment, but varying greatly in their degree of seriousness, both moral and artistic.

As I have indicated in Chapter IV, the overlaying of plays with moral sententiousness—and there is a good deal of this—does not help us much in assessing the didactic aim, for we can rarely tell how honest it is, or how superficial; how much it is a concession to Puritan criticism, how much a matter of ingrained taste and habit. And it may not affect the essential form of the play at all. The same difficulty is encountered with the chauvinistic sentiment that is rampant in so many plays of chronicle type (though that is more apt to affect the structure), not only in the crude form found in such plays as Heywood's on the troubles of Queen Elizabeth (*If You Know Not Me, You Know Nobody,* Parts I and II), but as well in the rhetorical splendors of Shakespeare's *Henry V.*

The case for a shaping moral intention in popular drama has been most plausibly made for domestic tragedies, those plays based on actual crimes committed by men of mean estate and without political implication. Professor Henry H. Adams [2] has shown that most tragedies of this sort follow a recognizable theological pattern of crime instigated by passion, of discovery, of repentance, and of temporal punishment combined with hope of eternal salvation; this pattern was traditionally familiar in morality plays on the Prodigal Son theme, and more immediately familiar in homiletic warnings against adultery and murder, the twin crimes so often seen as consequences of one another. Without questioning the presence of the ethical pattern from the moralities and the homilies, I do, however, question Mr. Adams' conclusion that the plays generally are dramatized sermons. The tendency to exploitation of brutality and sentiment in at least the poorer ones suggests quite as much that the stories were designed as stage thrillers. There are difficulties, of course, in assessing "intentions." One is that a not very intelligent or responsible author might not be aware of the contradiction of two such motives. The other is that anyone dramatizing a home-bred story of crime, unless he had something of Marlowe's original and questioning spirit, would almost certainly fall into the conventional way of thinking about it and treating it. Indeed, there would be a commercial advantage in his doing so. The general run of popular story-telling, on the stage or off, then as now, combines the exciting or the affecting with the most conventional morality. An Elizabethan draper's wife, sitting in breathless suspense right up to Alice Arden's savage stabbing of her husband, and then shedding tears over her edifying end, was not so different, we may suppose, from her twentieth-century counterpart. Your honest citizen always likes to get a bit of titillation without any prejudice to his morals; he wants to be thrilled, but not shocked. The sensational accounts of murders in pamphlet and ballad form, from which sources most of the domestic tragedies drew their plots, were always heavily moralized. I fancy that an Elizabethan audience which should see a stage-murderer going to the gallows defiant and unrepentant would have felt itself both cheated and outraged.

The important question is what the moralistic element does to the form of the plays. In the poorer ones, like *Two Lamentable Tragedies* and *A Warning for Fair Women*, it seriously clogs the action; hence these plays offer the best case for being regarded as dramatized sermons. In the better plays, the dramatic interest is dominant. The ethical point of view from which the action is regarded moves harmoniously with the fable in *A Woman Killed with Kindness* and in *The Witch of Edmonton*. Speculation about didactic intentions in these plays therefore becomes idle. Whether or not Heywood intended to preach a sermon on Christian forbearance in *A Woman Killed with Kindness,* the important thing is that he wrote a good play. Especially interesting is *Arden of Feversham;* just because there is in it no fully harmonious realization of aims, it clearly reveals the conflicting pulls of *prodesse* and *delectare*. A careful examination of the play will show that the focus of attention is on the exciting story of murderous intention on Alice Arden's and her lover's part, and of narrow escapes on her husband's, leading finally up to the nightmarishly bungled murder and the swift discovery of the participants. Indications of the moral are fitful and inconsistent. Alice, during the action, is handled in a detached way, in and for herself as a passionate and wayward woman. Arden, as Alice's husband, is shown as worried over her suspected infidelity, anxious to make her happy and to give her every chance to prove her attachment to him, not behaving at all like the conventional jealous husband. As a landholder, on the other hand, he is shown as grasping and unscrupulous; but this is a motive from the story as told in Holinshed necessary to bring Greene into the plot, and not given any emphasis in the play until the strange appearance of Reed to curse Arden and so prepare for us to accept his murder as righteous punishment. The author is clearly not working out in his play any consistent piece of moral reasoning, any more than he is trying to give us a character study of Arden. He is dramatizing an exciting murder story. If anyone needs to be reassured, he makes it touch superficially at different times various elements in the conventional theological scheme, and rounds it off soundly with the expected pregallows speech of Alice, the repentant murderess, and a moral judgment on Arden, the victim. In spite of its undeniable power, chiefly in the characterization of Alice, and in the management of exciting scenes, the play is episodic and structurally weak. The author has not seen his problems as a whole, either his story-telling problem or his moral problem. He has kept too much from his historical source and written scenically and rhapsodically.

If judgments on didactic purpose and its effect on the plays are difficult for these domestic tragedies with their homiletic background, how much more so for the romantic tragedies which are less bound by the conventions of bourgeois morality? It should be apparent that we have to rephrase our problem. What we have to look for is whether a play stays on the level of story for its own sake, that is for diversion solely, or whether it moves to a level of greater thoughtfulness, where questions of value are raised; and if it does, whether story and value coöperate, so that artistic design and meaning are one and the same thing. On that level the question of moral purpose tends to resolve itself. For serious dramatic art, if in some sense of Aristotle's terms it is an imitation of action and of life, must throw into relief human problems and purposes. It need not be, and generally is not, didactic in the directive sense of the Horatian doctrine, since the greater the artist and the deeper his perception, the less likely is he to give categorical answers to the questions raised, the less likely to wish to propel his listeners to any particular course of action. Yet, this serious dramatic art is moral in the profounder sense that it raises questions of meaning and behavior that men must as men be concerned with—in tragedy, the question of man's relation to his destiny, to the unknowable purposes of the universe; in comedy, the question of man's relation with his fellows in daily social living. In other words, it is meaningful. It has the element Aristotle called "thought" (*dianoia*). The artistic question, then, is how well a dramatist has realized within the resources of drama his ethical insights.[3]

A useful distinction can be made. Sometimes the central idea of a play is relatively simple and clear, and then we tend to feel, though perhaps erroneously, that the play was written with a moral purpose in mind. But the richer the play and the less simple and the less explicit its meanings, the less relevant becomes the question of didacticism. *The Atheist's Tragedy* appears to mean that to be an atheist is, on the whole, a bad thing. But what does *King Lear* mean?

Throughout the book, in the discussion of the major types of Elizabethan drama (Chapters V–VIII), in the discussion of character (Chapter IX), in the discussion of the various problems of organization of the fable (Chapters X and XI), this artistic question —the achievement of a form adequate to the meaning—has been central. The answers are at hand; they only need pointing up, and to that I shall devote a separate section. I shall consider only romantic tragedy (as distinct from domestic tragedy), comedy, and a special group of "tragi-comedies."

Form and Meaning

I do not propose to line up the major dramatists and give out marks. That would savor too much of arrogant confidence in my own taste. But my impression, with the reasons given, of the general strengths or weaknesses of the Elizabethan drama together with some judgments on the success or failure of particular plays should not give offense.

FIRST FOR tragedy. Senecanism had its merit in helping early Elizabethan tragedy find a language and a shape. *Gorboduc, Jocasta, The Misfortunes of Arthur, Gismond of Salerne* are well organized and move in a piece. They are outwardly serious, even desperately so, but it is hard to judge how much that is really meaningful for tragedy lurks in the Tartarean gloom of conventional literary motive and rhetoric. Kyd in *The Spanish Tragedy* keeps the Senecan enclosing framework of initial motivation by a ghost in a Stygian setting, but this frame has little to do with his more inwardly conceived tragic purpose—Hieronimo's heartbreak and revenge. Marlowe shakes off the dead weight of literary Senecanism and speaks in his own idiom, usually with certainty and direction. And the early Shakespeare, after first adapting Senecan techniques to his own clear ends (in *Richard III*), does likewise (in *Romeo and Juliet* and *Richard II*). But their contemporaries and imitators (Greene, Peele, the authors of *Selimus*, of *Locrine*, etc.) in conqueror plays and historical tragedies tend to violence and disorganization.

By the turn of the century, however, tragedy generally has grown up and found its own grim and wonderful voice. The originality and power last through Ford. Senecanism, assimilated and transmuted, is no longer in the rhetoric and does not invite labeling. Yet my own impression of Jacobean tragedy is that, apart from Shakespeare, its glory is splendid and fitful. It is endlessly arresting—for its intensity of passion and gesture, its richness of poetic texture, its flashes of profound insight into human feeling and human dilemma—yet it seldom fully satisfies. And this, I think, is because, like much sixteenth-century tragedy, it so often lacks coherence or hesitates in emphasis, sometimes in a part, sometimes in the whole. The ethical implications may be either vague, or at variance with one another, because action and statement, action and character, or different parts of the action, pull in different directions. The dramatic result of such inattention or confusion is both ambiguity of ethical implication and disjointedness of form.

An excellent illustration of what I mean is furnished by Webster's *Devil's Law-Case,* though it is a tragi-comedy rather than a tragedy. A complicated plot of rivalries in love, duels, and disappearances leads up to a fine trial scene in which the conscienceless Leonora's revengeful intentions against her own son are exposed and thwarted. But Webster does not let the findings of the trial govern the outcome of the play. He winds it up with a solution of affairs directly athwart every sympathy he has created, all sense of justice, and what might be called the "leading" of the plot. Instead of the double ending one expects from such a plot, with the virtuous rewarded and the abductors and traducers at least shamed if not punished, there is an obviously contrived and anticlimactic "happy" ending. Everyone gets a mate; even Leonora is rewarded with the man she had tried to take away from her own daughter, and the unoffending daughter has her second and less favored suitor fobbed off on her.

I have given other examples of this sort of thing elsewhere in the book—Chapman's handling of Byron (at the same time innocent and perjured); Chapman's, of Bussy (both the adulterous dishonorer of Montsurry and the self-righteous injured party when Montsurry seeks revenge on him); Webster's, of Vittoria (both accomplice in murder and innocent victim of her persecuting judges); Tourneur's, of Vindici (both justified revenger and deserving of death for his revenge). These instances are ambiguities not merely in character, but also in the movement of the action and in the response expected from the audience. I have suggested, of course, that we may find some of these apparent contradictions more disconcerting than an Elizabethan or Jacobean audience would, operating on somewhat different assumptions about consistency of character, and more used to accept, anyhow, what came in the story. But making all allowances, I think we still find many failures of direction. Plays like *Othello, The Duchess of Malfi,* or *The Changeling* demonstrate the possibility of an integration of fable, character, "thought," and style in a tragic meaning that is as convincing to us as to their original audiences.

These failures of direction may arise from several causes, operating separately or together.

One, clearly revealed in the instance of Vittoria, is the emphasis put on the single scene for immediate striking effect even at the expense of the total design. We know she is at best a passive accomplice in the murder of her husband and of her lover's wife; yet somehow we are made to feel, by her superb courage in the trial scene, that she, rather than her accusers, is being put upon. In this inveterate habit of emphasis on good theater at the expense of artistic consistency, or on vivid sympathetic insights at the expense of ethical coherence, English renaissance drama has some affinity with the much-admired Euripides. I am thinking of plays like *Orestes, Andromache,* or *Iphigeneia at Aulis,* not of structural masterpieces like *Hippolytus* or *Bacchae.* Shakespeare is perhaps no less prone than his fellows to fall into such temptations. The only difference may be that he better knows how to get himself out of trouble. Like feathered Mercury he vaults on Pegasus and is away, while poor Chapman, full of earnestness and oratory, stands taboring on a theme while his play slips out from under his nose.

Another cause for failure of coherence may be in the failure to motivate a character very clearly or at all, especially in some change of attitude. I have given in other chapters (especially in IX) many examples of this sort of thing and suggested explanations, both in psychological theory and in dramatic habit. Even if the explanations may be quite adequate, they do not necessarily lessen what may seem to us a flaw in the design. I pleaded earlier the relative point of view that if we understood Elizabethan expectations we should ourselves better understand the plays. And that is true. We have a right, however, in the final judgment of this art to apply more timeless standards of comparison, and to say that some plays are lesser than others because they do not transcend the limitations imposed by the conventions of their time. Our response to Marlowe's Isabella (in *Edward II*), perhaps to Beaumont and Fletcher's Evadne, possibly even to Webster's Vittoria, is uncertain in a way it is not to Shakespeare's Cleopatra, who, no more explicable than they, gives us more of an illusion of identity in her variousness.

Still another cause for failure of direction may lie in the thoroughly ingrained habit of the debate and disputation, discussed in Chapter XI. Opposing points of view may be equally well sustained and never resolved. Or they may lead to a conclusion that is contrary to the demands of the story. Chapman's Byron plays are the most conscipuous examples of the structural damage and the confusion in the reader this habit can lead to. Here again Shakespeare was subject to the weakness of the technique, as shown in small in *Troilus and Cressida,* in large in the histories, especially *King John,* and in *Julius Caesar.* On the whole, however, he was successful in overcoming it, probably because he had to a greater degree than most of his contemporaries the power of entertaining various points of view and of making them reënforce or qualify each other without mutual self-destruction: for example, the several responses to honor in *1 Henry IV* on the part of Hotspur, Prince Hal, and Falstaff; or the various responses to experience in *The Tempest* on the part of the conspirators, Gonzalo, the young lovers, and Prospero.

There is, finally, something deeper and harder to define. I think it consists in a failure always to provide an adequate frame of reference in which to view the characters in action. The motives and actions of Byron seem to us not fully enough realized to allow us both to sympathize with and to blame him (as we can Macbeth) while at the same time not losing our own firm basis of judgment. This is not the same as the second cause given above. It is not a matter of a psychological theory of character different from ours, or of the difference of a dramatic convention which accepts lack of motivation; it has to do with something much more fundamental, that is with the author's awareness of his own values. I do not, of course, mean that he should state a philosophy of life; such statements, in fact, are suspect, since they only too often run counter to the true implications of the fable. I mean that as the story moves from point to point and as the characters speak we should get a firm sense of the author's sympathies and of his moral judgment, so that we know where we stand. We can hardly reduce the "philosophy" of *Lear* to a statement; but we are in no doubt where our sympathies lie, what there is of good for us to admire, what of evil to reject.

This failure to establish an adequate frame of reference may arise from the author's uncertainty as to his own values. I have illustrated the point at length in Chapters VI and XI from Chapman, who tried to work out his own intuitions about the dignity of man, not altogether clearly, but movingly and honestly. Chapman seems to me earnest and deeply troubled and unsure. I think what may often happen is that an author fails to assimilate conventionally accepted ethical attitudes to his own more original responses; he may be handicapped with a set of terms inadequate to his feeling. That is, he may make to the situation in his story stock responses that inhibit his deeper insights, or that overlay them and conflict with them, or that conflict with each other. Webster betrays a conflict between the Christian ethics that lie on the surface of his tragedies, and a deeper, hardly definable, more defiant and more despairing response to the human condition. Tourneur, in *The Atheist's Tragedy,* keeps the fable moving so closely according to an unexamined ethical formula that its full possibilities are never realized. In *The Revenger's Tragedy,* if it be his, he keeps a motive from Senecan tragedy, but discards the machinery and drains the motive of its implications; he substitutes incompletely a Christian scheme of ethics, hence ultimately puzzles our response to his protagonist.

Since this play is in the main stream of one of the major tragic motives, it invites fuller comment and comparison with *Hamlet.* On the one hand, Vindici suggests the Senecan avenger, since, though apparently freely willing his revenges, he operates as if under some undefined compulsion; his instrumental character is suggested by the generic name Tourneur gives him.

> Vengeance, thou murder's quit-rent, and whereby
> Thou show'st thyself tenant to Tragedy,
> Oh keep thy day, hour, minute, I beseech,
> For those thou hast determined. Hum! who e'er knew
> Murder unpaid? Faith, give Revenge her due;
> Sh'as kept touch hitherto.

But what is Vindici the instrument of? There is here no family curse, no ghost, no Ate or Megaera. When he has finished his gruesome, self-appointed course, he is destroyed; but a rather lame piece of business, needing the introduction of a hitherto passive character, Antonio, is improvised to carry through the matter. On the other hand, there are suggestions in the play of the Christian pattern of sin providentially punished by an instrumental revenger who must himself be destroyed. The dramatic use of the skull of Vindici's dead mistress to point the *memento mori* theme and the appearance of portents, a blazing star and thunder, as Vindici arrives at the last stage of revenge on the foul "nest of dukes" both strongly suggest the Christian scheme. But Vindici does not wholly fit the picture; he is not himself moved by evil impulses, like Alice and Mosby, for instance, in *Arden,* or like Richard III in any of the tragedies about him. Vindici is moved by righteous motives and does more moralizing than anyone else in the play. Moreover, Antonio's judgment on Vindici and his brother is purely political: since they have killed the old duke, they are apt to kill a new one, namely himself. And Vindici's last speech is not one of conventional repentance. Although he passes a moral judgment on himself and Hippolito in remarking that "time will make the murderer bring forth himself," his last words are in unrepentant and self-satisfied justification:

> And now, my Lord, since we are in forever,
> This work was ours, which else might have been slipt.
> And if we list we could have nobles clipt
> And go for less than beggars; but we hate
> To bleed so cowardly. We have enough!
> Yfaith, we're well—our mother turn'd, our sister true;
> We die after a nest of dukes,—adieu!

Perhaps this failure to assimilate different attitudes arises from the fact that Tourneur is not really interested in how a man may be drawn into doing wrong to right wrong, that is with the fundamental tragic problem that revenge raises, but simply in the mordant depiction of a vicious and ugly world; if so, revenge for him may be just a technique for making a play. In contrast, Shakespeare translated the old-fashioned revenge theme into a fundamental tragic dilemma. For on Hamlet, guiltless of the evil done by Claudius, is placed unsought the obligation to set it right; yet he must bear the consequences of whatever may follow his taking up arms. Crying out in bitter protest at the trap,

> O cursed spite!
> That ever I was born to set it right!

he circles round and round his problem during the play. He gains his freedom, paradoxically, only by the acceptance—not the same impulsive and ignorant acceptance as at the beginning of the play under the spell of the Ghost's horror, but a philosophical acceptance —of his responsibility and whatever fate it brings. The Senecan frame of motivation by ghost and fury has been transmuted into a more emotionally credible Christian ghost and Hamlet's "sore distraction." And in the ethical implications of the play there is no conflict between "Senecan" and "Christian" because action does not stay on the surface of stock responses and conventional attitudes. The philosophic assumptions of Stoic and Christian ethics, so often assimilated in their long history, are assimilated here in a problem of human destiny that is valid in whatever terms it may be put.

This discussion has been concerned with the uncertainties of dramatic form that are consequent on the deeper uncertainties of the ethical bases of tragedy. I discussed in Chapter VI the two different ethical patterns that operate in English renaissance tragedy—one placing responsibility for the hero's fall on the unpredictable world of circumstance, the other on his free choice of the dictates of passion rather than of reason; I discussed how they were sometimes reconciled, and how different dramatists tended more to one emphasis or the other. I think it is clear that a failure either to make a choice between the two schemes or to assimilate them is what led to some of the confusions we are discussing. In varying degrees, Chapman, Tourneur, Webster, and Ford all illustrate these uncertainties and confusions. If Shakespeare shows less uncertainty than they, I think it is not because he chooses between one scheme or another or even makes a conscious philosophic resolution. His own emphasis, in point of fact, varies, being more Stoic in *Hamlet,* more Aristotelian in *King Lear.* I think it is because he may actually be freer of schemes and terms than his contemporaries. He sees clearly into the heart of all ethical problems, the distinction between motives and deeds. His tragedies seem to me to grow from his perception that we must judge men by their motives, but that they are judged in the scheme of things, nevertheless, by their deeds. He does not have to decide the degree to which men are free, the degree to which they are bound.

The basis for great tragedy lies in the perception that however little control a man may have over his fate he must nevertheless bear the responsibility for the effects of his actions. This is the assumption of the *Oresteia* and of *Oedipus Tyrannus.* As I have said above, it seems to me to be the assumption of *Hamlet*. Orestes chose freely to avenge his father by killing his mother; but he would have had to pay the price of a negative decision in ignominy, as he had to pay the price in being hounded by the Furies, of a positive one. Nothing he had done brought this inescapable choice between two evils upon him. Hamlet's dilemma is similar. The same assumption, with a difference, lies behind *Macbeth*. Whether the Weird Sisters are genuine fates which control Macbeth's decision or are merely symbols of an evil which is suggestive but not compulsive has been much disputed. Who can know? They are symbols of an ambiguous universe. In either case the tragic fact remains: he cannot escape the penalty of his decision. The further assumption of the *Oresteia* and of *Oedipus at Colonus,* the mitigating assumption that by facing his evil destiny a man may in some measure convert it to good, seems to me to be made in *Hamlet* and in *King Lear*.

There is no confusion in *Macbeth*, as in *Bussy* and *Byron,* in which Chapman cannot decide whether his heroes are responsible or not for their actions; for Shakespeare shifts emphasis from the cause to the inexorable effects of Macbeth's decision. Yet neither is there the rather limiting explicitness of Jonson, who in *Sejanus* makes a precise adjustment between the rôles of circumstance and free will. Sejanus himself, a skeptic and a cynic, admits Fortune as his only goddess. When in his fall he has been deserted by the senators who so fawned on him in the days of his glory, the "choric" characters point the irony in terms of Fortune:

> *Lepidus.*   O, violent change,
> And whirl of men's affections!
>   *Arruntius.*   Like as both
> Their bulks and souls were bound on Fortune's wheel,
> And must act only with her motion!

But this is not the last word. A refining comment makes clear that Sejanus has failed in the use of intelligence and so shares responsibility for his failure. When Arruntius asks, "Who would trust slippery chance?" Lepidus replies,

>   They that would make
> Themselves her spoil: and foolishly forget,
> When she doth flatter, that she comes to prey.
> Fortune, thou hadst no deity, if men

Had wisdom: we have placed thee so high
By fond belief in thy felicity.

The moral of the play, stated in the last speech, is an interesting
combination of tragic motives—Greek *hybris,* Christian pride, and
the Mirror theme:

Let this example move the insolent man
Not to grow proud and careless of the gods:
It is an odious wisdom to blaspheme,
Much more to slighten, or deny their powers.
For, whom the morning saw so great, and high,
Thus low, and little, 'fore the even doth lie.

Professor Farnham suggests that "though the shifting lines of
newly revived classic philosophies, of Christian asceticism, and of
Renaissance rationalism weave much confusion, they also make for
a new subtlety and breadth of moral order." [4] It is perhaps not so
important for tragedy that an age have an entirely coherent philosophy as that it give its writers an intense awareness of the stress between man and the universe he lives in, with a recognition of the
value of man's purposes as well as a recognition of his failures in
executing them. Elizabethan and Jacobean England evidently provided the conditions for that awareness. Lesser and greater artists
alike had it. For the lesser artists the conflicting explanations of
man's destiny sometimes got in the way of their more immediate sympathetic perceptions of human character and resulted in what may
have been for them unperceived failures of artistic coherence; these
are there for us, in an analytical after-age, to discover. For the greater
artists, this variety became the complex mystery of a universe which
hides its face from man, yet demands of him knowledge of good
and evil.

In a very few great tragedies of the period, profound ethical implication comes naturally from character and event, so that the artistic
design itself carries the meaning. One thinks at once of *Faustus,* of
The Duchess of Malfi, of *The Changeling.* It is a pity that each should
be marred by other characteristic renaissance weaknesses of form—
Faustus by the trivial horseplay, *The Duchess of Malfi* by excessive
looseness of time and place, *The Changeling* by a silly secondary
plot. Of all the greater tragic dramatists Shakespeare best learned
to sustain his tragic themes without running after false lures and

consistently to make his dramatic fable and his meaning one. In his great tragedies there is in him no failure of informing purpose.

IN COMEDY, one seldom finds so damaging a conflict of aims as in tragedy. That may be partly because social norms of behavior are easier to manage than philosophical assumptions about the universe. It may also be because we expect less, are more willing to take implausible action for the sake of a lively story, more willing to accept any mixture in an *olla podrida* of fun. Even at the time, the didactic view was not always pressed so hard for comedy as for tragedy; the moral function of comedy could quite as easily be, and often was, interpreted as purgation of melancholy as instruction in manners and morals. And of course the purging of melancholy is synonymous with being agreeably diverted.[5] Nevertheless, even if we are apt to take a more relaxed standard of judgment for comedy than for tragedy, we must be impressed by the degree of success with which English comic dramatists, from Udall to Brome, realized the variety and vitality of their insights. Their formal accomplishment has received much less attention than it deserves.

I discussed in Chapters VII and VIII the range of comedy—from fairy-tale fantasy like the *Old Wives' Tale* to intense satire, like *Volpone;* or, on another scale, from light-hearted romance like *Friar Bacon and Friar Bungay* to serious romance like *The Winter's Tale.* I considered the ways in which moral implication and social criticism were realized in it—in portraits of social types, in realistic treatments of manners in romance as well as in critical comedy, in humours (more of this in Chapter IX), in satire overlaid on a romantic plot, in satire structurally worked out. I also considered, in a discussion of Arcadianism and the pastoral (in VII and VIII) and in a comparison of the denouement in Jonson and Shakespeare (in Chapter XI), the ways in which Shakespearean romantic comedy had a meaningfulness of a different sort from Jonsonian critical comedy. Here I shall suggest clues to the failures in realization of aim we do sometimes find.

I think the failures in intention are more often apparent than real. That is, I think our puzzlement sometimes arises from our having simply lost the key, an easy thing to do in comedy, since much of its concern is with social manners and attitudes that so readily change from age to age. The classic case is *The Merchant of Venice*, which the modern attitude towards Shylock pulls in a direction quite contrary to the direction of the story. No attempt of historical imagination to force Shylock back into his proper context can ever make the play quite the happy one it was intended to be. Another example is *Measure for Measure,* where the reverse has happened in the direction of our sympathy; poor Isabella has been excoriated as a prig for not saving her brother's life at the expense of a little thing like her virtue. In our scheme of values, honor, certainly not when it takes the form of chastity, seldom transcends life.[6]

Examples may most frequently be found, probably, in romantic comedy, where we have lost touch with the romantic conventions of another age, as with Valentine's offer of his sweetheart to Proteus in what was then an eminently right choice between love and friendship. We may, too, be somewhat disquieted by a businesslike conduct of marriage arrangements which seems to belie the romantic speeches, as in Sebastian's willingness in *Twelfth Night* to accept marriage, as an obviously good thing, with a rich woman whom he has never laid eyes on before; or as in Bassanio's wooing of the rich heiress of Belmont; and as in many another love story in Chapman, Middleton, and Massinger, of poor gentlemen and rich heiresses. It has recently been suggested that in *Much Ado about Nothing* Shakespeare is making a purposeful break with the conventions of literary romance and showing in the Claudio-and-Hero affair a realistic Elizabethan matrimonial arrangement, in which family position is the important thing, love not in question, and liking on the man's part, acceptance on the girl's, quite enough.[7] Such a view explains plausibly the denunciation of Hero, who appears to have made a contract under false pretences; it also explains Claudio's immediate willingness to accept her "sister" as a substitute when he finds he was wrong about Hero. While I agree to the realism of the manners shown, I think we do not have to deny Hero and Claudio all romance or hold Shakespeare up to such a clearly defined and narrow purpose. This realism of manners with a wash of romance is common in Jacobean comedies, especially in those dealing with penniless gentlemen seeking well-to-do brides. The romance is a pleasant thing, a mitigation of the harsh commercial realities, a touch, on the right side, of sympathy and hope.

There are a number of comedies, of course, that face the issue squarely, and make love triumph over family objections. They may seem to us formally more satisfying. They are usually plays with some realism of setting, for example, Dekker's *Shoemaker's Holiday,* the Anne Page plot in Shakespeare's *Merry Wives,* the anonymous *Merry Devil of Edmonton.* One of the very best of these is Porter's *Two Angry Women of Abingdon.* It is thoroughly grounded in the realism of domestic manners, and its romance is no fairy-tale dream of true love overriding differences of rank or wealth. The two young people in love, who finally overcome the determined opposition of their mothers, are of the same station in life and the same town, and have every reason to expect as much—or as little—harmony in wedlock as their respective parents.

There are, however, occasional failures of coöperation of story and intention that can be laid to the author. And these may be similar to some of the faults that cause trouble in tragedy, such as the habit of arguing too well both sides of a question. Shakespeare has to share responsibility for the contrary pulls of *The Merchant of Venice,* since if he had not given Shylock so eloquent a plea in his own defence, we could not distort the play towards tragedy in our presentation of it. We might find its representation of a merely villainous Shylock distasteful, but we could not on our own stages convert the play into Shylock's tragedy and so leave the fifth act dangling as an anticlimax.

Too much motivation of character is perhaps liable to give more trouble in romantic comedy than too little. That is, the conventions of romantic story can be taken for their own sakes, without much explicit motivation in character. Shakespeare most frequently creates difficulties, as I have pointed out earlier in the chapter, by making some of his characters come alive so fully (like Julia in *The Two Gentlemen,* Helena and the Countess in *All's Well;* Shylock, too) that they burden the light frame in which they must move.

Again, we might expect to find the expressed moral of a play at odds with its more fundamental implications. And there are doubtless examples of this sort of thing; an author's profession of intentions is not always to be trusted. I do not recall, however, plays in which this causes any serious confusion. In Middleton's comedies, for example, there is a certain amount of conventional moralizing, but in the plays themselves little feeling of genuine reproof. His best comedies have much of the spirit of Plautus in his most bawdy farcical moods and of the Italians who were Plautus' successors. Compare *A Chaste Maid in Cheapside,* full of complacent cuckoldry, for instance, with Plautus' *Casina* or Cecchi's *L'Assiuolo* (*The Little Horned Owl*), in both of which a philandering old husband is ridiculously gulled. In Middleton's fantastically contrived plots, sharpers milk gullible heirs, amorous old men are made fools of, cuckoldry is rampant, all in as witty a way as possible, and nobody takes these matters very seriously, either Middleton or his characters. But the plots and the tone of the play are so well controlled that the moralizing, if any, lies lightly on them. The moral tags don't fool us, and aren't meant to.

Jonson can give more trouble, not because his moralizing is at odds with his plots, but because it can too easily take over and ruin them as good plays. When Jonson's didactic spirit runs away with him, as in an early play like *Every Man out of his Humour,* but especially as in late ones like *The Devil Is an Ass* and *The Staple of News,* he can be intolerably dull. The good fun and wit which does exist in these latter plays is quite overborne by their moral purpose. Not only does he tell us too often what he means; but also he makes the moral force the fable. I have already pointed out (in Chapter IX) the not too happy mixture in *The Staple of News* of satire on contemporary manners with morality play abstractions. In *The Devil Is an Ass* comic situation is wrested from its expected direction. The familiar cuckolding theme is given an unfamiliar moral turn. If anyone deserves to wear horns it is Fitzdottrel, who takes every course to provide himself with them. Middleton or Chapman would have let him wear them, in the best spirit of medieval farce and *fabliau;* but Jonson preserves the wife's virtue in order that she may the better teach her husband to be ashamed of himself. Fortunately, in his great comedies, Jonson is better than his profession. There is no want of fun in *Epicoene, The Alchemist, Bartholomew Fair,* or even *Volpone,* despite the tendency of modern critics to view the latter as so close to tragedy. No want of bawdry, either; one wonders just what kind he considered "unwashed." In these plays, more thoroughly than any other contemporary dramatist, he makes his satire integral to his plots. The gullibility and greed of the characters are the traps they unwittingly set for their own undoing. He has no need for explicit teaching, as the merry endings of *The Alchemist* and *Bartholomew Fair* reveal that he himself knows. Moral implication becomes part of the artistic design.

Jonson's trouble is the reverse of that of most of his contemporaries; he finds it hard not to be more instructive than he needs to be. His frequent enunciation of the Horatian aim leaves us in no doubt as to the seriousness with which he held it. And he implies that one reason for his scorn of much of the romantic comedy of his day was what seemed to him its lack of corrective purpose. Jonson knew that the corrective purpose must be through artistic means; unfortunately for his art, he did not always let himself trust them sufficiently. We admire him all the more, therefore, for the great comedies; his artistic victory in these plays cannot have been easy to win.

FINALLY, WE must consider a group of comedies, or tragi-comedies, that really do present a grave problem of adapting means to ends. In the discussion of tragi-comedy in Chapter VIII, I remarked briefly on a number of plays that are quite different in tone from Fletcherian romance or tragi-comedy. I mean, especially, Dekker's *Honest Whore,* Part II, Marston's *Dutch Courtesan,* Chapman's *Gentleman Usher,* Shakespeare's *Measure for Measure;* and there are others. They do not fall into an easily defined class. Shakespeare's *Measure for Measure* is usually called a "problem" comedy and drawn into uneasy alliance with *All's Well,* which has no serious problem, and with *Troilus and Cressida* and *Timon,* which have problems, certainly, but are hardly comedies. There are "problems," besides, in many plays we call something else, tragedy or comedy or history. Professor Tillyard adds *Hamlet* to the group,[8] and one might certainly agree that *Hamlet* is the eternal problem play—in more senses than one. But it makes a satisfactory tragic resolution, and the crucial difficulty with the plays I have in mind is that they do not seem to us to be satisfactorily resolved in the conventional happy ending of comedy.

Apart from the structural problem, there is some justification in calling them "problem plays." Different in many respects, the plays in the first list above are similar to one another in having an action tending to tragedy but fortunately solved, in giving a serious emphasis to a moral problem, and in containing a certain amount of realism or satire in the portrayal of city or court life. None of the plays is wholly satisfactory from a formal point of view, not so much because of the mingling of tones of satire, realistic comedy, romantic sentiment, and moral earnestness, but because of the working out of a serious moral problem in an action built of improbable device and lucky coincidence. The result is only too often to make the solutions seem trivial or forced.

The difficulty with these plays is that the problems are realistically viewed, the endings are not. Fortuitous solutions do not usually come to moral problems. Modern dramatists have worked out the technique of the ambiguous ending; mere development of the moral issue to a sharp focus may constitute the play. We are never told, for instance whether the mine-owner and the striking miners solve their difference in Galsworthy's *Strife*. Solution in a modern play may be simply in the hero's arrival at a state of mind which breaks the dilemma created by the moral issue and suggests the possibility of forward movement either towards a solution or towards new problems. Norah, in *The Doll's House,* neither kills herself nor, we suppose, lives happy ever after; she walks out of her husband's house. She has solved her problem by the adoption of a new attitude and a course of action consonant with it. The Elizabethans had no technique either for such suspended, or for such wholly mental, solutions. They grafted the problem on the pattern of complication and solution of romantic comedy. But the manipulation of intrigue and lucky chance to bring about the conventional happy ending gives the effect of an evasion of the serious issue of the play. Shakespeare tried something else in *Troilus and Cressida,* to the discontent of critics ever since. But how else should such a play end?

> Hector is dead; there is no more to say.

The true problem play among the early types of drama was the morality. Its solutions were adequate to its problems. The hero of a morality is always in imminent danger not only of death, but of damnation, and when he wins his battle against evil, salvation may still be at the cost of his life. If he lives, as in the Prodigal Son plays generally, it is by the skin of his teeth, as it were; and what he has achieved is not romantic happiness, but a sober reformation of life. The domestic tragedies which borrowed the morality pattern of sinning, repentance, punishment, and forgiveness, especially *A Woman Killed, The Miseries of Enforced Marriage,* and *The Witch of Edmonton,* may seem more satisfying to us as problem plays than the more romantic ones we are considering. But the morality play was restricted in range and attitude. It had pretty much only one story to tell. It had really only one problem, the problem of sin, and one way to solve it. There was every reason, in order to exploit a wider variety of interests, to keep to the theatrically successful techniques of romantic comedy and try to enlarge the content and implications ' of the story one had chosen.

An example or two will clarify my point. Everyone knows of the general critical dissatisfaction with the ending of *Measure for Measure*. Actually, I think Shakespeare has been at some pains to give it a formally satisfying ending, in the happily ironic reversal of the "measure for measure" theme. Early in the play, Angelo answers Isabella's plea that he temper justice with mercy, with his announced intention to carry out justice in the strictest sense of measure for measure. With their rôles reversed at the end of the play, Isabella is faced with the same problem with respect to him, and after a struggle she solves it by according him mercy. His measure should be death, but she asks the Duke that he be given life. Angelo's act, it is true, did not wholly overtake his bad intent, in that Isabella was not seduced and Claudio was not executed. But Angelo had nevertheless broken the severe law of the city against fornication, the same law for which he had held Claudio to strict account, and broken it without Claudio's intention of marriage; moreover, he had forsworn himself in breaking his promise to Isabella to let her brother go free. It must be remembered, too, that Isabella did not know, at the moment she sought to excuse Angelo, that her brother was still alive. The whole point is that she can generously find an excuse for Angelo (though he had meant her very ill indeed), as he could not find for Claudio, who had meant no ill at all. The eloquent words of her plea to Angelo come back to our minds with great ironic force as he stands to be judged at the end of the play:

> Why, all the souls that were were forfeit once;
> And He that might the vantage best have took,
> Found out the remedy. How would you be,
> If He, which is the top of judgment, should
> But judge you as you are? O! think on that,
> And mercy then will breathe within your lips,
> Like man new made.

There is another problem in the play, however, the problem of Isabella's choice between her brother's death and the sacrifice of her chastity; and we are troubled by the evasion of it through the device of the substituted woman common in the *novelle*.[9] I think a careful reading of the play shows that Shakespeare meant to put the primary emphasis on the problem of the exercise of power, the problem he solves, and not on the problem of Isabella's chastity. Nevertheless, we cannot wholly exorcise the difficulty that is inherent in housing problems like these in what H. Harvey Wood, speaking of Marston's plays, calls "the gimcrack erections of improbable situation."

The psychological-moral problem of Malheureux in *The Dutch Courtesan,* a highly moral and innocent young man who falls so hard for a courtesan that he is heading for ruin, is developed by Marston with very great perceptive subtlety. The issue is not evaded, for Malheureux is finally brought to his senses, but the solution is wholly contrived. His rescue is effected by the most incredible devices of intrigue and disguise on the part of his friend Freevill. And to make the ending properly theatrical, he is brought to the foot of the gallows before he is saved. The serious problem of Bellafront's struggle in *The Honest Whore,* Part II, to maintain her new-found chastity is set in the usual frame of Italianate intrigue. Matheo, her high-flying rogue of a husband, is made to reform, and Hippolito, her would-be lover, is cured of his infatuated pursuit of her through the elaborate scheming of her father in disguise. The final "lived happy ever after" ending is too easy to be true.

I doubt if this method of working out a moral problem seemed as unsatisfactory to the Renaissance as to us. A romantic plot made for variety and for lively action on the stage, and a happy solution that tied up all the ends made a play conform to the pattern of comedy—which should begin in trouble and end in happiness—without seeming to impair its moral function. Oddi justified even the fortuitous solution on moral grounds: by showing that young lovers in the extreme of human misery may be made blessed in an instant, Comedy teaches them not to do anything unworthy of themselves through desperation; she consoles and instructs the unhappy. This, of course, does not get at the heart of the difficulty. Use of the manipulated comedy plot undoubtedly prevented the development of a wholly satisfactory form for the realistic problem play, or "drama," as we should call it.

Completely romantic tragi-comedy probably succeeded better in achieving a definable form because it could move all in one piece, without conflict of emphasis. It is not, therefore, more interesting; for though Fletcherian tragi-comedy makes great play with moral problems of fidelity and honor, they are felt to be hollow. What counts is the manipulation of the story, the brilliance of the stage tricks, and the facility of the expression. The impulse to the heroic tale of imaginary dangers and noble sentiments is of course contrary to the realistic; it is not an attempt to show life with all its mixture of silliness and sadness, wisdom and folly, charm and horror, but an attempt to mitigate its harshness by rendering its dangers innocuous, its ugliness fascinating. That is possible, of course, only in a world of fairy tale, where the giant is always destroyed, the witch's spell is always broken, the kitchen drudge always turns out to be a princess, and the prince is always rewarded with her hand. Fletcherian tragicomedy does not have quite the air of fairy tale, of course, for it lacks its innocence, but it has its purpose: to create a world in which the virtuous can have security without tedium.

Shakespeare's romantic tragi-comedy is fairy tale with a difference. Indeed, Shakespeare's imaginary world of the last plays is a more successful way of coming at "problems" than was his way in *Measure for Measure*. That was direct and explicit; this is oblique and symbolic. The two emphases, on serious problem and on romantic story, are combined and their formal conflicts resolved in the complex attitudes of *The Winter's Tale* and *The Tempest*.

Multiple Unity and Narrative Technique

A final word that will bring us back to the beginning. In the introductory chapter I suggested the usefulness of Wölfflin's term of "multiple unity" to describe English renaissance drama at its best. I shall close the book with another analogy to the graphic and plastic arts, not as a speculation about influences, but only as a clarifying illustration.

A painter or a sculptor who finds his subjects in literary themes may treat his material in either a dramatic or a narrative way, or with a mixture of both ways. The method of representing a single incident or episode of a story at a significant moment of action—for example, Christ driving the money-changers from the Temple—we might call a dramatic method. This is the characteristic method of the artists of the high Renaissance, though of course it was not new with them. A method common in medieval and early renaissance

illumination, painting, and sculpture of representing various incidents in a story within a single compositional frame or picture space
is, by contrast, a primarily narrative method. For example, in Sassetta's "Meeting of St. Anthony and St. Paul," [10] St. Anthony is
shown three several times in the progressive stages of his journey to
find the other renowned hermit: first, in the upper left corner, as he
starts out; next, on the right and further down, as he meets the
centaur; and finally, in the center at the bottom, as he embraces St.
Paul before the latter's cave. The glimpses through woods of the
diagonals of the path suggest the length of the journey.

To realize the literary interest of the subject in terms of the design is probably easier with the former method, the selection of a
significant moment. The artist can give the proper emphasis to his
subject by purely artistic means—design, color, modeling, and the
like. But in the more narrative technique which tries to tell a story
by depicting several incidents within a single frame, emphasis is
harder to come by. The treatment of event, of place, and of time,
is apt to be diffuse, episodic, and unemphatic.

There is a third method, which combines the two, that is to present
a story in a series of successive scenes, as in Giotto's scenes from the
life of St. Francis, or from the life of Christ. If one looks at individual
paintings, the dramatic emphasis may be strong, but the tendency of
such a series is of course to invite attention to narrative, and usually
the arrangement gives no emphasis to any one event, so that the
total effect is episodic. In many illuminations and in some early
paintings, both methods are combined, so that some members in a
series depict single moments of actions, others show several actions
within one frame.[11]

The narrative method of including several incidents within one
composition need not, of course, preclude excellence of structural
design. The style began early (examples may be found in Byzantine
art) and continued late (into the sixteenth century), and some of the
best masters of the early Renaissance used it, for example, Duccio,
Giotto, Fra Angelico, Giovanni di Paolo, Sassetta, and Botticelli.[12]
But unless design and subject combine to give significance to some
one event, the picture remains, in so far as one regards the subject,
narrative in feeling rather than dramatic. Fra Angelico, in a painting
in San Marco, Florence, of one of the trials of Saints Cosmas and
Damian,[13] has achieved a satisfying composition and yet has given

no element of the story particular emphasis. Successive events in the episode—in which the two saints are thrown by two adversaries from a high rock into the sea, appear to drown, and are rescued by an angel—are arranged in a beautiful circular design. The eye is invited to follow the sequence until it makes a pause, but no dramatic stop, with the angel; then it goes round again. Drowning and rescue and each intermediate figure are equally important in the design. The late users of the technique, like Botticelli in his fresco of episodes from the youth of Moses in the Sistine Chapel, are apt to concern themselves with design almost entirely and let the narrative successiveness disappear.

A conspicuous and interesting example of the perfect union of narrative and design is Giovanni di Paolo's painting in the Chicago Art Institute of St. John in the Desert. In the lower left St. John is shown emerging from a city gate. Before him, and retreating towards the center of the picture, lie the green and yellow squares of tidy cultivated farmland. From the left center and towards the upper right corner rise steeply from the plain the gray, jagged rocks of the wilderness, and the figure of St. John appears again as he mounts the path into them. In their bold, ascending lines they focus the whole meaning of the story of renunciation and aspiration. In this picture, though the two figures of the saint give narrative sequence, the whole composition gives dramatic emphasis to a climactic moment.

Now FOR THE connection of all this with the drama. The multiple stage of the Middle Ages, set with its mansions, each the center of action for a given episode in a play, is not unlike the more naïvely organized narrative in painting and sculpture, where all the incidents represented in the story are present to the eye at once. Of course, an actor must perform his part in sequence; all the times of a play cannot be equally present to the spectator, as all the places can be. Yet the movement of the actors from place to place on a multiple stage, and their localizing of a place by being at it, might not have seemed to spectators very different from a painting in which the Magi could be seen several times in their progress from the distant hills to the Manger.[14] Indeed, a set of miniatures by Caillaux illustrating the Valenciennes Passion Play frequently shows a progressive series of actions within one frame.[15] I am not, however, trying to establish influence either way. Certain characteristics of medieval dramatic and visual art suggest, rather, common habits of mind that found expression in different media. One characteristic is a greater emphasis on the narrative than the dramatic, and on a narrative that tends to be episodic, without climax. The other is probably a corollary of the first: time and space are treated extensively, not intensively. Simultaneity flattens and is diffuse; it is apt to mean lack of perspective depth and of emphasis. Painters, of course, continued to treat subjects narratively long after they had learned skill in perspective and emphasis in design. But the unity they gave the subject remained a multiple unity, and the narrative feeling often remained, as in Fra Angelico's "Saints Cosmas and Damian."

On the English stage the successive principle, of scene following scene, triumphed, so that the spectator no longer had before the eye itself, in the great days of the drama, this simultaneity. But scenic successiveness offered nothing to cure episodic looseness in the fable, and nothing to check diffuseness of time and place. Since dramatists rarely adopted the classic principle of the single climactic episode, in which the past is caught in the present moment of crisis, they had to master their problems of unity, coherence, and emphasis, in this rather different organization of sequentially presented story. We have seen how, in various ways, different dramatists did meet, or failed to meet, the problems inherent in the story-telling technique.

Some amusing instances of the narrative technique in graphic art occur in illustrations of the very stories used for plays. In Chapter VII, I called attention to the use of the style in the woodcuts for the Grüninger Terence (Strassburg, 1496). Favorite subjects for tragedy are illustrated in the Zainer edition of Boccaccio's *De claribus mulieribus* (Ulm, 1473).[16] The ones I have chosen for reproduction show rather crudely various methods of organizing graphically a literary theme: the "Portia," the method of several central episodes within a single picture space, no one episode given great emphasis in the design; the "Pyramus and Thisbe," the same method, with emphasis in the design enhanced at the expense of the separation and the clarity of the episodes, but even so combining with the story emphasis in making the tragic events at the tomb central; the "Veturia," the method of portraying the great climactic moment of the story. The "Cleopatra," the "Jocasta," and the "Clytemnaestra," in their depiction of only two episodes, the "before" and "after," illus-

The Tragedy of Portia, Daughter of Cato
The Tragedy of Thisbe, a Babylonian Virgin

374

The Meeting of Veturia with her Son Coriolanus
The Tragedy of Cleopatra, Queen of the Egyptians

trate especially well the organization of *De casibus* tragedy with its rise and fall, or its balancing of cause and consequence in revenge and counter-revenge.[17]

The important thing for us, in this digression into the graphic and plastic arts, has been, not to raise speculation about precise influence in either direction, but to illuminate a way English dramatists of the sixteenth and early seventeenth centuries inherited of looking at dramatic problems. The dramatists, like the artists, saw their subject-matter in the great fund of traditional stories of human experience, religious and secular. And, like the artists, they had to subdue the stories to the artistic medium in which they worked. In general, the artists of the high Renaissance abandoned the old-fashioned narrative style in favor of the single episode or moment of action. The academic dramatists did the same, and their way was to win out on the great stage of Corneille and Racine. But on the English popular stage of our period, the dramatists did not often try the classic method of the single climactic episode. They learned to succeed by shaping the narrative method to dramatic ends. In this respect, Shakespeare's formal success is less like Michelangelo's than like Giovanni di Paolo's.

APPENDIX

1 The *Proemii* of Giorgio Vasari, 1550

WITH THE CRITERIA of judgment commonly applied in the sixteenth century to literary art, it is interesting to compare the criteria Vasari applies to painting and sculpture; see his *proemii* to the three parts, especially to II and III, of the first edition of *Le Vite de' piu eccellenti architetti, pittori, et scultori italiani da Cimabue insino a' tempi nostri* (Florence, 1550; reprinted by Corrado Ricci, Milan-Rome: Bestetti e Tumminelli, n.d., 4 vols.; Vasari's second edition, revised, did not contain the introductions). Vasari praises the painters and sculptors of what he calls the second stage of *la rinascità* (Masaccio, Donatello, etc.) for having surpassed those of the first stage (Giotto, etc.) in imitation of nature. Masaccio and his contemporaries "sought to represent what they saw in nature and no more" ("cercaron far quel che vedevono nel naturale e non più."—Ricci, I, 233). They did so well "that little remained to reduce everything to perfection and to achieve an exact imitation of the truth of nature" ("in modo che poco ci resterà a ridurre ogni cosa al perfetto; e che elle imitino appunto la verità della natura."—I, 231). But the masters of the third stage (Lionardo, etc.) excelled those of the second in a total perfection— coming from a freedom, a resolute boldness ("gagliardezza risoluta"), a grace, a vitality   that went beyond studied imitation; the implication throughout is that they achieved that perfect imitation of the truth of nature which is more than literal representation.

The praise of Lionardo and of Raphael is instructive. "Besides the strength and dash of his drawing and the extreme subtlety with which he counterfeited the *minutiae* of nature just exactly as they are, [Lionardo,] with good rule, better order, right proportion, perfect drawing, and divine grace, abounding in richness and profoundly versed in art, may be truly said to have given his figures motion and breath" ("....oltra la gagliardezza et bravezza del disegno, et oltra il contraffare sottilissimamente tutte le minuzie della natura così a punto come elle sono; con buona regola; migliore ordine; retta misura, disegna perfetto; et grazia divina; abbondantissimo di copie, et profondissimo

379

di Arte; dette veramente alle sue figure il moto, et il fiato."—III, 6–7). As for Raphael, he is said to have achieved, by taking the best of old and modern masters, the perfection of the ancients; he vanquished nature by his colors; his painted stories were like written stories in their true representation of places, buildings, and people; he had a gift of imparting grace to the heads of young men, old men, and women; in his figures he showed perfect decorum, in reserving modesty for the modest, wantonness for the wanton, and for children now mischief in their eyes, now playfulness in their attitudes; his draped garments he handled neither too simply nor too intricately but in a way that appeared real. ("Ma più di tutti il graziosissimo Raffaello da Urbino, il quale studiando le fatiche de' maestri vecchi et quelle de' moderni; prese da tutti il miglio; et fattone raccolta, arricchì l'arte della pittura di quella intera perfezzione che ebbero anticamente le figure di Apelle, et di Zeusi, et più se si potessi dire o mostrare l'opere di quelli a questo paragone. Là onde la natura restò vinta dai suoi colore, et l'invenzione era in lui sì facile et propria quanto può giudicare chi vede le storie sue, la quali sono simili alli scritti; monstrandoci in quelle i siti simili, et gli edificii, così come nelle genti nostrali et strane, le cere, et gli abiti, secondo che egli ha voluto; oltra il dono della grazia delle teste, giovani, vecchi et femmine, riservando alle modeste la modestia, alle lascive la lascivia; et ai putti ora i vizi ne gli occhi, et ora i giuochi nelle attitudini. Et così suoi panni piegati, nè troppo semplici, nè intrigati, ma con una guisa che paion' veri."—III, 7).

Another way (already suggested in some of the passages quoted) in which the artists of the third period excel those of earlier periods is in copiousness, variety, and ornament. The order achieved in the second period "wanted an invention copious in everything, and a certain beauty carried through every littlest detail, that would set forth all that order with more ornament" ("Il quale aveva bisogna di una invenzione copiosa di tutte le cose, et d'una certa bellezza continuata in ogni minima cosa, che mostrasse tutto quel ordine con più ornamento."—III, 4; cf. I, 358–59). Like the literary critics, Vasari preferred richness to simplicity.

We have in Vasari, then, all the principles we have met with in considering literary art: imitation of nature (meaning both exactness in the representation of detail and the achievement of a sense of independent life), universality through the observance of decorum, imitation of the ancients, copiousness and variety to give ornamental richness to the structural form. The three introductions should be read in their entirety; they are missing from some modern translations of the *Lives,* but may be found in Bohn's Standard Library edition, translated by Mrs. Jonathan Foster, London, 1878–81, 5 vols.; and in the Medici Society edition, translated by Gaston du C. de Vere, London, 1912–15, 10 vols.

2 "Tragedy" and "Comedy" in Tudor and Early Stuart Dictionaries

SIR THOMAS ELYOT, *Bibliotheca Eliotae,* Latin-English, 1548: *tragedy,* "an interlude, wherein the personages do represent some history or fable lamentable for the cruelty and misery therein expressed"; *comedy,* "an interlude, wherein the common vices of men and women are apparently declared in personages."

THOMAS COOPER, *Thesaurus Linguae Romanae et Britannicae,* Latin-English, 1565: *tragedy,* "a kind of plays representing personages of great estate, and matters of much trouble"; *comedy,* "a play wherein common vices are noted in personages representing them."

HULOET-HIGGINS—Richard Huloet, *Huloet's Dictionary,* English-Latin-French, revised by John Higgins, 1572: *tragedy* not defined; *comedy,* "Comoedia secundum Graecos est & [*sic*] privatae civilisque fortunae sine periculo vitae comprehensio [from Diomedes], Comoedia secundum Cic. est imitatio vitae, speculum consuetudinis & imago veritatis."

JUNIUS-HIGGINS—Adrian Junius, *Nomenclator,* Latin-Greek-French, etc., Englished by John Higgins, 1585: *tragedy,* "poema sublime, à vulgi sermone avium, illustrium hominum fortunas infelici exitu hauriens.   . . . a lofty kind of poetry, shewing the rueful end of noble personages, and their fall from felicity"; *comedy,* "poema stylo humili. *dramaticum,* res impeditas laeto exitu finiens.   . . . a base kind of poetry which endeth troublesome matters merrily."

THOMAS THOMAS, *Dictionarum Linguae Latinae et Anglicanae,* Latin-English, 1588? (my quotations are from fifth ed., revised, 1596): *tragedy,* "being a lofty kind of poetry, and representing personages of great state and matter of much trouble, a great broil or stir: it beginneth prosperously, it endeth unfortunately and doubtfully, contrary to a comedy"; *comedy,* "a play, wherein as in a glass, the image of civil and private living is represented, an interlude. It beginneth sorrowfully, and endeth merrily, contrary to a tragedy."

JOHN FLORIO, *A World of Words*, Italian-English, 1598 (definitions fuller than in 1611 edition): *tragedy*, "a tragedy or mournful play being a lofty kind of poetry and representing personages of great state and matter of much trouble, a great broil or stir: it beginneth prosperously and endeth unfortunately or sometimes doubtfully, and is contrary to comedy"; *comedy*, "a merry play, an interlude"; *tragicomedy*, "beginning mournfully, and ending merrily, half a tragedy, and half a comedy."

ROBERT CAWDREY, *A Table Alphabetical*, English, 1604: *tragedy*, "a solemn play, describing murders and sorrows"; *comedy*, "stage play."

RANDLE COTGRAVE, *A Dictionary of the French and English Tongues*, 1611: *tragedy*, "a stately play whose conclusion is doleful, and doubtful"; *comedy*, "a play, or interlude (that begins in dissention, or sorrow, and ends with agreement or merriment)."

JOHN MINSHEU, *The Guide into Tongues*, etymological dictionary, 1617: a rich collection of most of the available speculation on derivations; see his items 2195 (comedy or interlude), 9328–2 ("a stage play, comedy or tragedy, or tragicomedy"), and 11684 (tragedy).

FRANCIS HOLYOKE, *Dictionarum Etymologicum Latinum*, 1617? (see BM catalogue; I have seen edition of 1633, the first listed in STC). Similar to Minsheu, though not apparently based on him; speculation on derivations mainly follows Scaliger (*Poetices*, I. v, vi).

With Minsheu and Holyoke compare Robert Estienne's scholarly *Thesaurus Linguae Latinae* (first published in Paris, 1531? See Brunet, Grässe, Bibliothèque Nationale catalogue; Huntington has Basel edition of 1576–78). Estienne gives the familiar etymologies of tragedy and of comedy, and descriptions of both from Diomedes; he sends his readers to Horace and to Donatus' preface to Terence; and he includes a list of phrases, with precise references, to the use of the words *comoedia* and *tragoedia* and their derivatives in classical writers.

The earliest dictionary printed in England, *Promptorium Parvulorum* (Pynson, 1499; from Galfridus Anglicus, compiled ca. 1440), does not include "tragedy" and "comedy." The next, *Hortus Vocabulorum* (Wynkyn de Worde, 1500) does: comedy is "a town song. villanus cantus vel villana laus"; and tragedy ("hircina laus vel hircinus cantus. id est fetidus") is given a lively description, based on direct reference to ancient tragedy, not echoed in any of the later dictionaries ("et est de crudelissimis rebus sicut quidam patrem vel matrem occidit vel comedit filium et econverso"). Other dictionaries printed in England during our period, if they contain the words at all, either repeat the definitions given above or merely give an equivalent of "tragedy" or "comedy" in another language, without definition. The only dictionaries I have seen which mention "tragicomedy" are Florio's, Minsheu's, and Holyoke's. For bibliography, consult M. M. Mathews, *A Survey of English Dictionaries* (London, 1933), and De Witt T. Starnes and Gertrude E. Noyes, *The English Dictionary from Cawdrey to Johnson, 1604–1755* (Chapel Hill, 1946).

3 The Sources of *Measure for Measure*

GIRALDI'S *novella* (*Ecatommithi*, VIII. v; Monreale, 1565): The Emperor Maximilian charges one Juriste to prosecute justice in Innsbruck. Juriste revives an old law against incontinence, and arrests and condemns to death a young man (Vico, brother of Epitia) who has got a young woman with child, but who has promised to marry her. Epitia, who has "una dolcissima maniera di favellare," pleads with Juriste for her brother, asking him to show mercy rather than strict justice. Juriste dismisses her, but asks her to return the next day, when he proposes that she yield to him in exchange for her brother's life; but he also promises to marry her. She does yield, but Juriste has already given orders for Vico's death. The next day he orders the body of her brother to be sent to her. She goes to the Emperor to claim justice; Juriste appears asking for mercy. The Emperor orders Juriste to marry her, then to be killed. But Epitia, moved by her natural kindness, judges it not worthy of her to let him die, since that act would be attributed to a desire for vengeance, not justice. Therefore, she pleads with the Emperor that since he has shown justice he ought now to show mercy, which is greater. The Emperor agrees and pardons Juriste.

GIRALDI'S play, *Epitia* (of unknown date, printed posthumously by his son in 1583): The story is the same as in the *novella* except that (1) Juriste now has a sister named Angela, who, believing in her brother's good intentions, acts as go-between in his offer of marriage to Epitia; (2) the brother Vico does not actually appear in the play, and so we do not have his plea to his sister to save him; (3) the Captain of the prison does not execute Vico, but knowing his good intentions and relying on the Emperor's approval substitutes for him a hopelessly evil criminal; (4) Epitia wants Juriste killed to avenge her brother and will not listen to Angela's plea that she soften her heart and intercede with the Emperor for him; (5) the Captain announces that Vico has not been executed; Epitia, now that the reason for the Emperor's death sentence on him has been lifted, does intercede for him, and the Emperor spares him for mercy's sake; (6) several new characters—"Segretario," "Podestà," and "Cameriar"—appear; they discuss Juriste's actions in reviving the harsh law, also more general questions of the exercise of authority, justice and mercy, etc.

WHETSTONE'S prose story in *An Heptameron of Civil Discourses* (1582) and play, *Promos and Cassandra* (1579): Stories nearly alike; Whetstone mainly follows the *novella,* but borrows some things from *Epitia.* The King leaves Promos as his lieutenant to prosecute justice in Julio in Hungary. Promos arrests and condemns to death a young man, Andrugio, for the same reason as in Giraldi's versions. The sister, Cassandra, pleads for her brother; Promos is smitten with her, and proposes to her (apparently on her first visit, in *Heptameron;* on her second, in *P & C*) that she yield to him in return for her brother's life; he does not, however, offer marriage. Her brother urges her to yield, saying that there will be no dishonor to her in saving her brother's life, rather honor in the greatness of what she is doing for him. She yields, and Promos orders her brother's execution *after* he has enjoyed her. The jailer, however (here closer to *Epitia* than to *Ecatommithi*) finds a substitute for him and sends the head to Cassandra (in *Hept.* a criminal, in *P & C* merely "a dead man's head"). The King returns to hear complaints against Promos, listens to Cassandra's, and orders Promos to marry her. Now that she is his wife, she suddenly feels affection for him and pleads for his life. The brother suddenly appears in a friar's costume, and joins his sister, for her sake, in pleading for Promos; the King, moved by Promos' repentance, pardons him.

SHAKESPEARE'S *Measure for Measure* (ca. 1604): No need for summary. Essential differences from all the versions: (1) Isabella does not yield to Angelo; (2) a new character, Mariana, Angelo's old betrothed, takes her place; (3) the Duke in disguise engineers the entire denouement; (4) the Duke orders Angelo to marry, not Isabella, of course, but Mariana. Differences in motivation throughout go with these changes.

Measure for Measure is generally closer, in many details sufficiently familiar, to Whetstone's versions than to *Epitia;* but it does show some significant correspondences with *Epitia* where Whetstone differs markedly. The relation of *Measure for Measure* to Giraldi's *novella* is ambiguous, since some of the correspondences to that might have come through Whetstone, some through *Epitia*. I note the significant resemblances below between *Measure for Measure* and *Epitia*.

1. *Measure for Measure:* the name "Angelo."
   Epitia: "Angela," the sister of Juriste (Shakespeare's Angelo).
   Ecatommithi: no such character or name.
   Whetstone (both versions, and so throughout summary): no such character or name.

2. *Measure for Measure:* scene laid in Austria (Vienna).
   Epitia and *Ecat.:* scene in Austria (Innsbruck).
   Whetstone: scene in Hungary (Julio).

3. *Measure for Measure:* Escalus expostulates with Angelo on the rigor of his prosecution of Claudio; generally more temperate in attitude than Angelo; also remarks on "man dressed in a little brief authority."
   Epitia: "Segretario" protests to "Podestà" (not to Juriste directly) the harshness of the law and the severity of its prosecution (I. iv); comments in soliloquy (I. v) on the rigor of those in power.
   Ecat.: no such characters or discussion.
   Whetstone: no such characters or discussion.

4. *Measure for Measure:* Isabella's eloquence commented on.
   Epitia and *Ecat.:* heroine's gift of eloquence singled out for praise.
   Whetstone: no such comment, though she does in fact speak eloquently.

5. *Measure for Measure:* unregenerate state of the criminal whose head is to be substituted for Claudio's is described. (Further complication in substitution of Ragozine's head in place of Barnardine's head as first intended.)
   Epitia: the substituted criminal hopelessly evil.
   Ecat.: no substitution made; the heroine's brother actually killed.
   Whetstone: nothing said about the character of the criminal.

388 APPENDIX

6. *Measure for Measure:* the motive of Isabella's plea for Angelo—
Mariana, now married to him, pleads with Isabella to beg for
Angelo's life; Isabella, thinking Claudio dead, consents, argues
that Claudio had but justice in doing the thing for which he died,
but that Angelo's act did not, with respect to her, overtake his
bad intent.

Epitia: Epitia, married to Juriste at the Emperor's command in
order to restore her honor (she had yielded to him), wants
Juriste killed to avenge her brother; Angela, Juriste's sister,
pleads with Epitia to soften her heart and intercede for him, but
in vain until the Captain announces that her brother has not
been executed; then she pleads for Juriste, saying that the reason
for his condemnation has been abrogated; the Emperor, in spite
of Juriste's bad faith, pardons him for mercy's sake.

Ecat.: Epitia, married to Juriste, moved by her natural benevolence
and judging it not worthy of her to pursue vengeance for her
brother now her honor has been righted, pleads with the Emperor to show mercy rather than strict justice, and pardon
Juriste.

Whetstone: No one urges Cassandra to plead for Promos, but she,
married to Promos on the King's order and still thinking her
brother dead, pleads for Promos because she is now his wife
and suddenly feels a great "natural" affection for him.

Measure for Measure is like Whetstone's versions in having a
character married to Angelo–Promos wish to save his life (but
not the same character) and in having the heroine make her
plea *before* she learns her brother is alive. It is like *Epitia* in
having a second woman plead with the heroine to soften her
heart and intercede for the evil-doer with the ruler; also like
Epitia in distinguishing between intentions and acts. It is like
Ecatommithi in the nobility of motive and in the precise logic
of argument (making distinctions between Angelo's two evil
deeds, between justice and mercy, etc.). It is different from all
versions, of course, in that Isabella has not in fact yielded to
Angelo.

7. *Measure for Measure:* the Provost announces that Claudio has
not been executed; Claudio appears muffled, reveals himself,
but does not speak.

Epitia: Captain of prison announces that brother has not been killed; brother does not actually appear.

Ecat.: completely different; brother has been executed.

Whetstone: brother appears disguised and reveals himself, without intermediary.

8. *Measure for Measure:* The themes of justice and mercy, of power and authority, are central in Shakespeare.

Epitia: these themes handled in more detail than in *Ecatommithi*, still more than in Whetstone.

Whether immediately, or through a lost play, Shakespeare appears to have been indebted to *Epitia* as well as to Whetstone's two versions; indebtedness to Giraldi's *novella* is possible, but less certain.

NOTES
INDEX

Notes

INCLUDED IN the following list are only those most commonly used abbreviations that may not be self-evident. The first reference to a book cited in the notes is always given in full, and may be located from the index. Shortened titles, when they are used in later references, are nearly always identified by the author's name, either in the text or in the note; the only exceptions are such familiar reference books as Chambers' *Elizabethan Stage* (*Eliz. Stage*). References to learned journals follow the standard style in the annual bibliographies in *Studies in Philology* and in *Publications of the Modern Language Association*.

BCL, Biblioteca classica latina.
Com. e trag., Delle comedie, e delle tragedie in G. B. Giraldi Cinthio's *Discorso....intorno al comporre de i romanzi, delle comedie, e delle tragedie*.
Com. graec. frag., Comicorum graecorum fragmenta, edited by Georgius Kaibel.
ECE, Elizabethan Critical Essays, edited by G. Gregory Smith.
EECT, Early English Classical Tragedies, edited by John W. Cunliffe.
LC, Literary Criticism: Plato to Dryden, edited by Allan Gilbert.
Rom., De i romanzi in G. B. Giraldi Cinthio's *Discorso* (see *Com. e trag.*, above).

Chapter 1

1 Translated from the 7th German edition (1929) by M. D. Hottinger (New York, 1932), p. 166.
2 *Ibid.,* p. vii.
3 *Ibid.,* Ch. IV.
4 *Ibid.,* p. 159.
5 Many of the critical passages from Plato are collected in Allan Gilbert's *Literary Criticism: Plato to Dryden* (New York, 1940). Professor Gilbert includes all of the *Poetics* (in his own translation from Gudeman's text) except for strictly linguistic passages, and all of the *Ars Poetica* in E. H. Blakeney's translation. Quintilian and Cicero are most readily available in the Loeb Classical Library, and my references (as to the classics generally, unless otherwise indicated) are to the Loeb editions.
6 For bibliographical notes, see Ch. II, n. 31, and Ch. V, n. 13, 14, 15.
7 For bibliographies of Italian criticism consult esp. Joel E. Spingarn,

History of Literary Criticism in the Renaissance (2d ed., Columbia Univ. Press, 1924), pp. 337–43; also Italian translation of first edition by Antonio Fusco (Bari, 1905); Vernon Hall, *Renaissance Literary Criticism* (Columbia Univ. Press, 1945), pp. 233–40. Della Porta, Giraldi, Guarini, Tasso, and Trissino are available in modern Italian editions. Fracastoro's *Naugerius* and Pontanus' *Actius Dialogus* have been translated by Ruth Kelso (*Univ. of Illinois Studies in Lang. and Lit.*, Vol. IX, No. 3, 1924); Vida, by Albert S. Cook (Boston, 1892); Scaliger (most of the parts pertinent to drama), by F. M. Padelford (*Yale Studies in English*, No. 26; New York, 1905). Substantial portions of Trissino, Giraldi, Minturno, Castelvetro, Mazzoni, Tasso, and Guarini have been translated by Gilbert in *LC;* since, however, I have used complete and original texts wherever possible, I have not usually attempted to give references to Gilbert as well. His book is well indexed. The translations are my own, unless otherwise indicated.

8 For a bibliography of French renaissance criticism, see Hall, *Ren. Lit. Crit.* Modern French editions are available of all the important French critics.

9 See Ch. II, n. 31, and Ch. V, n. 16.

10 *El arte nuevo de hacer comedias,* 1609; in English in *LC.*

11 For a bibliography of English criticism, consult Hall, pp. 233–40. Most of the important English criticism is collected in G. Gregory Smith, *Elizabethan Critical Essays* (Oxford: Clarendon Press, 1904; 2 vols.); I have modernized quotations from it, as from English texts generally. Important editions of Sidney are Feuillerat's, for text (*Sidney,* Cambridge Univ. Press, 1923, Vol. III); Cook's, for notes (Boston, 1890). All of the *Defense* and selections from Jonson, Heywood, Webster, and Massinger are given in *LC.* An indispensable edition, with useful introduction, of Puttenham (not complete in *ECE*) is that by Gladys Doidge Willcock and Alice Walker (Cambridge Univ. Press, 1936).

12 For descriptions and bibliography consult T. W. Baldwin, *Shakspere's Small Latine and Lesse Greeke* (Univ. of Illinois Press, 1944), index; Arthur F. Leach, *English Schools at the Reformation* (Westminster, 1896); Foster Watson, *The English Grammar Schools to 1660* (Cambridge Univ. Press, 1908).

13 Giuseppe Toffanin, "Il teatro del Rinascimento," in *Storia del teatro italiano* (ed. Silvio d'Amico, Milan, 1936), pp. 65 ff. For a reverse swing of the pendulum in English criticism, see Alwin Thaler, *Shakespeare and Sir Philip Sidney* (Harvard Univ. Press, 1947). Professor Thaler argues for the direct influence of the *Defense* on Shakespeare; his book at least makes evident general similarities traceable to the climate of artistic theory in which both worked.

14 See esp. Lewis Einstein, *The Italian Renaissance in England* (Columbia Univ. Press, 1903); Kenneth Orne Myrick, *Sir Philip Sidney as a Literary Craftsman* (Harvard Univ. Press, 1935).

15 For discussion and references, see Ch. X, pp. 266–69 and n. 11–26.

16 See Benedetto Varchi, *Della poetica* (in *Lezzioni,* Florence, 1590; composed 1553), Pt. I (pp. 571–72): Since poetry is a species of logic (taking logic as all of rational philosophy), "no one can be a poet who is not a logician: rather, to the extent to which each one is a better logician, to that extent will he be a more excellent poet" ("nessuno può essere poeta, il quale non sia loico: Anzi quanto ciascheduno sarà miglior loico, tanto sarà ancora piu eccellente poeta"). For a history of the changing conceptions of poetic, see J. W. H. Atkins, *English Literary Criticism: The Medieval Phase* (Cambridge Univ. Press, 1943); for changing conceptions of rhetoric, see Richard McKeon, "Rhetoric in the Middle Ages," *Speculum,* XVII (Jan., 1942), 1–32.

17 See Wallace K. Ferguson, *The Renaissance in Historical Thought* (Boston, 1948), esp. Chs. I–III, for a full discussion of renaissance ideas of the Renaissance.

18 Imitation as an ideal of literary practice was so commonplace that it is difficult to select references; one of the best statements of its importance as an educational tool is in Ascham's *Schoolmaster* (*ECE,* I, 1–45); of its place in composition and hence criticism, in Jonson's *Timber* (ed. Schelling, Boston, 1892), pp. 75–79; and in Giovambattista Giraldi Cinthio's *Discorsi....intorno al comporre de i romanzi, delle comedie, e delle tragedie* (Venice, 1554; composed 1549, 1543): *De i romanzi,* pp. 149–60. Text also in *Scritti estetici di G. B. Cintio* (Milan, 1864, 2 pts.). See also Harold O. White, *Plagiarism and Imitation during the English Renaissance* (Harvard Univ. Press, 1935); also discussion and references in Ruth Wallerstein's *Studies in Seventeenth-Century Poetic* (Univ. of Wisconsin Press, 1950), pp. 11–13 and n. 2.

19 For references, see Ch. X, n. 74.

20 Consult indices to James Bass Mullinger, *The University of Cambridge* (Cambridge Univ. Press, 1873–1911); Sir Charles Edward Mallett, *A History of the University of Oxford* (London, 1924–27); Baldwin, *Small Latine.*

21 See F. L. Lucas, *Euripides and his Influence* (Boston, 1923), pp. 103–12. The English translations were Gascoigne and Kinwelmersh's *Jocasta* (through Dolce's Italian version of a Latin translation of *Phoenissae*), acted 1566, publ. 1573, 1575; Lady Lumley's *Iphigeneia in Aulis* (in MS only); Peele's *Iphigeneia* (not extant; recorded as acted).

22 Julius Caesar Scaliger, in his *Poetices libri septem* (Lyons, 1561), III. xcvii, analyzes *Hecuba* as an example of a good action; so also does Antonio Minturno, *L'arte poetica* (Venice, 1563 [Harvard copy], 1564 [Huntington copy]), pp. 85–88; note Sidney's knowledge of it, *Defense,* sec. 48 (my references to Sidney are to the text in *LC,* because of the convenient division and numbering of the paragraphs).

23 Quintilian, *Institutio oratoria,* X. i. 65–69. Quintus Cicero, in a letter to Tiro (M. T. Cicero, *Epist. ad familiares,* XVI. viii. 2; tr. W. G. Williams, Loeb ed.) comments, after quoting from Euripides: "How much *you* believe in him I don't know. I, at any rate, regard all his lines, one after

the other, as so many declarations on oath." Lucas notes that Cicero, Caesar, and Ovid were all steeped in Euripides (*Euripides,* pp. 62–71).

24   For a fully expressed preference, see Giraldi's praise of the superiority of Seneca in *Troades* to Euripides in *Hecuba* (itself singled out for praise in the decorum of character); but, Giraldi says, no one of judgment will deny superiority to *Troades* in majesty, in the passions, in observation of character, and in the vivacity of the sentences, and that one can scarcely read the scene at the sepulchre between Andromache and Ulysses without weeping (*Trag. e com.,* p. 262).

25   The most important statements of Senecan influence are in J. W. Cunliffe, *The Influence of Seneca on Elizabethan Tragedy* (London, 1893); his introduction to *Early English Classical Tragedies* (Oxford, 1912); F. L. Lucas, *Seneca and Elizabethan Tragedy* (Cambridge Univ. Press, 1922); Hardin Craig, "The Shackling of Accidents," *PQ,* XIX (Jan., 1940), 1–19, and "Shakespeare and the History Play" in *Joseph Quincy Adams: Memorial Studies* (The Folger Shakespeare Library, 1948), pp. 55–64. The most important questioning of Senecan influence is in Theodore Spencer's *Death and Elizabethan Tragedy* (Harvard Univ. Press, 1936) and Howard Baker's *Induction to Tragedy* (Louisiana State Univ. Press, 1939). An interesting revaluation, which finds Seneca's influence in ideas and tone rather than in details of style, is made by Henry W. Wells, "Senecan Influence on Elizabethan Tragedy: A Re-Estimation," in *Shakespeare Assoc. Bull.,* XIX (April, 1944), 71–84.

26   Nashe certainly thought the early *Hamlet* was Senecan, for English Seneca, "if you entreat him fair in a frosty morning ... will afford you whole *Hamlets* ... of tragical speeches."—Preface to *Menaphon* (*ECE,* I, 312).

27   Cf. interesting introduction by Wm. A. Ringler and Walter Allen, Jr., to John Rainolds' *Oratio in laudem artis poeticae,* ca. 1572 (Princeton Univ. Press, 1940).

28   *Antony and Cleopatra,* V. ii. 2–8. My references to Shakespeare throughout are to the Oxford text, ed. W. J. Craig. For the philosophic and ethical background of this passage, cf. Hardin Craig, "The Shackling of Accidents," *PQ,* XIX, 1–19.

29   Discussed in Chs. V, VII, and IX. On the importance of Terence in the school curriculum see Baldwin, *Small Latine,* Vol. I, *passim,* and the same author's *William Shakspere's Five-Act Structure* (Univ. of Illinois Press, 1947).

30   See "Aristophanes" in the indices to Mallett, to Mullinger, and to Baldwin, *Small Latine.*

31   Erasmus was probably reflecting the value put on Menander by Quintilian (X. i. 69–72) and by Caesar, for whom Terence was half-Menander ("o dimidiate Menander"), according to verses attributed to him by Suetonius in "Vita Terenti" in *De poetis,* VI (*C. Suetoni ... reliquiae,* ed. Augustus Reifferscheid, Leipzig: Teubner, 1860, p. 34). This "Vita" appears in most early editions of Terence and is reprinted in many modern ones; cf. edition of Sidney G. Ashmore (2d ed., New York,

1908). I owe the Caesar reference to Professor C. F. Edson. The fragments of Menander were first published in 1553 and four times more by 1626, but no renaissance translation was published; see John Edwin Sandys, *History of Classical Scholarship* (Cambridge Univ. Press, 1903–8), II, 105, and index.

32 Professors Herford and Simpson emphasize this point in their estimate of Jonson.—*Ben Jonson* (Oxford: Clarendon Press, 1925–52), I, 121–22.

33 *Counter-Statement* (New York, 1931), pp. 157–61.

34 These distinctions are from Quintilian, IX. i. 1–8.

35 *Defense,* sec. 49.

36 Two other matters, necessary to complete the synthesis, cannot be handled within the compass of the present volume. One is the problem of act-division. This had been planned for treatment as a third chapter on plot structure. The second of these (XI) examines the essentials of the plot—complication and unraveling—qualitatively, that is, in respect to motivation, causal connection of the action, and the like; the third would have looked at these essentials quantitatively, that is, at how they were spaced in the play. It would have dealt with the "shape" of the plot (the rise and fall, the position of the turn, the time devoted to exposition and denouement) and with the possible relation of act-division to the spacing of these elements in the forward movement of a dramatic fable. But the handling of this crucial problem demands too various and tangled a mass of data (from renaissance editions of classical texts, from extant Elizabethan play texts in manuscript and in print, from many plays examined internally, and from much besides) and poses too tough a set of problems—such as whether act-intervals were related to act-structure, whether Elizabethan tragedy and comedy had any specially characteristic plot-movement—to be done both adequately and clearly within the length of a single chapter. Professor Baldwin's tremendous scholarship in his *William Shakspere's Five-Act Structure* hardly makes the problem easier to deal with; the more one knows about it, the more difficult it gets. The question of act-division must be saved for separate treatment. The other matter, a full examination of style in the Elizabethan drama, done against the background of rhetorical education and critical theory, is obviously a book's worth—or many books' worth. Some indications of the bearing of style will be given in the appropriate places, as in the chapter on character. Most attention must be given, however, to the major aspects of structure.

Chapter 2

1 Samson Lennard's translation, *Of Wisdom,* III. xliii (1670 ed., p. 523; 1st ed., n. d., but between 1606 and 1612; see *STC*).

2 Definition attributed to Cicero; see Ch. III, p. 72 and n. 47.

3   Hardin Craig, *The Enchanted Glass* (New York, 1936), Ch. VII, esp. pp. 176–81; cf. Geoffrey Tillotson, "Expression in Sixteenth Century Style," in *Essays in Criticism and Research* (Cambridge Univ. Press, 1942), pp. 5–15.

4   In John Lydgate, *The Fall of Princes* (ed. Henry Bergen, Washington, D.C., 1923), VI. 3382. For an interesting account of the importance of speech in humanist education, see B. L. Joseph, *Elizabethan Acting* (London: Oxford Univ. Press, 1951), esp. Ch. II; he there quotes, in a fuller context, this same line from Lydgate.

5   *Inst.*, II. xx. 9 (tr. H. E. Butler, Loeb ed.).

6   Alessandro Lionardi, *Dialogi....della inventione poetica* (Venice, 1554), p. 12: "per poter mostrare l'utilità, il danno, il giusto, l'ingiusto, l'honesto, et il deshonesto. Di che nasce poi la civiltà, et il governo publico, et privato." Cf. *De oratore*, I. viii. 32–34.

7   *Inst.*, II. xvi. 10.

8   Thomas Wilson, *Arte of Rhetorique*, revised ed., 1560 (ed. G. H. Mair, Oxford, 1909), Preface, Avii.

9   From *De optimo genere oratorum*, i. 3; cf. *Orator*, xxi. 69 (the eloquent man will be one able to speak so as to prove, to please, and to sway: "ita dicet, ut probet, ut delectet, ut flectat").

10   For discussions of moving as an aim for poetry see Murray W. Bundy's introduction to Ruth Kelso's edition and translation of Fracastoro's *Naugerius*, pp. 16–20; Scaliger, *Poetices*, I. i; III. xxv; VII. i. 3; Gilbert, appendix to Sidney's *Defense, LC*, pp. 459–61.

11   Pp. 52–57.

12   *L'arte poetica*, p. 76: "....l'ufficio del Tragico poeta....non è altro, che dir talmente in versi, che insegni, e diletti; e muova sì, che delle passioni habbia à purgare gli animi de' riguardanti."

13   *Defense* (*LC*, sec. 26).

14   Puttenham, *Art of English Poesy*, I. iii (*ECE*, II, 6–7).

15   *Naugerius* (tr. Kelso), pp. 65, 60.

16   Francesco de Sanctis, *Storia della letteratura italiana* (ed. Croce; Bari, 1912), II, 211: "Fu rettorica, cioè a dire menzogna, espressione pomposa di sentimenti convenzionale."

17   Craig, *Enchanted Glass*, pp. 176–77.

18   Henry Peacham, *The Garden of Eloquence* (rev. ed., 1593), ABiij.

19   *Naugerius*, pp. 68–69. See Professor Wallerstein's discussion (*Studies in Seventeenth-Century Poetic*, pp. 13–16 and n. 8) of the treatment of ornament in renaissance poetics. She makes the important point that the term "ornament" changes meaning with changing views of art, and sees in Boccaccio's and Fracastoro's echo of Cicero's passage (quoted below; ref. in n. 40) "the whole humanistic feeling for poetry as a fine art."

20   See H. O. Taylor, *Thought and Expression in the Sixteenth Century* (2d ed., New York, 1930), esp. Vol. I, Ch. III; Vol. II, Ch. XXXV.

21   See Baldwin, *Small Latine*, Vol. I, Chs. IV–XIII, for summaries of early plans of education; also Ch. I, above, n. 12.

22 Cicero, *Partitiones oratoriae*, xxiii, 79.

23 See Charles Waddington, *Ramus: sa vie, ses écrits, et ses opinions* (Paris, 1855), pp. 28–29.

24 Karl R. Wallace (*Francis Bacon on Communication and Rhetoric*, Chapel Hill, 1943, pp. 190–91) sees public debate late in the century as more important than I have allowed it to be.

25 In *Timber*, ed. Schelling, p. 30; cf. similar praise in Lennard's Charron.

26 For university declamations, cf. John Rainolds' *Oratio;* Milton's *Prolusiones quaedam oratoriae* (tr. Bromley Smith in the Columbia *Milton*, Vol. XII, and by P. B. Tillyard in *Milton: Private Correspondence and Academic Exercises,* Cambridge Univ. Press, 1932) on such topics as "Whether day is more excellent than night," "On the music of the spheres," "That sometimes sportive exercises are not prejudicial to philosophic studies."

27 *Art of English Poesy*, III. ii (*ECE*, II, 145).

28 Quoted from J. W. Hebel and H. H. Hudson, *Poetry of the English Renaissance, 1509–1660* (New York, 1929), pp. 279–80.

29 In a letter to Ammonius (P. S. Allen, *Erasmi epistolae,* I, 545) quoted in Ringler's introduction to Rainolds' *Oratio,* p. 20.

30 Basel: Froben, 1534 (Huntington Library copy; not in Grässe, *Trésor de livres rares et précieux,* or Brunet, *Manuel de libraire*). An edition published by Froben in 1532 contained Erasmus' essay on the meter, but the description in Grässe gives no indication of the Melanchthon analyses. I have not seen any of the earlier editions in which Melanchthon had a hand, either in preparing the text (Tübingen, 1516; Antwerp, 1526) or in providing *scholia* (Mainz, 1518, 1528; Hagenau, 1528: cf. Grässe). Baldwin (*Small Latine,* I, 641) speaks of Melanchthon as having worked out the great pedagogic edition of the century about 1524; in *Five-Act Structure* (pp. 169–72) he furnishes bibliographical evidence for this date.

This rhetorical emphasis of Melanchthon's is of course traditional; it appears strongly in the commentary of Eugraphius (fifth, or more probably, sixth century), printed first in G. Faernus' edition of Terence (Florence: Giunta, 1565); modern edition by Paul Wessner in his *Aeli Donati quod fertur commentum Terenti* (Bibl. script. graec. et rom. Teubneriana, Leipzig, 1902–8), Vol. III.

31 The fourth-century commentary of Donatus on five of the plays was published first separately, in an incomplete form, in Rome, 1472, and in Venice about the same time (see Brunet and Grässe, but esp. Wessner, *Donatus commentum Terenti,* I, xxxiii–xxxvii); an undated edition, published probably at Strassburg, is certainly derived from the Venice edition (though dated 1467 in Huntington Library catalogue); see Remigio Sabbadini, "Il commento di Donato a Terenzio" (*Studi italiani di filologia classica,* Vol. II, Florence-Rome, 1893), pp. 76–79. The Donatus commentary was published in a complete form together with the plays in many editions from Calphurnius' Venice edition of 1476 on; see Brunet,

Grässe, BM catalogue, N. E. Lemaire's edition of Terence (Paris, 1827) in BCL.

The detailed commentary of Willichius, with a line by line analysis both rhetorical and ethical, Melanchthon's analyses, and a number of essays by other humanists on the meter and language, appeared in the Terence variorum ed. (Paris: De Roigny, 1552). For accounts of other commentaries, see Baldwin, *Five-Act Structure.*

32 My brief summary is chiefly indebted to Atkins, *English Literary Criticism: The Medieval Phase.* Other important studies of rhetoric in the Renaissance, its history and its relation to poetic: Atkins, *English Literary Criticism: The Renascence* (London, 1947); Charles Sears Baldwin, *Medieval Rhetoric and Poetic* (New York, 1928) and *Renaissance Literary Theory and Practice* (Columbia Univ. Press, 1939); Donald Lemen Clark, *Rhetoric and Poetry in the Renaissance* (Columbia Univ. Press, 1922); Milton Boone Kennedy, *The Oration in Shakespeare* (Chapel Hill, 1942); G. D. Willcock and A. Walker, introduction to Puttenham's *Arte of English Poesie* (ref. in Ch. I, n. 11); Sister Miriam Joseph, *Shakespeare's Use of the Arts of Language* (*Columbia Univ. Studies in Engl. and Comp. Lit.,* No. 165, 1947), esp. Ch. I.

33 *De nuptiis* (ed. Adolfus Dick, Bibl. script. graec. et rom. Teub., Leipzig, 1925), beginning of Lib. V (passage cited by Atkins, *Med. Phase,* pp. 27–28):

> "Interea sonuere tubae raucusque per aethram
> cantus, et ignoto caelum clangore remugit:
>
> .   .   .   .
>
> sed dum talibus perturbatur multa terrestrium plebs deorum, ecce quaedam sublimissimi corporis ac fiduciae grandioris, uultus etiam decore luculenta femina insignis ingreditur, cui galeatus uertex ac regali caput maiestate sertatum, arma in manibus, quibus se uel communire solita uel aduersarios uulnerare, fulminea quadam coruscatione renidebant. subarmalis autem uestis illi peplo quodam circa humeros inuoluto Latiariter tegebatur, quod omnium figurarum lumine uariatum cunctorum schemata praeferebat, pectus autem exquisitissimis gemmarum coloribus subbalteatum. haec cum in progressu arma concusserat, uelut fulgoreae nubis fragore colliso bombis dissultantibus fracta diceres crepitare tonitrua; denique creditum, quod instar Iouis eadem posset etiam fulmina iaculari."

34 Lines 1060–62 (ed. Wm. E. Mead, EETS, 1928 [for 1927]), of 1517 ed.

34a *Sommario,* II. ii. Cf. esp. p. 19ᵛ: "Ivi il Poema, et il florido stile de Virgilio tanto eccedeva in ornamento, et eccellenza a gli altri canti, che somigliava fra gli uccelli il papagallo adorno della maggioranza delle piante penne" (quoted from 1586 ed.). According to Brunet the work is a translation of Alonso de la Torre's *Vision deleytable* . . . (Seville, 1526).

35 *Abbregé de l'art poétique françois* (Paris, 1565); reprinted in *Œuvres complètes* (ed. Prosper Blanchemain, Paris, 1866), VII, 317–26.

36 See L. S. Hultzén, *Aristotle's "Rhetoric" in England to 1600:* abstract of thesis, Cornell, 1932; extremely interesting and important. His findings are that the use of the *Rhetoric* throughout the period is largely incidental, dissociated from any rhetorical theory.

37 *Small Latine, passim;* Mallett, *Oxford;* Mullinger, *Cambridge.*

38 See Ringler and Allen edition of *Oratio,* pp. 48–49, and Introduction; cf. n. 49, below.

39 *Directions for Speech and Style* (ed. from Harleian MS. 4604 by H. H. Hudson, Princeton Univ. Press, 1935), p. 41.

40 *De oratore,* III. 178–80 (tr. Rackham, Loeb ed.). This passage was a favorite of both medieval and renaissance writers; cf. the use Fracastoro makes of it in the passage quoted from him earlier.

41 On the three styles, see *De oratore,* III. 199; *Orator,* v. 20–vii. 22, xxi. 69–xxxvi. 125; also *Rhet. ad Herennium,* IV. xi–xvi (ed. J. W. Rinn, *M. T. Ciceronis . . . Opera rhetorica et oratoria,* Vol. I [1831], in BCL); "la roue de Virgile" (*Bucolics,* simple; *Georgics,* middle; *Aeneid,* sublime) in Jean de Garlande (see important discussion of medieval conceptions of the three styles in Edmond Faral, *Les Arts poétiques du XII. et du XIII. siècles,* Paris, 1924, p. 86–89); Scaliger, *Poetices,* IV. ii; Puttenham, III. vi (*ECE,* II, 158–59); Jonson, *Timber,* "Structura et statura" (Schelling ed., p. 64); etc. The knowledge was commonplace.

42 *Essais,* II. x, "Des livres"; see also I. li, "De la vanité des paroles."

43 *Advancement of Learning,* Everyman ed., pp. 145–50; for further references in Bacon, consult Wallace.

44 P. A. Duhamel, "Sir Philip Sidney and the Traditions of Rhetoric," unpublished doctoral dissertation at the University of Wisconsin, 1945.

45 Gabriel Harvey's *Pierce's Supererogation* (*ECE,* II, 277); see whole of pamphlet and of *Four Letters* (in Vol. II); also Nashe, esp. Preface to *Menaphon* (*ECE,* Vol. I). Cf. Daniel, *Defence of Rhyme* (*ECE,* II, 371–72). On protests against Ciceronianism, see Morris Croll, "Attic Prose: Lipsius Montaigne, Bacon," *Schelling Anniversary Papers* (New York, 1923), pp. 117–50; Croll, "Muret and the History of 'Attic' Prose," *PMLA,* XXXIX (June, 1924), 254–309; Wallace, *Bacon,* esp. Ch. XI; Ringler and Allen's introduction to Rainolds' *Oratio.* For a full and important study of English style, see Veré L. Rubel, *Poetic Diction in the English Renaissance from Skelton through Spenser* (New York, 1941); cf. Gladys D. Willcock, "Shakespeare and Rhetoric," in *Essays and Studies by Members of the English Association,* XXIX (1943), 50–61.

46 *Audomari Talaei rhetorica e P. Rami . . . praelectionibus observata.* Perry Miller (*New England Mind,* New York, 1939, p. 495), gives 1567 as the date of Talaeus' work; W. G. Crane (*Wit and Rhetoric in the Renaissance,* Columbia Univ. Press, 1937), ?1544.

47 For a full treatment of the place of Ramus as the logical outcome of a long historical process, begun by medieval encyclopaedists and logicians and continued by Agricola, Vives, Melanchthon, Sturm, and Wilson, see

Duhamel, Thesis, Ch. IV; for a description and assessment of Ramus, see Duhamel, "The Logic and Rhetoric of Peter Ramus," *MP*, XLVI (Feb., 1949), 163–71.

48 From preface to his *Dialectique*, printed in Waddington, *Ramus*, pp. 373–74.

49 *Talaei rhetorica* (London ed., preface dated 1575), Cap. I, II; see also Charles Butler, *Rhetoricae libri duo* (Oxford, 1598), which follows Talaeus closely. In the *Gorgias* (463A–C), Plato had said that rhetoric was a branch of flattery (κολακεία), of which cookery (ὀψοποιική), personal adornment (κομμωτική), and sophistry (σοφιστική) were also branches. Cf. the comparison made by George Downame (sixteenth-century English commentator on Ramus) of invention, disposition, and memory to Hercules, of elocution (style) and delivery "to merely the Hydra and the skin of eloquence." Dialectic "affords as it were the body of oratory, rhetoric the clothing" (quoted in Miller, p. 326). For denunciations of rhetoric in terms similar to Plato's, cf. Henry Cornelius Agrippa, *Of the Vanity and Uncertainty of Arts and Sciences* (English transl., 1569, Cap. VI), in which it is called "the art of fawning flattery"; and Rainolds' *Oratio* (Ringler and Allen, pp. 48–49), in which it is said to be "singed with harlots' curling-irons, smeared with dripping perfumes, daubed with pigments," and is likened to Dead Sea fruit.

50 Cf. Miller, *New England Mind*, Chs. XI and XII.

51 *Rom.*, pp. 186–88; for full discussion of *energeia*, see Ch. IX, below. To supplement the very tentative discussion in these paragraphs of renaissance conceptions of the function of style, consult the fuller treatments by Miss Wallerstein in *Studies* (Ch. II) and by Rosamond Tuve, esp. in *Elizabethan and Metaphysical Imagery* (Univ. of Chicago Press, 1947), but also in "Imagery and Logic: Ramus and Metaphysical Poets," *JHI*, III (Oct., 1942), 365–400.

52 See quotations, pp. 28 and 30, above; for whole discussion see *Naugerius*, pp. 58–71.

53 Lionardi, p. 12; Jonson, *Timber*, p. 64 ("Oratio imago animi"); Charron, I. xi (pp. 40–41).

54 III. v (*ECE*, II, 154); contrast III. i (n. 56, below).

55 See esp. Tuve, *Eliz. and Met. Imagery, passim*.

56 With Puttenham, "as th'excellent painter bestoweth rich orient colours upon his table of portrait," etc. (III. i; *ECE*, II, 142–43) cf. Ronsard, *Abbregé* (quotation given above); Lionardi (pp. 14–15): "....la veste non dar'essere o forma delle cose, ma come trovamento artificiale vestirle, & ornarle" (pp. 14–15). Paolo Beni (*Comparatione di Homero, Virgilio, e Torquato*, Padua, 1607), though following the traditional disjunction, is disturbed by it; a poem is not like an armed, mounted man, in whom we can distinguish at once between the essential parts (head, arm, etc.) and the added parts (helmet, saddle, etc.), but like a picture or a garden in which it isn't clear about many things whether they belong to the constitution of the subject or to its embellishment

("ove molte cose possono portar dubbio se appartengano alla costitutione del soggetto, overo all'abbellimenti & a riempir il vano," p. 175). But note (pp. 213–14): "And just as Painting has two parts and offices, the one of designing, the other of coloring, wherefore she first 'shadows forth' ("adombra") the work with the design and then with colors brightens it ("l'illustra") and brings it to perfection; so Poetry also has her design and her colors, with which first she shadows forth the subject and then gives it perfection in so far as she imitates and represents." Beni includes fable and action under design; character, sentences, and style under coloring.

57 *Defense*, sec. 52.
58 *Naugerius*, p. 65.
59 *Defense*, sec. 15.
60 *Garden of Eloquence*, ABiiij.
61 See n. 45, above. Wallace (*Bacon*, Ch. VII) disagrees with the appellation and points out, justly, that Bacon wrote in more than one style. Nevertheless, even the more ornate of the essays maintain the patterns of syntax (built on a principle of balance and logical emphasis, tending to compound rather than complex sentences, eschewing the periodic) which were evidently associated with the Attic style. Cf. the prose oration Shakespeare gives to Brutus (*Julius Caesar*, III. ii. 12–47), known from Plutarch and Cicero to be the leading "Attic" orator of his time. And see discussion of the plain style by Demetrius (*Demetrius On Style*, tr. W. Rhys Roberts, Loeb ed.), esp. IV. 190–208, on clearness (use of conjunctions to consolidate the style, *epanalepsis* or resumptive repetition, avoidance of dependent clauses, etc.).
62 *Progymnasmata*, a fourth-century rhetoric; in Greek and Latin in Aldus' *Rhetores graeci*, 1508; in numerous Latin translations throughout the century; in Latin, with expansions and *scholia* by Reinhard Lorick, 1537, augmented 1542 (many times reprinted); in English, with extensive adaptations by Richard Rainolde, *The Foundacion of Rhetorike*, Cambridge, 1563.
63 From Crane, *Wit and Rhetoric*, pp. 65–69. See Francis R. Johnson's introduction to his edition of Rainolde (New York: Scholars' Facsimiles and Reprints, 1945) for a full description of Lorick's and of Rainolde's expansions of Aphthonius; Baldwin (*Small Latine*, I, 221–23) for Edward VI's use of Aphthonius in the composition of a *chreia*.
64 "non est aliud vel admirabilius, vel magnificentius quam oratio, divite quadam sententiarum verborumque copia, aurei fluminis instar, exuberans" (the translation is Professor B. H. Ullman's). My quotations are from *De copia*, I. i–ix (in *Opera omnia*, Leyden, 1703, Vol. I).
65 *Inst.*, II. iv. 6, 7.
66 For a description of these, see Crane, Ch. III.
67 *Art of Rhetoric*, pp. 194, 115, 114.
68 *English Secretary*, 1599 ed., p. 9.
69 *Love's Labour's Lost*, V. i. 9–15. Cf. the Dauphin's praise of his horse,

404   NOTES TO PAGES 50–56

Henry V, III. vii. 32 ff.: "Nay, the man hath no wit that cannot, from the rising of the lark to the lodging of the lamb, vary deserved praise on my palfrey: it is a theme as fluent as the sea." Note the precise rhetorical sense of *vary.* For serious use of "copy," see esp. the lamentation scenes in *Richard III,* and note the Duchess of York's charge to Queen Elizabeth: "be copious in exclaims" (IV. iv. 135).

70 *La spositione di M. Simon Fornario da Rheggio sopra l'Orlando Furioso* (Florence, 1549), p. 46: "De gli affetti, de i costumi, delle sentenze, delle parole, & de gli altri ornamenti, che per l'opera tutta sparse, come pretiose gemme, si veggono, chi volesse notare i luoghi, costui torrebbe impresa d'annoverar le stelle del cielo nella serena notte, & l'onde del mare, quando egli è più gonfio nel mezzo dell'horrido, & tempestoso verno." "Costumi" may mean merely "habits," "manners," as opposed to "affetti" or "passions"; but the critics generally use "costumi" in the derivative sense of "characters" in epic or drama.

71 *Rom.,* p. 26.

Chapter 3

1 The first series is in the Cluny Museum. See *Masterpieces of French Tapestry,* catalogue of the exhibit at the Art Institute of Chicago, 1948, for reproductions and bibliography; also *Art News Annual* for 1948.

2 Figures 207–9 in Erwin Panofsky's *Albrecht Dürer* (Princeton Univ. Press, 1943), Vol. II. See text, Vol. I, for illuminating discussion of the iconography. See F. F. Chambers, *Cycles of Taste* (Harvard Univ. Press, 1928), for the renaissance discovery of Hellenistic aesthetics and its taste in "gold-and-glitter"; also Tillotson, "Expression in Sixteenth Century Style" (ref. in Ch. II, above, n. 3) A fine collection of renaissance jewelry on display at the Chicago Art Institute several years ago illustrated this taste perfectly; the jewelry was characterized by brilliance (of gold and precious stones), by variety (in the use of many stones of different colors), by intricacy of design, and by frequent use of mythological or symbolic figures (such as a pelican).

3 On various interpretations see *inspiration* in the index to *LC;* Panofsky on the *furor divinus* and *furor melancholicus* (*Dürer,* I, 156–71). For renaissance theories of the imagination see Murray W. Bundy, "Fracastoro and the Imagination," in *Renaissance Studies in Honor of Hardin Craig* (*PQ,* Vol. XX, No. 3, 1941); " 'Invention' and 'Imagination' in the Renaissance," *JEGP,* XXIV (Oct. 1930), 535–45; *Theory of Imagination in Classical and Mediaeval Thought* (*Univ. of Illinois Studies in Lang. and Lit.,* Vol. XII, Nos. 2, 3; May, August, 1927); also Ruth Wallerstein, "To Madness near Allied: Shaftesbury and his Place in the Design and Thought of *Absolom and Achitophel,*" *Huntington Lib. Quart.,* VI (Aug., 1943), 456–69.

4 "For my part, I do not see of what avail is either study, when not enriched by Nature's vein, or native wit, if untrained; so truly does each

claim the other's aid, and make with it a friendly league."—*AP*, 409–11 (tr. H. R. Fairclough, Loeb ed.).

5 *Defense*, sec. 46.

6 *Della poetica*, Pt. II (pp. 590–91); cf. Du Bellay's *Deffence et illustration de la langue francoyse* (1549), II. iii (ed. Henry Chamard, Paris, 1948, pp. 103–6). Du Bellay agrees that "doctrine" without "esprit" is useless; but argues that it would be too easy (and even contemptible) to win eternal fame if the talent given to the most unlearned sufficed for them to produce anything worthy of immortality: "Qui veut voler par les mains & bouches des hommes, doit longuement demeurer en sa chambre: & qui desire vivre en la memoire de la posterité, doit comme mort en soymesmes suer & trembler maintesfois, & autant que notz poëtes courtizans boyvent, mangent & dorment à leur oyse, endurer de faim, de soif & de longues vigiles. Ce sont les esles dont les ecriz des hommes volent au ciel." Here he is borrowing, as Chamard notes, from Sperone Speroni, "Dialogo delle lingue" (*I dialogi*, Venice, 1542), fols. 105^v–131^r.

7 Giraldi, *Rom.*, pp. 73–76; Puttenham, III. xxv (see pp. 59–61, below).

8 Scaliger, *Poetices*, I. ii; Agnolo Segni, *Ragionamento....sopra le cose pertinente alla poetica* (Florence, 1581), Lez. III (pp. 42–43).

9 *Defense*, sec. 11.

10 From "To my most dearly loved friend, Henry Reynolds, Esquire, of poets and poesy," from *The Battle of Agincourt* (Hebel and Hudson, p. 307).

11 Part I, V. ii. 97–110 (ed. Una Ellis-Fermor in Case ed. of Marlowe, London, 1930–33).

12 Opening lines of *The Progress of Poesy*.

13 III. ii (*ECE*, II, 145).

14 Giraldi, *Rom.*; Daniel, *Defence of Rhyme;* Jonson, esp. Induction to *Every Man out of his Humour*, ll. 228 ff., and dedicatory preface to *Volpone*, ll. 104 ff. (references to Jonson, unless noted, are to ed. by C. H. Herford and Percy Simpson, Oxford: Clarendon Press, 1925). For statements of the rules of art as fixed and universal, see Minturno, *L'arte poetica*, pp. 32–33; Tasso, *Discorsi del poema eroico*, 1594, Lib. III (*Prose diverse*, ed. Cesare Guasti, Florence, 1875, I, 148–52).

15 From section on "Poesis et pictura" (ed. Schelling, p. 49).

16 *Conversations with Drummond*, sec. 19, ll. 692–93 (Oxford *Jonson*, I, 151).

17 A full study of the tradition has been made by T. W. Baldwin in his *Small Latine*, Ch. I.

18 " 'Invention' and 'Imagination' in the Renaissance," *JEGP*, XXIV, 543.

19 IV. vii; IV. xiii (tr. H. Rackham, Loeb ed.).

20 Gray, *Progress of Poesy*, II. ii.

21 Address "To the Reader," 1612 quarto; in *LC*, p. 551.

22 *LC*, p. 548.

23 *Defense*, sec. 52.

24 *Ibid.*, sec. 33.

25 For a thorough analysis of Sidney's style see Duhamel, "Sidney," Ch. V.

26 "La tragedia a chi legge," in *Le tragedie* (ed. Celso Giraldi, Venice, 1583), pp. 132–33 (each play separately paged); translation of the whole address in *LC*, pp. 243–46.

27 From Sir John Beaumont's dedicatory preface to *Bosworth Field*, 1629 (Hebel and Hudson, p. 548).

28 *Timber*, "Ingeniorum Discrimina" (ed. Schelling, pp. 26–27).

29 Lodge, from *The Life and Death of Wm. Longbeard*, 1593 (Hebel and Hudson, p. 158).

30 *Le stanze*, 1478 (ed. Giosuè Carducci, Florence, 1863), I. 72; "But never absent from there [the garden of Venus] is joyous Spring, who spreads her blonde and crisp locks to the breeze, and binds a thousand flowers in a garland."

31 *Amoretti*, xxxvii.

32 *Pericles*, Prologue to Act V.

33 *Cymbeline*, II. iv, 80–85; 69–72.

34 I. 119.

35 I. 9 ff. (ed. L. C. Martin; *Marlowe*, Case ed.)

36 *Stanze*, I. 90: "The little painted birds among the leaves make the air grow sweet with new verses."

37 *Muses Elysium*, "Sixth Nymphal," 1659 (Hebel and Hudson, pp. 325, 327).

38 Quoted in Rudolph Schevill's *Cervantes* (New York, 1919), p. 125; cf. also Cervantes' making fun of pastoralism in his *Colloquy of the Dogs* (quoted by Schevill, pp. 126–27).

39 Raleigh, "The nymph's reply to the shepherd," from *England's Helicon*, 1600 (Hebel and Hudson, pp. 137–38).

40 *Republic*, X (esp. 596E, 598A–E, 599A); *Sophist*, 264C–267A.

41 *Poetics*, I–IV and *passim*. *Character, feelings, actions* are expressed by Aristotle's terms: ἤθη, πάθη, πράξεις. According to Butcher (chapter on imitation in his edition of the *Poetics*), Aristotle implies all these in his "men in action," the objects of imitation in the fine arts. Segni (*Ragionamento*, Lez. II, pp. 24–27) interprets Aristotle to include actions, character or fixed habits (*costumi*), passions, and ideas (*concetti della mente*); Varchi, actions, passions (*affetti*), character (ref. in n. 43, below).

42 For an especially strong statement of this position, see E. Hoby's translation of Coignet's *Politique Discourses*, 1586, Ch. 35 (*ECE*, I, App., 341–44). For the most eloquent defense, see, of course, Sidney's *Defense*, secs. 9, 10, 21, 23, 24, 40. For further references see *LC*, index, s. v. *lies, false, truth*, etc.; *ECE*, index, s. v. *poetry*.

43 *Art*, I. i (*ECE*, II, 1); Puttenham distinguishes between making and imitating in his last chapter, III. xxv, already summarized. For a rigid, formal definition of imitation, scholastically handled, see Varchi, *Della poetica*, Pt. II (pp. 576, 578–90); *Della poesia*, Pt. I (pp. 602–8). For more thoughtful attempts to interpret Plato's and Aristotle's concepts of imitation, see Segni, *Ragionamento*, Lez. I, II; Lionardi, *Dialogi*, pp. 10–15—in discussion on difference between words and things, the latter

the object of invention, nearly equated by him with imitation: "imitare non è altro che seguire gli effetti delle cose, & ottimamente conoscergli, & osservargli, et bisognando, sapere ritrarli, & questi poi accommodare al proposito secondo i luoghi, & i tempi opportune, ò in parlamento, ò in attione" ("to imitate is nothing else than to note the effects of things, and to know them thoroughly, and to observe them; and, at need, to know how to depict these things and accommodate them to the subject according to places and fitting times, either in words or deeds"). Castelvetro is noteworthy (*Poetica d'Aristotele vulgarizzata et sposta,* 2d ed. revised, Basel, 1576; IV. i, pp. 68 ff.) in thinking that the poet's activity of invention, demanding experience, advice, judgment, self-conscious art, should not be called imitation, so different is it from the imitation of others that comes natural to men and by means of which they learn. See further Bundy's book and articles referred to in n. 3, above, for "the movement away from 'imitation' and toward 'invention' explained in terms of 'imagination'."

44 *The Schoolmaster (ECE,* I, 7).

45 Plutarch, *De aud. poetis,* 3; also in *De gloria Atheniensum,* 3, where he attributes the idea to Simonides. For its provenance and wide occurrence see Smith, *ECE,* I, 386, n. 8; Schelling's ed. of *Timber,* note to sec. 49³, p. 131; Gilbert, *LC,* p. 363, n. 9 and index. Cf. Horace's "ut pictura poesis" (a poem is like a picture), *AP,* 361; see W. G. Howard, "Ut pictura poesis," *PMLA,* XXIV (March, 1909), 40–123.

46 See *mirror* in index to *LC;* Willard Farnham, *The Medieval Heritage of Elizabethan Tragedy* (Univ. of California Press, 1936), Chs. VII and VIII; Ruth L. Anderson, "The Mirror Concept and its Relation to the Drama of the Renaissance," *Northwest Missouri State Teachers College Studies,* Vol. III, No. 1 (1939).

47 From an essay attributed to Donatus, "De tragoedia et comoedia," frequently printed in renaissance editions of Terence; see below, Chs. V, n. 13, 14, and VI, n. 8a.

48 *Poetics,* (1) IX. 1451a37–1451b32; (2) XXIV. 1460a11–1460b2, XXV (whole chapter); (3) II. 1447b30–1448a6, V. 1449a31–36, 1449b9–10; (4) XV. 1454a16–33, 1454b8–15; (5) VI. 1449b24–31, XXII (whole chapter).

49 The importance of the passage in *Timon* was pointed out to me by Professor Craig. On the subject of these criteria applied to painting, see G. Vasari's introductions to Parts II and III of his *Vite* (in 1st ed., Florence, 1550); see App. I, below.

50 *Defense,* sec. 15.

51 *Poetics,* IX. 1451a37–39. In another place (XXV. 1460b33–36), Aristotle says that poets may defend departure from fact in description by saying, "But the objects are as they ought to be," just as Sophocles drew men as they ought to be, Euripides as they are. But the implication of *ought* is certainly conformity to a type or universal conception, less certainly conformity to a moral ideal.

52 *Sophist,* 235D–236D, 264C–267A. Cf. discussion of the distinction by

Jacopo Mazzoni (*Della difesa della "Commedia" di Dante*, 1587, esp. introduction and Lib. III) and by Torquato Tasso (*Del poema eroico*, II).

53 Cf. Giraldi, *Rom.*, pp. 54–59; Guarini, *Compendio della poesia tragicomica*, 1601, in G. Brognoligo's ed. of *Il Pastor Fido* (Bari, 1914), pp. 219–20.

54 *Dialogi*, pp. 63–64, 67: "Tutti le cose insieme deono essere corrispondenti, & piu tosto impossibili, & verisimili, che possibili, et non verisimili."

55 *L'arte poetica*, pp. 41–42: "Trovasi un modo d'approvare, nel quale il parer dell'humano intelletto s'inganna. Percioche, come che alquante cose tra loro sien talmente congiunte; che, se l'una avviene, è necessario, che l'altra ne segua, si come veggiamo all'apparir del sole necessariamente venirne il giorno: nondimeno alquante altre ne sono; che, benche sogliano senza necessità inanzi, ò dopo alcuna cosa avvenire, pur l'attissimo loro contesto, e la somiglianza del vero, e la vertù del mentitore parer le fà simile à quelle che necessariamente accadono. Ingannasi adunque il nostro intelletto, ov'egli delle cose, che avvengono, questa differenza non conosca. Ma laude grande è del Poeta, che alle cose finte acquista mirabil fede." Minturno here distinguishes between those things which are joined together by cause and effect and those which only appear to be because they occur in sequence; the power of the deceiver or simulator is to make the latter seem like the former. "Our intellect is deceived, therefore, when it does not recognize this difference between things. But great praise is due the poet who wins for feigned things a faith filled with wonder" (the sense of the passage seems to require *wondering* rather than *wonderful*).

56 See esp. his commentary on Aristotle's Ch. XXIV (*Poetica*, IV. iv., pp. 559–78).

57 *Naugerius*, pp. 69–70.

58 *Poetics*, XV. 1454a23–24 (tr. Butcher); Bywater translates, "But it is not appropriate in a female character to be manly, or clever."

59 References in Ch. IX, n. 49, 50.

60 Full discussion in Ch. VIII, pp. 194–97.

61 References on levels of style in Ch. II, n. 41.

62 *Rom.*, p. 12; *Com. e trag.*, pp. 208, 226–27; prologue to *Altile* and apology for *Orbecche* (in *Le tragedie*); see n. 26, above.

63 *Difesa* (*LC*, pp. 388–89).

64 *Defense*, sec. 23.

65 *Rom.*, p. 15.

66 *Naugerius*, pp. 68–70.

67 *Difesa* (tr. Gilbert, *LC*, p. 390).

68 *Comparatione*, Discorso II, pp. 82–83.

69 *Rom.*, p. 57.

70 θαυμαστόν (XXIV–XXV, 1460a11 ff.): Butcher translates "the wonderful"; Bywater, "the marvelous"; Gilbert, "the astonishing."

71 Giraldi, *Rom.*, pp. 55–57.

72   *Difesa* (tr. Gilbert, *LC*, p. 371).
73   *Del poema eroico* (ed. Guasti, I, 104–9, esp. 108–9): "Attribuisca il poeta alcune operazioni che de gran lunga eccedono il poter degli uomini a Dio, a gli angioli suoi, a' demoni, o a coloro a' quali da Dio o da' demoni è conceduta potestà; quali sono i santi, i magi e le fate. Queste opere, se per se stesse saranno considerate, meravigliose parranno; anzi miracoli sono chiamati nel commune uso di parlare. Queste medesime, se si averà riguardo a la virtù ed a la potenza di chi l'ha operate, verisimile saranno giudicate: perchè avendo gli uomini nostri bevuta nelle fasce insieme col latte questa opinione, ed essendo poi in loro confermata da i maestri della nostra santa fede, cioè che Dio e i suoi ministri, e i demoni, e i magi, permettendolo lui, possano far cose sovra le forze della natura meravigliose; e leggendo e sentendo ogni di ricordare nuovi essempi, non parrà loro fuori del verisimile quello che credono non solo esser possibile, ma stimano spesse fiate esser avvenuto e poter di nuovo molte volte avvenire...."

Chapter 4

1   Among the commendatory verses prefixed to Heywood's *An Apology for Actors*, 1612 (ed. R. H. Perkinson, New York: Scholars' Facsimiles and Reprints, 1941), sig. a3.
2   Gabriel Harvey's phrase, in *Four Letters*, 1592 (*ECE*, II, 231).
3   omne tulit punctum qui miscuit utile dulci,
             lectorem delectando pariterque monendo;

"He has won every vote who has blended profit and pleasure, at once delighting and instructing the reader."—*AP*, 343–44 (tr. H. R. Fairclough, Loeb ed.).
4   "or to utter words at once pleasing and helpful to life (*AP*, 334).
5   *De rerum naturae*, I. 936–50, IV. 11–25; cf. Tasso, *Del poema eroico*, p. 78; Nashe, *Anatomy of Absurdity*, 1589 (*ECE*, I, 328–29). See also *LC*, index, s.v. *medicine, poetry as pleasant; ECE*, notes on passage (I, 172, 390).
6   *Defense*, sec. 27.
7   Varchi, *Della poetica*, I. i–iii (pp. 571–78, esp. p. 574); II (pp. 585–89).
8   See *Defense, passim*, but esp. secs. 8–11, 15–29. For Sidney's debt to the Italian critics, consult Myrick, *Sidney as a Literary Craftsman*, Ch. III, and notes to the *Defense* in *ECE* and *LC*.
9   *Defense*, sec. 51 (contrast praise of religious and heroic lyrics in sec. 33). Puttenham appears somewhat apologetic, when he says his handbook is "for the learning of Ladies and young Gentlewomen, or idle Courtiers, desirous to become skilful in their own mother tongue, and for their private recreation to make now and then ditties of pleasure"

NOTES TO PAGES 88-91

(III. x; *ECE*, II, 164). English Protestant bias against the old romances is too well known to need references. Although not puritanical, Puttenham dismisses them as recreation for the common people at Christmas dinners and bride ales and in alehouses and taverns (II. x; *ECE*, II, 87). Italian critics, having Ariosto before them, had to face the romance as a serious poetic fact (see Ch. X, below).

10 Giasone De Nores, *Discorso intorno a' que' principii, cause e accrescimenti, che la comedia, la tragedia, et il poema eroico ricevono dalla philosophia morale, & civile, & da' governatori delle republiche* (Padua, 1587), *passim; Poetica* (Padua, 1588), introduction; *Apologia contra l'Auttor del Verato* (Padua, 1590), pp. 1ᵛ–3ᵛ.

11 *Apology for Actors,* sig. F3, F3ᵛ.

12 *Poetica,* I. ii, summary (p. 9ᵛ); III. i, summary (p. 121).

13 De Nores' word is *republica;* but the theory is of course applicable to any form of renaissance state. On the strongly social and political bias of renaissance criticism, see Hall, *Ren. Lit. Crit.*

14 *Defense,* sec. 48.

15 Giraldi, *Com. e trag.,* pp. [206, 207] (misnumbered 207, 208), 217–19; Minturno, *L'arte poetica,* pp. 76–78. See *LC,* index, s.v. *catharsis.*

16 *Poetica,* III. i (p. 117, ll. 5 ff.): "....con l'essempio suo, & con la spessa rappresentatione fa i veditori di vili magnanimi, di paurosi sicuri, & di compassionevoli severi...." Gilbert (*LC,* p. 315) translates: "with its example [i.e., of tragedy] and its frequent representation, it changes the spectators from vile to magnanimous, from fearful to firm, from over-pitying to strict."

17 *Compendio,* pp. 233–42; see below, Ch. VIII, n. 48, for summary.

18 *Della poesia,* Pt. IV (p. 660).

19 *Ragionamento,* Lez. III (pp. 47–55).

20 *Defense,* sec. 32. See Gilbert's appendix to the *Defense* (*LC,* pp. 459–61) for a discussion of "admiration and commiseration," evidently Aristotle's fear and pity.

21 *Compendio,* pp. 234–35.

22 *Poetica,* III. i, summary (p. 121).

23 See esp. Erwin Panofsky, *Studies in Iconology: Humanistic Themes in the Art of the Renaissance* (New York, 1939) and *Albrecht Dürer,* cited in Ch. III, above, n. 2.

24 *Naugerius,* p. 70; whole discussion of the useful, pp. 68–72; see Ch. III, pp. 76–77, above.

25 The morality play itself, being unclassical, was generally disregarded. Sebillet, however, compared it, because of its moral purpose, to classical tragedy (see Hall, pp. 103–4).

26 *Poetica,* I. iv (p. 29, ll. 31 ff): "L'ufficio....di buono poeta....è di speculando rassomigliare la verita de gli accidenti fortunosi degli huomini, e di porgere per rassomiglianza diletto agli ascoltatori lasciando il trovamento della verita nascosa delle cose naturali o accidentali al philosopho, & all'artista con la loro propria via di dilettare molto lontano da quella

del poeta, o del giovare." Professor Gilbert translates (p. 307) *artista* as *scientist*. But Castelvetro keeps a careful distinction between *philosopho* and *artista* through several pages of discussion; he speaks in the customary traditional way of the *science* of natural things (included as part of philosophy), but of the *art* (i.e., *technē*) of music, medicine, or agriculture. His *philosopher*, therefore, would seem to include theoretical scientist; his *artist*, craftsman and technician, or what we might call practical scientist.

27 *Poetica*, IV. i (p. 505, ll. 38 ff.): "Coloro, che vogliono, che la poesia sia trovata principalmente per giovare, o per giovare, & per dilettare insieme, veggano, che non s'oppongano all'autorita d'Aristotele, il quale qui, & altrove non par, che le assegni altro, che diletto, &, se pure le concede alcuno giovamento, gliele concede per accidente, come è la purgatione della spavento, & della compassione per mezzo della tragedia." "Incidentally" for "per accidente" is Professor Gilbert's translation (*LC*, p. 353).

28 *Naugerius*, pp. 68–70.

29 *Poetices*, I. ii.

30 *Art*, I. xxiii (*ECE*, II, 47).

31 *Ibid.*, I. xxiv (*ECE*, II, 49).

32 Jonson, prefaces, prologues, *Timber* (ed. Schelling, pp. 74–75, 79, 81–83). Chapman, dedicatory letter to *The Revenge of Bussy D'Ambois*, 1613; dedication and preface to *Achilles' Shield*, 1598 (*ECE*, II, 297–307). Heywood, *Apol. for Actors*, esp. Bk. III; Heywood gives one of the fullest statements of the moral aim of each type of play. Massinger, *The Roman Actor*, I. i. 1–26; I. iii. 31–141 (cf. Wm. L. Sandidge Jr.'s critical ed., Princeton Univ. Press, 1929; these passages are reprinted in *LC*, pp. 568–73). See also Whetstone on the usefulness of comedy in his dedication to *Promos and Cassandra* (*ECE*, I, 58–60).

33 Middleton is noteworthy for never claiming anything but delight for his plays (in spite of the moralizing tags sometimes found in the text). Cf. esp. Prologue to *No Wit, No Help like a Woman's* (ed. A. H. Bullen, London and Boston, 1885, Vol. IV); dedicatory letter to *The Witch* (Vol. V): ". . . bears no other charms about her but what may tend to your recreation"; Prologue to *The Roaring Girl* (Vol. IV; with Dekker):

> O roaring girl, whose notes till now ne'er were,
> Shall fill with laughter our vast theatre,
> That's all which I dare promise: tragic passion,
> And such grave stuff, is this day out of fashion;

and preface to the same, headed "To the Comic Play-Readers, Venery and Laughter," and continuing with an interesting comment on taste in 1611. The editors of the Oxford *Jonson* (IX, 408–10) point out Marston's anti-Horatian emphasis on delight in his Induction to *What You Will* (see epigraph to Ch. XII, below) and Prologue to *The Dutch Courtesan*.

34 Beeston's verses quoted as epigraph to this chapter.

35 From Nashe's *Pierce Penniless* (*Works,* ed. R. B. McKerrow, London, 1904–10, I, 213). For English treatises in the controversy over the stage, consult *ECE;* W. C. Hazlitt's *English Drama and Stage . . . 1543–1664* (Roxburghe Library, No. 4, 1869) for many treatises not in *ECE;* and *CHEL* Bibliography.

36 Wm. Webbe, *A Discourse of English Poetry,* 1586 (*ECE,* I, 251).

36a A counter-reply, ca. 1582, to Lodge's *Defence of Poetry, Music, and Stage Plays* (1579), itself a reply to Gosson's *School of Abuse* (1579). Text of *Plays Confuted,* in the liveliest and wittiest vein of Elizabethan controversy, is in Hazlitt, *English Drama and Stage,* pp. 157–218; the passages I have quoted are all from the "Second Action." Gosson denies, observantly (pp. 179–80), that the familiar definition of comedy ("imitatio vitae," etc.) Lodge gives as if from Cicero, ever came from Cicero; see above, Ch. III, n. 47; see below, Ch. VI, n. 8a.

37 Jonson and Chapman are possible exceptions. Jonson's charge against other playwrights of "immodest and obscene writing" (Induction to *Cynthia's Revels,* Oxford ed., ll. 175–76) and of profaneness and "foul and unwashed bawdry" (dedication, l. 46, *Volpone*) can be reconciled with his own hardly squeamish practice and his frank admission that in *Bartholomew Fair* "the language somewhere savours of Smithfield, the booth, and the pig-broth" (Induction, ll. 148–53) only by supposing that he made a distinction between others' practice and his own according to the end to which these means were put. Chapman's Prologue to *All Fools* (*Plays and Poems: The Comedies,* ed. T. M. Parrott, London, 1910) also suggests such critical awareness, esp.:

> Who can show cause why quick Venerian jests
> Should sometimes ravish, sometimes fall far short
> Of the just length and pleasure of your ears,
> When our pure dames think them much less obscene,
> Than those that win your panegyric spleen?

38 Massinger, *The Roman Actor,* I. iii. 96–106.

Chapter 5

1 Cf. epigraph to this chapter. Cf. Marston's "nocturnal" as a class of play (Induction to *What You Will,* pr. 1607, quoted in Ch. VIII, below, n. 5); "nocturnal" also in Dekker's *Seven Deadly Sins of London* (ed. Alexander Grosart, *Non-Dramatic Works,* II, 41). One must have great temerity to question W. J. Lawrence's identification of the "nocturnal" (*Pre-Restoration Stage Studies,* Harvard Univ. Press, 1927, Ch. VI) as specifically and only a type of comedy (like *The Two Angry Women of Abingdon* or *A Midsummer Night's Dream*) which uses night scenes

for at least one act of the play to increase the comic imbroglio. But "nocturnal" in Dekker, though, as Lawrence rightly observes, a substantive not an adjective, appears to be synonymous with "dismal tragedy": "all the City lookt like a private playhouse, when the windows are clapt down, as if some *Nocturnal* or dismal *Tragedy* were presently to be acted before all the tradesmen"; the point about the gloom of the city when the shutters go up at nightfall would be confused if "nocturnal" were understood here as comedy. Cf. "night-piece" in *The White Devil*, where Lodovico's last words are, "I limn'd [*text reads* limb'd] this night-piece and it was my best" (V. vi. 299). To the conventional classes of "tragedy," "comedy," and "pastoral," *Histriomastix* (ca. 1589, revised probably by Marston, 1599; text in Richard Simpson's *School of Shakespeare,* London, 1878, Vol. II) adds, in obvious parody of classifying, "nocturnal" and "infernal" (II. 217–21). One is tempted to call Marston's own *Sophonisba* both of these; there is a plethora of scenes calling for the appearance of characters in "night-gowns" and the scene with Erictho (IV. i) is one of the murkiest in the whole of Elizabethan drama.

2 Prologue to *The Comedy of the most virtuous and godly Susanna,* by Thos. Garter, pr. 1578, and also possibly earlier; see W. W. Greg's Introduction to Malone Society Reprint, 1936 (1937).

3 *Defense,* sec. 49. Cf. Florio's *Second Fruits,* 1591, pp. 22–23 (conversation given first in Italian and then in English):

   G. And then after dinner we will go see a play.
   H. The plays that they play in England are not right comedies.
   T. Yet they do nothing else but play every day.
   H. Yea, but they are neither right comedies, nor right tragedies [ne vere comedie, ne vere tragedie].
   G. How would you name them then?
   H. Representations of histories, without any decorum.

4 John M. Manly, "The Miracle Play in Mediaeval England," in *Essays by Divers Hands,* Trans. Royal Soc. of Lit. of the United Kingdom (London, 1927), N.S., VII, 133–52. I owe to Professor Craig the reference to this most important article and the appreciation of its significance in enabling us to see the development of Elizabethan drama in a truer light; see also Professor Craig's General Introduction (pp. 14–25, esp. pp. 18–19) to *The Complete Works of Shakespeare* (Chicago, 1951).

5 Texts and descriptive introductions in *Sacre rappresentazioni dei secoli XIV, XV e XVI,* ed. Alessandro d'Ancona (Florence, 1872), Vol. III; outlines of plots in Joseph Spencer Kennard, *The Italian Theatre from its Beginning to the Close of the Seventeenth Century* (New York, 1932), I, 61–63, n. 18. For further discussion see D'Ancona, *Origini del teatro italiano* (2d ed., Torino, 1891), I, 435–39; II, 58–60, and index.

6 *Patient Grissell* by John Phillips, ca. 1558–61 (Malone Soc., 1909); *Common Conditions,* ca. 1576 (ed. Tucker Brooke, Elizabethan Club Re-

prints, No. 1, Yale Univ. Press, 1915); *Clyomon and Clamydes,* same date or earlier (Malone Soc., 1913). Chambers includes with these romantic survivals *Cambises* and *Horestes* (*Eliz. Stage,* III, 37–41). For titles of nonextant romantic plays see *Eliz. Stage,* III, 178 and n. 2; Vol. IV, App. B for court plays, App. L for printed plays, App. M for lost plays. Also Introduction to James Paul Brawner's ed. of *The Wars of Cyrus* (Univ. of Illinois Press, 1942), pp. 64–66.

7 Gosson, *Plays Confuted* (ed. Hazlitt, pp. 181, 189; passages quoted in Ch. IV, above); Sidney, *Defense,* sec. 48; Whetstone, dedication to *Promos and Cassandra* (*ECE,* I, 59); Jonson (see references in Ch. VII, below, n. 26, 27). See Charles Read Baskervill, "Some Evidence for Early Romantic Plays in England" (*MP,* XIV [Aug. and Dec., 1916], 229–51, 467–512), for abundant evidence of a deep-rooted romantic tradition in both France and England in various types of dramatic performance, both in folk and court festival. These articles are as important as Professor Manly's.

8 On this point, see Professor Farnham's interesting discussion in *Medieval Heritage,* pp. 65–68, 173–76.

9 See below, p. 108 and n. 21.

10 Farnham, *passim.*

11 On elements of comedy in dramatic form in the Middle Ages, see Chambers, *Med. Stage, passim;* for farce, particularly, see Vol. I, Ch. IV; Vol. II, Ch. XXV. Also Allardyce Nicoll, *Development of the Theatre* (London and New York, 3d ed., 1946), pp. 60–62, 76–80; Nicoll, *Masks, Mimes, and Miracles* (London, 1931), pp. 171–75, 179–92.

12 Nicoll, *Theatre,* pp. 81–83, and *Masks,* pp. 152–58, for discussion and further references; also Chambers, *Med. Stage,* II, 206–8.

13 In Calphurnius' edition (Venice, 1476, and Treviso, 1477) and in many subsequent ones, often continuous with the "Terenti vita ex Donati commentariis excerpta" and without separate heading. Reprinted in Lemaire's *Terence,* I, xliv–1; in Wessner, *Donatus commentum Terenti,* I, 13–31; in Georgius Kaibel, *Comicorum graecorum fragmenta* (Berlin, 1899), Vol. I, fasc. 1, pp. 62–71.

14 See Lemaire's variorum notes, Vol. I. Erasmus attributed the first essay to Cornutus or Asper; Lindenbrogius (Paris *Terence* of 1602) denied this ascription and attributed it to Evanthius; see Franciscus Hackius' variorum *Terence* (Leyden, 1662), sig.*** 2–3.

14a See esp. *Com. graec. frag.,* "De comoedia graeca commentaria vetera," *passim.*

15 See Grässe under *Grammatici;* also Edmund Keil, *Grammatici latini* (Leipzig, 1857), I, 298 for list of editions; I, 487–92 for section of Diomedes on drama. Text of Diomedes also in *Com. graec. frag.,* pp. 53–61, and in Reifferscheid, *Suetoni reliquiae,* pp. 4–16. References to and quotations from Diomedes are common; see App. II, below, for Huloet's definition of comedy, and cf. John Minsheu (*The Guide into*

Tongues, 1617), who draws on Diomedes, as well as on Athenaeus and others, in his etymologies of *tragedy* and *comedy;* see also his entry 9328–2, *stage play.*

16 See the De Roigny *Terence* (Paris, 1552) for humanist treatises on drama. Marvin T. Herrick, in his *Comic Theory in the Sixteenth Century (Univ. of Illinois Studies in Lang. and Lit.,* Vol. XXXIV, Nos. 1–2, 1950), has stressed the importance of the grammarians and of the commentators on Terence in the formulation of renaissance comic theory and has quoted liberally from the texts.

17 *Ars grammatica,* III. viii, ix (ed. Kaibel, *Com. graec. frag.,* pp. 57–58): "Tragoedia est heroicae fortunae in adversis comprehensio. a Theofrasto ita definita est: τραγῳδία ἐστὶν ἡρωικῆς τύχης περίστασις. . . . Comoedia est privatae civilisque fortunae sine periculo [vitae] comprehensio, apud Graecos ita definita: κωμῳδία ἐστὶν ἰδιωτικῶν πραγμάτων ἀκίνδυνος περιοχή. . . . Comoedia a tragoedia differt, quod in tragoedia introducuntur heroes duces reges, in comoedia humiles atque privatae <personae>, in illa luctus exilia caedes, in hac amores, virginum raptus [nuptiae *add. Reifferscheid*]; deinde quod in illa frequenter et paene semper laetis exitus tristes ‡et liberorum fortunarumque priorum in peius adgnitio‡."

My rendering from the semicolon ("deinde quod . . .") to the end of the sentence is faithful to what I think must have been the intention of the passage. The difficult phrase "et liberorum . . ." (marked by daggers in Kaibel) has been variously emended: see critical apparatus in Keil, Reifferscheid, and Kaibel. No solution is more usual in New Comedy than the happy recognition of a lost son or daughter, and the balanced structure of the passage as a whole requires a statement on the catastrophe of comedy to match that on tragedy, as the editors have recognized either by marking a lacuna or by suggesting an addition. But Kaibel alone has coped with the difficulty of "et liberorum adgnitio" by attaching it to a missing phrase on comedy; he suggests "fortunarumque priorum in peius <commutatio succedunt, in hac tristibus rebus exitus laeti velut nuptiae> et liberorum adgnitio."

18 *De fabula hoc est de comoedia,* IV. 2 (*Com. graec. frag.,* p. 66): "Inter tragoediam autem et comoediam cum multa tum inprimis hoc distat, quod in comoedia mediocres fortunae hominum, parui impetus periculorum laetique sunt exitus actionum, at in tragoedia omnia contra, ingentes personae, magni timores, exitus funesti habentur; et illic prima turbulenta tranquilla ultima, in tragoedia contrario ordine res aguntur; tum quod in tragoedia fugienda uita, in comoedia capessenda exprimitur; postremo quod omnis comoedia de fictis est argumentis, tragoedia saepe de historica fide petitur."

19 *Apology for Actors,* Bk. III, sig. F 1ᵛ.

19a *De comoedia,* V. 1–2 (*Com. graec. frag.,* p. 67); quoted below, Ch. VI, pp. 116–17 and n. 8a.

20   Philip Whaley Harsh, *A Handbook of Classical Drama* (Stanford Univ. Press, 1944), p. 410.

21   See Dante's own explanation of the title in his letter of dedication of the *Paradiso* to Can Grande della Scala (tr. Gilbert, *LC,* pp. 203–4). Dante follows, with misunderstandings, the essential distinctions of the grammarians: Comedy "differs from tragedy in its matter in this respect, that tragedy in the beginning is good to look upon and quiet, in its end or exit is fetid and horrible [from *tragos,* hence goatish, or fetid in the manner of a goat]. . . . Comedy, however, at the beginning deals with the harsh aspect of some affair, but its matter terminates prosperously. . . . Likewise the two differ in their mode of speaking: tragedy speaks in an elevated and sublime fashion, but comedy in a lowly and humble way. . . . From this it is clear why the present work is called *Comedy.* For if we consider the material, at the beginning it is horrible and fetid, since it begins with Hell, but at the end it is attractive and pleasing, since it ends with Heaven. As to mode of expression, its mode is lowly and humble, since it is the speech of the masses in which even womenfolk converse." Cf. also for further medieval definitions, *Med. Stage,* II, 209–11, and references; and documents in *Com. graec. frag.,* esp. Tzetzes and *Tractatus Coislinianus.*

22   Quoted by Hall, *Ren. Lit. Crit.,* p. 106. Note that Scaliger (*Poetices,* I. vi), in explicitly differing from Aristotle, moves in the direction of the grammarians: "I do not wish to attack this definition [i.e., Aristotle's] other than by adding my own: A tragedy is the imitation of the adversity of a distinguished man; it employs the form of action, presents a disastrous *dénouement,* and is expressed in impressive metrical language" (tr. Padelford, p. 40). Cf. his full definitions of tragedy and comedy in III. xcvii.

23   Puttenham, I. xiii–xv. Webbe (*Discourse, ECE,* I, 249): "There grew at last to be a greater diversity between tragedy writers and comedy writers, the one expressing only sorrowful and lamentable histories, bringing in the persons of gods and goddesses, kings and queens, and great states, whose parts were chiefly to express most miserable calamities and dreadful chances, which increased worse and worse, till they came to the most woeful plight that might be devised. The comedies, on the other side, were directed to a contrary end, which, beginning doubtfully, drew to some trouble or turmoil, and by some lucky chance always ended to the joy and appeasement of all parties." For definitions in contemporary dictionaries, see App. II of this book.

24   For a full study of the morality play, see E. N. S. Thompson, *The English Moral Plays* (*Trans. Connecticut Acad. of Arts and Sciences,* XIV, 291–414; March, 1910); also W. Roy Mackenzie, *The English Moralities from the Point of View of Allegory* (Boston, 1914).

25   Chambers' date; Harbage (*Annals of English Drama, 975–1700,* Univ. of Pennsylvania Press, 1940) identifies the play with the old *Prodigality* of 1567–68.

Chapter 6

1 One of many renaissance versions of the passage from *Thyestes;* cf. Jasper Heywood's translation, *Thyestes,* III, Chorus (1560; in Newton's ed. of *Seneca His Tenne Tragedies,* 1581; Tudor Translations, 1927); also Epilogue to *The Misfortunes of Arthur,* ll. 40–41 *(EECT).*

2 See esp. Lily Bess Campbell, *Shakespeare's Histories: Mirrors of Policy* (Huntington Library, 1947); E. M. W. Tillyard, *Shakespeare's History Plays* (London, 1944; New York, 1946). For an important older treatment, see Wm. D. Briggs, Introduction to *Marlowe's Edward II* (London, 1914).

3 See pp. 143–44, below; cf. Florio's *Second Fruits,* quoted in Ch. V, n. 3.

4 See discussion of this point in Ch. XI. I cannot agree with Professor Tillyard (esp. Pt. I, Ch. II) that Shakespeare's design was clearly envisaged from the start, that it was all-controlling in the composition of the plays, and that, viewed all together, they present an Aeschylean completeness. My point of view on the first tetratology is closer to that of E. K. Chambers *(Shakespeare: A Survey,* London, 1925): "Certainly the unity so obtained is more a formal than a real one; an acknowledgment of the need for some such principle in the chronicle history, rather than a solution of the problem of attaining it" (p. 7); in discussing the second tetralogy Chambers likewise makes a comparison to Aeschylus, (pp. 136–38), but with many qualifications.

5 On origins see Harsh, *Handbook,* p. 4, and bibliography.

6 *Poetics,* III (1448a36–b1; Diomedes, III. ix. 2 (ed. Kaibel, p. 58); Evanthius, I. 3 (ed. Kaibel, p. 62). Webbe, interestingly enough for his time, follows the derivation from κωμάζειν *(ECE,* I, 248). For speculation on these and other derivations, consult Scaliger, *Poetices,* I. v, vi; also the etymological dictionaries of Estienne, Minsheu, and Holyoke (see App. II, below).

7 See esp. Nicoll, *Theatre,* pp. 19, 49, 106; *Masks,* pp. 20–37 (on the Dorian Mime), 50–65 (on the Rhintonicae and Phlyakes).

8 V. 2–6 (ed. Kaibel, pp. 67–68). Kaibel and Wessner give the genitive singular ἀπὸ τῆς κώμης; Lemaire and Reifferscheid *(Suetoni reliquiae,* p. 8, note) the genitive plural ἀπὸ τῶν κωμῶν.

8a "Comoedia est fabula diuersa instituta continens affectuum ciuilium ac priuatorum, quibus discitur quid sit in uita utile, quid contra euitandum. hanc Graeci sic definiuerunt: [quotes Greek definition from Diomedes; see Ch. V, above, n. 17]. comoediam esse Cicero ait imitationem uitae, speculum consuetudinis, imaginem ueritatis" (V. 1; *Com. graec. frag.,* p. 67).

9 *Poetics,* XIII. 1453a7–12, Bywater's translation; Butcher agrees. Gilbert translates "because of some error of the kind found in men of high reputation," etc.

10 *Poetics*, II. 1447b30–48a5, 48a16–18; V, 1449a31–33. Aristotle's word for the persons of tragedy is σπουδαῖοι (persons morally noble). If higher rank is implied, it is because nobility of character and position were not thought of as separable; see Butcher's commentary, pp. 228–39, for the complex implications of these distinctions. Professor Herbert Howe suggests a comparison with the history of the word *liberal;* only men who were free could engage in liberal pursuits.

11 *Poetics*, IV. 1448b25–27.

12 Illustrations of this point are conveniently assembled in Hall, *Ren. Lit. Crit., passim;* I have taken a different line from his in the interpretation of Aristotle.

13 *Poetica*, I. x (p. 50, marginal note): "....qui si deve notar, che le in-imicitie delle persone Illustri, et Tragiche si convertono in morti, & uccisioni; la dove quelle di privati si convertono in feste, & allegrezze." Cf. the allusion to this commonplace of decorum in Nathan Field's *A Woman Is a Weathercock* (1609–10), in which a gentlewoman slandered at the church door vows to her newly wedded husband that unless he vindicates her honor he will never enjoy her as a wife:

> Nay I'll think
> As abjectly of thee, as any mongrel
> Bred in the city; such a citizen
> As the plays flout still, and is made the subject
> Of all the stages. Be this true or no,
> 'Tis thy best course to fight.
> ... if thou be'st still,
> And like an honest tradesman eat'st this wrong:
> Oh, may thy spirit and thy state so fall,
> Thy first-born child may come to the hospital.
> (II. i. 273–84. *Plays*, ed. Wm. Peery, Univ. of Texas Press, 1950).

14 *Defense*, sec. 31.

15 *Ibid.*, sec. 32.

16 See interesting discussion of this in Farnham, Ch. II, pp. 54–68. See also Émile Mâle, *L'Art religieux de la fin du Moyen Age en France* (Paris, 1908), Pt. II, Ch. II, "La Mort"; Florence Warren's edition of the fifteenth-century English *Dance of Death* (EETS, 1931, for 1929), esp. App. V and Beatrice White's Introduction; Leonard P. Kurtz, *The Dance of Death and the Macabre Spirit in European Literature* (Columbia Univ. Press, 1934); Theodore Spencer, *Death and Eliz. Trag.*, pp. 29–34.

17 Farnham's thesis; cf. *Medieval Heritage*, pp. 363–67, and elsewhere. My debt to Professor Farnham, in the treatment of *De casibus*, or, as he also calls it, "Gothic," tragedy, is very great; I owe the division of the two major types of romantic tragedy—the tragedy of power and the tragedy of romantic intrigue—to him.

18 *Timon of Athens,* I. i. 74–89.
19 *Art,* I. xv (*ECE,* II, 35).
20 *Troades,* 1–6 (tr. F. J. Miller, Loeb ed.): "Whoever trusts in sovereignty and strongly lords it in his princely hall, who fears not the fickle gods and has given up his trustful soul to joy, on me let him look and on thee, O Troy. Never did fortune give larger proof on how frail ground stand the proud."
21 For an excellent statement of all the moralizing commonplaces, Stoical and Christian, in the tragedy of power, consult *The Misfortunes of Arthur,* esp. the choruses; also *Jocasta* (see n. 24, below). For a clear statement of the Stoical position, see Charron (tr. Lennard, p. 184), I. xlix: "It falleth out many times, that they make a miserable end, not only tyrants and usurpers, for it belongs to them, but such as have a true title to the crown. . . . It seemeth that as lightning and tempest oppose themselves against the pride and height of our buildings, so there are likewise spirits that envy and emulate greatness below upon the earth."
22 Discussed in Ch. IX, pp. 234–39.
23 For an important discussion of the variations of emphasis—Aristotelian, Christian, and Stoical—to be found in Elizabethan tragedy, see Professor Craig's "The Shackling of Accidents"; also Allan Gilbert, "Fortune in the Tragedies of Giraldi Cintio," in *Renais. Studies in Honor of Hardin Craig* (*PQ,* XX, 32–43).
23a Lennard's Charron, I. xx (pp. 70–71); whole chapter on ambition important; cf. I. xlix on sovereignty.
24 *Jocasta* (in *EECT*), epilogue and choruses, esp. the last, beginning

> Example here, lo take by Oedipus,
> You Kings and Princes in prosperity. . . .

25 "The Shackling of Accidents," *PQ,* XIX, 16–17.
26 Bussy in *Bussy D'Ambois,* V, iv. 94–98; cf. the deaths of Clermont, Byron, Cato, and Chabot. Cf. discussion of "Denouement" in Ch. XI.
27 See F. T. Bowers, *Elizabethan Revenge Tragedy, 1587–1642* (Princeton Univ. Press, 1940), *passim.* The importance of revenge for plot-building is discussed in Ch. XI, pp. 306–8, below. For references to Senecanism, see Ch. I, n. 25.
28 Farnham, pp. 391 ff.
29 *Gismond of Salerne* extant only in MSS (ed. Cunliffe, *EECT*); *Tancred and Gismond,* pr. 1591–92 (Malone Soc., 1914).
30 For an excellent brief account of the Italian *novella* and its spread, see "Novella," sections by Ferdinando Neri and by Salvatore Rosati, in *Enciclopedia italiana;* also article on Bandello by Letterio di Francia. For influence of *novelle* in England, consult John Dunlop, *History of Prose Fiction,* new ed., revised by Henry Wilson (London, 1896), esp. Chs. VII, VIII; Emil Köppel, "Studien zur Geschichte der italienischen Novelle in der englischen Litteratur des sechzehnten Jahrhunderts," *Quellen und Forschungen* (Strassburg, 1892), H. 70; Adèle Ott, *Die*

italienische Novelle im englischen Drama von 1600 bis zur Restauration (Zürich, 1904); Arundell Esdaile, *A List of English Tales and Prose Romances printed before 1740* (London: For the Bibliographical Society, 1912); Mary Augusta Scott, *Elizabethan Translations from the Italian* (Boston and New York, 1916), secs. I, IV, XII—detailed information both on contents of collections and on analogues in drama; Ernest A. Baker, *History of the English Novel* (London, 1929), Vol. II; René Pruvost, *Matteo Bandello and Elizabethan Fiction* (Paris, 1937).

31 Dependence on Giraldi's prose tale in *Ecatommithi* (VIII. v) is hesitatingly recognized by editors; actually there are more significant resemblances to Giraldi's play *Epitia*, which editors dismiss, perhaps following Julius L. Klein (*Geschichte des Dramas,* Leipzig, 1865–76, IV, 354–55). Klein notes as fortuitous Shakespeare's use of the name "Angelo" (not in either of Whetstone's versions or in the *novella*) and the use of "Angela" in *Epitia* for the name of the sister of Juriste (Shakespeare's Angelo). He did not notice other significant agreements between *Epitia* and *Measure for Measure* where the other sources differ; see App. III.

32 On the subject of the influence of Italian drama on English renaissance drama, see R. Warwick Bond, Introduction to *Early Plays from the Italian* (Oxford: Clarendon Press, 1911); Winifred Smith, *The Commedia dell' Arte* (Columbia Univ. Press, 1912), esp. Ch. VI, App. B, and Bibliography; Scott, *Eliz. Transl. from the Italian,* secs. III, XII; Kathleen M. Lea, *Italian Popular Comedy* (Oxford: Clarendon Press, 1934), Vol. II, Ch. VI, Bibliography and Appendices. The bibliography of the subject is extensive; the older German scholarship (Klein, Creizenach, Köppel, etc.—see bibliographies in *Shakespeare Jahrbuch*) should not be neglected. For further special studies on comedy, see Ch. VII, below, n. 5.

33 *Decameron,* IV. ix; De Nores, *Poetica,* I. x (pp. 48ᵛ ff.).

34 *Decameron,* IV, i.

35 See Harsh, *Handbook,* pp. 404–5.

36 Giraldi, *Com. e trag.,* pp. 222–24; prologue to *Orbecche* (*Tragedie,* and in *LC,* p. 245). On the importance of *Orbecche* for renaissance Senecanism, see Cunliffe, Introduction to *EECT,* pp. xxx ff.

37 For references to this and to differing points of view see Ch. I, n. 25. On the sources of *Titus Andronicus* see H. de W. Fuller, "The Sources of *Titus Andronicus,*" *PMLA,* XVI (1901), 1–65; R. A. Law, "The Roman Background of *Titus Andronicus,*" *SP,* XL (April, 1943), 145–53.

38 Baskervill ("Some Evidence for Early Romantic Plays in England," *MP,* XIV, 488) thinks the story is from an old play rather than from the *novella;* he says the same story is in the French *miracle de Notre Dame* "La Femme du roi de Portugal," and repeated in Louvet's first miracle, 1536.

39 Henry Hitch Adams, *English Domestic or Homiletic Tragedy* (Columbia Univ. Press, 1943), pp. 168–69.

40 *Ibid.,* pp. 177–83. The story is from Rosset, *Histoires tragiques,* No. 5.

41 *Com. e trag.,* pp. 219–25; full discussion in Ch. VIII, below, pp. 199–200, and references in Ch. VIII, n. 29, 30.

42 *Novelle,* I. xxii; see further discussion of *Much Ado,* Ch. VII, below, pp. 178–79.

43 For these figures I am indebted to D. P. Rotunda, "A Tabulation of Early Italian Tales," in *Univ. of California Publ. in Mod. Philology,* Vol. XIV, No. 4 (1930). Unfortunately he does not break down his figures for tales of illicit love into comic and tragic treatment.

44 For an interesting discussion of the tragedy of evil see Henry W. Wells, *Elizabethan and Jacobean Playwrights* (Columbia Univ. Press, 1939), Ch. II.

45 *The Duchess of Malfi,* III. ii. 127–29, 160–63 (*Works,* ed. F. L. Lucas, London, 1927).

46 *The White Devil,* III. ii. 215–18 (ed. Lucas).

47 *The Duchess of Malfi,* V. v. 125–26. Cf. Lennard's Charron, I. xxxv (p. 108): "Our present life is but the entrance and end of a Tragedy, a perpetual issue of errours, a web of unhappy adventures, a pursuit of divers miseries inchained together on all sides; there is nothing but evil that it distilleth, that it prepareth; one evil drives forward another evil, as one wave another; torment is ever present, and the shadow of what is good deceiveth us; blindness and want of sense possesseth the beginning of our life, the middle is ever in pain and travel [i.e., travail], the end in sorrow; and beginning, middle, and end in errour."

48 *The Revenge of Bussy D'Ambois,* V. v. 162–93 (*The Tragedies,* ed. Parrott).

49 *Caesar and Pompey,* V. i. 259–63.

50 *The Changeling,* V. iii. 178–80, 115–21 (ed. Bullen).

51 Adams, *Domestic Tragedy,* esp. Ch. IV.

52 To these Professor Adams (Ch. V) adds plays from legend and history, including both R. B.'s *Appius and Virginia* and the one attributed to Webster (ca. 1564 and 1608 respectively), *The Life and Death of Jack Straw* (1591), Dekker's *Old Fortunatus* (1599), Daborne's *A Christian Turned Turk* (1610), ?Heywood's *Edward IV* (ca. 1592–99) for the Jane Shore story.

53 In Farmer's Old English Drama: Students' Facs. Ed., 1912.

54 Alfred Harbage, *Shakespeare's Audience* (Columbia Univ. Press, 1941), Ch. III.

55 My view is not quite like that of Mr. Adams, who (pp. 185–89) finds domestic tragedy not sentimental.

56 A note on Elizabethan social structure is worth making here. Bellafront's father and her husband, apparently poor "gentlemen," get a living in the service of others and belong somewhere along that hierarchical chain of master-servant relationships, starting with the queen and ending with a charwoman, which had no place in it for precisely a "middle class." Craftsmen—masters, journeymen, and apprentices—formed a similar

hierarchy; younger sons of gentlemen were often apprentices to a craft. "Middle class" is a modern term retrospectively applied, with accuracy only to the growing city merchant class.

Chapter 7

1 *Handbook,* pp. 351, 363.
2 Professor Kittredge in his introduction to *Comedy of Errors* (*Complete Works of Shakespeare,* Boston, 1936) suggests stylistic indebtedness to Plautus. For a different point of view, see Bond's treatment of the meters of *Bugbears* and other early plays in his Introduction to *Early Plays from the Italian,* pp. lxxxi–xc; he speaks of the persistence of native meters and native accentual verse *despite* "the influence of Latin comedy, and of the Dutch Education–drama with its attention to Latin comic metres."
3 See Lea, *Italian Popular Comedy,* II, 408–13.
4 From Thomas Tomkis, *Albumazar, 1615* (ed. Hugh G. Dick, *Univ. of California Pub. in English,* Vol. XIII, 1944), IV. xiii. 2305–6.
5 On identifiable Italian plots used in English plays, see Winifred Smith, *Commedia dell'Arte,* App. B; further bibliography in Ch. VI, above, n. 32. For the influence of Italian motives and techniques on Shakespearean comedy see O. J. Campbell's studies: on *Love's Labour's Lost* and *The Two Gentlemen* in *Studies in Shakespeare, Milton, and Donne* (New York, 1925), pp. 1–63; on *The Merry Wives* in *Essays and Studies in Eng. and Comp. Lit.* (Univ. of Michigan Press, 1932), pp. 81–117.
6 See "Note on Italian Influence in Lyly's Plays," in R. Warwick Bond's *Lyly* (Oxford: Clarendon Press, 1902), II, 473–85.
7 V. i. 11–16.
8 Apuleius, *Florida,* xvi; he is describing the plays of Philemon, rival of Menander. The translator of *Florida* in Bohn's Classical Library (London, 1872) renders *amica inludens* as "wheedling mistress," *uxor inhibens* as "peremptory wife."
9 Cf. Harsh, pp. 331 ff., esp. p. 336. "Fabula palliata" (i.e., dressed in a pallium or cloak) was applied to comedy from Greek sources as distinct from "fabula togata," on Roman subjects.
10 This suggestion is most fully developed by E. E. Stoll in *Shakespeare Studies* (New York, 1927), Ch. VIII.
11 I. xiv. (*ECE,* II, 33).
12 *Elegies,* I. 15 (Ben Jonson's revision, in Marlowe's *All Ovid's Elegies,* n. d.; also in *Poetaster,* I. i).
13 For a stimulating study of the effect of profound economic changes on the drama, see L. C. Knights, *Drama and Society in the Age of Jonson* (London, 1937), esp. Chs. III, IV, V.
14 See Ch. III, n. 47; Ch. VI, n. 8a.
15 Basel: Froben, 1534 (ref. in Ch. II, n. 30).

16 *The Governour,* I. xiii (Everyman ed., p. 58). Passage in *Eunuchus* (ll. 930–33) reads:

> id verost quod ego mihi puto palmarium,
> me repperisse, quo modo adulescentulus
> meretricum ingenia et mores posset noscere,
> mature ut quom cognorit perpetuo oderit.

Sargeaunt's translation (Loeb Library): "my veritable masterpiece I consider it, in having found means to let a stripling into the characters and ways of that class so early in life that his acquaintance with them will lead to a lifelong loathing."

17 See esp. Bond, Introduction to *Early Plays from the Italian,* pp. xci–cx.

18 See Harbage, *Annals.* Texts of *Nice Wanton, Disobedient Child* in Farmer's Students' Facs. Ed.; of *Misogonus* in *Early Plays from the Italian.*

19 I. i. 153–55, 156–58.

20 "Fourth Intermeane," after Act IV. The terms used by the postclassical grammarians (Evanthius, IV. 5, in *Com. graec. frag.,* p. 67; Donatus, VII. 1–4, *ibid.,* p. 69) for the movement of the fable—*protasis* (the setting forth, or exposition), *epitasis* (increase of tension, hence thickening of the plot), and *catastrophe* (lit., a sudden turn, hence ending or solution)—were also familiar through commentaries on Terence; see esp. Melanchthon's analysis of the plays in Erasmus' school edition of 1534 (ref. in Ch. II, n. 30, above). Jonson uses all these terms precisely (see esp. Choruses to *The Magnetic Lady*) and adds *catastasis* from Scaliger (his source for the term unknown), defined in *Poetices,* I. ix, as "vigor, ac status fabulae" and placed after the *epitasis;* defined by Dryden (*Essay of Dramatic Poesy, LC,* sec. 18) as "the height and full growth of the play; . . . the counterturn."

21 *The Fortunes of Falstaff* (Cambridge Univ. Press, 1944). Testimony to the continued popularity of the Prodigal Son plays is found in the parody of one in *Histriomastix,* II. 86–142, 281–88 (ed. Simpson); passages probably from old part of play, ca. 1589 (see *Eliz. Stage,* IV, 17–18).

22 "Grex," ll. 231–33. Professor Baskervill suggested (in his *English Elements in Jonson's Early Comedies, Univ. of Texas Bull.,* No. 178 [1911], pp. 7, 212–13) that Jonson might possibly be referring here to the old style in English comedy, that is to morality plays, and cited Jonson's use of the phrase with that sense in *Conversations with Drummond,* sec. 16, ll. 409–15 (Oxford *Jonson,* I, 143–44). Knights (*Drama and Society in the Age of Jonson,* p. 188 and n. 2) makes this identification categorically. But the tenor of the discussion in *Every Man Out* better fits Aristophanic comedy; the Oxford editors so take it (*Jonson,* I, 376; IX, 421, note to l. 232).

22a "To the Reader," ll. 186–92 (Oxford *Jonson,* IV, 323). Jonson is compared to Aristophanes as well as to Menander and Horace in J. Cleveland's "Ode to Ben Jonson upon his Ode to Himself" (text in Wm. Gifford's

Jonson, accompanying *The New Inn*); Jonson is "English Horace," "our whole Menander," and not less than the witty, sharp, and salty Aristophanes:

> He got the start of thee in time and place,
> But thou hast gain'd the goal in art and grace.

23 *Poetices,* I. vii (Padelford, p. 43). For the belief that Roman satire and Old Comedy were closely connected, see Oxford *Jonson,* IX, 396–99.

24 *Satire* I. 85–86 (tr. G. G. Ramsay, Loeb ed.): "All the doings of mankind, their vows, their fears, their angers and their pleasures, their joys and goings to and fro, shall form the motley subject of my page."

25 See Herford and Simpson's introduction to *Volpone* (*Jonson,* II, 49–53). Jonson has transferred tŏ modern Italy the vice of legacy-hunting (*captatio*) satirized by Horace, Juvenal, Pliny, Petronius, and Lucian; the two latter tell stories of *captatores* caught by their own greed which form the basis of the action in *Volpone.*

26 From ode in defense of *The New Inn* (Oxford *Jonson,* VI, 492); cf. *"Tales, Tempests,* and such like *Drolleries"* in *Bartholomew Fair,* Induction, l. 130.

27 Choric comment on Act I of *The Magnetic Lady,* ll. 15–24.

28 *Every Man in his Humour,* Prologue, ll. 21–24.

29 *Volpone,* Prologue, ll. 31–32.

30 *Epicoene,* second prologue.

31 *Alchemist,* Prologue, ll. 15–18.

32 Cf. esp. Ch. V, above, pp. 102–4.

33 *Theagenes and Chariclea,* tr. Thomas Underdowne (as *An Aethiopian History*), 1569?, 1577, 1587, etc. *Clitophon and Leucippe,* tr. W. B[urton], 1597 (ed. S. Gaselee, Oxford, 1923); Italian translation by L. Dolce, 1546, by Angelo Coccio, 1550; French, by Belleforest, 1568, and by others. *Daphnis and Chloe,* tr. Angel Day, 1587 (ed. J. Jacobs for Tudor Library, London, 1890); French tr. by Amyot, 1547 (BM cat.). For bibliographical details see Loeb editions of the Greek texts; also Samuel Lee Wolff, *The Greek Romances in Elizabethan Prose Fiction* (Columbia Univ. Press, 1912).

34 Ashley H. Thorndike, *English Comedy* (New York, 1929), pp. 32, 63.

35 The editions described were seen at the Huntington Library. For *Andria* illustration see frontispiece, and with its narrative and romantic style compare the handsome woodcuts (designs attributed to Dosso Dossi) in the Valgrisi ed. of *Orlando Furioso* (Venice, 1556; Huntington copy, 1566 ed.; see item 12 in *La raccolta Ariostea della biblioteca municipale di Reggio d'Emilia,* Reggio d'Emilia: Scuola di bibliog. ital., 1933).

36 Cf. Ch. XII, below, and illustrations.

37 In Ch. VI, above, pp. 133–35 and n. 33.

38 *Poetica,* III. ix (pp. 144^v ff.).

39 See Ch. VIII, below, p. 192 and n. 10, 49.

40 In *Giambattista della Porta: Le commedie* (ed. Vicenzo Spampanato,

Bari, 1911), Vol. II. Date of *Gli duoi fratelli rivali* unknown; Ireneo
Sanesi (*La commedia*, Milan, 1911; I, 352) conjectures it to be any time
between Oddi's work (written in the 70's) and end of century; printed
1601, and in collected ed. of plays, 1714 (F. Neri, *Encic. ital.*), 1726
(Brunet).

41 *Orlando Furioso*, cantos iv–vi. Note Paolo Beni's praise of this story as
excellent for tragi-comedy, *Comparatione*, p. 289. I note that D. J.
Gordon (*"Much Ado about Nothing:* A Possible Source for the Hero-
Claudio Plot," *SP*, XXXIX [April, 1942], 279–90) has independently
made the suggestion of the similarity between *Much Ado* and Della
Porta's play. The theme of slander of an innocent heroine is not uncommon; cf. Secchi's *Interesse*, in which someone impersonates the
heroine at her chamber door; this play has other motifs and situations
similar to *Twelfth Night*. Themes of calumny and vindication lead naturally to tragi-comic treatment; cf. another tragi-comedy of Della Porta's,
Il Moro, also based on the Ariodante and Ginevra story; Nathan Field's
A Woman is a Weathercock (pr. 1612); Shakespeare's *Winter's Tale*,
etc.

Since this chapter was written, Charles T. Prouty's *Sources of "Much
Ado about Nothing"* (Yale Univ. Press, 1950) has appeared. Professor
Prouty reprints Peter Beverley's *Ariodanto and Jenevra* (ca. 1566), an
expanded adaptation in verse of the Ariosto story, and gives an account
of all the known versions of the tale. Mr. Prouty's book is valuable for
its study of the different ways in which the source stories in Ariosto
and Bandello underwent elaboration and change of purpose in Beverley
and Belleforest, and interesting for its speculation on the effect these
changes may have had on Shakespeare's own particular emphasis.

42 Literally, the spirit of the soul which animates it and gives it motion:
"spirito dell'anima che l'avviva e le [*sic*] dá moto" (ed. Spampanato, II,
197).

43 "Ché se non fossi cosí cieco degli occhi dell'intelletto come sei, vedresti
l'ombre di Menandro, di Epicarmo e di Plauto vagar in questa scena e
rallegrarsi che la comedia sia gionta a quel colmo e a quel segno dove
tutta l'antichitá fece bersaglio" (II, 198).

44 First ed., Venice?, 1537; a score of editions appeared in the sixteenth
century, and the play was widely known and imitated in France, Spain,
and England: see edited text and bibliographical note in *Commedie del
Cinquecento*, ed. Ireneo Sanesi (Bari, 1912), Vol. I. Latin version,
Laelia (through Étienne's *Les Abusez*), played at Queens' College, Cambridge, 1595, is a possible line of influence on *Twelfth Night.—Eliz.
Stage*, IV, 375–76.

45 "Epistre du Traducteur" (in *Les Abusez. Comedie faite à la mode des
anciens comiques, premierement composee en langue Tuscane ... depuys
traduite en Françoys par Charles Estienne ... à Paris ... 1552*): "... au lieu
desquelles folies, trouverent la Comedie, qu'ilz apelloient nouvelle, en
laquelle n'introduisoyent que villageoys, ou personnages de vile qualité:

ne parlans d'autre cas que de mariages, amours, & semblables choses: lesquelles à fin qu'elles fussent delectables aux auditeurs, deduysoient en telle sorte, & si commodement, avecq' changemens de propos, choses inopinées, celées, & puys descouvertes, laissans un propos pour entrer à l'autre, puis reprenants le premier poinct, le faisans convenir au dernier avecq' si grande dexterité & maniere, que cela rendoit un plaisir incredible aux spectateurs."

With this taste for the complexity of the fable in New Comedy contrast Montaigne's disapproval (II. x, "Des livres"), precisely because it forced attention to the story, of the modern habit of making plots from several plays of Terence or Plautus or from five or six tales of Boccaccio; he liked Terence because the grace of his style makes the reader lose interest in his subject: "sa gentillesse et sa mignardise nous retiennent partout; il est partout si plaisant ... et nous remplit tant l'âme de ses graces, que nous en oublions celles de sa fable."

46   *Poetices,* III. xcvii (tr. Padelford, p. 69); cf. Scaliger's stress on importance of plot in New Comedy, I. v; I. vii. In connection with his emphasis on the romantic element, it is important to remember Jonson's acquaintance with him.

47   See quotations in Ch. V, above, pp. 106–7 and n. 17–19a; Ch. VI, n. 8a.

48   *Bartholomew Fair,* Induction, ll. 127–28.

49   See epigraph to this chapter.

50   On history of English pastoral drama, see W. W. Greg, *Pastoral Poetry and Pastoral Drama,* London, 1906.

51   I. iv. 40–56. "Kit" and "crowd" mean fiddle; "tabret," drum.

52   Cf. Jonson's claim in *Conversations,* sec. 16, ll. 393–401, about his *May Lord:* "Contrary to all other pastorals, he bringeth the clowns making mirth and foolish sports."

53   See esp. Panofsky, *Studies in Iconology,* Ch. II and illustrations.

Chapter 8

1   I use this epithet without prejudice to the question of Shakespeare's precedence with *Cymbeline,* or Beaumont and Fletcher's with *Philaster,* the two plays which appear to have begun the vogue for a certain style of sophisticated romantic tragi-comedy, with considerable emphasis on theatrical device. The question as to which was first is probably a false alternative; for the suggestion that Shakespeare and the two younger playwrights may well have developed the new style jointly for the courtly audience at the Blackfriars, acquired by the King's Men in 1608, and that the similarity of *Philaster* and *Cymbeline* comes from their common purpose and environment, not from imitation, see the important article by Gerald Eades Bentley, "Shakespeare and the Blackfriars Theatre," *Shakespeare Survey,* No. 1 (Cambridge Univ. Press, 1948), pp. 38–49.

2   A distinction is sometimes made in the use of these two terms (see Wells, *Eliz. and Jacob. Playwrights,* p. 145); it is a modern subtlety, often rightly enough felt, very difficult to apply consistently. Professor Wells's book is valuable, however, precisely because it does not follow rigid conventional classifications, but throws plays into new groupings suggestive of tone and sentiment.

3   "I do not offer this play to you as comedy, for it does not observe the comic mode in all things; I do not wish you to believe it a tragedy, although you will see in it a chorus of Nymphs. Whatever it is, fable or history, I offer it to you, and not as gold" [lit., "not for the excellence of gold]."—Quoted by D'Ancona in *Origini,* II, 6.

4   Mabbe mistranslates, "the author himself." On the complicated bibliography and authorship of *Celestina,* see H. Warner Allen's App. II to his edition of Mabbe's version for the Broadway Translations (London, [1908]). This dramatic novel comes into the discussion because it was known as a play in its shortened English form (published by Rastell, n. d.; reprinted for the Malone Society as *Calisto and Melebea,* 1908), and because Rojas' calling it a tragi-comedy may have helped give the term currency.

5   Cf. esp. the Induction to Marston's *What You Will* (ca. 1601), in which Doricus asks of the play about to be given, "Is't comedy, tragedy, pastoral, moral, nocturnal, or history?" and Phylomusus answers, "Faith, perfectly neither, but even *What You Will,* a slight toy, lightly composed, too swiftly finished, ill plotted, worse written, I fear me worst acted, and indeed *What You Will."*

6   See Ch. V, above, p. 103 and n. 5. Toffanin (in *Storia del teatro italiano,* pp. 65 ff.) takes issue with D'Ancona's view that the *sacra rappresentazione* never issued, as did the religious drama in England and Spain, in a great romantic theater, because it was poisoned in its cradle by classical imitation; Toffanin thinks that the Christian and the classical are inextricably involved.

7   D'Ancona, *Origini,* II, 1–60.

8   See Ch. VI, above, n. 31; also App. III.

9   See Sanesi, *La commedia,* I, 301–3, 347–49.

10 Guarini's *Compendio,* first published separately in 1601, then as an appendix to *Il Pastor Fido* in 1602, should be read; available in Italian in Brognoligo's ed. of the play (ref. in Ch. III, above, n. 53) and, in part, in English in *LC.* For summaries of the controversy, see Frank Humphrey Ristine, *English Tragi-Comedy: Its Origin and History* (Columbia Univ. Press, 1910), pp. 33–45; V. Rossi, *Battista Guarini ed Il Pastor Fido* (Torino, 1886), pp. 238–52; Greg, *Pastoral Poetry and Pastoral Drama,* pp. 206–10. For dating of *Pastor Fido,* see Greg, pp. 194, 206–7. Note Jonson's amusing reference to Guarini's play in *Volpone* (III. iv. 86–92):

> Lady Politic. Here's *Pastor Fido. . . .*
> . . . All our English writers,

> I mean such as are happy in th'Italian,
> Will deign to steal out of this author, mainly;
> Almost as much as from Montagnie:
> He has so modern, and facile a vein,
> Fitting the time, and catching the court-ear.

11 See Ristine, *English Tragi-Comedy*, pp. 8–9.

12 Prologue, tr. Paul Nixon (Loeb ed., Vol. I).

13 Mythological travesty had a long tradition behind it in the Dorian mimes, in the *phlyakes* (*phlyax* is the Dorian word for *phlyaros*, silly talk or foolery, hence a kind of farce, probably travestied tragedy: Liddell and Scott, *Greek-English Lexicon*) or dramatic entertainments of Sicilian Greeks, and in the Latin Atellan farces, probably connected with the *phlyakes*. Rhinton of Tarentum had called his *phlyax* plays *hilaro-tragoediae*, and they were evidently mythological burlesques, "tragedy" in the sense of having gods as subject matter. Some of the Sicilian vases clearly illustrative of *phlyax* comedies show Zeus with a ladder and about to climb into Alcmena's window.—Nicoll, *Masks*, Ch. I.

14 I am indebted to Professor Ristine's valuable and detailed *English Tragi-Comedy* for a number of references used in this section of the chapter. My distinctions of meaning for the term "tragi-comedy" are similar to his, but are either fortified or qualified by new interpretations of the Italian critics. And the tenor of my discussion, which stresses the artificiality of the term and regards Fletcherian tragi-comedy as only the sophisticated end product of an old taste, is rather different from his. Cf. also H. C. Lancaster's important *The French Tragi-Comedy*, Baltimore, 1907. Since this chapter was written Professor Eugene M. Waith's *The Pattern of Tragicomedy in Beaumont and Fletcher* (Yale Univ. Press, 1952) has appeared. Although we traverse in part a similar background (see his Chs. I and II), what each of us sees, or chooses to explore further, is often enough different to make our several journeys hardly repetitive. Sometimes our observations are quite at variance, but often they are mutually reënforcing, and I am grateful for so much corroboration in his book of my point of view.

15 Quoted by Ristine, p. 55, with reference to Lancaster, p. xii.

16 *Defense*, sec. 49. Cf. Florio, *Second Fruits* (quoted in Ch. V, above, n. 3).

16a Text in *Chief Pre-Shakespearean Dramas*, ed. Joseph Quincy Adams (Boston, 1924).

17 Minturno (*L'arte poetica*, pp. 83–89, 122, 125–26) is typical.

18 Quoted in part by Ristine, p. 90; from *Virgidemiarum* (1597), I. iii (*Collected Poems*, ed. A. Davenport, Liverpool Univ. Press, 1949).

19 *Amphitryon* cited as an authority in Giraldi, *Com. e trag.*, pp. 219–20; in Guarini, *Compendio*, pp. 226, 246–47. *Amphitryon* deplored in De Nores, *Apologia*, fols. 5ᵛ–6, 29–29ᵛ, 32–[33], 38–38ᵛ; in Scaliger, VI. iii;

in Daniel Heinsius, "Ad Horatii de Plauto et Terentio iudicium dissertatio," in Hackius' *Terence,* Leyden, 1662; also in Lemaire, Vol. I.

20 *Com. e trag.,* pp. 219–20.

21 *Ibid.,* p. 220: "Questo modo di tragedia (alla quale diede Aristotile il nome di mista) ci mostrò Plauto nel prologo del suo Anfitrione, quando disse che in essa eran persone men nobile mescolato con le grandi e reali. La qual cosa tolse però dalla Poetica di Aristotile, ove egli di questa sorte di tragedia favella. La quale di sua natura è più grata agli spettatori, per finire ella in allegrezza." See n. 30, below.

22 *Compendio,* pp. 255–62.

23 De Nores, *Apologia,* fols. 6ᵛ–8ᵛ.

24 *Compendio,* pp. 267–76.

25 The implication fits *Damon and Pythias,* though we cannot know if Edwards intended it. The social implication is applicable to *Appius and Virginia* (also called a "tragicall comedie") only in the sense that it fits *Celestina* and in a sense opposite to *Amphitryon,* that is, in the sense that a *tragic* action is based on the private affairs of citizens, which are appropriate only to comedy. H. H. Adams suggests this usage for *Appius and Virginia,* in *English Domestic Tragedy,* p. 76.

26 From "Epistola Nuncupatoria," tr. Ristine, p. 23; he treats at length this kind of drama (pp. 18–25) and the tradition it established. The Latin text may be found in L. R. Merrill, *The Life and Poems of Nicholas Grimald* (*Yale Studies in English,* No. LXIX, 1925), p. 108: "Quemadmodum enim quò res ipsa nomen tueatur suum, primum Actum Tragico moerori cedere, quintum uerò & ultimum iucunditatibus adcommodari & gaudijs: ita quô uarietas satietati occurrat, caeteris omnibus intermedijs, nunc lugubria, nunc festiua interseri." Grimald also claims that he has observed the decorum of comedy in other matters, notably in trying to imitate Terence's meters ("numeros Comicos & ferè Terentianos obseruari") and in interweaving great things with small, happy with sad, obscure with clear, incredible with probable ("& magna paruis, laeta tristibus, obscura dilucidis, incredibilia probabilibus intexuisse").

27 Ristine's suggestion, pp. 62–63.

28 "Tr. Com." appears after the title on a manuscript title page of a contemporary quarto, dated 1598; see Ristine, pp. 79–80.

29 Plays with double endings—*Selene* and *Altile;* with happy endings for all—*Epitia, Arrenopia, Euphimia, Gli Antivalomeni;* his *Tragedie* were published posthumously at Venice in 1583.

30 *Poetics,* XIII. 1453a30–39; Butcher's translation. Minturno (pp. 79, 84–85) associates this passage with the one which describes the best kind of situation with respect to the deed of horror (XIV. 1453b36–54a9), that is for someone to be about to do an irreparable deed through ignorance and make the discovery before it is done, e.g., as in *Iphigeneia in Tauris.*

31 *Compendio,* pp. 255–62.

32   *L'Art poétique*, III. 163–74 (ed. Georges Pellissier, Paris, 1885); quoted in part by Ristine, p. 55.

33   *Apologia*, fols. 4ᵛ–5. Appeals to Euripides as authority for tragi-comedy in Giraldi, *Com. e trag.*, pp. 221–22; in Minturno, pp. 83–88; in Guarini, pp. 226, 246–47, 285.

34   See Ristine, p. 147.

35   Evanthius, III. 5 (*Com. graec. frag.*, p. 65); cf. Lope de Vega, *Arte nuevo* (*LC*, p. 543).

36   Diomedes, III. xii (*Com. graec. frag.*, p. 60): "Satyrica est apud graecos fabula in qua item tragici poetae non heroas aut reges sed satyros induxerunt ludendi causa iocandique, simul ut spectator inter res tragicas seriasque satyrorum iocis et lusibus delectaretur, ut Horatius sensit his versibus...." (quotes Horace, *AP*, ll. 220–24). Cf. Scaliger, I. viii; III. xcvii; Guarini, pp. 246–47. Minturno (pp. 161–66) follows Aristotle in thinking comedy and tragedy both derived from satyr drama, but discusses the latter only in the form of satyric tragedy, since the only surviving example is Euripides' *Cyclops*.

37   Evanthius, II. 4–7 (*Com. graec. frag.*, pp. 63–64); Puttenham, I. xiv. (*ECE*, II, 33–34).

38   Diomedes, III. x. 5, 9 (*Com. graec. frag.*, pp. 59, 60); see also Minturno, p. 161.

39   *Satire*, L. *satira* or *satura*, is a specific application to poetry of *satura*, medley, according to the grammarians elliptical for *lanx satura*, a dish filled with a mixture of fruits, from *satur*, full or sated: *Harper's Latin Dict.*; *NED*. On the confusion with satyr, see *NED*. Cf. Scaliger, III. xcvii; Puttenham, I. xi, xiii–xv (*ECE*, II, 27, 32–36): satires were "recitals of rebuke, uttered by the rural gods out of bushes and briars."

40   *Compendio*, pp. 271–72.

41   The pastoral or "satiricall" scene is represented in S. Serlio, *Architettura* (Venice, 1551); English translation, *The First* [*-Fifth*] *Book of Architecture* (1611), Bk. II. The scene is reproduced in *Eliz. Stage*, IV, 362, in an extract from Serlio; in Nicoll, *Theatre*, fig. 81; in L. B. Campbell, *Scenes and Machines*, p. 38. Consult the last (pp. 123, 164) for influence of setting on pastoral drama. But see Perrault's edition of Vitruvius (Paris, 1684) for doubt that the ancient satyr play, more farcical than poetical, and the modern pastoral were the same (p. 178, n. 1), though Perrault allows it to be proper for the pastoral to use the rustic scene; this edition is accompanied by excellent notes and illustrations. With the classical tradition, cf. the tradition of the "woodwose" or "woodhouse" (wild man or satyr) in English masques and pageants; see *Eliz. Stage*, index.

42   Minturno, pp. 84, 163–66; Guarini, pp. 226, 246–47.

42a   Reproduced in the Oxford *Jonson*, Vol. IV, frontispiece; described in IX, 15–16.

43   Prologue partially quoted in Sanesi, *Commedia*, I, 349: "Et nell'amarezza delle lagrime ancora sta nascosta la dolcezza del diletto; et io che in

ogni maniera dilettar voglio, fo cosí spesso e di lagrime, e di riso una vaghissima mescolanza, e l'amaro del pianto fa più gioconda la dolcezza del riso."

44 *Com. e trag.*, pp. 210–15, 221–22, 224–25; on the importance of Giraldi, see P. Bilancini, *Giambattista Giraldi e la tragedia italiana nel sec.* XVI (Aquila, 1890). On Della Porta, see discussion in Ch. VII, above, pp. 179–80 and n. 42, 43.

45 *Compendio,* p. 282. This is of course an adaptation to tragi-comedy of Aristotle's formula for tragic wonder (IX. 1452a1–11); cf. Minturno's definition (p. [118], misnumbered 119) and his application of it to Terence's comedies.

46 *Compendio,* p. 227: "Può dunque stare non dico l'allegrezza e 'l dolore, ma la pietá col riso in una favola stessa. E cosí tutta la somma di questa contradizione si verrebbe a ridurre ad una sola differenza, cioè il terribile, la quale non può mai stare se non in favola tragica, né seco mai alcuna comica mescolarsi, perciocché il terrore mai non s'induce se non per mezzo delle gravi e funeste rappresentazioni; e, dove questo si truova, non v'ha luogo riso né scherzo."

47 *Ibid.,* p. 233: "....il temperamento del diletto tragico e comico, che non lascia traboccar gli ascoltanti nella soverchia né malinconia tragica né dissoluzione comica. Da che risulta un poema di eccellentissima forma e temperatura...." For "dissoluzione comica" I have borrowed Professor Gilbert's excellent "comic relaxation" (*LC,* p. 512).

48 *Compendio,* p. 243: "E quale è il diletto tragico? L'imitare azion grave di persona illustre con accidenti nuovi e non aspettati. Or lievisi il terrore e riducasi al pericolo solo, fingasi nuova favola e nuovi nomi, e tutto sia temperato col riso: resterá il diletto dell'imitazione, che sará tragico in potenza, ma non in atto, e rimarráne la scorza sola, ma non l'affetto, che è il terribile, per purgare; il quale non si può inducere se non con tutte le parti tragiche...." The clause "e rimarráne....per purgare" is difficult; an alternative translation might be: "and there will remain only the husk [of the terrible], not the emotion [of terror] to be purged (or, for purging)." But I think the translation I have adopted, which was suggested to me by Mr. De Vitis, is nearer Guarini's intention; it is understandable in the context of his whole interesting discussion of tragic catharsis (pp. 233–47). In attempting to explain Aristotle's "through pity and fear effecting the proper purgation of these emotions," Guarini distinguishes between the emotions of pity and fear which purge and those which are purged: those which are the purging agents are the good aspects of these emotions—the fear of shame and of internal death, the pity for the afflictions of the soul; the emotions purged are the debasing forms of the emotions—the fear of bodily death, the pity for those afflictions of the body which are good for the soul. Professor Gilbert (*LC,* p. 522) translates the passage in question: "and only the outside of it will remain, but not the tendency for purging which resides in the terrible."

49 *Apologia*, folios [36]–38 (36 misnumbered 40). De Nores says that the story of Giannole and Minghino, which he selected in his *Poetica* as a plot suitable for comedy, does not present the danger of death without the terror, for it contains only some dissensions and light troubles ("alcune dissioni e brighe leggiere") and these are resolved at one stroke in jests and pleasant things ("in un tratto si risolvono in burle, e in piacevolezze, ma non si fatti pericoli"). But as told in Boccaccio the tale would easily lend itself to tragi-comic treatment; see above, Ch. VII, pp. 176–78.

50 *Compendio*, pp. 276 ff.

51 The use of a riddle or an oracle in tragedy (as in *Oedipus* or *Macbeth*) creates the same expectation of fulfillment, but the situation and the terms of the oracle lead one to expect an ironic reversal in the opposite direction from that of comedy or tragi-comedy.

52 *Compendio*, pp. 248–55.

53 *Ibid.*, p. 231: "Cosí fa chi compone tragicommedia, perciocché dall'una prende le persone grandi e non l'azione; la favola verisimile, ma non vera; gli affetti mossi, ma rintuzzati; il diletto, non la mestizia; il pericolo, non la morte; dall'altra il riso non dissoluto, le piacevolezze modeste, il nodo finto, il rivolgimento felice, e sopratutto l'ordine comico.... Le quali parti, in questa guisa corrette, possono stare insieme in una favola sola, quand'elle massimamente sono condite col lor decoro e con le qualitá del costume che lor convengono." (In this context, "dissoluto" might, as Mr. De Vitis suggests, be translated "enervating." The usual connotation of "dissolute" as immoral may also not be absent, as shown by Guarini's discussion of the licence of Old Comedy before New Comedy introduced more modest humor.) For whole discussion of tragi-comic mixture, see pp. 222–33. Cf. discussion of the same topic in Dryden, *Essay of Dramatic Poesy:* Lisideius doubts if mirth and compassion can be mingled (*LC*, sec. 30); Neander defends the mixture as natural (sec. 45) and by the rule of contraries in logic—each sets off the other. On the decorum of manners claimed by Guarini, note that Jonson did not agree: "That Guarini, in his Pastor Fido, kept not decorum in making Shepherds speak as well as himself could."—*Conversations*, sec. 4, ll. 64–65; also sec. 18, ll. 610–13 (Oxford *Jonson*, I, 134, 149).

54 *Compendio*, p. 246: "In modo che l'imitare, il qual è fine strumentale, è quel ch'è misto, rappresentando egli cose tragiche e comiche mescolate. Ma il purgare, ch'è fine architettonico, non è se non un solo, riducendosi il misto delle due qualitá sotto un soggetto solo: di liberar gli ascoltanti dalla malinconia."

55 Translated in *LC* (pp. 540–48).

56 For other evidence, see Ristine, pp. 109–10, 146–49.

57 *Compendio*, pp. 222–33, esp. pp. 225–29.

58 *Arte nuevo* (*LC*, p. 544).

59 Middleton's figure; quotation at head of Ch. V.

60 Introduction to Vol. III of *The Plays of John Marston* (Edinburgh, 1934–39), p. xxv.

61 *Art,* I. xviii (*ECE,* II, 39–40). For a brief but fair summary of various interpretations of Virgil's *Eclogues,* see E. V. Rieu's introduction and critical essays in his recent translation for the Penguin Classics (*Virgil: The Pastoral Poems,* 1949). Dr. Rieu is disinclined to press the topicality of the Eclogues very far, and prefers to regard them first of all as what they seem to be, sophisticated nature poetry. But Puttenham's view is of course standard in the Renaissance.

62 See n. 41, this chapter.

Chapter 9

1 See Ch. III, above, pp. 77–79.

2 Puttenham, III. xxiv (*ECE,* II, 181).

3 XV. 1454a16ff.; cf. Horace, *AP,* ll. 153–78.

4 *Rhetoric,* II. xii–xvii; III. vii. 6–7.

5 *De inventione,* I. xxiv–xxv. The Loeb translator, E. M. Hubbell, translates *affectio* in this list as "feeling" (examples here are "laetitia, cupiditas, metus, molestia, morbus, debilitas"); in II. ix, where the examples are "amor, iracundia, molestia," he translates "feeling or emotion." It is hard to find a word in English that covers *morbus* as well as *iracundia;* it is evident that what Cicero has in mind is an unstable or temporary condition as opposed to *habitus,* which he says (in II. ix) "in aliqua perfecta et constanti animi aut corporis absolutione consistit, quo in genere est virtus, scientia et quae contraria sunt" ("... habit consists of a complete and stable constitution [lit., perfection] of mind or of body, in which class are moral worth [also, capacity, courage, etc.], knowledge, and their opposites"). The Ciceronian "places" or attributes recur constantly in the later rhetorics and poetics; a very full list, for instance, is in Lionardi, pp. 33–34.

6 *Inst.,* V. x. 23–31; Quintilian calls them "accidents of persons."

7 Wilson, p. 179; cf. pp. 12–13, 91.

8 Text reads *for.*

9 *ECE,* I, 59–60. Cf. Prologue (ll. 14–26) to *Damon and Pythias* (pr. 1571; in *Pre-Sh. Dramas*):

> In comedies the greatest skill is this: rightly to touch
> All things to the quick, and eke to frame each person so
> That by his common talk you may his nature rightly know.
> A roister ought not to preach—that were too strange
>   to hear,—
> But, as from virtue he doth swerve, so ought his words
>   appear.

The old man is sober; the young man rash; the lover
  triumphing in joys;
The matron grave; the harlot wild, and full of wanton
  toys:
Which all in one course they no wise do agree,
So correspondent to their kind their speeches ought to be.

10 *Rom.*, pp. 65–69; *Com. e trag.*, pp. 259–63, 271–76. Cf. Minturno,
    L'arte poetica, pp. 118–20.
11 *The Honest Whore*, Pt. II, IV. i. 377 ff. (ed. E. H. C. Oliphant in
    Shakespeare and his Fellow Dramatists, New York, 1929, Vol. I).
12 *Com. e trag.*, pp. 245–46.
12a "Hent," act of seizing.
13 Tasso, *Del poema eroico* (ed. Guasti, I, 115): "Si ritrova in Enea l'eccel-
    lenza della pietà; della fortezza militare in Achille; della prudenza in
    Ulisse." Cf. Scaliger, *Poetices*, III. xii (on Aeneas "perfectissimus");
    VII. i. 3 (poet teaches mental disposition—*affectus*—through action);
    cf. also Spenser's letter to Raleigh on *The Faerie Queene*, and Chapman,
    Revenge of Bussy, II. iv. 14–25:

> When Homer made Achilles passionate,
> Wrathful, revengeful, and insatiate
> In his affections, what man will deny
> He did compose it all of industry,
> To let men see that men of most renown,
> Strong'st, noblest, fairest, if they set not down
> Decrees within them, for disposing these,
> Of judgment, resolution, uprightness,
> And certain knowledge of their use and ends,
> Mishap and misery no less extends
> To their destruction, with all that they priz'd,
> Than to the poorest, and the most despis'd.

14 *Defense*, secs. 9–10.
15 *Ibid.*, sec. 23.
16 Ed. Hudson, pp. 41–42.
17 *Poetica*, III. iii (p. 140): "....se la favola è il fine della tragedia, & per
    conseguente d'ogni maniera di poema....& non sia cosa accessoria a
    costumi, ma per lo contrario i costumi non tengono il luogo finale, &
    sono cosa accessoria alla favola, seguita, che molti autori di gran grido
    di lettere degli antichi, & de' moderni, tra quali è anchora Giulio Cesare
    dalla Scala, o Scaligero, habbiano gravemente errato, li quali vogliono,
    che l'intentione di buoni poeti, come d'Homero, & di Virgilio nelle loro
    piu famose opere, quali sono l'Iliada, & l'Odissea, & l'Eneida, sia stata
    di dipingere, & di dimostrare al mondo, pogniamo, un capitano sdegnato
    nella piu eccellente maniera, che sia possibile, o un valoroso conduttiere,
    o un savio huomo, & la natura loro, & simili ciancie, conciosia cosa che,

se questo fosse vero, i costumi non sarebbono stati presi da poeti per secondare l'attione, come dice Aristotele, ma l'attione sarebbe stata presa per secondare i costumi, senza che non s'aveggono, che, se simile materia fosse principale, & non accessoria, non potrebbe essere materia poetica, essendo naturalmente philosophica, & trattata da molti philosophi, & spetialmente da Aristotele, & da Theophrasto.... Adunque i buoni poeti, quali sono Homero, & Virgilio nelle loro famose opere, & gli altri simili a loro hanno inteso a comporre una bella favola, per cagione della quale hanno prese le persone, e i costumi convenevoli, accioche riesca piu bella, cio è maravigliosa, & verisimile."

18   Especially in Ch. VII, in the discussion of "Manners and types," and of "Moral instruction."

19   Appendix to Erasmus' *Terence* (1534), sig. x–[x3] (misnumbered x5): "... cordati senes, Davus veterator, honesta ac pia mente praeditus adolescens Pamphilus"; "... nihil moderatum in hoc, nihil consilii: contra in illo moderatiora omnia penè, quàm vel aetas poscit, vel sinit amor."

20   *Andria, the first Comoedie of Terence, in English.... Carefully translated out of Latin, by Maurice Kyffin...* (London, 1588), sig. Bii^v–Biij.

21   *Defense,* sec. 31.

22   On the importance attached to the poet's knowledge of these formal aspects or oratory for the representation of character, see Lionardi, pp. 24–29 (poets need to know all the things treated of in the demonstrative and deliberative oration, and though they use the judicial oration less, still tragic and heroic poets need to know how to accuse and defend). I do not treat the major forms of oratory in this chapter, since they have been so thoroughly done recently, notably by Kennedy, *The Oration in Shakespeare* (see Ch. II, above, n. 32).

23   On the subject which follows, the relation of the minor rhetorical forms to character drawing, see Benjamin Boyce, *The Theophrastan Character in England to 1642* (Harvard Univ. Press, 1947), esp. Ch. II. I am greatly indebted to him for the discussion of the figures of thought contributory to character-drawing and for their distinctions in meaning, but I have not followed him closely; my discussion of *ethopoeia* and *prosopopoeia* is wholly independent of his. He should be consulted for fuller reference. See also Blanchard W. Bates, *Literary Portraiture in the Historical Narrative of the French Renaissance* (New York, 1945).

24   For Cicero, see n. 5 above; also *Topica,* xxii. 83. For later usage, see Matthieu de Vendôme, *Ars versificatoria,* esp. secs. 74–77 (in Faral, *Les Arts poétiques*); Scaliger, *Poetices,* III. ii, xii–xxiv. Matthieu gives examples of individuals (e.g., Davus, Caesar, Helen), but insists that their portraits be held to precise laws of decorum (see secs. 78–92, and Faral's discussion, pp. 75–81). See also discussion and references in Boyce, Ch. II.

25   IV. l–li (text in Rinn's *Cicero,* Vol. I).

26   Wilson, p. 187; Erasmus, *De copia,* (1703 ed., I, 80–81).

27 *Inst.*, IX. ii. 29–37, 58–63; cf. *evidentia* (vivid illustration), 40–44.

28 *Ibid.*, VI. ii. 17; cf. I. ix. 3. In the passage quoted, the Loeb translator's *ethos* represents Quintilian's plural ἤθη; "moral character," his *mores*.

29 Text in Aldine *Rhetores graeci* (see Ch. II above, n. 62): *ethopoeia*, fol. 159ᵛ; *descriptio*, fol. 160; my references are to 1523 ed.

30 *Aphthonii Sophistae Progymnasmata ... cum luculentis in eadem scholiis Reinhardi Lorichii Hadamarii* (Frankfort, 1553): *ethopoeia*, fols. 176ᵛ– 191ᵛ; *descriptio*, 191ᵛ–195ᵛ.

31 *Foundation of Rhetoric*, sig. xlix–liij.

32 See Boyce, pp. 112–18 and n. 117.

33 For an excellent summary of the native background of character-writing, consult Boyce, Ch. III; also Baskervill, *English Elements in Jonson's Early Comedies*, Chs. II, III.

34 See esp. Hardin Craig, *The Enchanted Glass*, Ch. V; Ruth L. Anderson, *Elizabethan Psychology and Shakespeare's, Plays* (*Univ. of Iowa Humanistic Studies*, Vol. III, No. 4, 1927); Lily Bess Campbell, *Shakespeare's Tragic Heroes, Slaves of Passion* (Cambridge Univ. Press, 1930); and the references given in these books. Cf. also Paul Kreider, *Elizabethan Comic Character Conventions as revealed in the Comedies of George Chapman* (Univ. of Michigan Press, 1935), Ch. VII, "Employment of Elizabethan Psychology for Purposes of Characterization."

35 *Tamburlaine*, Pt. I, II. i. 6 ff.; "What stature wields he, and what personage? ..." (mainly *effictio*). See Carroll Camden, "Marlowe and Elizabethan Psychology," *PQ*, VIII (Jan., 1929), 69–78; Professor Camden does not cite this particular passage.

36 Cf. Hogarth's distinction between *character* and *caracatura* in an engraving of a number of heads issued to accompany *Marriage à la Mode* in 1743 (*Life and Works*, ed. John Lafarge, Philadelphia, 1900, V, 1–6); see also his *Character, or the Bench*, in which, although he decried caricature, his sketches of judges show how a strong satiric conception of a type can be individualized by caricature. This print and his explanation "Of the different Meanings of the Words *Character, Caracatura,* and *Outré* in Painting and Drawing" occasioned a retort by "B" in the *Monthly Review* for 20 Sept., 1758, which provides us with a useful set of definitions: "*Character* therefore is true resemblance; *Caracatura* is exaggerated ridiculous resemblance; and *Outré* is exaggeration with or without resemblance."—*Biographical Anecdotes of Wm. Hogarth* (in Lafarge ed., III, 85–94).

37 See App. XIX in the Oxford *Jonson* (IX, 391–95) for extracts from sixteenth-century medical books on the physiological theory of the humours. Professor Baskervill (in *English Elements*, Ch. III) has a valuable study on the development and extension of the term "humour" from its early purely physiological sense, through its psychological sense, to its late sense as whim or affected behavior; he does not, however, treat the lengthy passage in *Every Man Out* as a whole, and so seems to me to miss its emphasis. Jonson not only gives the metamorphosis in meaning

of "humour" and condemns the current trivial sense as a false one, but also especially indicates that he is going to satirize this very usage; actually, he includes in his play humour characters in two senses— (1) those with an excess in passion or disposition, (2) those with an affectation in behavior.

38 Ch. VII, pp. 164–65.

39 See discussion below, under "Concepts of style."

40 Kenneth Burke's term, defined in Ch. I, above, pp. 21, 22.

41 This is the familiar position developed by Professor Stoll in his *Shakespeare Studies* and in subsequent critical books.

42 Thomas Wright, *The Passions of the Mind* (1601), Ch. XV, p. 114. Pierre de la Primaudaye (*The French Academy*, tr. T. B., 1586; *The Second Part . . .* , tr. T. B., 1594) and F. N. Coeffeteau (*A Table of Humane Passions*, tr. Edward Grimeston, 1621) treat the passions pretty much *per se* with no more than perfunctory attention to differences in temperament.

43 The Friar in *Bussy d'Ambois*, II. ii. 140–41. Cf. La Primaudaye, *Second Part*, Ch. XLII (1594 ed., p. 245) and Ch. XLIII (p. 247): ". . . there are not so many sorts of winds, whirlwinds, or tempests in the sea, as there is variety of motions that come from the affections in our hearts. Therefore we ought to be very careful, that when we see and perceive any beginnings in our souls, we straightways give not ourselves over into the power and swinge [note this characteristic word of Chapman's] of our affections. But we are so far from looking to this, that we throw ourselves into the middest of the tempest, that it may carry us, not whither we would, but whither that will. For seeing we enterprise our affairs, not by the appointment and decree of an upright judgment directed by reason, but at the judgment and lust of our corrupt and crooked nature, we are so much moved as our nature hath power. . . . But it is clean contrary with a prudent and wise man." Cf. similar metaphor of the tempest in Coeffeteau, Ch. III (pp. 70–71).

44 Cf. Cicero's definition of *affectio* (*De inv.*, I. xxv) as "animi aut corporis ex tempore, aliqua de causa, commutatio" ("a sudden change. for some reason, in mind or body"); Quintilian's definition of *commotio* (V. x. 28) as "temerarius animi motus, sicut ira, pavor" ("a temporary motion of the mind, such as anger or fear"). See notes 5, 6, this chapter.

45 *Bussy d'Ambois*, II. ii. 100.

46 *Rhetoric*, $\tilde{\eta}\theta\eta$, II. xii–xvii, III. xvi. 8–9; $\pi\acute{a}\theta\eta$, II. i. 8 ff., III. xvii. 8.

47 *Inst.*, VI. ii. 8–24. Quintilian makes rather more qualifications than I have indicated.

48 Aphthonius (*Rhetores graeci*, ed. Aldus), fol. 159^v; Priscian (*ibid.*), fol. 154^v (under the head of "allocutio").

49 *L'arte poetica*, pp. 45–64, 426–29. Cf. Scaliger's distinction between $\tilde{\eta}\theta os$ (*mores*) and $\delta\iota\acute{a}\theta\epsilon\sigma\iota s$ (*affectus*), VII. i. 3: "Itaque non est quaerendum, doceátne, $\tilde{\eta}\theta os$ poeta, an $\pi\rho\hat{a}\gamma\mu a$: sed utrum $\delta\iota\alpha\theta\acute{\epsilon}\sigma\epsilon\iota s$, an eventa. nam tametsi praeter morem fiunt multa: non tamen sine affectu fiunt" ("So

our inquiry is not as to whether the poet teaches character or action, but as to whether he teaches a mental disposition, or the outward expression of it. Though many things are done contrary to character, they are not done without our being disposed to do them"; tr. Padelford, pp. 82–83. For "διαθέσεις, an eventa" Professor Howe suggests "inclination, or the result of that inclination.") Orestes' murder of his mother is given as an example; no question here of character, since the murder was not a characteristic action. But Aegistheus was a murderer in character— "at suo more fecit Aegisthus." For illustrations in Elizabethan rhetorics of this distinction and of the figures used to achieve it, see Sister Miriam Joseph, *Shakespeare's Use of the Arts of Language,* Chs. V and IX.

50 *L'arte poetica,* pp. 92–96; cf. treatment of persons of comedy, pp. 115–20, 127–30.

51 *Inst.,* VI. ii. 20. Professor George Sensabaugh (in *The Tragic Muse of John Ford,* Stanford Univ. Press, 1944) argues that Ford's treatment of the problems of tragedy is passionate rather than ethical, with a deterministic premise, and on this basis differentiates him from earlier dramatists. My distinction is not quite the same as his; I am not ruling out ethical considerations from tragedy, only pointing out a normal shift of emphasis from the study in comedy of fixed characters to the study in tragedy of states of passion; the extent of perception of a background of character against which the passion is set varies with different dramatists.

52 Wright, *Passions of the Mind,* Ch. I (1601 ed., pp. 7–9); also Ch. III, (p. 26), on *philautia,* self-love or "old Adam, law of the flesh, sensuality." La Primaudaye's strong ethical emphasis tends to this same generalized view of human nature.

53 The heroes both of *The Castle of Perseverance* and of *Mankind* face the same situation as Faustus. Mankind in the former dies appealing to God's mercy and is saved from Hell after death; Mankind in the latter, though in despair and unable to see how God's mercy can be great enough to save him, is rebuked by Mercy for his presumption and is finally saved through submission.

54 Kreider, *Comic Character Conventions in Chapman,* gives a useful classification of conventions in comedy (direct self-identification, autobiographical self-identification, direct self-characterization, direct self-characterization supplemented by a chorus, etc.), but he does not study origins and influences.

55 For early formal usage, see *The Spanish Tragedy* (ed. F. S. Boas, *Works of Thomas Kyd,* Oxford: Clarendon Press, 1901), II. v. 1 ff.; III. ii. 1 ff.; III. vii. 1 ff., 40 ff.; III. xiii. 1 ff. Cf. in *Damon and Pythias* the *notationes* (portraits of traits) of Aristippus (Adams, *Pre-Sh. Dramas,* p. 573), of Carisophus (p. 575), of Damon and Pythias (p. 577), of the true and false courtiers (p. 591). Cf. the formal speeches of grief in *Gorboduc* (III. i, IV. i, IV. ii) and *Cambises* (Adams, p. 653). That my qualification is necessary, however, is shown by Professor Waith's

new book (see Ch. VIII, above, n. 14) on the rhetorical tradition of
Roman declamation in the plays of Beaumont and Fletcher; it has
come too late to be made use of in my own book.

56 Many examples in Jonson, Webster, Beaumont and Fletcher, Ford. Note
Jonson, in *The Magnetic Lady* (I. ii) introducing a doctor and a parson
each with a formal "character" so labeled (ll. 14, 34).

57 *Twelfth Night*, III. i. 62–70; *As You Like It*, II. vii. 12–87; IV. i. 10–19.

58 *Richard II*, I. iv. 23–36.

59 *Antony and Cleopatra*, III, viii. 18–33.

60 *King Lear*, IV. iii. 19–24.

61 II. ii. 457 ff. See Professor Craig's comments on this speech in "Shakespeare's Bad Poetry," in *Shakespeare Survey*, No. 1 (1948), p. 54.

62 III. xi. 2–4.

63 *Inst.: energeia*, VIII. iii. 89; *enargeia*, IV. ii. 63–65; VIII. iii. 61–71. Cf.
definitions in Liddell and Scott's *Greek Lexicon*: ἐνέργεια—act, action,
operation, opp. to ἕξις, habit, in Arist. *Ethics;* energy, life in description,
Arist. *Rhet.;* v. ἐνεργέω to be in operation, active, to work. ἐνάργεια, clearness, distinctness, bright or vivid appearance, in Plato, *Politics;* vivid
description in rhetoricians; from ἐναργής, distinct, visible, in bodily shape.
But note that Aristotle (see n. 62) uses *energeia* of description which
"sets things before the eyes"—exactly as Quintilian uses *enargeia.*

64 *On Style* (tr. W. Rhys Roberts, Loeb ed.). ἐνάργεια, IV. 209–20; δεινότης,
V.

65 "....sia da cercare questa anima del Poema, che non è altro per ora che
quella forza, e quella virtù dell'orazione, onde entrino gli affetti nel core,
a chi legge, come se fosse una viva voce che parlasse" (pp. 160–61); cf.
p. 62: "Perchè la Energia nel Poeta....appresso i Latini e appresso noi
non sta (come si ha creduto il Trissino) nel minutamente scrivere ogni
cosuccia, qualunque volta il Poeta scrive eroicamente, ma nelle cose che
sono degne della grandezza della materia che ha il Poeta per le mani
e la virtù dell'Energia, la quale noi possiamo dimandare efficacia, si
asseguisce qualunque volta non usiamo nè parole, nè cose oziose." "Efficacia" is Giraldi's translation of *energeia;* cf. Scaliger, *Poetices*, III.
xxv.

66 "....che sono come nate insieme colla cosa" (p. 161). Giraldi's "voci
proprie" are Aristotle's κύρια (*Rhet.*, III. ii. 2), established, vernacular
words, as opposed to foreign, figurative, or archaic words; the former
give perspicuity rather than elevation or adornment.

67 Aristotle, *Rhet.*, II. ii–xi; III. vii. Cicero, *De orat.*, II. xliv–liii; *Part. orat.*,
xv–xvii (peroration and amplification); *De inv.*, I. lii–lvi (peroration;
note esp. treatment of *indignatio*, arousing of hatred, and *conquestio*,
lament or complaint). Quintilian, *Inst.*, VI. i (peroration), VI. ii (*ethos*
and *pathos*), VIII. iv (amplification). Cf. Lionardi, pp. 36–40, 53–57
(note especially his praise of the poet for his Protean ability to compose
many and diverse discourses, so fittingly expressing various passions,
p. 67).

68. *Spanish Tragedy*, II. v. 1 ff.; III. ii. 1 ff.
69. Cf. *Sejanus*, V. 5–9:

> Great, and high,
> The world knows only two, that's Rome and I.
> My roof receives me not; 'tis air I tread:
> And, at each step, I feel my advanced head
> Knock out a star in heav'n!

70 Giraldi, *Com. e trag.*, pp. 204–5, 227–36; see also *Rom.*, pp. 88–89, and apology for *Dido* (*Tragedie*, pp. 132–34). Neither Minturno nor Giraldi approves of prose for comedy, though they disagree on the types of verse appropriate.

71 *L'arte poetica*, pp. 426–51.

72 See Ch. II, above, p. 38 and n. 41.

73 For an example of an inflexible use according to a pattern see Dekker's *Shoemaker's Holiday*. The comic action of Eyre, his wife, and workmen, is always in prose; the two love stories are pretty consistently in verse. This distinction also corresponds, with a significant exception, to a social distinction between the artisans on one hand and the gentry and nobles on the other. The exceptions are Eyre's apprentice Ralph and Ralph's sweetheart Jane, who, apparently because they are the center of a love story, nearly always speak in verse, even if the situation at the moment is not romantic. The pattern is thus partly social, but primarily thematic, the themes rather rigidly identified with certain characters. For a full discussion of Shakespeare's use of prose and for briefer accounts of its use by other dramatists, see Milton Crane's *Shakespeare's Prose* (Univ. of Chicago Press, 1951). My account of *Shoemaker's Holiday* does not follow his.

74 Virginia Woolf, *Mr. Bennett and Mrs. Brown* (London: Hogarth Press, 1924): "It is the prevailing sound of the Georgians—rather a melancholy one if you think what melodious days there have been in the past, . . . if you think of the language, and the heights to which it can soar when free, and see the same eagle captive, bald, and croaking."

75 *The Dutch Courtesan*, V. iii. 137–42 (act and scene division as in S. H. Bullen's ed.; text checked in Wood's *Marston*, not divided).

76 Cf. the present writer's "Imagery in *Richard II* and *Henry IV*," *MLR*, XXXVII (April, 1942), esp. 121–22.

77 *Romeo and Juliet*, III. ii. 20–25; IV. v. 49 ff.

78 *Antony and Cleopatra*, V. ii. 79 ff.

79 *Decameron* (tr. J. M. Rigg, Everyman ed.), III. ix.

80 Apology for *Dido* (*Tragedie*, p. 152).

81 Cf. Cicero's *natura* and *habitus*, p. 219, above, and notes 4, 5.

> *Regan.* 'Tis the infirmity of his age; yet he hath ever but slenderly known himself.
>
> *Goneril.* The best and soundest of his time hath been but rash; then, must we look to receive from his age, not alone the imperfections

of long-engraffed condition, but therewithal the unruly waywardness that infirm and choleric years bring with them. (I. i. 294–300).

82 On the background of sources, see Wilfred Perrett, *The Story of King Lear from Geoffrey of Monmouth to Shakespeare* (*Palaestra*, No. 35), Berlin, 1904; also Robert Adger Law, "Holinshed's *Leir* Story and Shakespeare's," *SP*, XLVII (Jan., 1950), 42–50.

83 "So much as thou hast, so much art thou worth."

84 Cf. Virtue, Vice, and Fortune in Dekker's *Old Fortunatus* (esp. their respective attempts to win Andelocia in IV. i (act division as in Rhys, Mermaid ed.); also the Evil Angel and the Good Angel who appeal to Jonas in *A Looking-Glass for London and England*.

85 Cf. the use of a ghost as a device of conscience in *The Atheist's Tragedy*, in *The Changeling*, and, much more subtly handled, in *The White Devil*.

86 *King Lear*, I. iv. 266–72.

Chapter 10

1 *LC*, sec. 15.

2 *Ibid.*, sec. 12.

3 For a clear statement of these relative strengths and weaknesses, see Dryden's comparisons both of ancient and of modern drama, and of contemporary French and English drama, *ibid., passim*, but esp. secs. 11–15, 23, 30–38, 46–50. Cf. Thomas Raysor, "The Aesthetic Significance of Shakespeare's Handling of Time," *SP*, XXXII (April, 1936), 197–209.

4 *Play of the Sacrament* in *Non-Cycle Mystery Plays* (ed. Osborn Waterhouse, EETS, 1909) and in Adams, *Pre-Sh. Dramas*. *Mary Magdalene* in *The Digby Mysteries* (ed. F. J. Furnivall, London, 1882); only the first half in Adams.

5 See Ch. V, above, p. 103 and n. 4, 5.

6 Text in *Drammi spirituali inediti di Giovanmaria Cecchi* (ed. Raffaelo Rocchi, Florence, 1895, 1900), Vol. I. Cf. his similar handling of another Biblical story, the rebellion of Core (Korah) in his *Datan e Abiron* (*Drammi spirituali*, Vol. II); the classicism here extends to the introduction of Megaera, who inflames Korah against Moses. On Cecchi's *drammi spirituali* consult Sanesi (*La commedia*, I, 325–28), who indicates that they came from Cecchi's later period; he wrote from about 1542 to about 1585.

6a Text in D'Ancona, *Sacre rapp.*, I, 97 ff.; the names here are "Tobbia" and "Tobbiuzo."

7 A good deal of the newer point of view is indicated in Professor Gilbert's illuminating notes and introductions in *LC;* see also his article on Giraldi, cited in Ch. VI, above, n. 23.

8 *Poetics*, VI. 1450a16–17.

 9 *Ibid.*, VI. 1450a37–38.
10 *Ibid.*, VIII. 1451a30–36.
11 *L'arte poetica*, pp. 28–29; for whole discussion, pp. 24–35.
12 For a summary of these different points of view, see Minturno, p. 28.
13 *La spositione....sopra l'Orlando Furioso* (1549), esp. pp. 31–48, "Apologia brieve sopra tutto l'Orlando Furioso."
14 *Comparatione*, Disc. VII (esp. p. 256); Ariosto's lines read:

> Le donne, i cavallier, l'arme, gli amori,
> Le cortesie, l'audaci imprese io canto.

For whole discussion and for refutation of Da Rheggio's position, see Beni, pp. 251–70, 281–83. Cf. the very similar position taken by De Sanctis (ed. Croce, II, 19), who comments on the futility of making any of the three actions the central one. The undertaking of Agramante is the fixed point around which "il mondo cavalleresco" unfolds. The madness of Orlando and the loves of Ruggiero are not episodes, "appunto perchè non ci è un'azione unica e centrale, ma parti importanti di quell'immensa totalitá che dicesi 'mondo cavalleresco'. L'unitá è dunque non questa o quella azione e non questo o quel personnaggio, ma è tutto esso mondo nel suo spirito e nel sviluppo nel tal luogo e nel tempo."
15 Giraldi, *Rom.*, pp. 11–12; Giovan Battista Pigna, *I romanzi* (Venice, 1554), *passim.*, but esp. pp. 44–45: "....& perchè d'erranti persone è tutto il poema, egli altresì errante è, inquanto che piglia & intermette infinite volte cose infinite: & sempre con arte" ("and because the poem is about wandering persons, it likewise is wandering, to the extent that it takes up and interrupts infinite things infinite times, and always with art"). Cf. De Sanctis (II, 20), who justifies the form for essentially the same reason, though his terms sound more sophisticated.
16 *Primitivism and Decadence* (New York, 1937), pp. 27, 77, 136–37.
17 *L'arte poetica,* p. 27: He says the defenders of the romances confess they haven't the form or the order of Homer and Virgil, or that commanded by Aristotle and Horace, "e nondimeno si ingeganino di questo errore difendere: anzi, percioche tal compositione comprende i fatti de' Cavalieri erranti, affermino ostinatamente non pur la Virgiliana & Homerica maniera di poetare non convenirle: ma esser le richiesto, ch'ella anco errante sia, passando d'una in altra materia, e varie cose in un fascio stringendo" ("yet they exercise their ingenuity to defend this error: thus, because such a composition comprehends the deeds of wandering knights, they obstinately affirm not merely that the Virgilian and Homeric manner of composition is not fitting to the romance, but that the form it ought to have should also be wandering, passing from one matter to another, and binding up various things together in one bundle"). See also p. 30: one should not attribute to the romance itself as a form the excellence which comes from the power of the most noble "ingegno" of Ariosto, who with his style made a thing which was in its own nature

so barbarous and so bare of any grace to appear so beautiful and so pleasing to everybody.

18 *Rom.,* pp. 41–43.

19 *Ibid.,* p. 43; cf. passage quoted above in Ch. II, pp. 50–51.

20 *Comparatione,* p. 288.

21 *Ibid.,* pp. 232–36; cf. eloquent passage on the way in which the maker of the heroic poem imitates the Supreme Maker in this very matter of creating variety within one frame, p. 180.

22 *Ibid.,* pp. 287–94.

23 *Rom.,* pp. 39–41; *Com. e trag.,* pp. 214–15, 224–25. Contrast Minturno's disapproval of this technique of interruption and of leaping from on♦ subject to another: *L'arte poetica,* p. 35. But cf. Harington's praise of *Orlando Furioso* both because it is "full of Peripet[e]ia, which I interpret an agnition of some unlooked for fortune either good or bad, and a sudden change thereof," and because the abrupt breaking off of the narrations "is a point of great art, to draw a man with a continual thirst to read out the whole work" (*ECE,* II, 216–17). He comments that if Sidney had counted this a fault, he would not have done the same thing in his *Arcadia.* Professor Myrick (*Sidney as a Literary Craftsman,* pp. 134–37) observes that in his second form of the *Arcadia* Sidney employed much less of this interruptive technique than in the first form, evidently reflecting Minturno's disapproval of Ariosto's method. Might he not have been in the old *Arcadia* deliberately following Ariosto's technique?

24 *Comparatione,* Disc. II (pp. 44–77); Disc. III (pp. 85–106), Disc. V (pp. 172–212). Tasso's poem was also attacked for the greater attention given to the episodes than to the central action; see summary of the controversy in De Sanctis, II, 150–52. For an interesting survey of the views of major Italian critics on the unities of action and of time in the epic, see Ralph Coplestone Williams, *The Theory of the Heroic Epic in Italian Criticism of the Sixteenth Century,* n.p. (Baltimore?), 1921. My treatment is independent of Professor Williams'.

25 Note Harington's comment, in n. 23, above. Professor Myrick has shown convincingly that Sidney rewrote the *Arcadia* in conformity with the idea of the heroic poem embodied in Minturno's *De poeta* and *Arte poetica.* Like the critics of *Orlando Furioso,* Professor Myrick and I would dispute what constitutes the central action of the "poem"; he would apparently make it the love stories of Pyrocles and Musidorus, I would make it the political action of King Basilius.

26 Passage quoted above in Ch. II, p. 50 and n. 70.

27 Giraldi, *Rom.,* pp. 19–25; Beni, *Comparatione,* pp. 106–34.

28 *Poetica,* IV. i (pp. 499 ff., esp. 504–5).

29 *Ibid.,* III. vi (pp. 173–79).

30 *Ibid.,* p. 178: "Ma non per tanto Aristotele qui, & altrove ostinatamente comanda, che l'attione riempiente la favola sia una, & d'una persona sola, &, se pure sono piu attioni, che l'una dipenda dall'altra ne di cio

adduce ragione, o pruova niuna, se non l'essempio di poeti tragichi, &
d'Homero che si sono attenuti alla singolarita dell'attione d'una persona
in comporre la favola."

31 Cf. Ch. I, above, p. 6.

32 Da Rheggio. The ambiguous attitude of Cervantes makes an interesting
parallel to that of the Italian critics. In *Don Quixote* (I. xlviii) Cervantes
reprehends Lope de Vega for not obeying the unities; yet he had himself, in his more romantic plays, been the most hopelessly episodic of
dramatists. And that he loved an errant and rich variety we have not only
his explicit statement in *Don Quixote* (I. xlvii) but the evidence of the
book itself.

33 XII. 1452b14–27.

34 IX. 1451b33–35.

35 XVII. 1455a34–b23.

36 XXIII. 1459a35–37.

37 *LC*, sec. 10.

38 Beni, pp. 56–57; Minturno, pp. 124–25.

39 Scaliger, III. xcvii; cf. Minturno's division (pp. 122–23) of episodes
into (1) persons introduced outside the fable and (2) persons within
the fable but taking part in actions not necessary to it or narrating something useful to it but not part of it.

40 *Poetica*, III. xii (pp. 260–61). Castelvetro says Aristotle uses *episode* in
four senses: things outside the action in time, things outside it in place,
things invented to show the details of the action as distinct from the
action in summary form (see n. 41), and the quantitative parts of the
tragedy between the choral odes.

41 *Ibid.*, III. xii (p. 260): Episodes are things "found" or invented ("cose
trovate") by the poet "per mostrare le particolarita del fatto, che non
si sa se non sommariamente, le quali, se non si confanne con quel, che
si sa del fatto, ne dipendono l'una dall'altra secondo verisimilitudine, o
necessita, sono riprese da Aristotele, la, dove disse, che la favola son
doveva ἐπεισοδιώδης."

42 Cf. Giraldi, *Com. e trag.*, pp. 2[50]–53; Minturno, pp. 103–6; Castelvetro,
III. xii (p. 260).

43 Cf. Giraldi, *Rom.*, pp. 25–26; Pigna, pp. 42–44; Minturno, pp. 35–36;
Castelvetro, IV. i (pp. 499 ff.); Beni, pp. 172–85, esp. p. 173: the reasons for joining episodes to the fable are as much to lengthen it as to
vary and ornament it ("sono tanto per alungar detta favola, quanto per
variarla & ornarla").

44 Minturno, pp. 124–25. Minturno and Dryden (*LC*, sec. 14) make the
principal action of *Eunuchus* the story of Chaerea and Pamphila;
Melanchthon (Erasmus' *Terence*, 1534, sig. x3ᵛ–x4) and T. W. Baldwin
(*Five-Act Structure*, pp. 12–14) make it the business of Thraso, Thais,
and Phaedria. Minturno himself hesitates over *Phormio*, whether to make
the subject all that treats of Phormio, or the love affair of Antipho; if
the latter, then all that touches on Phaedria, the old "beffati," and Nico-

strata [i.e., Nausistrata?] is for the "ornament" of the comedy and for delight.

45 Guarini, *Compendio*, pp. 224, 262–67 (intelligent discussion of structure of *Andria*, in which he explains just how the Charinus story functions); Giraldi, *Com. e trag.*, pp. 214–15. Cf. Beni's perception that skilfully handled episodes in a heroic poem cannot always be separated from the principal action as "unnecessary" (*Comparatione*, p. 175).

46 *Poetica*, III. vi (pp. 173–74).

47 *Ibid.*, pp. 178–79.

48 *Poetices*, III. xcvii; the disunity of *Hecuba* was recognized by Guarini (pp. 266–67). Minturno and Sidney apparently did not consider it disunified (see Ch. I, n. 22, above); a discussion of the attitudes of these two is in Myrick, pp. 105–7. But it should properly be noted that unity of action is not actually the point of the discussion of *Hecuba* in either, though it is evidently assumed. Minturno finds *Hecuba* single rather than double (Aristotle, *Poetics*, XIII. 1453a30–39) in having persons of one rank and an unhappy ending for all, and simple rather than complex (*ibid.*, X. 1452a12–21) in having recognition without reversal; Sidney finds that *Hecuba* does not violate the unities of time and place.

49 *Essay* (*LC*, sec. 52).

50 *Ibid.*, secs., 46, 47, 49.

51 *Defense*, sec. 48; cf. Whetstone, Dedication to *Promos and Cassandra* (*ECE*, I, 59); Jonson, Prologue to *Every Man In; Magnetic Lady*, Act I, Chorus, ll. 15–24. Cervantes (*Don Quixote*, I. xlviii) uses almost the same terms as Sidney's in his condemnation of the violation of the unities in contemporary Spanish drama.

52 *Poetica*, III. vi (pp. 178–79); see pp. 271–72 above.

53 The Italian critics consistently ignore the purely popular Italian theater, both plays and stage.

54 See n. 72, below.

55 *Comparatione*, pp. 113–14.

56 Detailed references here unnecessary. Consult the standard works: Wilhelm Creizenach, *Geschichte des neueren Dramas* (Halle, 1893–1916), esp. the translated and revised edition of Vol. IV: *The English Drama in the Age of Shakespeare* (London, 1916), Bk. VIII; E. K. Chambers, *Mediaeval Stage* (Oxford, 1925) and *Elizabethan Stage* (Oxford: Clarendon Press, 1923); Karl Young, *The Drama of the Medieval Church* (Oxford: Clarendon Press, 1933); D'Ancona, *Origini del teatro italiano;* Gustave Cohen, *Histoire de la mise en scène dans le théâtre religieux française du Moyen Age,* rev. ed. (Paris, 1926); *Le Théâtre en France au Moyen Age* (Paris, 1928)—the latter esp. useful for illustrations; Henry Carrington Lancaster, *A History of French Dramatic Literature in the Seventeenth Century* (Johns Hopkins Press, 1929–42); Karl Mantzius, *A History of Theatrical Art in Ancient and Modern Times* (tr. Louise von Cossel, London, 1903–21), Vol. II;

Nicoll, *The Development of the Theatre;* George K. Kernodle, *From Art to Theatre* (Univ. of Chicago Press, 1944).

57   See Nicoll, *Theatre,* figs. 56–62; Cohen, *Théâtre,* Vol. I (for Fouquet's illustrations); etc.

58   *Med. Stage,* II, 134, 417–19, 421; but esp. Hardin Craig, "Note on the Home of *Ludus Coventriae*" in *Univ. of Minnesota Studies in Lang. and Lit.,* No. 1 [1914], pp. 72–81. Professor Craig suggests that the plays in their present form were arranged for performance at Lincoln, where there is evidence of the acting of the Corpus Christi play, at least in part, on a fixed stage.

59   *Med. Stage,* II, 156; also Manly, "The Miracle Play in Medieval England" in *Essays by Divers Hands.*

60   For descriptions of the settings of both plays see *Med. Stage,* II, 136, 430, 156; diagrams for both in Adams, *Pre-Sh. Dramas,* pp. 225, 264.

61   See texts of this and the following plays in the EETS editions.

62   From inventories only; text not extant.—Hardin Craig, *Two Coventry Corpus Christi Plays* (EETS, London, 1902), App. II on the Cappers Company accounts.

63   The earliest editions of Vitruvius were without illustrations.

64   Sebastiano Serlio, *Il libro primo[-quinto] d'architettura* (Venice, 1551), Lib. II. Serlio's designs reproduced in *Eliz. Stage,* IV; Nicoll, *Theatre,* figs. 78–81; L. B. Campbell, *Scenes and Machines;* and elsewhere.

65   *The First [-Fift] Booke of Architecture, made by Sebastian Serly* (English trans., London, 1611), Bk. II, fols. 24–26.

66   Nicoll, *Theatre,* figs. 85, 86, 88, 89.

67   *Ibid.,* Ch. IV, secs. vi, vii, and references therein.

68   Reproductions in Nicoll, *Theatre,* figs. 72–76. Cf. Venice *Terence* of 1497, 1499; *Eliz. Stage,* frontispiece to Vol. III. Cf. Puttenham's ideas of ancient staging (I. xvii; *ECE,* II, 37–39) : tragedy acted on scaffolds, with "sundry little divisions by curtains as traverses to serve for several rooms where they might repair unto and change their garments and come in again, as their speeches and parts were to be renewed." The whole chapter should be read.

69   On shift from medieval to classic stage in France see Lancaster, Pt. I, Ch. XI; Pt. V, p. 17; see also his edition of Mahelot's *Mémoire pour la décoration des pièces* (Paris, 1920). Reproductions of some of Mahelot's designs in Cohen, *Théâtre;* Nicoll, *Theatre,* fig. 133 (*Pandòste*).

70   For controversy over staging of *Le Cid* see Lancaster, Pt. II, Ch. V, esp. pp. 125–26, 144; Corneille's defense in *Examen,* 1660 (ed. M. Ch. Marty-Laveaux [Paris, 1862], XIII, 97–101) and in *Discours des trois unités,* 1660 (I, 117–22); the latter partly translated in Gilbert, *LC,* pp. 577–79.

71   In this play time, or even place, cannot, of course, be reduced to consistency. Eumenides and the others do not age in Endymion's forty years of sleep, and the fountain is in one place (IV. ii. 67) spoken of as "hard by" the lunary bank; but even on the other side of the stage, it would be, in one sense, hard by.

72 *Eliz. Stage,* III, 32–46; cf. Miss Campbell (*Scenes and Machines,* pp. 127, 129), who speaks of the increasing freedom in regard to the observance of the unity of place after 1576, when the Theatre was built, and who cites Professor Boas as knowing of no violation of unity of place before that time. The difficulty is that only academic and court plays survive from the earlier period, and these are compared with popular plays of the later period.

73 "The Miracle Play in Medieval England."

74 Campbell, *Scenes and Machines,* Ch. IX; Nicoll, *Theatre,* Ch. VII, esp. sec. iv. A quite different theory of the origin of the Elizabethan stage façade is developed by Kernodle (*From Art to Theatre*): i.e., the tradition of the visual arts as adapted by the designers of the *tableaux vivants.* He will not allow that the multiple principle still surviving on the Elizabethan stage is connected with the multiple stage of the religious drama. The book is important in pointing out the similarities between the stages of various countries in the Renaissance.

75 Cf. Nicoll, *Theatre,* Chs. IV, VII (secs. vi, vii), VIII; Lancaster, Pt. III, Ch. XIV; Pt. IV, Ch. XV.

76 Discussed in Ch. IX, above, pp. 234–39, 254–56.

77 What Kenneth Burke calls "syllogistic form"; cf. Ch. I, above, pp. 21, 22.

78 Neander in *Essay* (*LC,* secs. 46, 47).

79 *Ibid.,* sec. 30.

80 Burke's term.

81 See discussion in Ch. VIII, above, p. 214.

82 Dated by Boas and Reed, ca. 1497 (ref. in Ch. XI, below, n. 26); by Chambers, before 1500.

83 Lope de Vega, *Arte nuevo* (*LC,* p. 544).

84 Alexander H. Sackton's *Rhetoric as a Dramatic Language in Ben Jonson* (New York, 1948) is an admirable study of Jonson's adaptation of rhetorical means to dramatic ends; it does little, however, with strictly poetic devices, like imagery and prosody. The same emphasis is in Knights, *Drama and Society in the Age of Jonson,* Chs. VI and VII. But see unpublished Harvard diss. (1950) by John Enck, "Ben Jonson's Imagery."

Chapter 11

1 Sec. 49 (*LC*).

2 Texts in Malone Soc. Reprints. See Guarini, *Compendio,* p. 287, on the importance of choice of the fable.

3 The story was much told: Livy, III. xliv–lviii; *Il Pecorone,* XX. ii; *Roman de la Rose,* ll. 5613 ff.; Gower, *Confessio Amantis,* VII. 5131 ff.; Chaucer, *Physician's Tale;* Painter, *Palace of Pleasure,* I. v. Giovanni Fiorentino, Gower, and Painter follow Livy; Chaucer, the simpler story in *Roman*

de la Rose. The much later play attributed to Webster restores the fuller motivation and complication of Livy.

4   The point is still good, even though Peele varies the story by having Paris tried before Jupiter for his partial choice among the three goddesses and sent off to Troy as a judgment; and by having the whole thing turned into a graceful compliment of the Queen, who is adjudged by Diana as the one really deserving the apple.

5   I owe this important suggestion to Professor Craig; see his *Complete Shakespeare,* introduction to *Romeo and Juliet,* pp. 394–95; also General Introduction, pp. 43–45. Cf. also Herford and Simpson, introduction to *Sejanus* (*Jonson,* II, 8–9), for importance of influence of Italian novels on structure of English tragedy and comedy.

6   Reference in notes 41, 43, below.

7   The introduction of Tybalt as a potential enemy at the Capulet party, the introduction of Paris as a suitor for Juliet before she even meets Romeo, above all the killing of Tybalt and Romeo's banishment before the wedding night and Capulet's acceptance of Paris as Juliet's husband on the very day of her wedding to Romeo, and finally the advance of the wedding day. It is possible that some of these changes had been made in the old play which Shakespeare may have known (cf. Brooke's preface, and see J. J. Munro, Introduction to *Brooke's "Romeus and Juliet"* in The Shakespeare Classics, London and New York, 1908, pp. xxxvi–xlvii), but judging from the naïve plotting of most early English drama, extremely unlikely. For a full study of the sources, see Olin H. Moore, *The Legend of Romeo and Juliet* (Ohio State Univ. Press, 1950); he finds new evidence for the direct use of Da Porto, and in Ch. XIV he attacks the common habit of assuming lost documents for every difference from known sources observed in Shakespeare.

8   For Jonson's use of many sources for these plays, consult the Oxford *Jonson,* introductions in Vol. II, commentaries in Vols. IX and X, and appendix to *Sejanus* (Vol. IV) containing Jonson's notes to the quarto edition. The editors remark (II, 8) that in Italy and France the histories of Caesar, Pompey, and Cleopatra were treated in the manner of Euripides and Seneca: ". . . antique scheme held its ground with even increased stringency, completely unaffected by the allurements of a complex historic plot." This only reënforces my point about English dramatists' being dominated by their sources.

9   Reference to texts in Ch. V, n. 6.

10   *Poetics,* XVIII (esp. 1455b24–33).

11   See *Med. Stage* (Vol. I, Chs. IX, X) on the "riding" or procession on St. George's Day, in which there is always a Dragon; not to be confused with the St. George or Mummers' Play, in which the constant feature is not St. George's victory over the Turkish Knight, since the latter sometimes wins, but the restoration to life at the hands of the Doctor.

12   Full discussion in Ch. XII.

13   *Mary Magdalene* discussed in Ch. X, above, pp. 263–64.

14 *Woman Killed,* V. iii. 200–1 (lines as in Oliphant, *Shakespeare and his Fellow Dramatists,* Vol. I).

15 *The Tragedy of Byron,* V. iv. 91–94; cf. Byron's charge against La Fin as an enchanter and agent of Hell in V. ii. 135 to the end.

15a I owe this important suggestion to my former graduate student, Professor Frank Nelick, now at the University of Kansas.

16 This is the title in early editions (*ed. pr.,* ca. 1480) and of Jasper Heywood's translation in *Seneca His Tenne Tragedies* (London, 1581); the Loeb translator (F. J. Miller) uses *Phoenissae,* but the play, though on the same subject, differs greatly from Euripides' *Phoenissae.*

17 Texts in Cunliffe, *EECT.* On *Gismond,* cf. Ch. VI, above, p. 130 and n. 29; p. 135 and n. 34.

18 Consult Bowers, *Elizabethan Revenge Tragedy,* esp. Ch. I.

19 Cf. discussion of lack of motivation in character in this type of story in Ch. IX, above, pp. 251–52.

20 *Euphues* (Bond's *Lyly*), I, 234, ll. 3–6.

21 *Campaspe* (Bond's *Lyly,* Vol. II), IV. i. 43–46.

21a *Ibid.,* II. ii. 45 ff.

22 Miss Jessie L. Weston's translation in *The Chief Middle English Poets* (London, 1913), p. 324.

23 On the *débat* generally, and the subjects and form of *débats, battailles, tençons,* and *jeux partis,* consult Gaston Paris, *La Littérature au Moyen Age* (Paris, 1888), secs. 110, 126, 155; L. Petit de Julleville, *Histoire de la langue et de la littérature française* (Paris, 1896), I, 348–88; II, 208–11; John Edwin Wells, introduction to his edition of *The Owl and the Nightingale* (Boston and London, 1909), sec. IV; *Les Jeux Partis d'Adam de la Halle,* ed. L. Nicod (Paris, 1917), both texts and introduction; *Receuil général des jeux-partis français,* ed. Arthur Långfors, A. Jeanroy, et L. Brandin (Paris, 1926, 2 vols.; in Société des Anciens Textes Français), both texts and introduction. For further references, see *Med. Stage,* I, 79–83, 187–88, and notes; II, 153.

24 *Dialogi,* p. 30.

25 Texts of four of the plays in R. de la Bère, *John Heywood, Entertainer* (London, 1937); summaries of the rest. Text of *A Play of Love* in Farmer's Tudor Facs. Texts, 1909.

26 Text in Henry E. Huntington Facsimile Reprints, no. 1 (New York, 1920); also in Tudor and Stuart Library, ed. F. S. Boas and A. W. Reed (Oxford, 1926). See discussion of play in their introduction; also by A. W. Reed in *Early Tudor Drama* (London, 1926), pp. 94–100; and by C. R. Baskervill in "Conventional Features of Medwall's *Fulgens and Lucres,*" *MP,* XXIV (May, 1927), 419–42.

27 Composed in 1428, dedicated to Carlo Malatesta, Lord of Rimini; English translation (of a French version) by John Tiptoft printed by Caxton in 1481. For details see Boas and Reed, ed. of *Fulgens and Lucres.*

28 *Med. Stage,* II, 201. See Baskervill, "Some Evidence for Early Romantic Plays" (*MP,* XIV, 229–51, 467–512), for abundant evidence of con-

tinuity with renaissance romantic drama of medieval folk and court festival entertainments, in which dramatic elements of dialogue, debate, and combat appeared.

29 Text in Malone Soc. Reprints, 1930.
30 Cf. his discussion in *Five-Act Structure*, pp. 209–12.
31 On background of morality debate themes, see ref. in n. 23, above.
32 In Ch. IX, pp. 238–39, 254–56.
33 II. ii. 184–93. For a different point of view of Hector's change of mind, see Robert K. Presson, "The Structural Use of a Traditional Theme in *Troilus and Cressida*," *PQ*, XXXI (April, 1952), 180–88; Professor Presson takes the about-face as a yielding of reason to will, different in degree but not in kind from similar defects in Troilus and Achilles, and part of Shakespeare's moral design in the play. I see a structural design in it, too, but not this one. Hector seems to me to be blameless, and Troilus a poignantly sympathetic study of a young man cruelly disillusioned in both love and war.
34 Ch. IX, pp. 252–53.
35 The issue discussed appears extensively throughout both plays, but see esp. *Conspiracy*, V. i, ii; *Tragedy*, III. i, ii; IV. ii; V. i.
36 The fact that the historical Byron, from the account of him Chapman followed in Grimeston's *General Inventory of the History of France* (Parrott, *Tragedies*, pp. 592–94), was nearly as puzzling and contradictory as the hero of the play does not fully absolve Chapman from the failure to give his character dramatic integrity; contrast Shakespeare's Cleopatra.
37 Mercury Theatre, 1937–38. In her production of the play in 1949, Miss Margaret Webster took a similar anti-Fascist line. Apparently to avoid anticlimax in the second half, she played up Octavius as a younger copy of Julius; dressed in a similar black uniform, and backed by the same red and black eagle standards (reminiscent of the Sportspalast), he mounted a rise on the battlefield after the death of Brutus and took the "Hail, Caesar's" of Antony and the other officers, just as Julius had taken them at the opening of the play. Caesar's revenge was indeed complete, but in what a cynical un-Shakespearean way!
38 Sextus Pompeius' phrase in *Antony and Cleopatra*, II. vi. 14–19:

> What was't
> That mov'd pale Cassius to conspire? and what
> Made the all-honour'd, honest Roman, Brutus,
> With the arm'd rest, courtiers of beauteous freedom,
> To drench the Capitol, but that they would
> Have one man but a man?

Cf. Cassius' speeches in *Julius Caesar*, I. ii; and the speeches of members of the Germanicus party in *Sejanus* (esp. Arruntius, I. 86–104; Cordus, III. 407–60).

39 Guarini, see below, n. 44, 46; Castelvetro, *Poetica,* III. xix (p. 389).

40 Aristotle, *Poetics,* XV. 1454a37–b8; Horace, *AP,* ll. 191–92.

41 *Poetics,* IX. 1452a1–11.

42 For the fullest discussions of plotting, see Giraldi, *Com. e trag.,* pp. 207–15 (one action, nexus and solution), 219–25 (tragedy with a happy ending), 240–42 (recognition); Castelvetro, *Poetica,* III. vi (unity of action, double plots), III. xii (episodes), III. xix (nexus and solution); Minturno, *L'arte poetica,* pp. 42–45 (types of fable: single, complex, etc.), 83–89 (tragic fable), 120–26 (comic fable); De Nores, *Poetica,* I. iii (tragic fable in general), I. viii (nexus and solution), I. ix (simple and double endings), III. ii (comic fable in general), III. viii (simple and double endings); Guarini, *Compendio,* pp. 265–88 (full analysis of plotting of *Il Pastor Fido*).

43 Minturno, *L'arte poetica,* pp. 40–42, 118; De Nores, *Poetica,* I. iii (pp. 12ᵛ–13), III. ii (pp. 123–123ᵛ); Guarini, *Compendio,* p. 282.

44 *Compendio,* p. 282: "E quinci passiamo al quinto [atto], nel quale, come nel capo risiede lo 'ntelletto dell'uomo, cosí è riposto il maggior nervo dell'artifizio drammatico; conciosiacosaché il sapere annodare è ben malagevole assai, ma tanto più è lo sciôrre, quanto questo nel mutarsi delle cose vuole avere il mirabile accompagnato col verisimile, del quale accompagnamento non ha l'arte drammatica cosa che sia né di maggior fatica né di più pregio."

45 See n. 42, above, and Ch. VIII, n. 44. The same tendency to assimilate the methods of tragedy to those of comedy is indicated in the quotation from Dryden at the head of this chapter.

46 *Compendio,* p. 280.

47 Gonzalo in V. i. 208–13.

48 *The Plays and Poems of William Cartwright,* ed. G. Blakemore Evans (Univ. of Wisconsin Press, 1951), p. 519. Also in Glover and Waller ed. of *Beaumont and Fletcher* (Cambridge Univ. Press, 1905–12), I, xxxvii–xxxviii; cf. the verses of John Webb (p. xxxi) in praise of Beaumont and Fletcher's "rare invention; conflicts that beget/ New strange delight." On the admiration of these authors in the seventeenth century see Lawrence B. Wallis, *Fletcher, Beaumont and Company* (New York, 1947), Chs. I and VII.

49 Ref. in n. 40, above.

50 For the argument, see Ch. IX, above, n. 53.

51 See T. S. Eliot, "The Stoicism of Seneca" in *Elizabethan Essays* (London, 1934), esp. his discussion (pp. 38–40), with which I take issue, of Othello's last speech. For references to Senecan influence consult Ch. I, above, n. 25, and Ch. VI, n. 23.

52 V. iv. 94–111; cf. discussion above, Ch. VI, pp. 127–28, 140–42.

53 Cf. the spirit of Hercules leaving Antony in IV. iii, but esp. "The shirt of Nessus is upon me," etc., IV. x. 56–62. Cf. Chapman's allusion to the poison of Nessus in *Chabot,* V. ii. 82–85, for a similar situation of suffering from a supposed betrayal.

54 Bosola in *The Duchess of Malfi*, V. v. 120–22.
55 *Shakespeare: A Survey*, pp. 5–6.

Chapter 12

1 Fifteen editions between 1598 and 1688. See list of editions and text in *The Shakespeare Apocrypha*, ed. C. F. Tucker Brooke, Oxford, 1918.
2 In *English Domestic Tragedy;* cf. discussion in Ch. VI, above, and ref. in Ch. VI, n. 39.
3 For an interesting and important discussion of this always difficult question of the way in which great nondidactic art is yet meaningful, see Alfred Harbage, *As They Liked It: An Essay on Shakespeare and Morality* (New York, 1947), *passim*. Professor Harbage's central point is that Shakespeare's drama is artistry, not morality, and that a play is as moral as the person who traverses its course, intensifying his moral convictions rather than altering or extending them; but "To say that Shakespearean drama is a highroad leading nowhere is not a paradoxical praise, once we recognize that *nowhere* means *home*—the fundamental convictions of men. Logically, one's estimate of this drama should be about as high as one's estimate of mankind. Shakespeare himself did not underestimate. . . . Shakespeare's drama *in toto* attests his high regard for his audience. Its most fundamental beliefs evoke his grandest utterances" (p. 55).
4 *Medieval Heritage*, p. 351.
5 See esp. Heywood, *Apology for Actors*, F3ʳ–F4; the subjects of comedy are "mingled with sportful accidents, to recreate such as of themselves are wholly devoted to melancholy, which corrupts the blood: or to refresh such weary spirits as are tired with labour, or study, to moderate the cares and heaviness of the mind, that they may return to their trades and faculties with more zeal and earnestness, after some small soft and pleasant retirement."
6 See esp. R. W. Chambers, "The Jacobean Shakespeare and *Measure for Measure*," British Academy Lecture for 1937 (in *Proc. of the Brit. Acad.*, Vol. XXIII).
7 See Prouty, *The Sources of "Much Ado about Nothing."*
8 *Shakespeare's Problem Plays*, Toronto, 1949.
9 For a subtle and provocative discussion of both these problems in the play, see Harbage, *As They Liked It*, pp. 83–84, 89–92, 126–31. Professor Harbage observes that the ending of the play metes out exactly "measure for measure" and is pragmatic justice, not mercy, since Angelo's evil intents have missed fire; perhaps so, but who is it in the play who most needs forgiveness, and who gets it?
    For a development, in a very different way, of a point on the structure

similar to mine, namely, that the artistic weakness of the "problem" comedies results from attempting to cast serious ethical problems in the mold of romantic comedy, see Virgil Whitaker, "Philosophy and Romance in Shakespeare's 'Problem' Comedies" (in *The Seventeenth Century: Studies in the History of English Thought and Literature from Bacon to Pope,* by Richard Foster Jones and others, Stanford University Press, 1951). I should, however, argue many of the particular points therein made about Shakespeare's intentions, methods, and meanings.

10   In the National Gallery, Washington, D.C.; reproduced in *Art News Annual* for 1944.

11   Cf. Duccio's altarpiece, the *Maestà,* parts of which are reproduced in *Italian Painting: The Creators of the Renaissance,* Geneva and Paris: Albert Skira, 1950.

12   For examples, see any good collection of reproductions of medieval and renaissance art, such as Georg Leidinger (ed.), *Meisterwerke der Buchmalerei aus Handschriften der Bayerischen Staatsbibliothek München* (Munich, 1920); Max Hauttman (ed.), *Die Kunst des frühen Mittelalters* (Berlin, 1929); Wilhelm Hausenstein (ed.), *Das Bild* (Munich, 1922), Bde. III–IV: *Die Malerei der frühen Italiener;* Raimond van Marle, *The Development of the Italian Schools of Painting* (The Hague, 1923–38), Vol. I, sixth to thirteenth centuries (1923); Arthur M. Hind, *An Introduction to a History of Woodcut* (London, 1935), Vol. II—especially interesting for illustrations of narrative, like *The Metamorphoses, The Golden Legend,* etc.

13   Reproduced in Hausenstein, No. 92.

14   The Adoration of the Magi was a favorite theme for this technique, doubtless because it offered interesting opportunities for perspective in the approach of their trains from a distance. Cf. esp. the treatments of the theme by Gentile da Fabriano in the Uffizi (Haustenstein, No. 84) and by Giovanni di Paolo (Hausenstein, No. 102).

15   Reproduced in Cohen, *Histoire de la mise en scène,* Pl. I; also in his *Théâtre en France au Moyen Age,* Vol. I, Pl. XL. A summary, with further references, of the case for the effect of the medieval stage on art will be found in Cohen's chapter on "Art et Mystère" in *Histoire.* Where there are actual signs of influence, mostly changes in iconography (as in some of the depictions in fresco painting and sculpture of the Last Judgment), they are almost all of the fourteenth century or later. Professor Cohen appears to agree with M. Mâle in attributing the style itself (that is of a progressive series of actions within one frame) to the influence of the stage; but the style existed before the full development of the multiple stage for the secularized mysteries of the fourteenth and fifteenth centuries, even before the simple beginnings of the liturgical plays in the ninth and tenth centuries. Carvings on sarcophagi, cathedrae, columns, reliquary crosses, and the like, of scenes from sacred history naturally gave rise to such a treatment; see examples from the

fourth century on in Hauttman, *Die Kunst des frühen Mittelalters*. See esp. No. 521, the charming relief on the bronze door of St. Zeno in Verona of the dance of Salome before Herod (11th c.).

16 A similar set of woodcuts appears in a Spanish edition, *Johan bocacio de las mujeres illustre en romance* (Saragossa, 1494); the designs have been reversed and evidently recut, much more crudely. The reversal plays havoc with the narrative design: Lucretia appears to be stabbing herself before Tarquin has ravished her, Antony and Cleopatra to be committing suicide before they have feasted, and so on.

17 For "Jocasta" and "Clytemnaestra" see p. 129. Note that in Boccaccio the mother of Coriolanus is "Veturia," not "Volumnia" as in Plutarch and Shakespeare.

Index

THE NOTES are indexed only for (1) full bibliographical references to a title; (2) names and titles not appearing in the text; and (3) additional matter that warrants treatment as if it were part of the text.

— *Volpone:* debt to Roman comedy in, 150; as nonromantic, 150; Mosca, 155, 168–69, 329; Volpone, 155, 158, 168–69, 329, 348; structural satire in, 169, 329, 365; classical sources of, 170; the denouement of, 329; good and evil in, 330; mentioned, 172, 427–28 *n10*

Joseph, B. L., *Elizabethan Acting,* 398 *n4*

Joseph, Sister Miriam, *Shakespeare's Use of the Arts of Language,* 400 *n32*

Juvenal: as influencing Jonson, 170; *Satires,* quoted by Marston, 170

KAIBEL, Georgius (ed.), *Comicorum graecorum fragmenta,* 414 *n13*

Keats, John, 53, 185

Keil, Edmund (ed.), *Grammatici latini,* 414 *n15*

Kelso, Ruth, ed. *Naugerius,* 28

Kennard, Joseph Spencer, *The Italian Theatre,* 413 *n5*

Kennedy, Milton Boone, *The Oration in Shakespeare,* 400 *n32*

Kernodle, George K.: *From Art to Theatre,* 446 *n56;* on origin of stage façade, 447, *n74*

Kittredge, G. L., intro. to *Comedy of Errors,* 422 *n2*

Klein, Julius L., *Geschichte des Dramas,* 420 *n31*

Knights, L. C., *Drama and Society in the Age of Jonson,* 422 *n13*

Köppel, Emil, "Studien zur Geschichte der italienischen Novelle," 419 *n30*

Kreider, Paul, *Elizabethan Comic Character Conventions in Chapman,* 436 *n34*

Kurtz, Leonard P., *The Dance of Death,* 418 *n16*

Kyd, Thos.: *Soliman and Perseda,* 130, 137; and Fletcher, 240; *Works,* ed. Boas, 438 *n55*

— *The Spanish Tragedy:* as Senecan, 15–16, 353; as Italianate tragedy

of intrigue, 130, 131, 289, 306; amplification in, 244–45; function of ghost in, 307; the play within the play, 332; mentioned, 137

Kyffin, Maurice: on character types in *Andria,* 225; *Andria . . . in English* (tr.), 435 *n20*

LA FRESNAYE, Jean Vauquelin de: against tragi-comedy, 200; *L'Art poétique* (ed. Pellisier), 430 *n32;* mentioned, 8

Lancaster, H. C.: *French Tragi-Comedy,* 428 *n14; History of French Dramatic Literature in the Seventeenth Century,* 445 *n56*

La Primaudaye, Pierre de, *The French Academy* (tr. T.B.), 437 *n42*

Larum for London, A, as history play, 114

La Taille, Jean de, 8

Laudun, Pierre de, 8

Laurentius Valla, *Elegantiae,* as school text, 49

Law, R. A.: "The Roman Background of *Titus Andronicus,*" 420 *n37;* "Holinshed's *Leir* Story and Shakespeare's," 441 *n82*

Lawrence, W. J.: on the "nocturnal," 12–13 *n1; Pre-Restoration Stage Studies,* 412 *n1*

Lea, Kathleen M., *Italian Popular Comedy,* 420 *n32*

Leach, Arthur F., *English Schools at the Reformation,* 394 *n12*

Legge, Thomas, *Richardus Tertius,* 125

Leidinger, Georg (ed.), *Meisterwerke der Buchmalerei,* 453 *n12*

Leir, King (pre-Shakespearean), on theme of power, 124

Lennard, Samson (tr.), *Of Wisdom,* 397 *n1. See* Charron, Pierre

Leonardo da Vinci, as example of renaissance style, 5. *See also* App. I

Liberality and Prodigality, The Contention between, 110

Lingua. See Tomkis, Thos.

63, 364; conflict of character and story in, 364

— *Midsummer Night's Dream, A:* Theseus' speech in, 58, 62–63; decorum of style in, 79; use of setting in, 293; story and character in, 325–26

— *Much Ado about Nothing:* as typical romantic comedy, 137, 178–80; and *Gli Duoi Fratelli Rivali,* 178–80; and *Susanna,* 188; and *Cymbeline,* 211; tragi-comic possibilities in, 268; Don John as evil adversary in, 304; chance in the denouement of, 330; Claudio-and-Hero relation, social conventions in, 363

— *Othello:* as example of successful form, 51, 355; as tragedy of intrigue, 130; and Jacobean tragedies of sex, 139; tragic irony in, 142; imagery of Devil, death, and hell in, 142, 239; and *Cymbeline,* 211; Othello, 238, 239, 240, 261, 302, 331, 334–35; Iago, 239, 261, 322; *ethopoeia moralis* in, 240; motivation in, 253, 261; "natural" order of action in, 261; setting in, 293; evil as adversative in, 304, 305, 337; denouement of, 334–35

— *Richard II:* history as tragedy in, 81, 114, 115; symbolic use of crown in, 99–100; Richard, 123, 126, 249; rise and fall theme in, 124, 288, 320–21, 337; dramatic use of rhetoric in, 240–41, 342–43; unresolved opposition in, 298, 318, 320–21; Bolingbroke *vs.* Richard, 306, 320

— *Richard III:* history as tragedy in, 81, 114, 115; rise and fall theme in, 124, 288, 337; Richard, 126, 128, 240, 255; Senecan techniques in, 130, 353; Anne, 221; soliloquies as *ethopoeiae,* 240; moral play debate technique in, 255; *décor simultané* in, 287; mentioned, 298, 336

— *Romeo and Juliet:* characters as examples of decorum, 78, 158, 220–21; and *Antony and Cleo-*

patra, lyric passages in, 249–50; comic relief in, 292; setting in, 293; structure in relation to source, 297; accident as a source of tragic irony in, 333; dramatic use of rhetoric in, 342; mentioned, 131, 132

— *Tempest, The:* art *vs.* nature in, 63, 64; Ferdinand and Miranda, 64, 185; Caliban, 64, 249; setting in, 293; Antonio as evil adversary, 304; function of Prospero in, 308, 327; "discovery" in, 327; the denouement, 330; mentioned, 343, 356

— *Timon of Athens:* Poet and Painter (qu), 72–74; sources of, 81; rise and fall theme in, 119–20, 124; mentioned, 213, 366

— *Troilus and Cressida:* romantic story and satire in, 213; effect of debate technique on, 317, 356; as a "problem" play, 366, 367

— *Twelfth Night:* debt to Roman comedy in, 150, 174; *Gl'Ingannati* as source of, 180; Sir Andrew Aguecheek, 229; *ethologia* in, 240; Viola, 240, 309, 326–27; story and character in, 257, 326–27; style as unifying, 290; setting in, 293; Feste *vs.* Malvolio, 302; and *Philaster,* 328; mentioned, 338, 363

— *Two Gentlemen of Verona, The:* lack of motivation in, 252; Julia and Proteus, 252, 325, 347; conflict of character and story in, 325, 347, 364; social conventions in, 363

— *Winter's Tale, The:* Polixenes (qu), 59; art *vs.* nature in, 59, 63; the oracle in, 206; pastoralism in, 215; Autolycus, 215; Leontes, 235, 253; and *Othello,* motivation in, 253; "natural" order of action in, 261; organization of, 279; setting in, 293; moral choice in, 316; chance in denouement, 327, 330; mentioned, 187, 285, 343, 370

Shelley, Percy Bysshe, *Adonais* (qu), 53

Sherry, Richard: *Treatise of the Figures of Grammar and Rhetoric,*